Sexualities in Anthropology

Blackwell Anthologies in Social and Cultural Anthropology

Series Editor: Parker Shipton, Boston University

Drawing from some of the most significant scholarly work of the nineteenth and twentieth centuries, the *Blackwell Anthologies in Social and Cultural Anthropology* series offers a comprehensive and unique perspective on the ever-changing field of anthropology. It represents both a collection of classic readers and an exciting challenge to the norms that have shaped this discipline over the past century.

Each edited volume is devoted to a traditional subdiscipline of the field such as the anthropology of religion, linguistic anthropology, or medical anthropology, and provides a foundation in the canonical readings of the selected area. Aware that such subdisciplinary definitions are still widely recognized and useful – but increasingly problematic – these volumes are crafted to include a rare and invaluable perspective on social and cultural anthropology at the onset of the twenty-first century. Each text provides a selection of classic readings together with contemporary works that underscore the artificiality of subdisciplinary definitions, and point students, researchers, and general readers in the new directions in which anthropology is moving.

Series Advisory Editorial Board:

Fredrik Barth, University of Oslo and Boston University
Stephen Gudeman, University of Minnesota
Jane Guyer, Northwestern University
Caroline Humphrey, University of Cambridge
Tim Ingold, University of Aberdeen
Emily Martin, Princeton University
Sally Falk Moore, Harvard Emerita
Marshall Sahlins, University of Chicago Emeritus
Joan Vincent, Columbia University and Barnard College Emerita

Sexualities in Anthropology

A Reader

Edited by

Andrew P. Lyons
and Harriet D. Lyons

A John Wiley & Sons, Ltd., Publication

Registered Office
John Wiley & Sons Ltd, The Atrium, Southern Gate, Chichester, West Sussex, PO19 8SQ, United Kingdom

Editorial Offices
350 Main Street, Malden, MA 02148-5020, USA
9600 Garsington Road, Oxford, OX4 2DQ, UK
The Atrium, Southern Gate, Chichester, West Sussex, PO19 8SQ, UK

For details of our global editorial offices, for customer services, and for information about how to apply for permission to reuse the copyright material in this book please see our website at www.wiley.com/wiley-blackwell.

Library of Congress Cataloging-in-Publication Data

Sexualities in Anthropology : A Reader / [edited by] Andrew P. Lyons and Harriet D. Lyons.
    p.   cm. – (Blackwell Anthologies in Social and Cultural Anthropology ; 15)
    Includes bibliographical references and index.
  ISBN 978-1-4051-9053-4 (pbk.) – ISBN 978-1-4051-9054-1 (hardcover)
  1. Sex customs–Cross-cultural studies.   I. Lyons, Andrew P. (Andrew Paul), 1944– , editor of compilation.   II. Lyons, Harriet D., 1943– , editor of compilation.   III. Weston, Kath, 1958– The bubble, the burn, and the simmer.
        GN484.3.S49 2011
        306.7–dc22
                      2010043547

A catalogue record for this book is available from the British Library.

Set in 9/11pt Sabon by SPi Publisher Services, Pondicherry, India.
Printed and bound in Malaysia by Vivar Printing Sdn Bhd
1   2011

In Memory of M. F. Ashley Montagu

Contents

Acknowledgments

We would like to acknowledge the encouragement of Parker Shipton who asked us to prepare this volume, Rosalie Robertson, Julie Kirk, and others at Wiley-Blackwell who guided us through the publication process, and many others who went out of their way to provide help and advice, including, most particularly, Kath Weston, Morgan Holmes, Susan Sperling, Kevin Nixon, Rachel Spronk, and Gilbert Herdt. They are all partially responsible for any virtues this collection possesses, but we alone are responsible for any errors and omissions.

The editors and publisher gratefully acknowledge the permissions granted to reproduce the copyrighted material in this book:

1   Kath Weston, The Bubble, the Burn, and the Simmer: Introduction: Locating Sexuality in Social Science, from *Long Slow Burn: Sexuality and Social Science*, by Kath Weston, London: Routledge, 1998, pp. 1–27, 213–215. Reprinted with permission of Taylor & Francis Group LLC.

2   Zine Magubane, Which Bodies Matter? Feminism, Poststructuralism, Race, and the Curious Theoretical Odyssey of the "Hottentot Venus," from *Gender and Society*, vol. 15, no. 6 (Dec 2001): 816–834. Reprinted by permission of SAGE Publications.

3   Extract from *The Origin of the Family, Private Property and the State*, by Friedrich Engels, trans. Alick West, pp 55–68. Reprinted with permission of Lawrence & Wishart UK.

4   Extracts from Andrew P. Lyons and Harriet D. Lyons, *Irregular Connections: A History of Anthropology and Sexuality*, University of Nebraska Press, 2004. By permission of the University of Nebraska Press. © 2004 by the Board of Regents of the University of Nebraska.

11   Extracts from Bronislaw Malinowski, *The Sexual Life of Savages*, reprint of 3rd edition, Boston: Beacon Press, 1987[1932], pp. 59–64. Reprinted with permission of Taylor & Francis UK.

12   Extracts from Margaret Mead, *Coming of Age in Samoa*, New York: Morrow, 1928, chap. 7, Formal Sex Relations, pp. 86–109. Copyright © 1928, 49, 55, 61, 73 by Margaret Mead. Reprinted by permission of HarperCollins Publishers USA.

13   Extract from Isaac Schapera, Premarital Pregnancy and Native Opinion, from *Africa*, vol. 6, no. 1 (1933): 59–89. Reprinted with permission of International African Institute IAI.

14   Extracts from John Messenger, Sex and Repression in an Irish Folk Community, from *Human Sexual Behavior*, Robert M Suggs and Donald Marshall, eds., New York: Basic Books, pp 3–37. Copyright © 1971 by The Institute for Sex Research Inc. Reprinted by permission of The Kinsey Institute for Research in Sex, Gender, and Reproduction, Inc.

15   Extracts from Bronislaw Malinowski, *The Sexual Life of Savages*, reprint of 3rd edition. Boston: Beacon Press, 1987[1932], pp. 153–172. Reprinted with permission of Taylor & Francis UK.

16   Ashley Montagu, *Coming into Being Among the Australian Aborigines*, 2nd edition, London: Routledge Kegan Paul, 1974, pp. 377–386. Reprinted with permission of Taylor & Francis Books UK.

17   Extracts from Edmund Leach's essay, Virgin Birth, from *Proceedings of the Royal Anthropological Institute*, 1966: 39–49. Reprinted with permission of Wiley-Blackwell.

18   Derek Freeman, Was Margaret Mead Misled or Did She Mislead on Samoa? Sex and Hoax in Samoa, from *Current Anthropology*, vol. 41, no. 4 (Aug–Oct 2000): 609–614. © 2000 by The Wenner-Gren Foundation for Anthropological Research. Reprinted with permission of The University of Chicago Press.

19   Penelope Schoeffel, Sexual Morality in Samoa and its Historical Transformations, from A Polymath Anthropologist: Essays in Honour of Ann Chowning, *Research in Anthropology and Linguistics*, vol. 6 (2005): 69–75, University of Auckland. Reprinted with permission of University of Auckland and the author.

20   Paul Shankman, Virginity and the History of Sex in Samoa, from *The Trashing of Margaret Mead: Anatomy of an Anthropological Controversy*, University of Wisconsin Press, 2009, *pp.* 175–189, 263–264. © 2009 by the Board of the Regents of the University of Wisconsin System. Reprinted by permission of The University of Wisconsin Press.

21   Harriet Lyons, Genital Cutting: The Past and Present of a Polythetic Category, from *Africa Today*, vol. 53, no. 4: 3–17. Reprinted with permission of Indiana University Press.

22   Esther Newton, Role Models, from *Mother Camp, Female Impersonators in North America*, University of Chicago Press, 1979, pp. 97–111. Reprinted with permission of The University of Chicago Press and the author.

23   Gilbert Herdt, Notes and Queries on Sexual Excitement in Sambia Culture, from *Etnofoor*, vol. 7, no. 2 (1994): 25–41. Slightly adapted/edited for this Reader. Reprinted with permission of Amsterdam Institute for Social Science Research (AISSR).

24   Don Kulick, Causing a Commotion: Public Scandal as Resistance Among Brazilian Transgendered Prostitutes, from *Anthropology Today*, vol. 12, no. 6 (Dec 1996): 3–7. Reprinted with permission of Wiley-Blackwell.

25   Tom Boellstorff, Between Religion and Desire, Being Muslim and *Gay* in Indonesia, from *American Anthropologist*, vol. 107, no. 4 (2005): 575–585. Reproduced by permission of the American Anthropological Association and the author. Not for sale or further reproduction.

26   Megan Sinnott, The Semiotics of Transgendered Sexual Identity in the Thai Print Media, from *Culture, Health and Sexuality*, vol. 4, no. 2 (2000): 425–440. Reprinted with permission of the publisher (Taylor & Francis Group http://www.informaworld.com).

27   David Valentine, The Categories Themselves, from *GLQ: A Journal of Lesbian and Gay Studies*, vol. 10, no. 2 (2004): 215–220. Copyright © 2004 Duke University Press. All rights reserved. Used by permission of the Publisher.

28   Pamela R. Stern and Richard G. Condon, A Good Spouse Is Hard to Find: Marriage, Spouse Exchange, and Infatuation Among the Copper Inuit, from *Romantic Passion*, William Jankowiak, ed., New York: Columbia University Press, 1995, pp. 196–218. Reprinted with permission of Columbia University Press.

29   Daniel Jordan Smith, Love and the Risk of HIV, from *Modern Loves*, Jennifer Hirsch and Holly Wardlow, eds., Ann Arbor: University of Michigan Press, 2006, pp. 135–154. Reprinted with permission of University of Michigan Press and the author. Photos © Daniel J Smith.

30   Rachel Spronk, Beyond Pain, Towards Pleasure in the Study of Sexuality in Africa, from *Sexuality in Africa Magazine*, vol. 4, no. 3 (2007): 3–6, 8–14. African Regional Sexuality Resource Centre, www.arsrc.or. Reprinted with permission of ARSRC.

Introduction: Problems in Writing About Sex in Anthropology

In her well-known essay, "The Bubble, The Burn, and The Simmer," reproduced in this Reader, Kath Weston remarks:

> In the early years of social science, researchers staked out a territory for fledgling disciplines based upon case studies, illustrations, and debates that prominently featured matters of sexuality. So it is not merely that there is a theoretical component to research on sexuality in the social sciences. There is also a sexual component to the most basic social science theory. Without it, there wouldn't be a social science. Or more precisely, there wouldn't be *this* social science. (See p. 13)

As practitioners of *this* social science for more than 40 years, we were pleased to be asked to assemble a Reader that reflects some of the topics we have recently written about. A mere 12 years ago, when her book *Long Slow Burn* appeared, Weston remarked that there was still a tendency to ghettoize the study of sexuality in social science. Anthropologists studying sexuality were still marginalized in the discipline, although from the 1970s to the 1990s there was a gradual but sustained increase in interest in the topic, nourished by some significant fieldwork in both Western and non-Western countries. Furthermore, outsiders might turn to anthropologists only for data rather than for theory – "flora and fauna" tidbits such as "how often per night?," "with whom?," and "where?." Perhaps, the appearance of this Reader is one more sign that sexuality is moving closer to center stage in anthropology.

This Reader incorporates short selections from the writings of key figures in the history of anthropology about sexualities, morality, and the family. It is easy for modern students of the anthropology of sexuality to ignore significant work that was done by our disciplinary ancestors and to misread that work even when they acknowledge it. Even the errors of our predecessors can be instructive. In the

Sexualities in Anthropology: A Reader, edited by Andrew P. Lyons and Harriet D. Lyons
© 2011 Blackwell Publishing Ltd.

nineteenth century debates about "race" and humanity's place in nature, and, from 1860 onwards, theories about the origin of the family, morality, religion, and private property, all involved speculations about sexuality.

Literature produced since the 1970s on both heterosexualities and same-sex sexualities is well represented in this book. Readers will note that to some degree anthropology has witnessed the birth/rebirth of two traditions (gay and straight) in sexuality studies, which don't always address each other. Until 2005, most of the significant new work was in gay, lesbian, bisexual, and transgender (GLBT) studies, but recently that picture has changed a little.

We incorporate material on controversies both past and present, including discussions of "primitive promiscuity" in the nineteenth and early twentieth centuries, supposed ignorance or "nescience" of physiological paternity and the "facts of life," clitoridectomy and other forms of "genital cutting," homosexualities and how we discuss them, the Mead–Freeman "debate" over whether Samoan adolescents enjoyed sexual freedom, and the usefulness of discussions of love in other societies.

And What Do We Mean by Sexuality?

"Sexuality" is not merely a loaded term, it is pre-eminently ambiguous, yet most of us (which means most anthropologists) are reasonably sure what "it" means. It might be said, like the word "game," to be an odd-job word, a signifier with numerous, sometimes contradictory, referents. It can be used to mean a biological given, whether a propensity or a drive; it may refer to individuals or groups; it may refer to "unconscious" or conscious impulses; it may describe behavior, whether indulged in, observed, desired, or related in narrative; it may be a concept in discourse which refers to some or all of the preceding.

The broadness of such a discursive concept may reflect the view that there is no verifiable reality beyond talk – that "sexuality" is best viewed as a social construct. "Sex" itself is similarly ambiguous. It can be seen as the biological "counterpoint" to socially constructed "gender," in which event either category could be and has been viewed as dependent on the other.[1]

The anthropologists whose work we have selected vary greatly according to time, place, interests, and ideology, so that it is hardly surprising that they do not, did not, or would not all agree as to the meaning and purview of "sex" and "sexuality." Most writing before the 1950s (or even perhaps the 1970s) assumed that "sexuality," albeit it was culturally mediated and to some extent variable, was at root a biological given. For example, Westermarck, Ellis, Malinowski, Messenger, and even Mead adhered to positions that would now be called *essentialist*. Some more contemporary writers on heterosexuality (e.g., Marjorie Shostak, William Jankowiak, and Thomas Gregor, and, in this volume, Pamela Stern and the late Richard Condon) might also be described as essentialist, inasmuch as they adhere to either modern Darwinian (sociobiological) or some Freudian viewpoints. Most but not all writers of the new gay, lesbian, and transgender anthropology (e.g., Weston, Boellstorff, Sinnott, and Valentine in this volume) may be described as constructionist. They are much less concerned with whether or not homosexuality is rooted in a "gay gene" than with the fact that different societies and different sectors of society classify (or fail to classify) minority sexualities in different ways. People may create classifications through talk and action, and they may seek to affirm or modify social classification by performing (or failing to perform) an expected role, or indeed by performing it in an exaggerated fashion (which is "camp"). Constructionism (or constructivism) is rooted in the mid-to-late twentieth-century movement in North American sociology known as symbolic interactionism, and the later philosophical writings of Michel Foucault and Judith Butler.

Some Problems Relating to the Anthropology of Sexuality

Arguably, all anthropologists are nosy parkers all of the time. As Margaret Mead, Donald Tuzin, and Ernestine Friedl noted (Mead 1961: 1434–5; Tuzin 1991: 270–4, 1995: 265, 266; Friedl 1994), with some very rare exceptions, the sex act is the most private of all acts in most societies, and sexuality in general is a field where boundaries are sharply drawn. Such a situation may present problems of both an evidentiary and an ethical nature even to the most resolute of nosy parkers. The problems are particularly acute where issues of power and inequality are involved. Arguably, sexuality is a topic around which such issues cluster with a greater frequency than is the case with most other areas of study, as Michel Foucault reminded us.

In the popular imagination most anthropological inquiries into sexuality are conducted in very cold or very steamy places, far removed from modern urban settings. Such a stereotype fits the imaginings of the cultural evolutionists and the early ethnographic work of Malinowski and Mead and the contemporary studies of scholars such as Gilbert Herdt. However, the Western metropolis was implicitly or explicitly present as a comparator in all of this work. In the late twentieth century much of the new lesbian and gay anthropology focused its attention on sexuality in contemporary urban contexts throughout the world.

Most discussions of sexuality in the academic literature have a moral or political, as well as a scientific, agenda. Recognizing this fact does not mean that anthropologists have discovered nothing of value, nothing new, or nothing "true" about sexuality, though critics of relativist approaches equate such recognition with just such denials. Anthropologists have sometimes disturbed outsiders by questioning supposed moral universals on the basis of ethnographic evidence; more recently, they are disturbing each other by questioning the premises that underlie the ethnographic enterprise, from the entry to the field to the inscription of data. Freeman's critique of Mead's portrayal of Samoan sexuality stirred the popular imagination in the 1980s, largely because it presented a challenge to a famous woman's reputation. A number of scholars, including anthropologists who had long been skeptical of some of Mead's conclusions, were disturbed by Freeman's attack. To them, it seemed to champion a discredited assumption that sexual behavior and gender roles were biologically determined, and to open the way for other biological determinisms, particularly with regard to race, although Freeman denied that his work was in any way about race.

The debate over sexuality in Samoa is one of the later controversies linking comparative studies of sexuality to pressing social issues. In our book *Irregular Connections* (Lyons and Lyons 2004), we discuss a long history of the "conscription" of sexuality, particularly the sexuality of relatively powerless populations, into debates about morality and hierarchy in the places where anthropological works were written and read and from which anthropologists set out for the field. The sexuality of aboriginal populations of Australia, the Pacific Islands, the Americas, and Africa has figured in debates about slavery in the US South, colonialism in Africa and elsewhere, and the appropriate treatment of women, homosexuals, and the working classes in Europe and North America.

From 1775 to 1900, including the years before 1860 when there was no academic discipline called social anthropology, there was a debate among academic and popular biologists, including some of the founders of physical anthropology, concerning the basis of racial hierarchy. There were discussions concerning the definition of species, and it should be noted that one of the contested criteria of species was sexual, the ability of matings to produce fertile offspring. Genitalia were given racial rankings along with every other part of the body. The findings of biological science were sustained by, and in turn helped to maintain, stereotypes about the sexuality of non-Western peoples as well as abject populations at home. Most commonly, there was an assumption that "primitive" peoples were oversexed both physically and socially. The story of Saartje Baartmann, the so-called Hottentot Venus, discussed in the paper by Magubane is a case in point (see Chapter 2).

Evolutionary social theory at its zenith, represented by the writings of Lewis Henry Morgan, Sir John Lubbock, John McLennan and Sir Edward Burnett Tylor, reflected the self-confidence of Victorian progressives who imagined a zero point of sexual promiscuity from which all peoples progressed at different paces on the road to monogamous, bourgeois marriages. Friedrich Engels, the revolutionary communist who borrowed his conjectural history of the family from Morgan, hoped for a better future, and for a while his theories were used as the basis for experiments in free love in the Soviet Union.

By the turn of the century, confidence had waned after an international economic depression. The Victorian family was under attack from feminists and evangelical Christians who wished to enforce male as well as female chastity, and occasionally from sexual libertarians like Richard Burton interested in more freedom, particularly for men. During this same period sexologists created typologies of normality and perversion, and the first stirrings of homosexual consciousness occurred. It was surely no coincidence that questionings of received morality were integrated into anthropological works that negated the grand narratives of social evolution, such as the denial by Westermarck, Ellis, and Crawley of universal primitive promiscuity. Burton, Westermarck, and Ellis all wrote about the cross-cultural incidence of homosexuality in such a way as to naturalize it, though Burton made disapproving comments while doing so.

Malinowski, who studied with Westermarck, furthered the rejection of social evolution, and portrayed Trobriand adolescence with its measured freedom as a useful training for marriage rather than as an instance of promiscuity. He urged anthropologists to advise colonial administrators and missionaries concerning sexual matters in order to prevent social instability. He also became active in the birth control movement in Britain. Mead's career as a popular expert on family issues began with her controversial portrait of Samoan adolescence.

From the late 1930s anthropological research on sexuality was largely subsumed in other projects such as kinship studies in Britain and the British Empire, and culture and personality studies in the United States. This continued till the 1970s.

In the 1960s a curious debate erupted when Sir Edmund Leach attacked some of his contemporaries for accepting Malinowski's assertions that the inhabitants of the Trobriand Islands had been ignorant of the facts of physiological paternity when Malinowski studied them during World War I. Although Malinowski rejected Victorian ideas of primitive matriarchy in studying this matrilineal people, Leach argued that accepting such "ignorance" at face value could not be separated from its roots in Victorian ideas of savages who were too promiscuous to be certain of their father's identity and too stupid to figure out the facts of life.

Issues of power and inequality and memories of a racist past also haunt current debates about female circumcision. The conflicts between anthropology's relativist tradition and its humanitarian and feminist commitments may be resolved by its ability to create dialogue and by attempts to empower women in communities that have practiced genital cutting.

Empowerment is necessarily a critical issue in GLBT anthropology, which played a leading role in reviving anthropological field studies of sexuality in the past three decades. Many of them have taken place in North American as well as non-Western settings. In the 1990s Weston observed in her article, "The Virtual Anthropologist," that the lesbian or gay anthropologist who studies lesbian or gay subcultures "at home" might be told that she was not doing "real" fieldwork, because she had not gone to a foreign place and was studying her own kind. Questions of categorization and conscription are encountered in gay and lesbian studies, most notably those conducted abroad. These are discussed in detail in our introduction to the section on GLBT studies (see Part X).

Curiously, "love" was not a common topic in anthropological studies of sexuality. When it was mentioned, it was often accompanied by denials of its social recognition outside Western society. Studies in this volume by Stern and Condon, Smith, and Spronk are part of a growing literature that suggests that such assumptions should be questioned and more attention paid to the cross-cultural study of love.

Despite the hopes of some anthropologists that our discipline would be able to point the way to a "healthy" or "normal" way for people to "do sex," such an outcome has not ensued. Rather, what we have learned is the *hubris* entailed in any assumption that such universal prescriptions are possible. What the anthropology of sexuality does tell us is that humans have lived under many different sexual regimes, each with its own unique internal dynamics. This knowledge does not provide solutions. Rather, it asks some very challenging questions.

NOTE

1   This paragraph and the previous one are taken from the Introduction to our book, *Irregular Connections* (Lyons and Lyons 2004: 12).

REFERENCES

Foucault, Michel
    1980[1976]   The History of Sexuality, vol. 1: An Introduction. Trans. Robert Hurley. New York: Vintage Books.
Friedl, Ernestine
    1994   Sex the Invisible. American Anthropologist 96(4):833–844.
Lyons, Andrew P. and Harriet D. Lyons
    2004   Irregular Connections: A History of Anthropology and Sexuality. Lincoln, NE: University of Nebraska Press.
Mead, Margaret
    1961   Cultural Determinants of Sexual Behavior. *In* Sex and Internal Secretions, vol. 2. 3rd edition. William C. Young, ed. Pp. 1433–1479. Baltimore: Williams and Wilkins Co.
Tuzin, Donald
    1991   Sex, Culture and the Anthropologist. Social Science and Medicine 33:867–874.
Tuzin, Donald
    1995   Discourse, Intercourse, and the Excluded Middle: Anthropology and the Problem of Sexual Experience. *In* Sexual Nature, Sexual Culture. Paul R. Abramson and Steven D. Pinkerton, eds. Pp. 257–275. Chicago: University of Chicago Press.
Weston, Kath
    1998   Long Slow Burn: Sexuality and Social Science. New York and London: Routledge.
Weston, Kath
    1997   The Virtual Anthropologist. In Anthropological Locations: Boundaries and Grounds of a Field Science. Akhil Gupta and James Ferguson, eds. Pp. 163–184. Los Angeles: University of California Press.

1

The Bubble, the Burn, and the Simmer: Locating Sexuality in Social Science

Kath Weston

Shortly before *The Lesbian and Gay Studies Reader* appeared on bookstore shelves in 1993, *Glamour* magazine produced a photo essay about two girls who accompanied one another as dates to their high school prom. *Redbook* published without fanfare a story about lesbian parenthood entitled, "My Two Moms." As the decade rolled on, television sitcoms began tossing bit parts to gay characters. A job ad appeared in the newsletter of the American Anthropological Association with "lesbian/gay issues" tucked away into a long list of potentially desirable specializations. Something called "queer theory" found its way into English departments and the pages of the *New York Times*. Publishers signed five-figure, even six-figure, book deals with researchers in the emerging field of lesbian/gay studies. Critics as well as supporters of the lesbian/gay/bisexual/ transgender (LGBT) movement asserted that the movement had encouraged the study of sexuality in general and homosexuality in particular. Professors began to lament that the social sciences had lagged behind the humanities in taking advantage of these new opportunities

(Stein and Plummer 1994). Sexuality had suddenly become a "hot," if not quite respectable, topic for investigation.[1]

Suddenly? In this popular truncated version of the history of scholarship on sexuality, an increasingly "open" social climate allows queer theory to "liberate" sexuality for study, with the humanities leading the way (cf. Seidman 1994). A narrative of progress if ever there was one. But in order to portray research on sexuality as a late-breaking development, the raconteurs of this tale have to pass quickly over widely publicized empirical studies of sexual behavior from mid-century by investigators such as Alfred Kinsey, William Masters, and Virginia Johnson. In order to portray social science as a latecomer to the party, they also have to minimize the contributions of an array of investigators who matched Kinsey in commitment, if not acclaim. During her lifetime the psychologist Evelyn Hooker (1965, 1967) received little more than a nod for bringing the study of homosexuality out from under the rubric of deviance. Over in sociology, William Gagnon and John Simon (1973)

Kath Weston, The Bubble, the Burn, and the Simmer: Introduction: Locating Sexuality in Social Science, from *Long Slow Burn: Sexuality and Social Science*, by Kath Weston, London: Routledge, 1998, pp. 1–27, 213–215. Reprinted with permission of Taylor & Francis Group LLC.

Sexualities in Anthropology: A Reader, edited by Andrew P. Lyons and Harriet D. Lyons
© 2011 Blackwell Publishing Ltd.

were developing their concept of "sexual scripts" while the parents of some of today's queer theorists were debating the merits of cloth versus disposable diapers. When W. H. R. Rivers embarked on a multidisciplinary expedition to the Torres Straits at the turn of the century, he wasn't just interested in mythology or gardening techniques. He also posed questions about marriage, erotic dreams, and conception (see Kuklick 1991).

A few of the earliest researchers, such as the anthropologist Bronislaw Malinowski, are remembered as pioneers in their fields, but rarely because they studied sexuality. Most are barely remembered at all. Yet the impact of their findings has extended beyond their respective disciplines to shape debates about sexuality and intimacy that still grip the popular imagination. Thus the long, slow character of the burn, or at least the simmer.

This forgotten legacy of sexuality within the social sciences intimates that the present resurgence of interest in the topic represents something more than an abrupt enlightenment or a newfound "openness" toward controversial issues. Nor can the latest burst of scholarship on sexuality be explained by allegations that multicultural politics have conspired with a "gay agenda" to foment sexual revolution in ivory tower offices and high school locker rooms. Within the social sciences, too much research predates the late-twentieth-century movements for social justice to legitimate such a contention, and even research conducted in conjunction with those movements has encountered formidable opposition. While activists have worked hard, against great odds, to clear a space for study, the latest round of graduate student papers on transgender identity, international gay organizing, and abstinence is just one installment in a much longer story. Queer studies, as an outgrowth of the LGBT movement, may have insisted upon stirring up the pot. But queer studies hasn't been the first to assemble the ingredients or turn up the fire.

[…] If sexuality is already deeply embedded in the topics and debates that constitute social science's stock-in-trade, then more explicit attention to those aspects of social life marginalized as "just sex" has the potential to reconfigure conventional analysis along more productive lines.[…]

What does the most recent surge of research on sexuality mean for business-as-usual in the social sciences? What does queer scholarship have to say to taken-for-granted ways of understanding bodies, relationships, and lives? What kind of scholarship can truly come to grips with the inequalities of our time? What will it take to bring research on sexuality out of the universities and into the streets or onto the airwaves? Are there contiguities between the new research and the old? The answers to these questions depend upon making a distinction between investigating sexuality *per se* and investigating the ways in which sexuality can become embedded in any and every topic constituted as an object for research. It's one thing to study sexuality as an entity unto itself; it's quite another to study the infusion of sexuality into the very pursuit of knowledge.

[…] A person cannot "just" study sexuality, because sexuality is never separate from history, "class," "race," or a host of other social relations. […] Once s/he begins paying attention to sexuality, social issues never appear in quite the same light again.

If sexuality is already integral to many of the topics examined by social scientists, it is equally integral to the history of social science disciplines. I mean this not just in the obvious sense that researchers have devoted long hours to analyzing the timing of orgasms, the social construction of impotence, the sexual metaphors in descriptions of trade wars or military maneuvers that hope to "penetrate," and the contrasting ways in which societies handle "adultery." I also mean that the classic debates which molded social science into a distinctive set of disciplines relied, often as not, on illustrative examples drawn from the "realm" of sexuality.

Go back to foundational studies of cognition and you will find "marriage classes" used to explain "primitive classification." Scratch the surface of the concept of social organization and you will lay bare speculative debates in which some scholars hypothesized sexual jealousy where others imagined an evolutionary stage of promiscuity. Look a few steps past the figures customarily associated with sex, and you will find Durkheim, Mauss, and Weber consorting with the likes of Darwin and

Doctor Freud. Nor are such instances confined to the past. Consider, for one, that eminently contemporary and highly contentious debate on reflexivity in social science. As researchers ponder whether or not to use "I" in their work, they are, in effect, grappling with aspects of cultural categories (narcissism, confession, self-indulgence, kiss-and-tell) that have become parceled off, boxed up, and increasingly marketed under the rubric of sex.

Put this way, the study of sexuality starts to look like the bread and butter of the social sciences, rather than the sure-fire prescription for academic suicide as it was described to me during my student days. Yet it is important to understand precisely how sexuality came to be construed as a compact and isolated subtopic, a matter of specialized study for the few renegade scholars foolish enough to pay it any mind. Only once sexuality becomes cordoned off in the professional imagination from the examination of religion, diaspora, voting behavior, interpersonal dynamics, community organization, and a million other facets of social life does the study of sexuality become a professional bridge-jump. Only then can it be said that a move to position sexuality at the heart of the disciplines does not describe social science as usual, or at least social science as most people have been trained to know it.

For all the attention recently garnered by queer theory, institutions of higher learning continue to ghettoize the study of sexuality. Best to pack it safely away, isolate it in the corner of a discipline, give it very limited standing as a subfield, maybe organize a lesbian/gay studies department, but preferably just revise the curriculum to offer a token course or two. Best not to let sexuality wander too much farther afield, lest it come into contact with subjects near and dear to the hearts of "mainstream" scholars, not to mention a wider public.

It wasn't always this way. What processes have obscured the links between the efflorescence of work associated with queer studies and earlier scholarship? What is the price of that forgetting? What allows researchers to sound credible when they insist that sexuality has little bearing on the rest of social science inquiry? How did sexuality come to be formulated as a fringe topic that can get any scholar's license to presumed heterosexuality revoked? One place to look for clues is on the hallowed ground where empiricism meets ethnography.

What Do They Do? Hunting the (Homo)Sexual in Early Ethnography

In some parts of Western Australia, wrote R. H. Mathews in 1900, a circumcised man would be allotted an uncircumcised brother of the woman he would later marry. "The boy is used for purposes of masturbation and sodomy, and constantly accompanies the man" (125). Mathews described the arrangement in matter-of-fact terms and followed his comments with an account of the uses of heated sand to keep warm during winter months in the desert. Thirty years later, in "Women and Their Life in Central Australia," G. Róheim progressed directly from a list of the foodstuffs gathered by women (tubers, fruit, lizards, birds' eggs, mice) to a description of a dance in which men sounded a musical instrument called an *ulpura*. "The woman who hears it follows [the player] when he goes hunting, and finally she elopes with him." On the same occasion, "the first lover of a woman will go up to the husband and ask him to give her back for one night, and he is expected to grant this wish" (1933: 208–209).

Like the chronicles from the voyages of exploration on which they were modeled, many early ethnographies adopted a flora-and-fauna approach to the study of sexuality (cf. Kuklick 1997). Details of social life that European and North American observers considered "sexual" provided nothing more and nothing less than additional data. In many accounts that took the form of a report back from the field, "sexual acts" did not seem to call for specialized examination, much less a disciplinary subfield. They merely constituted phenomena to be documented and integrated into monographs that compiled information on everything from edible plants to myths, from body painting to funerary practices.

Kava drinking, circumcision, "a special form of *nambas* or penis wrapper," hereditary chieftainship, and "a remarkable organization of male homosexuality" share a paragraph in A. Bernard Deacon's 1934 monograph, *Malekula* (14). Mutual masturbation and the removal of one or two upper front teeth (for aesthetic reasons) share a page in Melville Herskovits's *Dahomey* (1938: 289). In Papua New Guinea, young men were said to eat limes to prevent pregnancy from male-male intercourse during initiation ceremonies (F. E. Williams 1936: 200–201). And in the lowlands of northern Colombia, according to Julian Steward and Louis Faron, both rich men and chiefs practiced polygyny. After the authors duly noted the presence of female prostitutes and "a special class of male inverts who went from village to village selling their sexual services" among the Calamari, they moved on with the same deliberation to examine war patterns, cannibalism, and something called a "priest-temple-idol complex" (1959: 223).

Some observers offered thicker descriptions. Instead of cataloging "inverts" and acts, they explained how adults negotiated rights to children in cases of "adultery" or how children ignored adults when they wanted to engage in "sex play" (e.g., Evans-Pritchard 1951: 91; Berndt and Berndt 1951: 86–87). John Shortt (1873: 402) devoted an entire article to "the true Kojahs, or Eunuchs" left in charge of the women's quarters of "Mussulman nobles" in southern India. His essay contributed less to the establishment of sexuality as a subfield than to the ethnographic project that called upon social science to verify the existence of diverse "peoples" in order to place them firmly within the annals of discovery.

Nor was this documentary imperative some antiquated holdover from the turn of the century. In her study of Nyakyusa age-villages in Africa, Monica Wilson took the time to point out that the word for sex play between girls, *ubugalagala*, doubled as a word for the "wicked cleverness" of witches (1963: 94). Her reason for including the information in this context? The linguistic resonance had significance for other topics of interest to Wilson, including witchcraft and "mystical interdependence." Raymond Kelly followed a similar logic in his study of witchcraft by alluding to the Etoro belief that "heterosexual intercourse in a garden will cause the crops to wither and die" (1976: 45). When June Nash wrote up her research on tin miners in Bolivia, she included a description of Carnival that encompassed not only music, costume, and cosmology, but also the "perverse dance combinations where whites play blacks, men play women, and all the contradictions of their lot in life are transformed into the opposite and transcended" (1979: 318). Whatever one might think of the appeal to transcendence, crossdressing features in the account in such a way that it is simultaneously noted and brought to bear on a more extensive discussion of racial categories and oppression.

Of course, what these researchers busied themselves documenting (in a manner integral to the reports on kava drinking and taro cultivation) were phenomena they *perceived* to be sexual. The categories that framed their descriptions – perversion, inversion, adultery, norm, marriage, homosexuality, transvestism – came straight out of Euroamerica. Social scientists imported classificatory schemes that marked some things as erotic (and others as not) along with their rucksacks, typewriters, and steamer trunks. No wonder that ethnographies often made non-sense to the very people they were supposed to describe.

And a complex sort of nonsense it was, given the colonial situation that prevailed in most of the locations under study. Nationalist movements frequently stressed the "normality" of local practices in response to European characterizations of colonial subjects as sexually uncontrollable and perverse. In the context of domination, people could not always afford to undo the sexualizing logic of the colonial powers.

Anticolonialist movements ended up building certain arguments for home rule on the backs of European categories and, some would say, local women. Dress modestly. Clothe yourself to swim. No "obscene" dances. No drums. No daring backless blouses. Hands off the colonial equation of nudity with immorality and lust. Scrutinize your wives' and daughters' every gesture for "unbecoming" implications in order to demonstrate yourself fit to govern.

This was a rhetorical strategy that adopted the language of sexuality to speak propriety and decorum to power. Its consequences and its ironies are still in the process of being unraveled.[2]

So it is not quite correct to say that the notetakers and the about-to-be-annotated subscribed to independent, much less mutually incomprehensible, modes of "thinking sex" and thinking relationship.[3] Rather, they participated in the *inter*dependent exchanges of groups locked in struggle, in which sexualization offered both a rhetorical chip and a weapon. There is plenty that Samoans of Margaret Mead's time could have said (and did) about a book index in which "*Fa'atama* (tomboy)" succeeded "Elopement"; "*Lavalava* (loincloth)" found itself sandwiched between "Love affairs" and "Incest"; while an entry for "Sex" subdivided into "Sex (erogenous zones)," "Sex (experimentation)," "Sex (friendship)," "Sex (techniques)," "Sex (adventure)," and "Sex (American girl)."[4] But not without a political cost.

In the earliest days of ethnography, social scientists tended to conceive of sexuality as a self-evident, perhaps intriguing, perhaps disgusting, possibly trivial, but nevertheless unified object for inquiry.[5] This was no category with meanings shaped by class warfare and colonial struggle, but a force both primal and given. That Thing Called Sex might be forever molded and sculpted by social forces, leading to tremendous variety in the ways that people around the world "do it." But there "it" was, awaiting report or observation, firmly grounded in a biological substrate of hormones and drives. Only with the newer scholarship that followed in the wake of publications such as Erving Goffman's *Stigma* would researchers begin to see needs, identities, desires, and repulsions as themselves socially constructed, their power explicable only with reference to something larger than the individual and biology. After that, the mind became a contender for the most erogenous zone (Ross and Rapp 1983).

Meanwhile, cultural relativism had gained ground. In the absence of any serious analysis of history or colonialism, the tremendous variety in erotic practices appeared to be the product of localized preferences and localized "traditions." If Ojibwa etiquette demanded cross-cousin joking that could edge over into flirtation (Landes 1937) and young men undergoing initiation in parts of New Guinea had to "practise sodomy in order to become tall and strong" (Landtman 1927: 237), well, that seemed to represent no more and no less a range than could be found in matters of religion or diet.

Although many ethnographies professed not to judge what they described, a certain amount of evaluation was inevitably conveyed in the description. "Adultery" is hardly a nonjudgmental term and "invert" sounds like something your kid would hate to be called on the playground. "Homosexual" implied a life-long identification, yet researchers applied the word to rituals that lasted only months, years, or days. But even those like Malinowski who approached the topic of sexuality with a certain distaste argued strongly for its place within social science: "Man is an animal, and, as such, at times unclean, and the honest anthropologist has to face this fact" (1927: 6).

Of course, not all researchers approached the phenomena they dubbed "sexual" with equal aplomb. In some instances, sex appears as a "present absence" in ethnography. An investigator notes the "sexual" character of something observed and then either affirms his or her reluctance to discuss it, or simply moves on without comment. In his classic essay, "Religion as a Cultural System," for example, Clifford Geertz described a Rangda-Barong performance in Bali, in which the "witch" Rangda (taken by some as an incarnation of the Hindu goddess Durga) "evokes fear (as well as hatred, disgust, cruelty, horror, and, though I have not been able to treat the sexual aspects of the performance here, lust)" (1973: 118). At a later date, perhaps?

Over the years, entire articles on sexuality and even the occasional book did emerge within the ethnographic literature. Malinowski's *Sex and Repression in Savage Society* is among the best known, but there were also articles by Edward Westermarck on "Homosexual Love" (1906), Ruth Benedict on "Sex in Primitive Society" (1939), Ruth Landes on "A Cult Matriarchate and Male

Homosexuality" (1940), Ian Hogbin on "The Sexual Life of the Natives of Wogeo, New Guinea" (1946), Ronald Berndt and Catherine Berndt on "Sexual Behavior in Western Arnhem Land" (1951), Robert Suggs on "Marquesan Sexual Behavior" (1966), Alice Kehoe on "The Function of Ceremonial Sexual Intercourse Among the Northern Plains Indians" (1970), and Evans-Pritchard on "Sexual Inversion Among the Azande" (1970), to name only a few. A veritable cottage industry arose on Two-Spirits (formerly called by the pejorative *berdache*), a category applied across American Indian groups to describe people considered at once sacred, cross-gendered or multiply gendered, and therefore inadequately described by terms such as "homosexual" or "bisexual" (see Lang 1996: 92).

This deliberately eclectic collection of sources suggests that, when it comes to establishing a lineage for the study of sexuality, social scientists are not dealing with the odd article out. There are plenty more ethnographies where these came from, without even extending the search to anthropology's sister-disciplines of psychology and sociology. Yet the references to sexuality in early ethnographies are important for more than their ability to dispute the joanna-come-lately charges aimed at queer studies. The colonial "adventure" that informed these ethnographies has had a lasting impact on the way that researchers (and the public) approach the study of sexuality (Stoler 1995). So has the on-again, off-again alliance of social science with "hard" science. In the popular imagination, the social sciences have become associated with a reductive sort of empiricism that contemporary research on sexuality has yet to shake. Nowhere is this more evident than in the question that runs from the latest sex survey right back through early ethnographic accounts: What *do* they do?

"What *do* they do?" There is only so much to be gleaned from the information that Marquesan children live in fear of being reprimanded for masturbation, but that "the error appears to lie in being so inept as to be caught at any of these activities ... rather than in the activity itself" (Suggs 1966: 46). First of all, this isolated observation offers no context. Are we talking pre- or post-missionary? Who

asks and who answers, under what sorts of conditions? Whose category, this "masturbation"? How is the presentation of this decontextualized observation linked to a larger intellectual/political project? Yes, it's data, but never simply data. Data is selected and collected, used and abused by researchers who are always in some sense a product of their times.

Such a litany may approach methodological truism at this late date, but like good sex, it bears repeating. The point is not just that social science has more to contribute to the study of sexuality than forays into social life that bring back data in bits and relatively undigested pieces. The point is also that the long history of flora-and-fauna accounts of sexuality – a history coextensive with ethnography itself – has fostered a mistaken impression of social science research on sexuality as an overwhelmingly empirical project. Empirical it has been and must be, but not without an edge that is simultaneously moral, theoretical, political, and analytical.

To the extent that early ethnography has helped sustain a "just the facts, ma'am" approach to social science research on sexuality, ethnography's relevance exceeds the anthropological. Caricatures of social science as a data-spewing science were only reinforced when attention shifted from "Them" to "Us," from exotics abroad to misfits at home, from analyses that focused on difference to analyses that heralded deviance.[6] From the moment that "deviance" emerged as a topic for scholarship and a foil for "the norm," the topic was sexualized. College courses on deviance were much more likely to cover cross-dressing than political rebellion or the odd girl out who hated apple pie, refused to salute the flag, and resisted the postwar marketing imperative to consume. In the interim, Kinsey had arrived on the scene to tabulate interviews on sexuality into percentages: 37 (not 35, not 38) percent of American men had experienced homosexual sex to orgasm. Masters and Johnson showed up with electric leads to hook up volunteers to machines that monitored, measured, and ultimately condensed a host of bodily functions (heart rate, sweat) into a "human sexual response cycle" (J. Jones 1997; Robinson 1989).

Sexology's mid-century aspiration to scientific precision gelled well enough with the approach of turn-of-the-century expeditions that had taken the world as their lab. But a renewed emphasis on data entailed a diminished recognition for the importance of the analytic frameworks that give form to data itself. Cultural relativism, to take just one such framework, has had a tremendous impact on how people think about "nature," "sexuality," and human possibility.

For all their utility and appeal, then, flora-and-fauna approaches contributed mightily to the fantasy of the social scientist as documentarian, a purveyor of distilled data ready to be taken up into other people's theories and analyses. What is at stake when so much attention accrues to social science as a source of "facts," and so little to data's uses, derivation, or production? Why, when it comes to social science's *theoretical* contributions to the study of sexuality, do so many still feel compelled to avert their eyes?

Before I move to examine that question in greater depth, I want to consider another way in which social scientists have been writing about sexuality all along. The grab bag of erotic practices integrated into flora-and-fauna accounts is the least of what's lost when contemporary research on sexuality proceeds without an understanding of its heritage. In the early years of social science, researchers staked out a territory for fledgling disciplines based upon case studies, illustrations, and debates that prominently featured matters of sexuality. So it is not merely that there is a theoretical component to research on sexuality in the social sciences. There is also a sexual component to the most basic social science theory. Without it, there wouldn't be a social science. Or more precisely, there wouldn't be *this* social science.

How the Social Scientist Got Her Spots

Think about some of the founding concepts and debates in social science, the kind any aspiring researcher spends hours committing to memory in graduate school. Social organization. Families and kinship. Norms and roles. The incest taboo. Nature versus culture. Diffusion versus independent invention. Interpretations of myth. Reciprocity and the gift. Work. Ritual. Solidarity. Cognitive competence. Inheritance and resource transfers. Primitive promiscuity. Evolution. The division of labor. Gender differences. Social stratification. International relations. The Protestant ethic. Characteristics that distinguish homo sapiens from the rest of the animals. Society. Instinct. Culture. Change. Some (the incest taboo, primitive promiscuity) appear more explicitly sexual than others (the exchange of gifts). But each and every one of these pivotal concepts in the history of social science drafted sexuality into the service of some "larger" debate.

The move usually happened in one of two ways. In the more pedestrian instance, an aspect of the erotic occupied center stage not as an isolated datum point, but as evidence advanced to make an argument. To take just one example, in that founding document of social science, *The Protestant Ethic and the Spirit of Capitalism*, Max Weber groups "temptations of the flesh" with "idleness" in a discussion of Puritan reservations about the pursuit of wealth (1958: 157). Here the material related to sexuality is offered almost as an aside, a small matter duly noted, but one that buttresses the author's point. Something similar occurs when E. E. Evans-Pritchard includes "virility medicine" in a more extensive catalog of Azande medicines, or explains the resort to "good magic" by describing how a man might employ magic to determine who was sleeping with his wife. Readers learn that good magic can be used not only to find out "who has committed adultery," but also who has "stolen his spears or killed his kinsman" (1976: 183, 189). [...] The activity marked as sexual appears alongside nonsexual activities, but Evans-Pritchard offers it up as more than description or detail, because he uses the observation about "adultery" to support a particular analysis of witchcraft.

[...]

The second type of liaison between sex and analysis in social science was by far the more spectacular, and of more lasting consequence. In this case, authors treated sexual relations as a paradigmatic instance that offered either the best illustration of a concept or the best means of adjudicating an argument. "Puberty" (initiation) rites, with their implicit reference to sexual maturation, almost came to define the general category of ritual in both the popular and scholarly imagination.[7] Researchers interested in cognition did not just ask people to narrate inkblots, explain their reasoning, and fit odd shapes into boxes. They also gravitated toward a highly sexualized form of the $64,000 question: Was it possible that Those Savages understood the mechanics of human conception? (Show that you can give a biological accounting for fatherhood and you too can be granted mental acuity, accompanied by a fair-to-middling post on the evolutionary ladder.)[8] Likewise, when social scientists began to develop the concept of a norm, it was heavily indebted to contrasts drawn with the practices of "Others" imagined to fall outside the norm's parameters. These Others, pictured as deviant or exotic or both, were supposed to be recognizable in part by sexual excess (cf. Bleys 1995).

In each case, the analytic turn toward sexuality sought out material that would prove exemplary rather than interesting of its own accord. When Marcel Mauss developed his analysis of gift-giving as a device that created social solidarities, he took from Malinowski's work on the Trobriand Islands the notion that relations between husband and wife constituted the "pure" gift. "One of the most important acts noted by the author," declared Mauss, "and one which throws a strong light on sexual relationships, is the *mapula*, the sequence of payments by a husband to his wife as a kind of salary for sexual services" (1967: 71).[9] When Mauss teamed up with Emile Durkheim (1963) to study so-called primitive classification, "marriage classes" (moieties) provided a key component of their analysis. They contended that the division of some societies into two camps (the eligible and the off-limits) had provided researchers with a way of understanding different kinds of logic and basic modalities of human thought. In most of the societies they examined, what

they referred to as "marriage" had its erotic dimensions, although sex did not necessarily feature as the centerpiece that it is often assumed to be in a society that claims "a good sex life" as a birthright.

Shadowing these discussions are philosophical treatises about human nature and fantasies about human beings in a primeval state. When it came to inquiry into what, if anything, humans universally share, the linchpin of debate often as not turned out to involve sexuality. One still hotly contested concept, the incest taboo, became a stepping-stone to the theorization of social relations. Does *everyone* (at least officially) find it repugnant to sleep with their children and their parents? What about siblings? Half-siblings? What to make of the coexistence of groups that forbid cousin marriage and groups that enjoin it (see Wolf 1995)? At stake for many writers was not an understanding of eroticism *per se*. More to the point were questions about the degree to which biology dictates the ordering of human relationships. The move to push back the claims for biology in turn created room for new analytic concepts such as "society" and "culture."

The culture concept has accrued a range of meanings over the years, including "high" art, custom, collective invention, the constructedness of practically everything, and the possibility of multiple cultures. In a global economy where very little seems discretely bounded, the notion of culture has undergone sustained critique, but at the time that it first circulated widely within the social sciences, scholars explained culture in part by opposing it to "instinct." Seemingly inevitably, the path to instinct led through sex. Instinct paired birds with birds, bees with bees, and humans with other humans, but only humans went a step beyond instinct to give rules, regulations, and irate relatives a say in how they mated. Or so said the wisdom of the day.[10]

The work of Sigmund Freud, who wrote extensively on the topic of instinct, was also tremendously influential in moving sexuality to a position of prominence within social science. Before literary critics struck up their latter-day flirtation with psychoanalysis, psychologists and anthropologists tried their hand at the game. But Freud was not some Ur-source who accomplished this feat single-handedly. He himself was in the habit of citing ethnography to make his points, not only in the celebrated *Totem and Taboo* (1918), but also in essays such as "The Sexual Aberrations" (1975). And writing well before Freud were authors who pitched their arguments on the terrain of sexuality without becoming known as scholars of sex. Among them were Lewis Henry Morgan, Frederick Engels, Henry Maine, John McLennan, Emile Durkheim, and Charles Darwin.

Back in the emphatically pre-Freudian days of the nineteenth century, scholars endlessly debated the theory that societies progress through a number of developmental stages, the first being "primitive promiscuity." In his 1865 study, *Primitive Marriage*, McLennan speculated that men in the earliest societies had originally mated indiscriminately with women of the group. Under such conditions, no one could trace biological fatherhood with any hope of certainty. Darwin vociferously disagreed, contending that "sexual jealousy was a fundamental emotion, and that it must have contributed to the early establishment of orderly mating arrangements amongst men" (Kuper 1988: 40). Engels picked up where McLennan left off, arguing that primitive promiscuity was obviously unsuitable for a system of private property. How would men know who stood to inherit? Something must have succeeded "the horde" once large-scale agriculture made the accumulation of surpluses possible. Engels, who drew heavily upon Lewis Henry Morgan's research on Iroquois Indians, proposed that this something was "the family." The family as Engels envisioned it restricted access to women in a way that allowed for the institutionalization of private property and control over its now regularized transmission.

What was at issue in the debate about primitive promiscuity? Not so much the "mating practices" of a bygone era, but an understanding of power relations: who owns, who inherits, who controls. The same debate provided an opportunity to elaborate theories of development and social evolution. Few, if any, of the authors who participated in the debate on primitive promiscuity set out to

write about sexuality. Typically they came at sexuality from another angle, beginning with ostensibly asexual topics for investigation. How do you explain the logic for property transfers? The division of labor? Social organization? Changing modes of production? The rise of the state? They ended up writing page after page about marriage alliances, sexual jealousy, promiscuity, and the like.

In these speculative accounts, the way that a group handles eroticism becomes a marker of social (dis)organization and evolutionary advance. Joseph Marie Degérando, writing during the French Enlightenment, reflected on the state of "savage" society by asking, among other things, if "savages" focused love on one person alone and whether "such a degree of brutalization" existed among them that "the women ... go [naked] in front of men without blushing" (Stocking 1968: 25). How different were his concerns from those raised by Darwin, Engels, Maine, and McLennan more than half a century later? Given that many turn-of-the-century writers on evolution attributed darker skin to "savages" and "barbarians" as a matter of course (Stocking 1968: 132), the hypersexualization that was integral to the invention of the primitive would reappear in some of the most patently offensive stereotypes associated with the emerging concept of "race."

Out-and-out racism characterized the decades-long search for a "missing link." And where did social scientists go to seek this putative bridge between human and ape? To sexual relations generally and Africa specifically. In the many spurious accounts of African women who mated with orangutans or chimpanzees, heterosexual intercourse symbolized a continuity between humans and animals, in sharp contrast to tool use and the acquisition of language, which figured as tropes for a reassuring division of "man" from beast. When Europeans caged and exhibited a Khoi woman as "The Hottentot Venus," her lasciviousness was assumed, while the size of her genitalia became a matter for public comment and censure (Comaroff and Comaroff 1991: 104, 123; Gilman 1985).[11]

The eroticization of the search for a missing link cannot be understood apart from the concomitant search for a rationale for domination. As many have pointed out, social science lends itself admirably to the uses of intervention.[12] Terms such as "primitive promiscuity" may have been speculative, but they were not without worldly effect. Maine's *Ancient Society*, which followed Darwin's position on "sexual jealousy" in the primitive promiscuity debates, can also be read as a pseudo-historical polemic against Indian independence (cf. Kuper 1988: 18–20). So long as colonial subjects lived lives of sexual immorality, the product of a rudimentary ("patriarchal") stage of social evolution, who were they to take up agitation in the name of Home Rule?

After Captain Cook returned from his first voyages, European romantics tethered dreams of free love to the South Sea islands (Stocking 1992: 307). Their less romantic peers gazed into the same mirror and walked away aghast at the image of a sexuality so "out of control" it seemed to beg for European "civilization" to set it to rights. Of course, bare skin that intimated lust to colonial eyes could signify very differently to people who thought the colonizers fools for fainting away in the monsoon heat in their button-downs.

These fevered fantasies of the colonial imagination came down hard on people under even nominal European or American control. Clothes, music, art, and anything else judged "obscene" by imported standards frequently became hybridized, displaced, or forced underground. Rampant eroticization also had a boomerang effect, both upon social science and upon the societies that proposed to rule. International relations emerged as a subfield from a shuffle of papers that attributed impotence, effeminacy, and enervation to countries, if not entire climates. Sociological studies of immigrant communities in the United States helped establish government standards for housing. When the state stepped in to assume custody of children in cases of neglect, judgments about "overcrowding" (based upon whose standard, what manner of living?) reflected fears that kids might see adults "doing it," not just safety issues regarding tenements in disrepair.

Social science also had a hand in producing the relief that some readers feel when they learn that neither a proclivity for nipples nor an 8.5-centimeter penis falls outside the (social-science-produced) "norm" (see Masters and Johnson 1966: 191). Some bad psychology and even worse incarceration programs have been developed in search of "cures" for departures from that norm. And it's a sure bet that adolescents who tease their friends about a sexual repertoire limited to "the missionary position" seldom have in mind the centuries of violence and religious/political repression interred in that phrase. Nor need they be conscious of the debt that the aspiration to master an elaborate array of sexual techniques owes to colonialist escapades.[13]

Even methodological debates could turn on issues of sexuality. In anthropology, the Mead/Freeman controversy was fought out (in part) over the issue of forcible rape. Freeman attacked Mead's reputation with the claim that forcible rape had, indeed, taken place on Samoa during the years when Mead heralded its virtual absence (see Stocking 1992: 332). Did forcible rape occur on Samoa or not? Was it common? […] In this case, sex offered a site for testing out the reliability of a method and the limits of professional credibility.

Researchers who presumed "sexual acts" to be abstractable and so in principle available for scholarly inspection ran into problems when they tried to employ the methodological staples of the social science arsenal. If they used surveys, they found that sexuality again offered a paradigmatic case, this time regarding a methodological issue called the problem of self-report. How could social scientists gauge the veracity of retrospective testimony about something like sex without subjecting it to first-hand investigation (Lewontin 1995)? That left the methodological techniques of observation and, yes, participation.[14] What means were justified to gain knowledge of sexuality? What ethics should prevail? The turn to examine sexuality as a discrete object for inquiry threatened to lay bare the voyeurism (not to mention the romanticism) embedded more generally in the documentary project.

[…] From the very beginning, assumptions about sexuality infused social science concepts such as normality, evolution, progress, organization, development, and change.

Likewise, judgments about sexuality remain deeply embedded in the history of scholarly explanations for who acquires power, who deserves it, and who gets to keep it. The same can be said for a multitude of theories about cognition, reciprocity, gender, race, and many other stock concepts in social science. These are not just abstractions; they are abstractions with a past. Over years of application, they have proven as concrete in their effects as they have proven convenient in the hands of those who seek to justify domination. [...]

There are many ways to tell a tale, and the social scientist is not the only animal in the forest. I have chosen for the moment to make the social scientist central to an intellectual narrative that highlights sexuality. In this telling, researchers engaged in the study of everything from ritual to social change have cut their eye-teeth on documents that locate eroticism at the heart of the darkness that becomes a discipline. Many a researcher has gone on to save her professional hide by penning a manuscript dotted with arguments that appeal to "sexuality" to make a case. And that, best beloved colleagues, is how the social scientist got his spots.

Data on the Half-Shell

Social science researchers who come into this inheritance find themselves in a real quandary. On the one hand, they know they bring concerns and convictions to their projects, which means that their data is always produced, usually analyzed, and frequently theorized, just-so. Even the concepts they use to frame questions can carry an erotic charge. On the other hand, they go to work in a world that treats social scientists as the bringers of data. In this view, data figures as pure content, waiting for collection like cans on the street or driftwood on the beach. Forget the theory and analytics. With researchers cast as data-bearers, the contribution of social science to an understanding of sexuality diminishes in the mind's eye to the documentation of "acts" and "beliefs," little more.

Malinowski, a leading exponent of getting it "right" when it comes to the fauna, can be thought of as a data collector, or he can be remembered as someone who made sexuality into the terrain of an early foray into interdisciplinarity. In *Sex and Repression in Savage Society*, Malinowski held up Freudian models for cross-cultural inspection, pausing along the way to reflect about the implications of his analysis for class relations in Europe. (How does the mother's brother, ever-important in the Trobriand Islands, fit into the Oedipal triangle? The answer: He doesn't, because psychoanalytic theory can't do justice to his relationship with his sister's son. The conclusion? Time for psychoanalysis to moderate some of its universalist pretensions.) Malinowski's book does much more than report back on research findings. The point is to read Malinowski for *how* he studies as well as *what* he studies. But that sort of reading would be incompatible with the marginalization of the study of sexuality taking place within the social sciences today, a marginalization that casts "sexuality studies" as a subfield and a "strictly empirical" project, with little bearing on theory or other aspects of social life.

Under these conditions, when something becomes marked as sexual, it looms large. So large, in effect, that it can overpower the rest of a writer's points. Margaret Mead "was amazed that the students of a professor at a Tennessee teachers' college should have thought that her book *Coming of Age in Samoa* was 'mainly about sex education and sex freedom,' when 'out of 297 pages there are exactly sixty-eight which deal with sex'" (Stocking 1992: 318). Even in passages that directly addressed sexuality, Mead analyzed and theorized, oftentimes in the description. Having noted that Tchambuli women engaged in sex play with the female masks worn by male dancers, she remarked upon "the double entendre of the situation, the spectacle of women courting males disguised as females" (Mead 1963: 256). In this instance Mead's comments have a contemporary, almost cultural studies, ring. Passing, reversals, and mimesis are obvious components of the story, but they can scarcely be discerned in the erotic haze that descended upon her work.

To say that *Coming of Age in Samoa* is a book about sexuality is like saying that Evans-Pritchard's *The Nuer* is a book about cattle. Both statements have a certain logic, but evaluation can't stop there. *The Nuer* may be a book about cattle, but it sets up the feeding and decoration and exchange of cattle as a device for understanding lineage and alliance. Likewise with Mead. Her observations about sexuality provide a point of entree to other issues about which she cared deeply, such as childhood development and the limits of human malleability. To imagine otherwise is to employ a familiar combination of seeing and refusing to recognize, like parents who know that their son has a boyfriend but somehow refuse to find out.[15]

A cursory review of the ways that literary critics, historians, and cultural studies scholars have taken up social science research into their own accounts reveals the latter principle in action. Passages on initiation ceremonies and seconds-to-orgasm tend to be cited uncritically, presented as truths bereft of politics or theory, in a way that literary theory strongly counsels against. Nor are social scientists themselves immune to the ironies and seductions of "discovery." "You'll never guess how they do it in New Guinea!" "You'll never believe what this survey tells us about the difference between what Americans say they do and what they actually do when they close the bedroom door!" Got the facts, ma'am. Just the facts.[16]

Flora-and-fauna accounts remain a useful but limited form of investigation, dangerous to the degree that they brook no accounting. When social science goes under to the uses of documentation, it never has to acknowledge the desire for mastery bound up in the written word. It never has to call attention to the selection or interpretation of what it "finds." It can overlook the multiple ways in which "data-bearers" carry with them the histories of disciplines. It can indulge in the convenience of forgetting that the notion of (pure) data works behind the scenes to make someone's perceptions, someone else's pet theory, more palatable. The utopian fantasy of ordering your data raw depends upon the illusion that the world is your oyster.

To the degree that social science lags behind the humanities in contemporary research on sexuality, something more must be involved than mere prudishness or a recalcitrance that inexplicably afflicts social scientists more frequently than their counterparts in literature and history. Within academic divisions of labor, the notion of the social scientist as a collector of other people's data has demoted social science to a kind of unskilled labor in the fields of sexuality studies. (Honestly, Paulo, how much skill can it take to go out and observe?) Yet the history of social science disciplines testifies not so much that sexuality is good to collect, but that sexuality is good to think. For centuries scholars have used what passes for "the erotic" to work their way out of intellectual dead-ends and back into vigorous debate. To highlight the empirical here, at the expense of the analytic, places social scientists in an untenable position, because in their research the two are already one. In the food for thought served up by any scholar, data is already cooked, and in the hands of some, about to become highly spiced.

How did it happen that, by the late twentieth century, sexuality had become associated with a flora-and-fauna style of analysis, then isolated and disparaged as a fringe topic? What gives staying power to the mistaken belief that social science research on sexuality speaks for itself without offering theory or interpretation? The issues here are complex. Certainly the erasure of the intellectual history described in these pages, along with the assimilation of that history into ostensibly "asexual" topics for study, has not helped. Responsibility might also be laid at the door of an impoverished conception of the science in social science, in which knowledge appears as certitude, as fact. The kind of science most often (mis)attributed to research on gay friendship networks or fidelity in marriage is one in which the world stops turning for the observer-explorer. This is hardly the science of black holes, bubble universes, and mutable genes. But even these explanations beg the question of why an outdated conception of social science should regulate discussions of sexuality more than other areas of investigation.

There may be another culprit: an unholy alliance between the deskilling of social scientists in the popular imagination and the packaging of eroticism into a separate and distinct sphere. Following Foucault, Steven Seidman (1991) has argued that the imaginative segregation of sexuality from other aspects of social life is a relatively recent historical development that preceded the emergence of the LGBT movement. But the erotic sphere, once established, came to signify a domain of pleasure, frivolity, and fluff, a domain ostensibly peripheral to social life and therefore hardly a matter for serious investigation. No easy route to tenure here!

These historical developments are critical to understanding how sexuality, once ensconced in debate at the disciplinary center, became sidelined with respect to the simmering controversies and burning issues of the present day. Under such conditions, "sexuality studies" and "lesbian/gay studies" – like the ethnic studies programs that these would-be fields took as their model – tended to assume the shape of a bounded area of scholarship. Coincidentally (or not), the emergence of lesbian/gay studies as a discrete field of study corresponded with a move away from discrete, canonical academic subfields such as political sociology or economic anthropology. Once bounded, the study of sexuality was bound to resemble an intellectual backwater in a society increasingly preoccupied with themes of displacement, border-crossing, and change.

While many social scientists today are busy talking diaspora, race, territoriality, civil society, secularism, transnationalism, capitalist restructuring, and global relations, when it comes to sexuality people want to know what "the X" *really* do in the privacy of the shack, the hut, or the boudoir. This is the language of ethnonostalgia, a language of false certitude and mystified connection.[17] It is part of the mechanism by which flora-and-fauna studies pretend to be the whole of what social science can contribute to an understanding of sexuality, as well as the mechanism by which the sexuality embedded in workaday social science concepts is minimized or disappeared. Easy then to ghettoize the study of sexuality, making it fit for queers or for no study at all. How far is this scholarly marketing practice, really, from

the retailing of a video such as *Sacred Sex*, which promises to instruct the buyer, in return for her contribution to public television, in "Tantric techniques" that will "prolong lovemaking pleasure"?[18] Both are exoticizing, orientalizing, portable, importable, eminently collectible, and oh so convenient on the replay.
[...]

NOTES

Acknowledgments: Rosemary Coombe and Geeta Patel generously agreed to read and comment upon an early draft of this introduction. [...]

1   For the articles in *Glamour* and *Redbook*, see Cunningham (1992) and Salter (1992), respectively. Despite these developments, research funding and job opportunities remained limited for scholars who named "sexuality" as their topic. Sociologists and anthropologists who have called for the social sciences to "open up" to the study of sexuality are well aware of the obstacles, both inside and outside academic institutions, that continue to block such research (see Lewin and Leap 1996; Namaste 1994; Newton 1993c). Relatively few social scientists, such as Rosalind Morris (1995), have attempted to bridge the disciplinary divide by acknowledging the impact of humanities scholarship (e.g., performance theory) on the study of sex and gender within the social sciences.

2   See Basu (1993); Bleys (1995); Chow (1995); J. Kelly (1991); Nandy (1983); Patel (1997b); Sarkar (1994); Sinha (1995).

3   The phrase "thinking sex" derives from Gayle Rubin's (1984) classic article by the same name.

4   Entries appear in the index for Mead's *Coming of Age in Samoa* (1961).

5   Gilbert Herdt (1991a, 1991b) refers to this phenomenon as the conceptualization of sexuality as an "it-entity."

6   Of course, one could argue that the bulk of social science research has always referred back to a Euro-American "Us." In this sense, the most culturally relative account of erotic practices "over there" becomes an implicit comparison with and commentary upon the situation "back here" (see Gupta and Ferguson 1997). Ruth Benedict, for example, famously observed that Zuni could effectively

accomplish "divorce" by setting a husband's belongings "on the doorsill" (see Stocking 1992: 299, who notes Benedict's emphasis on "the ease of sexuality" that prevailed in matrilineal pueblos). Widespread quotation of this particular observation by Benedict can be attributed, at least in part, to the fact that she wrote during an era in which divorce remained notoriously difficult to obtain under the jurisdiction of United States courts. By way of contrast, David Damrosch's (1995) reading of Lévi-Strauss's *Tristes Tropiques* notes the gap between Lévi-Strauss's positive description of Nambikwara male-male sex and the pejorative language applied later in the book to the gay male residents of Fire Island's Cherry Grove. In Cherry Grove, wrote Lévi-Strauss, "sterile couples can be seen returning to their chalets pushing prams (the only vehicles suitable for the narrow paths) containing little but weekend bottles of milk that no baby will consume" (quoted in Damrosch 1995: 9).

7   In *The Rites of Passage*, Arnold van Gennep categorized "puberty rites" as rites of separation "whose sexual nature is not to be denied and which are said to make the individual a man or a woman, or fit to be one.... they are followed by rites of incorporation into the world of sexuality and, in all societies and all social groups, into a group confined to persons of one sex or the other" (1960: 67).

8   See Delaney (1991). Like Lévy-Bruhl (1923: 438–439), Malinowski (1927: 19 *passim*) found himself preoccupied with the question of whether "savages" understood the details of conception. He found it "extraordinary" (given his belief in an ordered evolutionary hierarchy) that Melanesians should share the Australian aborigines' reputed ignorance of "the natural connection between intercourse and birth." Malinowski's own ignorance, willful or otherwise, of the complexities of colonial relations comes through in his choice of anecdotes to illustrate his argument. In one, a young Papuan who has been away for two years becomes angry when a white man intimates that the recent birth of a child to the Papuan's wife demonstrates her infidelity (recounted in Stocking 1992: 255). The young man's response speaks as much or more to the economy of race and indentured labor in which he found himself than it does to any timeless "cultural" unfamiliarity with the facts of conception.

The plantation system placed numerous strictures on sexuality; moreover, a situation in which a representative of the colonial powers made such an innuendo at the expense of the colonized could easily double as provocation.

9   Malinowski (1966: 40) later revised his analysis, noting that he had taken this particular exchange out of context by overlooking its place in a longer chain of transactions.

10 On changes in the meaning of "culture," see Sapir (1963) and Wagner (1981). Freud was not the only writer who opposed culture (or "civilization") to instinct. Malinowski, following his lead, included an entire section on "Instinct and Culture" in *Sex and Repression in Savage Society*, where he argued that "between the human parent and child under conditions of culture there must arise incestuous temptations which are not likely to occur in animal families governed by true instincts" (1927: 164). According to Jeffrey Weeks (1986: 47), "The Darwinian revolution in biology, which demonstrated that man was part of the animal world, encouraged the search for the animal in man, and found it in his sex." For a critique of the utility of the culture concept for the analysis of social relations in the late twentieth century, see Abu-Lughod (1991); Coombe (1997); Thomas (1991); and Wagner (1981).

11 European explorers kidnapped Native Americans, too, and brought them back to Europe for profit and display (Takaki 1993: 30–31).

12 See, for a start, Asad (1973), Behar (1996), Diamond (1992), and Wolf (1996) on the politics of alliances between the social sciences and goverments, power elites, reformers, employers, and social movements.

13 A debt evident across the decades, from Richard Burton's and F. F. Arbuthnot's (1995) early translation of the *Kama Sutra* to Foucault's (1978: 57) attribution of a static *ars erotica* to "China, Japan, India, Rome, [and] the Arabo-Moslem societies." Foucault postulated the *ars erotica* as a counterpoint to the West's *scientia sexualis*, both mechanisms for producing "the truth of sex."

14 For the accounts that sparked the initial controversy over the impact of erotic attraction

on a researcher's perceptions and agenda, see Malinowski (1989) and Rabinow (1977). For more recent discussion of the same topic, see Kulick and Willson (1995). On the question of whether sleeping with people "in the field" can constitute an ethical research practice, see Altork (1995); Bolton (1991, 1995); and Murray (1991, 1996).

15 Interesting, too, that Mead – unlike Malinowski or Evans-Pritchard, who also wrote explicitly about "sex" – is the one more likely to be remembered as a chronicler of sexuality. Although it is common to cite Mead's reputation as a "popularizer" for the disregard in which her work came to be held by colleagues, reading practices that eroticized her work by reading it back through her body may also have contributed to her loss of stature well before the onset of the Mead/Freeman controversy. [...]

16 The citational practices described here are so widespread that to hold up one or two examples for censure would unfairly single out their authors. Some historians have credited social scientists such as McIntosh (1981) or Gagnon and Simon (1973) with giving them a greater sense of the variability and constructedness of the erotic (see Bleys 1995: 6). For the most part, however, humanities scholarship on sexuality continues to turn to social science for ostensibly factual data and evidentiary support.

17 "Ethnonostalgia" is a term coined by Diane Nelson in association with Mario Loarca (1996: 289) to describe the lingering power of "the primitive-modern divide." Nelson studied Mayan activists in Guatemala who used their skills as computer hackers to further political organization. She credits ethnonostalgia for the chuckles elicited by the very notion of a "Maya hacker" from friends and colleagues back in the States.

18 The video in question appeared in the "WGBH Boston Video" catalogue for Summer 1997, p. 38.

BIBLIOGRAPHY

Abu-Lughod, Lila
1991 "Writing Against Culture." In *Recapturing Anthropology*, ed. Richard G. Fox, pp. 137–162. Santa Fe, N.M.: School of American Research.

Altork, Kate
1995 "Walking the Fire Line: The Erotic Dimension of the Fieldwork Experience." In *Taboo: Sex, Identity, and Erotic Subjectivity in Anthropological Fieldwork*, ed. Don Kulick and Margaret Willson, pp. 107–139. New York: Routledge.

Asad, Talal, ed
1973 *Anthropology and the Colonial Encounter*. New York: Humanities Press.

Basu, Amrita, ed
1993 "Women and Religious Nationalism in India." Special issue of the *Bulletin of Concerned Asian Scholars* 25 (4).

Behar, Ruth
1996 *The Vulnerable Observer: Anthropology That Breaks Your Heart*. Boston: Beacon Press.

Benedict, Ruth
1939 "Sex in Primitive Society." *American Journal of Orthopsychiatry* 9 (3): 570–573.

Berndt, Ronald M. and Catherine H. Berndt
1951 *Sexual Behavior in Western Arnhem Land*. New York: The Viking Fund.

Bleys, Rudi C.
1995 *The Geography of Perversion: Male-to-Male Sexual Behavior Outside the West and the Ethnographic Imagination, 1750–1918*. New York: New York University Press.

Bolton, Ralph
1991 "Mapping Terra Incognita: Sex Research for AIDS Prevention – An Urgent Agenda for the 1990s." In *The Time of AIDS: Social Analysis, Theory, and Method*, ed. Gilbert Herdt and Shirley Lindenbaum, pp. 124–158. Newbury Park, Calif.: Sage.

Bolton, Ralph
1992 "AIDS and Promiscuity: Muddles in the Models of HIV Prevention." *Medical Anthropology* 14: 145–223.

Bolton, Ralph
1995 "Tricks, Friends, and Lovers: Erotic Encounters in the Field." In *Taboo: Sex, Identity, and Erotic Subjectivity in Anthropological Fieldwork*, ed. Don Kulick and Margaret Willson. New York: Routledge.

Burton, Richard and F. F. Arbuthnot, trans
1995 (originally published 1883). *The Kama Sutra of Vatsyayana*. Ware, Hertfordshire: Wordsworth Editions.

Chow, Rey
  1995   *Primitive Passions: Visuality, Sexuality, Ethnography, and Contemporary Chinese Cinema.* New York: Columbia University Press.
Comaroff, Jean and John Comaroff
  1991   *Of Revelation and Revolution: Christianity, Colonialism, and Consciousness in South Africa.* Chicago: University of Chicago Press.
Coombe, Rosemary J.
  1997   "Contingent Articulations: A Critical Cultural Studies of Law." In *Law in the Domains of Culture*, ed. Austin Sarat and Thomas R. Kearns. Ann Arbor: University of Michigan Press.
Cunningham, Amy
  1992   "Not Just Another Prom Night." *Glamour*, June, 222–225, 259–262.
Damrosch, David
  1995   "The Ethnic Ethnographer: Judaism in *Tristes Tropiques*." *Representations* 50: 1–13.
Deacon, A. Bernard
  1934   *Malekula: A Vanishing People in the New Hebrides.* London: George Routledge & Sons.
Delaney, Carol
  1991   *The Seed and the Soil: Gender and Cosmology in Turkish Village Society.* Berkeley: University of California Press.
Diamond, Timothy
  1992   *Making Gray Gold: Narratives of Nursing Home Care.* Chicago: University of Chicago Press.
Durkheim, Emile and Marcel Mauss
  1963   *Primitive Classification.* Trans. Rodney Needham. Chicago: University of Chicago Press.
Engels, Frederick
  1970   *The Origin of the Family, Private Property and the State.* New York: International Publishers.
Evans-Pritchard, E. E.
  1951   *Kinship and Marriage among the Nuer.* Oxford: Oxford University Press.
Evans-Pritchard, E. E.
  1970   "Sexual Inversion among the Azande." *American Anthropologist* 72 (6): 1428–1434.
Evans-Pritchard, E. E.
  1976   *Witchcraft, Oracles, and Magic among the Azande.* Oxford: Clarendon Press.
Foucault, Michel
  1978   *The History of Sexuality.* Vol. 1. New York: Vintage.

Freud, Sigmund
  1918   *Totem and Taboo.* London: Hogarth Press.
Freud, Sigmund
  1975[1962]   *Three Essays on the Theory of Sexuality*, trans. and ed. James Strachey. New York: Basic Books.
Gagnon, John H. and William Simon
  1973   *Sexual Conduct: The Social Sources of Human Sexuality.* Chicago: Aldine.
Geertz, Clifford
  1973   *The Interpretation of Cultures.* New York: Basic Books.
Gilman, Sander L.
  1985   "Black Bodies, White Bodies: Toward an Iconography of Female Sexuality in Late Nineteenth Century Art, Medicine and Literature." *Critical Inquiry* 12: 204–242.
Gupta, Akhil and James Ferguson
  1997   *Anthropological Locations: Boundaries and Grounds of a Field Science.* Berkeley: University of California Press.
Herdt, Gilbert H.
  1991a   "Representations of Homosexuality: An Essay on Cultural Ontology and Historical Comparison, Part I." *Journal of the History of Sexuality* 1 (3): 481–504.
Herdt, Gilbert H.
  1991b   "Representations of Homosexuality: An Essay on Cultural Ontology and Historical Comparison, Part II." *Journal of the History of Sexuality* 1 (4): 603–632.
Herskovits, Melville J.
  1938   *Dahomey: An Ancient West African Kingdom.* New York: J. J. Augustin.
Hogbin, H. Ian
  1946   "Puberty to Marriage: A Study of the Sexual Life of the Natives of Wogeo, New Guinea." *Oceania* 16 (3): 185–209.
Hooker, Evelyn
  1965   "Male Homosexuals and Their 'Worlds.'" In *Sexual Inversion*, ed. Judd Marmor, pp. 83–107. New York: Basic Books.
Hooker, Evelyn
  1967   "The Homosexual Community." In *Sexual Deviance*, ed. John H. Gagnon and William Simon, pp. 167–184. New York: Harper & Row.
Jones, James H.
  1997   *Alfred C. Kinsey: A Public/Private Life.* New York: W. W. Norton.

Kehoe, Alice B.
1970 "The Function of Ceremonial Sexual Intercourse Among the Northern Plains Indians." *Plains Anthropologist* 15: 99–103.

Kelly, John D.
1991 *A Politics of Virtue: Hinduism, Sexuality, and Countercolonial Discourse in Fiji*. Chicago: University of Chicago Press.

Kelly, Raymond C.
1976 "Witchcraft and Sexual Relations: An Exploration in the Social and Semantic Implications of the Structure of Belief." In *Man and Woman in the New Guinea Highlands*, ed. Paula Brown and Georgeda Buchbinder. Washington, D.C.: American Anthropological Association.

Kuklick, Henrika
1991 *The Savage Within: The Social History of British Anthropology, 1885–1945*. Cambridge: Cambridge University Press.

Kuklick, Henrika
1997 "After Ishmael: The Fieldwork Tradition and Its Future." In *Anthropological Locations: Boundaries and Grounds of a Field Science*, ed. Akhil Gupta and James Ferguson. Berkeley: University of California Press.

Kulick, Don and Margaret Willson, eds
1995 *Taboo: Sex, Identity, and Erotic Subjectivity in Anthropological Fieldwork*. New York: Routledge.

Kuper, Adam
1988 *The Invention of Primitive Society: Transformations of an Illusion*. New York: Routledge.

Landes, Ruth
1937 *Ojibwa Society*. New York: Columbia University Press.

Landes, Ruth
1940 "A Cult Matriarchate and Male Homosexuality." *Journal of Abnormal and Social Psychology* (35): 386–397.

Landtman, Gunnar
1927 *The Kiwai Papuans of British New Guinea: A Nature-Born Instance of Rousseau's Ideal Community*. London: Macmillan.

Lang, Sabine
1996 "Traveling Women: Conducting a Fieldwork Project on Gender Variance and Homosexuality Among North American Indians." In *Out in the Field: Reflections of Lesbian and Gay Anthropologists*, ed. Ellen Lewin and William I. Leap. Urbana: University of Illinois Press.

Lévy-Bruhl, Lucien
1923 *Primitive Mentality*. Boston: Beacon Press.

Lewin, Ellen and William L. Leap, eds
1996 *Out in the Field: Reflections of Lesbian and Gay Anthropologists*. Urbana: University of Illinois Press.

Lewontin, Richard
1995 "Sex, Lies, and Social Science." *New York Review of Books* (April 20): 24–29.

Malinowski, Bronislaw
1927 *Sex and Repression in Savage Society*. New York: Meridian.

Malinowski, Bronislaw
1966 *Crime and Custom in Savage Society*. Totowa, N.J.: Littlefield, Adams & Co.

Malinowski, Bronislaw
1989 *A Diary in the Strict Sense of the Term*. Stanford: Stanford University Press.

Masters, William H. and Virginia E. Johnson
1966 *Human Sexual Response*. Boston: Little, Brown and Company.

Mathews, R. H.
1900 "Native Tribes of Western Australia." *Proceedings of the American Philosophical Society* 39: 123–125.

Mauss, Marcel
1967 *The Gift*. New York: W. W. Norton.

McIntosh, Mary
1981 "The Homosexual Role." In *The Making of the Modern Homosexual*, ed. Ken Plummer, pp. 30–44. Totowa, N.J.: Barnes & Noble.

McLennan, John M.
1865 *Primitive Marriage: An Inquiry into the Origin of the Form of Capture in Marriage*. Edinburgh: Black.

Mead, Margaret
1961 *Coming of Age in Samoa: A Psychological Study of Primitive Youth for Western Civilization*. New York: Dell.

Mead, Margaret
1963 *Sex and Temperament in Three Primitive Societies*. New York: Morrow.

Morris, Rosalind C.
1995 "All Made Up: Performance Theory and the New Anthropology of Sex and Gender." *Annual Review of Anthropology* 24: 567–592.

Murray, Stephen O.
1991   "Sleeping with the Natives as a Source
of Data." *Society of Lesbian and Gay
Anthropologists Newsletter* 13 (3): 49–51.
Murray, Stephen O.
1996   "Male Homosexuality in Guatemala:
Possible Insights and Certain Confusions from
Sleeping with the Natives." In *Out in the Field:
Reflections of Lesbian and Gay Anthropo-
logists*, ed. Ellen Lewin and William L. Leap, pp.
236–260. Urbana: University of Illinois Press.
Namaste, Ki
1994   "The Politics of Inside/Out: Queer
Theory, Poststructuralism, and a Sociological
Approach to Sexuality." *Sociological Theory*
12 (2): 220–231.
Nandy, Ashis
1983   *The Intimate Enemy: Loss and Recovery
of Self Under Colonialism*. Delhi: Oxford
University Press.
Nash, June
1979   *We Eat the Mines and the Mines Eat
Us*. New York: Columbia University Press.
Nelson, Diane M.
1996   "Maya Hackers and the Cyberspatialized
Nation-State: Modernity, Ethnonostalgia,
and a Lizard Queen in Guatemala." *Cultural
Anthropology* 11 (3): 287–308.
Newton, Esther
1993   "Lesbian and Gay Issues in
Anthropology: Some Remarks to the Chairs of
Anthropology Departments." Paper read at the
annual meetings of the American Anthro-
pological Association, Washington, D.C.
Patel, Geeta
1997   "Homely Housewives Run Amok."
Unpublished ms.
Rabinow, Paul
1977   *Reflections on Fieldwork in Morocco*.
Berkeley: University of California Press.
Robinson, Paul
1989   *The Modernization of Sex: Havelock
Ellis, Alfred Kinsey, William Masters and
Virginia Johnson*. Ithaca, N.Y.: Cornell
University Press.
Róheim, G.
1933   "Women and their Life in Central
Australia." *Journal of the Royal Anthropological
Institute of Great Britain and Ireland* 63:
207–265.
Ross, Ellen and Rayna Rapp
1983   "Sex and Society: A Research Note
from Social History and Anthropology." In

Powers of Desire: The Politics of Sexuality, ed.
Ann Snitow, Christine Stansell, and Sharon
Thompson, pp. 51–73. New York: Monthly
Review Press.
Rubin, Gayle
1984   "Thinking Sex: Notes for a Radical
Theory of the Politics of Sexuality." In *Pleasure
and Danger*, ed. Carole S. Vance, pp. 267–319.
New York: Routledge & Kegan Paul.
Salter, Stephanie
1992   "My Two Moms: Ryan's Parents Want
Only the Best for Him. Should It Make Any
Difference That They're Lesbians?" *Redbook*,
May, 64–66, 70.
Sapir, Edward
1963   *Selected Writings of Edward Sapir
in Language, Culture, and Personality*.
Ed. D. G. Mandelbaum. Berkeley: University of
California Press.
Sarkar, Tanika
1994   "Bankimchandra and the Impossibility
of a Political Agenda." *Oxford Literary Review*
16 (1/2): 177–204.
Seidman, Steven
1991   *Romantic Longings: Love in America,
1830–1980*. New York: Routledge.
Seidman, Steven
1994   "Symposium: Queer Theory/Sociology:
A Dialogue." *Sociological Theory* 12 (2):
166–177.
Shortt, John
1873   "The Kojahs of Southern India."
*Journal of the Anthropological Institute of
Great Britain and Ireland* 2: 402–407.
Sinha, Mrinalini
1995   "Nationalism and Respectable Sexuality
in India." *Genders* 21: 30–57.
Stein, Arlene and Ken Plummer
1994   "I Can't Even Think Straight: Queer
Theory and the Missing Sexual Revolution
in Sociology." *Sociological Theory* 12 (2):
178–187.
Steward, Julian H. and Louis C. Faron
1959   *Native Peoples of South America*.
New York: McGraw-Hill.
Stocking, George W., Jr.
1968   *Race, Culture, and Evolution: Essays in
the History of Anthropology*. New York: Free
Press.
Stocking, George W., Jr.
1992   *The Ethnographer's Magic and
Other Essays in the History of Anthropology*.
Madison: University of Wisconsin Press.

Stoler, Ann Laura
1995 *Race and the Education of Desire: Foucault's History of Sexuality and the Colonial Order of Things.* Durham, N.C.: Duke University Press.
Suggs, Robert C.
1966 *Marquesan Sexual Behavior.* New York: Harcourt, Brace & World.
Takaki, Ronald
1993 *A Different Mirror: A History of Multicultural America.* Boston: Little, Brown.
Thomas, Nicholas
1989 *Out of Time: History and Evolution in Anthropological Discourse.* Cambridge: Cambridge University Press.
van Gennep, Arnold
1960 *The Rites of Passage.* Trans. Monika B. Vizedom and Gabrielle L. Caffee. Chicago: University of Chicago Press.
Wagner, Roy
1981 *The Invention of Culture.* Chicago: University of Chicago Press.
Weber, Max
1958 *The Protestant Ethic and the Spirit of Capitalism.* New York: Charles Scribner's Sons.
Weeks, Jeffrey
1986 *Sexuality.* New York: Tavistock Publications.
Weeks, Jeffrey
1987 "Questions of Identity." In *The Cultural Construction of Sexuality*, ed. Pat Caplan, pp. 30–51. New York: Tavistock.
Westermarck, Edward
1906 *The Origin and Development of the Moral Ideas.* London: Macmillan.
Williams, F. E.
1936 *Papuans of the Trans-Fly.* Oxford: Clarendon Press.
Wilson, Monica
1963 *Good Company: A Study of Nyakyusa Age-Villages.* Boston: Beacon Press.
Wolf, Arthur P.
1995 *Sexual Attraction and Childhood Association: A Chinese Brief for Edward Westermarck.* Stanford: Stanford University Press.
Wolf, Diane L., ed.
1996 *Feminist Dilemmas in Fieldwork.* Boulder, CO: Westview Press.

Part I
Sex, Race and Gender in Anthropological History

Introduction

There can be little doubt that social and cultural anthropology in Britain and North America (and, for that matter, the Durkheimian tradition in French anthropology that was influential in Britain for so long) was built on the rejection or the willful neglect of "race" as an explanation for human difference. Earlier, however, between 1775 and 1860, the notion that physical difference, cultural difference, and differences in mental ability and emotional maturity were all closely correlated was taken for granted by scholars and laymen alike. Disagreements concerned the degree of those differences and their malleability. In the last 150 years the notions of "culture" and "society" have replaced "race" in social science, but older notions persist among a minority of physical anthropologists, geneticists, and an unknown percentage of the general public.

Race has always been an imprecise concept. In the nineteenth century it was used to refer to major supposed divisions of humanity, distinguished by visible features such as skin color, stature, and color of hair and eyes. Smaller supposed divisions were also invented, as in the work of the French (originally Jamaican) anthropologist William-Frédéric Edwards, who divided the French into the Celts and the Cymri, and Harvard anthropologist W. Z. Ripley, who, a half century later, divided Europeans into three races: Nordic, Alpine, and Mediterranean. These smaller racial divisions were often confounded with language, class, and status divisions among national groups. During the nineteenth century, a plethora of criteria were used in race classification, with the result that raciologists, who all thought that race determined culture, art, and morality, could not agree on racial criteria and, accordingly, on the number of races. The list of potential criteria included skin color, hair color, hair texture, color of eyes, breadth of nose, straightness of facial profile (does the jaw jut forward?), size of skull, ratio of breadth to length of skull, position of foramen

Sexualities in Anthropology: A Reader, edited by Andrew P. Lyons and Harriet D. Lyons
© 2011 Blackwell Publishing Ltd.

magnum (affecting the way the skull articulates with the rest of the body), length of arms and forearms versus length of legs, and size of genitals. Racial hierarchies that were constructed using these criteria usually placed those with the smallest brains, the darkest skin, and *supposedly* less evolved genitalia at the bottom.

In the period before Darwin, as the new science of biology grew in importance, there was much dispute as to whether races were separate, unchangeable species (*polygenesis*) or varieties of a single species (*monogenesis*). Members of the same species were expected to share a significant number of inherited anatomical and physical characteristics so that they resembled each other much more than they resembled members of other species. A second criterion of species that was not always invoked was directly sexual – that males could produce fertile offspring with females of the same species. Polygenists tended to look for greater racial differences. They asserted that races were "fixed" types. They either cast doubt on interfertility as a criterion by pointing to mammalian anomalies, or even by telling stories of male apes in amorous pursuit of African women, or more commonly invoked it by asserting that mulattoes were reproductively disadvantaged and (in some accounts) insane or mentally handicapped. Many but not all polygenists supported slavery. Monogenists sometimes claimed biblical authority, but they always relied on their understanding of the biology of the day, pointing out physical and sometimes mental similarities between all human races. They tended to assume that mental and physical variation between human groups was the result of variation in climate, diet, and "mode of life" (i.e., technology, ecology, and culture, generally) and asserted that it had developed over thousands (rather than millions) of years through the inheritance of acquired characteristics, and that it was to some degree reversible. Some but not all monogenists were "liberal" on racial issues, inasmuch as they thought that good treatment of the less fortunate might cause them to improve, and that slavery was immoral. Those monogenists who stuck to the pre-Darwinian timescale had a job explaining how raciation could have occurred in a short period. The revived, originally medieval notion of the *Great Chain of Being* was supported by some of these writers (such as the monogenists Petrus Camper and Georges-Louis Leclerc, Comte de Buffon, and the polygenists Charles White and Edward Long) but opposed by some of the most prominent biologists (Carl Linnaeus, and the monogenists Johan Friedrich Blumenbach and Georges Cuvier). It asserted that a continuous, unbroken gradation from highest to lowest had characterized God's Creation since the time of Adam, from whites to blacks, to apes and monkeys, to mammals, to reptiles, etc., down to slugs and stones. There were no missing rungs in the ladder, no missing links in the chain. In the work of racists, such as the polygenist Charles White, blacks were as close to apes as to whites with respect to characteristics like the length of forearm, woolliness of hair, gait, and reproductive characteristics. White had a single black penis in his collection that was 12 inches long, he informed his readers in Latin, and this scientific sample sufficed to prove all rumors about black sexuality correct (Lyons and Lyons 2004: 29).

The hierarchical racial stereotypes that were common in biology and early physical anthropology between 1775 and 1860 rarely contradicted more diffuse and less scientific ideas of primitivity and sexual alterity or "otherness" that were to be found in much travel writing of the time and which underpinned the matriarchal evolutionary theories of the 1860s and 1870s. The hypothesis of primitive promiscuity fitted in very well with notions that "primitives" were oversexed. As the editors of this volume have already pointed out (Lyons and Lyons 2004: 20–50), sexual alterity in fact took three forms: (1) the most common image was that of the "oversexed" savage; (2) some Polynesian societies, like Tahiti at the time of contact in the eighteenth century, are portrayed as sexually free in a positive way; (3) a few North American peoples such as the Iroquois were negatively portrayed because they respected female honor and were therefore considered undersexed. It will be noted that while most ideas about primitive sexuality were negative, different stereotypes were entertained about different groups.

The last point is perhaps illustrated by some of the stories that were told about Africans. The Bantu and other "black" inhabitants of sub-Saharan Africa were portrayed as "oversexed" in many eighteenth- and nineteenth-century writings, and stories of male excess, the evils of polygamy, and the drudgery of women abounded (see Lyons and Lyons 2004: 62–70 and 131–54 for a discussion of authors like Winwood Reade, Richard Burton, and Harry Johnston). Practices like male circumcision and clitoridectomy were seen as indexes of sexual pathology and moral difference. In eighteenth- and nineteenth-century raciology, hunting and gathering peoples like the Hottentots and Bushmen were sometimes seen as similar to Bantu, but at other times their racial distinctiveness was stressed: San males were portrayed as possessing horizontal penises; it was unclear to some whether some Hottentot males removed one testicle or were monorchids at birth – it seems that after 1800 most of them possessed two testicles; the appearance of a labial flap caused by an enlargement of the *labia minora*, invisible to the unhappy voyeur when people were clothed, and huge buttocks supposedly demarcated and distinguished San and Hottentot women, such as Saartje Baartmann, the "Hottentot Venus" (see Gordon 1992 and 1998).

Ideas about the sexuality of others are obviously linked to the complex relationships between colonizers and the colonized at different points in imperial history. Post-contact stereotypes differ usually from pre-contact stereotypes. Demography and the variability of culture and history play a role in their formation. The degree to which stereotypes are fed by the "misreading" of other cultures cannot be exaggerated. In *White Over Black* (1968) Winthrop Jordan specifically connected some of the doctrines of early scientific racism with the realities of American slavery and sentiments about miscegenation in the plantation, the farm, and the slave-owner's home.

The connection between these images of race and images of class in the nineteenth century is not a figment of historians' imagination. Henry Mayhew's *London Labour and the London Poor*, which appeared in 1861/2, caused something of a scandal in Victorian England. The first three volumes are given over to vivid depictions of the ordinary lives of working-class people. The fourth volume is on Vice, which includes thieves, swindlers, beggars, and a global survey of prostitution. The category, "prostitution," seems to include pre-marital and extra-marital sex. Here, all of a sudden, we meet primitives (as well as Greeks and Romans) in a section of 120 pages that was actually written mainly by Mayhew's friend, Bracebridge Hemyng, who used second-hand material rather than the direct observation evident in the rest of the book. We meet lustful African males who treat their women like reptiles, naked and depraved Amazonian Indians, Australian aborigines who are as bad as the Africans, and undersexed but honorable North American braves. The Maori are a cut above the savages; their immorality is planned: "[I]t is the appetite of the sensualist, deliberately gratified, and by means similar in many respects, to those adopted among the lowest classes in Europe" (Mayhew 1861/2: 71).

The late nineteenth century saw the rise of Darwinism and of social anthropology, which were two variants on the evolutionary idea. In the subject area that was to become physical anthropology, the idea of polygenesis as an idea slowly disappeared, but scientific racism did not. Over hundreds of thousands of years substantial differences could arise between members of the same species. Furthermore, the struggle for survival was an uneven process. Urbanization and misguided charity might promote the survival of degenerate types, evolutionary atavisms or throwbacks, new savages in the city.

All of this should give us some background to a 1985 article by Sander Gilman (there were two different versions with different titles), who argues that Hottentot, properly *Khoi*, women (equated with African women generally) were depicted as icons of extreme lust (the inverse of Victorian chastity) and equated with prostitutes in London and other European cities. Gilman, who is a historian of psychiatry and anti-Semitism, compared images of the sexuality of Hottentot women, such as the "Hottentot Venus," with an assortment of pictures and photographs: those of black women in paintings such as Manet's *Olympia*; fat Parisian prostitutes described by Parent-Duchatelet in 1836; Pauline Tarnowsky's late nineteenth-century representations of Russian prostitutes who had wild eyes and misshapen noses; and Cesare Lombroso's prostitutes who combine some of Tarnowsky's stigmata with enlarged labia. We believe that the concept of the article was brilliant, but it was full of historical inaccuracies and anachronisms, which, surprisingly, were left unquestioned by Gilman's many critics, as noted in the formidable article by Zine Magubane (reproduced here – see Chapter 2) on the case of the "Hottentot Venus."

Saartje Baartmann, who was at least in part Khoi, traveled from the Eastern Cape to Capetown, where she worked for a British officer and his colored employees. They arranged for her transportation to London in 1810, where she was exhibited in what we would now call a "freak show," because of her steatopygia (huge buttocks). Anti-slavery abolitionists tried to stop the public shows, but a court procedure failed when Baartmann, who spoke three languages, convinced the court that she fully consented to what was going on. In 1814, the show moved to Paris. Georges Cuvier, the world's greatest anatomist at that time, and his assistant Henri de Blainville arranged to see Baartmann, but to their dismay, de Blainville merely glimpsed her genitalia (she had a tablier or "Hottentot apron," albeit not the most extreme in nature). They got their chance to do so after her premature death in 1815. Her brains and genitals were preserved in the Musée de l'Homme along with Cuvier's brains, but, after an outcry, what was left of Baartmann was returned to South Africa in 2002.

Gilman's article was one of a number produced in the 1980s and 1990s by anti-racist male scholars in cultural studies, anthropology, and biology (such as Robert Gordon in 1992 and 1998 and Stephen Jay Gould in 1985) that dealt with the Baartmann case in detail. What perhaps distinguished the piece and caused some offence were particular illustrations of genitalia that Gilman had reproduced from the late nineteenth-century criminal anthropologists, Cesare Lombroso and Guglielmo Ferrero. Mary Louise Pratt (1992: 232) noted that Gilman had "been rightly criticized for reproducing the very pornographic dimension he is seeking to condemn." Anne Fausto-Sterling (1995) refused to print any illustrations in her article on the case, because the subject matter was not to be Baartmann's wrongly pathologized genitals but, rather, the impersonal, objectivizing, taxonomizing science of Cuvier and his kind. Yvette Abrahams (1997), who claims some Khoi ancestry, accused the white, male scholars who had written about Baartmann in the 1980s and 1990s of perpetuating rather than obliterating colonial racial stereotypes. This is the very last thing these scholars intended, and the criticism is unfair, but the case does illustrate that these historical issues are not abstract. Racism leaves raw wounds, and, because those wounds hurt, there are questions about authorial positioning – in other words, who has the right to tell Saartje Baartmann's full story.

REFERENCES AND FURTHER READING

Abrahams, Yvette
    1997   The Great Long National Insult: "Science," Sexuality and the Khoisan in the 18th and Early 19th Century. Agenda 32:34–47.
Fausto-Sterling, Anne
    1995   Gender, Race and Nation: The Comparative Anatomy of "Hottentot" Women in Europe, 1815–1817. In Deviant Bodies: Critical Perspectives on Difference in Science and Popular Culture. Jennifer Terry and Jacqueline Urla, eds. Pp. 19–48. Bloomington, IN: Indiana University Press.
Gilman, Sander L.
    1985   The Hottentot and the Prostitute: Toward an Iconography of Female Sexuality. In Difference and Pathology: Stereotypes of Sexuality, Race and Madness. Pp. 76–108. New York and London: Cornell University Press.
Gilman, Sander L.
    1986   Black Bodies, White Bodies: Toward an Iconography of Female Sexuality in Late Nineteenth-Century Art, Medicine and Literature. In "Race," Writing and Difference. Henry Louis Gates, Jr., ed. Pp. 222–261. Chicago: University of Chicago Press.
Gordon, Robert J.
    1992   The Venal Hottentot Venus and the Great Chain of Being. African Studies 51(2):185–201.
Gordon, Robert J.
    1998   The Rise of the Bushman Penis: Germans, Genitalia and Genocide. African Studies 57(1):27–54.
Gould, Stephen Jay
    1985   The Hottentot Venus. In The Flamingo's Smile: Reflections in Natural History. Pp. 291–305. New York: Norton.
Holmes, Rachel
    2007   African Queen: The Real Life of the Hottentot Venus. New York: Random House.
Jordan, Winthrop D.
    1968   White Over Black: American Attitudes Toward the Negro. Baltimore: Penguin Books.
Levy, Anita
    1991   Other Women: The Writing of Class, Race and Gender, 1832–1898. Princeton: Princeton University Press.
Lyons, Andrew P. and Harriet D. Lyons
    2004   Irregular Connections: A History of Anthropology and Sexuality. Lincoln: University of Nebraska Press.
Lyons, Harriet
    1981   Anthropologists, Moralities and Relativities: The Problem of Genital Mutilations. Canadian Review of Sociology and Anthropology 18(4):499–518.

Magubane, Zine
   2001   Which Bodies Matter? Feminism, Poststructuralism, Race, and the Curious Theoretical Odyssey of the "Hottentot Venus." Gender and Society 15(6):816–834.
Mayhew, Henry
   1861/2 London Labour and the London Poor: A Cyclopaedia of the Condition and Earnings of Those That Will Work, Those That Cannot Work, and Those That Will Not Work. 4 vols. London: Griffin, Bohn.
Pratt, Mary Louise
   1992   Imperial Eyes: Travel Writing and Transculturation. London: Routledge.
Qureshi, Sadiah
   2004   Displaying Sara Baartman, The Hottentot Venus. History of Science 62:233–257.

2

Which Bodies Matter?
Feminism, Poststructuralism,
Race, and the Curious
Theoretical Odyssey of the
"Hottentot Venus"

Zine Magubane

Any scholar wishing to advance an argument on gender and colonialism, gender and science, or gender and race must, it seems, quote Sander Gilman's (1985) "Black Bodies, White Bodies: Toward an Iconography of Female Sexuality in Late Nineteenth-Century Art, Medicine, and Literature." First published in a 1985 issue of *Critical Inquiry*, the article has been reprinted in several anthologies. It is cited by virtually every scholar concerned with analyzing gender, science, race, colonialism, and/or their intersections (Abrahams 1997; Crais 1992; Donald and Rattansi 1992; Fausto-Sterling 1995; Gordon 1992; Haraway 1989; hooks 1992; Lindfors 1999; Loomba 1998; McClintock 1995; Pieterse 1995; Schiebinger 1993; Sharpley-Whiting 1999; Stoler 1995;

Strother 1999; Thomson 1997; Vaughan 1991; Wiss 1994).

In the article, Gilman uses Sarah Baartmann,[1] the so-called Hottentot Venus, as a means of showing how medical, literary, and scientific discourses work to construct images of racial and sexual difference. Baartmann, a Khoikhoi[2] woman, was taken from the Cape Colony in South Africa and exhibited at the Piccadilly Circus in London because of the purported abnormality of her sexual organs. She was said to suffer from both steatopygia (an enlargement of the buttocks) and an elongation of the labia (thus named the "Hottentot Apron"). Baartmann suffered the indignity of public exhibition and became the subject of popular lore and political

Zine Magubane, Which Bodies Matter? Feminism, Poststructuralism, Race, and the Curious Theoretical Odyssey of the "Hottentot Venus," from *Gender and Society*, vol. 15, no. 6 (Dec 2001): 816–834. Reprinted by permission of SAGE Publications.

Sexualities in Anthropology: A Reader, edited by Andrew P. Lyons and Harriet D. Lyons
© 2011 Blackwell Publishing Ltd.

lampooning before her premature death
and subsequent dissection at the hands of
Georges Cuvier, a French anatomist. The basic
premise of Gilman's argument is summed up
in this frequently quoted passage:

> The antithesis of European sexual mores and
> beauty is embodied in the Black, and the
> essential Black, the lowest rung on the great
> chain of being, is the Hottentot. The physical
> appearance of the Hottentot is, indeed, the
> central nineteenth-century icon for sexual dif-
> ference between the European and the Black.
> (Gilman 1985, 231)

Gilman's analysis of Baartmann was the genesis
for a veritable theoretical industry. After the
publication of Gilman's article, Baartmann was,
in the words of Z. S. Strother (1999, 1), "recapitulated to fame" and became "an academic
and popular icon." The theoretical groundswell
her story precipitated cannot be separated from
the growing popularity of poststructuralist
analyses of race and gender. The ways in which
science, literature, and art collectively worked
to produce Baartmann as an example of racial
and sexual difference offered exemplary proof
that racial and sexual alterity are social constructions rather than biological essences. Thus,
her story was particularly compelling for anyone interested in deconstructing difference and
analyzing the "othering" process.

The fact that Gilman's article has been
"instrumental in transforming Baartman into
a late-twentieth-century icon for the violence
done to women of African descent" (Strother
1999, 37) makes it even more critical that we
reconsider the ways in which Baartmann, as
both subject and object, has been deployed
theoretically. In the pages that follow, I will
argue that although most studies that discuss
Baartmann (or Gilman's analysis of her) are
scrupulous in their use of words like *invented,
constructed*, and *ideological*, in their practice,
they valorize the very ground of biological
essentialism they purport to deconstruct.

Thus, in this article, I examine the parameters
of inquiry that have structured how scholars
have posed their research questions. I am particularly interested in looking at what assumptions about racial and sexual difference inform
the theoretical orthodoxy about Baartmann. I

argue that most theorists have, following
Gilman's theoretical lead, focused obsessively
on Baartmann's body and its difference. As a
result, they have accepted, without question,
his core assertion that "by the eighteenth century, the sexuality of the Black, both male and
female, becomes an icon for deviant sexuality
in general" (Gilman 1985, 228). They have
not, however, asked what social relations determined which people counted as Black, and for
which people did Blacks become icons of sexual
difference and why? Neither have they investigated the important differences that marked
how social actors in different structural locations saw and experienced Baartmann – in particular her very different interpellation into
French versus British medicine and science.
As a result, their work has actually placed
Baartmann *outside* history.

In the interest of placing Baartmann (and
racial and sexual alterity) back within history,
the remainder of this article will take issue
with, and disprove, three of Gilman's core
assertions. The first assumption I disprove
is that Europeans' fears of the "unique and
observable" physical differences of racial and
sexual "others" was the primary impetus for
the construction and synthesis of images of
deviance. The second assumption I challenge is
that ideas about Blackness remained relatively
static and unchanged throughout the nineteenth century. The final assumption I critique
is that Baartmann evoked a uniform ideological response, and her sexual parts represented
the "core image" of the Black woman in the
nineteenth century. The article will conclude
with a discussion of the theoretical lapses that
precipitated Baartmann's recent theoretical
fetishization.

Ways of Seeing: Hierarchies
of Value and the Social
Construction of Perceptions

Long before the first poststructuralist put pen
to paper, Emile Durkheim (1982, 34) argued
that "social life is made up entirely of representations." His strongest criticisms were
directed against social theorists who naturalized these representations, treating them as the

result of universal sensory impressions rather than historically specific cultural creations. He thus argued that

> consciousness allows us to know them [representations] well up to a certain point, but only in the same way as our senses make us aware of heat or light, sound or electricity. It gives us muddled impressions of them, fleeting and subjective, but provides no clear, distinct notions or explanatory concepts. (P. 36)

Durkheim argued that representations must be analyzed like social facts (1982, 36). Viewing representations as social facts, he explained, "is not to place them in this or that category of reality; it is to observe towards them a certain attitude of mind." He was essentially arguing that analyses of psychic impressions must give way to analyses of social relations if the theorists are to arrive at a sophisticated understanding of how we perceive and order our world.

It appears that Gilman (1985, 231) was determined not to repeat the mistakes of a generation of theorists before and after Durkheim when he began his essay with this compelling question: "How do we organize our perceptions of the world?" His analysis suggests that he sees differences as "myths" that are "perceived through the ideological bias of the observer" (1985, 223). However, the ahistorical perspective he adopts on how human beings perceive difference and organize hierarchies of value belies this seemingly radical constructivist stance. Gilman essentially argues that ideas about difference are the unmediated reflex of psychic impressions. In his analysis, the visible stigmata of racial and corporeal abnormality – what he terms "unique and observable physical differences" – are of key importance (1985, 231). He argues that the scientific discourse of degeneracy, which was key in pathologizing the Other, devolved primarily in relation to non-European peoples as an expression of fears about their corporeal difference.

> It is the inherent fear of the difference in the anatomy of the Other that lies behind the synthesis of images. The Other's pathology is revealed in anatomy. The "white *man's* burden" thus becomes his sexuality and its

control, and it is this which is transferred into the need to control the sexuality of the Other. ... This need for control was a projection of inner fears; thus, its articulation in visual images was in terms which described the polar opposite of the European male. (Gilman 1985, 256)

Despite his ahistoricism and psychological determinism, a number of feminist scholars wholeheartedly embraced Gilman's analysis. Several, following Gilman's theoretical lead, argued that Cuvier's dissection was an expression of his inner fears of Baartmann's anatomical difference and his need for control (Fausto-Sterling 1995; Haraway 1989; Schiebinger 1993; Sharpley-Whiting 1999). Fausto-Sterling (1995, 42) was clearly drawing on Gilman when she argued,

> Cuvier most clearly concerned himself with establishing the priority of European nationhood; he wished to control the hidden secrets of Africa and the woman by exposing them to scientific daylight. ... Hence he delved beneath the surface, bringing the interior to light; he extracted the hidden genitalia and defined the hidden Hottentot. Lying on his dissection table, the wild Baartmann became the tame, the savage civilized. By exposing the clandestine power, the ruler prevailed.

Anne McClintock (1995, 41) also employed Gilman in support of her claim that

> it was necessary to invent visible stigmata to represent – as a commodity spectacle – the historical atavism of the degenerate classes. As Sander Gilman has pointed out, one answer was found in the body of the African woman, who became the prototype of the Victorian invention of primitive atavism.

In following Gilman's lead, and analyzing the discourse of degeneracy as a product of psychological dispositions, these accounts cannot explain the paradoxical stance of the founder of the science of degeneracy, Augustine Benedict Morel. Morel argued "between the intellectual state of the wildest Bushman and that of the most civilized European, there is *less difference* [emphasis added] than between the intellectual state of the same European and that of the degenerate being" (Pick 1989, 26).

Morel's comments become even more striking when we recall that many scientists and travelers believed that Baartmann was a female member of the so-called Bushman tribe.

Morel's comments become much more understandable if we proceed from the assumption that social relations, rather than psychological dispositions, provide the background and context for human encounters. Degeneration, as an explanatory framework, did not develop in response to external others and their corporeal alterity. Rather, the discourse was a response to fears about the blurring of class and status differences within the European polity. This was considered far more threatening than the racial and sexual alterity of non-European peoples. Malik (1996, 112) explained that "for the ruling classes equality and democracy were themselves symptoms of degeneracy." What was distinctive about the idea of degeneration was that external features were *not* reliable indicators of its existence. Degeneration was not always (or even primarily) associated with unique and observable physical differences. As Pick (1989) explained, degeneration was considered so dangerous precisely because it was a process capable of usurping all boundaries of discernible identity. Degeneracy was marked by its slow, invidious, and *invisible* proliferation.

The importance of analyzing social relations, rather than enumerating psychological dispositions, is nowhere more evident than in Georges Cuvier's stance on the Great Chain of Being. The Great Chain of Being was a theory that speculated all creatures could be arranged on a continuous scale from the lowliest insect to the most highly evolved human. After the publication of Gilman's article, Cuvier became popularly (and erroneously) associated with the Great Chain of Being (Gordon 1992; Sharpley-Whiting 1999; Strother 1999). Wiss (1994, 29), for example, asserts that "Cuvier, by fractioning the gradual continuities of the 'great chain of being' was able to divide humanity into four distinct races."

What these analyses do not and cannot account for is Cuvier's stubborn and enduring *resistance* to the doctrine. As Appel (1987, 50–51) explained,

Of all the speculative theories, the one that most aroused Cuvier's passions was the eighteenth-century doctrine of the chain of being. It became in effect his *bete noire*.... Cuvier's main stated objection to the chain was that it was a speculative *a priori* scheme that went beyond the facts.... By 1812 Cuvier had already renounced even the possibility of arranging classes along a scale of perfection.

Cuvier's stance can be better understood if it is analyzed in relation to nineteenth-century European class dynamics, rather than simply concluding that his actions reflect the generalized psychological dispositions and fears of European men. Indeed, his disaffection for the notion of a Great Chain of Being stemmed equally from sociopolitical as it did from scientific or psychological sources.

In Cuvier's day, it was commonly believed that speculative philosophies had been the source behind the French Revolution. During the Revolution, scientific theories had been intensely politicized. Thus, Cuvier was acutely aware of the power that unregulated ideas, political or scientific, could have on the masses. The ideas of Mesmer, for example, had been joined to the revolutionary ideas of Rousseau, as were Felix Pouchet's ideas about spontaneous generation. Cuvier associated speculative theories with materialism and feared that the two taken in tandem could be used to promote social unrest. Speculative theories could, in his opinion, be more easily exploited by the masses who were intent on overturning the social order.

Thus, although Cuvier's observations about Baartmann suggest that he viewed her as sharing a number of affinities with apes, it is important to note that he never explicitly stated that she was the "missing link." His reluctance to do so tells us less about his attitudes toward racial and sexual alterity than it does about his attitudes toward class. It demonstrates his profound aversion to any action that could potentially endow the "dangerous classes" claims to equality any legitimacy. This aversion was strong enough to prevent him from drawing the "logical" conclusion about Baartmann, based on his own empirical observations. As strong as Cuvier's fears about Baartmann's corporeal difference were, it appears his fears about the potential political equality of his fellow Frenchmen were even greater.

The actions of Cuvier demonstrate that the social relations of nineteenth-century France tell us far more about the process of constructing boundaries between Self and Other than do blanket generalizations about the psychological dispositions of European men. His behavior makes evident the truth of Barbara Fields's (1982, 148) claim that "the idea one people has of another, even when the difference between them is embodied in the most striking physical characteristics, is always mediated by the social context within which the two come into contact."

Sex and Savagery: Africa in the Historical Imagination

The ahistorical and psychologically determinist perspective Gilman adopts in his discussions about degeneration and the Great Chain is even more pronounced in his discussions about race. The publication of "Black Bodies, White Bodies" (Gilman 1985) in the anthology *"Race," Writing, and Difference*, edited by Henry Louis Gates Jr., was instrumental in securing the article's place as a foundational text in a postfoundationalist world. The anthology soon became one of the most cited texts in the fields of poststructuralism, feminism, critical race studies, and postcolonial studies. It is not difficult to ascertain why. In the introduction, Gates explains that the purpose of the text was "to deconstruct the ideas of difference inscribed in the trope of race" (Gilman 1985, 2). The title's use of quotation marks around the word *Race* announced the volume's emphasis on critically engaging race as a discursively and socially constructed phenomenon. The characterization of race as a trope, and thus similar to any other kind of figurative language, was clearly meant to decisively and permanently disrupt any notion of race as referring to innate biological or physical differences. Race, as a trope, is the ultimate empty signifier.

Although Gilman's intention is to argue that perceptions of difference are socially constructed, he focuses on Baartmann's "inherent" biological differences. He argues that "her physiognomy, her skin color, the form of her genitalia label her as inherently different" (1985, 232). Gilman argues that because of her "unique and observable" physical differences, Baartmann "represented Blackness in *nunce*" (1985, 225). He thus concludes that "while many groups of African Blacks were known to Europeans in the nineteenth century, the Hottentot remained representative of the essence of the Black, especially the Black female" (225).

Gilman's theoretical adherents, with little question and much enthusiasm, took up the idea that Baartmann's physical stigmata transformed her into a representation of "Blackness in nunce" (Fausto-Sterling 1995; McClintock 1995; Schiebinger 1993; Sharpley-Whiting 1999; Wiss 1994). Donna Haraway (1989, 402), for example, uses Gilman to support her claim that because of their perceived biological differences, "Black women were ontologically the essence of animality and abnormality."

Most scholars, in accepting Gilman's declaration about Baartmann's racial representativeness, have neither historicized nor problematized the idea of Blackness. They have made "the assumption that race is an observable physical fact, a thing, rather than a notion that is profoundly and in its very essence ideological" (Fields 1982, 144). However, as Wacquant (1997, 223) observed, American conceptions of race are better thought of as "folk conceptions" that reflect the "peculiar schema of racial division developed by one country during a small segment of its short history." The fact that many Baartmann scholars have unthinkingly reproduced commonsense understandings of Blackness as it exists in the contemporary United States is evidenced by two historically untenable assumptions they make about race. The first assumption is that Baartmann's color and sexual difference not only marked her as different but also rendered her fundamentally the same as all other Black people. The second assumption is that ideas about what constitutes Africanity and Blackness have remained relatively unchanged over time.

The assumption that Khoikhoi people were considered broadly representative of Africans as a whole is central to Gilman's argument. It allows him to move from a discussion about Baartmann to making much broader claims about perceptions of African people as a whole. This theoretical maneuver allows him to argue that Baartmann "represented Blackness *in nunce.*" However, the reports of nineteenth-century travelers show that this particular assertion also does not withstand historical scrutiny.

Travelers made much of the fact that the Khoikhoi were not Black or brown but yellow or tawny and thus different in important respects from Africans living further North, as well as those on the West Coast (Barrow 1801; Burchell [1827] 1953; Lichtenstein 1812; Pringle 1834; Thompson 1827). Travelers and naturalists also drew sharp divisions between different classes of Khoikhoi people, based on their color, culture, geographic location, and appearance. Barrow (1801, 151), for example, distinguished between the so-called colonial Hottentots or bastard Hottentots, who lived inside the colony, and those in the outlying regions ("savage Hottentots" who "retained more of their original character"). He went on to note that although the "elongated nymphae [Hottentot Apron] are found in all Hottentot women ... in the bastard Hottentot it ceases to appear" (1801, 281). Other travelers testified to the existence of different "races" within the "Hottentot nation." George Thompson (1827, 269), for example, remarked that "in personal appearance the Korannas are superior to any other race of Hottentots. Many of them are tall with finely shaped heads and prominent features."

Even those travelers who did not make such fine distinctions between individual Khoikhoi people drew sharp distinctions between the Khoikhoi and other Black ethnic groups within the Cape Colony. It was widely agreed that the Xhosa (called variously Kaffirs, Caffirs, and Caffers) and the San (pejoratively referred to as Bushmen) were wholly unlike the Khoikhoi. An article in *The Quarterly Review* remarked that "no two beings can differ more widely than the Hottentot and the Caffre" (Review of *Lichtenstein's Travels* 1812, 388). Barnard Fisher (1814, 7) likewise commented that "three races more distinct and unlike than the

Hottentot, Caffre, and Bushman cannot possibly be." James Prior (1819, 14) echoed Fisher when he marveled at the "marked differences as appear in the three races of Kaffir, Hottentot, and Bushman."

The fact that historical evidence suggests that the Khoikhoi did *not* represent Blackness *in nunce* is important because it forces us to return to the central question posed earlier: "How do we organize our perceptions of the world?" Gilman (1985, 250) imputes a timeless stability to the idea of race. He argues that "the primary marker of the Black is his or her skin color." However, skin color and hair textures were not stabilized as markers of racial difference until fairly late in the nineteenth century. Barrow (1801, 168), for example, observed that the Xhosa were "dark glossy brown verging on black." He also described them as having "short curling hair." Nevertheless, he concluded that they had "not one line of the African Negro in the composition of their persons" (1801, 205). Lichtenstein (1812, 303) concurred with Barrow that "the Kaffirs have in many respects a great resemblance to Europeans. Indeed they have more resemblance to them than either to Negroes or Hottentots." Thomas Pringle (1834, 413) echoed Barrow when, after describing the Xhosa as being "dark brown" and having "wooly hair," he declared them as having features that "approached the European model." What these historical observations suggest is that Blackness is less a stable, observable, empirical fact than an ideology that is historically determined and, thus, variable.

The profoundly ideological nature of Blackness becomes even more apparent when we consider that as Englishmen continued to speculate as to whether the dark-skinned (by contemporary standards) Xhosa should be classified as Negroes, they were convinced that the pale-skinned (again by contemporary standards) Irish most definitely *should* be. As Cheng (1995, 26) noted, "the Irish/Celtic race was repeatedly related to the Black race not merely in terms of tropes, but insistently as *fact*, as literal and biological relatives." Indeed, much was made of the "unique and observable physical differences" (to borrow a phrase from Gilman) that separated the Anglo-Saxons from the Celts. Dr. John Beddoe, founding member of the British Ethnological Society, devoted most of his career to establishing that the Irish Celts were not only genetically distinct from, and inferior to, Anglo-Saxons but also bore biological affinity to Negroes. His work served to "confirm the impressions of many Victorians that the Celtic portions of the population in Wales, Cornwall, Scotland, and Ireland were considerably darker or more melanous than those descended from Saxon and Scandinavian forbears" (Curtis 1997, 20). Beddoe was by no means alone in his estimation of the "Africanoid" origin of the Irish (Bentham 1834; Price 1829; Prichard 1857).

I have gone to such lengths to demonstrate (1) the Khoikhoi were not considered representative of Africans, (2) not all Africans were thought of as Negroes, and (3) not all Negroes were Black for two reasons. My first objective is to challenge Gilman's core assertions and thus unsettle the theoretical orthodoxy about Baartmann. My second objective is to make a larger sociological point about ideologies concerning racial differences (or any other kind of differences for that matter).

As the above selections from British travel writing, missionary reports, and related ephemera so graphically illustrated, there was not a uniform opinion on the Khoikhoi or other Africans with regard to sexuality, appearance, habits, or otherwise. This is because "race is not an idea but an ideology. It came into existence at a discernible historical moment for rationally understandable historical reasons and is subject to change for similar reasons" (Fields 1990, 101). Races are not clearly demarcated and bounded groups existing "out there" in the world, prior to the process of categorization. English perceptions of the Irish make it clear that the characteristics that we currently identify as important for establishing difference (i.e. dark skin) were not preexisting in the world, simply waiting for someone (scientists, colonialists, travelers, Europeans) to come along and construct a hierarchy of value. Rather, what we see when we look at each other is profoundly mediated by social context. Whether we are looking at the source of discourses of degeneration or impressions of biological characteristics, the end result is the same. An analysis that does not go beyond psychological impressions to consider the importance of social relations will do nothing more than produce theories that explain "not the facts ... but the preconceptions of the author before he [sic] began his research" (Durkheim 1982, 38).

When and How Do Bodies Matter? Science, Sex, and Ideological Struggle

There is no doubt that the express aim of poststructuralist scholarship on Baartmann has been to critique racism and biological essentialism. The question must be asked, therefore, why the theoretical orthodoxy has reproduced the very assumptions it purports to destabilize. Part of the problem stems from the fact that despite theorists' claims that race is a notion that is essentially ideological, their analyses fail to actually treat it as such. This fact becomes especially clear when we subject Gilman's most popular theoretical claim to a rigorous sociological analysis.

Writing almost a decade and a half after the article was first published, Strother (1999, 38) observed that Gilman's assertion that Baartmann's sexual parts "serve as the central image for the Black female throughout the nineteenth century" remains its most frequently cited statement. This assertion, perhaps more than any other, was taken up without question (Crais 1992; Fausto-Sterling 1995; Haraway 1989; McClintock 1995; Pieterse 1995; Sharpley-Whiting 1999). Londa Schiebinger (1993, 159), for example, argued that "African women were seen as wanton perversions of sexuality.... They served as foils to the Victorian ideal of the passionless woman, becoming, as Sander Gilman has written, the central icon for sexuality in the nineteenth century." bell hooks (1992, 62) also cites Gilman in support of similar claims, writing that "Gilman documents the development of this image ... he emphasizes that it is the Black female body that is forced to serve as an icon for sexuality in general."

Although writing about ideology, these scholars fail to appreciate the very essence of ideology – what makes them so *ideological* – is the fact they are riddled with contradictions and marked by continuous conflicts and struggles over meaning. As Mannheim (1936, 9) explained in *Ideology and Utopia*:

It is with this clashing of modes of thought, each of which has the same claims to representational validity, that for the first time there is rendered possible the emergence of the question which is so fateful, but also so fundamental in the history of thought, namely, *how is it possible that identical human thought-processes concerned with the same world produce divergent conceptions of that world* [emphasis added]. And from this point it is only a step further to ask: Is it not possible that the thought processes which are involved here are not at all identical? May it not be found, when one has examined all the possibilities of human thought, that there are numerous alternative paths which can be followed?

Theorists who contend that there was a single ideology, central icon, or core image about Blackness and sexuality in the nineteenth century make two mistakes. First, they discount the extent to which ideas about Blackness were still emerging. Second, their analysis implies that this particular ideology magically escaped the types of conflicts that all other ideologies are subject to. Only by underplaying the existence and importance of ideological conflict can they sustain Gilman's argument that people from such widely different social locations as French aristocrats, English merchants, displaced peasants, gentlemen scientists, and factory workers held a singular and unified opinion about, and image of, Black women and sexuality.

The available historical evidence strongly contradicts Gilman's claims about the alleged ideological unanimity of such diverse social actors. Historical sources demonstrate quite clearly that the issue of whether or not steatopygia was a general attribute of Khoikhoi women, and whether Baartmann was considered a typical example of a Khoikhoi person, remained open to debate. Fisher (1814, 8), who compiled a compendium of his journey to the Cape, noted that

there is something like symmetry in the person of a Hottentot, their limbs being neatly turned, but they are for the most part of a diminutive stature, and no just idea of them can be formed from the specimens seen in this country [England], particularly that singular character the Hottentot Venus.

William Burchell (1822, 216) made a similar observation in his *Travels in the Interior of Southern Africa*. After describing a Khoikhoi woman with "a very large and protuberant behind," he hastened to add that this was not a general condition of the Khoikhoi people:

The exhibition of a woman of this description, in the principal countries of Europe has made the subject well known to all those who are curious in such matters. ... I ought not to allow this occasion to pass by without endeavoring to correct some erroneous notions. ... It is not a fact that the whole of the Hottentot race is thus formed. Neither is there any particular tribe to which this steatopygia, as it may be called, is peculiar. Nor is it more common to the Bushman tribe than to other Hottentots. It will not greatly mislead if our idea of its frequency be formed by comparing it with the corpulence of individuals among European nations.

It might be tempting to conclude that some people are simply more prescient observers than others are or, alternatively, that some people simply harbor less racial prejudice. Although important differences marked the standpoints of travelers in Africa versus pseudoscientists and lay people in England, the access to a wider array of empirical evidence is not the only reason that opinions varied so widely. Rather, what these examples make clear is that ideologies about racial and sexual alterity display the same basic characteristics as other ideologies do. They are internally inconsistent, they are constantly subject to struggle, and they reflect the structural locations of their adherents.

Most studies of Baartmann, following Gilman, have focused their attention on the role of science in establishing her sexual alterity (Fausto-Sterling 1995; Haraway 1989; McClintock 1995; Sharpley-Whiting 1999;

Wiss 1994). However, because scholars have so readily accepted Gilman's claim that the mere sight of Baartmann produced a uniform and unvarying ideological response, few have noticed or been motivated to investigate the important differences between British and French representations of her. None have questioned Gilman's (1985, 235) assertion that Baartmann's "genitalia and buttocks summarized her essence for the nineteenth century observer." Thus, they have neither noticed nor analyzed Baartmann's relatively weak interpellation into British medical and scientific discourses as compared to French. However, as Fausto-Sterling (1995, 33) observed (but did not analyze), "Although a theater attraction and the object of a legal dispute about slavery in England, *it was only in Paris* [emphasis added], before and after her death, that Baartmann entered into the scientific accounting of race and gender."

A second key question that goes unremarked and unanalyzed is how and why Baartmann came to reside in Paris at all. Despite the importance of this move, most scholars, following Gilman's lead, do not take up the issue at all (McClintock 1995; Schiebinger 1993; Wiss 1994). Strother (1999, 33), for example, simply stated that "Baartmann moved to Paris in 1814." Likewise, Fausto-Sterling (1995, 29) took note of it only to comment that after 1814, she "somehow ended up in Paris." However, Baartmann didn't simply move to or end up in Paris. Writing to the *Morning Chronicle*, Baartmann's original captor, Henrik Cezar, explained that he quickly sold her to "an Englishman" because his "mode of proceeding at the place of public entertainment seems to have given offense to the Public" (23 October 1810). According to Baartmann's own testimony, she was subsequently abandoned in Paris "by another Englishman" and thus came to be the property of a showman of wild animals.

We might ask why a commodity of such value to the English, both commercially and ideologically, passed through so many hands before she had to be taken out of the country and abandoned. Why didn't British theaters of anatomy, schools of medicine, or museums jump at the chance to examine and display this

bit of curiosity from their newest imperial outpost? Science was critical for rescripting conquest as both a necessary and essentially humanitarian act. Why, then, didn't British science make greater use of Baartmann's alterity?

It is important to note that at the time of Baartmann's exhibition in London, medical science was no less developed or commercialized than in France. There were many large medical hospitals and "theaters of anatomy" wherein the nongentlemanly members of the British scientific community earned their livelihoods. A large portion of these scholars combined medical practice with teaching as a form of economic support. Furthermore, the popularity of medical and anatomical lectures among the lay community was even *more* pronounced in Britain than it was in France. French scientists were employed by secular public institutions and wrote mainly for other scientists. In London, however, the line between science and show business was easily and often traversed. As Hays (1983, 106) explained, "Lectures on biological subjects could draw on another London resource in addition to the talent of the medical community. They could exploit London's position as the center of entertainment, spectacle, and display."

The fact that Baartmann failed to arouse commensurate amounts of scientific interest in England and France illustrates my earlier point that social relations, rather than biological essences, are critical for determining what individuals see when they look at one another. I maintain that Baartmann represented far more in the European imagination than a collection of body parts. Indeed, closer examination of the furor that ensued in the wake of her exhibition demonstrates that what she represented varied (as ideologies are wont to do) according to the social and political commitments of the interested social actors. Baartmann's exhibition provoked varying and contradictory responses. These responses can be better understood if they are analyzed as part and parcel of larger debates about liberty, property, and economic relations, rather than seeing them as simple manifestations of the universal human fascination with embodied difference.

Despite the popularity of contemporary claims that Baartmann was seen "only in terms of her buttocks" (Wiss 1994, 31), a substantial portion of the British public actually saw her as representing much more. When many people looked at Baartmann, they saw not only racial and sexual alterity but also a personification of current debates about the right to liberty versus the right to property. For many, Baartmann's captivity encapsulated the conflict between individual freedom and the interests of capital.

The contemporary debates about slavery provided the context to the Baartmann controversy, and it is within their parameters that it must be understood. Many individuals who opposed slavery on humanitarian grounds, nevertheless, were reluctant to infringe on the property rights of slaveholders. Reformers also balked at ideas of personhood that had the potential to complicate the relationship between capital and "free" labor. There was "a wish to attack slavery but not to infringe upon legally acquired property rights or to question long term indenture or even service for life" (Malik 1996, 64). Thus, Lindfors (1985, 138) incorrectly characterizes the legal battle that occurred about Baartmann's exhibition as "a classic confrontation between heated humanitarianism and commerce, between the abolitionist conscience and the entrepreneurial ideal, between love and money." There is a clear connection between the legal furor over the exhibition and how the British envisioned incorporating the Cape into the British Empire.

It is important to note that the society that sued Henrik Cezar, Baartmann's captor, on her behalf was called "The African Association for Promoting the Discovery of the Interior of Africa" and sought to play a leading role in opening a new phase in the exploitation of the continent. It was to this end that subscriptions were paid that were then used to subsidize sending travelers and explorers to Africa. Thus, the pertinent contest was never *between* love and money. Humanitarianism, as expressed in the actions of the African Association, served the interests of the landed and mercantile elite. These men were concerned with securing the global expansion of capitalist relations of production. Commercially minded men recognized the importance of Africa as a place where tropical products such as tea, coffee, tobacco,

sugar, and rice, desired by the growing middle-class market, might successfully be grown at less cost. They also saw Africa as a potential market for British manufactures.

High hopes were held out that the Cape Colony could be transformed to meet the objectives of both the merchant and landed elites. However, this transformation was contingent on a proletarianization of the indigenous labor force. This proletarianization required that slavery, the existing system of labor relations, be overturned in favor of a capitalist legal order wherein the Khoikhoi would be legally "free" but more completely open to subjugation as laborers in the developing frontier economy (Keegan 1996). As John Philip (1828, 365), director of the London Missionary society, explained,

By raising all the Hottentots of the colony … a new and extensive market would be created for British goods. We say nothing of the increased consumption of British manufactures … or the increase of our exports which would necessarily arise from the additional stimulus which would be given to the industry of the Hottentots by the increase of their artificial wants.

Thus, it was no accident that the goals of progressively minded landed elites, the mercantile and commercial classes, and humanitarians coalesced so readily in the goals of the African Association. Despite the many points of disagreement between merchants, missionaries, and explorers about how it would be accomplished, most agreed that the Khoikhoi would eventually be proletarianized and made to understand the value (and responsibility) of self-commodification. Humanitarianism readily and easily embraced the cause of economic liberalization, particularly in the areas of productive and commercial relations. The rhetoric of antislavery (which provided a critical backdrop to the opposition to Baartmann's forced captivity) merged (almost) seamlessly with that of imperial expansion.

The discussions concerning the Khoikhoi at the Cape thus paralleled the legal furor over Baartmann's exhibition. The question of the ownership of labor power took center stage in both. The immediate concern of the African Association (which sued Baartmann's captor, Henrik Cezar, on her behalf) was to ascertain whether she owned her own labor. As Macauley stated in the affidavit filed on her behalf, his purpose was to determine "whether [Baartmann] was made a public spectacle with her own free will and consent or whether she was compelled to exhibit herself" (quoted in Strother 1999, 43). Those opposed to Baartmann's exhibition debated less about whether her confinement represented a moral blight than about whether she was owned by someone else, and hence subject to forced exhibition, or if she belonged to herself, and thus was acting freely. For example, the *Morning Chronicle* (12 October 1810) argued,

The air of the British Constitution is too pure to permit slavery in the very heart of the metropolis, for I am sure you will easily discriminate between those beings who are sufficiently degraded to shew [sic] themselves for their own immediate profit where they act from their own free will and this poor slave.

Thus, in a number of ways, the Baartmann exhibition encapsulated in miniature the debates that were occurring about the labor more generally. Henrik Cezar, her brutal Dutch master, represented the old economic order at the Cape, based on enslavement, forced captivity, and despotism. The African Association represented the coming of a new colonial order based on a "voluntary" commodification of the self and a "willing" capitulation to the dominant logic of capital.

I have explored the widely divergent actions and reactions of the African Association, British travelers, missionaries, and the British viewing public at such length to demonstrate that when Europeans looked at Sarah Baartmann, it was not that they saw *only* her buttocks. Although her body represented sexual alterity, that was not all it represented. Some observers looked at her and her captivity and saw a particular system of productive relations they wanted to overthrow. Others saw a new area of the world ripe for exploitation and a new way to exploit it. And still others looked and saw the aesthetic antithesis of themselves.

Most probably saw a combination of these and more. Although the members of the African Association, no less than Cuvier, Cezar, and the hordes of British and French citizens who came to gawk at Baartmann's most intimate parts, no doubt took notice of her difference and believed in some notion of white supremacy, it is a mistake to take their actions as expressions of a *single, trans-historical, and unidimensional* ideology. If that were the case, it would be impossible to explain why Baartmann's alterity led one group of social actors to fetishize her exhibition and another to call for its immediate cessation.

Baartmann's exhibition also makes clear that white supremacy was never the simple expression of color prejudices. Each group of social actors, whether its particular interest was in looking at Baartmann, dissecting her, or sending her home, had its particular brand of racialist ideology, which was reflected in its political program. These political programs, in turn, reflected the social positions of their advocates. Thus, the only way French scientists (or any other group of social actors for that matter) could have imposed their exact understanding of Baartmann, Black women, and Black sexuality on any other group would have been if they could have transformed the lives and social relations of the relevant actors into exact replicas of their own.

Conclusion: Whose Bodies Matter?

Artist/scholar Jean Young (1997, 699) wrote that Sarah Baartmann has been "re-objectified" and "re-commodified." Yvette Abrahams (1997, 46), a South African scholar, also argues that "the genital encounter is not over. It may be seen in much recent scholarship on Sara Bartmann." The question must be asked why *this* woman has been made to function in contemporary academic debates as *the* preeminent example of racial and sexual alterity. This question becomes even more compelling when we consider that Sarah Baartmann was one of thousands of people exhibited and transformed into medical spectacles during the course of the nineteenth century (Altick 1978; Corbey 1993;

Lindfors 1999). Examples abound of women with excessive hair (who were primarily of European and Latin American ancestry) that were exhibited in circuses and "freak shows." These women were not only believed to be the "missing links" between the human and animal worlds but also hermaphrodite hybrids, caught between the male and female worlds (Bogdan 1988; Thomson 1997). However, none of these women (nor the category of excessively hairy women more generally) have been made to stand as "icons" of racial or sexual difference.

We might also return to the example of the Irish. Londa Schiebinger (1993, 156) maintains that "male skulls remained the central icon of racial difference until craniometry was replaced by intelligence testing in the late nineteenth and early twentieth centuries." Nancy Stepan (1990, 43) has also argued that the systematic study and measurement of male skulls was "especially significant for the science of human difference and similarity." We might also add that nineteenth-century ethnologists speculated about the biological basis for the "effeminancy" of the Celtic male. As Curtis (1968, 61) explained, "There was a curiously persistent and revealing label attached to the Irish, namely their characterization as a feminine race of people. This theme of Celtic femininity appears repeatedly." Yet, to my knowledge, the Irish male skull has *never* had the dubious distinction of being the central nineteenth-century image for racial and sexual difference between the European and the Black. The fact that Irish male skulls have not been thus characterized reflects less about the available historical evidence than about scholars' abilities to free themselves from contemporary understandings about what, historically, has constituted a Black experience. For if we compare the amount of ink spilled, the volume of studies done, and the number of corpses examined, it becomes apparent that Irish male skulls were of far more interest, and caused far more speculation about the nature of racial and gender differences, than steatopygious African backsides ever did.[3]

Some critics of postfoundationalist theories, like postmodernism and poststructuralism, have argued that they "simply appropriate the expe-

rience of 'Otherness' to enhance the discourse" (hooks 1994, 424). The lacunae and lapses that mark much of the contemporary feminist scholarship on Baartmann make us pause and ask, Is this simply another case of what Margaret Homans (1994) identified as the tendency for feminist theory to make Black women function as "grounds of embodiment in the context of theoretical abstractions?" Although some might argue that this is the case, this argument fails to consider the diverse strands within feminist theory and the long and intensely varied tradition of feminist thought and praxis. It also discounts the contributions of the many feminists of color that employ postmodernism and poststructuralism in their work (Carby 1999; hooks 1994; Spillers 1987).

Sarah Baartmann's curious and problematic "theoretical odyssey" cannot simply be explained as stemming from a lack of theoretical fit between postfoundationalist theory and the historical experiences of African and African American women. Rather, the ways in which she has been constructed as a theoretical object highlight the inherent dangers in the deployment of *any* theory without due attention to historical specificity. In particular, Baartmann's curious theoretical odyssey points to the problems that occur when race and gender are universalized and, thus, reified; or, in other words, when "commonsense understandings of these categories as they exist in the United States are elevated to the status of social scientific concepts" (Loveman 1999, 894).

Baartmann's curious theoretical odyssey also points to the dangers of analyzing the construction and perception of human difference as primarily a product of inner psychological drives. Gilman's pronouncements about Baartmann (and the theoretical "industry" that emerged therefrom) would not have been possible had her exhibition not been largely abstracted from its political and historical context. It was this theoretical abstraction (coupled with a healthy amount of psychological determinism) that made it easier for scholars to momentarily forget that Blackness, as an ideological construction, could not possibly have inspired a singular and uniform response. Privileging psychological dispositions over social relations also allowed scholars to give

Baartmann's corporeal alterity the power to produce history while momentarily forgetting this alterity was, at the same time, an historical product. Thus, in the final analysis, the theoretical lapses of contemporary social scientists, rather than the actions of nineteenth-century pseudoscientists, are the ones that threaten to finally succeed in transforming "the Hottentot Venus" into the central nineteenth-century icon for racial and sexual difference between the European and the Black.

NOTES

AUTHOR'S NOTE: *I would like to thank Emily Ignacio, Wanda Pillow, Yoon Pak, and Juliana Cheng for their helpful comments in preparing this article. I would also like to thank the Center for Advanced Study, University of Illinois Urbana–Champaign, where I was a fellow during the completion of this article.*

1 Sarah Baartmann is also sometimes referred to as Saartji Bartman or Baartman.

2 The Khoikhoi are also sometimes referred to as Khoisan and Khoi.

3 By Fausto-Sterling's (1995) estimate, there were a mere seven articles published between 1816 and 1836 (including Cuvier and de Blainville's dissection reports on Baartmann) on the subject of Khoikhoi women and steatopygia. There is not a single book-length monograph. Compare this with the hundreds of monographs and articles, published both in Britain and the United States, that used craniology to establish the racial inferiority and Negroid ancestry of the Irish Celt. These articles appeared in journals such as the *Journal of the Anthropological Institute of Great Britain* and *The Anthropological Review*.

REFERENCES

Abrahams, Yvette
1997 The great long national insult: "Science," sexuality, and the Khoisan in the 18th and early 19th century. *Agenda* 32:34–48.

Altick, Richard
1978 *The shows of London*. Cambridge, MA: Harvard University Press.

Appel, Tony
1987 *The Cuvier-Geoffroy debate*. Oxford, UK: Oxford University Press.

Barrow, John. [1801]
1968 *Travels in the interior of southern Africa*. Reprint, London: Johnson Reprint Co.

Bentham, William
1834 *The Gael and the Cymbri*. Reprint, London.

Bogdan, Robert
1988 *Freak show*. Chicago: University of Chicago Press.

Burchell, William. [1822]
1953 *Travels in the interior of southern Africa*. Reprint, with a foreword by Isaac Schapera. London: Batchworth Press.

Carby, Hazel
1999 *Cultures in Babylon: Black Britain and African America*. London: Verso.

Cheng, William
1995 *Joyce, race, empire*. Cambridge, UK: Cambridge University Press.

Corbey, Raymond
1993 Ethnographic showcases, 1870–1930. *Cultural Anthropology* 8 (3): 338–69.

Crais, Clifton
1992 *The making of the colonial order*. Cambridge, UK: Cambridge University Press.

Curtis, Perry
1968 *Anglo-Saxons and Celts: A study of anti-Irish prejudice in Victorian England*. Berkeley: University of California Press.

Donald, James, and Ali Rattansi
1992 *"Race," culture, and difference*. London: Sage.

Donald, James, and Ali Rattansi
1997 *Apes and angels: The Irish in Victorian caricature*. Washington, DC: Smithsonian Institution.

Durkheim, Emile
1982 *The rules of sociological method*. New York: Free Press.

Fausto-Sterling, Anne
1995 Gender, race, and nation: The comparative anatomy of "Hottentot" women in Europe, 1815–1817. In *Deviant bodies*, edited by Jennifer Terry and Jacqueline Urla. Bloomington: Indina University Press.

Fields, Barbara
1982 Slavery, race, and ideology in American history. In *Region, race, and reconstruction*, edited by J. Morgan Kousser and James M. McPherson. New York: Oxford University Press.

Fields, Barbara
1990   Slavery, race, and ideology in the United States of America. *New Left Review* 181: 95–118.

Fisher, Richard Barnard
1814   *The importance of the Cape of Good Hope*. London.

Gilman, Sander
1985   Black bodies, white bodies: Toward an iconography of female sexuality in late nineteenth century art, medicine, and literature. In *Race, writing, and difference*, edited by Henry L. Gates Jr. Chicago: University of Chicago Press.

Gordon, Robert
1992   The venal Hottentot Venus and the great chain of being. *African Studies* 51 (2): 185–201.

Haraway, Donna
1989   *Primate visions*. London: Routledge.

Hays, J. N.
1983   The London lecturing empire, 1800–50. In *Metropolis and province: Science in British culture, 1780–1850*, edited by Ian Inkster and Jack Morrell. Philadephia: University of Pennsylvania Press.

Homans, Margaret
1994   Women of color, writers, and feminist theory. *New Literary History* 25:73–94.

hooks, bell
1992   *Black looks: Race and representation*. Boston: South End.

hooks, bell
1994   Postmodern blackness. In *Colonial discourse and postcolonial theory*, edited by Patrick Williams and Laura Chrisman. New York: Columbia University Press.

Keegan, Timothy
1996   *Colonial South Africa and the origins of the racial order*. Cape Town, South Africa: David Philip.

Lichtenstein, Henry
1812   *Travels in southern African in the years 1803, 1804, 1805, and 1806*. London.

Lindfors, Berth
1985   Courting the Hottentot Venus. *Africa* 40:133–48.

Lindfors, Berth
1999   *Africans on stage*. Indiana: University of Indiana Press.

Loomba, Ania
1998   *Colonialism postcolonialism*. New York: Routledge.

Loveman, Mara
1999   Is race essential? *American Sociological Review* 64:891–98.

Malik, Keenan
1996   *The meaning of race*. New York: New York University Press.

Mannheim, Karl
1936   *Ideology and utopia*. New York: Harcourt.

McClintock, Anne
1995   *Imperial leather*. London: Routledge.

Philip, John. [1828]
1969   *Researches in South Africa*. Reprint, New York: Negro Universities Press.

Pick, D.
1989   *Faces of degeneration: A European disorder, C. 1848–1918*. Cambridge, UK: Cambridge University Press.

Pieterse, Jan N.
1995   *White on Black*. New Haven, CT: Yale University Press.

Price, Thomas
1829   *An essay on the physiognomy and physiology of the present inhabitants of Britain*. Reprint, London.

Prichard, James C.
1857   *The eastern origin of the Celtic nations*. Reprint, London.

Pringle, Thomas. [1834]
1964   *African sketches*. Reprint, Cape Town: C. Struik.

Prior, James
1819   *Voyage along eastern coast of Africa*. London: Richard Philips Co.

Review of *Travels in southern Africa in the years 1803–1806*, by Henry Lichtenstein. 1812. *The Quarterly Review* 7 (16): 374–395.

Schiebinger, Londa
1993   *Nature's body*. Boston: Beacon.

Sharpley-Whiting, Tracey Denean
1999   *Black Venus*. Durham, NC: Duke University Press.

Spillers, Hortense
1987   Mama's baby, Papa's maybe: An American grammar book. *Diacritics* 17:65–81.

Stepan, Nancy
1990   Race and gender: The role of analogy in science. In *Anatomy of racism*, edited by David Theo Goldberg. St. Paul: University of Minnesota Press.

Stoler, Anne
1995   *Race and the education of desire*. Durham, NC: Duke University Press.

Strother, Z. S.
1999 Display of the body Hottentot. In *Africans on stage*, edited by Berth Lindfors. Bloomington: University of Indiana Press.

Thompson, George
1827 *Travels and adventures in southern Africa*. London.

Thompson, Rosmarie
1997 *Extraordinary bodies: Figuring physical disability in American culture and literature*. New York: Columbia University Press.

Vaughan
1991 *Curing their ills*. Cambridge, MA: Polity.

Wacquant, Loic
1997 Towards an analytic of racial domination. *Political Power and Social Theory* 11:221–34.

Wiss, Rosemary
1994 Lipreading: Remembering Saartjie Baartman. *Australian Journal of Anthropology* 5:11–40.

Young, Jean
1997 The re-objectification and re-commodification of Saartjie Baartman in Suzan Lori Parks's Venus. *African American Review* 31:699–708.

Part II

Primitive Promiscuity and Matriarchal Theory ("Oversexed Savages")

Introduction

With the exception of the Cambridge and Oxford law professor, Henry Sumner Maine, virtually all the major evolutionary anthropologists of the late nineteenth century believed that the family had evolved from a pre-cultural zero point where there was no sexual regulation, not even an incest taboo, and promiscuity was normal. The idea of primitive promiscuity fed on the stereotypes of "oversexed savages," which we have already discussed, although it was conceded that total promiscuity no longer existed anywhere. The reports of missionaries and travelers in South America, California, and sub-Saharan Africa were all utilized to construct this representation, but it was (then) contemporary Australia, whose aboriginal inhabitants supposedly represented the living kindergarten of the human race, that most closely approximated the zero point. Primitive promiscuity supposedly evolved into some form of "mother right" (matriarchy, what we would now call "matriliny," misconstrued). Matrilineal descent was logical when one could always presumably trace the mother, but the father might be one of several different people. Matriarchy evolved into patriarchy in more advanced farming societies, and was eventually succeeded by modern monogamy. On these matters, J. J. Bachofen in Switzerland, John F. McLennan and John Lubbock in Britain, and Lewis Henry Morgan in the US all agreed, but they disagreed vociferously on the details.

Bachofen called the primal stage "hetaerism," in other words "whoredom," assuming, like many of his contemporaries, an equivalence between prostitutes everywhere and the earliest savages. "Exhausted" by male lusts, women revolted and established the first social order, "mother right" (Bachofen 1967 [1861]: 93–95). Eventually, as agriculture, property rights, and morality developed, "mother right" was succeeded by the more spiritual institution of patriarchy.

Sexualities in Anthropology: A Reader, edited by Andrew P. Lyons and Harriet D. Lyons
© 2011 Blackwell Publishing Ltd.

McLennan described a movement from promiscuity to forms of regulated matriliny that involved an exchange of women between social groups (exogamy). In the primal state there had been a Hobbesian state of chaos. Endemic warfare and shortages of food may have caused a preference for males over females that resulted in female infanticide. As a consequence there was a shortage of women in many groups which could be remedied by raiding expeditions. Noting that savages were not known for delicacy of feeling in sexual matters, McLennan described an Australian marriage ceremony: "Among the Australians, according to one account, when a man sees a woman whom he likes, he forces her to accompany him by blows, ending by knocking her down and carrying her off" (1970[1865]: 31–2). Eventually, negotiated exchanges and regular alliances were substituted for warfare. Endogamous groups succeeded exogamous groups and patriliny succeeded matriliny (we leave out the details of an elaborate scheme second stage of marriage by capture).

The clue that this institution was once universal was the worldwide occurrence of ceremonies of symbolic capture that often accompanied marriage in many societies, particularly some in Central Asia. The bride is the victim of a fake abduction by the groom and his friends, traveling on horseback in order to sweep her off her feet. Sir John Lubbock, McLennan's contemporary, was also a believer in marriage by capture. As Sir Edmund Leach remarked 45 years ago (see Chapter 17 in this volume), such fantasies tell us a lot about the mindset of Victorian patriarchs, but very little about the history of marriage and sexual morality.

In *Systems of Consanguinity and Affinity* and *Ancient Society*, Lewis Henry Morgan developed a much more sober account of moral evolution, correlating the development of the family with the evolution of modes of property and the development of technology. What we would now called band societies were succeeded by societies based on the lineage or clan ("gentile" society after the Roman *gens* or clan/lineage), a change that corresponded with the development of pottery and early horticulture. The earliest changes in band societies corresponded to a movement from total promiscuity involving incest (the consanguineous family) to group marriage which was simultaneously polyandry and polygyny (one's parents and siblings were now off limits). A late form of group marriage that, in Morgan's imagination, had recently existed in Hawaii, involved the linking of a set of brothers ("the Smiths," we might say) with a set of sisters ("the Browns") who were not members of their (the Smiths') kin group. Such groups were still matrilineal, and matriliny was also typical of more evolved groups like the Iroquois, with whom Morgan became familiar (he was raised in upstate New York, practiced law there, and was introduced to the Seneca by the young chief, Ely Parker). The Iroquois had no group marriage; they had a system of clan exogamy, whereby it was necessary for a man to select his partner from any clan but his own (there were up to eight clans in number). Although Iroquois women could not become chiefs, they could and still do help select them. Up until this stage of social evolution ("The Lower Status of Barbarism"), property in both things and people was communal, and the society was egalitarian. The development of irrigation agriculture in the Western Hemisphere (along with adobe houses) and the domestication of animals in Europe and Asia resulted in a surplus of resources, and the creation of inheritable forms of property. Animal husbandry in Eurasia had a lot to do with the creation of patriarchal institutions and systematic forms of inequality (gender and various social groups – castes, estates, etc.) based on differential access to property. The invention of iron technology and the development of writing brought further advances in Eurasia only.

In order to prove his hypotheses, Morgan relied heavily on the data he accumulated over a period of 20 years, beginning in 1858, regarding kinship terminologies in various societies from missionaries and other correspondents. The fact that the Iroquois called some cousins by the same terms as they did their siblings, but distinguished others from them (B = MZS = FBS ≠ MBS ≠ FZS; Z = MZD = FBD ≠ MBD ≠ FZD; MBS = FZS; MBD = FZD),[1] was perhaps evidence that they once had Punaluan marriage. Such a union would mean that one's parallel cousins (FBC, MZC) might also be one's siblings. In Hawaii, the Iroquoian relationship terminology was not found, but instead there was a set of terms which equated one's father with one's uncles on both sides of the family, etc. The generations were kept distinct. Morgan thought that the Hawaiian terminology pointed back to a very early stage of human social evolution. His mistake was to assume that "kinship" terms always describe blood relationships – they can denote membership of larger groups, honorary or fictional links, age- or generation-related status, etc.

Friedrich Engels and his friend Karl Marx read Morgan and the matriarchal theorists with great interest. They felt that Morgan had clearly demonstrated the probability of primitive communalism which, despite its many disadvantages, was basically fair, that he had further used a materialistic scheme to show how changes in technology affected social and moral evolution, and that he had correctly seen that progress had made victims both of women and those groups that occupied the bottom rung of society at various stages of evolution. Socialism would eventually free women, just as it would free the workers. Engels's book, *The Origin of the Family, Private Property and the State*, is a remarkably clear summary of Morgan's work. It was for many years assigned reading in the USSR, where it represented anthropological orthodoxy, thereby perpetuating one particular interpretation of a very "Victorian" book.

As we have already indicated, Maine disagreed strongly with matriarchal theory, because the societies whose past he could trace with written records (Rome, Greece, India) had stronger forms of the patriarchal family, the further back one went, and he was loath to indulge in speculation about the unrecorded past. Although Lubbock was his friend and neighbor, Darwin was unsure about theories of matriarchy and primitive promiscuity, because the limited evidence of social behavior among apes pointed in a very different direction, to groups dominated by jealous, older males (Lyons and Lyons 2004: 105).

NOTE

1 B = brother, D = daughter, F = father, M = mother, S = son, Z = sister, C = child, so that MBD = FZD means that we refer to both mother's brother's daughter and father's sister's daughter (both *cross* cousins) by the same term.

REFERENCES

Bachofen, J. J.
  1967[1861] Myth, Religion and Mother Right, Selected Writings of J. J. Bachofen. Trans. Ralph Manheim. Bollingen Series, 84. New York: Princeton University Press.

Lubbock, Sir John
  1978[1870]   The Origin of Civilization and the Primitive Condition of Man. Ed. and with
  an introduction by Peter Riviere. Chicago: University of Chicago Press.
Lyons, Andrew P., and Harriet D. Lyons.
  2004   Irregular Connections: A History of Anthropology and Sexuality. Lincoln, NE:
  University of Nebraska Press.
Maine, Sir Henry
  1883   Dissertation on Early Law and Custom. London: John Murray.
McLennan, John F.
  1970[1865]   Primitive Marriage: An Inquiry into the Origin of the Form of Capture in
  Marriage Ceremonies. Ed. and with an introduction by Peter Riviere. Chicago: University
  of Chicago Press.
Morgan, Lewis Henry
  1870   Systems of Consanguinity and Affinity of the Human Family. Washington:
  Smithsonian Institution.
Morgan, Lewis Henry
  1963[1877]   Ancient Society. Ed. and with an introduction and annotations by Eleanor
  Burke Leacock. Cleveland and New York: World Publishing Company.

3

Origins of the Family

Friedrich Engels

The Family

Morgan, who spent a great part of his life among the Iroquois Indians – settled to this day in New York State – and was adopted into one of their tribes (the Senecas), found in use among them a system of consanguinity which was in contradiction to their actual family relationships. There prevailed among them a form of monogamy easily terminable on both sides, which Morgan calls the "pairing family." The issue of the married pair was therefore known and recognized by everybody: there could be no doubt about whom to call father, mother, son, daughter, brother, sister. But these names were actually used quite differently. The Iroquois calls not only his own children his sons and daughters, but also the children of his brothers; and they call him father. The children of his sisters, however, he calls his nephews and nieces, and they call him their uncle. The Iroquois woman, on the other hand, calls her sisters' children, as well as her own, her sons and daughters, and they call her mother. But her brothers' children she calls her nephews and nieces, and she is known as their aunt. Similarly, the children of brothers call one another brother and sister, and so do the children of sisters. A woman's own children and the children of her brother, on the other hand, call one another cousins. And these are not mere empty names, but expressions of actual conceptions of nearness and remoteness, of equality and difference in the degrees of consanguinity: these conceptions serve as the foundation of a fully elaborated system of consanguinity through which several hundred different relationships of one individual can be expressed. What is more, this system is not only in full force among all American Indians (no exception has been found up to the present), but also retains its validity almost unchanged among the aborigines of India, the Dravidian tribes in the Deccan and the Gaura tribes in Hindustan. To this day the Tamils of southern India and the Iroquois Seneca Indians in New York State still express more than two hundred degrees of consanguinity in the same manner. And among these tribes of India, as among all the American Indians, the actual relationships arising out of the existing form of the family contradict the system of consanguinity.

Extract from *The Origin of the Family, Private Property and the State*, by Friedrich Engels, trans. Alick West, pp 55–68. Reprinted with permission of Lawrence & Wishart UK.

Sexualities in Anthropology: A Reader, edited by Andrew P. Lyons and Harriet D. Lyons
© 2011 Blackwell Publishing Ltd.

How is this to be explained? In view of the decisive part played by consanguinity in the social structure of all savage and barbarian peoples, the importance of a system so widespread cannot be dismissed with phrases. When a system is general throughout America and also exists in Asia among peoples of a quite different race, when numerous instances of it are found with greater or less variation in every part of Africa and Australia, then that system has to be historically explained, not talked out of existence, as McLennan, for example, tried to do. The names of father, child, brother, sister are no mere complimentary forms of address; they involve quite definite and very serious mutual obligations which together make up an essential part of the social constitution of the peoples in question.

The explanation was found. In the Sandwich Islands (Hawaii) there still existed in the first half of the nineteenth century a form of family in which the fathers and mothers, brothers and sisters, sons and daughters, uncles and aunts, nephews and nieces were exactly what is required by the American and old Indian system of consanguinity. But now comes a strange thing. Once again, the system of consanguinity in force in Hawaii did not correspond to the actual form of the Hawaiian family. For according to the Hawaiian system of consanguinity all children of brothers and sisters are without exception brothers and sisters of one another and are considered to be the common children not only of their mother and her sisters or of their father and his brothers, but of all the brothers and sisters of both their parents without distinction. While, therefore, the American system of consanguinity presupposes a more primitive form of the family which has disappeared in America, but still actually exists in Hawaii, the Hawaiian system of consanguinity, on the other hand, points to a still earlier form of the family which, though we can nowhere prove it to be still in existence, nevertheless must have existed; for otherwise the corresponding system of consanguinity could never have arisen.

The family [says Morgan] represents an active principle. It is never stationary, but advances from a lower to a higher form as society advances from a lower to a higher condition. ... Systems of consanguinity, on the contrary, are passive; recording the progress made by the family at long intervals apart, and only changing radically when the family has radically changed. [Morgan 1877: 444]

"And," adds Marx, "the same is true of the political, juridical, religious, and philosophical systems in general." While the family undergoes living changes, the system of consanguinity ossifies; while the system survives by force of custom, the family outgrows it. But just as Cuvier could deduce from the marsupial bone of an animal skeleton found near Paris that it belonged to a marsupial animal and that extinct marsupial animals once lived there, so with the same certainty we can deduce from the historical survival of a system of consanguinity that an extinct form of family once existed which corresponded to it.

The systems of consanguinity and the forms of the family we have just mentioned differ from those of today in the fact that every child has more than one father and mother. In the American system of consanguinity, to which the Hawaiian family corresponds, brother and sister cannot be the father and mother of the same child; but the Hawaiian system of consanguinity, on the contrary, presupposes a family in which this was the rule. Here we find ourselves among forms of family which directly contradict those hitherto generally assumed to be alone valid. The traditional view recognizes only monogamy, with, in addition, polygamy on the part of individual men, and at the very most polyandry on the part of individual women; being the view of moralizing philistines, it conceals the fact that in practice these barriers raised by official society are quietly and calmly ignored. The study of primitive history, however, reveals conditions where the men live in polygamy and their wives in polyandry at the same time, and their common children are therefore considered common to them all – and these conditions in their turn undergo a long series of changes before they finally end in monogamy. The trend of these changes is to narrow more and more the circle of people comprised within the common bond of marriage, which was originally very wide, until at last it includes only the single pair, the dominant form of marriage today.

Reconstructing thus the past history of the family, Morgan, in agreement with most of his colleagues, arrives at a primitive stage when unrestricted sexual freedom prevailed within the tribe, every woman belonging equally to every man and every man to every woman. Since the eighteenth century there had been talk of such a primitive state, but only in general phrases. Bachofen – and this is one of his great merits – was the first to take the existence of such a state seriously and to search for its traces in historical and religious survivals. Today we know that the traces he found do not lead back to a social stage of promiscuous sexual intercourse, but to a much later form – namely, group marriage. The primitive social stage of promiscuity, if it ever existed, belongs to such a remote epoch that we can hardly expect to prove its existence directly by discovering its social fossils among backward savages. Bachofen's merit consists in having brought this question to the forefront for examination.[1]

Lately it has become fashionable to deny the existence of this initial stage in human sexual life. Humanity must be spared this "shame." It is pointed out that all direct proof of such a stage is lacking, and particular appeal is made to the evidence from the rest of the animal world; for, even among animals, according to the numerous facts collected by Letourneau (Evolution du manage et de la faults, 1888), complete promiscuity in sexual intercourse marks a low stage of development. But the only conclusion I can draw from all these facts, so far as man and his primitive conditions of life are concerned, is that they prove nothing whatever. That vertebrates mate together for a considerable period is sufficiently explained by physiological causes – in the case of birds, for example, by the female's need of help during the brooding period; examples of faithful monogamy among birds prove nothing about man, for the simple reason that men are not descended from birds. And if strict monogamy is the height of all virtue, then the palm must go to the tapeworm, which has a complete set of male and female sexual organs in each of its 50–200 proglottides, or sections, and spends

its whole life copulating in all its sections with itself. Confining ourselves to mammals, however, we find all forms of sexual life – promiscuity, indications of group marriage, polygyny, monogamy. Polyandry alone is lacking – it took human beings to achieve that. Even our nearest relations, the quadrumana, exhibit every possible variation in the grouping of males and females; and if we narrow it down still more and consider only the four anthropoid apes, all that Letourneau has to say about them is that they are sometimes monogamous, sometimes polygamous, while Saussure, quoted by Giraud-Teulon, maintains that they are monogamous. The more recent assertions of the monogamous habits of the anthropoid apes which are cited by Westermarck (The History of Human Marriage, London, 1891), are also very far from proving anything. In short, our evidence is such that honest Letourneau admits: "Among mammals there is no strict relation between the degree of intellectual development and the form of sexual life." And Espinas (Des societes animates, 1877), says in so many words:

The herd is the highest social group which we can observe among animals. It is composed, so it appears, of families, but from the start the family and the herd are in conflict with one another and develop in inverse proportion.

As the above shows, we know practically nothing definite about the family and other social groupings of the anthropoid apes; the evidence is flatly contradictory. Which is not to be wondered at. The evidence with regard to savage human tribes is contradictory enough, requiring very critical examination and sifting; and ape societies are far more difficult to observe than human. For the present, therefore, we must reject any conclusion drawn from such completely unreliable reports.

The sentence quoted from Espinas, however, provides a better starting point. Among the higher animals the herd and the family are not complementary to one another, but antagonistic. Espinas shows very well how the jealousy of the males during the mating season loosens the ties of every social herd or temporarily breaks it up.

When the family bond is close and exclusive, herds form only in exceptional cases. When on the other hand free sexual intercourse or polygamy prevails, the herd comes into being almost spontaneously.... Before a herd can be formed, family ties must be loosened and the individual must have become free again. This is the reason why organized flocks are so rarely found among birds.... We find more or less organized societies among mammals, however, precisely because here the individual is not merged in the family.... In its first growth, therefore, the common feeling of the herd has no greater enemy than the common feeling of the family. We state it without hesitation: only by absorbing families which had undergone a radical change could a social form higher than the family have developed; at the same time, these families were thereby enabled later to constitute themselves afresh under infinitely more favorable circumstances. [Espinas, op. cit., quoted by Giraud-Teulon, Origines du mariage et de la famille, 1884, pp. 518–20].

Here we see that animal societies are, after all, of some value for drawing conclusions about human societies; but the value is only negative. So far as our evidence goes, the higher vertebrates know only two forms of family – polygyny or separate couples; each form allows only one adult male, only one husband. The jealousy of the male, which both consolidates and isolates the family, sets the animal family in opposition to the herd. The jealousy of the males prevents the herd, the higher social form, from coming into existence, or weakens its cohesion, or breaks it up during the mating period; at best, it arrests its development. This alone is sufficient proof that animal families and primitive human society are incompatible, and that when primitive men were working their way up from the animal creation, they either had no family at all or a form that does not occur among animals. In small numbers, an animal so defenseless as evolving man might struggle along even in conditions of isolation, with no higher social grouping than the single male and female pair, such as Westermarck, following the reports of hunters, attributes to the gorillas and the chimpanzees. For man's

development beyond the level of the animals, for the achievement of the greatest advance nature can show, something more was needed: the power of defense lacking to the individual had to be made good by the united strength and co-operation of the herd. To explain the transition to humanity from conditions such as those in which the anthropoid apes live today would be quite impossible; it looks much more as if these apes had strayed off the line of evolution and were gradually dying out or at least degenerating. That alone is sufficient ground for rejecting all attempts based on parallels drawn between forms of family and those of primitive man. Mutual toleration among the adult males, freedom from jealousy, was the first condition for the formation of those larger, permanent groups in which alone animals could become men. And what, in fact, do we find to be the oldest and most primitive form of family whose historical existence we can indisputably prove and which in one or two parts of the world we can still study today? Group marriage, the form of family in which whole groups of men and whole groups of women mutually possess one another, and which leaves little room for jealousy. And at a later stage of development we find the exceptional form of polyandry, which positively revolts every jealous instinct and is therefore unknown among animals. But as all known forms of group marriage are accompanied by such peculiarly complicated regulations that they necessarily point to earlier and simpler forms of sexual relations, and therefore in the last resort to a period of promiscuous intercourse corresponding to the transition from the animal to the human, the references to animal marriages only bring us back to the very point from which we were to be led away for good and all.

What, then, does promiscuous sexual intercourse really mean? It means the absence of prohibitions and restrictions which are or have been in force. We have already seen the barrier of jealousy go down. If there is one thing certain, it is that the feeling of jealousy develops relatively late. The same is true of the conception of incest. Not only were brother and sister originally man and wife; sexual intercourse between parents and children is still permitted among many peoples today. Bancroft (The Native Races of the Pacific States of North America, 1875, Vol. I), testifies to it among the Kadiaks on the Behring Straits, the Kadiaks near Alaska, and the Tinneh in the interior of British North America; Letourneau compiled reports of it among the Chippewa Indians, the Cucus in Chile, the Caribs, the Karens in Burma; to say nothing of the stories told by the old Greeks and Romans about the Parthians, Persians, Scythians, Huns, and so on. Before incest was invented – for incest is an invention, and a very valuable one, too – sexual intercourse between parents and children did not arouse any more repulsion than sexual intercourse between other persons of different generations, and that occurs today even in the most philistine countries without exciting any great horror; even "old maids" of over sixty, if they are rich enough, sometimes marry young men in their thirties. But if we consider the most primitive known forms of family apart from their conceptions of incest – conceptions which are totally different from ours and frequently in direct contradiction to them – then the form of sexual intercourse can only be described as promiscuous – promiscuous in so far as the restrictions later established by custom did not yet exist. But in everyday practice that by no means necessarily implies general mixed mating. Temporary pairings of one man with one woman were not in any way excluded, just as in the cases of group marriages today the majority of relationships are of this character. And when Westermarck, the latest writer to deny the existence of such a primitive state, applies the term "marriage" to every relationship in which the two sexes remain mated until the birth of the offspring, we must point out that this kind of marriage can very well occur under the conditions of promiscuous intercourse without contradicting the principle of promiscuity – the absence of any restriction imposed by custom on sexual intercourse. Westermarck, however, takes the standpoint that promiscuity "involves a suppression of individual inclinations," and that therefore "the most genuine form of it is prostitution." In my opinion, any understanding of primitive society is impossible to

people who only see it as a brothel. We will return to this point when discussing group marriage.

According to Morgan, from this primitive state of promiscuous intercourse there developed, probably very early:

The Consanguine Family, The First Stage of the Family

Here the marriage groups are separated according to generations: all the grandfathers and grandmothers within the limits of the family are all husbands and wives of one another; so are also their children, the fathers and mothers; the latter's children will form a third circle of common husbands and wives; and their children, the great-grandchildren of the first group, will form a fourth. In this form of marriage, therefore, only ancestors and progeny, and parents and children, are excluded from the rights and duties (as we should say) of marriage with one another. Brothers and sisters, male and female cousins of the first, second, and more remote degrees, are all brothers and sisters of one another, and precisely for that reason they are all husbands and wives of one another. At this stage the relationship of brother and sister also includes as a matter of course the practice of sexual intercourse with one another.[2] In its typical form, such a family would consist of the descendants of a single pair, the descendants of these descendants in each generation being again brothers and sisters, and therefore husbands and wives, of one another.[3]

The consanguine family is extinct. Even the most primitive peoples known to history provide no demonstrable instance of it. But that it must have existed, we are compelled to admit: for the Hawaiian system of consanguinity still prevalent today throughout the whole of Polynesia expresses degrees of consanguinity which could only arise in this form of family; and the whole subsequent development of the family presupposes the existence of the consanguine family as a necessary preparatory stage.

NOTES

1   Bachofen proves how little he understood his own discovery, or rather his guess, by using the term "hetaerism" to describe this primitive state. For the Greeks, when they introduced the word, hetaerism meant intercourse of men, unmarried or living in monogamy, with unmarried women, it always presupposes a definite form of marriage outside which this intercourse takes place and includes at least the possibility of prostitution. The word was never used in any other sense, and it is in this sense that I use it with Morgan. Bachofen everywhere introduces into his extremely important discoveries the most incredible mystifications through his notion that in their historical development the relations between men and women had their origin in men's contemporary religious conceptions, not in their actual conditions of life.

2   In a letter written in the spring of 1882, Marx expresses himself in the strongest terms about the complete misrepresentation of primitive times in Wagner's text to the Nibelangen: "Have such things been heard, that brother embraced sister as a bride?" To Wagner and his "lecherous gods" who, quite in the modern manner, spice their love affairs with a little incest, Marx replies: "In primitive times the sister was the wife, and that was moral."

3   NOTE in Fourth edition: A French friend of mine who is an admirer of Wagner is not in agreement with this note. He observes that already in the Elder Edda, on which Wagner based his story, in the OEgisdrekka, Loki makes the reproach to Freya: "In the sight of the gods thou didst embrace thine own brother." Marriage between brother and sister, he argues, was therefore forbidden already at that time. The OEgisdrekka is the expression of a time when belief in the old myths had completely broken down; it is purely a satire on the gods, in the style of Lucian. If Loki as Mephisto makes such a reproach to Freya, it tells rather against Wagner. Loki also says some lines later to Niordhr: "With thy sister didst thou breed son." (vidh systur thinni gaztu slikan mog) Niordhr is not, indeed, an Asa, but a Vana, and says in the Ynglinga saga that marriages between brothers and sisters are usual in Vanaland, which was not the case among the Asas. This would seem to show that the Vanas were more ancient gods than the Asas. At any rate, Niordhr lives among the OEgisdrekka is rather a proof that at the time when the Norse sagas of the gods arose, marriages between brothers and sisters, at any rate among the gods, did not yet excite any horror. If one wants to find excuses for Wagner, it would perhaps be better to cite Goethe instead of the Edda, for in his ballad of the God and the Bayadere Goethe commits a similar mistake in regard to the religious surrender of women, which he makes far too similar to modern prostitution.

SELECT BIBLIOGRAPHY

Bachofen, Johann Jakob
    1861   Das Mutterrecht: eine Untersuchung über die Gynaikokratie der alten Welt nach ihrer religiösen und rechtlichen Natur. Stuttgart: Krais & Hoffman.
Bancroft, Hubert H.
    1875   Native Races of the Pacific States of North America. New York: D. Appleton and Company.
Espinas, Alfred
    1877   Les Sociétés animales. Paris.
Letourneau, Charles Jean M.
    1888   L'Evolution du mariage et de la famille. Paris.
Morgan, Lewis Henry
    1877   Ancient Society: or, Researches in the Lines of Human Progress from Savagery through Barbarism to Civilization. London: Macmillan.
Westermarck, Edward
    1891   The History of Human Marriage. London: Macmillan.

Part III

Against Primitive Promiscuity
(Fear of Sex)

Introduction

In this set of readings we examine the slow disappearance of an idea that was integral to many racial theories of the eighteenth and nineteenth centuries and also formed the basis of the matriarchal theories we have discussed. That notion was the primitive promiscuity of the oversexed savage. Chapter 4 (taken from our own book) deals with the critical period between the late 1880s and 1910 when matriarchal theory suffered many blows. It had always had powerful opposition from scholars such as Henry Maine, who insisted that the patriarchal family could be traced back to the earliest days of Greek, Roman, and Hindu civilization. There were now new opponents such as Charles Staniland Wake, Northcote Thomas, the first government anthropologist in West Africa as well as an expert in Australian kinship, the lawyer J. J. Atkinson, and a trio of scholars who read each other's work with some approval: the sociologist and anthropologist Edward Westermarck, the classicist and amateur anthropologist Ernest Crawley, and the reclusive sexologist Havelock Ellis. Westermarck was to teach the young Bronislaw Malinowski, whose doctoral thesis, *The Family among the Australian Aborigines* (1913), endorsed his belief in the primordial existence of the family unit. We show that the work of these scholars may in part have reflected the availability of new data from missionaries, travelers, and early ethnographers, but we are unsure whether or not that evidence was the fundamental reason for the change. In the case of Westermarck, adherence to Darwinian principles played a key role, insofar as he thought that the reproductive pressures on the family were consistent throughout human history. Some of the "advances" in knowledge about primitive sexuality had a downside: a belief that primitive peoples were undersexed rather than oversexed, and resembled non-human mammals inasmuch as they went in and out of heat.

Sexualities in Anthropology: A Reader, edited by Andrew P. Lyons and Harriet D. Lyons
© 2011 Blackwell Publishing Ltd.

We suggest that the social climate of the late nineteenth century may have had a profound influence on the formation of these ideas. As Elaine Showalter (1991) has noted, there was a general "crisis in masculinity" reflected in the fiction of authors like Rider Haggard (*She*), Robert Louis Stevenson (*Dr. Jekyll and Mr. Hyde*), and J. M. Barrie (*Peter Pan*), as well as in the life and writings of Oscar Wilde (*The Picture of Dorian Gray*). That crisis reflected a questioning of Victorian patriarchal institutions. In Britain, there was a feminist and humanitarian outcry concerning trafficking in girls and women and dissatisfaction with attempts to control venereal disease without fundamentally altering the double standard. Prostitutes who had previously been regarded as a deplorable but necessary evil, subjected to medical inspection and confinement, came to be seen by many as victims of a corrupt system. In both Britain and the United States the social purity movement supported temperance and the control of male sexuality for religious as well as feminist reasons. Demands for change put new pressure on middle-class marriages as husbands and wives were increasingly expected to fill each other's sexual needs at home. This culminated in early twentieth-century advocacy of trial marriage and companionate marriage by "advanced" thinkers.

New anxieties were raised by advocates of eugenics, who worried about the erosion and degeneration of creative sectors in society, fearful that the best elements of society were not breeding enough, while the lower orders were breeding too much. Birth control remained highly controversial during this period, but despite legal and moral conflicts its use was gradually increasing. Some eugenicists were socially conservative, while others supported a variety of schemes for social betterment, the advancement of women, and sexual liberation.

The fin de siècle (1885–1910) was a period when the new science of sexology focused its attention on homosexuality and assorted so-called "perversions." We do not think it a coincidence that two out of the three most prominent critics of theories of primitive promiscuity and matriarchy (Westermarck and Ellis) were, in one way or another, sexual outsiders who did not accept the Victorian status quo. There has been a tendency to misread their work as advocating heteronormativity, but in fact both of them strongly advocated better treatment for sexual minorities.

The short extracts from the work of Ellis and Crawley are intended to give a flavor of their writing, and through it the sensibilities of the now distant period they represented.

REFERENCES

Malinowski, Bronislaw
    1963[1913]   The Family among the Australian Aborigines. New York: Schocken Books.
Showalter, Elaine
    1991   Sexual Anarchy: Gender and Culture at the Fin de Siècle. New York: Penguin.

4

The Reconstruction of "Primitive Sexuality" at the Fin de Siècle

Andrew Lyons and Harriet Lyons

In the eighteenth century, when savage tribes in various parts of the world first began to be visited, extravagantly romantic views widely prevailed as to the simple and idyllic lives led by primitive peoples. During the greater part of the nineteenth century, the tendency of opinion was to the opposite extreme, and it became usual to insist on the degraded and licentious morals of savages....

In reality, however, savage life is just as little a prolonged debauch as a protracted idyll.

Havelock Ellis,
Analysis of the Sexual Impulse

The period we are now to examine is one in which anthropology is institutionalized in the United States (the American Anthropological Association is founded) and is taught in universities for the first time in the United States and Great Britain, ethnography in the true sense is first written, Australian kinship studies mature, and Durkheim's school flourishes

in France. This is the time when the British imperium in Africa is solidified, and at home the welfare state is making its first tentative appearance during a period of class struggle. It is the period of jingoism, the Spanish-American War, the Boer War, and World War I. The eugenics movement flourished on both sides of the Atlantic, in the academy and in the halls of power. Psychoanalysis was born, and there also appeared several works of sexology or, as Michel Foucault would say, *scientia sexualis*. These included Richard von Krafft-Ebing's *Psychopathia Sexualis* (1886); *Das Weib* by Hermann Ploss (1885); John Gregory Bourke's *Scatologic Rites of All Nations* (1891); Havelock Ellis and John Addington Symonds's *Sexual Inversion* (1897); Ellis's *The Evolution of Modesty* (1899), *Analysis of the Sexual Impulse* (1903), and *Sex in Relation to Society* (1910); Edward Westermarck's *The History of Human Marriage* (1891) and *The Origin and Development of Moral Ideas* (1906–8); Sigmund Freud's report of his analysis of "Dora" (1905); and Ernest Crawley's

Extracts from Andrew P. Lyons and Harriet D. Lyons, *Irregular Connections: A History of Anthropology and Sexuality*, University of Nebraska Press, 2004. By permission of the University of Nebraska Press. © 2004 by the Board of Regents of the University of Nebraska.

Sexualities in Anthropology: A Reader, edited by Andrew P. Lyons and Harriet D. Lyons
© 2011 Blackwell Publishing Ltd.

The Mystic Rose (1902). Crawley's *Studies of Savages and Sex* (1929) is a posthumous work that re-creates the Zeitgeist of the world preceding Mead and Malinowski.

According to Foucault, discourse in this period validated and naturalized the status of the heterosexual, procreating couple and created a buzz around the figures of the perverse adult, the masturbating child, the Malthusian couple, and the hysterical woman (1980:105). In Britain there was doubtless less stigmatization of the Malthusian couple than in France, but contraceptive advice remained a matter of controversy. Foucault did not consider a fifth sexual Other, "the differently sexed savage," nor did he examine the place of the anthropologist in the structures of knowledge and power he so famously elaborated. In this chapter we shall attempt, among other things, to undertake these tasks.

Anthropologists' representations of the sexuality of primitives underwent radical changes in the years between 1885 and the Great War. Ellis, Westermarck, and Crawley did more than anyone else to revise widely held opinions on such matters. Andrew Lang and Northcote Thomas also made their contributions. Evolutionary fantasies about primitive promiscuity, marriage by capture, and exotic forms of sexual abuse were already suspect by the time the first classics of modern ethnography were written, though we have long since learned not to expect any simplistic replacement of fantasy by "truth." Historians of social anthropology have dealt relatively little with the circumstances that led to the disappearance of these illusions. To a degree, the works of these three thinkers were informed by new data, but they were also fictions of the fin de siècle, refractions of ideas concerning racial and sexual difference, sexual freedom, and restriction. Furthermore, the late Victorian and Edwardian eras saw a series of attacks on the familial institutions and gender concepts of the mid-Victorian era. It is our contention that those attacks, which came from both the advocates of social purity and the proponents of sexual liberty, paralleled a refashioning of the images of primitive strangers so that such images could continue to serve as foils for a new generation.

The reader of textbooks in anthropology, whether they are historical compendia or introductory surveys, will learn little of these five thinkers, whose contributions have been largely obliterated from our collective memory. Ellis, the author of the seven volumes of *Studies in the Psychology of Sex,* which originally appeared between the 1890s and the 1920s, is regarded as a quaint but interesting scholar, overshadowed by his great contemporary, Freud, and as such has been the subject of two excellent biographies (Brome 1979; Grosskurth 1980). He is not usually regarded as an anthropologist. Westermarck is known to regional specialists as an early ethnographer of Morocco and to most anthropologists as the inventor of one or two theories concerning incest that are dimly recalled from their oversimplified and garbled traduction in introductory textbooks. Most anthropologists today will complete their careers without reading a word he wrote. Brief summaries of *The Mystic Rose* appear in a few modern sources (Honigmann 1976:185–187; Evans-Pritchard 1965:35–37), but little is said of the book's author. During their lifetimes, both Ellis and Westermarck enjoyed intellectual celebrity and, in Ellis's case, some notoriety. Crawley, an Anglican churchman who briefly was headmaster of a public school and subsequently wrote articles of general scientific interest for *Nature,* received plaudits from many of his contemporaries, including Edwin Sidney Hartland, Arnold van Gennep, and Westermarck (Theodore Besterman in Crawley 1931:vii), and from one distinguished successor (Malinowski 1962). Crawley's primary success was outside academe. He was a player of lawn tennis and a sportswriter. His obituary notice in the *Times* (October 25, 1924) contains the remark: "He was also known as an anthropologist." As for Lang, he is best remembered as a folklorist. Thomas is remembered as an interesting footnote in the history of the armchair anthropology of kinship and social organization, though, as we shall see in the next chapter, he played a not dishonorable role as the first ever government anthropologist.

One can only surmise the reasons for such oblivion. The modern academic is easily bored by the lengthy compilations of data that were so beloved by both practitioners of the older physical anthropology and exponents of the comparative method. Yet many still read Lewis Henry Morgan and Edward Tylor. A more telling point is that historical memory is always shaped by current concerns, for example, intellectualist versus sociological theories of religion, the evolution of social organization, and, more recently, "the invention of kinship" as well as, for that matter, the invention of nearly everything else (see Kuper 1988). Only latterly did human sexuality and sexual or gender difference reemerge as *acknowledged* problematics within anthropology. Last but not least, transition points in the history of any discipline are notoriously difficult to comprehend. Paradigms erode slowly and in ways that often elude the consciousness of innovators. Transitional perspectives frequently appear as wrongheaded to modern readers as the paradigms they replace; nonetheless, they are both the products and the agents of changed intellectual and social climates. Sensitivity to the nuances of change can bridge the apparent chasms of difference that emerge when recent systems of truth and error are compared to older ones.

The movement from social evolutionism to historical particularism and cultural relativism has been well explored by some historians of American anthropology (e.g., Harris 1969; Stocking 1968). On the other hand, the parallel movement toward relativism and functionalism (as well as the hyperdiffusionist detour) in British anthropology has been less exhaustively detailed (apart from Stocking 1995 and Langham 1981). Insofar as this movement encompassed changes in our view of kinship and marriage, it both drew upon and contributed to changes in broad cultural understandings of sexuality. The very replacement of "sex" as a category of understanding by the more neutral "kinship and marriage" during the years when functionalism dominated British anthropology has helped to erase the importance of fin de siècle debates about primitive and modern sexuality from the collective memory of anthropologists. It is our contention that challenges to notions of sexual morality in fin de siècle society contributed to a tendency to replace fictive images of lascivious savages with representations of primitives

as either less highly sexed than civilized men and women, less imaginative in their exercise of the sexual function, or blocked by taboo or environmental restraints from the full exercise of their libidos.

Background

There were not one but several discourses about sexuality in 19th-century anthropology but the highly sexed primitive was a figure common to most of them. Iconography and popular culture also employed images of oversexualized primitives. Sander Gilman's essay "The Hottentot and the Prostitute: Towards an Iconography of Female Sexuality" (1985:76–108) commences with an account of Édouard Manet's painting *Olympia* (1862–63), which shows a naked white female attended by a black female servant. The reader is then introduced to other 19th-century images of oversexualized females, including the exhibitions involving Saat-Jee, the "Hottentot Venus," and photographs and plates from volumes by Pauline Tarnowsky and by Cesare Lombroso and Guglielmo Ferrero that depict genital anomalies and peculiarly atavistic facial features in both Hottentot females and modern European prostitutes. The images that Gilman analyzes are used to establish links between the sexualized female body, primitivity, behavioral excess, biological degeneracy, and the underclass of those times. Ideas of degeneracy and evolutionary atavism had become particularly prominent by the fin de siècle. A current of pessimism about urbanization, industrialism, and social instability was reflected in the belief that modern society could unwittingly defeat the forces of natural selection and allow the undesirable elements that flourished in its unhealthy cities to reverse the tide of progress. The equation between "savages" and real and imagined "enemies within" became even more specifically concerned with bodies and physiology as the new sciences of sexology and criminology were brought to bear on social crises and moral panics. Homosexuals, Jews, criminals, prostitutes, artists, and the insane were all seen as threats to the entire community (Gilman 1985).

Several feminist historians (see, e.g., Russett 1989; Levy 1991) have discussed the oversexualizing of the female body during the Victorian era, noting that wanton savage women were often depicted as warnings of the need to control all female sexuality. Such authors, however, pay little if any attention to the parallel treatment of primitive males. John and Robin Haller, in *The Physician and Sexuality in Victorian America* (1974), discuss 19th-century ideas of male sexual evolution but say relatively little about the treatment of primitive women. Susan Kingsley Kent, in *Sex and Suffrage in Britain, 1860–1914* (1987), provides an excellent account of the social and political ramifications of the Victorian double standard but is not concerned with the anthropological literature. In truth, the processes described by all of these authors reinforced each other in the creation of the tropic portrait of the oversexed savage.

Men of the Victorian middle classes were allowed more sexual indulgence than respectable women. Despite this, men were believed to be characterized by a higher mental development, making them less subject to the demands of their reproductive systems than their wives, provided they had not obstructed their mental development at an early age by indulgence in the "solitary vice." Images of primitive sexuality that saw male and female alike as debauched shored up a number of planks in the construction of the Victorian sexual and gender system. Such images underscored a belief in greater sexual differentiation the higher one went up the evolutionary ladder. Men, confronted with lecherous savage ancestors, might excuse their visits to prostitutes as inevitable expressions of male nature while at the same time congratulating themselves on hours spent in the study, the office, or the laboratory. Women, on the other hand, whose lives were centered mainly upon marriage and reproduction, might, as Levy suggests, be warned that their elevation above the primitive was tenuous at best and depended upon strict adherence to domestic norms. When norms came under attack at the fin de siècle, differentiations between men and women, savage and civilized remained salient, but some of

the terms of the comparisons changed their value, and new tropes emerged.

There were early criticisms of the hypothesis of primitive promiscuity. That notion clearly contradicted Sir Henry Maine's opinions concerning the early patriarchal family, and, not surprisingly, he attacked it (1883:208). Others were more reserved as to their opinions. In correspondence with Westermarck Tylor requested that Westermarck, who was preparing a second edition of *The History of Human Marriage*, ensure that "I am put right in the Introduction, as an unbeliever in 'communal marriage'" (December 15, 1893, in Wikman 1940:12). His opposition had not been very public.

Sir Charles Darwin gave the theory a lukewarm endorsement in *The Descent of Man*. He was disturbed because his own reading suggested that higher apes (e.g., gorillas) were characterized by small families headed by jealous males. The gregarious, promiscuous commune conjured into being by the "matriarchal" theorists contradicted the principle of continuity in evolution. Furthermore, it would not allow for the individual choice on which his theory of sexual selection depended. However, Sir John Lubbock was his friend, neighbor, and ally, and Darwin did not regard himself as an expert in the new social anthropology. He thought that the marriage tie was very loose in many primitive societies and that there was much sexual license, but he doubted the necessity for "believing in absolutely promiscuous intercourse" (Darwin 1981:360).

In his discussion of sexual selection Darwin remarks that women, unlike men, do not delight in competition but are tender, unselfish, and nurturant. However, he noted: "It is generally admitted that with woman the powers of intuition, of rapid perception, and perhaps of imitation, are more strongly marked than in man; but some, at least, of these faculties are characteristic of the lower races, and therefore of a past and lower state of civilisation" (Darwin 1981:326, 327). Furthermore, as Francis Galton had noted, few women had excelled in the arts, history, philosophy, and science. *Overall,* "the average of mental power in man must be above that of woman" (Darwin 1981:327).

Charles Staniland Wake's book *The Development of Marriage and Kinship* (1889) laid waste to the theory of primitive promiscuity, John F. McLennan's views on marriage by capture, and Lubbock's ideas on hetaerism. Wake's book was neither a commercial nor an academic success. It was cited but seldom, and its author later died in Chicago, an obscure and forgotten figure.

It was Darwin rather than Maine or Wake who inspired a revival of "patriarchal" theory during the first decade of the 20th century. His views on the family organization of the higher apes furnished a model to J. J. Atkinson, whose *Primal Law* was published in 1903, at which time Sigmund Freud was beginning to develop the theory of psychoanalysis in Vienna. For many scholars during the first half of the last century and in some small circles even today, psychoanalytic theory is the primary source of speculation on the evolution of sexuality and the family. Few scholars of any kind and few devotees of psychoanalytical theory read *Primal Law*, the book that was the foundation stone of Freud's theory of the origin of religion, the incest taboo, and the Oedipus complex, as expressed in *Totem and Taboo* (1913). All of these phenomena, and with them culture itself, were imagined by Freud to have been born of the guilt felt by a horde of young men after an uprising during which they killed their fathers and subsequently married their mothers.

That Atkinson's work ever saw the light of day was due to his own cousin Andrew Lang, the distinguished folklorist, who published the work together with his own *Social Origins* after the author's death. Lang explained the origin of exogamy with reference to Crawley's theory of the need to avoid harmful contact with females and to his cousin's theory. Atkinson's argument was a compote of patriarchal theory (but not Maine's version of it), common ideas of primitive brutality, Darwin's observations on gorilla family organization, as well as the projections of his own imagination. Atkinson postulated the existence of an archaic family, headed by a senior male, who had sole access to the women of the group, including his own daughters. Bands of exiled young males seized women by force from other family groups. Eventually, mothers demanded that

their sons be allowed to remain in the group, but, in exchange, the patriarchs demanded that the sons renounce access to their own mothers. [...]

To Atkinson's theory, Freud added just a few key elements: parricide, mother–son incest, guilt, and totemism. Briefly, Freud argued that men invented totemism and the incest taboo out of guilt stemming from a mass slaying of fathers by sons followed by the sexual appropriation of the murderers' mothers. The memory of the father, displaced onto totemic animals, could be both honored and erased by taboos surrounding the killing and eating of the totems. Interestingly, Freud's theory of totemism is entirely based on male desire, male agency (parricide, war between the brothers, instigation of totemism). He does not consider why women in such societies also believe in totemism. In this he differs from Atkinson's original version of the primal horde theory: Atkinson thought that the driving out of the young males had ended because the mothers insisted on it once human ancestors had evolved enough for long, close relationships between mothers and children to develop. Atkinson's theory, though it is a crucial part of a general trend away from matriarchal theory (though some, like Robert Briffault, continued to believe in it), continues to allow female agency and affective relationships between men and women that are other than sexual. There is little if anything in Freud's version of patriarchal origins theory to explain why women should also believe in totemism. Matrilineally inherited totems (and hence exogamous matrilineal clans) are explained simply as a way of rendering the mother taboo.

When Freud adapted Atkinson's theory, he added to the notion of the primal, brutal primitive his own speculations concerning Australians, whose myths, he believed, revealed a more recent consciousness of incestuous desires than could be attributed to healthy, civilized adults. Adapting the popular recapitulation hypothesis ("ontogeny recapitulates phylogeny"), he compared totemism to childhood animal phobias. Such phobias are characterized by a psychic strategy whereby ambivalent sentiments toward the same-sex parent are displaced onto animals. By identifying totemism with childhood animal phobias, Freud was able to view primitives as being simultaneously childlike, irrational, guilt ridden, and closer to unsocialized sexuality than civilized adults. In this analysis of totemism lies the explanation for the fact that Freud saw primitives as simultaneously taboo ridden and sexually lascivious. This is exactly the position Freud attributes to the child late in the Oedipal phase, a point where significant limits have already been placed on the gratification of desire. It should be noted that the zero points of Atkinson's and Freud's stories of social evolution begin not with primitive promiscuity as such but with a "family" of sorts in which at least some restrictions on sexual access are maintained by the jealousy of the senior male. It requires little speculation on our own part to descry the link between Freud's assassinated patriarch, Atkinson's primal males, and, indeed, the corn god of Sir James Frazer's *The Golden Bough,* sacrificed annually only to rise again – they are all transformations of phallic worship.

Lang died just a year before the appearance of *Totem and Taboo,* so we can only surmise what he would have thought of Freud's adaptation of Atkinson's ideas. In *Social Origins* Lang suggested that the younger males who were cast out of the primal group (we must recall that in this version of the hypothesis the patriarchs stay alive and keep their women) obtained sexual partners by raiding other family groups. At some point members of such groups somehow got the notion of arranging themselves into pairs to facilitate the peaceful exchange of women. These newly created exogamous moieties would use animal sobriquets to insult each other, which eventually led to the emergence of totemic ideology. In *The Secret of the Totem* Lang, perhaps in an attempt to reach a compromise with some critics, suggested that phratry exogamy was given a religious meaning through the introduction of totemic taboos (1905:125). In short, instead of commencing with the "undivided commune" (which did not resemble "the family" in any sense we would recognize), social evolution commences with family bands dominated by patriarchs. Moiety and clan exogamy were thus not the product of an "unconscious reformation" that led to the

dividing of the original group but were instead the product of conscious alliance between formerly warring groups. Given that Lang rejected the evolutionary sequence embraced by Morgan, Lorimer Fison, A. W. Howitt, and Baldwin Spencer, it is not surprising that he also rejected the idea of universal ignorance of paternity among primitives. He was willing to concede that the Arunta denied the father's role in procreation. However, he observed that other Australian groups who were as primitive as or more primitive than the Arunta were perfectly aware of physiological paternity. For this reason he suspected that such nescience was a unique product of Arunta dogmas about reincarnation rather than simple ignorance (Lang 1905:190–193). In no way did Lang wish totally to deny distance and differentiation between Australian Aborigines and ourselves, but he did see the differences as being less radical than did some of his contemporaries. [...]

[Northcote Thomas's book] *Kinship Organisations and Group Marriage in Australia* (1906) contained a long and precise exposition of what was known about Australian section systems. After completing this task Thomas launched an attack on assumptions that relationship terminologies referred to biological connection rather than "duties and status." Given that the Arunta term *unawa* covered a whole category of women whom a man might have married in addition to the person he did marry, it could not be translated into any single term in English such as "wife" (Thomas 1966:123). One would not say that "the fact that *femme* in French means both wife and woman is an argument for the existence of promiscuity in France in Roman or post-Roman times" (Thomas 1966:129). [...]

Thomas had previously discussed the advantages and admitted disadvantages of Westermarck's definition of "marriage" as "a more or less durable connection between male and female, lasting beyond the mere act of propagation till after the birth of the child" (1966:105). He felt that it was the best definition anthropologists had at that time. Many societies permitted forms of "gamic union" that were not perduring and did not impose the same rights and confer the same duties as marriage (Thomas 1966:106). [...]

What Thomas displayed was an ability to talk about Australian Aboriginal sexual mores and marriage rules in a language that attempted "scientific" precision. Such language may indeed deprive Australian social life of flesh and blood, but it does try to avoid the ethnocentric excesses still so widespread in the first years of the 20th century. Such language was common in social anthropology 20 to 30 years later. By that time ideas of group marriage and primitive promiscuity were to be found only on the fringes of the discipline.

The Demise of Primitive Promiscuity

In 1889 Westermarck's doctoral thesis, which was to constitute the first six chapters of *The History of Human Marriage,* was accepted by his university in Finland. Two years later the complete book appeared in print. Nearly 40 years later the author described how his research led him to dispute the theory of primitive promiscuity.

From Darwin's book I discovered that several scientists held the view that primitive man lived in a state of promiscuity – in other words, that in the earliest ages of our race individual marriage relations did not exist and all men had access to all women without distinction. He himself thought that in those times the men's jealousy would prevent such a condition, but took for granted – on the ground of Morgan's, McLennan's, and Lubbock's investigations – that promiscuity or something similar had, at a later date, been general amongst the human race. I went to the authorities he quoted, and thus at last – at twenty-five years of age – found it necessary to learn to read an English book. In the material I collected concerning the manners and customs of different peoples, I also thought I could trace remnants of earlier promiscuity; thus I began by supporting a theory which I was to dispute later on. But I had not got far before I found that I was on the wrong track. I perceived that marriage must primarily be studied in its connection with biological conditions, and that the tendency to interpret all sorts of customs

as social survivals, without a careful investigation into their existing environment, is apt to lead to the most arbitrary conclusions. (Westermarck 1929:68)

Many of Westermarck's disagreements with the author of *The Descent of Man* arose from the simple fact that in many ways he was more Darwinian than Darwin himself. [...] He firmly believed that some form of lasting pair bonding was part of the human inheritance from our primate ancestors. Such marriages had to last sufficiently long to ensure that children, few in number, might be nurtured until such time as they could fend for themselves. In that sense, "marriage" had a biological as well as a cultural base. He believed that monogamy was probably the prevalent form of marriage in primitive societies. Polygamous institutions were special adaptations. Polygyny was most common among advanced savages and barbarians; its causes included differentials in power, boredom on the part of men, barrenness, and the premature aging of females (Westermarck 1906–8, vol. 2:388–390). The "higher forms of civilization" favored monogamy, in part because the supply of animal milk reduced suckling time, the number of wars decreased, pregnancy taboos declined, and there was a less intense need for offspring. Additionally, civilization had made female beauty more durable. Social evolution had also resulted in changes that had favored women who benefited from monogamy: "Moreover, the sentiment of love becomes more refined, the passion for one more absorbing. The feelings of the weaker sex are frequently held in higher regard. And the better education of women enables them to live comfortably without the support of a husband" (Westermarck 1906–8, vol. 2:391). [...]

Westermarck used several arguments to attack the theories of McLennan, Morgan, and Lubbock:

1   The theory of primitive promiscuity was based on unreliable reports by missionaries and travelers. Very often data were misinterpreted. The absence of a word for marriage in a foreign language did not entail that the institution did not exist

among its speakers. New data from reliable sources, for example, E. H. Man on the Andamanese and John Mathew on the Australian Aborigines, indicated that supposedly promiscuous peoples were simply not promiscuous (Westermarck 1901:49–61).

2   Even if promiscuity did exist among some primitive peoples, no proof was available that it had always been present. Culture contact, slavery, and colonization often caused a collapse in morality and a decline in the birthrate (Westermarck 1901:66–69).

3   McLennan and Lubbock were wrong to suggest that the condition of women in very primitive communities was particularly degraded. The ethnographic evidence did not point in that direction (Westermarck 1901). Furthermore, if women had to labor hard in primitive communities, the same was true of their menfolk (Westermarck 1904:408–421).

4   The fact that a people permitted premarital sexual relations did not mean that they permitted promiscuity. The two concepts were not the same (Westermarck 1901:61–66).

5   Primitives tended to marry early in life, and few were left unmarried. More advanced peoples tended to favor late marriage, and a number of individuals were left on the shelf. For a variety of reasons the latter condition was more conducive to promiscuity than the former: "Irregular connexions between the sexes have on the whole established a tendency to increase along with the progress of civilization" (Westermarck 1901:69).

6   Lubbock had contended that institutions such as the lending of wives to strangers and the jus primae noctis demonstrated that individuals asserting their own privileges had to make a ceremonial concession to the group. Such practices were, therefore, survivals of group marriage and primitive promiscuity. Westermarck suggested some more prosaic interpretations such as the observance of rules of hospitality (1901:72–81).

7   There was little evidence of ignorance of physiological paternity in any existing group (Westermarck 1901:105–107).

8   Morgan's analysis of relationship terminologies was faulty. McLennan had been correct to suggest that they were merely terms of address rather than accurate reflections of marriage patterns past or present (Westermarck 1901:82–96).

9   Ethnographic evidence did not indicate that matriliny inevitably preceded patriliny (Westermarck 1901:96–105).

10 Male jealousy was a biological and cultural universal in human societies. This very fact rendered it unlikely that systematic promiscuity could ever have been the rule (Westermarck 1901:115–133).

In *Analysis of the Sexual Impulse,* originally published in 1903 as volume 3 of his *Studies in the Psychology of Sex,* Ellis gave his loyal support to Westermarck on the question of primitive promiscuity. He observed that the conclusion that primitive peoples were "abandoned to debauchery" often rested on misunderstandings of customs such as wife lending and ritual intercourse (Ellis 1942a, pt. 2:260–262). Sometimes a genuine increase in promiscuity could be the consequence of interference by missionaries with established cultural practices [...] Like Westermarck but in a much more cursory fashion, Ellis examined the ethnographic record of the time and claimed that it failed to support the hypothesis of primitive promiscuity. [...]

Westermarck's Darwinism led him to consider that many features of human behavior, for example, marriage, maternal and paternal care, and maidenly coyness, were rooted in instinct and therefore "normal." In his review of the fifth edition of *The History of Human Marriage,* which was first published in 1928 in the seventh volume of *Studies in the Psychology of Sex,* Ellis was pleased to note that "the two main points in this [Westermarck's] method are its biological basis and its inductive collection of comparative facts" (1942b, pt. 2:495).

In the 1913 edition of *Analysis of the Sexual Impulse* Ellis cites Freud and Crawley. A gradual rapprochement developed between Crawley and Ellis, albeit they started from very different premises. Although Crawley was not among those who viewed primitives as slaves to excessive sexual drives, he did subscribe to that school of opinion that saw them as entrapped by superstition and taboo.

In The *Mystic Rose* Crawley developed a theory of marriage origins with highly individualistic premises. Primitive individuals lived in a state of fear. Contagion was a dreaded result of contact with any other thing or person. This net of primitive irrationalism was exemplified by the fear of sexual contagion, a terror on the part of each sex of that which was opposite and alien to it. Sexual intercourse was, needless to say, a requirement for the continued existence of any society. Accordingly, it was performed but at times and in a manner stipulated by taboo. Hedges were always necessary against the dangers caused by the crossing of ritual boundaries. Not surprisingly, Crawley was hostile to all theories of religion, kinship, and sexuality that were based in assumptions of human gregariousness. He devoted much of his time to attacking McLennan, noting that marriage by capture could well be the very thing McLennan said it was not, a cultural expression of sexual coyness.

[...]

Seasonal Stories: Periodicity, Coyness, and "No Means Yes"

In an early conference paper (Lyons and Lyons 1981) we suggested that one consequence of the work of Ellis and Crawley was the substitution of the image of the "undersexed" for that of the "oversexed" savage. Those remarks were exaggerated, but they had a point. Westermarck, Ellis, and Crawley were all convinced that primitive humans had a mating season, a "rutting" time just like many other mammals. At other times they were sexually inactive.

Traces of periodicity were to be found even in civilized European countries [...] In general it appeared that conceptions peaked in May and June, which fact was reflected in a February–March peak in the birthrate (Westermarck 1901:32). While Westermarck did not adequately explore nonbiological explanations for the alleged phenomenon, his

European data were at the very least more than anecdotal. However, when he endeavored to substantiate the existence of a rutting season among primitives, he relied on a kind of evidence that he would never have entertained from a proponent of primitive promiscuity: "Speaking of the Watch-an-dies in the western part of Australia, Mr. Oldfield remarks, 'Like the beasts of the field, the savage has but one time for copulation in the year. About the middle of spring ... the Watch-an-dies begin to think of holding their grand semi-religious festival of Caa-ro'" (Westermarck 1901:28).

Westermarck entertained various reasons for the timing of rutting. It was noteworthy that among non-European as well as European peoples "we find ... the sexual instinct increasing at the end of the spring" (Westermarck 1901:33). This was true, for instance, of India, and it was at this time that the festival of Holi was held. However, the main festival time in some parts of India was in January, a fact Westermarck found problematic, because he felt that saturnalian festivals and the mating season should coincide. Sexual periodicity could not be explained simply in terms of the position of the heavenly bodies. Nor was it adequate to suggest that the mating season occurred when there was a plenitude of food, because May and June in Scandinavia were "rather hard" months. Conditions at the time of birth and infancy were critical. Clearly, the mating season had to be timed so that births could take place during the season that was optimal for the survival of progeny (Westermarck 1901:34–35). The principle of natural selection was at work.

In Westermarck's opinion there was a simple reason why the mating season had nearly disappeared among civilized populations. Progress had enabled humans to escape the rigors of the seasons, thus permitting more "variations as to the pairing time," a pattern that was preserved and transmitted from generation to generation. A similar pattern was to be found among a few primitive groups such as the Yahgans of Tierra del Fuego, who had an adequate food supply all year round.

It is to be noted that Westermarck made no direct observations about the sexual potency of primitives, although the notion of periodicity implies such, and Ellis and Crawley were to make some very unambiguous remarks. Certainly, he did not believe that primitive peoples were always consumed by sexual desire, and that is perhaps one reason why he embraced a theory of incest that is the very opposite of Freud's inasmuch as he assumed that groups with an innate aversion to incest would have been favored by natural selection (Westermarck 1901:290–355). He thought that such an aversion did not come into play when close relatives were reared apart and were unaware of the relationship, so he was, in fact, speaking of a behavioral trait triggered by contiguity: "What I maintain is that there is an innate aversion to sexual intercourse between persons living very closely together from early youth, and that, as such persons are in most cases related, this feeling displays itself chiefly as a horror of intercourse between near kin" (Westermarck 1901:320).

Crawley at first eschewed biological explanations for primitive sexual restraint as surely as Westermarck rejected ritual determinism. The disagreement extended to the explanation of brief periods of license. Whereas Westermarck noted the coincidence of saturnalia and the supposed mating season and implied that nature in some way dictated its desires to culture, Crawley explained these festivals, which we would now call liminal rites or rituals of reversals, as magical ways to bridge the barriers that taboos had created between humans.

Ellis reconciled the biological and ritual positions on the origin of sexual restraint by suggesting that taboos could only take hold where the sexual instinct was fundamentally weak (1942a, pt. 2:263, 264). This weakness was often correlated with an underdevelopment of the sexual organs and certain psychic manifestations, for example, lack of jealousy (something Westermarck would not have credited). The sexual urge, rather than being constant, ebbed and flowed. At its peak it burst forth in violent manifestations of sexual energy, feasts, orgies, and saturnalia (Ellis 1942a, pt. 2:266). Ellis accepted many of Westermarck's notions concerning periodicity and the rutting season and added more ethnographic data about their salience in primitive societies as well as statistical data that demonstrated that such phenomena were still significant in contemporary societies. He relied on some colorful and dubious travelers' tales such as the suggestion by Dr. Frederick Cook of the Peary North Greenland expedition that among the Eskimo, secretions, passions, and muscular activities diminish over the winter but that "soon after the sun appears a kind of rut affects the young population. They tremble with the intensity of sexual passion" (Ellis 1942a, pt. 1:126). Such violent but occasional outbursts of the sexual instinct were, in Ellis's opinion, the reason why so many mistakenly believed that savages possessed a particularly powerful sex drive.

Crawley accepted many of Ellis's arguments and modified others. He wrote an essay on "Chastity and Sexual Morality" that appeared in a posthumous volume edited by Theodore Besterman, *Studies of Savages and Sex*. Crawley's intent in his essay was to write a minihistory of the "biological, economic and psychological causes of sexual morality" and, concomitantly, a study of "distribution of the habit of chastity, and the natural curve of its development" (1928:2). The reader is informed that, "roughly speaking, the sexual impulse is a psychical outgrowth from the nutritive, corresponding to it as physiological reproduction corresponds to physiological nutrition" (Crawley 1928:2). The undernourished primitive had "underdeveloped" sexual organs and manifested "difficulty in attaining sexual excitement" (Crawley 1928:3). Accordingly, notions of primitive sexual communism were absurd. Crawley enthusiastically repeated some of the arguments of Ellis and Westermarck (1928:6–9). Unlike Ellis and Westermarck, Crawley was insistent that there was no primitive mating season in the strict biological sense. However, cultural institutions fulfilled the same role, inasmuch as they had a latent biological function. Group gatherings and festivals, whose overt purpose was merrymaking, were the occasions for sexual arousal and were often followed by long periods of natural chastity. "Thus we have a cultural as well as a physiological rhythm of periodicity" (Crawley 1928:10).

Overall, Westermarck's attacks on the promiscuity hypothesis served to elevate the primitive Other; Crawley's theories had a very different effect. He informed his readers that the higher races not only had greater sexual potency but could concentrate on higher things because their young took longer to mature and the "associational centres of the brain" could develop even after puberty. The savage child was as intelligent as the European up until puberty, but "subsequently he 'runs to seed,' or rather 'to sex'" (Crawley 1928:32).

The reader of the above account might be excused the thought that there is one human physiological process, menstruation, that is undeniably periodic but that is not directly linked to any mating season. Indeed, menstrual taboos commonly prohibit mating. A close reading of the texts, particularly Ellis's *The Evolution of Modesty*, leaves one with the feeling that Ellis confused menstruation with heat. He answered his own inquiry as to why intercourse was prohibited during menstruation with the remark that "the whole of religion is a ... remolding of nature, a repression of natural impulses, an effort to turn them into new channels" (Ellis 1942a, pt. 1:98–99).

Thomas Laqueur has recently observed that the hormonal basis of ovulation was not understood until the 1930s and that women who read medical advice books were once told to restrict intercourse to the twelfth to sixteenth days after menstruation if they wished to avoid pregnancy (1990:9)! Furthermore, the relationship between menstruation and the cycle of ovulation was not understood. Nineteenth-century writers frequently confused menstruation with heat (Laqueur 1990:218–220).

The imagery involved in medical accounts of menstruation was quite vivid. According to Laqueur, Walter Heape, an antifeminist reproductive biologist who taught at Cambridge, used language "redolent of war reportage" to describe the "destruction" of the uterine lining, referring to it as a severe and devastating periodic action (1990:221). In *Man and Woman*, the first edition of which appeared in 1894, Ellis lamented that women were "periodically wounded in the most sensitive spot in their organism" (1930:335). The behavioral effects of menstruation, which allegedly included a rise in the suicide rate of females, were bemoaned: "They emphasize the fact that even in the healthiest woman a worm, however harmless and unperceived, gnaws periodically at the roots of life" (Ellis 1930:347). [...] Ellis tentatively tried to extend the concept of periodicity to men, claiming that there was evidence of this phenomenon in the timing of nocturnal emissions (1942a, pt. 1:144). Of course, there is no suggestion of "wounds" or "disease" in his description of male periodicity.

The shift from presumed moral hierarchies to interpretations of partially understood physiological evidence left primitives both closer to lower animals than civilized folk and less sophisticated in their sexual attainments. It is fair to note, however, that Westermarck is far less pejorative in his descriptions of primitives than is Ellis, though the underlying logic of his arguments is similar, as both men see natural selection working its effects more clearly and directly upon the uncivilized.

[...] Ellis believed that women were naturally passive in sexual intercourse (Grosskurth 1980:231). Westermarck observed that, in point of fact, women in primitive societies sometimes played an active role in the choice of mates and frequently had the chance of refusing. Both Westermarck and Ellis drew attention to the role played by modesty in courtship. Westermarck observed that nudity was not a sign of immorality among those groups such as the Australians and Tasmanians who wore no clothing (Westermarck 1901:187–188). Clothing that might originally be adopted for several reasons, including decoration, warmth, a new sense of modesty, or perhaps the desire of husbands to hide their wives' bodies from rivals, served as a source of temptation or sexual excitement. Coyness and coquetry on the part of females now became possible (Westermarck 1901:195–198; Ellis 1942a, pt. 1:54–64).

[...]

Ellis somewhat infamously (see, e.g., Jackson 1987:56–58) postulated that women might enjoy their own violation or feign reluctance, a speculation that offends current sensibilities to such an extreme degree that we forget that it also contained, implicitly, a new acknowledgment of female desire and sexual agency. Of marriage by capture, for example, Ellis says: "While this is sometimes a real capture, it is more often a mock capture; the lover perhaps pursues the beloved on horseback, but she is as fleet and as skillful as he is, cannot be captured unless she wishes to be captured, and in addition, as among the Kirghiz, she may be armed with a formidable whip; so that 'marriage by capture,' far from being a hardship imposed on women, is largely a concession to their modesty and a gratification of their erotic impulses" (1918:6). More radically, Ellis makes a similar observation of women of the middle class. Westermarck quotes him as repeating the following remark, made by one lady to another in front of a painting by Rubens of *The Rape of the Sabine Women*: "I think the Sabine women enjoyed being carried off like that" (1906–8, vol. 1:658).

[...]

It is fitting now that we say more about the extent to which the work of our three thinkers was influenced by the social currents of their day. Neither Ellis nor Westermarck had a conventional marriage. Ellis's marriage to Edith Lees was described by him as "semi-detached." Westermarck was a bachelor and may have been a homosexual. Westermarck (1929) avoids the issue of his personal sexuality in his autobiography, where he mentions no intimate relationships with women and describes several close friendships with men.

A dislike for certain varieties of Christianity is evident in the works of Crawley and Ellis. Crawley, as we remarked, condemned the Catholic Church's attitudes toward celibacy. Westermarck attacked the Catholic Church because its obsession with female impurity, from the time of the church fathers to the present, had resulted in the degradation of women (1906–8, vol. 2:661–666). [...]

Westermarck has been accused of being a defender of conventional Victorian monogamy (Coward 1983:57, 70, 72). If he helped to naturalize what Foucault has described as the heterosexual, procreating couple, it was because of an addiction to the Darwinian paradigm. In any event, he explicitly denied any conservative intent (Westermarck 1934:332). He believed that some sort of monogamy was part of our primate inheritance and that from the woman's point of view it was preferable to polygyny. He felt, however, that monogamy in its modern form was an institution in need of improvement. [...]

Westermarck did not say that all primitive groups permitted premarital sex but rather showed that there was much variability in this respect. He did not advocate a return to primitive sexual institutions. He believed that conjugal love had probably grown more intense with the advance of civilization. He conclusively rejected the mid-Victorian equation between the primitive female and the prostitute. [...]

Changing Images of the Primitive and the Crisis in Masculinity

Prostitution was at the core of many of the discourses of both feminism and social purity. The old Victorian double standard, which saw men and women as having fundamentally different sexual natures and some women as being irretrievably fallen and thus acceptable vessels for male lust, was not tolerable to participants in the feminist, social purity, and social hygiene movements. Although many were content to concentrate on women's economic condition as a cause of prostitution, there was a growing belief that greater sexual satisfaction would have to be found within marriage if prostitution were to be combatted. There was thus a growing concern with the diagnosis and treatment of sexual blocks. Freud's work is a case in point, although he did not have much influence in England until after the Great War. Medical notions of mental and sexual inadequacy, whether labeled as hysteria, neurasthenia, neurosis, or perversion, represent an inward turning of the ideas of degeneracy we discussed earlier in this chapter. In *Sexual Anarchy* (1991) Elaine Showalter has examined the crisis in masculinity at the fin de siècle that was reflected in the writings of figures as diverse as Wilde, Rider Haggard, and Robert Louis Stevenson and in popular and scientific notions of degeneracy, perversion, madness, inadequacy, and neurosis.

The work of Ellis, Crawley, and Westermarck was certainly a part of this discourse, which may help explain the emergence of the "undersexed savage." "Primitive" sexuality was imagined in terms that either opposed or exaggerated the civilized condition. Hence, a society troubled by promiscuity and seduction had asserted a fundamental closeness between oversexed primitives and the seductive women and oversexed men of the lower classes. When men of the middle classes came to be troubled by their own perceived (or perhaps imagined) repressions and sexual disabilities, similar disorders, often in exaggerated form, began to crop up in their representations of primitives. Alternatively, insofar as primitives as well as sex itself rose in the Western estimation, primitives were portrayed as more natural and sensible than their civilized counterparts. Westermarck, more than Ellis and Crawley, inclined to the latter view.

Continuations

While Crawley's work quickly passed into obscurity, the work of Ellis and Westermarck did exercise some influence on the direction of anthropology during their own later years and for a short time afterward. Westermarck's pupil, Malinowski, turned to Ellis after he became disillusioned with Freud, made detailed notes on Ellis's writings, and used themes from Ellis's *Studies in the Psychology of Sex* as chapter headings in *The Sexual Life of Savages in Northwestern Melanesia* (1929). Ellis was pleased to write the introduction to that work. If one reads it closely, one may notice references to periodicity, which Malinowski considered to be a purely cultural phenomenon, insofar as it existed.

We believe that the "undersexed savage" or "occasionally sexed savage" of Ellis and Crawley is best seen as a transitional model, bridging the gap between Victorian images of savage lechery and portraits that represent South Sea Islanders, whether Trobrianders or Samoans, as having passionless and boring but stable and sexually well-adjusted marriages.

REFERENCES

Atkinson, J. J.
1903 Primal Law (published along with Social Origins by Andrew Lang). London: Longmans, Green, & Co.

Bourke, John Gregory
1891 Scatologic Rites of All Nations. Washington.

Brome, Vincent
1979 Havelock Ellis, Philosopher of Sex: A Biography. London and Boston: Routledge and Kegan Paul.

Crawley, Ernest
1902 The Mystic Rose: A Study in Primitive Marriage. London: Macmillan.

Crawley, Ernest
1929 Studies of Savages and Sex. Theodore Besterman, ed. London: Methuen.

Crawley, Ernest
1931 Dress, Drinks and Drums: Further Studies of Savages and Sex. Theodore Besterman, ed. London: Methuen.

Darwin, Sir Charles
1871 The Descent of Man and Selection in Relation to Sex, 2 vols. New York: Appleton.

Darwin, Sir Charles
1981 The Descent of Man, and Selection in Relation to Sex. Reprint of First English Edition, [1871] London: J. Murray, with an Introduction by J. T. Bonner and R. M. May. Princeton, NJ: Princeton University Press.

Ellis, Havelock
1910a[1899] The Evolution of Modesty. Third Edition. Studies in the Psychology of Sex, I (originally published as Vol. II). Philadelphia: P. A. Davis and Co.

Ellis, Havelock
1910b Analysis of the Sexual Impulse. Vol. III of Studies in the Psychology of Sex. Philadelphia: P. A. Davis and Co.

Ellis, Havelock
1910c Sex in Relation to Society, Vol. VI of Studies in the Psychology of Sex. Philadelphia: P. A. Davis and Co.

Ellis, Havelock
1942[I] Studies in the Psychology of Sex. Volume 1. Part 1 is a reprint of The Evolution of Modesty [previously Vol. I, orig. published in 1899 as Vol. II]. Part 2 is a reprint of the second edition [1913] of Analysis of the Sexual Impulse [previously Vol. III]. Part 3 is a reprint of Sexual Selection in Man [1905, previously

Vol. IV]. Part 4 is a reprint of the third edition [1910] of Sexual Inversion [previously Vol. II, originally published in 1897 as Vol. 1 by the so-called "Watford University Press"]. Two-volume edition. New York: Random House.

Ellis, Havelock
1942[II] Studies in the Psychology of Sex. Part I is a reprint of the third edition [1910] of Erotic Symbolism [orig. Vol. V]. Part 2 is a reprint of the first edition [1928] of Eonism and Other Supplementary Studies (previously Vol. VIII]. Part 3 is a reprint of the first edition [1910] of Sex in Relation to Society [originally Vol. VI]. New York: Random House.

Ellis, Havelock in collaboration with J. A. Symonds
1897 Sexual Inversion. London: Wilson & Macmillan.

Evans-Pritchard, Sir E. E.
1965 Theories of Primitive Religion. Oxford: The Clarendon Press.

Foucault, Michel
1980[1976] The History of Sexuality. Vol. I: An Introduction. Robert Hurley, trans. New York: Vintage Books.

Freud, Sigmund
1953[1905] Fragment of an Analysis of a Case of Hysteria. *In* Standard Edition of the Complete Psychological Works of Sigmund Freud. James Strachey, ed. Pp. 130–243. London: Hogarth Press.

Freud, Sigmund
1959[1913] Totem and Taboo. The Standard Edition of the Complete Psychological Works of Sigmund Freud, vol. 13. Pp. ix–162. New York: Macmillan.

Gilman, Sander L.
1985 Difference and Pathology: Stereotypes of Sexuality, Race and Madness. Ithaca and London: Cornell University Press.

Grosskurth, Phyllis
1980 Havelock Ellis: A Biography. Toronto: McClelland and Stewart.

Haller, John, and Haller, Robin
1974 The Physician and Sexuality in Victorian America. Urbana: University of Illinois Press.

Harris, Marvin
1969[1968] The Rise of Anthropological Theory. London: Routledge & Kegan Paul.

Honigmann, John
1976 The Development of Anthropological Ideas. Homewood, Illinois: Dorsey Press.

Jackson, Margaret
1987 "Facts of Life" or the Eroticization of Women's Oppression? Sexology and the Social Construction of Heterosexuality. *In* The Cultural Construction of Sexuality. Pat Caplan, ed. Pp. 52–81. London: Tavistock Publications Ltd.

Kent, Susan Kingsley
1990[1987] Sex and Suffrage in Britain, 1860–1914. London: Routledge.

Krafft-Ebing, Richard von
1892[1886] Psychopathia Sexualis. Philadelphia and London: F. A. Davis.

Kuper, Adam
1988 The Invention of Primitive Society. London: Routledge.

Lang, Andrew
1903 Social Origins (published along with Primal Law by J.J. Atkinson). London: Longmans, Green, & Co.

Lang, Andrew
1905 The Secret of the Totem. London: Longmans, Green, & Co.

Langham, Ian
1981 The Building of British Social Anthropology: W. H. R. Rivers and His Cambridge Disciples in the Development of Kinship Studies, 1898–1931. Dordrecht, Boston and London: D. Reidel Publishing Company.

Laqueur, Thomas
1990 Making Sex: Body and Gender from the Greeks to Freud. Cambridge, Mass. and London: Harvard University Press.

Levy, Anita
1991 Other Women: The Writing of Class, Race and Gender, 1832–1898. Princeton: Princeton University Press.

Lubbock, Sir John
1885 On the Customs of Marriage and Systems of Relationship Among the Australians. Journal of the Anthropological Institute of Great Britain and Ireland 14:292–300.

Lubbock, Sir John
1978 [1870] The Origin of Civilization and the Primitive Condition of Man. Edited and with an Introduction by Peter Riviere. Chicago: University of Chicago Press.

Maine, Sir Henry
1883 Dissertation on Early Law and Custom. London: John Murray.

Malinowski, Bronislaw
1962 Sex, Culture and Myth. A. Valetta Malinowski, ed. London: Rupert Hart-Davies.

McLennan, John F.
  1970 [1865] Primitive Marriage: An Inquiry Into the Origin of the Form of Capture in Marriage Ceremonies. Edited and with an Introduction by Peter Rivière. Chicago: University of Chicago Press.
Ploss, Hermann H.
  1935[1885] Woman: An Historical, Gynaecological and Anthropological Compendium (Orig. Das Weibe). E. J. Dingwall, ed. London: Heinemann Medical Books, Ltd.
Russett, Cynthia Eagle
  1989 Sexual Science: The Victorian Construction of Womanhood. Cambridge and London: Harvard University Press.
Showalter, Elaine
  1991 Sexual Anarchy: Gender and Culture at the Fin De Siècle. New York: Penguin.
Stocking, George W., Jr.
  1968 Race, Culture and Evolution. New York: The Free Press.
Stocking, George W., Jr.
  1995 After Tylor: British Social Anthropology 1888–1951. Madison, Wisconsin: University of Wisconsin Press.

Thomas, Northcote W.
  1966[1906] Kinship Organizations and Group Marriage in Australia. New York: Humanities Press.
Wake, Charles Staniland
  1967[1889] The Development of Marriage and Kinship. Edited and with an Introduction by Rodney Needham. Chicago: University of Chicago Press.
Westermarck, Edward
  1901[1891] The History of Human Marriage, 3rd edn. London: Macmillan and Co.
Westermarck, Edward
  1904 The Position of Women in Early Civilization. American Journal of Sociology 10:408–442.
Westermarck, Edward
  1906–8 The Origin and Development of the Moral Ideas, 2 vols. London: Macmillan.
Westermarck, Edward
  1929 Memories of My Life. London: Allen and Unwin.
Wikman, K.R.V., ed.
  1940 Letters from Edward B. Tylor and Alfred Russell Wallace to Edward Westermarck. Acta Academiae Aboensis.

5

The Sexual Instinct in Savages

Havelock Ellis

I

In the eighteenth century, when savage tribes in various parts of the world first began to be visited, extravagantly romantic views widely prevailed as to the simple and idyllic lives led by primitive peoples. During the greater part of the nineteenth century the tendency of opinion was to the opposite extreme, and it became usual to insist on the degraded and licentious morals of savages.[1]

In reality, however, savage life is just as little a prolonged debauch as a prolonged idyll. The inquiries of such writers as Westermarck, Frazer, and Crawley are tending to introduce a sounder conception of the actual, often highly complex, conditions of primitive life in its relations to the sexual instinct.

At the same time it is not difficult to account for the belief, widely spread during the nineteenth century, in the unbridled licentiousness of savages. In the first place, the doctrine of evolution inevitably created a prejudice in favor of such a view. It was assumed that modesty, chastity, and restraint were the finest and ultimate flowers of moral development;

therefore at the beginnings of civilization we must needs expect to find the opposite of these things. Apart, however, from any mere prejudice of this kind, a superficial observation of the actual facts necessarily led to much misunderstanding. Just as the nakedness of many savage peoples led to the belief that they were lacking in modesty, although, as a matter of fact, modesty is more highly developed in savage life than in civilization,[2] so the absence of our European rules of sexual behavior among savages led to the conclusion that they were abandoned to debauchery. The widespread custom of lending the wife under certain circumstances was especially regarded as indicating gross licentiousness. Moreover, even when intercourse was found to be free before marriage, scarcely any investigator sought to ascertain what amount of sexual intercourse this freedom involved. It was not clearly understood that such freedom must by no means be necessarily assumed to involve very frequent intercourse. Again, it often happened that no clear distinction was made between peoples contaminated by association with civilization, and peoples not so contaminated. For instance,

Havelock Ellis, *Studies in the Psychology of Sex*. Random House, 1942. 2-volume edition. Vol. 1, part 2, Analysis of the Sexual Impulse. Appendix A, pp. 259–266.

Sexualities in Anthropology: A Reader, edited by Andrew P. Lyons and Harriet D. Lyons
© 2011 Blackwell Publishing Ltd.

when prostitution is attributed to a savage people we must usually suppose either that a mistake has been made or that the people in question have been degraded by intercourse with white peoples, for among unspoilt savages customs that can properly be called prostitution rarely prevail. Nor, indeed, would they be in harmony with the conditions of primitive life.

It has been seriously maintained that the chastity of savages, so far as it exists at all, is due to European civilization. It is doubtless true that this is the case with individual persons and tribes, but there is ample evidence from various parts of the world to show that this is by no means the rule. And, indeed, it may be said – with no disregard of the energy and sincerity of missionary efforts – that it could not be so. A new system of beliefs and practices, however excellent it may be in itself, can never possess the same stringent and unquestionable force as the system in which an individual and his ancestors have always lived, and which they have never doubted the validity of. That this is so we may have occasion to observe among ourselves. Christian teachers question the wisdom of bringing young people under free-thinking influence, because, although they do not deny the morals of free-thinkers, they believe that to unsettle the young may have a disastrous effect, not only on belief, but also on conduct. Yet this dangerously unsettling process has been applied by missionaries on a wholesale scale to races which in some respect are often little more than children. When, therefore, we are considering the chastity of savages we must not take into account those peoples which have been brought into close contact with Europeans.

In order to understand the sexual habits of savages generally there are two points which always have to be borne in mind as of the first importance: (1) the checks restraining sexual intercourse among savages, especially as regards time and season, are so numerous, and the sanctions upholding those checks so stringent, that sexual excess cannot prevail to the same extent as in civilization; (2) even in the absence of such checks, that difficulty of obtaining sexual erethism which has been noted as so common among savages, when not overcome by the stimulating influences

prevailing at special times and seasons, and which is probably in large measure dependent on hard condition of life as well as an insensitive quality of nervous texture, still remains an important factor, tending to produce a natural chastity. There is a third consideration which, though from the present point of view subsidiary, is not without bearing on our conception of chastity among savages: the importance, even sacredness, of procreation is much more generally recognized by savage than by civilized peoples, and also a certain symbolic significance is frequently attached to human procreation as related to natural fruitfulness generally; so that a primitive sexual orgy, instead of being a mere manifestation of licentiousness, may have a ritual significance, as a magical means of evoking the fruitfulness of fields and herds.[3]

When a savage practises extraconjugal sexual intercourse, the act is frequently not, as it has come to be conventionally regarded in civilization, an immorality or at least an illegitimate indulgence; it is a useful and entirely justifiable act, producing definite benefits, conducing alike to cosmic order and social order, although these benefits are not always such as we in civilization believe to be caused by the act. Thus, speaking of the northern tribes of central Australia, Spencer and Gillen remark: "It is very usual amongst all of the tribes to allow considerable license during the performance of certain of their ceremonies when a large number of natives, some of them coming often from distant parts, are gathered together – in fact, on such occasions all of the ordinary marital rules seem to be more or less set aside for the time being. Each day, in some tribes, one or more women are told off whose duty it is to attend at the corrobboree grounds, – sometimes only during the day, sometimes at night, – and all of the men, except those who are fathers, elder and younger brothers, and sons, have access to them.... The idea is that the sexual intercourse assists in some way in the proper performance of the ceremony, causing everything to work smoothly and preventing the decorations from falling off."[4]

It is largely this sacred character of sexual intercourse – the fact that it is among the things that are at once "divine" and "impure," these two conceptions not being differentiated in primitive thought – which leads to the frequency with which in savage life a taboo is put upon its exercise. Robertson Smith added an appendix to his *Religion of the Semites* on "Taboo on the Intercourse of the Sexes."[5] Westermarck brought together evidence showing the frequency with which this and allied causes tended to the chastity of savages.[6] Frazer has very luminously expounded the whole primitive conception of sexual intercourse, and showed how it affected chastity.[7] Warriors must often be chaste; the men who go on any hunting or other expedition require to be chaste to be successful; the women left behind must be strictly chaste; sometimes even the whole of the people left behind, and for long periods, must be chaste in order to insure the success of the expedition. Hubert and Mauss touched on the same point in their elaborate essay on sacrifice, pointing out how frequently sexual relationships are prohibited on the occasion of any ceremony whatever.[8] Crawley, in elaborating the primitive conception of taboo, has dealt fully with ritual and traditional influences making for chastity among savages. He brings forward, for instance, a number of cases, from various parts of the world, in which intercourse has to be delayed for days, weeks, even months, after marriage. He considers that the sexual continence prevalent among savages is largely due to a belief in the enervating effects of coitus; so dangerous are the sexes to each other that, as he points out, even now sexual separation of the sexes commonly occurs.[9]

There are thus a great number of constantly recurring occasions in savage life when continence must be preserved, and when, it is firmly believed, terrible risks would be incurred by its violation – during war, after victory, after festivals, during mourning, on journeys, in hunting and fishing, in a vast number of agricultural and industrial occupations.

It might fairly be argued that the facility with which the savage places these checks on sexual intercourse itself bears witness to the weakness of the sexual impulse. Evidence of another order which seems to point to the undeveloped state of the sexual impulse among savages may be found in the comparatively undeveloped condition of their sexual organs, a condition not, indeed, by any means constant, but very frequently noted. As regards women, it has in many parts of the world been observed to be the rule, and the data which Ploss and Bartels have accumulated seem to me, on the whole, to point clearly in this direction.[10]

At another point, also, it may be remarked, the repulsion between the sexes and the restraints on intercourse may be associated with weak sexual impulse. It is not improbable that a certain horror of the sexual organs may be a natural feeling which is extinguished in the intoxication of desire, yet still has a physiological basis which renders the sexual organs – disguised and minimized by convention and by artistic representation – more or less disgusting in the absence of erotic emotion.[11] And this is probably more marked in cases in which the sexual instinct is constitutionally feeble. A lady who had no marked sexual desires, and who considered it well bred to be indifferent to such matters, on inspecting her sexual parts in a mirror for the first time in her life was shocked and disgusted at the sight. Certainly many women could record a similar experience on being first approached by a man, although artistic conventions present the male form with greater truth than the female. Moreover, – and here is the significant point, – this feeling is by no means restricted to the refined and cultured. "When working at Michelangelo," wrote a correspondent from Italy, "my upper gondolier used to see photographs and statuettes of all that man's works. Stopping one day before the Night and Dawn of S. Lorenzo, sprawling naked women, he exclaimed: 'How hideous they are!' I pressed him to explain himself. He went on: 'The ugliest man naked is handsomer than the finest woman naked. Women have crooked legs, and their sexual organs stink. I only once saw a naked woman. It was in a brothel, when I was 18. The sight of her "natura" made me go out and vomit into the canal. You know I have been twice married, but I never saw either of my wives without clothing.' Of very rank cheese he said one day: 'Puzza come la natura d' una donna.'" This man, my correspondent added, was entirely normal and robust, but seemed to regard sexual congress as a mere evacuation, the sexual instinct apparently not being strong.

It seems possible that, if the sexual impulse had no existence, all men would regard women with this *horror feminæ*. As things are, however, at all events in civilization, sexual emotions begin to develop even earlier, usually, than acquaintance with the organs of the other sex begins; so that this disgust is inhibited. If, however, among savages the sexual impulse is habitually weak, and only aroused to strength under the impetus of powerful stimuli, often acting periodically, then we should expect the *horror* to be a factor of considerable importance.

The weakness of the physical sexual impulse among savages is reflected in the psychic sphere. Many writers have pointed out that love plays but a small part in their lives. They practise few endearments; they often only kiss children (Westermarck notes that sexual love is far less strong than parental love); love-poems are among some primitive peoples few (mostly originating with the women), and their literature often gives little or no attention to passion.[12] Affection and devotion are, however, often strong, especially in savage women.

It is not surprising that jealousy should often, though not by any means invariably, be absent, both among men and among women. Among savages this is doubtless a proof of the weakness of the sexual impulse. Spencer and Gillen note the comparative absence of jealousy in men among the Central Australian tribes they studied.[13] Negresses, it is said by a French army surgeon in his *Untrodden Fields of Anthropology*, do not know what jealousy is, and the first wife will even borrow money to buy the second wife. Among a much higher race, the women in a Korean household, it is said, live together happily, as an almost invariable rule, though it appears that this was not always the case among a polygamous people of European race, the Mormons.

The tendency of the sexual instinct in savages to periodicity, to seasonal manifestations, I do not discuss here, as I have dealt with it in the first volume of these *Studies*.[14] It has, however, a very important bearing on this subject. Periodicity of sexual manifestations is, indeed, less absolute in primitive man than in most animals, but it is still very often quite clearly marked. It is largely the occurrence of these violent occasional outbursts of the sexual instinct – during which the organic impulse to tumescence becomes so powerful that external stimuli are no longer necessary – that has led to the belief in the peculiar strength of the impulse in savages.[15]

II

The facts thus seem to indicate that among primitive peoples, while the magical, ceremonial, and traditional restraints on sexual intercourse are very numerous, very widespread, and nearly always very stringent, there is, underlying this prevalence of restraints on intercourse, a fundamental weakness of the sexual instinct, which craves less, and craves less frequently, than is the case among civilized peoples, but is liable to be powerfully manifested at special seasons. [...] Travelers, and too often would-be scientific writers, have been so much impressed by the absence among savages of the civilized ideal of chastity, and by the frequent freedom of sexual intercourse, that they have not paused to inquire more carefully into the phenomena, or to put themselves at the primitive point of view, but have assumed that freedom here means all that it would mean in a European population.

[...]

NOTES

1   Thus, Lubbock (Lord Avebury), in the *Origin of Civilization,* fifth edition, 1889, brings forward a number of references in evidence of this belief. More recently Finck, in his *Primitive Love and Love-stories*, 1899, seeks to accumulate data in favor of the unbounded licentiousness of savages. He admits, however, that a view of the matter opposed to his own is now tending to prevail.

2   See "The Evolution of Modesty" in the first volume of these *Studies*.

3   The sacredness of sexual relations often applies also to individual marriage. Thus, Skeat, in his *Malay Magic,* shows that the bride and bridegroom are definitely recognized as sacred, in the same sense that the king is, and in Malay States the king is a very sacred person. See also, concerning

the sacred character of coitus, whether individual or collective, A. Van Gennep, *Rites de Passage, passim.*

4 Spencer and Gillen, *Northern Tribes of Central Australia*, p. 136.

5 *Religion of the Semites*, second edition, 1894, p. 454 *et seq.*

6 *History of Marriage*, pp. 66–70, 150–156, etc.

7 *Golden Bough*, third edition, part ii, *Taboo and the Perils of the Soul.* Frazer has discussed taboo generally. For a shorter account of taboo, see art. "Taboo" by Northcote Thomas in *Encyclopædia Britannica*, eleventh edition, 1911. Freud has lately (*Imago*, 1912) made an attempt to explain the origin of taboo psychologically by comparing it to neurotic obsessions. Taboo, Freud believes, has its origin in a forbidden act to perform which there is a strong unconscious tendency; an ambivalent attitude, that is, combining the opposite tendencies, is thus established. In this way Freud would account for the fact that tabooed persons and things are both sacred and unclean.

8 "Essai sur le Sacrifice," *L'Année Sociologique*, 1899, pp. 50–51.

9 *The Mystic Rose*, 1902, p. 187 *et seq.*, 215 *et seq.*, 342 *et seq.*

10 *Das Weib*, vol. i, section 6.

11 This statement has been questioned. It should, however, be fairly evident that the sexual organs in either sex, when closely examined, can scarcely be regarded as beautiful except in the eyes of a person of the opposite sex who is in a condition of sexual excitement, and they are not always attractive even then. Moreover, it must be remembered that the snake-like aptitude of the penis to enter into a state of erection apart from the control of the will puts it in a different category from any other organ of the body, and could not fail to attract the attention of primitive peoples so easily alarmed by unusual manifestations. We find even in the early ages of Christianity that St. Augustine attached immense importance to this alarming aptitude of the penis as a sign of man's sinful and degenerate state.

12 Lubbock, *Origin of Civilization*, fifth edition, pp. 69, 73; Westermarck, *History of Marriage*, p. 357; Grosse, *Anfänge der*

Kunst, p. 236; Herbert Spencer, "Origin of Music," *Mind*, Oct., 1890.

13 Spencer and Gillen, *Native Tribes of Central Australia*, p. 99; *cf.* Finck, *Primitive Love and Love-stories*, p. 89 *et seq.*

14 "The Phenomena of Sexual Periodicity." The subject has also been more recently discussed by Walter Heape, "The 'Sexual Season' of Mammals," *Quarterly Journal of Microscopical Science*, vol. xliv, 1900. See also F. H. A. Marshall, *The Physiology of Reproduction*, 1910.

15 This view finds a belated supporter in Max Marcuse ("Geschlechtstrieb des Urmenschens," *Sexual-Probleme*, Oct., 1909), who, on grounds which I cannot regard as sound, seeks to maintain the belief that the sexual instinct is more highly developed among savage than among civilized peoples.

SELECT BIBLIOGRAPHY

Bloch, Iwan
    1903   Beiträge zur Aetiologie der Psychopathia Sexualis. 2 vols. Dresden: Dohrn.

Crawley, Ernest
    1902   The Mystic Rose, A Study of Primitive Marriage. London: Macmillan & Co.

Ellis, Havelock
    1910[1899]   Studies in the Psychology of Sex. Vol. 1: The Evolution of Modesty; The Phenomena of Sexual Periodicity; Auto-Erotism. Philadelphia: F. A. Davis.

Finck, Henry Theophilus
    1899   Primitive Love and Love Stories. New York: Scribner's Sons.

Frazer, Sir James G.
    1911–1915   The Golden Bough: A Study in Magic and Religion. 12 vols. London: Macmillan.

Freud, Sigmund
    1919   Totem and Taboo. London: Routledge.

Grosse, Ernst
    1894   Die Anfänge der Kunst. Freiburg: J. C. B. Mohr.

Heape, Walter
    1900   The 'Sexual Season' of Mammals and the Relation of the 'Pro-oestrum' to Menstruation. Quarterly Journal of Microscopical Science 44:1–70.

Hubert, Henri and Marcel Mauss
1898 Essai sur la nature et la fonction de sacrifice. L'Année sociologique 2:29–138.

Lubbock, Sir John, Lord Avebury
1889 The Origin of Civilization and the Primitive Condition of Man. London: Longmans, Green.

Marcuse, Max
1909 Geschlechtstrieb und Liebe des Urmenschen. Sexual-Probleme: Zeitschrift für Sexualwissenschaft und Sexualpolitik 5:921–940.

Marshall, F. H. A.
1910 The Physiology of Reproduction. London: Longmans, Green.

Ploss, Hermann Heinrich, and Maximilian Karl A. Bartels
1895 Das Weib in der Natur- und Völkerkunde. Leipzig.

Skeat, Walter William
1900 Malay Magic: Being an Introduction to the Folklore and Popular Religion of the Malay Peninsula. London: Macmillan.

Smith, W. Robertson
1894 Lectures on the Religion of the Semites. London: Adam & Charles Black.

Spencer, Baldwin, and F. J. Gillen
1904 The Northern Tribes of Central Australia. London: Macmillan & Co.

Spencer, Herbert
1890 The Origin of Music. Mind 16 (October): 375–386.

Thomas, Northcote W.
1911 Taboo. In Encyclopaedia Britannica, Eleventh Edition. Cambridge: Cambridge University Press.

van Gennep, Arnold
1909 Les Rites de passage. Paris: É. Nourry.

Westermarck, Edward
1894 The History of Marriage. London: Macmillan.

X, Jacobus
1898 Untrodden Fields of Anthropology. Paris: Librairie de médecine, folklore et anthropologie.

6

The Mystic Rose: Selections

Ernest Crawley

"In the beginning, when Twashtri came to the creation of woman, he found that he had exhausted his materials in the making of man, and that no solid elements were left. In this dilemma, after profound meditation, he did as follows. He took the rotundity of the moon, and the curves of creepers, and the clinging of tendrils, and the trembling of grass, and the slenderness of the reed, and the bloom of flowers, and the lightness of leaves, and the tapering of the elephant's trunk, and the glances of deer, and the clustering of rows of bees, and the joyous gaiety of sunbeams, and the weeping of clouds, and the fickleness of the winds, and the timidity of the hare, and the vanity of the peacock, and the softness of the parrot's bosom, and the hardness of adamant, and the sweetness of honey, and the cruelty of the tiger, and the warm glow of fire, and the coldness of snow, and the chattering of jays, and the cooing of the *kókila*, and the hypocrisy of the crane, and the fidelity of the *chakrawáka*, and compounding all these together, he made woman and gave her to man. But after one week, man came to him and said: Lord, this creature that you have given me makes my life miserable. She chatters incessantly and teases me beyond endurance, never leaving me alone; and she requires incessant attention, and takes all my time up, and cries about nothing, and is always idle; and so I have come to give her back again, as I cannot live with her. So Twashtri said: Very well; and he took her back. Then after another week, man came again to him and said: Lord, I find that my life is very lonely, since I gave you back that creature. I remember how she used to dance and sing to me, and look at me out of the corner of her eye, and play with me, and cling to me; and her laughter was music, and she was beautiful to look at, and soft to touch; so give her back to me again. So Twashtri said: Very well; and gave her back again. Then after only three days, man came back to him again and said: Lord, I know not how it is; but after all I have come to the conclusion that she is more of a trouble than a pleasure to me; so please take her back again. But Twashtri said: Out on you! Be off! I will have no more of this. You must manage how you can. Then man said: But I cannot live with her. And Twashtri replied: Neither could you live without her. And he

Selections from Ernest Crawley, *The Mystic Rose*, London: Macmillan, 1902, pp. 33–37, 204–207, 213–223.

Sexualities in Anthropology: A Reader, edited by Andrew P. Lyons and Harriet D. Lyons

turned his back on man, and went on with his work. Then man said: What is to be done? for I cannot live either with her or without her."[1]

This extract from a beautiful Sanscrit story illustrates a conception of the relations of man and woman, which often recurs in literature. The same conception, due ultimately to that difference of sex and of sexual characters which renders mutual sympathy and understanding more or less difficult, is characteristic of mankind in all periods and stages of culture. Woman is one of the last things to be understood by man; though the complement of man and his partner in health and sickness, poverty and wealth, woman is different from man, and this difference has had the same religious results as have attended other things which man does not understand. The same is true of woman's attitude to man. In the history of the sexes there have been always at work the two complementary physical forces of attraction and repulsion; man and woman may be regarded, and not fancifully, as the highest sphere in which this law of physics operates; in love the two sexes are drawn to each other by an irresistible sympathy, while in other circumstances there is more or less of segregation, due to and enforced by human ideas of human relations.

The remarkable facts which follow show the primitive theory and practice of this separation of the sexes. Both in origin and results the phenomena are those of Taboo, and hence I have applied to these facts the specific term of Sexual Taboo. At first sight this early stage of the relations of men and women may cause surprise, but when one realises the continuity of human ideas, and analyses one's own consciousness, one may find there in potentiality, if not actualised by prejudice, the same conception, though perhaps emptied of its religious content.

In Nukahiva if a woman happens to sit upon or even pass near an object which has become *tabu* by contact with a man, it can never be used again, and she is put to death. In Tahiti a woman had to respect those places frequented by men, their weapons and fishing implements; the head of a husband or father was *sacred* from the touch of woman, nor might a wife or daughter touch any object that

had been in contact with these *tabued* heads, or step over them when their owners were asleep. In the Solomon Islands a man will never pass under a tree fallen across the path, because a woman may have stepped over it before him. In Siam it is considered unlucky to pass under women's clothes hung out to dry. It is *degrading* to a Melanesian chief to go where women may be above his head; boys also are forbidden to go underneath the women's bed-place. Amongst the Karens of Burmah going under a house when there are females within is avoided; and in Burmah generally it is thought an *indignity* to have a woman above the head; to prevent which the houses are never built with more than one storey. This explanation of an architectural peculiarity is doubtless *ex post facto*. Amongst the people of Rajmahal, if a man be detected by a woman sitting on her cot and she complains of the impropriety, he pays her a fowl as fine, which she returns; on the other hand, if a man detects a woman sitting on his cot, he kills the fowl which she produces in answer to his complaint, and sprinkles the blood on the cot to purify it, after which she is pardoned. In Cambodia a wife may never use the pillow or mattress of her husband, because "she would hurt his happiness thereby." In Siam the wife has a lower pillow "to remind her of her inferiority." This reason is possibly late. Amongst the Barea man and wife seldom share the same bed, the reason they give is, that if they sleep together the breath of the wife will render her husband weak. Amongst the Lapps no grown woman may touch the hinder part of the house, which is sacred to the sun. No woman may enter the house of a Maori chief. Amongst the Kaffas of East Africa husband and wife see each other only at night, never meeting during the day. She is secluded in the interior portion of the house, while he occupies the remainder. "A public resort is also set apart for the husband, where no woman is permitted to appear. A penalty of three years' imprisonment attaches to an infringement of this rule." Observers have noted "the haughty contempt" shown by Zulus for their wives. Men and women rarely are seen together; if a man and his wife are going to the same place, they do not walk together. In some Redskin tribes and amongst the Indians of California a man never enters his wife's wigwam except under cover of the darkness; and the men's club-house may never be entered by women. The Bedouin tent is divided into two compartments for the men and women respectively. No man of good reputation will enter the women's part of the tent or even be seen in its shadow. In Nukahiva the houses of important men are not accessible to their own wives, who live in separate huts. Amongst the Samoyeds and Ostyaks a wife may not tread in any part of the tent except her own corner; after pitching the tent she must fumigate it before the men enter. In Fiji husbands are as frequently away from their wives as with them; it is not, in Fijian society, thought well for a man to sleep regularly at home. [...]

What, then, are the chief female properties the transmission of which is feared as deleterious? First of all, mere difference is regarded by the savage as dangerous, simply because it is unknown. In the second place, the difference is specialised as inferiority of physical strength and stature, relatively, that is, to the male standard. It is a universal conception amongst men of all stages of culture that woman is weaker than man. As a rule, man forgets the *relativity* of this characteristic, and regards woman as more or less absolutely weak. That this idea is practically inherent in human male nature, as a physiological inference of the simplest kind, is proved by its regular expression in the life and literature of all ages. The use and connotation of the word "effeminate" illustrates this well. This evidence taken with that of ethnology is overwhelming. Primitive man agrees with the most modern of the moderns, for instance, with a Nietzsche, who regards woman as a slight, dainty, and relatively feeble creature. The ethnological evidence for this masculine belief is very extensive. General inferiority is sometimes found as a secondary result.

[...]

This characteristic and that of weakness are the complement of masculine courage and strength, and are connected with a physical subconscious fear of men. When associated with hysterical phenomena, timidity is merged in another conception of woman, as a "mysterious" person. The mystery is based on sexual differentiation, in particular on the sexual phenomena of menstruation and child-birth. As we have seen, this mystery is deepened by further ideas it creates, such as the ascription of taboo properties to woman, and the beliefs that woman has intercourse with the spiritual world at menstruation, and that she is more or less of a potential witch. The whole reasoning is clinched by the fact of a temporary depression, identified with loss of strength, following upon intercourse with this weak but mysterious creature, and the imperious demands of nature which enforce association with the female sex, inevitably cause a continuous repetition of sexual taboo and of the ideas which underlie it. These organic characteristics not only make woman peculiarly susceptible to religious influences, but have fitted her to be a useful medium for priestcraft, and often to hold the priestly authority herself. The priestess is a frequent feature of savage worship. Here is to be found the explanation of one set of cases of priests dressing as women. For example, amongst the Sea Dyaks some of the priests pretend to be women, or rather dress as such, and like to be treated as females. Patagonian sorcerers, who are chosen from children who have St. Vitus' dance, wear women's clothes. Amongst the Kodyaks there are men dressed as women who are regarded as sorcerers and are much respected. Doubtless the idea is to assume such emotional peculiarities of women as are useful to the priest. To the savage mind, the donning of another's dress is more than a token of the new position: it completes identity by communicating the qualities of the original owner. There is also the desire to command attention by eccentricity if not by mystery, for both of which ends change of sex is a time-honoured method.

It remains to add direct evidence for the belief, which is the chief factor in sexual taboo, that contact with women causes transmission of female characteristics, femininity, effeminancy, weakness, and timidity.

In South Africa a man must not, when in bed, touch his wife with his right hand; "if he did so, he would have no strength in war, and would surely be slain." If a man touch a woman during menstruation, "his bones become soft, and in future he cannot take part in warfare or any other manly exercise." Stepping over another's person is highly improper; while if a *woman* steps over her husband's stick "he cannot aim or hit any one with it. If she steps over his *assegai*, it will never kill or even hit an enemy, and it is at once discarded and given to the boys to play and practise with." The Galela and Tobelorese are continent during war, "so as not to lose their strength." The Seminoles believed that "carnal connection with a woman exercised an enervating influence upon men, and rendered them less fit for the duties of the warrior." [...]

To savages who do not know the use of salt, blood is an excellent substitute. In the Central Australian tribes "blood may be given by young men to old men of any degree of relationship, and at any time, with a view to strengthening the latter." Again, blood is not infrequently used to assuage thirst and hunger; indeed, when under ordinary circumstances a black-fellow is badly in want of water, what he does is to open a vein in his arm and drink the blood. Other Australian tribes "have no fear of blood or of the sight of it"; they drink it freely to acquire strength. The Wachaga and Koos delight in drinking warm blood fresh from a slaughtered animal. At the Dieri ceremony of *Wilyaru* blood drawn from men is poured on the novice's back "to infuse courage, and to show him that the sight of blood is nothing." The latter reason is secondary. Woman's blood is feared or desired, just as are other parts of woman, because it is a part of woman and contains feminine properties.

The contagion of woman during the sexual crises of menstruation, pregnancy, child-birth, is simply intensified, because these are occasions when woman's peculiar characteristics are accentuated, these are feminine crises when a woman is most a woman. This is the only difference between contact then and contact in ordinary states, a difference of degree only.

We may now conclude the description of the ideas which have produced sexual taboo. We have traced its origin from sexual differentiation, difference of occupation, and a resulting solidarity in each sex; this biological material is then informed by religious ideas concerning human relations, which are regulated by contact. Thus the usual working motive in sexual taboo is that the properties of the one sex can be transmitted to the other by all methods of contact, transmission, or contagion, and by various vehicles. Animal-like, the savage fears weakness more than anything else. Two remarkable facts have emerged – first, that it is dangerous, and later, wrong, for men to have anything to do with women; intercourse commensal and sexual being especially dangerous because especially intimate, but there is a tendency against all living together; and secondly, that sexual intercourse, even when lawful morally and legally, is dangerous first, and later, sinful. To primitive thought all intercourse has one connotation of material danger, which later split into ideas of sins, such as incest and fornication, for any intercourse is the breaking of a personal taboo and a sexual taboo, and the material results of such breaking develop into moral sin.

Sexual taboo would seem to have had the useful results not only of assisting Nature's institution of the family and of producing the marriage system, by preventing licence both within and without the family limits, keeping men from promiscuity and incest, degradations which were never primitive – the early efforts of human religious thought being in the direction of assisting, not of checking, Nature – but also of emphasising the characteristic qualities of each sex by preventing a mixture of male and female temperaments through mutual influence and association, and, as the complement to this, of accentuating by segregation the charm each sex has for the other in love and married life, the charm of complementary difference of character. Man prefers womanliness in woman, and woman prefers manliness in man; sexual taboo has enhanced this natural preference.

Where sexual taboo is fully developed, the life of husband and wife is a sort of divorce *a mensa et thoro*, and the life of men and women is that of two divided castes. The segregation is naturally emphasised as between young persons of the opposite sex, most of all between those who, as living in the somewhat close contact of the family, are more strictly separated, both because parents prevent the dangerous results obviated by sexual taboo with all the more care since their own children are in danger, and because, subsequently, a feeling of duty in this regard is combined with the natural affection of brothers and sisters, which is due to early association. The biological basis of this separation is the universal practice by which boys go about with the father as soon as they are old enough, and the girls remain with the mother. This is the preparatory education of the savage child, beginning about the age of seven. Girls and boys till the age of seven or eight, and sometimes till puberty, are often classed as "children," with no distinction of sex, as amongst the Kurnai. In Leti, Moa, and Lakor children are brought up together till about ten years old. The girls then begin to help the mother, and the boys go about with the father. So in the Babar Islands. Amongst the Kaffirs, as amongst most peoples, boys and girls till seven or eight live with the mother. As soon as they are old enough, the boys are taken under the father's charge.

In Samoa the boys leave their mother's care at seven years of age, and come under the superintendence of their father and male relatives. They are now circumcised and receive a new name. This case combines an "initiation" ceremony placed at a date earlier than usual. In Patagonia the sons begin to go about with the father at ten, and the girls with the mother at nine. Amongst the Jaggas boys have to live together as soon as they can do without a mother's care. Of some Australian tribes Mr. Curr reports that "from a very early age the boys begin to imitate their fathers, and the girls their mothers, in their everyday occupations. When the boy is four or five years of age the father will make him a miniature shield, spear, and *wommera*, with which the little fellow fights his compeers and annoys his mother and the dogs. About seven or eight years of age commences in earnest the course of education. At eight or ten the boy has to leave the hut of his father and sleep in one common to the young men and boys of the tribe."

The following cases show how sexual taboo emphasises this. In the Society and Sandwich Islands "as soon as a boy was able to eat, his food was kept distinct from that of his mother, and brothers and sisters might not eat together from the earliest age." In Uripiv boys from a few days after birth are supposed to eat with the male sex only, else "death would mysteriously fall upon them. The fact of suckling, however, is overlooked." In Fiji brothers and sisters may not speak to each other, nor eat together. The boys sleep in a separate room. The relationship between brothers and sisters is termed *ngane*, which means "one who shuns the other." In some Australian tribes brother and sister are not allowed even to converse. Amongst all the Indian tribes of California brothers and sisters scrupulously avoid living together. In Melanesia there is a remarkable avoidance between a boy and his sisters and mother, beginning when he is first clothed, and in the case of the sister when she is first tatooed. He is also forbidden to go underneath the women's bed-place, just as a Melanesian chief thinks it a degradation to go where women may be above his head. In Fiji, again, brothers and sisters may not converse, the boys' sleeping-room is separated from that of the girls, and boys may not eat with a female. In New Caledonia brothers and sisters after having reached years of maturity are no longer permitted to entertain any social intercourse with each other; they are prohibited from keeping each other's company, even in the presence of a third person, and if they casually meet, they must instantly go out of the way, or, if that is impossible, the sister must throw herself on the ground with her face downwards. Yet, if a misfortune should befall one of them, they assist each other to the best of their ability through the medium of a common friend. In Japan young princes are prohibited from all intercourse with the opposite sex. According to the moral code of the same country, "parents must teach their daughters to keep separate from the other sex. The old custom is: man and woman shall not sit on the same mat, nor put their clothing in the same place, shall have different bathrooms, shall not give or take anything directly from hand to hand. On walking out, even in the case of families, the men must keep separate from their female relatives." In the Hervey Islands the first-born son is forbidden to kiss his sister; "she may not cross his path when the wind which has passed over her is likely to touch his most sacred person." Amongst the Nairs of Malabar a man honours his eldest sister; he may never stay in the same room with his other sisters, and his behaviour to them is most reserved. In the Nanbúri caste of Travancore "women are guarded with more than Moslem jealousy; even brothers and sisters are separated at an early age." In Tonga a chief pays the greatest respect to his eldest sister, and may never enter her house. In Ceylon a father is forbidden to see his daughter at all after she has arrived at puberty, so also in the case of mother and son. Amongst the Todas near relations of different sexes consider it a "pollution" if even their garments should touch, and a case is mentioned of a girl expressing horror when handled by her father. A Corean girl is taught that the most disgraceful thing a woman can do is to allow herself to be seen or spoken to by any man outside her own family circle. After the age of eight, she is never allowed to enter the men's quarters of her own home. "The boys in the same way are told that it is unbecoming and undignified to enter the portion of the house set apart for females. The men and the women have their meals separately, the women waiting on their husbands. Thus family life as we have it is utterly unknown in Corea."

With the approach of puberty, the sexual question appears which emphasises the separation, both natural and taboo, and at the ceremonies of initiation boys are formally taken away, as they have practically already been taken away, from the mother's sphere and female associations. The danger, now enhanced by a new instinct, produces the very common custom that from this time boys may not sleep even in the house or with the family. A common form of this custom is the institution of public buildings, which combine the features of a dormitory and a club, for the use of the young men. In Annam these are called *morongs*. The custom is found, for instance, amongst the Niamniam and Bongos, the Dyaks, in the islands between Celebes and New Guinea, in New Guinea, Tonga, the Andaman Islands, South and West Africa, and amongst the Pueblos, in the New Hebrides, and Indo-China.

The separation of the young outside the family is a fairly regular social rule. On Fraser's Island "a young man will not sit down on the same stool or box, or in fact anywhere where a young woman has been sitting at any time. They imagine that the young man would sicken and die. The shadow of young women must not pass over the sleeping-places of young men." Among the Iroquois young men could have no intercourse with girls, nor even conversation; and amongst most North American tribes, "the chastity of girls is carefully guarded." "The separation of the immature youth of the two sexes is a feature strongly insisted upon in the social practice of all the North-Western American tribes." Amongst the Northern Indians "girls are from the early age of eight or nine years prohibited by custom from joining in the most innocent amusements with children of the opposite sex. When sitting in their tents, or even when travelling, they are watched and guarded with such an unremitting attention as cannot be exceeded by the most rigid discipline of an English boarding-school." Amongst the Omahas a girl may not speak to a man, except very near relations. In Madagascar the tribes of the forest and East Coast have a higher morality than the Hovas, girls being scrupulously kept from any intercourse with the male sex until marriage. Amongst the Greenlanders single persons of both sexes have rarely any connection; for instance, a maid would take it as an affront were a young fellow to offer her a pinch of snuff in company. Eusofzye women consider it indecent to associate with the men. In Loango a youth dare not speak to a girl except in her mother's presence. Amongst the Hill Dyaks the young men are carefully separated from the girls. In New South Wales unmarried youths and girls may not speak to each other. In some Victorian tribes the unmarried adults of both sexes are kept carefully apart. Amongst the same people the seducer of an unmarried girl is beaten to death, and the girl is punished and sometimes killed. In South Nias both the seducer and the girl are put to death. In the Tenimber Islands (Timorlaut) it is taboo for a boy to touch a girl's breast or hand, and for her to touch his hair. Amongst the Leh-tas of Burma boys and girls "when they may have occasion to pass each other, avert their gaze, so that they may not see each other's faces." In Cambodia the girls are carefully secluded, and the reserve which they show is remarkable. "The stringency of custom prevents the intercourse of the young. Accordingly, the *rôle* of village Don Juan is scarcely possible." In the Andaman Islands bachelors may only eat with men, spinsters with women. In Tasmania "the young men and lads moved early from the camp in the morning so as not to interfere with female movements at rising. Unmarried men never wandered in the bush with women; if meeting a party of the other sex, native politeness required that they turned and went another way." An Australian woman, in most tribes, is not allowed to converse or have any relations with any adult male save her husband. Even with a grown-up brother she is almost forbidden to exchange a word. Here the proprietary jealousy of husbands is a factor in the rule; but the common Australian custom, as in the Central tribes, where no man as a general rule may go near the *Erlukwirra* ("women's camp") and no woman may approach the *Ungunja* ("men's camp"), brings us back to sexual taboo, and reminds us that this separation of the young is due to all the ideas of this taboo, and not to the fear of sexual intercourse only. Such rules as usual become further causes, and have perpetuated the separation of the sexes.

In the examples of separation of brother and sister, we have been really reviewing the process of preventing "incest," and in those of the separation of young persons generally, the process of preventing "promiscuity." Neither of these needed prevention, for neither was ever anything but the rarest exception in any stage of human culture, even the earliest; the former is prevented by the psychological difficulty with which love comes into play between persons either closely associated or strictly separated before the age of puberty, a difficulty enhanced by the ideas of sexual taboo, which are intensified in the closeness of the family circle, where practical as well as religious considerations cause parents to prevent any dangerous connection. We saw that in many cases, not merely is the intercourse of husband and wife not practised in the house, but even the performance of ordinary functions, such as eating, is prohibited there, as in New Zealand and the Sandwich Islands.

Parents bring up their children by the same rule, which is, put briefly, that all close connection between the sexes is dangerous, and especially between those who are in close contact. Marriage of man and woman is theoretically a forbidden thing, both outside and inside the family circle. The very word "incest" originally meant simply "unchaste," connoting a merely general infringement of sexual taboo, such infringement being more reprehensible between those who are not likely to make it. As to the fictions of primitive "incest" and "promiscuity," both in popular tradition and scientific theories of primitive marriage, it is natural that marriage systems should be explained as intended to put a stop to a prevailing practice, by those who do not know how religion simply assists nature, but the explanation does not at all go to show that these practices ever existed.

Lastly, as will be discussed hereafter, it is the application of sexual taboo to brothers and sisters, who, because they are of opposite sexes, of the same generation, and are in close contact, and for no other reasons, are regarded as potentially marriageable, that is the foundation of exogamy and the marriage system.

NOTE

1 *A Digit of the Moon*, trans. by F. W. Bain, 13–15.

SELECT BIBLIOGRAPHY

Aymonier, Étienne
    1883   Notes sur les coutumes et croyances superstitieuses des Cambodgiens. Saigon.
Bain, Francis William
    1905   A Digit of the Moon and Other Love Stories from the Hindoo. Trans. F. W. Bain. New York: G. P. Putnam's Sons.
Bastian, Adolf
    1860   Der Mensch in der Geschichte. 3 vols. Leipzig: Otto Wigand.
Brooke, Charles, Rajah of Sarawak
    1866   Ten Years in Sarawak. 2 vols. London: Tinsley.

Codrington, Robert Henry
1891   The Melanesians: Studies in their Anthropology and Folklore. Oxford: Clarendon Press.

Curr, Edward M.
1886/1887   The Australian Race. 4 vols. Melbourne: J. Ferres.

Dobrizhoffer, Martin
1822   Account of the Abipones, an Equestrian People of Paraguay. London: John Murray.

Dumont d'Urville, Jules-Sébastien-César
1834   Voyage pittoresque autour du monde. Paris: Tenré et Dupuy.

Ellis, Havelock
1914   Man and Woman: A Study of Human Secondary Sexual Characters. London: Walter Scott.

Ellis, William
1853   Polynesian Researches During a Residence of Eight Years in the Society and Sandwich Islands. London: Bohn.

Elphinstone, Mountstuart
1842   An Account of the Kingdom of Caubul and its Dependencies in Persia, Tartary and India. 2 vols. London: Bentley.

Fison, Lorimer, and A. W. Howitt
1880   Kamilaroi and Kurnai: Group Marriage and Relationship, and Marriage by Elopement, drawn chiefly from the Usage of the Australian Aborigines. Melbourne: G. Robertson.

Guppy, Henry Brougham
1887   The Solomon Islands and their Natives. London: Sonnenschein, Lowrey.

Krapf, Johann L.
1860   Travels, Researches and Missionary Labours During an Eighteen Years' Residence in East Africa. London: Trübner and Co.

Letourneau, Charles
1893   Sociology Based on Ethnography. Trans. H. M. Trollope. London: Chapman Hall.

Melville, Herman
1846   Narrative of a Four Months' Residence Among the Natives of a Valley of the Marquesas. London: J. Murray.

Munzinger, Werner
1864   Ostafrikanische Studien. Schaffhausen: Hurter.

Ploss, Herman Heinrich
1899   Das Weib in der Natur- und Völkerkunde. Anthropologische Studien. 2 vols. Leipzig: Grieben.

Powers, Stephen
1877   Tribes of California. Washington, DC: Government Printing Office.

Reade, W. Winwood
1863   Savage Africa. London: Smith, Elder & Co.

Schoolcraft, Henry R.
1851–1857   Historical and Statistical Information Respecting the History, Condition and Prospects of the Indian Tribes of The United States. 6 vols. Philadelphia: Lippincott.

Schweinfurth, Georg August
1873   The Heart of Africa, Three Years' Travels and Adventures in the Unexplored Regions of Central Africa. 2 vols. Trans. E. E. Frewer. London: Sampson Low, Marston, Low and Searle.

Spencer, Baldwin, and F. J. Gillen
1899   The Native Tribes of Central Australia. London: Macmillan.

Taylor, Richard
1870   Te Ika a Maui OR New Zealand and its Inhabitants. London: W. Macintosh.

Tregear, Edward
1891   The Maori-Polynesian Comparative Dictionary. Wellington, New Zealand: Lyon and Blair.

Williams, Thomas, and James Calvert
1860   Fiji and the Fijians. New York: Appleton.

Part IV

Early Work on Homosexualities

Introduction

In the century after the discovery of the New World, reports of varying reliability began to appear concerning male homosexuality and/or ritual transvestism among the Aztecs, the Cueva of Panama, the Timacuans of Florida, and other peoples. By the mid-nineteenth century quite a substantial literature had accumulated about the institution of the *berdache*, as it was then known. The word "berdache" is French and probably of Persian origin. It describes a form of ritual transvestism that was found among many North American peoples, and could occasionally involve female to male as well as male to female transvestism. There were also a number of reports about the ambiguous gender of shamans among the Inuit and northeast Asian peoples. If one added data from classical and biblical studies concerning homosexualities in Sparta, Athens, Canaan, and the Roman world, there was enough information to initiate cross-cultural analysis of same-sex sexualities.

The establishment of social anthropology first as an armchair and, a few decades later, as a fieldwork discipline coincided with the emergence of "homosexuality" as a biological/social category that was explored in sexology, early gay literature, and the legal realm. The term "homosexual" was first used by the Hungarian Károly M. Kertbeny in 1869, but initially the term "Uranian" (in German *Urning*), which was invented by the gay writer Karl Heinrich Ulrichs in 1865, was more popular. It was during the latter part of the nineteenth century that Walt Whitman's "Leaves of Grass" went through a number of editions, and in the last two decades of the century Oscar Wilde became first a celebrity and later a prisoner. In England, the Criminal Law Amendment Act of 1885 lowered penalties for consensual sex ("gross indecency") between men, with the paradoxical effect of encouraging prosecution. The Cleveland Street scandal involving messenger boys and, allegedly, members of the aristocracy occurred four years after the Act was passed. Censorship was always

Sexualities in Anthropology: A Reader, edited by Andrew P. Lyons and Harriet D. Lyons
© 2011 Blackwell Publishing Ltd.

a consideration, and contemporary readers of texts from this period must sometimes read a few things between the lines. At least two of the four authors included in this section were fearful of censorship. Sir Richard Burton was rightfully fearful that the authorities might seize copies of his 10-volume edition of the Arabian Nights, because it contained risqué stories, explicit footnotes, and a *Terminal Essay* that included a brief section on homosexualities in Arabia and elsewhere. The volumes were privately printed, extremely expensive, and available by subscription only. That way, Burton avoided prosecution. However, on the urging of the National Vigilance Association, the publisher Henry Vizetelly was prosecuted and imprisoned in 1889 for publishing a translation of works by Émile Zola. In 1898 the bookseller, publisher, and radical George Bedborough received a sentence for offering Havelock Ellis's *Sexual Inversion* to the general public. As a result, Ellis arranged for the remaining six volumes of his *Studies in the Psychology of Sex* to be published and distributed by F. A. Davis, a medical publisher, in Philadelphia.

Burton translated *The Thousand Nights and One Night* (Arabian Nights), *The Perfumed Garden*, *The Kama Sutra*, and other erotica, as well as writing a number of books concerning his travels and explorations. He was a soldier in India, a pilgrim to Mecca (wearing a disguise), and a diplomat in West Africa, Brazil, Damascus, and Trieste. In the 1860s he was vice-president of the Anthropological Society of London. Burton's publications demonstrate some anthropological understanding of both Arab and African cultures, but they are marred by his racism, extreme even for his time, and anti-Semitism. After many sexual adventures, Burton was married for about 30 years to Isobel Arundell, who burned many of his papers after his death in order, she thought, to preserve his reputation. The papers included a more complete translation of *The Perfumed Garden*, enlarged to include a section on pederasty. She could not understand his interest in homosexuality: "Why did he wish the subject of unnatural crime to be so largely aired and expounded – he had such an unbounded contempt for the Vice and its votaries?"[1] Burton's interest in "the Vice" dated back to the 1840s when, as a young officer in India, he produced a report on male brothels (lupanars) in Karachi for the British Commanding Officer, General Sir Charles Napier, who was concerned about the welfare of his officers. Burton's thoroughness and enthusiasm in carrying out this assignment led to a suspicion of "participant observation" which may have damaged his career in India. In the extract from the *Terminal Essay* reproduced here, he notes that homosexuality is worldwide in occurrence, but seems to be most frequent in a belt that includes both the coastal and nearby mountain areas to the north and south of the Mediterranean and extends eastwards through the mountains of Western and Central Asia, as well as the South Seas and the Americas. His inference is that there is some kind of connection between geographical environment and sexuality. This would imply that in certain circumstances homosexuality is "natural." Whatever his intent, Burton had shifted the ground of the argument. However, the "Sotadic Zone" was mere invention.

Havelock Ellis's *Sexual Inversion* contained details of his case studies, based on letters he had received and solicited from various correspondents, and selections from the writings of the literary critic, John Addington Symonds, on homosexuality in Greece and elsewhere. Symonds died before the first publication of the manuscript in German. In order to placate his family, Ellis withdrew Symonds's name (but not the writing) from the English edition. In *Sexual Inversion* Ellis argued that homosexuality was a sport of nature more than it was a product of the environment. The implication was that one could not be blamed for being homosexual. Indeed, homosexuals had made many contributions in art, literature, and politics. Ellis believed that both male and female same-sex relations (between adults) should be legalized, provided that they were conducted in private, but thought that the public would not be able to tolerate public displays of homosexual love. Biographers like Phyllis Grosskurth have drawn attention to Ellis's own personal life, including his never-consummated first marriage to Edith Ellis, who was publicly lesbian, his impotence that lasted till his 60th birthday and his *urolagnia* (he was sexually aroused by the sight of women urinating). Whatever the case, Ellis exhibited quite a lot of courage by publishing his work and facing the possible consequences (as it happens, Bedborough, whom he assisted, was tried and pleaded guilty, but, as an individual with a medical degree publishing a medical work, Ellis escaped prosecution).

The anthropological consideration of homosexuality in the second volume of Edward Westermarck's *The Origin and Development of the Moral Ideas* (extracted here) was detailed, scholarly, and thoughtful, and is still of some value today. Westermarck's supporting data cover the entire ethnographic spectrum (for reasons of space we had to omit the elaborate footnotes that are longer than the main text). He was particularly well informed about homosexuality among Islamic scribes in Morocco, a country where he had a vacation home and conducted ethnographic research. Note his statement that homosexuality is "probably no abnormality at all, only a feature in the ordinary sexual constitution of man." Westermarck is the first anthropologist to attack the pathologization and medicalization of same-sex relations. In his opinion, homosexuality could be innate (in the case of many shamans). However, he felt that Ellis neglected some of the environmental triggers that might encourage same-sex relationships, such as confinement to single-sex institutions like monastic orders and the military.

Edward Carpenter, writer, sometime priest, lecturer, socialist, and pacifist, was a member of the 1880s Fellowship of the New Life, a socialist group, and accordingly knew Havelock Ellis, Olive Schreiner, Eleanor Marx Aveling, George Bernard Shaw, and the future prime minister of Britain, Ramsay MacDonald. For many years Carpenter lived with his working-class lover, George Merrill, in the Yorkshire countryside. He was the author of *The Intermediate Sex* (1908) and *Intermediate Types among Primitive Folk* (1914), a chapter of which is extracted here. Carpenter was well versed in the anthropology of his day, and some chapters in *Intermediate Types* appeared in a French anthropology journal. The book is both a brief catalogue, what Kath Weston would call an exercise in *ethnocartography*, of what was then known about gays around the world, and also a rudimentary typology. In the first part of the book Carpenter describes shamans in the Arctic, berdaches (whom we now call "two-spirit people") in North America, and male temple prostitutes in Palestine, and then discusses religious representations of bisexuality in the Greek and Hindu pantheons. In the second part of the book he examines forms of homosexuality in military environments, concentrating first on the idealization of "comrade-love" among Dorian Greek soldiers in the middle of the first millennium BC (the Dorians had settled in Sparta and most of the Peloponnese, as well as Crete and Mytilene in the early part of the millennium). In another chapter he discusses comrade-love among Japanese Samurai. Little is said here about lesbianism, although there is a brief mention of Sappho in a discussion of the positive relationship between tolerance or encouragement of male homosexuality and the status of women that is demonstrated in Greek history. When tolerance of homosexuality declined (500–200 BC), women's status was also degraded.

A graduate of Barnard College in New York, with a PhD from Columbia, Elsie Clews Parsons was the wealthy wife of a Republican congressman, a feminist who advocated companionate marriage (or no marriage at all) in her early writing, some of which was published under a male pseudonym. She was initially a sociologist. After becoming an anthropologist and folklorist around 1910, she did fieldwork among the Hopi, Tewa, and Zuni. Because of her work, she was able to fund the fieldwork of other women who worked with Franz Boas, such as Ruth Bunzel and Ruth Benedict. Her account of the Zuni *Lamana* that is reproduced here is one of the first journal articles based on fieldwork study of transgender roles. Note that, while most *Lamana* are male–female transvestites, Parsons says that a few are female–male.

NOTE

1   Letter from Isobel Burton to Leonard Smithers, July 17, 1892. Burton Papers, Huntington Library, San Marino, California.

REFERENCES AND FURTHER READING

Burton, Sir Richard Francis
    1885–7   A Plain and Literal Translation of the Arabian Nights' Entertainment, Now Entitled the Book of The Thousand Nights and a Night. With Introduction, Explanatory Notes on the Manners and Customs of Moslem Men and a Terminal Essay upon the History of the Nights. 10 vols. London and Benares: Kamashastra Society.
Carpenter, Edward
    1930[1916]   The Intermediate Sex: A Study of Some Transitional Types of Men and Women. Reprint of 4th edition (1st edition published 1908). London: George Allen & Unwin.
Ellis, Havelock
    1897   Sexual Inversion. Initially published by "Watford University Press" (George Bedborough). Later editions published as Volume Two of Studies in the Psychology of Sex by F. A. Davis, Philadelphia.
Grosskurth, Phyllis
    1980   Havelock Ellis: A Biography. Toronto: McClelland and Stewart.
Kennedy, Dane
    2005   The Highly Civilized Man: Richard Burton and the Victorian World. Cambridge, MA: Harvard University Press.
Lyons, Andrew P.
    2007   Missing Ancestors and Missing Naratives. Histories of Anthropology Annual 3:148–166. (About the anthropology of Richard Burton.)
Rowbotham, Sheila
    2008   Edward Carpenter: A Life of Liberty and Love. London: Verso.

7

Pederasty

Richard Burton

The "execrabilis familia pathicorum" first came before me by a chance of earlier life. In 1845, when Sir Charles Napier had conquered and annexed Sind, despite a fraction (mostly venal) which sought favour with the now defunct "Court of Directors to the Honourable East India Company," the veteran began to consider his conquest with a curious eye. It was reported to him that Karáchi, a townlet of some two thousand souls and distant not more than a mile from camp, supported no less than three lupanars or borders, in which not women but boys and eunuchs, the former demanding nearly a double price, lay for hire. Being then the only British officer who could speak Sindi, I was asked indirectly to make enquiries and to report upon the subject; and I undertook the task on express condition that my report should not be forwarded to the Bombay Government, from whom supporters of the Conqueror's policy could expect scant favour, mercy or justice. Accompanied by a Munshi, Mirza Mohammed Hosayn of Shiraz, and habited as a merchant, Mirza Abdullah the Bushiri passed many an evening in the townlet, visited all the porneia and obtained the fullest details, which were duly despatched to Government House. But the "Devil's Brother" presently quitted Sind leaving in his office my unfortunate official: this found its way with sundry other reports to Bombay and produced the expected result. A friend in the Secretariat informed me that my summary dismissal from the service had been formally proposed by one of Sir Charles Napier's successors, whose decease compels me parcere sepulto. But this excess of outraged modesty was not allowed.

Subsequent enquiries in many and distant countries enabled me to arrive at the following conclusions:

1   There exists what I shall call a "Sotadic Zone," bounded westwards by the northern shores of the Mediterranean (N. Lat. 43°) and by the southern (N. Lat. 30°). Thus the depth would be 780 to 800 miles including meridional France, the Iberian Peninsula, Italy and Greece, with the coast-regions of Africa from Marocco to Egypt.
2   Running eastward the Sotadic Zone narrows, embracing Asia Minor, Mesopotamia and Chaldæa, Afghanistan, Sind, the Punjab and Kashmir.

Extracts from the Terminal Essay in Richard Burton's *Arabian Nights*, 1885–1887, vol. 10, pp. 207, 208.

Sexualities in Anthropology: A Reader, edited by Andrew P. Lyons and Harriet D. Lyons

3 In Indo-China the belt begins to broaden, enfolding China, Japan and Turkistan.

4 It then embraces the South Sea Islands and the New World where, at the time of its discovery, Sotadic love was, with some exceptions, an established racial institution.

5 Within the Sotadic Zone the Vice is popular and endemic, held at the worst to be a mere peccadillo, whilst the races to the North and South of the limits here defined practice it only sporadically amid the opprobrium of their fellows who, as a rule, are physically incapable of performing the operation and look upon it with the liveliest disgust.

Before entering into topographical details concerning pederasty, which I hold to be geographical and climatic, not racial, I must offer a few considerations of its cause and origin. We must not forget that the love of boys has its noble, sentimental side. The Platonists and pupils of the Academy, followed by the Sufis or Moslem Gnostics, held such affection, pure as ardent, to be the beau idéal which united in man's soul the creature with the Creator. Professing to regard youths as the most cleanly and beautiful objects in this phenomenal world, they declared that by loving and extolling the chef-d'oeuvre, corporeal and intellectual, of the Demiurgus, disinterestedly and without any admixture of carnal sensuality, they are paying the most fervent adoration to the Causa causans. They add that such affection, passing as it does the love of women, is far less selfish than fondness for and admiration of the other sex which, however innocent, always suggest sexuality; and Easterns add that the devotion of the moth to the taper is purer and more fervent than the Bulbul's love for the Rose. Amongst the Greeks of the best ages the system of boy-favourites was advocated on considerations of morals and politics. The lover undertook the education of the beloved through precept and example, while the two were conjoined by a tie stricter than the fraternal. Hieronymus the Peripatetic strongly advocated it because the vigorous disposition of youths and the confidence engendered by their association often led to the overthrow of tyrannies. Socrates declared that "a most valiant army might be composed of boys and their lovers; for that of all men they would be most ashamed to desert one another." And even Virgil, despite the foul flavour of Formosum pastor Corydon, could write:

Nisus amore pio pueri.

The only physical cause for the practice which suggests itself to me and that must be owned to be purely conjectural, is that within the Sotadic Zone there is a blending of the masculine and feminine temperaments, a crasis which elsewhere occurs only sporadically. Hence the male *féminisme* whereby the man becomes patiens as well as agens, and the woman a tribade, a votary of mascula Sappho, Queen of Frictrices or Rubbers. Prof. Mantegazza claims to have discovered the cause of this pathological love, this perversion of the erotic sense, one of the marvellous list of amorous vagaries which deserve, not prosecution but the pitiful care of the physician and the study of the psychologist. According to him the nerves of the rectum and the genitalia, in all cases closely connected, are abnormally so in the pathic, who obtains, by intromission, the venereal orgasm which is usually sought through the sexual organs. So amongst women there are tribads who can procure no pleasure except by foreign objects introduced a posteriori. Hence his threefold distribution of sodomy; (1) Peripheric or anatomical, caused by an unusual distribution of the nerves and their hyperæsthesia; (2) Luxurious, when love a tergo is preferred on account of the narrowness of the passage; and (3) the Psychical. But this is evidently superficial: the question is what causes this neuropathy, this abnormal distribution and condition of the nerves.

As Prince Bismarck finds a moral difference between the male and female races of history, so I suspect a mixed physical temperament effected by the manifold subtle influences massed together in the word climate. Something of the kind is necessary to explain the fact of this pathological love extending over the greater portion of the habitable world, without any apparent connection of race or media, from the polished Greek to the cannibal Tupi of the Brazil. Walt Whitman speaks of the ashen grey faces of onanists: the faded colours, the puffy features and the unwholesome complexion of the professed pederast with his peculiar cachetic expression, indescribable but once seen never forgotten, stamp the breed, and Dr. G. Adolph is justified in declaring "Alle Gewohnneits-paederasten erkennen sich einander schnell, oft met einen Thick." This has nothing in common with the féminisme which betrays itself in the pathic by womanly gait, regard and gesture: it is a something sui generic; and the same may be said of the colour and look of the young priest who honestly refrains from women and their substitutes. Dr. Tardieu, in his well-known work, "Étude Medico-régale sur les Attentats aux Moeurs," and Dr. Adolph note a peculiar infundibuliform disposition of the "After"

and a smoothness and want of folds even before any abuse has taken place, together with special forms of the male organs in confirmed pederasts. But these observations have been rejected by Caspar, Hoffman, Brouardel and Dr. J. H. Henry Coutagne (Notes sur la Sodomie, Lyon, 1880), and it is a medical question whose discussion would here be out of place.

The origin of pederasty is lost in the night of ages; but its historique has been carefully traced by many writers, especially Virey, Rosenbaum and M. H. E. Meier. The ancient Greeks who, like the modern Germans, invented nothing but were great improvers of what other races invented, attributed the formal apostolate of Sotadism to Orpheus, whose stigmata were worn by the Thracian women.

8

Homosexual Love

Edward Westermarck

Our review of the moral ideas concerning sexual relations has not yet come to an end. The gratification of the sexual instinct assumes forms which fall outside the ordinary pale of nature. Of these there is one which, on account of the *rôle* which it has played in the moral history of mankind, cannot be passed over in silence, namely, intercourse between individuals of the same sex, what is nowadays commonly called homosexual love.

It is frequently met with among the lower animals. It probably occurs, at least sporadically, among every race of mankind. And among some peoples it has assumed such proportions as to form a true national habit.

In America homosexual customs have been observed among a great number of the native tribes. In nearly every part of the continent there seem to have been, since ancient times, men dressing themselves in the clothes and performing the functions of women, and living with other men as their concubines or wives. Moreover, between young men who are comrades in arms there are *liaisons d'amitié*, which, according to Lafitau, "ne laissent aucun soupçon de vice apparent, quoiqu'il y ait, ou qu'il puisse y avoir, beaucoup de vice réel."

Homosexual practices are, or have been, very prominent among the peoples in the neighbourhood of Behring Sea. In Kadiak it was the custom for parents who had a girl-like son to dress and rear him as a girl, teaching him only domestic duties, keeping him at woman's work, and letting him associate only with women and girls. Arriving at the age of ten or fifteen years, he was married to some wealthy man and was then called an *achnuchik* or *shoopan*. Dr. Bogoraz gives the following account of a similar practice prevalent among the Chukchi: "It happens frequently that, under the supernatural influence of one of their shamans, or priests, a Chukchi lad at sixteen years of age will suddenly relinquish his sex and imagine himself to be a woman. He adopts a woman's attire, lets his hair grow, and devotes himself altogether to female occupation. Furthermore, this disowner of his sex takes a husband into the *yurt* and does all the work which is usually incumbent on the wife in most unnatural and voluntary subjection. Thus it

Selections from Edward Westermarck, *Origin and Development of the Moral Ideas*, 2nd edition, vol. 2, London: Macmillan, 1917, pp. 456–471 (footnotes and some of this text are omitted).

frequently happens in a *yurt* that the husband is a woman, while the wife is a man! These abnormal changes of sex imply the most abject immorality in the community, and appear to be strongly encouraged by the shamans, who interpret such cases as an injunction of their individual deity." The change of sex was usually accompanied by future shamanship; indeed, nearly all the shamans were former delinquents of their sex. Among the Chukchi male shamans who are clothed in woman's attire and are believed to be transformed physically into women are still quite common; and traces of the change of a shaman's sex into that of a woman may be found among many other Siberian tribes. In some cases at least there can be no doubt that these transformations were connected with homosexual practices. [...]

In the Malay Archipelago homosexual love is common, though not in all of the islands. It is widely spread among the Bataks of Sumatra. In Bali it is practised openly, and there are persons who make it a profession. The *basir* of the Dyaks are men who make their living by witchcraft and debauchery. They "are dressed as women, they are made use of at idolatrous feasts and for sodomitic abominations, and many of them are formally married to other men." [...] Homosexual love is reported as common among the Marshall Islanders and in Hawaii. From Tahiti we hear of a set of men called by the natives *mahoos*, who "assume the dress, attitude, and manners, of women, and affect all the fantastic oddities and coquetries of the vainest of females. They mostly associate with the women, who court their acquaintance. With the manners of the women, they adopt their peculiar employments. ... The encouragement of this abomination is almost solely confined to the chiefs." [...]

Among the natives of the Kimberley District in West Australia, if a young man on reaching a marriageable age can find no wife, he is presented with a boy-wife, known as *chookadoo*. In this case, also, the ordinary exogamic rules are observed, and the "husband" has to avoid his "mother-in-law," just as if he were married to a woman. The *chookadoo* is a boy of five years to about ten, when he is initiated. [...] There is no doubt they have connection, but the natives repudiate with horror and disgust the idea of sodomy." Such marriages are evidently exceedingly common. As the women are generally monopolised by the older and more influential men of the tribe, it is rare to find a man under thirty or forty who has a wife; hence it is the rule that, when a boy becomes five years old, he is given as a boy-wife to one of the young men. According to Mr. Purcell's description of the natives of the same district, "every useless member of the tribe" gets a boy, about five or seven years old; and these boys, who are called *mullawongahs*, are used for sexual purposes. [...]

Homosexual practices are common among the Banaka and Bapuku in the Cameroons. But among the natives of Africa generally such practices seem to be comparatively rare, except among Arabic-speaking peoples and in countries like Zanzibar, where there has been a strong Arab influence. [...] they are frequent among the peasants of Egypt and universal among the Jbâla inhabiting the Northern mountains of Morocco. On the other hand, they are much less common or even rare among the Berbers and the nomadic Bedouins, and it is reported that the Bedouins of Arabia are quite exempt from them.

Homosexual love is spread over Asia Minor and Mesopotamia. It is very prevalent among the Tartars and Karatchai of the Caucasus, the Persians, Sikhs, and Afghans; in Kaubul a bazaar or street is set apart for it. Old travellers make reference to its enormous frequency among the Muhammedans of India. In China, where it is also extremely common, there are special houses devoted to male prostitution, and boys are sold by their parents about the age of four, to be trained for this occupation. In Japan pederasty is said by some to have prevailed from the most ancient times, whereas others are of opinion that it was introduced by Buddhism about the sixth century of our era. The monks used to live with handsome youths, to whom they were often passionately devoted; and in feudal times nearly every knight had as his favourite a young man with whom he entertained relations of the most intimate kind, and on behalf of whom he was always ready to fight a duel when occasion occurred. Tea-houses with male *gheishas* were found in Japan till the middle of the nineteenth century. [...]

No reference is made to pederasty either in the Homeric poems or by Hesiod, but later on we meet with it almost as a national institution in Greece. [...] At the close of the sixth century, Polybius tells us, many Romans paid a talent for the possession of a beautiful youth. During the Empire [...] formal marriages between men were introduced with all the solemnities of ordinary nuptials. Homosexual practices occurred among the Celts, and were by no means unknown to the ancient Scandinavians. [...]

Of late years a voluminous and constantly increasing literature on homosexuality has revealed its frequency in modern Europe. No country and no class of society is free from it. In certain parts of Albania it even exists as a popular custom, the young men from the age of sixteen upwards regularly having boy favourites of between twelve and seventeen.

[...] Among the American aborigines there are not only men who behave like women, but women who behave like men. Thus in certain Brazilian tribes women are found who abstain from every womanly occupation and imitate the men in everything, who wear their hair in a masculine fashion, who go to war with a bow and arrows, who hunt together with the men, and who would rather allow themselves to be killed than have sexual intercourse with a man. "Each of these women has a woman who serves her and with whom she says she is married; they live together as husband and wife." So also there are among the Eastern Eskimo some women who refuse to accept husbands, preferring to adopt masculine manners, following the deer on the mountains, trapping and fishing for themselves. Homosexual practices are said to be common among Hottentot and Herero women. [...] In Egyptian harems every woman is said to have a "friend." In Bali homosexuality is almost as common among women as among men, though it is exercised more secretly; [...] From Greek antiquity we hear of "Lesbian" love. The fact that homosexuality has been much more frequently noticed in men than in women does not imply that the latter are less addicted to it. For various reasons the sexual abnormalities of women have attracted much less attention, and moral opinion has generally taken little notice of them.

Homosexual practices are due sometimes to instinctive preference, sometimes to external conditions unfavourable to normal intercourse. A frequent cause is congenital sexual inversion, that is, "sexual instinct turned by inborn constitutional abnormality toward persons of the same sex." It seems likely that the feminine men and the masculine women referred to above are, at least in many instances, sexual inverts; though, in the case of shamans, the change of sex may also result from the belief that such transformed shamans, like their female colleagues, are particularly powerful. [...] Even between inversion and normal sexuality there seem to be all shades of variation. Professor James [William James, the famous American psychologist] thinks that inversion is "a kind of sexual appetite, of which very likely most men possess the germinal possibility." This is certainly the case in early puberty.

A very important cause of homosexual practices is absence of the other sex. There are many instances of this among the lower animals. [...] The West Australian boy-marriage is a substitute for ordinary marriage in cases when women are not obtainable. Among the Bororó of Brazil homosexual intercourse is said to occur in their men-houses only when the scarcity of accessible girls is unusually great. [...] In Muhammedan countries they are no doubt largely due to the seclusion of women, preventing free intercourse between the sexes and compelling the unmarried people to associate almost exclusively with members of their own sex. Among the mountaineers of Northern Morocco the excessive indulgence in pederasty thus goes hand in hand with great isolation of the women and a very high standard of female chastity, whereas among the Arabs of the plains, who are little addicted to boy-love, the unmarried girls enjoy considerable freedom. Both in Asia and Europe the obligatory celibacy of monks and priests has been a cause of homosexual practices, though it must not be forgotten that a profession which imposes abstinence from marriage is likely to attract a comparatively large number of congenital inverts. The temporary separation of the sexes involved in a military mode of life no doubt accounts for the extreme prevalence of homosexual love among warlike races. [...]

Dr. Havelock Ellis justly observes that when homosexual attraction is due simply to the absence of the other sex we are not concerned with sexual inversion, but merely with the accidental turning of the sexual instinct into an abnormal channel, the instinct being called out by an approximate substitute, or even by diffused emotional excitement, in the absence of the normal object. But it seems to me probable that in such cases the homosexual attraction in the course of time quite easily develops into genuine inversion. [...] But how is it that in some parts of Morocco such a very large proportion of the men are distinctly sexual inverts, that is, persons who for the gratification of their sexual desire prefer their own sex to the opposite one? It may be that in Morocco and in Oriental countries generally, where almost every individual marries, congenital inversion, through the influence of heredity, is more frequent than in Europe, where inverts so commonly abstain from marrying. But that this could not be an adequate explanation of the fact in question becomes at once apparent when we consider the extremely unequal distribution of inverts among different neighbouring tribes of the same stock, some of which are very little or hardly at all addicted to pederasty. I take the case to be, that homosexual practices in early youth have had a lasting effect on the sexual instinct, which at its first appearance, being somewhat indefinite, is easily turned into a homosexual direction. In Morocco inversion is most prevalent among the scribes, who from childhood have lived in very close association with their fellow-students. Of course, influences of this kind "require a favourable organic predisposition to act on"; but this predisposition is probably no abnormality at all, only a feature in the ordinary sexual constitution of man. It should be noticed that the most common form of inversion, at least in Muhammedan countries, is love of boys or youths not yet in the age of puberty, that is, of male individuals who are physically very like girls. [...] Moreover, in normal cases sexual attraction depends not only on sex, but on a youthful appearance as well; and there are persons so constituted that to them the latter factor is of chief importance, whilst the question of sex is almost a matter of indifference.

In ancient Greece, also, not only homosexual intercourse but actual inversion, seems to have been very common; and although this, like every form of love, must have contained a congenital element, there can be little doubt, I think, that it was largely due to external circumstances of a social character. [...] According to Plato, the gymnasia and common meals among the youth "seem always to have had a tendency to degrade the ancient and natural custom of love below the level, not only of man, but of the beasts." Plato also mentions the effect which these habits had on the sexual instincts of the men: when they reached manhood they were lovers of youths and not naturally inclined to marry or beget children, but, if at all, they did so only in obedience to the law. Is not this, in all probability, an instance of acquired inversion? But besides the influence of education there was another factor which, co-operating with it, favoured the development of homosexual tendencies, namely, the great gulf which mentally separated the sexes. Nowhere else has the difference in culture between men and women been so immense as in the fully developed Greek civilisation. The lot of a wife in Greece was retirement and ignorance. She lived in almost absolute seclusion, in a separate part of the house, together with her female slaves, deprived of all the educating influence of male society, and having no place at those public spectacles which were the chief means of culture. [...] They had reached a stage of mental culture at which the sexual instinct normally has a craving for refinement, at which the gratification of mere physical lust appears brutal. [...] So also it seems that the ignorance and dullness of Muhammedan women, which is a result of their total lack of education and their secluded life, is a cause of homosexual practices; Moors are sometimes heard to defend pederasty on the plea that the company of boys, who have always news to tell, is so much more entertaining than the company of women. [...]

SELECT BIBLIOGRAPHY

Bancroft, Hubert Howe
  1875   The Native Races of the Pacific States of North America. London.
Bastian, Adolf
  1860   Der Mensch in der Geschichte. 3 vols. Leipzig: Otto Wigand.
Burckhardt, John Lewis
  1819   Travels in Nubia. London: John Murray.
Burckhardt, John Lewis
  1827   Travels in Arabia. 2 vols. London: Henry Colburn.
Burton, Sir Richard F.
  1885–1887   Terminal Essay. *In* A Plain and Literal Translation of the Arabian Nights' Entertainment, Now Entitled the Book of The Thousand Nights and a Night. With Introduction, Explanatory Notes on the Manners and Customs of Moslem Men and a Terminal Essay Upon the History of the Nights. London and Benares: Kamashastra Society.
Catlin, George
  1841   Letters and Notes on the Manners, Customs, and Condition of the North American Indians. 2 vols. London: published by the author.
Coreal, François (Francisco)
  1722   Voyages de François Coreal aux Indes Occidentales, contenant ce qu'il a vû de plus remarquable pendant son séjour depuis 1666, jusqu'en 1697. 3 vols. Amsterdam: Bernard.
De la Vega, Garcilaso
  1609   First Part of the Royal Commentaries of the Incas. Vol. 2. Lisbon: Pedro Crasbeek.
De Landa Calderón, Diego
  1566   Relación De Las Cosas De Yucatán. Spain.
Dorsey, J. O.
  1884   Omaha Sociology. Bureau of American Ethnology, Third Annual Report, 205–270.
Ellis, Havelock, and John Addington Symonds
  1896   Das konträre Geschlechtsgefühl. Lepizig: G. H. Wigand.
Ellis, Havelock
  1910   Sexual Inversion. Vol. 2. Philadelphia: F. A. Davis.
Fison, Lorimer and A. W. Howitt
  1880   Kamilaroi and Kurnai: Group Marriage and Relationship, and Marriage by Elopement, drawn chiefly from the Usage of the Australian Aborigines. Melbourne: G. Robertson.

Hardman, E. T.
  1891   Notes on Some Habits and Customs of the Natives of the Kimberley District, Western Australia. Proceedings of the Royal Irish Academy, Series 3, Vol. 1:70–75.
Howitt, A. W.
  1884   Some Australian Ceremonies of Initiation. Journal of the Anthropological Institute 13:432–459.
Jochelson, Waldemar (Vladimir)
  1905   Koryak Religion and Myth. New York and Leiden.
Karsch (or Karsch-Haack), Ferdinand
  1900   Päderastie und Tribadie bei den Tieren, auf Grund der Literatur. Jahrbuch für sexuelle Zwischenstufen 2:126–154.
Karsch (or Karsch-Haack), Ferdinand
  1901   Uranismus oder Päderastie und Tribadie bei den Naturvölkern. Jahrbuch für sexuelle Zwischenstufen 3:72–181.
Lafitau, Joseph-François
  1724   Mœurs des sauvages Ameriquains, comparées aux mœurs des premiers temps. Vol. 2. Paris: chez Saugrain l'aîné.
Purcell, H.
  1893   Rites and Customs of Australian Aborigines. Zeitschrift für Ethnologie 25: 286–289.
Schoolcraft, Henry Rowe
  1851–1857   Historical and Statistical Information Respecting the History, Condition and Prospects of the Indian Tribes. 6 vols. Philadelphia: Lippincott.
Schweinfurth, Georg August
  1873   The Heart of Africa, Three Years' Travels and Adventures in the Unexplored Regions of Central Africa. 2 vols. Trans. E. E. Frewer. London: Sampson Low, Marston, Low and Searle.
Steinmetz, Sebald Rudolf
  1903   Rechtsverhältnisse von eingeborenen Völkern in Afrika und Ozeanien. Berlin: J. Springer.
Torday, E. and T. A. Joyce
  1905   Notes on the Ethnography of the Ba-Mbala. Journal of the Anthropological Institute 35:398–426.
von den Steinen, Karl
  1894   Unter den Naturvölken Zentral-Brasiliens. Berlin: D. Reimer.
von Spix, J. B., and C. F. P. von Martius
  1824   Travels in Brazil. Vol. 2. London: Longman, Hurst, Rees, Orme, Brown and Green.

9

Hermaphrodism Among Gods and Mortals

Edward Carpenter

[…] Jacobus Le Moyne, who travelled as artist with a French Expedition to Florida in 1564, left some very interesting drawings[1] representing the Indians of that region and their customs; and among them one representing the "Hermaphrodites" – tall and powerful men, beardless, but with long and abundant hair, and naked except for a loin-cloth, engaged in carrying wounded or dying fellow-Indians on their backs or on litters to a place of safety. He says of them that in Florida such folk of double nature are frequent, and that being robust and powerful, they are made use of in the place of animals for the carrying of burdens. For when their chiefs go to war the hermaphrodites carry the food; and when any of the tribe die of wounds or disease they construct litters … of wood and rushes … and so carry the dead to the place of burial. And indeed those who are stricken with any infectious disease are borne by the hermaphrodites to certain appointed places, and nursed and cared for by them, until they may be restored to full health."

Similar stories are told by Charlevoix,[2] de Pauw,[3] and others; and one seems to get a glimpse in them of an intermediate class of human beings who made themselves useful to the community not only by their muscular strength, but by their ability and willingness to act as nurses and attendants on the sick and dying.

It is needless, of course, to say that these were *not* hermaphrodites in the strict sense of the term – *i.e.,* human beings uniting in one person the functions both of male and female – since such beings do practically not exist. But it is evident that they *were* intermediate types – in the sense of being men with much of the psychologic character of women, or in some cases women with the mentality of men; and the early travellers, who had less concrete and reliable information on such subjects than we have, and who were already prepossessed by the belief in the prevalence of hermaphroditism, leapt easily to the conclusion that these strange beings were indeed of that nature. De Pauw, indeed, just mentioned, positively refuses to believe in the explanation that they were men dressed as women, and insists that they *were* hermaphrodites!

In 1889, a certain Dr. A. B. Holder, anxious to settle positively the existence or non-existence of hermaphrodites, made some investigations

Edward Carpenter, Hermaphrodism Among Gods and Mortals, from *Intermediate Types Among Primitive Folk*, 2nd edition, 1919, chap. 4, pp. 66–83.

Sexualities in Anthropology: A Reader, edited by Andrew P. Lyons and Harriet D. Lyons

among the Crow-Indians of Montana – among whom the Bardaches were called "Boté."[4] And Dr. Karsch, summarising his report, says[5]: "This word, bo-té, means literally 'not man, not woman.' A corresponding Tulalip-word which the Indians of the Washington region make use of is, according to Holder, 'burdash,' which means 'half man, half woman' – and that without necessarily implying any anomalous structure of the sex-organs ... The Crow-tribe, in 1889, included five such Boté, and possessed about the same number before. They form a class in every tribe, are well-known to each other, and knit friendly relations with their likes in other tribes, so that they become well acquainted with the Uranian relationships also in the neighbour tribes. They wear female attire, part their hair in the middle, and plait it in womanly style; they possess or cultivate feminine voices and gestures, and live continually in association with the women, just as if they belonged to that sex. All the same their voices, features, and figure never lose their masculine quality so completely as to make it hard for a careful observer to distinguish a Boté from a woman. Such a Boté among the Crows carried on women's work, like sweeping, scrubbing, dish-washing, with such neatness and willingness that he would often obtain employment among the white folk. Usually the feminine attire is adopted in childhood, and the corresponding ways of life at an early age, but his special calling is not exercised by the Boté till the age of puberty. A young scholar of an educational establishment – a boys' school in an Indian Agency – was often caught dressing himself in secret in women's clothes; and although punished on each occasion, he nevertheless, after leaving school, transformed himself into a Boté – to which calling he has ever since remained true. A certain Boté, well accredited among the Crow-tribe, who belonged to the scouting-party of Dr. Holder, was a Dakota Indian; he is described as a splendidly built young man of pleasing features, perfect health, brisk alertness, and the happiest disposition. Holder attached him to his own service, and finally persuaded him – though only after much unwillingness on his part – to allow himself to be personally examined." The result of the examination was to prove him to be physically a complete man – and, moreover, an exceedingly modest one!

The Père Lafitau, whom I have quoted before, and who was a keen observer and a broad-minded man, says, in one passage of his *Sauvages Américains:* "The spectacle of the men disguised as women surprised the Europeans who first landed in America. And, as they did not at all understand the motives of this sort of metamorphosis, they concluded that these were folk in whom the two sexes were conjoined: as a matter of fact our old records always term them hermaphrodites." He goes on to say that though the spirit of religion which made these men embrace this mode of life caused them to be regarded as extraordinary beings, yet the suspicions which the Europeans entertained concerning them took such hold upon the latter "that they invented every possible charge against them, and these imaginations inflamed the zeal of Vasco Nugnes de Vabra, the Spanish captain who first discovered the Southern Sea (*la mer du Sud*), to such an extent that he destroyed numbers of them by letting loose upon them those savage dogs, of whom his compatriots indeed made use for the purpose of exterminating a large proportion of the Indians."

On the cruelties of the Spanish conquerors among the Indian tribes – only paralleled apparently by those of modern Commercialism among the same – we need not dwell. What interests us here is the evidence of the widespread belief in hermaphroditism current among the early European travellers. That a similar belief has ruled also among most primitive peoples is evident from a consideration of their gods. *Why* it should so have ruled is a question which I shall touch on towards the conclusion of this chapter. The whole matter, anyhow, belongs to the subjects we are discussing in this book. For clearly bisexuality links on to homosexuality, and the fact that this characteristic was ascribed to the gods suggests that in the popular mind it must have played a profound and important part in human life. I will, therefore, in concluding this portion of the book, give some instances of this divine bisexuality.

Brahm, in the Hindu mythology, is often represented as two-sexed. Originally he was the sole Being. But, "delighting not to be alone he wished for the existence of another, and at once he became such, as male and female embraced (united). He caused this his one self to fall in twain."[6] Siva, also, the most popular of the Hindu divinities, is originally bi-sexual. In the interior of the great rockhewn Temple at Elephanta the career of Siva is carved in successive panels. And on the first he appears as a complete full-length human being conjoining the two sexes in one – the left side of the figure (which represents the female portion) projecting into a huge breast and hip, while the right side is man-like in outline, and in the centre (though now much defaced) the organs of both sexes. In the second panel, however, his evolution or differentiation is complete, and he is portrayed as complete male with his consort Sakti or Parvati standing as perfect female beside him.[7] There are many such illustrations in Hindu literature and art, representing the gods in their double or bi-sexual role – e.g., as Brahma Ardhanarisa, Siva Ardhanarisa (half male and half female).[8] And these again are interesting in connection with the account of Elohim in the 1st chapter of Genesis, and the supposition that he was such an androgynous deity. For we find (v. 27) that "Elohim created man in his own image, in the image of Elohim created he him, *male and female* created he them." And many commentators have maintained that this not only meant that the first man was hermaphrodite, but that the Creator also was of that nature. In the Midrasch we find that Rabbi Samuel-bar-Nachman said that "Adam, when God had created him, was a man-woman (androgyne);" and the great and learned Maimonides supported this, saying that "Adam and Eve were created together, conjoined by their backs, but God divided this double being, and taking one half (Eve), gave her to the other half (Adam) for a mate." And the Rabbi Manasseh-ben-Israel, following this up, explained that when "God took one of Adam's ribs to make Eve with," it should rather be rendered "one of his sides" – that is, that he divided the double Adam, and one half was Eve.[9]

In the Brihadaranyaka Upanishad (1 Adhyaya, 4th Brahmana) the evolution of Brahm is thus described[10] – "In the beginning of this [world]

was Self alone, in the shape of a person. ... But he felt no delight. ... He wished for a second. He was so large as man and wife together [i.e., he included male and female]. He then made this his Self to fall in two; and thence arose husband and wife. Therefore, Yagnavalkya said: We two are thus (each of us) like half a shell [or as some translate, like a split pea]." The singular resemblance of this account to what has been said above about the creation of Adam certainly suggests the idea that Jehovah, like Brahm (and like Baal and other Syrian gods), was conceived of as double-sexed, and that primitive man was also conceived as of like nature. The author (Ralston Skinner) of *The Source of Measures* says (p. 159) "The two words of which Jehovah is composed make up the original idea of male-female of the birth-originator. For the Hebrew letter Jod (or J) was the *membrum virile*, and Hovah was Eve, the mother of all living, or the procreatrix Earth and Nature."[11]

The tradition that mankind was anciently hermaphrodite is world-old. It is referred to in Plato's *Banquet*, where Aristophanes says: – "Anciently the nature of mankind was not the same as now, but different. For at first there were three sexes of human beings, not two only, namely male and female, as at present, but a third besides, common to both the others – of which the name remains, though the sex itself has vanished. For the androgynous sex then existed, both male and female; but now it only exists as a name of reproach." He then describes how all these three sorts of human beings were originally double, and conjoined (as above) back to back; until Jupiter, jealous of his supremacy, divided them vertically "as people cut apples before they preserve them, or as they cut eggs with hairs" – after which, of course, these divided and imperfect folk ran about over the earth, ever seeking their lost halves, to be joined to them again.

I have mentioned the Syrian Baal as being sometimes represented as double-sexed (apparently in combination with Astarte). In the Septuagint (Hos. ii. 8, and Zeph. i. 4) he is called ή Baal (feminine) and Arnobius tells us that his worshippers invoked him thus[12] "Hear us, Baal! whether thou be a god or goddess." Similarly Bel and other Babylonian gods were often represented as androgyne.[13] Mithras among the Persians is spoken of by the Christian controversialist Firmicus as two-sexed, and by Herodotus (Bk. i., c. 131) as identified with a goddess, while there are innumerable Mithraic monuments on which appear the symbols of two deities, male and female combined.[14] Even Venus or Aphrodite was sometimes worshipped in the double form. "In Cyprus," says Dr. Frazer in his *Adonis, etc.* (p. 432, note), "there was a bearded and masculine image of Venus (probably Astarte) in female attire: according to Philochorus the deity thus represented was the moon, and sacrifices were offered to him or her by men clad as women, and by women clad as men (see Macrobius *Saturn* iii. 7, 2)." This bearded female deity is sometimes also spoken of as Aphroditus, or as Venus Mylitta. Richard Burton says[15]: – "The Phœnicians spread their androgynic worship over Greece. We find the consecrated servants and votaries of Corinthian Aphrodite called Hierodouloi (Strabo, viii. 6), who aided the 10,000 courtesans in gracing the Venus-temple. ... One of the headquarters of the cult was Cyprus, where, as Servius relates (Ad. Aen. ii. 632), stood the simulacre of a bearded Aphrodite with feminine body and costume, sceptred and mitred like a man. The sexes when worshiping it exchanged habits, and here the virginity was offered in sacrifice."

The worship of this bearded goddess was mainly in Syria and Cyprus. But in Egypt also a representation of a bearded Isis has been found, – with infant Horus in her lap;[16] while again there are a number of representations (from papyri) of the goddess Neith in androgyne form, with a male member (erected). And again, curiously enough, the Norse Freya, or Friga, corresponding to Venus, was similarly figured. Dr. von Römer says[17]: – "Just as the Greeks had their Aphroditos as well as Aphrodite so the Scandinavians had their Friggo as well as their Friga. This divinity, too, was androgyne. Friga, to whom the sixth day of the week was dedicated, was sometimes thought of as hermaphrodite. She was represented as having the members of both sexes, standing by a column with a sword in her right hand, and in her left a bow."

In the Orphic hymns we have: –

Zeus was the first of all, Zeus last, the lord of the lightning;
Zeus was the head, the middle, from him all things were created;
Zeus was Man, and again Zeus was the Virgin Eternal.

And in another passage, speaking of Adonis: –

Hear me, who pray to thee, hear me O many-named and best of deities,
Thou, with thy gracious hair ... both maiden and youth, Adonis.

Again, with regard to the latter, Ptolemaeus Hephaestius (according to Photius) writes: – "They say that the androgyne Adonis fulfilled the part of a man for Aphrodite, but for Apollo the part of a wife."[18]

Dionysus, one of the most remarkable figures in the Greek Mythology, is frequently represented as androgyne. Euripides in his *Bacchae* calls him "feminine-formed" ($\Theta\eta\lambda\acute{\nu}\mu\rho\rho\phi\rho\varsigma$) or thelumorphos, and the Orphic hymns "double-sexed" ($\delta\iota\phi\acute{\nu}\eta\varsigma$) or diphues; and Aristides in his discourse on Dionysus says: – "Thus the God is both male and female. His form corresponds to his nature, since everywhere in himself he is like a double being; for among young men he is a maiden, and among maidens a young man, and among men a beardless youth overflowing with vitality." In the museum at Naples there is a very fine sculptured head of Dionysus, which though bearded has a very feminine expression, and is remindful of the traditional head of Christ. "In legend and art," says Dr. Frazer,[19] "there are clear traces of an effeminate Dionysus, and in some of his rites and processions men wore female attire. Similar things are reported of Bacchus, who was, of course, another form of Dionysus. Even Hercules, that most masculine figure, was said to have dressed as a woman for three years, during which he was the slave of Omphale, queen of Lydia. "If we suppose," says Dr. Frazer,[20] "that queen Omphale, like queen Semiramis, was nothing but the great Asiatic goddess, or one of her Avatars, it becomes probable that the story of the womanish Hercules of Lydia preserves a reminiscence of a line or college of effeminate priests who, like the eunuch priests of the Syrian goddess, dressed as women in imitation of their goddess, and were supposed to be inspired by her. The probability is increased by the practice of the priests of Heracles at Antimachia in Cos, who, as we have just seen, actually wore female attire when they were engaged in their sacred duties. Similarly at the vernal mysteries of Hercules in Rome the men were draped in the garments of women."

Such instances could be rather indefinitely multiplied. Apollo is generally represented with a feminine – sometimes with an extremely feminine – bust and figure. The great hero Achilles passed his youth among women, and in female disguise. Every one knows the recumbent marble Hermaphrodite in the Louvre. There are also in the same collection two or three elegant bronzes of Aphrodite-like female figures in the standing position – but of masculine sex. What is the explanation of all this?

It is evident that the conception of a double sex, or of a sex combining the characters of male and female, haunted the minds of early peoples. Yet we have no reason for supposing that such a combination, in any complete and literal sense, ever existed. Modern physiological investigation has never produced a single case of a human being furnished with the complete organs of both sexes, and capable of fulfilling the functions of both. And the unfortunate malformations which do exist in this direction are too obviously abortive and exceptional to admit of their being generalised or exalted into any kind of norm or ideal. All we can say is that – though in the literal sense no double forms exist – certainly a vast number of intermediate forms of male and female are actually found, which are double in the sense that the complete organs of one sex are conjoined with some or nearly all of the (secondary) characters of the other sex; and that we have every reason to believe that these intermediate types have existed in considerable numbers from the remotest antiquity. That being so, it is possible that the observation or influence of these intermediate types led to a tentative and confused idealisation of a double type.

Anyhow the fact remains – that these idealisations of the double type are so numerous.

And it is interesting to notice that while they begin in early times with being merely grotesque and symbolical, they end in the later periods by becoming artistic and gracious and approximated to the real and actual. The Indian Siva, with his right side masculine and his left side feminine, is in no way beautiful or attractive; any more than Brahma with twenty arms and twenty legs. And the same may be said of the bearded Egyptian Isis or the bearded Syrian Aphrodite. These were only rude and inartistic methods of conveying an idea. The later spirit, however, found a better way of expression. It took its cue from the variations of type to be seen every day in the actual world; and instead of representing the Persian Mithra as a two-sexed monster, it made him a young *man*, but of very feminine outline. The same with the Greek Apollo; while on the other hand, the female who is verging toward the male type is represented by Artemis or even by the Amazons.

It may be said: – we can understand this representation of intermediate forms from actual life, but we do not see why such mingling of the sexes should be ascribed to the gods, unless it might be from a merely fanciful tendency to personify the two great powers of nature in one being – in which case it is strange that the tendency should have been so universal. To this we may reply that probably the reason or reasons for this tendency must be accounted quite deep-rooted and anything but fanciful. One reason, it seems to me, is the psychological fact that in the deeps of human nature (as represented by Brahm and Siva in the Hindu philosophy, by Zeus in the Orphic Hymns, by Mithra in the Zend-avesta, etc.) the sex-temperament *is* undifferentiated;[21] and it is only in its later and more external and partial manifestations that it branches decidedly into male and female; and that, therefore, in endeavoring through religion to represent the root facts of life, there was always a tendency to cultivate and honor hermaphroditism, and to ascribe some degree of this quality to heroes and divinities. The other possible reason is that as a matter of fact the great leaders and heroes *did* often exhibit this blending of masculine and feminine qualities and habits in their actual lives, and that therefore at some later period, when exalted to divinities, this blending of qualities was strongly ascribed to them and was celebrated in the rites and ceremonies of their religion and their temples. The feminine traits in genius (as in a Shelley or a Byron) are well marked in the present day. We have only to go back to the Persian Bâb of the last century[22] or to a St. Francis or even to a Jesus of Nazareth, to find the same traits present in founders and leaders of religious movements in historical times. And it becomes easy to suppose the same again of those early figures – who once probably were men – those Apollos, Buddhas, Dionysus, Osiris, and so forth – to suppose that they too were somewhat bi-sexual in temperament, and that it was really largely owing to that fact that they were endowed with far-reaching powers and became leaders of mankind. In either case – whichever reason is adopted – it corroborates the general thesis and argument of this paper.

NOTES

1   *Indorum Floridam provinciam inhabitantium eicones,* etc. (Frankfurt, 1591). Also translation of the same with heliotypes of the engravings (Boston, J. R. Osgood & Co., 1875.)
2   P. F. X. de Charlevoix, *La Nouvelle France,* 2 vols. (Paris, 1744).
3   De Pauw, *Recherches sur les Américains,* 2 vols. (Berlin, 1768).
4   See for his Report, *The New York Medical Journal,* vol. L., No. 23 (7th Dec., 1889).
5   *Jahrbuch für s.Z.,* vol, iii., p. 138.
6   Quoted from the Yajur-Veda. See *Bible Folklore*: a study in Comp. Mythology (London, 1884), p. 104.
7   See *Adam's Peak to Elephanta,* by E. Carpenter (1903), p. 308.
8   See drawings in *Ancient Pagan and Modern Christian Symbolism,* by Thomas Inman (London, 1874).
9   These and some other references are taken from the learned and careful study "Ueber die androgynische Idee des Lebens," by Dr. von Römer, of Amsterdam, which is to be found in vol. v. of the *Jahrbuch für Sexuelle Zwischenstufen* (Leipzig, 1903).
10 *Sacred Books of the East,* vol. xv., p. 85.

11 See H. P. Blavatsky, *Secret Doctrine,* vol. ii., p. 1: quoted in vol. v., *Jahrbuch für* S. Z., p. 76.
12 Inman's *Ancient Pagan and Modern Christian Symbolism* (Trubner, 1874), p. 119.
13 *Pagan Christs,* by John M. Robertson (1908), p. 308.
14 *Ibid.,* p. 307.
15 *The Thousand Nights and a Night* (1886), vol. x., p. 231.
16 See illustration, *Jahrbuch für* S. Z., vol. v., p. 732.
17 See his study already quoted, *Jahrbuch,* pp. 735–744.
18 See *Jahrbuch,* as above, pp. 806, 807 and 809.
19 *Adonis,* etc., p. 432.
20 *Ibid,* p. 431.
21 Compare the undifferentiated sex-tendencies of boys and girls at puberty and shortly after.
22 Ali Muhammed, who called himself the Bâb (or Gate), was born at Shiraz in 1820. In 1844 he commenced preaching his gospel, which was very like that of Jesus, and which now has an immense following. In 1850 he was shot, at Tabriz, as a malefactor, and his beloved disciple Mirza Muhammed Ali, refusing to leave him, was shot with him.

SELECT BIBLIOGRAPHY

Blavatsky, Helena Petrovna
    1888   The Secret Doctrine. 2 vols. London.
Burton, Sir Richard F.
    1885–1887   A Plain and Literal Translation of the Arabian Nights' Entertainment, Now Entitled the Book of The Thousand Nights and a Night. With Introduction, Explanatory Notes on the Manners and Customs of Moslem Men and a Terminal Essay Upon the History of the Nights. 10 vols. London and Benares: Kamashastra Society.
Carpenter, Edward
    1892   From Adam's peak to Elephanta: Sketches in Ceylon and India (1892). London: S. Sonnenschein & Co.
Charlevoix, Pierre François Xavier de
    1744   Histoire et description générale de la Nouvelle-France. Paris.
Frazer, Sir James G.
    1906   Adonis, Attis, Osiris: Studies in the History of Oriental Religion. London and New York: Macmillan.

Holder, A. B.
1889 The Bote: Description of a peculiar sexual perversion found among American Indians. New York Medical Journal 50 (7 Dec.): 623.

Karsch-Haack, Ferdinand
1901 Uranismus oder Päderastie and Tribadie bei den Naturvölkern. Jahrbuch für sexuelle Zwischenstufen 3: 72–181.

Le Moyne de Morges, Jacobus
1591 Indorum Floridam provinciam inhabitantium eicones, primum ibidem ad vivum expressae, addita ad singulas brevi earum declaratione. Frankfurt.

Muller, Friedrich, Max
1884 Sacred Books of the East. Volume 15, The Upanishads. Oxford: Clarendon Press.

De Pauw, Cornelius
1768 Recherches philosophiques sur les Américains, ou Mémoires intéressants pour servir à l'Histoire de l'Espèce Humaine. Avec une Dissertation sur l'Amérique & les Américains. 2 vols. Berlin.

Rogers, James Edwin Thorold
1884 Biblical Folklore: A study in comparative mythology, by the Author of Rabbi Jeshua. London: Kegan Paul.

Robertson, John M.
1903 Pagan Christs: Studies in Comparative Hierology. London: Watts & Co.

Von Romer, L. S. A. M.
1903 Ueber die androgynische Idee des Lebens. Jahrbuch für sexuelle Zwischenstufen 5: 711–939.

10

The Zuñi Ła'mana

Elsie Clews Parsons

Of these "men-women" there are today in Zuñi three or, one might almost say, three and a half – there is a boy about six years old qualifying, so to speak, for the status. An elderly Zuñi with whom I talked, a man over seventy, had known during his lifetime of nine *la'mana*. Mrs. Stevenson mentions five.[1] The three adults now living are about the same age, in the late thirties and early forties. Their names are Kasineli, Tsalatitse, and U'k.[2] Kasineli I watched repeatedly in the audience of a five-day rain dance; Tsalatitse was pointed out to me in the street; U'k I failed to see or rather recognize during my first visit to Zuñi in August, he was taking part in the *ko'kokshi* when I began to look for him, in the last two of the five days' dance, and then I had to leave Zuñi. On my second visit in December, U'k was dancing again, but this time I saw him without a mask. The child, Laspeke (for Las Vegas), I had several opportunities to watch. Far from adequate, my observations may be nevertheless worth recording, so very little has been recorded at all about the Indian berdache. I hope to continue the study.

To begin with the little boy, he is still dressed as a male, wearing trousers and a shirt; but his shirt is of a considerably longer cut than that of the other little boys, nor is it tucked into the trousers as they sometimes tuck in theirs. Around his neck is a bead necklace, a mixture of commercial and of stone beads, an ornament not altogether commonplace for either little boys or girls. His hair-cut is the usual all round short cut for boys – girls of his age would be growing a lock at the back of the neck. His features are unusually fine and delicate, unusual even in a Zuñi girl, and his facial expression unusually gentle, mild of expression as is the Zuñi of either sex. Whenever I saw him playing about he was with a girl, although boys of his age begin to gang together. "He talks like a girl," I was told. And by that I learned was meant that he used the "expressions" of a girl,[3] their exclamations and turns of speech.[4] A few of these differentiations in the speech of the sexes I collected:

	Oh, dear!
Girl:	*Hia an'na!* or *An'na!*
Boy:	*Cha an'na!*
	Oh, lovely or bully!

Elsie Clews Parsons, The Zuñi Ła'mana, from *American Anthropologist*, vol. 18, no. 4 (Oct–Dec 1916): 521–528.

Sexualities in Anthropology: A Reader, edited by Andrew P. Lyons and Harriet D. Lyons
© 2011 Blackwell Publishing Ltd.

Girl: *Ho ĕlu!*
Boy: *Cha ĕlu!*
　　　Outch!
Girl: *Hia atu!*
Boy: *Cha kochi'!*
　　　Stop!
Girl: *elesma!*
Boy: *Lesma!*
　　　I don't want to! I'm shy!
Girl: *Hia ati!*
Boy: *Cha ati!*
　　　Oh, I'm so tired!
Girl: *Hish atu ho utechika.*
Boy: *Hish kochi' ho utechika.*
　　　It's awfully cold!
Girl: *Hish itsu' tetse.*
Boy: *Cha itsu' hish tetse.*
　　　Oh, it's very good!
Girl: *Hish ali hekwa alitecha.*
Boy: *Hish ali alitecha.*

Kasineli has the facial expression and the stature of a man. He has the longer stride of a man, but it is slow and ponderous like the Zuñi woman's. During the rain dances he always stood on the roof top behind the old woman who is the head of his household. He did not wear the American calico petticoat so many of the Zuñi women wear but his dress was in every particular as far as I could see like a woman's, and he wore his black blanket in woman fashion, up around the back of the head, irrespective of the temperature, and falling to the knees.[5] Next him on the roof top were standing or sitting three or four kinswomen. One of them was an informant of mine. To the *ła'mana* in her family she would never refer, although we talked of the subject in general from time to time and we worked together on her family genealogy. Nor would she take me to the house where he lived, the house of her father's sister where her own little son was living and where she had grown up. Her people had tried very hard to dissuade the lad from becoming a *ła'mana,* I was told,[6] and I got the impression that in general a family would be somewhat ashamed of having a *ła'mana* among its members. In regard to the custom itself there seemed to be no reticence in general and no sense of shame.

Kasineli is a first-class plasterer. So is Tsalatitse – he had been called in to plaster the chimney-place of the room I lived in, by the way. Kasineli is especially good too at pottery. Among the other six *ła'mana* my old man informant had known during his lifetime two were noted as skilful weavers of blankets, and two as skilful potters.[7]

It is the *ła'mana*, Mrs. Stevenson states, whose special function it is to fetch from To'wa Yalenĕ the clay used in making pottery. This is certainly not so today; anyone may fetch the clay. My elderly informant declared it was never the function of the *ła'mana*. At two periods during his memory, however, have the Priests of the Bow endeavored to give a sacred character to the pottery-making, confining it to the first four days of the summer solstice ceremonial, prescribing the firing for the fourth night. Mrs. Stevenson describes this custom without mentioning, however, that it is an innovation.[8] It is possible, it occurs to me, that limiting the fetching of the clay to the *ła'mana* may have been prescribed also by these inventive Bow priests. It is possible, but very doubtful I must say until I hear of other religious or quasi-religious functions attaching distinctively to the *ła'mana*. I heard of none.

There are myths, however, in regard to "men-women." In a myth reported by Mrs. Stevenson[9] it is the *chaakwena*, a god captured by the *kia'nakwe*, who puts on the *kor'koshi* (*ko'kokshi*), a woman's dress to break his spirit – he is rebelling against taking part in a dance to celebrate his capture. This was the first appearance of a male, say the Zuñi, in women's dress. The *kor'koshi* mask in the *kia'nakwe* dramatization is in woman's dress and is called the *ko'thlama* (*ko'łama*).[10] Cushing gives a different account of the first appearance of the "man-woman." The first born of the incestuous couple, Siweluhsina and Siweluhsita, the couple who figure so prominently in Zuñi mythology, was "a woman in fullness of contour, but a man in stature and brawn" – a fairly accurate description of the hermaphrodite. And the Zuñi explanation is that

from the mingling of too much seed in one kind, comes the two-fold kind, *'hláhmon,* being man and woman combined – even as from a kernel of corn with two hearts, ripens an ear that is neither one kind nor the other, but both!

According to Cushing then this "man-woman of the Kâ'kâ"[11] is the elder sister of the *ko'yemshi*, those sacred antic personages of Zuñi ceremonial, sexually abnormal too, we recall, because "seedless."

I was unable to verify these myths. It was positively denied that the *ko'łamana* was the offspring of *awăn tsita* (their mother) as Sewiluhsita is called. He came up with the others (Siweluhsita and Sewiluhsina came up in advance) and he was among those who were lost crossing the river and with them went to *koluwala* to stay there as a *ko'ko* (god). "He was the first *ła'mana*, so there would be others." He figures in the *kia'nakwe* dance because together with other *ko'ko* he was taken prisoner by the *kia'nakwe*.

These myths are, I take it, *a posteriori* explanations of the *ła'mana*. They may give a sanction to the transformation custom; they do not originate it. But this matter of possible relationship between the *ła'mana* and supernatural function or office needs further study.[12] Meanwhile we should note that the part of the *ko'łamana* appears to be usually taken by a *ła'mana*. We'wha took it. Kasineli has taken it. In recent years,[13] however, it has been played by one who is not a *ła'mana*, not a "man-woman," but rather a "woman-man" so to speak. Nancy is called in fact, in a teasing sort of way, "the girl-boy," *katsŏtsĕ* (*ka'tsiki*, girl, *ŏtsĕ*, male). Of the *katsŏtsĕ* I saw quite a little, for she worked by the day in our household. She was an unusually competent worker, "a girl I can always depend on," said her employer. She had a rather lean, spare, build and her gait was comparatively quick and alert. It occurred to me once that she might be a *ła'mana*. "If she is," said her employer, "she is not so openly like the others. Besides she's been too much married for one." She was, I concluded, a "strong-minded woman," a Zuñi "new woman," a large part of her male, as Weininger would say.

It is because they like woman's work, is the reason that has always been given me both in Zuñi and among the Rio Grande pueblos for the existence of the "man-woman." At Zuñi I

was also told, one of my informants being the woman interpreter I have already referred to, that if the household were short on women workers a boy would be more readily allowed to became a *ła'mana*. It is always insisted upon that there is never any compulsion upon him to become one.

Of the nine *ła'mana* known to my aged interpreter, two had married men, *i.e.*, lived with men as their wives. One of these *ła'mana* had been known to my younger Zuñi acquaintances. He was described as effeminate looking – "pretty," like a woman. The families of both parties were said to have objected to the "marriage." The "marriage" was discussed with me as an economic arrangement, and with not the slightest hint of physical acts of perversion on the part of either "husband" or "wife." It seemed to me at the time that the utter obliviousness to that point of view was due to ignorance or innocence, not to reticence.[14] On questions of sexual intercourse the Zuñi, I would say, is naturalistic, not reticent. Nevertheless it is not at all unlikely that this oblivious manner was assumed to check further discussions – for reasons I do not know.

Although the *ła'mana* U'k was, I gathered on my first visit, somewhat effeminate looking, he was not married. (Here I should say that Tsalatitse is not effeminate looking. Like Kasineli he is tall and walks with a long, heavy stride.) U'k was teased, I was told, by the children, and he would answer them back like a child. He walks too more like a child than either an adult man or an adult woman, "flighty like," with short, nervous steps. In short he is an undeveloped kind of person. A careful and reliable woman described him as a simpleton.

He is, nevertheless, one of the dancers, for he was initiated into the *ko'tikili*,[15] as are all *ła'mana*, just like other boys.[16] The night I saw U'k dancing during the *sha'lako* ceremonial he was in the *chaakwena* dance, that is with the set of dancers from the *uptsana kiwitsine*.[17] He was clothed in the ordinary woman's dress and buckskin leggings plus the usual Hopi dance blanket. He had a downy white feather in his hair, otherwise his hair was dressed in the regular woman's style, bang and turned up queue. He came in to the house fourth in the line of dancers but soon fell out of line and danced separately, opposite the line. Representing a female personage, as I was told he did – that is the position he would naturally take. Before the dancers withdrew, he took a place in the line again, number six. His dance step was much less vigorous than the others; but that is true too of normal males personating "goddesses." U'k is not as tall as the other *ła'mana*, his stature is more that of a woman than a man. His features, however, are masculine. Their expression in this dance was that of animal-like dumb patience.

When U'k fell out of line the audience, an audience mostly of women with their children, girls, and a few old men, grinned and even chuckled, a very infrequent display of amusement during these *sha'lako* dances.[18] "Did you notice them laughing at her?" my Cherokee hostess asked me on my return. "She is a great joke to the people – not because she is a *ła'mana*, but because she is half-witted."

Neither U'k nor the other two *ła'mana* are members of any of the esoteric fraternities. Of the other *ła'mana* my aged informant had known one, and one only belonged to a fraternity, the Bed-bug fraternity.

When prepared for burial the corpse of a *ła'mana* is dressed in the usual woman's outfit, with one exception, under the woman's skirt a pair of trousers are put on.[19] "And on which side of the graveyard will he be buried?"[20] I asked, with eagerness of heart if not of voice, for here at last was a test of the sex status of the *ła'mana*. "On the south side, the men's side, of course. *Kwash lu*[21] *ŏtsě tea'mě* (Is this man not)?" And my old friend smiled the peculiarly gentle smile he reserved for my particularly unintelligent questions.

NOTES

1 "The Zuñi Indians," *Twenty-first Annual Report Bureau American Ethnology*, p. 37. Three of them became *ła'mana* after 1890.

2 U'k "sounds like a man's name," I was told; *ditse* is the ending of a girl's name.

3 The Hopi woman's word of thanks is *eskwali*, the man's *kwa kwi*. (Hough, W., *The Hopi Indians*, p. 115. Cedar Rapids, 1915.)

4 Lowie notes that Assiniboine berdaches "employed the affirmative and imperative particles peculiar to women's speech." (*Anthropological Papers, American Museum of Natural History*, IV, 1, p. 42. New York, 1910.) See too Fletcher, A. C. and La Flesche, F., "The Omaha Tribe," p. 132, Twenty-seventh *Annual Report Bureau of American Ethnology* (1905–6).

5 A Zuñi man wears his blanket in summer only when it is chilly and well up over his head and above his knees. In winter it falls lower, leaving his head bare. Indoors as well as out it stays in place around his neck and across his face up to his nose or even eyes. It is a mode of wearing his blanket as irrespective of temperature and as conventional as that of a woman.

6 Mrs. Stevenson who seems to have known his family pretty well states that his mother and grandmother were quite complaisant, but that the grandfather, the elder brother Bow priest, tried to shame the boy out of his intent. (*The Zuñi Indians*, p. 38.)

7 One of them was undoubtedly We'wha, a notable character. (See Stevenson, *The Zuñi Indians*, pp. 37, 310–13, 374.)

8 *Ib.*, p. 150.

9 *Ib.*, p. 37.

10 *Ib.*

11 "Zuñi Creation Myths," *Thirteenth Annual Report Bureau American Ethnology*, pp. 401–413.

12 Suggestive in this connection is Jochelson's theory of the "transformed men" of the Chukchee and Koryak. "I think abnormal sexual relations [of five *irka*[8] *la'ul* among the 3,000 Kolyma Chukchee, two were "married to other men"] have developed under the influence of the ideas concerning shamanistic power, which the 'metamorphosed' men obtain from the spirits at whose bidding and with whose help the change of sex is accomplished. These beliefs have found fertile soil in individuals of abnormal physical and psychical development." ("The Koryak," pp. 754–5. *Memoirs American Museum Natural History*, vol. VI, pt. II. Leiden and New York, 1908.) See too Parsons, E. C. (Main, John), *Religious Chastity*, pp. 310–1. New York, 1913.

The Franciscan Fathers refer quite incidentally to the Navajo *na'dle* (he changes) men skilled in the arts and industries of both men and women. (*An Ethnologic Dictionary of the Navaho Language*, p. 292. St. Michaels, Arizona, 1915.) Of any supernatural function or trait attaching to these "hermaphrodites" there is no mention.

13 The *kia'nakwe* ceremonial is quadrennial. It was last performed in November, 1915. On November 17 the *kia'nakwe* prepared their plumes, on November 18 they came in from the south and danced in front of their *kiwitsine*, the *chu'pawa*, where they spent the night. November 19 they danced until the following sunrise.

14 It is a pity Mrs. Stevenson felt called upon to be so reticent. "There is a side to the lives of these men which must remain untold" is all she vouchsafes. (*The Zuñi Indians*, p. 38.) The *la'mana* who was married to a man she mentions, but she refers to the couple merely "as two of the hardest workers in the Pueblo and among the most prosperous." Stating that the *la'mana* never marry women and seldom, it is understood, have any sexual relations with them, she reports that We'wha was reputed to be the father of several children, his paternity in one case at least being undoubted.

15 The initiation takes place between seven and eleven, the age falling necessarily uncertainly because the ceremonial takes place quadrennially. At any rate this age is prior to that when female dress is definitely assumed, about twelve. Nevertheless, judging from the youngster now qualifying as a *la'mana*, a boy is marked down for one year sooner, and he is initiated into the *ko'tikili* in the knowledge that he is to become a *la'mana*.

16 Girls are not initiated as a regular thing into the *ko'tikili*. There are only four women in it now – a married woman with children, two older widows, a much married but now husbandless woman, the *katsŏtsĕ* I have already referred to.

Two reasons for not initiating girls as well as boys were given me at different times by my old man informant. Girls would not talk as boys would of what they saw. So there was no need to initiate them to keep their mouths shut. So much for his offhand bit of rationalism. When I pressed him for his tradition he related that in the first days women were taken into the *ko'tikili*. These were the days when the *ko'ko* themselves came and went between the Pueblo and *ko'luwala*. The women among the *ko'ko* fell in love with them and unwilling to be left behind accompanied them to *ko'luwala*. Lonesome there, they wanted to be brought back to the *ashiwi*. Such flightiness was too much for the *ko'ko* and so the women were no longer admitted into the *ko'tikili*.

The reason for taking women into the *ko'tikili* is to me still obscure. In her earliest publication on Zuñi Mrs. Stevenson states that the female initiates have to take a vow of celibacy for life and that as a woman member grows old she chooses her successor. In her later publication Mrs. Stevenson omits these statements. I have been told that if a girl were frightened by a bad dream she might be initiated, or, if sick, she might choose to go into the *ko'tikili* instead of one of the fraternities. (*Cf. The Zuñi Indians*, p. 65.) If not initiated under these circumstances, she would die.

17 To that *kiwitsine* he therefore belongs.

18 Aside from the merriment produced by the *ko'yemshi*, the only other show of amusement I saw was called forth by the little boys in the *hemishi'kwe* dance, boys who had their faces painted white and wore a *pitone* to represent female figures.

19 Noted too by Mrs. Stevenson, *The Zuñi Indians*, pp. 312–3.

20 In the center of the graveyard, one of the few Spanish relics in Zuñi, stands a large wooden cross. It forms the boundary line for this mortuary division of the sexes. "Why do you make the division?" I asked my old man informant. "Because we do not pray to the women for rain, only to the men."

21 Personal pronouns showing sex are lacking in Zuñi.

Part V

Heterosexual Freedoms (Elsewhere)

Introduction

In the 1920s a series of books appeared that revisited the topic of "primitive promiscuity" with changed social, theoretical, and methodological perspectives. In much of
the Western and Western-influenced world the 1920s were a time when experiments
with new sexual mores reached beyond the avant-garde to the middle classes. Even
those who continued to lead very conventional lives were made aware by the media
of Flappers, young people "petting" in cars, and public debates over changes to the
laws governing birth control, marriage, divorce, and illegitimacy. A generation of
anthropologists with professional training had emerged, along with expectations of
empirical research "in the field" with people of "different" cultures. Cultural evolutionism and scientific racism were no longer fashionable, so that cross-cultural differences in sexual norms required explanations other than evolutionary backwardness
or racial difference; moreover, metropolitan debates about sexuality made some writers inclined to wonder if the sexual behavior of "others" had some lessons for "us"
beyond self-congratulation about how far we'd come. Additionally, although activism
against both colonialism abroad and internal colonialism on Indian reservations in
the US was still nascent at most, the practical necessities of governance required that
authorities confront such issues as divorce rates, prostitution, illegitimacy, and changes
in patterns of marriage, premarital sex, and adultery. It was in this context that
Bronislaw Malinowski, Margaret Mead, and Isaac Schapera wrote pioneering ethnographic studies in the anthropology of sexuality, which are extracted in this section.[1]

Malinowski and Mead wrote library dissertations in anthropology before setting
out to conduct ethnographic research, Malinowski under the supervision of Edward
Westermarck and Mead under that of Franz Boas, although Mead's degree was
actually awarded in 1929, after she published *Coming of Age in Samoa*. Malinowski
worked in the Trobriand Islands off the coast of New Guinea between 1915 and

Sexualities in Anthropology: A Reader, edited by Andrew P. Lyons and Harriet D. Lyons
© 2011 Blackwell Publishing Ltd.

1918 and Mead visited the island of Ta'u in American Samoa for several months in 1925 and 1926. Malinowski attempted to immerse himself in the entirety of Trobriand culture through participant observation, while Mead undertook a much more focused project, namely the personal adjustment of adolescent girls. They wrote major works in which they described sexual freedoms accorded to unmarried youths in the South Pacific islands they studied. Both authors found some features to admire in such customs and both argued forcefully that limited tolerance of pre-marital sexual experimentation did not amount to "primitive promiscuity" and that stable marriages generally ensued. Mead's 1928 book *Coming of Age in Samoa: A Psychological Study of Primitive Youth for Western Civilization* received great attention from a mass audience (and mixed reviews from other anthropologists) while Malinowski's 1929 work *The Sexual Life of Savages in North-Western Melanesia: An Ethnographic Account of Courtship, Marriage, and Family Life among the Natives of the Trobriand Islands, British New Guinea* enjoyed relatively large sales for an English academic book. Malinowski's work on Trobriand sexuality influenced such British intellectuals as the philosopher Bertrand Russell, as well as anthropologists.

The Trobriand Islands appealed to Malinowski because they seemed to share many of the characteristics which the nineteenth-century evolutionists had diagnosed as "primitive matriarchy" and survivals of primitive promiscuity. Malinowski insisted throughout his work that matriliny did not amount to matriarchy: that men in general and fathers in particular played important roles in Trobriand society, even though their role in paternity was not recognized (see below, Introduction to Part VII, "Virgin Birth"). Malinowski wrote at length about the treatment of sex in myth, making the important point that ethnographers needed to distinguish between narrative and reality, and that stories of insatiable women and wild orgies were likely to be instructive contrasts with normal behavior, not depictions of it. He noted that strict incest taboos limited sexual freedom, and that children's sex play, adolescent trysts, and visits of girls to the communal bachelors' houses were part of a gradual process by which young people were prepared for sexually satisfying marriages. He described Trobriand sexual techniques and positions in some detail, noting that Trobrianders believed that they were more pleasurable to women than the European "missionary position." He asserted that though adultery, jealousy, and divorce did occur, marital infidelity was not unduly frequent and, for the most part, Trobrianders were able to deal with it without marital breakdown. These assertions led Bertrand Russell to cite Malinowski in his book *Marriage and Morals,* which advocated trial marriage and more realistic attitudes toward adultery for Europeans.

In various venues, Malinowski himself advocated birth control and better preparation for marriage for people in the modern world. He maintained important contacts with Marie Stopes and Margaret Sanger, the British and American birth control pioneers. Malinowski was, however, decidedly against experiments in "free love." He believed that Trobriand sexual customs had made homosexuality unknown there. In a posthumously published work (1962) he suggested that homosexuals in Europe might be provided with some safe location, where they could fulfill their sexual needs without "infecting" others. The topics covered in *The Sexual Life of Savages* mirrored the major topics in the work of Havelock Ellis, and Ellis wrote a laudatory introduction to it.

Although Malinowski noted that some Trobriand women had slept with European traders and that Trobrianders were reluctant to accept European theories of conception and missionary interference, he didn't really interrogate the significance of colonialism for Trobriand sexuality. Malinowski's functionalist theoretical position caused him to emphasize the interconnection between different aspects of bounded social systems, including marriage and sexuality, and, when he advised missionaries and government officials about such things as circumcision and initiation schools in Africa, he suggested caution about interference. He may have been oblivious to the degree to which such interference was already present in the Trobriands. Recently, works have been published (e.g., Reed 1997) indicating that at the time of Malinowski's fieldwork Australian authorities had attempted to take unpopular measures against adultery and other matters related to venereal disease and a supposed decline in population. More than 20 years after his death, a private diary which Malinowski kept while he was in the Trobriands appeared in print (1967), indicating that Malinowski struggled with his own attraction to Trobriand women, one of whom he had "pawed," leading to some questions about the "observer effect" on ethnographic findings about sexuality.

In *Coming of Age in Samoa* (1928) Margaret Mead described a culture in which adolescence was not a time of emotional distress, arguing for cultural influence on the experience of maturation, which many had believed to be entirely governed by biology. Among the causes to which she attributed this outcome, Mead included a de-emphasis on competition in Samoan socialization, a predictable adult career path for everyone, and a "casual" rather than an emotionally charged attitude to family and sexual relationships. Many readers of the book experienced it as largely a laudatory account of "love under the palm trees," though Mead later pointed out that sex was not the primary topic of the book. Controversies generated by *Coming of Age in Samoa* in the 1980s, after Mead's death, are discussed in Part IX. In this section Mead's work is considered in the social and intellectual context of its time.

Like the Trobrianders, Mead's Samoans were said to enjoy a period of adolescent sexual experimentation that was to be distinguished from earlier depictions of primitive promiscuity and that also was said to teach young people about sex before marriage. Unlike the Trobrianders, the Samoans were said to place a high value on virginity, but only a few girls of high rank, the *taupous*, or ceremonial virgins, were described by Mead as having to reflect that value in their conduct. Some girls who lived with the local pastor were also said to be restricted in their sexual relations, but such residence was usually temporary. For other girls sexual experience, though permitted, was not presented as free of restriction. Codes of politeness and discretion, for both boys and girls, are described, incest taboos had to be observed, and an open elopement, not sanctioned by a subsequent marriage, could bring disgrace on a girl. Nonetheless, Mead claimed that these rules allowed sufficient freedom for all Samoans to become proficient in sexual techniques, so that frigidity and impotence were unknown, except in cases of physical illness. Mead also claimed that early same-sex encounters were tolerated, but that adult "perversion" was virtually unknown, an outcome she noted with approval. She acknowledged the existence of *fa'afafine*, traditional cross-dressers, but she seems to have encountered only one effeminate male, not a full-fledged cross-dresser, in Ta'u. As Malinowski did in the Trobriands, Mead saw stable marriages as resulting from premarital sexual experimentation in Samoa, and noted that relatively easy divorce made marriage more satisfactory, not less.

Mead did not view Samoa as a tropical paradise, though she has been stereotyped as having done so. In a chapter written at the suggestion of her publisher, she argued that Samoan life was rather lacking in creativity and excitement, and challenged "Americans" to educate their youth in a way which would bring them some of the benefits enjoyed by Samoans without sacrificing these vital aspects of American culture. For the rest of her life Mead compared various cultures to America, both in her books and scholarly articles, and in writings and media appearances aimed at popular audiences. In the 1930s she studied a range of cultures with very different regimes of sex and gender, including the Manus, in New Guinea, whom she portrayed as sexually repressed (Mead 1930), the Arapesh, also in New Guinea, where she said that men and women valued tenderness and nurturance more than genital pleasure (Mead 1935), and two other New Guinea societies, who, she said, had very different ideas of masculinity and femininity both from each other and from Americans (Ibid). She used these experiences to argue throughout her life for more attention to families, childrearing, and maternity in both scholarly research and government policy. She certainly believed that women should be allowed to have both careers and sexual pleasure, but she stressed their alleged need for loving relationships and the experience of bearing and rearing children. She served on numerous government committees concerned with sexuality and the family, and used such positions to advance these views. She opposed the Kinsey Report for not paying enough attention to love (Mead 1948).

Like Malinowski, Mead studied in colonial societies, in Samoa, New Guinea, and Bali, and did not interrogate colonialism as a factor in sexuality, though she did sometimes acknowledge "change." In her one field study in the US, a brief stay with the Omaha in Nebraska, she encountered a situation where various forms of sexual "delinquency" such as prostitution and promiscuity were occurring in an abjected population which had previously set a high store on chastity. She found the experience highly distressing, and did not want to repeat it. In her 1932 book *The Changing Culture of an Indian Tribe* she acknowledged that political mobilization against white injustice could be therapeutic for Native Americans, a relatively novel idea at the time, but she didn't go so far as to support such actions.

Mead's attitudes toward sex and gender have appeared conservative to some who advocated change in the US and radical to those who supported what they believed to be "traditional" values. Mead may have had to toe a careful and sometimes obfuscating line because of her own, somewhat unconventional, personal life: she had three husbands and a number of male and female lovers, the latter fact coming to light only after her death.

Isaac Schapera, a South African Jew who had served as Malinowski's assistant during the writing of *The Sexual Life of Savages*, published *Married Life in an African Tribe* in 1940, based on fieldwork in Bechuanaland (present-day Botswana) in the 1930s. Malinowski wrote an introduction to the book, which dealt with many of the same topics as *Sexual Life of Savages*, including courtship, sexual positions, theories of conception, adultery, and marital stability and divorce. Unlike Malinowski (and Mead), however, Schapera did not describe a "primitive" society with a few glimpses of change and contact allowed the reader. He wrote about the Kgatla people as a part of the sexual mix of Southern Africa in the 1930s, although he did include elders' accounts of a more chaste past without questioning their veracity (see Thomas 2009; Lyons and Lyons 2004). He also included material that was distinctly "modern": love letters and accounts of the interconnection of labor migration and urbanization with patterns of courtship and marriage. In the 1933 paper included in this volume, Schapera discusses premarital sexual relations, the status of children born out of wedlock, and changing definitions of marriage itself. He quotes Tswana, who told him that in the past illegitimate children were highly stigmatized (if not actually killed), while their mothers were subject to ostracism and shaming, especially by means of much-feared insulting songs sung by female elders. By the 1930s such songs were a thing of the past, and unmarried mothers had become common. To some degree Schapera describes this situation as the combined result of the banning of polygamy by Christian missionaries, making husbands harder to come by, and the difficulty of amassing sufficient bride wealth for traditional marriage. Movements of both men and women out of rural areas in search of employment and excitement was also said to have had an effect. Poverty was a pervasive problem, and elders frequently said that things were better in the old days.

Schapera's account is neither a story of promiscuity nor one of simple social decay. There were opportunities for sex outside marriage in the past, so long as pregnancy did not result, and the present was not devoid of structure and solidarity, despite poverty, discrimination, and forced culture loss. Schapera also portrays family strength and love between couples, as well as a world in which some men and women seem to benefit from new freedoms, even if they also cause new hardships. It should be noted (Thomas 2009: 37, 40) that Schapera's work was regarded as obscene and as painting Tswana in a bad light by the Bamangwato Regent Tshekedi Kama and his white supporters, although the same leader had encouraged Schapera to write about things "as they were" rather than portray idealized and exotic primitivism. Schapera can fairly be said to have been a pioneer in avoiding such primitivism, and his work is enjoying new attention because of that fact.

NOTE

1   Other contributions to the anthropology of sexuality at this time included Firth's discussion of Tikopian sexuality in *We the Tikopia* (1957[1936]), Devereux's 1937 account of gender-crossing men and women among the Mohave, and Elwin's book, *The Muria and their Ghotul* (1991[1947]), which discussed sexual partnerships between adolescents in age-specific dormitories among a tribal population in India.

REFERENCES AND FURTHER READING

Devereux, George
    1937   Institutionalized Homosexuality of the Mohave Indians. Human Biology 9: 498–527.
Elwin, Verrier
    1991[1947]   The Muria and their Ghotul. Delhi: Oxford University Press.
Firth, Sir Raymond
    1957[1936]   We, the Tikopia: A Sociological Study of Kinship in Primitive Polynesia. London: George Allen & Unwin.

Lyons, Andrew, and Harriet Lyons
    2004   Irregular Connections: A History of Anthropology and Sexuality. Lincoln: University
    of Nebraska Press.
Malinowski, Bronislaw
    1962   Sex, Culture and Myth. A. Valetta Malinowski, ed. London: Rupert Hart-Davies.
Malinowski, Bronislaw
    1967   A Diary in the Strict Sense of the Term. Trans. N. Guterman. London: Routledge &
    Kegan Paul.
Mead, Margaret
    1930   Growing up in New Guinea: A Comparative Study of Primitive Education.
    New York: William Morrow.
Mead, Margaret
    1935   Sex and Temperament in Three Primitive Societies. New York: William Morrow.
Mead, Margaret
    1948   An Anthropologist Looks at the Report. In Proceedings of a Symposium on the First
    Published Report of a Series of Studies of Sex Phenomena by Professor Alfred C. Kinsey,
    Wardell B. Pomeroy and Clyde E. Martin. Pp. 58–69. New York: American Social Hygiene
    Association.
Mead, Margaret
    1966[1932]   The Changing Culture of an Indian Tribe. New York: Capricorn Books.
Reed, Adam
    1997   Contested Images and Common Strategies: Early Colonial Sexual Politics in the
    Massim. In Sites of Desire, Economies of Pleasure: Sexualities in Asia and the Pacific.
    L. Manderson and M. Jolly, eds. Pp. 48–71. Chicago: University of Chicago Press.
Russell, Bertrand
    1929   Marriage and Morals. New York: Horace Liveright.
Schapera, Isaac
    1940   Married Life in an African Tribe. London: Faber and Faber.
Thomas, Lynn M.
    2009   Love, Sex and the Modern Girl in 1930s Southern Africa. In Love in Africa. J. Cole
    and L. M. Thomas, eds. Pp. 31–57. Chicago: University of Chicago Press.

11

Prenuptial Intercourse Between the Sexes

Bronislaw Malinowski

The Bachelors' House

The most important feature of this mode of steering towards marriage, through gradually lengthening and strengthening intimacies, is an institution which might be called "the limited bachelors' house", and which, indeed, suggests at first sight the presence of a "group concubinage". It is clear that in order to enable pairs of lovers permanently to cohabit, some building is needed which will afford them seclusion.[...]

To meet this need, tribal custom and etiquette offer accommodation and privacy in the form of the *bukumatula*, the bachelors' and unmarried girls' house. In this a limited number of couples, some two, three, or four, live for longer or shorter periods together in a temporary community. It also and incidentally offers shelter for younger couples if they want amorous privacy for an hour or two.

[...]

At present there are five bachelors' establishments in Omarakana, and four in the adjoining village of Kasana'i. Their number has greatly diminished owing to missionary influence. [...] Whatever the reason, it is needless to say that this state of affairs does not enhance true sex morality.

The internal arrangements of a *bukumatula* are simple. The furniture consists almost exclusively of bunks with mat coverings. Since the inmates lead their life in association with other households in the day-time, and keep all their working implements in other houses, the inside of a typical *bukumatula* is strikingly bare. It lacks the feminine touch, the impression of being really inhabited.

In such an interior the older boys and their temporary mistresses live together. Each male owns his own bunk and regularly uses it. When a couple dissolve their liaison, it is the girl who moves, as a rule, to find another sleeping-place with another sweetheart. The *bukumatula* is, usually, owned by the group of boys who inhabit it, one of them, the eldest, being its titular owner. I was told that sometimes a man would build a house as a *bukumatula* for his daughter, and that in olden days there used to be unmarried people's houses owned and

Extracts from Bronislaw Malinowski, *The Sexual Life of Savages*, reprint of 3rd edition, Boston: Beacon Press, 1987[1932], pp. 59–64. Reprinted with permission of Taylor & Francis UK.

Sexualities in Anthropology: A Reader, edited by Andrew P. Lyons and Harriet D. Lyons
© 2011 Blackwell Publishing Ltd.

tenanted by girls. I never met, however, any actual instance of such an arrangement.

At first sight, as I have said, the institution of the *bukumatula* might appear as a sort of "Group Marriage" or at least "Group Concubinage", but analysis shows it to be nothing of the kind. Such wholesale terms are always misleading, if we allow them to carry an extraneous implication. To call this institution "Group Concubinage" would lead to misunderstanding; for it must be remembered that we have to deal with a number of couples who sleep in a common house, each in an exclusive liaison, and not with a group of people all living promiscuously together; there is never an exchange of partners, nor any poaching nor "complaisance". In fact, a special code of honour is observed within the *bukumatula*, which makes an inmate much more careful to respect sexual rights within the house than outside it. The word *kaylasi*, indicating sexual trespass, would be used of one who offended against this code; and I was told that "a man should not do it, because it is very bad, like adultery with a friend's wife."

Within the *bukumatula* a strict decorum obtains. The inmates never indulge in orgiastic pastimes, and it is considered bad form to watch another couple during their love-making. I was told by my young friends that the rule is either to wait till all the others are asleep, or else for all the pairs of a house to undertake to pay no attention to the rest. I could find no trace of any "voyeur" interest taken by the average boy, nor any tendency to exhibitionism. Indeed, when I was discussing the positions and technique of the sexual act, the statement was volunteered that there are specially unobtrusive ways of doing it "so as not to wake up the other people in the *bukumatula*."

Of course, two lovers living together in a *bukumatula* are not bound to each other by any ties valid in tribal law or imposed by custom. They foregather under the spell of personal attraction, are kept together by sexual passion or personal attachment, and part at will. The fact that in due course a permanent liaison often develops out of a temporary one and ends in marriage is due to a complexity of causes, which we shall consider later; but even such a gradually strengthening liaison is not binding until marriage is contracted. *Bukumatula* relationships, as such, impose no legal tie.

Another important point is that the pair's community of interest is limited to the sexual relation only. The couple share a bed and nothing else. In the case of a permanent liaison about to lead to marriage, they share it regularly; but they never have meals together; there are no services to be mutually rendered, they have no obligation to help each other in any way, there is, in short, nothing which would constitute a common ménage. Only seldom can a girl be seen in front of a bachelors' house, and this as a rule means that she is very much at home there, that there has been a liaison of long standing and that the two are going to be married soon. [...]

In the Trobriands two people about to be married must never have a meal in common. Such an act would greatly shock the moral susceptibility of a native, as well as his sense of propriety. To take a girl out to dinner without having previously married her – a thing permitted in Europe – would be to disgrace her in the eyes of a Trobriander. We object to an unmarried girl sharing a man's bed – the Trobriander would object just as strongly to her sharing his meal. The boys never eat within, or in front of, the *bukumatula*, but always join their parents or other relatives at every meal.

The institution of the *bukumatula* is, therefore, characterized by: (1) individual appropriation, the partners of each couple belonging exclusively to one another; (2) strict decorum and absence of any orgiastic or lascivious display; (3) the lack of any legally binding element; (4) the exclusion of any other community of interest between a pair, save that of sexual cohabitation.

[...]

12

Formal Sex Relations

Margaret Mead

The first attitude which a little girl learns towards boys is one of avoidance and antagonism. She learns to observe the brother and sister taboo towards the boys of her relationship group and household, and together with the other small girls of her age group she treats all other small boys as enemies elect. After a little girl is eight or nine years of age she has learned never to approach a group of older boys. This feeling of antagonism towards younger boys and shamed avoidance of older ones continues up to the age of thirteen or fourteen, to the group of girls who are just reaching puberty and the group of boys who have just been circumcised. These children are growing away from the age-group life and the age-group antagonisms. They are not yet actively sex-conscious. And it is at this time that relationships between the sexes are least emotionally charged. Not until she is an old married woman with several children will the Samoan girl again regard the opposite sex so quietly. When these adolescent children gather together there is a good-natured banter, a minimum of embarrassment, a great deal of random teasing which usually takes the form of accusing some little girl of a consuming passion for a decrepit old man of eighty, or some small boy of being the father of a buxom matron's eighth child. Occasionally the banter takes the form of attributing affection between two age mates and is gaily and indignantly repudiated by both. Children at this age meet at informal *siva* parties, on the outskirts of more formal occasions, at community reef fishings (when many yards of reef have been enclosed to make a great fish trap) and on torch-fishing excursions. Good-natured tussling and banter and co-operation in common activities are the keynotes of these occasions. But unfortunately these contacts are neither frequent nor sufficiently prolonged to teach the girls co-operation or to give either boys or girls any real appreciation of personality in members of the opposite sex.

Two or three years later this will all be changed. The fact that little girls no longer belong to age groups makes the individual's defection

Extracts from Margaret Mead, *Coming of Age in Samoa*, New York: Morrow, 1928, chap. 7, Formal Sex Relations, pp. 86–109. Copyright © 1928, 49, 55, 61, 73 by Margaret Mead. Reprinted by permission of HarperCollins Publishers USA.

Sexualities in Anthropology: A Reader, edited by Andrew P. Lyons and Harriet D. Lyons
© 2011 Blackwell Publishing Ltd.

less noticeable. The boy who begins to take an active interest in girls is also seen less in a gang and spends more time with one close companion. Girls have lost all of their nonchalance. They giggle, blush, bridle, run away. Boys become shy, embarrassed, taciturn, and avoid the society of girls in the daytime and on the brilliant moonlit nights for which they accuse the girls of having an exhibitionistic preference. Friendships fall more strictly within the relationship group. The boy's need for a trusted confidante is stronger than that of the girl, for only the most adroit and hardened Don Juans do their own courting. There are occasions, of course, when two youngsters just past adolescence, fearful of ridicule, even from their nearest friends and relatives, will slip away alone into the bush. More frequently still an older man, a widower or a divorced man, will be a girl's first lover. And here there is no need for an ambassador. The older man is neither shy nor frightened, and furthermore there is no one whom he can trust as an intermediary; a younger man would betray him, an older man would not take his amours seriously. But the first spontaneous experiment of adolescent children and the amorous excursions of the older men among the young girls of the village are variants on the edge of the recognised types of relationships; so also is the first experience of a young boy with an older woman. But both of these are exceedingly frequent occurrences, so that the success of an amatory experience is seldom jeopardised by double ignorance. Nevertheless, all of these occasions are outside the recognised forms into which sex relations fall. The little boy and girl are branded by their companions as guilty of *tautala lai titi* (presuming above their ages) as is the boy who loves or aspires to love an older woman, while the idea of an older man pursuing a young girl appeals strongly to their sense of humour; or if the girl is very young and naïve, to their sense of unfitness. "She is too young, too young yet. He is too old," they will say, and the whole weight of vigorous disapproval fell upon a *matai* who was known to be the father of the child of Lotu, the sixteen-year-old feeble-minded girl on Olesega. Discrepancy in age or experience always strikes them as comic or pathetic according to the degree. The theoretical punishment which is meted out to a disobedient and runaway daughter is to marry her to a very old man, and I have heard a nine-year-old giggle contemptuously over her mother's preference for a seventeen-year-old boy. Worst among these unpatterned deviations is that of the man who makes love to some young and dependent woman of his household, his adopted child or his wife's younger sister. The cry of incest is raised against him and sometimes feeling runs so high that he has to leave the group.

Besides formal marriage there are only two types of sex relations which receive any formal recognition from the community – love affairs between unmarried young people (this includes the widowed) who are very nearly of the same age, whether leading to marriage or merely a passing diversion; and adultery.

Between the unmarried there are three forms of relationship: the clandestine encounter, "under the palm trees," the published elopement, *Avaga*, and the ceremonious courtship in which the boy "sits before the girl"; and on the edge of these, the curious form of surreptitious rape, called *moetotolo*, sleep crawling, resorted to by youths who find favour in no maiden's eyes.

In these three relationships, the boy requires a confidant and ambassador whom he calls a *soa*. Where boys are close companions, this relationship may extend over many love affairs, or it may be a temporary one, terminating with the particular love affair. The *soa* follows the pattern of the talking chief who makes material demands upon his chief in return for the immaterial services which he renders him. If marriage results from his ambassadorship, he receives a specially fine present from the bridegroom. The choice of a *soa* presents many difficulties. If the lover chooses a steady, reliable boy, some slightly younger relative devoted to his interests, a boy unambitious in affairs of the heart, very likely the ambassador will bungle the whole affair through inexperience and lack of tact. But if he chooses a handsome and expert wooer who knows just how "to speak softly and walk gently," then as likely as not the girl will prefer the second to the principal. This difficulty is occasionally anticipated by employing two or three *soas* and setting them to spy on each other. But such a lack of trust is likely to inspire a similar attitude in the agents, and as one over-cautious and disappointed lover told me ruefully, "I had five *soas*, one was true and four were false."

Among possible *soas* there are two preferences, a brother or a girl. A brother is by definition loyal, while a girl is far more skilful for "a boy can only approach a girl in the evening, or when no one is by, but a girl can go with her all day long, walk with her and lie on the mat by her, eat off the same platter, and whisper between mouthfuls the name of the boy, speaking ever of him, how good he is, how gentle and how true, how worthy of love. Yes, best of all is the *soafafine*, the woman ambassador." But the difficulties of obtaining a *soafafine* are great. A boy may not choose from his own female relatives. The taboo forbids him ever to mention such matters in their presence. It is only by good chance that his brother's sweetheart may be a relative of the girl upon whom he has set his heart; or some other piece of good fortune may throw him into contact with a girl or woman who will act in his interests. The most violent antagonisms in the young people's groups are not between ex-lovers, arise not from the venom of the deserted nor the smarting pride of the jilted, but occur between the boy and the *soa* who has betrayed him, or a lover and the friend of his beloved who has in any way blocked his suit.

In the strictly clandestine love affair the lover never presents himself at the house of his beloved. His *soa* may go there in a group or upon some trumped-up errand, or he also may avoid the house and find opportunities to speak to the girl while she is fishing or going to and from the plantation. It is his task to sing his friend's praise, counteract the girl's fears and objections, and finally appoint a rendezvous. These affairs are usually of short duration and both boy and girl may be carrying on several at once. One of the recognised causes of a quarrel is the resentment of the first lover against his successor of the same night, "for the boy who came later will mock him." These clandestine lovers make their rendezvous on the outskirts of the village. "Under the palm trees" is the conventionalised designation of this type of intrigue. Very often three or four couples will have a common rendezvous, when either the boys or the girls are relatives who are friends. Should the girl ever grow faint or dizzy, it is the boy's part to climb the nearest palm and fetch down a fresh cocoanut to pour on her face in lieu of *eau de cologne*. In native theory, barrenness is the punishment of promiscuity; and, *vice versa*, only persistent monogamy is rewarded by conception. When a pair of clandestine experimenters whose rank is so low that their marriages are not of any great economic importance become genuinely attached to each other and maintain the relationship over several months, marriage often follows. And native sophistication distinguishes between the adept lover whose adventures are many and of short duration and the less skilled man who can find no better proof of his virility than a long affair ending in conception.

Often the girl is afraid to venture out into the night, infested with ghosts and devils, ghosts that strangle one, ghosts from far-away villages who come in canoes to kidnap the girls of the village, ghosts who leap upon the back and may not be shaken off. Or she may feel that it is wiser to remain at home, and if necessary, attest her presence vocally. In this case the lover braves the house; taking off his *lavalava*, he greases his body thoroughly with cocoanut oil so that he can slip through the fingers of pursuers and leave no trace, and stealthily raises the blinds and slips into the house. The prevalence of this practice gives point to the familiar incident in Polynesian folk tales of the ill fortune that falls the luckless hero who "sleeps until morning, until the rising sun reveals his presence to the other inmates of the house." As perhaps a dozen or more people and several dogs are sleeping in the house, a due regard for silence is sufficient precaution. But it is this habit of domestic rendezvous which lends itself to the peculiar abuse of the *moetotolo*, or sleep crawler.

The *moetotolo* is the only sex activity which presents a definitely abnormal picture. Ever since the first contact with white civilisation, rape, in the form of violent assault, has occurred occasionally in Samoa. It is far less congenial, however, to the Samoan attitude than *moetotolo*, in which a man stealthily appropriates the favours which are meant for another. The need for guarding against discovery makes conversation impossible, and the sleep crawler relies upon the girl's expecting a lover or the chance that she will indiscriminately accept any comer. If the girl suspects and resents him, she raises a great outcry and the whole household gives chase. Catching a *moetotolo* is counted great sport, and the women, who feel their safety endangered, are even more active in pursuit than the men. One luckless youth in Luma neglected to remove his *lavalava*. The girl discovered him and her sister succeeded in biting a piece out of his *lavalava* before he escaped. This she proudly exhibited the next day. As the boy had been too dull to destroy his *lavalava*, the evidence against him was circumstantial and he was the laughing stock of the village; the children wrote a dance song about it and sang it after him wherever he went. The *moetotolo* problem is complicated by the possibility that a boy of the household may be the offender and may take refuge in the hue and cry following the discovery. It also provides the girl with an excellent alibi, since she has only to call out "*moetotolo*" in case her lover is discovered. "To the family and the village that may be a *moetotolo*, but it is not so in the hearts of the girl and the boy."

Two motives are given for this unsavoury activity, anger and failure in love. The Samoan girl who plays the coquette does so at her peril. "She will say, 'Yes, I will meet you to-night by that old cocoanut tree just beside the devilfish stone when the moon goes down.' And the boy will wait and wait and wait all night long. It will grow very dark; lizards will drop on his head; the ghost boats will come into the channel. He will be very much afraid. But he will wait there until dawn, until his hair is wet with dew and his heart is very angry and still she does not come. Then in revenge he will attempt a *moetotolo*. Especially will he do so if he hears that she has met another that night." The other set explanation is that a particular boy cannot win a sweetheart by any legitimate means, and there is no form of prostitution, except guest prostitution in Samoa. As some of the boys who were notorious *moetotolos* were among the most charming and good-looking youths of the village, this is a little hard to understand. Apparently, these youths, frowned upon in one

or two tentative courtships, inflamed by the loudly proclaimed success of their fellows and the taunts against their own inexperience, cast established wooing procedure to the winds and attempt a *moetotolo*. And once caught, once branded, no girl will ever pay any attention to them again. They must wait until as older men, with position and title to offer, they can choose between some weary and bedraggled wanton or the unwilling young daughter of ambitious and selfish parents. But years will intervene before this is possible, and shut out from the amours in which his companions are engaging, a boy makes one attempt after another, sometimes successfully, sometimes only to be caught and beaten, mocked by the village, and always digging the pit deeper under his feet. Often partially satisfactory solutions are relationships with men. There was one such pair in the village, a notorious *moetotolo*, and a serious-minded youth who wished to keep his heart free for political intrigue. The *moetotolo* therefore complicates and adds zest to the surreptitious love-making which is conducted at home, while the danger of being missed, the undesirability of chance encounters abroad, rain and the fear of ghosts, complicate "love under the palm trees."

Between these strictly *sub rosa* affairs and a final offer of marriage there is an intermediate form of courtship in which the girl is called upon by the boy. As this is regarded as a tentative move towards matrimony, both relationship groups must be more or less favourably inclined towards the union. With his *soa* at his side and provided with a basket of fish, an octopus or so, or a chicken, the suitor presents himself at the girl's home before the late evening meal. If his gift is accepted, it is a sign that the family of the girl are willing for him to pay his addresses to her. He is formally welcomed by the *matai*, sits with reverently bowed head throughout the evening prayer, and then he and his *soa* stay for supper. But the suitor does not approach his beloved. They say: "If you wish to know who is really the lover, look then not at the boy who sits by her side, looks boldly into her eyes and twists the flowers in her necklace around his fingers or steals the hibiscus flower from her hair that he may wear it behind his ear. Do not think it is he who whispers softly in her ear, or says to her, 'Sweetheart, wait for me to-night. After the moon has set, I will come to you,' or who teases her by saying she has many lovers. Look instead at the boy who sits afar off, who sits with bent head and takes no part in the joking. And you will see that his eyes are always turned softly on the girl. Always he watches her and never does he miss a movement of her lips. Perhaps she will wink at him, perhaps she will raise her eyebrows, perhaps she will make a sign with her hand. He must always be wakeful and watching or he will miss it." The *soa* meanwhile pays the girl elaborate and ostentatious court and in undertones pleads the cause of his friend. After dinner, the centre of the house is accorded the young people to play cards, sing or merely sit about, exchanging a series of broad pleasantries. This type of courtship varies from occasional calls to daily attendance. The food gift need not accompany each visit, but is as essential at the initial call as is an introduction in the West. The way of such declared lovers is hard. The girl does not wish to marry, nor to curtail her amours in deference to a definite betrothal. Possibly she may also dislike her suitor, while he in turn may be the victim of family ambition. Now that the whole village knows him for her suitor, the girl gratifies her vanity by avoidance, by perverseness. He comes in the evening, she has gone to another house; he follows her there, she immediately returns home. When such courtship ripens into an accepted proposal of marriage, the boy often goes to sleep in the house of his intended bride and often the union is surreptitiously consummated. Ceremonial marriage is deferred until such time as the boy's family have planted or collected enough food and other property and the girl's family have gotten together a suitable dowry of tapa and mats.

In such manner are conducted the love affairs of the average young people of the same village, and of the plebeian young people of neighbouring villages. From this free and easy experimentation, the *taupo* is excepted. Virginity is a legal requirement for her. At her marriage, in front of all the people, in a house brilliantly lit, the talking chief of the bridegroom will take the tokens of her virginity.[1] In former days should she prove not to be a virgin, her female relatives fell upon and beat her with stones, disfiguring and sometimes fatally injuring the girl who had shamed their house. The public ordeal sometimes prostrated the girl for as much as a week, although ordinarily a girl recovers from first intercourse in two or three hours, and women seldom lie abed more than a few hours after childbirth. Although this virginity-testing ceremony was theoretically observed at weddings of people of all ranks, it was simply ignored if the boy knew that it was an idle form, and "a wise girl who is not a virgin will tell the talking chief of her husband, so that she be not shamed before all the people."

The attitude towards virginity is a curious one. Christianity has, of course, introduced a moral premium on chastity. The Samoans regard this attitude with reverent but complete scepticism and the concept of celibacy is absolutely meaningless to them. But virginity definitely adds to a girl's attractiveness, the wooing of a virgin is considered far more of a feat than the conquest of a more experienced heart, and a really successful Don Juan turns most of his attention to their seduction. One youth who at twenty-four married a girl who was still a virgin was the laughing stock of the village over his freely related trepidation which revealed the fact that at twenty-four, although he had had many love affairs, he had never before won the favours of a virgin.

The bridegroom, his relatives and the bride and her relatives all receive prestige if she proves to be a virgin, so that the girl of rank who might wish to forestall this painful public ceremony is thwarted not only by the anxious chaperonage of her relatives but by the boy's eagerness for prestige. One young Lothario eloped to his father's house with a girl of high rank from another village and refused to live with her because, said he, "I thought maybe I would marry that girl and there would be a big *malaga* and a big ceremony and I would wait and get the credit for marrying a virgin. But the next day her father came and said that she could not marry me, and she cried very much. So I said to her, 'Well, there is no use now to wait any longer. Now we will run away into the bush.'" It is conceivable that the girl would often trade the temporary prestige for an escape from the public ordeal, but in proportion as his ambitions were honourable, the boy would frustrate her efforts.

Just as the clandestine and casual "love under the palm trees" is the pattern irregularity for those of humble birth, so the elopement has its archetype in the love affairs of the *taupo*, and the other chiefs' daughters. These girls of noble birth are carefully guarded; not for them are secret trysts at night or stolen meetings in the day time. Where parents of lower rank complacently ignore their daughters' experiments, the high chief guards his daughter's virginity as he guards the honour of his name, his precedence in the kava ceremony or any other prerogative of his high degree. Some old woman of the household is told off to be the girl's constant companion and duenna. The *taupo* may not visit in other houses in the village, or leave the house alone at night. When she sleeps, an older woman sleeps by her side. Never may she go to another village unchaperoned. In her own village she goes soberly about her tasks, bathing in the sea, working in the plantation, safe under the jealous guardianship of the women of her own village. She runs little risk from the *moetotolo*, for one who outraged the *taupo* of his village would formerly have been beaten to death, and now would have to flee from the village. The prestige of the village is inextricably bound up with the high repute of the *taupo* and few young men in the village would dare to be her lovers. Marriage to them is out of the question, and their companions would revile them as traitors rather than envy them such doubtful distinction. Occasionally a youth of very high rank in the same village will risk an elopement, but even this is a rare occurrence. For tradition says that the *taupo* must marry outside her village, marry a high chief or a *manaia* of another village. Such a marriage is an occasion for great festivities and solemn ceremony. The chief and all of his talking chiefs must come to propose for her hand, come in person bringing gifts for her talking chiefs. If the talking chiefs of the girl are satisfied that this is a lucrative and desirable match, and the family are satisfied with the rank and appearance of the suitor, the marriage is agreed

upon. Little attention is paid to the opinion of the girl. So fixed is the idea that the marriage of the *taupo* is the affair of the talking chiefs that Europeanised natives on the main island, refuse to make their daughters *taupos* because the missionaries say a girl should make her own choice, and once she is a *taupo*, they regard the matter as inevitably taken out of their hands. After the betrothal is agreed upon the bridegroom returns to his village to collect food and property for the wedding. His village sets aside a piece of land which is called the "Place of the Lady" and is her property and the property of her children forever, and on this land they build a house for the bride. Meanwhile, the bridegroom has left behind him in the house of the bride, a talking chief, the counterpart of the humbler *soa*. This is one of the talking chief's best opportunities to acquire wealth. He stays as the emissary of his chief, to watch over his future bride. He works for the bride's family and each week the *matai* of the bride must reward him with a handsome present. As an affianced wife of a chief, more and more circumspect conduct is enjoined upon the girl. Did she formerly joke with the boys of the village, she must joke no longer, or the talking chief, on the watch for any lapse from high decorum, will go home to his chief and report that his bride is unworthy of such honour. This custom is particularly susceptible to second thought on the part of either side. Does the bridegroom repent of the bargain, he bribes his talking chief (who is usually a young man, not one of the important talking chiefs who will benefit greatly by the marriage itself) to be oversensitive to the behaviour of the bride or the treatment he receives in the bride's family. And this is the time in which the bride will elope, if her affianced husband is too unacceptable. For while no boy of her own village will risk her dangerous favours, a boy from another village will enormously enhance his prestige if he elopes with the *taupo* of a rival community. Once she has eloped, the projected alliance is of course broken off, although her angry parents may refuse to sanction her marriage with her lover and marry her for punishment to some old man.

So great is the prestige won by the village, one of whose young men succeeds in eloping with a *taupo*, that often the whole effort of a *malaga* is concentrated upon abducting the *taupo*, whose virginity will be respected in direct ratio to the chances of her family and village consenting to ratify the marriage. As the abductor is often of high rank, the village often ruefully accepts the compromise.

This elopement pattern, given meaning by the restrictions under which the *taupo* lives and this inter-village rivalry, is carried down to the lower ranks where indeed it is practically meaningless. Seldom is the chaperonage exercised over the girl of average family severe enough to make elopement the only way of consummating a love affair. But the elopement is spectacular; the boy wishes to increase his reputation as a successful Don Juan, and the girl wishes to proclaim her conquest and also often hopes that the elopement will end in marriage. The eloping pair run away to the parents of the boy or to some of his relatives and wait for the girl's relatives to pursue her. As one boy related the tale of such an adventure: "We ran away in the rain, nine miles to Leone, in the pouring rain, to my father's house. The next day her family came to get her, and my father said to me, 'How is it, do you wish to marry this girl, shall I ask her father to leave her here?' And I said, 'Oh, no. I just eloped with her for public information.'" Elopements are much less frequent than the clandestine love affairs because the girl takes far more risk. She publicly renounces her often nominal claims to virginity; she embroils herself with her family, who in former times, and occasionally even to-day, would beat her soundly and shave off her hair. Nine times out of ten, her lover's only motive is vanity and display, for the boys say, "The girls hate a *moetotolo*, but they all love an *avaga* (eloping) man."

The elopement also occurs as a practical measure when one family is opposed to a marriage upon which a pair of young people have determined. The young people take refuge with the friendly side of the family. But unless the recalcitrant family softens and consents to legalise the marriage by a formal exchange of property, the principals can do nothing to establish their status. A young couple may have had several children and still be classed as "elopers," and if the marriage is finally legalised after long delay, this stigma will always cling to them. It is far more serious a one than a mere accusation of sexual irregularity, for there is a definite feeling that the whole community procedure has been outraged by a pair of young upstarts.

Reciprocal gift-giving relations are maintained between the two families as long as the marriage lasts, and even afterwards if there are children. The birth of each child, the death of a member of either household, a visit of the wife to her family, or if he lives with her people, of the husband to his, is marked by the presentation of gifts.

In premarital relationships, a convention of love making is strictly adhered to. True, this is a convention of speech, rather than of action. A boy declares that he will die if a girl refuses him her favours, but the Samoans laugh at stories of romantic love, scoff at fidelity to a long absent wife or mistress, believe explicitly that one love will quickly cure another. The fidelity which is followed by pregnancy is taken as proof positive of a real attachment, although having many mistresses is never out of harmony with a declaration of affection for each. The composition of ardent love songs, the fashioning of long and flowery love letters, the invocation of the moon, the stars and the sea in verbal courtship, all serve to give Samoan love-making a close superficial resemblance to our own, yet the attitude is far closer to that of Schnitzler's hero in *The Affairs of Anatol*. Romantic love as it occurs in our civilisation, inextricably bound up with ideas of monogamy, exclusiveness, jealousy and undeviating fidelity does not occur in Samoa. Our attitude is a compound, the final result of many converging lines of development in Western civilisation, of the institution of monogamy, of the ideas of the age of chivalry, of the ethics of Christianity. Even a passionate attachment to one person which lasts for a long period and persists in the face of discouragement but does not bar out other relationships, is rare among the Samoans. Marriage, on the other hand, is regarded as a social and economic arrangement, in which relative wealth, rank, and skill of husband and wife, all must be taken into consideration. There are many marriages in which both individuals, especially if they are over thirty, are completely faithful. But this must be attributed to the ease of sexual adjustment on the one hand, and to the ascendency of other interests, social organisation for the men, children for the women, over sex interests, rather than to a passionate fixation upon the partner in the marriage. As the Samoans lack the inhibitions and the intricate specialisation of sex feeling which make marriages of convenience unsatisfactory, it is possible to bulwark marital happiness with other props than temporary passionate devotion. Suitability and expediency become the deciding factors.

Adultery does not necessarily mean a broken marriage. A chief's wife who commits adultery is deemed to have dishonoured her high position, and is usually discarded, although the chief will openly resent her remarriage to any one of lower rank. If the lover is considered the more culpable, the village will take public vengeance upon him. In less conspicuous cases the amount of fuss which is made over adultery is dependent upon the relative rank of the offender and offended, or the personal jealousy which is only occasionally aroused. If either the injured husband or the injured wife is sufficiently incensed to threaten physical violence, the trespasser may have to resort to a public *ifoga*, the ceremonial humiliation before some one whose pardon is asked. He goes to the house of the man he has injured, accompanied by all the men of his household, each one wrapped in a fine mat, the currency of the country; the suppliants seat themselves outside the house, fine mats spread over their heads, hands folded on their breasts, heads bent in attitudes of the deepest dejection and humiliation. "And if the man is very angry he will say no word. All day he will go about his business; he will braid cinet with a quick hand, he will talk loudly to his wife, and call out greetings to those who pass in the roadway, but he will take no notice of those who sit on his own terrace, who dare not raise their eyes or make any movement to go away. In olden days, if his heart was not softened, he might take a club and together with his relatives go out and kill those who sit without. But now he only keeps them waiting, waiting all day long.

The sun will beat down upon them; the rain will come and beat on their heads and still he will say no word. Then towards evening he will say at last: 'Come, it is enough. Enter the house and drink the kava. Eat the food which I will set before you and we will cast our trouble into the sea.'" Then the fine mats are accepted as payment for the injury, the *ifoga* becomes a matter of village history and old gossips will say, "Oh, yes, Lua! no, she's not Iona's child. Her father is that chief over in the next village. He *ifod* to Iona before she was born." If the offender is of much lower rank than the injured husband, his chief, or his father (if he is only a young boy) will have to humiliate himself in his place. Where the offender is a woman, she and her female relatives will make similar amends. But they will run far greater danger of being roundly beaten and berated; the peaceful teachings of Christianity – perhaps because they were directed against actual killing, rather than the slightly less fatal encounters of women – have made far less change in the belligerent activities of the women than in those of the men.

If, on the other hand, a wife really tires of her husband, or a husband of his wife, divorce is a simple and informal matter, the non-resident simply going home to his or her family, and the relationship is said to have "passed away." It is a very brittle monogamy, often trespassed and more often broken entirely. But many adulteries occur – between a young marriage-shy bachelor and a married woman, or a temporary widower and some young girl – which hardly threaten the continuity of established relationships. The claim that a woman has on her family's land renders her as independent as her husband, and so there are no marriages of any duration in which either person is actively unhappy. A tiny flare-up and a woman goes home to her own people; if her husband does not care to conciliate her, each seeks another mate.

Within the family, the wife obeys and serves her husband, in theory, though of course, the hen-pecked husband is a frequent phenomenon. In families of high rank, her personal service to her husband is taken over by the *taupo* and the talking chief but the wife always retains the right to render a high chief sacred personal services, such as cutting his hair. A wife's rank can never exceed her husband's because it is always directly dependent upon it. Her family may be richer and more illustrious than his, and she may actually exercise more influence over the village affairs through her blood relatives than he, but within the life of the household and the village, she is a *tausi*, wife of a talking chief, or a *faletua*, wife of a chief. This sometimes results in conflict, as in the case of Pusa who was the sister of the last holder of the highest title on the island. This title was temporarily extinct. She was also the wife of the highest chief in the village. Should her brother, the heir, resume the higher title, her husband's rank and her rank as his wife would suffer. Helping her brother meant lowering the prestige of her husband. As she was the type of woman who cared a great deal more for wire pulling than

for public recognition, she threw her influence in for her brother. Such conflicts are not uncommon, but they present a clear-cut choice, usually reinforced by considerations of residence. If a woman lives in her husband's household, and if, furthermore, that household is in another village, her interest is mainly enlisted in her husband's cause; but if she lives with her own family, in her own village, her allegiance is likely to cling to the blood relatives from whom she receives reflected glory and informal privilege, although no status.

NOTE

1 This custom is now forbidden by law, but is only gradually dying out.

13

Premarital Pregnancy and Native Opinion: A Note on Social Change

Isaac Schapera

Legitimacy in Bantu Society

In his recent writings on the subject of marriage and kinship, Malinowski has repeatedly emphasized what he terms the 'principle of legitimacy'.[1] By this he means the rule, found in all human societies, that a woman has to be married before she is allowed legitimately to conceive. 'Roughly speaking, an unmarried mother is under a ban, a fatherless child is a bastard. This is by no means only a European or Christian prejudice; it is the attitude found amongst most barbarous and savage peoples as well.' Where prenuptial intercourse is regarded as illicit and immoral, marriage is obviously the essential prelude to the birth of legitimate children, i.e. children having full social status in the community. But even where prenuptial intercourse is tolerated, this tolerance does not extend to liberty of conception. The unmarried boys and girls may indulge freely in sex, but there must be no issue. An unmarried mother will be subjected to punishment and become the object of scorn, her child possibly killed or aborted, while often the putative father is also penalized unless he marries the girl. Almost universally, a child born out of wedlock has a different status from the legitimate offspring, usually very much to his disadvantage. Facts such as these show that the group of mother and child is considered incomplete in the eyes of the community, and that the sociological position of husband and father is everywhere felt to be indispensable.

This intimate association between marriage and the right to bear children is as true of the South African Bantu as it is of other peoples. Marriage amongst them is accomplished by the transfer of [...] material wealth [*boxadi*], such as cattle, by the bridegroom, or his family acting on his behalf, to the bride's father or guardian. [...] All children born to a woman for whom *boxadi* has been transferred or promised are considered to be the legal offspring of her husband, even although he may not actually be their physiological father.

Extract from Isaac Schapera, Premarital Pregnancy and Native Opinion, from *Africa*, vol. 6, no. 1 (1933): 59–89. Reprinted with permission of International African Institute IAI.

On the other hand, children born to a woman for whom *boxadi* has not been transferred or contracted are regarded as illegitimate. They belong to their mother's family and clan, their physiological father having no claim to them unless he makes a special payment, and even then they are subordinated to his legitimate children in social and economic rights and privileges.

In their attitude towards premarital sex relations these tribes differ widely. [...] But no matter what their conventional attitude may be in this respect, all the Southern Bantu agree in demanding that an unmarried girl must not become pregnant. Should she do so, she is penalized, together with her lover and child. The penalties exacted also vary widely, but the most common usage is that the lover is fined, while the girl and her child, where it is allowed to live, both suffer social degradation and other indignities. In no case is premarital pregnancy found to occur without coming under the ban of the community.

Recent Modifications of Native Custom

Of recent years it has often been a matter of comment that the South African tribes are no longer as strict in their attitude towards premarital pregnancy as they formerly were. [...] It is no longer so serious an offence as it was for an unmarried girl to have a child, and, correspondingly, the treatment meted out to her has grown less severe. [...] It is easy enough to say, as is often done, that the disintegration of the old morality is due to the effects of contact with the Europeans. But this facile conclusion, although it is largely true, is nevertheless seldom based upon adequate investigation, with the result that it fails to reveal fully how the change actually came about. [...]

To illustrate concretely the transformation of native opinion in regard to premarital pregnancy, we may contrast the original and the modern attitudes towards it prevailing amongst the BaKxatla baxaKxafêla of Bechuanaland Protectorate, a tribe belonging to the Sotho-Tšwana cluster. As in all the other tribes of this cluster, marriage involves the transfer of cattle, known as *boxadi*, from the bridegroom's family to that of the bride. The amount of *boxadi* is not fixed, but an odd number is considered unlucky and is therefore not generally acceptable. As a rule, any even number from two upwards is given, the actual amount depending upon the status and means of the bridegroom. The bride's family must take whatever is offered to them, and there is none of the preliminary bargaining characteristic of the Zulu-Xhosa tribes. The boy's parents, after they have agreed with their son as to whom his future wife should be, send special messengers to the girl's family to try and arrange a betrothal. If the latter consent, the boy's people send them goods of various kinds (nowadays chiefly blankets and dress material) to be given to the girl. Her parents, in return, brew beer which is ceremonially drunk by the messengers. Once the betrothal has been confirmed in this way, the wedding may take place at any time. Generally, an interval of one or two years elapses before it is celebrated. During this period the boy has the right to visit the girl's home whenever he pleases, and food is always prepared for him there; but the girl is not permitted to visit her fiancé's home.

The essentials of the marriage contract are mutual agreement between the two families concerned, and the payment of the *boxadi*. The latter is considered by the BaKxatla primarily as serving to establish a bond of special intimacy between the two families, and as a register of the marriage. But they say, also, that it transfers the reproductive power of a woman from her own family into that of the man. This point is of special importance, for upon it rests the whole Kxatla conception of legitimacy. It should be made clear at once that the people realize that the man plays some part in the physiology of procreation. They believe that the foetus in the womb of the woman is built up out of a mixture of her menstrual blood with the semen of the man; and, accordingly, they are able to associate pregnancy with the cessation of the menses. But although the physiological paternity of a man may be admitted, this does not imply that he is necessarily regarded as the sociological father of the child. Summarizing their legal conceptions briefly, it may be said that no form of cohabitation between a man and a woman is held to be a marriage unless it is accompanied by the transfer of, or the formal contract to transfer, the *boxadi*. No man can claim, for any purposes, the children he has by any woman, until he and his family have agreed to pay, and under certain circumstances until they have actually paid, the *boxadi*. On the other hand, all the children borne by a married woman, no matter who their real father may be, are held to be the legitimate offspring of the man on whose behalf the *boxadi* for that woman was paid. These facts must be remembered if the Kxatla attitude towards premarital pregnancy, both formerly and at the present time, is to be fully understood.

Contact with the Europeans has in many ways modified the traditional laws and customs of the BaKxatla. The most pronounced change of all came about when the chief Lentswe became converted to Christianity about forty years ago. [...] Associated with this conversion was the abandonment for a while of the payment of *boxadi* at marriage. The missionaries regarded the practice as a form of wife-purchase, and the chief, in his zeal for the new religion, agreed to do away with it. But it was found that this led to confusion and dissatisfaction, and Lentswe's successor, the regent Isang, impressed upon the Church authorities that the absence of the *boxadi* payments was tending to make marriages very unstable. As a result they agreed to the restoration of the practice, and at the present time the payment of *boxadi* is an essential element in the Church marriage, as well as in the heathen marriages which still take place. But the missionaries have consistently opposed the practice of polygyny, which the BaKxatla shared with the other South African Bantu, and no man is allowed to be a member of the Church who has more than one wife.

Another important effect of Christianity which still survives, was the abolition of the traditional initiation ceremonies at puberty. These ceremonies were held at intervals of several years apart, boys and girls being separately initiated. All the eligible children of the same sex and of about the same age were subjected, as a group, to a lengthy series of rites, involving their seclusion away from the rest of the community for a period of about three months or so, circumcision in the case of the boys and an analogous operation on the girls, hardships and strenuous physical tests of various kinds, and formal instruction in tribal lore and sexual behaviour. At the end of the ceremony, all those who had passed through it together were incorporated into a *mophatô* (regiment), which was given a distinctive name. They remained members of this *mophatô* for the rest of their lives, and in their capacity as such had to render various services to the chief. At the present time the regimental organization still flourishes, but the preliminary initiation ceremonies have lost much of their former character. Circumcision, with its associated rites and taboos, has been completely abandoned, nor is the secrecy, which was so marked an element of the old ceremonies, any longer maintained. It is not even compulsory nowadays for a boy to pass through the initiation rites before he is accepted into a regiment. These modifications of the old initiation system have inevitably affected the marriage regulations, and also the whole aspect of premarital sexual life.

Premarital Pregnancy in Former Times

Marriage in the olden days was permitted only to those who had been admitted into a *mophatô*, i.e. to those who had been through the initiation ceremonies. The girls were generally married soon after they came out of the initiation 'school'. The boys, however, were expected to marry, not into the *mophatô* of girls roughly contemporaneous with themselves, but into the one formed after that. This meant, in effect, that they had to wait anywhere from four to seven years after initiation before they could marry. Even then not all of them would be successful in obtaining wives immediately, for, owing to the practice of polygyny, many of the newly-initiated girls would become the junior wives of elderly or middle-aged men. It was an accepted practice, however, that such boys should be allowed secret access to the younger wives of their male relatives in the same *kxôrô* (lineage group). In particular, the boy's *rangwane* (father's younger brother) was expected to grant him this privilege. Any children born of such a union would, of course, be regarded as the legitimate offspring of the woman's husband, in accordance with the rights established by the transfer of *boxadi*. This practice, so far from being looked upon in the light of adultery, was held to be highly justifiable, especially when the husband was old and impotent. The main idea underlying it was that the boy should 'raise up seed' in the junior 'house' of his relative. My informants, however, also stressed the fact that it gave these boys an opportunity for acquiring sexual experience which, if denied to them, now that they were old enough to marry, might have led to frequent attempts at seduction and other illicit means of obtaining sexual satisfaction.

These privileges were allowed only to boys who had been admitted into their *mophatô*, and the women are said to have thought it shameful to sleep with anybody who was not circumcised. Before they had been initiated the young people of both sexes were expected to live chastely. I found it very difficult to obtain satisfactory information regarding premarital sexual relations. All my informants insisted that boys and girls were not allowed to mix together freely. The boys were sent out to the cattle-posts away from the villages, and were kept there as long as possible, sometimes even after they had been initiated. A boy's first wife was chosen for him by his parents, who after making all the necessary arrangements, would call him home to marry her. This might be the first sight he had ever had of her. But in spite of this sexual segregation at adolescence, and although my informants maintained that premarital sexual intercourse in the olden days was an 'unheard-of thing', it is obvious from what follows that chastity was not universally observed.

My informants could not tell me of the treatment meted out to youthful lovers who managed to avoid conception (and therefore in all probability discovery as well). On the other hand, they were able to describe to me, rather sketchily it is true, what happened to an unmarried girl who had conceived. But they all emphasized that such cases were very infrequent. It was regarded as a profound disgrace by her family if an unmarried girl became pregnant, and every effort was made to conceal the fact. If the matter ever became general knowledge, the unfortunate girl was subjected to every possible humiliation. She was stripped of all her decorations and no longer allowed to wear them; she might not cut her hair, but had to wear it long as a sign of disgrace; she was not allowed to mix with the other girls, lest she pollute them as well; she might not wash her head, nor smear her face and body with the usual ointment of fat; and if she had not yet been initiated she was not sent to the *bôjale* (girls' initiation school) with the rest of her coevals, but was separately treated. It was even said that attempts would be made to bewitch her, so that she might die together with the child in her womb. She was called by all sorts of opprobrious names, such as *seaka* (whore), and above all she was publicly mocked by the other girls and women, who would gather at night round her *lapa* (household enclosure) and sing obscene songs reviling her and her people. [...]

Their mockery is said to have been the most powerful sanction against premarital pregnancy, for it was the one thing which the girls feared above all else.

The child of an unmarried woman, when it was not aborted, was usually killed at birth by her parents. [...] In the rare instances where convention was defied and the child permitted to live, it could not be carried about in a *thari* (skin cradle) on its mother's back, it might not mix with the other children, and above all, it dare not sit with other people round the fireplace at the *kxotla* (men's gathering-place).

Concerning the treatment of the girl's lover I could obtain but little information. It was said that the girl was forced by her mother to reveal his name, and the matter would then be reported to his parents. There was a conflict of opinion as to whether he would be expected to marry the girl. Some informants said that under no circumstances would her parents consent to the match. Others insisted that he was forced to do so if he was eligible for marriage, i.e. if he was already the member of a *mophatô*, and that if he was not, one of his father's younger brothers would be asked to do so instead. In any case, it was agreed that his conduct was regarded as extremely disgraceful, and that he would be violently reproached for dishonouring his family and his tribe. If he had not yet been initiated, he was treated with special severity when he went to the *boxwêra* (boy's initiation school), and one old man hinted that it was by no means unusual for such a boy to be killed during the course of the ceremonies.

The evidence, slight as it is, shows clearly enough that in the olden days the BaKxatla regarded premarital pregnancy with pronounced abhorrence. The humiliation of the girl, the killing of her child lest it bring evil upon the members of the community, and the revulsion of feeling against her lover, all indicate that the people strongly condemned an occurrence of this nature. At the present time there is still a noticeable discrimination between premarital and marital pregnancies, but the whole attitude towards the former has become so very much milder that comparatively little disgrace is suffered by the people concerned.

Premarital Sex Relations of To-day

First of all it should be noted that premarital sexual intercourse, so far from being exceptional, has become a very widespread practice. Few of the BaKxatla, whether men or women, are still virgins at marriage. From the time when they are about seven or eight years old they begin to acquire sexual experience. The small boys and girls who play about together in the villages have a game called *mantlwane*. In this they build miniature huts of branches and leaves, and mimic the life of their parents. They pair off in couples as 'husband' and 'wife', and most of their play lies in dancing and singing, eating together, and celebrating mock 'marriages'. Frequently enough, however, the game takes on a definitely sexual character. In the intimacy of their huts the small boys will persuade their 'wives' to remove the tiny fringe which is their sole garment, and as they lie next to each other naked, they will

rub their genitals together, without, of course, achieving actual penetration. This is all part of the game of doing as their parents do, for the young children sleep in the same huts as their parents, and therefore have ample opportunity of spying upon their embraces. The boys boast to one another about their successes in this love-making, and taunt others with their failures. Sometimes they keep the same girl as 'wife' for a couple of weeks, but generally they change fairly rapidly from one to another. It is all regarded as play, but, at the same time, they attempt to conceal its true nature from the adults, who whip them whenever it is discovered what is actually going on.

From such beginnings it is not long before the adolescent children indulge in full intercourse. The *maxwane* (boys who are to be incorporated in the next *mophatô*) are notoriously addicted to sexual licence. These boys spend most of their time at the cattle-posts, where they talk a good deal about sex and prepare their *meratisô*, the love medicines with which they hope to win the favour of the girls. [...] Sometimes they will seize upon any girl whom they fancy, and ask her to sleep with them. She is by no means always unwilling, but, if she refuses, they whip her with the canes which they habitually carry and force her to comply with their wishes. Often two *maxwane* will copulate in succession with the same girl; they catch her when she is out alone, and compel her to accept their advances, or bribe her with gifts of beads and wooden spoons. At night they dance and sing in the open spaces of the village to the accompaniment of a girls' chorus. The songs, which they compose themselves, are often obscene and contain many insulting references to the girls with whom they have slept. At such gatherings I have often seen one of the boys, at the end of his dance, take a girl out of the chorus and walk away with her into the neighbouring bushes. Nobody takes any particular notice of this. If the girl resists he thrashes her, and, unless she succeeds in running away, she will be forcibly violated. She may afterwards complain to her parents, but apparently this is not often done, as she feels 'too ashamed'. But even if she does, little can be done, for the *maxwane* are allowed unbridled licence. [...] At most, the girl's father, if he catches the boy, may thrash him severely, but the opportunity for doing so seldom occurs, as the boys take good care to keep out of reach.

The sex relations just described are sporadic and casual, and in effect consist of the violation of a more or less unwilling girl. But many of the older *maxwane* and, above all, the unmarried men of the junior regiments, have their regular concubines (*dinyatsi*). By means of various small gifts, and also, they affirm, by the use of their love medicines, they win the favour of the girl, and then appear to have little difficulty in ultimately persuading her to sleep with them. At first she may be reluctant, partly because it is not 'good form' to accept a boy the first time he proposes cohabitation, but mainly owing to the fear of becoming pregnant. By promising to be careful, however, the boy will generally succeed in his object, and he will use the girl as a mistress as long as their mutual attraction lasts. He visits her at night in her hut (the older girls have separate huts of their own), and remains there alone with her until it is very late. Few of the unmarried young men whom I got to know well were without their mistresses, and they all asserted that the practice was very common. In fact, a boy who has not a *nyatsi* will be treated as a laughing-stock by the others. Such relationships often last for several months before the couple drift apart, although sometimes the affection between them deepens and they ultimately get married. Nowadays it is seldom that a boy's parents still choose his wife for him. He courts the girl himself and then tells his parents, who, if they approve of her, will enter into the necessary negotiations on his behalf.

In some cases unmarried girls are the concubines of men who are already married. Formerly such girls would probably have become the junior wives of these men, and very occasionally they still do; but the strong attitude taken up by the Church against polygyny has led to an obvious decay of the institution. Concubinage of this sort is a more lasting affair than where the two persons concerned are both unmarried, and the girl is, to all intents and purposes, the wife of the man in all but law. For the most part, however, married men take as their concubines young widows, who, in the olden days, would have been inherited by their deceased husband's brother, or else they visit the married women whose husbands have been away for a long time in the European centres of employment.

Social Attitude Towards Premarital Unchastity

In their attitude towards concubinage in general the BaKxatla vary a great deal. Some of my older informants, who were pillars of the Church, condemned the practice as indecent and shameful, but admitted that it had become very widespread and generally tolerated, and spoke sadly of moral degeneration. Others not only regarded it lightly, but even defended it, for reasons which will be discussed later on. The younger men, naturally enough, tended to approve of it, and cheerfully boasted of their *dinyatsi*. On the whole, it may be said that concubinage is now an accepted practice, although it is not officially admitted in Kxatla law, especially in the case of unmarried people.

The same variation is found in the care exercised by the people over the chastity of their daughters. Some parents encourage their daughters to receive male visitors, and give them every facility for being alone with the boys. The mothers will even teach their girls what love medicines to use in order to attract the young men to remain with them. Sometimes they act in this way because they are pleased that their daughters prove more attractive than those of other women. Sometimes they hope that one of the boys will ultimately marry the girl. Some are even more mercenary still, and, in effect, prostitute their daughters so as to be able to claim the fine of cattle which must be paid if she becomes pregnant. A few of them also believe that, if their daughter is still a virgin at marriage, she will hurt the back and thighs of her husband when he has intercourse with her, and are therefore willing to see her deflowered beforehand. [...]

Other parents, said to be in a minority nowadays, are more strict about the morals of their daughters. They discourage male visitors, and, if possible, never allow them to be alone in her hut with the girl. There is no legal redress for seduction when it is not followed by pregnancy, and the tribal courts will refuse to judge a case of this nature. But the father or guardian of the girl has the admitted right, if he catches the seducer red-handed, to inflict bodily hurt upon him. [...] The girl may also be whipped, but more often than not she is simply scolded. [...]

Pregnancy in Unmarried Women

It is only when pregnancy ensues that the girl's people have an actionable claim against her seducer. The BaKxatla practise several methods of avoiding conception. The majority of these consist in the woman's drinking or washing her body with herbal decoctions, either before or after intercourse; and they can scarcely be considered as in any way efficacious. The only practicable method known to them, and the one most generally employed, is *coitus interruptus*. Even this is not particularly reliable, especially as some of the young men admitted that after a while they tended to become rather careless about carrying it out properly. In consequence, it is not surprising that many of the girls sooner or later find themselves pregnant. [...]

A few of the girls, when they realize their condition, resort to abortion. Sometimes they make use of native roots and bulbs, but for the most part they fall back upon the rather crude expedient of drinking a mixture of ink and the pulverized heads of matches! A strong solution of 'washing blue', also obtained at the trader's store, is another favourite abortifacient. These girls are in some cases helped by their mothers, who want their daughters to make a good match. It is said that the men are not so ready to marry a girl who has already got a child, unless they are themselves responsible for its existence. If the abortion is reported to the *kxotla*, the girl's father is fined a few head of cattle. Generally, the matter is hushed up as far as possible, and unless a formal report is lodged with the *kxotla* no official notice may be taken of it. But the girl's action is often condemned by her relatives and friends, who feel that she has been rather foolish. Most of the girls allow their

children to be born, and there has been no case within recent times of an illegitimate child's being killed at birth, itself a most striking illustration of the great change that has taken place.

The general attitude nowadays towards girls who have been 'spoiled' is one of mild disapproval. There are still some families which look upon such an occurrence as disgracing them, but this is not generally the case. [...] The songs of mockery are a thing of the past; the girl observes no special taboos or usages to distinguish her from other pregnant women; her child is born with the same ceremonial as in the case of ordinary legitimate births; and she proudly nurses and walks about with it. If she is a Church member, however, she falls under the public censure of the Church authorities, and, as we have already noted, she is not considered as good a match as an 'unspoiled' woman. But so many of the unmarried young women are mothers that none of them need feel herself deeply shamed or humiliated. [...]

Treatment of the Girl's Lover

The boy who causes a girl to conceive has to pay her father a fine of cattle, which is fixed at four head. [...]

As soon as the girl is seen to be pregnant, she is asked by her mother to reveal the name of her lover. Her father then reports the fact of her pregnancy to the boy's people. If the boy admits his responsibility for her condition, the matter is often enough settled between them out of court, by the boy, or his father on his behalf, simply paying over the accepted number of cattle. [...] The cattle go, as a rule, to the father of the girl, the idea being that they compensate him for the damage he has suffered by the seduction of his daughter. But there is a growing tendency nowadays to regard them as providing rather for the maintenance of the child, and I was told of several instances in which a girl had claimed that she was entitled to them. The chief, in such cases, awarded the girl three of the cattle, allowing her father to keep the fourth as *mabula lebati*, the payment for 'opening the door' of his house.

Should the girl's lover desire to marry her, and she also is willing, he is not called upon to pay the fine, but he must give the usual *boxadi*. [...] Such marriages, in which the bride is either pregnant or already a mother, differ from the ordinary marriage in that none of the customary wedding feasts are held, nor are the couple allowed to get married in the tribal church unless the girl has first been formally readmitted to the fold.

When a boy, accused of having impregnated a girl, denies his guilt and refuses to pay the fine, the matter is brought before the *kxôsana* (headman) of his *kxôrô*. The headman tells the parents on both sides to await the birth of the child. When this occurs, it is reported to the local *kxotla* (court) by the girl's father. After two or three months all the people concerned, together with the child, come to the *kxotla*, where the headman now hears the case. The child is produced and inspected to see if it bears any resemblance to its putative father. If the latter still denies his paternity, the girl must produce witnesses to testify that he has often visited her at night, e.g. another girl who may have been present in the hut at such a time. If the boy is then found guilty, he is made to pay the customary fine, all of which goes to the girl's people. [...] No pressure is brought upon him to marry the girl, nor is he the object of the scorn occasionally directed against her by the older women.

Should a girl who has once given birth to an illegitimate child become pregnant again, whether by the same or another lover, no action can be brought before the *kxotla* by her father if he received payment of the normal fine on the first occasion. It is felt that, were this allowed, some parents would deliberately encourage their daughters to lead a loose life, in effect prostitute them, for the sake of the cattle, which could then be claimed whenever pregnancy ensued. [...]

In the olden days a man's cross-cousin was expected to be his first choice for a wife, a practice now falling away, although still kept up to some extent by the more conservative elements of the tribe. But even if a boy does not marry his cross-cousin, he is allowed to associate with her on terms of the greatest intimacy. It is said: *motswalao ke mosadi wa xaxo, xa xo rone le xe o ka robala naê*, 'your cross-cousin is your wife, there is no shame even though you sleep with her'.

Should he cause her to become pregnant, her parents have the right to claim the customary fine, but actually they seldom do so unless they are on bad terms with his side of the family.

The same leniency is practised when a girl is made pregnant by the boy to whom she is betrothed. He has the right to remain alone with her late at night, and it has become a common practice for them to sleep together during the period of betrothal, without any objection being raised by her parents. If she then becomes pregnant nothing is done as a rule, so long as the boy shows that he still intends to marry her. It is only when he tries to abandon her that pressure is brought to bear upon him to keep to his engagement, and should he refuse to do so he is severely penalized. [...]

Should a betrothed girl conceive by someone else than her fiancé, as is sometimes the case, her parents must report the fact to the boy and his people. The latter then have the right to state whether they wish to cancel the engagement, or are still willing to accept the girl into their family. If the boy decides that he no longer wants to marry her, her lover, in addition to paying the customary fine to her father, must also recompense the boy for the presents he made to the girl at betrothal. If, however, the fiancé agrees to go on with the match in spite of all that has happened, nothing is done to the lover unless the fiancé's people insist that the girl's father take up the matter against him. The fine that must then be paid all goes to the girl's father, the boy's people having no claim at all to any share of it. At marriage, too, the fiancé must state whether he wishes to take over the child as well as its mother. He is entitled to claim the child, in accordance with the rights he obtains over the girl's reproductive power by paying *boxadi* for her, but if he refuses to exercise his claim the child remains with its mother's people.

Status of Premarital Children

The child of an unmarried woman is known variously as *ngwana wa dikxora*, 'child of a full stomach', or *ngwana wa marêbana*, 'child who was born outside', or *ngwana wa dinyatsi*, 'child of concubines'. On the whole such children appear to be held in little respect, and are seldom shown any consideration, except by their mothers. They play about with the other children, but should any quarrel arise they will be taunted with their illegitimate birth. [...] The old people shake their heads sadly at the presence of such children, whom they believe to be partly responsible for the general decline in the health of the tribe. 'These children', they say, 'sit round the fire at the *kxotla* with our chiefs and our headmen, and make them weak so that they easily become sick and die.' But the younger generation regards this belief as old-fashioned superstition and prejudice. They have no scruples or fears about associating with illegitimate children, although, at the same time, they rather despise them for being fatherless. [...]

If the child is a girl, the *boxadi* paid when she becomes married goes to her mother's father or mother's brother, and not to her own father. [...] In this particular instance, the payment of the *boxadi* to the child's maternal relatives shows that they are held to be her guardians, and that her own father has no claim at all upon her. In other words, although the physiological fact of his paternity may be acknowledged, he is not regarded as the sociological or lawful father of the child.

But, as we have seen, the girl's lover has the right to marry her, and, if he does so, he takes the child as well. [...] Sometimes the lover wishes to take the child without marrying the mother, but in such cases every effort is made to induce him to make her his wife. In law, however, he has the admitted right to claim the child alone, by paying one or two head of cattle in addition to the normal fine of four cattle. [...]

As we have seen, it occasionally happens that a married man takes another woman as his concubine, and visits her regularly. This is done especially by men who have no children by their wives. It seldom happens that such a man is called upon to pay the usual fine if he causes the woman to conceive. Her people acquiesce in the relationship, so long as the lover feeds and clothes the woman and the children he has by her, helps her to cultivate her garden, and so on. Again, a boy too poor to find the *boxadi* cattle will sometimes be allowed by the girl's parents to visit her regularly at their home or even to take her to his own home, a small feast being first celebrated. Should the girl then bear him a child no action is taken against him.

In both cases the relationship between the man and the woman is considered regular, in that it meets with the approval of her people. But it is not regarded as a true marriage, owing to the fact that *boxadi* has not been given for the woman. [...]

If the union is accepted by the girl's people, then even although the *boxadi* has not been paid and she is, in consequence, not fully married, her children no longer suffer from the same stigma of being fatherless. It is the offspring of casual and unrecognized liaisons who are despised, not those of standing unions which meet with the sanction of the girl's family.

[...]

Factors Underlying the Modern Attitude

Reviewing the position generally, it will be seen that there has been a decided change in the Kxatla attitude towards premarital pregnancy. The old severity with which the woman was treated has given place to what may be described as at most a mild form of contempt; there is no longer the same conspicuous disgrace attaching to her, and the dreaded songs of mockery are a thing of the past. The unfortunate children are no longer killed at birth, but are allowed to take full part in the normal tribal life, although, as long as their mother remains unmarried, they labour under the stigma of being 'bastards'. Her subsequent marriage, however, restores her to a respectable status, and her children too are freed from their invidious position. The fine imposed upon the woman's lover is admitted by the people to be an innovation, and shows that they themselves were fully aware of the fact that the old moral sanctions were proving inadequate or had already become obsolete.

It should be emphasized, however, that although the general tribal attitude towards premarital pregnancy has grown so much more tolerant, such an occurrence is not yet altogether condoned. It is true that the woman suffers comparatively little, but she must still be married before she is fully restored to respectability. The fine imposed upon her lover likewise indicates that the community regards the impregnation of an unmarried woman as a punishable offence. In the case of the children, again, they labour under a social disadvantage which clings to them until their mother is married, and even then they do not always attain to equal rights with legitimate children in regard to succession and inheritance. All this shows that amongst the BaKxatla the principle of legitimacy still prevails, although the sanctions reinforcing it have grown very much milder. [...]

All my informants said that in the olden days no such licence was permitted. But they found it difficult to say why conditions have changed so markedly in this respect. Most of them declared with resignation that it was part of the general moral decay noticeable throughout the tribe. A few who regarded the matter with more interest suggested that it might be attributed to the abolition of the old initiation ceremonies, where the emphasis placed upon the sexual purity of the initiates had acted as a safeguard of chastity. Parents in the olden days would exercise every possible control over the behaviour of their children, lest the latter be disgraced in the initiation schools and suffer more severely in consequence. Nowadays there is no longer the same intimate connexion between initiation and the sexual life of the adolescent children, and as a result parental control has gradually grown weaker. Chastity is not demanded from those who have not yet been initiated, and accordingly the young people have not the same scruples about taking advantage of the opportunities that come their way.

The more intelligent natives with whom I discussed the whole problem attributed the greater sexual freedom of the present time to the fact that so many of the young men go out of the tribal reserve to work for the Europeans in rural and industrial centres. The boys periodically return home, but remain there for short intervals only before going out again to earn money for their taxes and newly-acquired economic necessities. In the towns they have numerous opportunities of indulging in sex, and in this way become accustomed to regarding sex relations lightly. On their return, well dressed and perhaps with money to spend, they appear desirable to the girls, whom they are generally able to seduce fairly easily, especially by promising at the same time to marry them. But often enough as soon as the girl becomes pregnant, the boy disappears again to the white centres of employment where he cannot be found.

Moreover, the absence of so many young men in the towns, a large number of whom drift away permanently from the tribe, has led to a surplus of marriageable women in the reserve. This means that as a rule a girl may have to wait several years after puberty before she is married. At the present time, the average age of marriage in the case of the men is from twenty-five to thirty, and in that of the girls from nineteen to twenty-six. 'It is against nature', as one of my informants put it, for the girls to remain chaste all this time, and most of them yield sooner or later to the advances of the young men. Some are never married at all, but remain *mafêtwa*, 'those who have been passed by', and it is amongst them that the married men often find their concubines. There is even a growing tendency, in spite of the opposition of the chief, for the girls to slip away into European areas, since at home there are not enough men to go round. They lose all hopes of getting married soon, and prefer the freedom of life away from the tribal control to the restrictions surrounding them if they remain.

By thus drawing away the young men to the labour centres, European civilization has unquestionably affected the pattern of sexual behaviour in the tribal reserve. In other respects, too, its influence has worked in the same direction. Education in the schools erected within the reserve, and the general infiltration of European cultural forces, have given the younger generation a greater sense of freedom than they formerly enjoyed. They no longer look to their parents for guidance in everything, but are tending to act more and more upon their own responsibility. [...]

The modern Kxatla girl, with her short European skirts and irresponsible behaviour, often herself takes the initiative in love-making. There has developed amongst them what might almost be termed a class of flappers. [...]

Still another contributory influence may be found in the fact that the Dutch Reformed Church, now the official religious body of the tribe, does not permit polygyny amongst its members. The Bechuanaland Protectorate Administration, by imposing an additional tax upon polygynists, has also assisted in the noticeable decline of the institution. [...] In consequence, many of the young women who would formerly have become the junior wives in a polygynous household now have to wait until the young men are able to marry them. The inevitable result has been the spread of concubinage. The older men have only one official wife, but many of them also keep one or more concubines whom in the olden days they would have married; while the girls, realizing that not all of them can be married, grow reconciled to living in this way. [...] There seems to be a general impression amongst the people that their rate of increase is dying down, and the men who keep concubines are said to help the tribe by giving it more children. [...]

The early missionaries are also said to have been responsible for the disappearance of the dreaded songs of mockery, which in the olden days were the most powerful sanction against premarital pregnancy. Objection was taken to their obscenity, and pressure exerted upon the chief to do away with them. The weight of his influence, together with the general change in attitude towards premarital sex relations, led in time to the complete abandonment of the songs. [...] 'These songs used to sadden the tribe, and they also helped to save many girls from becoming pregnant; they saddened the tribe because it felt grieved at so much cursing, they helped the girls and boys by making them fear the insults, so that they said, we shall be careful, they feared to sleep with the girls. And to-day the children do just as they please, they conceive in groups day by day and year by year. The only thing which they have to fear now is religion, and that is not so severe as the curses which they used to fear formerly' (free translation). The censure of the Church is a far less effective sanction than these songs used to be; it cannot affect the large section of the tribe which still clings to its heathenism, and public opinion in general is not too intolerant.

NOTE

1   His latest discussion appears in the essay: 'Parenthood, the Basis of Social Structure' (pp. 113–68 in *The New Generation*, edited by V. F. Calverton and S. D. Schmalhausen. London, 1930), which refers also to his previous writings on the subject.

Part VI

Sexual Repression: A Test Case

Introduction

The selection which follows, "Sex and Repression in an Irish Folk Community," by John Messenger, was published in a volume which appeared in 1971, but which drew on papers submitted to conferences of the American Anthropological Association in 1961 and the Central States Anthropological Society in 1965 (Marshall and Suggs 1971). The fieldwork on which it was based took place about 10 years before the collection was published (though Messenger and his wife continued visiting the island until 1966). In the essay, Messenger notes that the introduction of television and travel to the remote Irish island he called "Inis Beag" had greatly altered the culture described in the article, which refers only to the period between 1959 and 1960. This history is significant, because the article refers to a level of sexual repression which many found it hard to believe could exist in Western Europe in the middle of the twentieth century.

The sexual culture of Inis Beag has frequently been cited in the anthropological literature as a puzzling anomaly: what would cause a contemporary European culture to be so negative in its attitudes toward sexuality that marriage is late (with strict chastity for the unmarried), young people are given no sex education, husbands and wives make love fully clothed and without much pleasure, speech is highly censored to avoid any sexual innuendo, children are beaten for masturbating, and even dogs are punished for licking their genitals? The answers which have been given to this conundrum are in some ways an exercise in anthropological theory in microcosm. The culture and personality school, which had not yet lost its influence at the time the article appeared, suggested lack of maternal warmth as a reason for sexual inadequacy, particularly in males. This argument was found in a variety of works in the middle of the twentieth century. It was applied to cultures beyond Ireland, including the US, but Inis Beag seemed to be an extreme case. The bleak, chilly climate of

Sexualities in Anthropology: A Reader, edited by Andrew P. Lyons and Harriet D. Lyons
© 2011 Blackwell Publishing Ltd.

the island and the difficulty of earning a living by agriculture might suggest an eco-logical basis for a lack of interest in sensual indulgence. Inis Beag could also be seen as simply an extreme example of a tendency to late marriage (or lifelong bachelor-hood and spinsterhood), with a low incidence of out-of-wedlock births which had been noted elsewhere in Ireland. This had been explained by some as a direct result of the power of particularly ascetic orders of priests in the Irish Catholic Church, and by others as the result of a need to avoid dividing parcels of family land between multiple heirs. Still another suggestion Messenger considers is that Inis Beag is sim-ply a late example of a pattern of peasant culture which was once more general in Europe, a last outpost of pre-modernity. Messenger considers all of these possibili-ties, without definitively rejecting any of them, but not choosing any single explana-tion as "the" answer.

What should a contemporary student of anthropology learn from the curious case of Inis Beag? First, one might reflect on why we find such a culture worthy of com-ment, why a "deficiency" of sexual desire is something we think needs explanation. Secondly, we might reflect on the tendency of something we can't fully understand to become a kind of Rorschach test, telling us as much about our (or our culture's) attitudes to mothers, sex, Ireland, the Catholic Church, and rural life as it does about a vanished moment in the sexual history of a place which is at once remote and uncomfortably close.

REFERENCE

Marshall, Donald S. and Robert C. Suggs, eds.
   1971   Human Sexual Behavior. *In* Human Sexual Behavior: Variations in the Ethnographic Spectrum. Studies in Sex and Society. New York: Basic Books.

14

Sex and Repression
in an Irish Folk Community

John C. Messenger

In this chapter I will discuss sexual repression
– its manifestations in behavior and beliefs,
its causes, its inculcation, and its broader
historical and cultural implications – in a
small island community of the Gaeltacht that
I will call Inis Beag.[1] My wife and I conducted
ethnographic research there for nineteen
months, between 1958 and 1966, which
included a one-year stay and eight other visits
of from one to seven weeks – at Christmas or
during the summer. Ours is the only holistic
ethnographic study of this community,
although archeologists, linguists, philologists,
folklorists, geographers, anthropometricians,
and other scientists have undertaken research
there for over a century. We collected a large
body of culture and personality data on three
other Irish islands for the purposes of making
comparisons and testing hypotheses concerning culture and personality concomitants
of island living. Inis Beag is ideally suited
to ethnographic and folklore research in that
its population possesses a tradition which

is less acculturated than that of any other
local Irish group.

According to anthropological definition
(Lewis 1960: 1–2), the islanders qualify as folk
people in almost every respect. The community
has maintained its stability for at least 200
years; there is a strong bond between the peasants and their land, and agriculture provides
them with the major source of their livelihood;
production is mainly for subsistence and is
carried on with a simple technology, using the
digging stick, spade, and scythe as primary
implements; the island folk participate in a
money economy, but barter still persists; a low
standard of living prevails, and the birth rate is
high; the family is of central importance, and
marriage figures prominently as a provision of
economic welfare; the island is integrated into
the county and national governments and is
subject to their laws; the people have long been
exposed to urban influences and have borrowed
cultural forms from other rural areas on the
mainland, integrating them into a relatively

Extracts from John Messenger, Sex and Repression in an Irish Folk Community, from *Human Sexual
Behavior*, Robert M Suggs and Donald Marshall, eds., New York: Basic Books, pp 3–37. Copyright © 1971
by The Institute for Sex Research Inc. Reprinted by permission of The Kinsey Institute for Research in Sex,
Gender, and Reproduction, Inc.

Sexualities in Anthropology: A Reader, edited by Andrew P. Lyons and Harriet D. Lyons
© 2011 Blackwell Publishing Ltd.

stable system; and, finally, the experience of living under English rule for centuries has created in the islanders an attitude of dependence on – yet hostility toward – government which continues to this day. The only conditions in Inis Beag which run counter to those found in most other peasant communities are low death and illiteracy rates and bilateral, rather than unilineal, descent (although inheritance is patrilineal).

Inis Beag culture also characterizes people of nearby islands, and the traditions of the several together might be regarded as forming a subculture of the total Irish system. Many island customs are shared with rural peasants on the mainland (where numerous regional subcultures exist), and some are part of a broader European matrix. The island has experienced considerable cultural change since the establishment of the Congested Districts Board (forerunner of the Gaeltacht) in 1891 and the growth of tourism in this century. But conditions there still approximate those which must have prevailed two generations ago, and earlier, throughout this region of peasant Ireland.

Inis Beag has a population of approximately 350 persons living in seventy-one "cottages" distributed among four settlements, called "villages." Bordering a "strand" and a large tract of common land on the northeastern side of the island are a series of limestone terraces, separated by water-bearing shales and faced by small cliffs, on which the villages are situated. Most of the arable land is found on this side, where the shales have been broken down by weathering and alien soils deposited by wind and by ice of the Weichsel glacier. Over many generations, the islanders have deepened these soils and created new soils on rock surfaces by adding seaweed, sand, and human manure. On the southwestern side of Inis Beag, known as the "back of the island," limestone pavements slope rather evenly, almost as the gentle dip of the strata, from the crest of the highest terrace to the sea a mile away. The bared surfaces are intersected in all directions by crevices, which contain a large portion of the natural flora – herbs and shrubs – of the island. Stone fences delimit many hundreds of plots which compose most of the two-square-mile land surface of Inis Beag.

The island boasts a post office with radio-telephone facilities, a "national school" in which three teachers instruct ninety pupils in the seven "standards," two provision shops with attached "pubs," a former coast guard station now housing the nurse and a knitting industry which employs local girls, a lighthouse, and a chapel served by a curate who resides nearby. Inis Beag lacks electricity and running water, and the only vehicles are several ass-drawn carts which are able to travel the narrow, fence-bordered trails. A small "steamer" carrying supplies, passengers, and mail to and from a mainland port visits the island at least once each week. That Inis Beag has experienced far less cultural change than other island communities of Ireland is largely due to the fact that, in absence of a deep water quay, the steamer has had to stand off the strand and be met by "canoes." Most of the tourists who come to the island stay only for the hours that the steamer is anchored and go ashore mainly for the thrill of riding in the canoes, which the island men row with consummate skill. Insofar as I can discover, the inhabitants of Inis Beag are less prone to visit the mainland than are the peoples of other Irish islands.

Inis Beag History and Culture[2]

[...]

More important than the formal political structure of Inis Beag are the local informal system and social control techniques of gossip, ridicule, satire, and the like. Crime is rare in Inis Beag, and there are no "guards" stationed there. The island is seldom visited by politicians, and many inhabitants are either apathetic or antagonistic toward the county and national governments. Those asked to account for their antigovernment attitude cite widespread nepotism and corruption among officials, the slight differences between the platforms of the two major parties, and "foolish" government schemes in Inis Beag – usually instituted without consulting the islanders. Government aid is sought and even expected as a "right," but it is seldom considered adequate. Taxation in any form, especially of tobacco and stout, is bitterly opposed.

The informal political system is dominated by the curate, the "headmaster" of the national school, and a self-appointed local "king." In the past, the amount of influence exerted by curates has varied; some have been concerned mostly with fulfilling spiritual responsibilities, while others have attacked by sermon, threat, and even physical action such activities as courting, dancing, visiting, gossiping, and drinking spirits. Anticlerical sentiment (seldom manifested in overt acts) is as strong as, or stronger than, its antigovernment counterpart. The clergy are said to interfere too much in secular affairs, to live too "comfortably," to be absent from the island too often, and to act overly aloof and supercilious. The most outspoken anticlerics assert that curates have employed informers, allocated indulgences, withheld the sacraments, and placed curses ("reading the Bible at") in their efforts to regulate the secular life of Inis Beag. The headmaster, appointed and rigidly supervised by the parish priest and curate, presides over social events and serves as an adviser to the islanders in many matters, in addition to carrying out his official duties.

Inis Beag lacks a class system, and the status symbols which affect human relationships are few. There is, in fact, little difference in the style of life between the most and the least prosperous of the islanders. The web of kinship rather than the possession of status attributes, for the most part, determines who will interact with whom and in what manner. Land and money are the principal symbols, with formal education and influential relatives (particularly priests, nuns, and teachers), on the mainland and abroad, becoming more important. Two generations ago, strength, courage, economic skills, and musical and storytelling abilities were highly regarded as well, but acculturation has lessened their significance.

Although there are fifty-nine nuclear families, only thirteen surnames exist today. There is much inbreeding, as might be expected, and the church carefully checks the genealogies of prospective spouses to ascertain their degree of consanguinity. Courtship is almost nonexistent, and most marriages are arranged with little concern for the desires of the young people involved. Late marriage and celibacy are as prevalent in Inis Beag as elsewhere in Ireland.

The average marriage age for men is thirty-six and for women twenty-five, and 29 percent of those persons eligible for marriage are single.[3] The functions of the family are mainly economic and reproductive, and conjugal love is extremely rare. A sharp dichotomy exists between the sexes; both before and after marriage men interact mostly with men and women with women. The average family has seven offspring, and many women are unhappy about being forced by the unauthorized decree of local priests to produce as many children as possible. They feel that the constant bearing and rearing of offspring increase their work, restrict their freedom, and perpetuate the poverty of their families. Jealousy of the greater freedom of men is commonly expressed by women who have many young children. Mothers bestow a considerable amount of attention and affection on their offspring, especially on their sons. However, tensions between fathers and sons which develop in childhood often flare into scarcely repressed hostility later on, particularly in those families where competition for the inheritance of property is engendered among siblings by the fathers' attempts to ensure favored treatment in old age.

Men are far more active socially than are women. The latter are restricted by custom mostly to visiting, attending parties during the winter, and participating in church-associated activities. Many women leave their cottages only to attend mass, wakes, and funerals or to make infrequent calls on relatives; my wife and I talked with some elderly women who had not visited other villages or walked to the back of the island for thirty or more years. Men not only attend parties with their womenfolk but go to dances during the summer, frequent the pubs, play cards almost nightly during November and December (the period when once people congregated to hear storytellers), visit the homes of kin and friends or meet along the trails at night, and range the entire island and the sea about it in their economic pursuits. Before the age of benevolent government, women shared many economic tasks with men, such as collecting seaweed, baiting lines, and gutting fish. But now they tend to household chores and only milk cows and perform some of the lighter farming jobs with their fathers and husbands.

The island folk are devout Catholics, despite the fact that they are critical of their priests and hold pagan religious beliefs. Youth of Inis Beag overtly disallow the existence of other than church-approved supernatural entities. However, their elders cling to traditional pagan beliefs and practices (many of which are Druidic in origin) about which they are extremely secretive for fear of being ridiculed by outsiders and their more skeptical neighbors. [...] The only form of witchcraft practiced today is the casting of the evil eye. At least three persons, suitably ostracized, are believed to be able to perpetrate evil by the act of complimenting their victims. Other religious retentions found in Inis Beag are a multitude of taboos, divination through the seeking of omens, magical charms and incantations of a protective nature, and an emphasis on "natural" foods, folk medicines, and other products impinging on the human body.

It is believed by many people in Ireland that the Catholicism of the islanders embodies an ideal unattained on the mainland, where the faith is thought to set an example for the world. In fact, the worship of the folk is obsessively oriented toward salvation in the next world, with a corresponding preoccupation with sin in this world; there is a resemblance to polytheism in the manner in which they relate to the Blessed Virgin and Irish saints; Christian as well as pagan rituals and religious artifacts are often employed to serve magical ends; and many beliefs that they hold to be orthodox Catholic are in reality idiosyncratic to Inis Beag or Ireland. Christian morality in its "outward" manifestations is realized to a remarkable degree. This can be attributed, in part, to the emphasis placed on good works as a means of gaining salvation; but, more importantly, it results from the already-mentioned techniques of social control exercised by the clergy, based on an overwhelming fear of damnation.

Research Procedures

[...]

My wife and I devoted most of our research to documenting the contemporary culture of Inis Beag: its economic, political, social, religious, esthetic, and recreational aspects. We also described formal and informal education and the personality traits formed by it, reconstructed Inis Beag history of the past century by examining historical materials of many types and probing the memories of aged island respondents, and recorded cultural change in process over an eight-year period. The standard ethnographic research techniques that we employed include guided and open-ended interviews, external and participant observation, collection of life histories, cross-checking, photography, and phonography. The sample for much of our data was the total universe of 350 inhabitants.

It is extremely difficult to obtain information in Inis Beag about such matters as amounts and sources of income, disputes, pagan religious retentions and reinterpretations, and sex. [...]

Our data on sex came from my involvement as a participant-observer in personal and often intimate conversations with men and my wife's counseling of women who were bothered by such matters as explaining and coping with menstruation, menopause, mental illness, the sexual curiosity of their children, and "excessive" sexual demands of their spouses. Our sexual knowledge and sympathy coupled with their needs and inquisitiveness gave rise to a "counselor-client" relationship between many of the folk and ourselves. They came to speak freely, albeit indirectly at times, with each of us about this sphere of behavior which arouses so much anxiety and fear. I must mention that the relationship arose partly out of our desire to alleviate distress and not solely to collect information. We had performed the same role seven years earlier among primitive Nigerians, and for similar reasons. However, the Africans were uninhibited, talked freely with us about sex, and were not offended by what we subsequently wrote.

Another important source of information on sex was the island nurses, who supplied us with accounts of their own observations over an eight-year period and gave us access to pertinent medical records. My wife and I believe that our information is, for the most part, reliable, but that some of it may well be erroneous. This report will, we are afraid, offend and alienate some of our Inis Beag friends, for whom we hold deep affection; they do not comprehend the aims and values of anthropology and may regard our reporting of sexual beliefs and behavior as a breach of friendship and trust. Certainly our findings will be denied by many Irish readers. [...]

Sexual Repression: Its Manifestations

Both lack of sexual knowledge and misconceptions about sex among adults combine to brand Inis Beag as one of the most sexually naive of the world's societies. Sex never is discussed in the home when children are about; only three mothers admitted giving advice, briefly and incompletely, to their daughters. We were told that boys are better advised than girls, but that the former learn about sex informally from older boys and men and from observing animals. Most respondents who were questioned about sexual instructions given to youths expressed the belief that "after marriage nature takes its course," thus negating the need for anxiety-creating and embarrassing personal confrontation of parents and offspring. We were unable to discover any cases of childlessness based on sexual ignorance of spouses, as reported from other regions of peasant Ireland. Also, we were unable to discover knowledge of the sexual categories utilized by researchers in sex: insertion of tongue while kissing, male mouth on female breast, female hand on penis, cunnilingus, fellatio, femoral coitus, anal coitus, extramarital coitus, manifest homosexuality, sexual contact with animals, fetishism, and sado-masochistic behavior. Some of these activities may be practiced by particular individuals and couples; however, without a doubt they are deviant forms in Inis Beag, about which information is difficult to come by.

Menstruation and menopause arouse profound misgivings among women of the island, because few of them comprehend their physiological significance. My wife was called on to explain these processes more than any other phenomena related to sex. When they reach puberty, most girls are unprepared for the first menstrual flow and find the experience a traumatic one – especially when their mothers are unable to provide a satisfactory explanation for it. And it is commonly believed that the menopause can induce "madness"; in order to ward off this condition, some women have retired from life in their mid-forties and, in a few cases, have confined themselves to bed until death, years later. Others have so retired as a result of depressive and masochistic states. Yet the harbingers of "insanity" are simply the physical symptoms announcing the onset of menopause. In Inis Beag, these include severe headaches, hot flashes, faintness in crowds and enclosed places, and severe anxiety. Mental illness is also held to be inherited or caused by inbreeding (or by the Devil, by God punishing a sinner, or by malignant pagan beings) and stigmatizes the family of the afflicted. One old man came close to revealing what is probably the major cause of neuroses and psychoses in Ireland, when he explained the incarceration of an Inis Beag curate in a mental institution for clerics as caused by his constant association with a pretty housekeeper, who "drove him mad from frustration." This elder advocated that only plain-appearing older women (who would not "gab" to "our man") be chosen for the task. Earlier, according to island opinion, the same priest had caused to be committed to the "madhouse" a local man who publicly challenged certain of his actions. The unfortunate man was released six months later, as per law, since he was not mentally ill.

Sexual misconceptions are myriad in Inis Beag. The islanders share with most Western peoples the belief that men by nature are far more libidinous than women. The latter have been taught by some curates and in the home that sexual relations with their husbands are a "duty" which must be "endured," for to refuse coitus is a mortal sin. A frequently encountered assertion affixes the guilt for male sexual strivings on the enormous intake of potatoes of the Inis Beag male. (In Nigeria, among the people whom my wife and I studied, women are thought to be more sexually disposed than men and are the repositories of sexual knowledge; it is they who initiate coitus and so pose a threat to their spouses. Nigerian men place the blame on clitoridectomy performed just prior to marriage.) Asked to compare the sexual proclivities of Inis Beag men and women, one mother of nine said, "Men can wait a long time before wanting 'it,' but we can wait a lot longer." There is much evidence to indicate that the female orgasm is unknown – or at least doubted, or considered a deviant response. One middle-aged bachelor, who considers himself wise in the ways of the outside world and has a reputation for making love to willing tourists, described one girl's violent bodily reactions to his fondling and asked for an explanation; when told the "facts of life" of what obviously was an orgasm, he admitted not realizing that women also could achieve a climax, although he was aware that some of them apparently enjoyed kissing and being handled.

Inis Beag men feel that sexual intercourse is debilitating, a common belief in primitive and folk societies. They will desist from sex the night before they are to perform a job which will require the expenditure of great energy. Women are not approached sexually during menstruation or for months after childbirth, since they are considered "dangerous" to the male at these times. Returned "Yanks" have been denounced from the pulpit for describing American sexual practices to island youths, and such "pornographic" magazines as *Time* and *Life*, mailed by kin from abroad, have aroused curates to spirited sermon and instruction.

The separation of the sexes, started within the family, is augmented by separation in almost all segments of adolescent and adult activity. Boys and girls are separated to some extent in classrooms, and completely in recess play and movement to and from school. During church services, there is a further separation of adult men and women, as well as boys and girls, and each of the four groups leaves the chapel in its turn. The pubs are frequented only by men or by women tourists and female teachers who have spent several years on the mainland while training and thus are "set apart" (and, of course, by inquisitive female ethnographers). Women occasionally visit the shops to procure groceries, but it is more common for them to send their children to do so, since supplies and drinks are proffered across the same counter, and men are usually to be found on the premises. Even on the strand during summer months, male tourists tend to bathe at one end and women at the other. Some swimmers "daringly" change into bathing suits there, under towels and dresses – a custom practiced elsewhere in Ireland which has overtones of sexual catharsis.

It is often asserted that the major "escape valve" of sexual frustration among single persons in Ireland is masturbation; frustration-aggression theorists, however, would stress the ubiquity of drinking, alcoholism, disputes, and pugnacity as alternative outlets. Pugnacity can also be linked to the widespread problem of male identity. Our study revealed that male masturbation in Inis Beag seems to be common, premarital coitus unknown, and marital copulation limited as to foreplay and the manner of consummation. My wife and I never witnessed courting – "walking out" – in the island. Elders proudly insist that it does not occur, but male youths admit to it in rumor. The claims of young men focus on "petting" with tourists and a few local girls, whom the "bolder" of them kiss and fondle outside of their clothing. Island girls, it is held by their "lovers," do not confess these sins because they fail to experience pleasure from the contact. The male perpetrators also shun the confessional because of their fear of the priest.

We were unable to determine the frequency of marital coitus. A considerable amount of evidence indicates that privacy in the act is stressed and that foreplay is limited to kissing and rough fondling of the lower body, especially the buttocks. Sexual activity invariably is initiated by the husband. Only the male superior position is employed; intercourse takes place with underclothes not removed; and orgasm, for the man, is achieved quickly, almost immediately after which he falls asleep. (I must stress the provisional nature of these data, for they are based on a limited sample of respondents and relate to that area of sexual behavior least freely discussed.)

Many kinds of behavior disassociated from sex in other societies, such as nudity and physiological evacuation, are considered sexual in Inis Beag. Nudity is abhorred by the islanders, and the consequences of this attitude are numerous and significant for health and survival. Only infants have their entire bodies sponged once a week, on Saturday night;

children, adolescents, and adults, on the same night, wash only their faces, necks, lower arms, hands, lower legs, and feet. Several times my wife and I created intense embarrassment by entering a room in which a man had just finished his weekly ablutions and was barefooted; once when this occurred, the man hurriedly pulled on his stockings and said with obvious relief, "Sure, it's good to get your clothes on again." Clothing always is changed in private, sometimes within the secrecy of the bedcovers, and it is usual for the islanders to sleep in their underclothes.

Despite the fact that Inis Beag men spend much of their time at sea in their canoes, as far as we could determine none of them can swim. Four rationales are given for this deficiency: the men are confident that nothing will happen to them, because they are excellent seamen and weather forecasters; a man who cannot swim will be more careful; it is best to drown immediately when a canoe capsizes far out in the ocean rather than swim futilely for minutes or even hours, thus prolonging the agony; and, finally, "When death is on a man, he can't be saved." The truth of the matter is that they have never dared to bare their bodies in order to learn the skill. Some women claim to have "bathed" at the back of the island during the heat of summer, but this means wading in small pools with skirts held knee-high, in complete privacy. Even the nudity of household pets can arouse anxiety, particularly when they are sexually aroused during time of heat. In some homes, dogs are whipped for licking their genitals and soon learn to indulge in this practice outdoors. My wife, who can perform Irish stepdances and sing many of the popular folk songs, was once requested to sing a seldom-heard American Western ballad; she chose "The Lavendar Cowboy," who "had only two hairs on his chest." The audience response was perfunctory and, needless to say, she never again was "called out" to sing that particular song.

The drowning of seamen, who might have saved themselves had they been able to swim, is not the only result of the sexual symbolism of nudity; men who were unwilling to face the nurse when ill, because it might have meant baring their bodies to her, were beyond help when finally treated. While my wife and I were on the island, a nurse was assaulted by the mother of a young man for diagnosing his illness and bathing his chest in the mother's absence. (In this case, Oedipal and sexual attitudes probably were at work in tandem.)

It must be pointed out that nudity is also shunned for "health" reasons, for another obtrusive Inis Beag character trait is hypochondria. In some cases, however, it is hard to determine whether concern with modesty or health is dominant in a particular behavioral response. Fear of colds and influenza is foremost among health concerns; rheumatism and related muscular joint ailments, migraine headaches and other psychosomatic disorders, tooth decay, indigestion ("nervous stomach"), and hypermetropia are other widespread pathologies which cause worry among the folk – not to mention those of supernatural origin.

Secrecy surrounds the acts of urination and defecation. The evacuation of infants before siblings and strangers is discouraged, and animals that discharge in the house are driven out. Chickens that habitually "dirty" their nests while setting are soon killed and eaten. Although some women drink spirits privately, they seldom do so at parties. In part this is because of the embarrassment involved in visiting the outside toilet with men in the "street" looking on. One of the most carefully guarded secrets of Inis Beag, unreported in the many works describing island culture, is the use of human manure mixed with sand as a fertilizer. We were on the island eight months before we discovered that compost is not "street drippings" and "scraw," but decomposed feces. With "turf" becoming more difficult to procure from the mainland, some islanders have taken to importing coal and processed peat and burning cattle dung. The dung is prepared for use in difficult-to-reach plots at the back of the island when tourists are few in number it is burned covertly because of the overtones of sex and poverty. Another custom that my wife and I learned of late in our research, due to the secrecy surrounding it, concerns the thickening of wool; men are required to urinate in a container and tread the wool therein with their bare feet.

Other major manifestations of sexual repression in Inis Beag are the lack of a "dirty joke" tradition (at least as the term is understood by ethnologists and folklorists) and the style of dancing, which allows little bodily contact among participants. I have heard men use various verbal devices – innuendoes, puns, and asides – that they believed bore sexual connotations; relatively speaking, they were pallid. In the song that I composed,[4] one line of a verse refers to an island bachelor arising late in the day after "dreaming perhaps of a beautiful mate"; this is regarded as a highly suggestive phrase, and I have seen it redden cheeks and lower glances in a pub. Both step- and set-dancing are practiced in Inis Beag, although the former type is dying out. This rigid-body dancing, from which sex is removed by shifting attention below the hips, appears to have originated in Ireland during the early nineteenth century. The set patterns keep partners separated most of the time; but, even so, some girls refuse to dance, because it involves touching a boy. Inis Beag men, while watching a woman step-dance, stare fixedly at her feet, and they take pains to appear indifferent when crowding at a party necessitates holding women on their laps and rubbing against them when moving from room to room. But they are extremely sensitive, nevertheless, to the entire body of the dancer and to these casual contacts, as are the women. Their covert emotional reactions (which become overt as much drink is taken) are a form of catharsis.

Sexual Repression: Its Historical Causes

Analysts of Irish character have put forth various hypotheses to account for sexual repression, ranging from the sophisticated to the absurd. The former can be classified under three rubrics: historical (e.g., the influence of ascetic monasticism, Augustinianism, and Jansenism),[5] sociocultural (e.g., the Oedipus complex in the Irish family and male solidarity), and psychological (e.g., masochism). Beyond serious scientific consideration are such hypotheses as the loss of the Irish tongue, lack of a Catholic aristocracy, fear of Protestant libertinism, and the ever-appealed-to factors of race, climate, and the famine. In the following

paragraphs, I will quote excerpts from Irish authors and from critical observers of the Irish scene. [...]

Paul Blanshard, in his polemical but insightful (and, in my estimation, often understated) work, *The Irish and Catholic Power*, says that "whatever the explanation, the total sexual expression of the Irish people is much less than it is in other countries, and that the Catholic crusade against normal sexual life has actually created a nation of men and women who try to drown their fundamental instincts." In attempting to account for sexual repression on such a scale, he writes:

Ireland was ... one of the world's most ascetic countries, and the monastic ideal has undoubtedly left a deep mark on the Irish mind. Although Irish priests were permitted to have wives as late as the eighth century, sexual renunciation came to be identified with virtue and distinction in the community, and thousands of the best men and women lived apart from each other. Kevin Devlin in his *Christus Rex* article on "Single and Selfish" ... says of the ancient Irish that "when they 'fell in love with Christianity' ... they took to the ideal of virginity with a Pauline enthusiasm unknown elsewhere. St. Patrick himself noted this with an inflection of surprise in the *Confessions* ..." (Blanshard 1954: 160–161).

Several Irish scholars since 1955 have expressed the opinion in personal conversations that the rapidity of Irish conversion to monasticism in the early medieval period can be attributed, in large measure, to masochism. This ancient character trait is most evident in the projective system of early Irish verbal art, if one discounts the possibility of widespread distortion through the actions of Celtic defense mechanisms and later revisionists. [...]

Granted the profound influence social structure has on such a basic matter, a purely structural-functional analysis is hard put to explain adequately the quite ascetic sexual morality of the Irish countryside.... [An] attitude similar to that of the countryman is far from uncommon in a city such as Dublin – and among New Dubliners and Old Dubliners to boot – whose social structure differs so radically from that of the countryside. Structural-functional explanations of attitudes do hold up to a point. But world-views and their ethical consequences also have their special effect (Humphreys 1966: 24–27).

Monasticism and Augustinianism certainly "set the stage" for later Jansenism, although all three probably are connected with basic Irish culture and personality traits of long standing.

Jansenism is succinctly placed in its historical context in Ireland by Joe McCarthy.

Like most everything in Ireland, the severe strictness of the old-time Catholic clergymen was rooted in historical events of the country's past. During the dark era of the anti-Catholic Penal Laws in the 18th Century, young Irishmen had to study for the priesthood on the Continent. In the early 1790's, the British Government became alarmed by the rise of Theobald Wolfe Tone's Irish Protestant revolutionary movement and made hurried bids of appeasement to Irish Catholics in an effort to win their loyalty. One of these conciliatory moves was the establishment of the Catholic theological seminary at Maynooth in 1795. Perhaps not entirely by accident, the faculty of the new college was staffed by refugees from the French Revolution, promonarchy theologians who hated Tone's republican ideas. Most of these theologians had been influenced by Jansenism – the rigid and gloomy doctrine, denounced as Calvinistic by the Jesuits, that man is a helplessly doomed being who must endure punishing soul-searching and rigorous penances to prove his love of God. Mere faith and constant church-going ... are not enough to win salvation [...] (McCarthy 1964: 78).

Our research reveals that in some areas of Ireland "the last vestiges of the doctrine" are still associated with Irish Catholicism. In fact, one Dublin social scientist with whom I correspond asserts that Jansenism as manifested in sexual repression probably reached its zenith in the 1930s and has gradually been dying out since then. However, it is still very apparent, even among "emancipated" Dubliners of the middle and upper classes.

A much harsher evaluation of Jansenism, again in an historical context, is found in Bryan McMahon's chapter in *The Vanishing Irish*, edited by Fr. John O'Brien, a collection which also includes pertinent essays by Arland Ussher and the editor himself. McMahon says:

Associated with the heresy of Jansenism were the principles of an exaggerated moral and disciplinary rigorism under the pretext of a return to the primitive Church. [...] The penances of the early Celtic monks were severity itself.... Significant in this context is the presence of four refugee doctors of the Sorbonne on the staff of Maynooth College in its early and formative years. [Their] teachings ... cannot but have in some measure colored ... the whole course of Irish seminary life and consequently the whole body of Irish lay thought (O'Brien 1953: 215–216).

[...]

The impact of the Oedipus complex on Irish character has been explored by cultural analysts and writers almost from the time Freud first conceptualized the phenomenon. Indeed, Freud might have been describing Ireland rather than a particular class in Austria at the turn of the century (just as Marx might have had Ireland in mind when positing religion as the opiate of the oppressed masses). Two recent controversial novels use the Oedipus complex as a focus. *Michael Joe*, by William Murray, examines the role of the emasculating Irish mother, and John McGahern, in *The Dark*, probes the conflict between father and son so characteristic of Irish society.

One of the most penetrating studies of this sociocultural configuration, which has such momentous psychological consequences, is that of Marvin Opler and Jerome Singer, conducted among first, second, and third generation Irish male schizophrenic patients in New York hospitals. The intent of these social scientists was to determine how psychotic syndromes are culturally patterned. For a year they observed their respondents to obtain total psychiatric, anthropological, and psychological profiles. Their observations included ward scrutiny, interviews, the collection of life histories and case histories, and the administration of thirteen tests, among them the Rorschach, Thematic Apperception, Sentence Completion, and Porteus Maze. The investigators conclude that there is a continuity of Irish (and Italian) culture and personality forms among immigrants for at least three generations; their psychological findings are buttressed by research data collected in Irish and English mental institutions. My wife and I visited one of these hospitals and interviewed several Irish psychiatrists both there and in America. Our own conclusions support many of those reported by Opler, Singer, and the psychiatrists interviewed. Opler and Singer have the following to say about the Oedipus complex in Ireland:

> Normative cultural standards led to the hypothesis that the central female figure in the Irish family, the mother, could instil primary anxiety and fear toward female figures.... This hypothesis grew out of anthropological observations that the central figure in Irish families is more likely to be a controlling figure on the distaff side, while fathers, especially in straitened economic circumstances, are frequently by contrast shadowy and evanescent.... An Irish male patient beset with anxiety and fear of female figures early in life, and lacking possibilities of firm male identification with a father, would later experience the sexual repressions and socio-religious definitions of marriage and sexuality for which his culture, with its high celibacy rates, protracted engagements, and sin-guilt emphases, is justly famous.... all this spells a final anxious and fearful lack of positive sexual identification, varying in a continuum from repressed and latent homosexual balances through to added displacements and distortions that are either pallid asexuality or fearful and bizarre misidentifications. Since the culture does not condone sexual expression or postpones and then rigidly defines it in marriage ... latent homosexual balances [were hypothesized] for this group, no overtly sought interpersonal manifestations, and a facade of asexual misogyny varied only by the most personalized and bizarre female identifications.... [The] basic personality has stamped into it such feelings as male inadequacy, the masculine protest, hostility toward females, and the kind of latent homosexual feelings

which produce a further sense of sin and guilt (Opler and Singer 1956: 15–18).

Among the seven diagnostic variables utilized by the researchers, the Irish patients ranked highest in the "Sin, Sex, and Guilt Ideology" (93 percent of the sample) and "Homosexuality Types" (90 percent of the sample latent, none overt) categories.

Complementing the Oedipus complex in the etiology of sexual puritanism is male solidarity. It has a long history in Ireland – revealed in legend and modern literature alike – and is instrumental in delaying marriage and making for marital maladjustment. Freudian psychologists see it as one of the many possible by-products of the "universal" Oedipus complex – "male inadequacy, the masculine protest, hostility toward females, and ... latent homosexual feelings"; but many anthropologists (especially structural-functionalists) analyze it as a sociocultural phenomenon, for it is found in societies in which the Oedipal configuration appears not to exist. [...]

Sexual Repression: Its Inculcation

The inculcation of sexual puritanism in Inis Beag must be examined in four contexts: the role of the curate, the influence of visiting missions, enculturation in the home, and what I will term "secular social control" – the behavioral regulations imposed on themselves by Inis Beag adolescents and adults. It is through these agencies that Jansenism, masochism, the Oedipus complex, male solidarity, and other inextricably linked factors shape the severe sexual repression which gives rise to the cultural manifestations discussed in the last section of the chapter.

Priests of Jansenist persuasion have had subtle means of repressing the sexual instincts of the islanders in addition to the more extreme methods of controlling behavior – "clerical social control," such as employing informers, allocating indulgences, and refusing the sacraments to, and placing curses on, miscreants. Through sermons and informal classroom talks, the pulpit and the national school have served as effective vehicles of church discipline. The talks are especially telling, since they take advantage of the personality malleability of the formative years. The adult Irish person is rare who, although anticlerical, and even agnostic or atheistic, can transcend these early enculturative experiences, particularly in times of social crisis or personality disorganization. Erring islanders have often been sought out by priests and talked to privately after their ways have become known through gossip, informers, or the confessional. Some curates have suppressed courting, dancing, visiting, and other behavior either directly or "indirectly" (widely interpreted in Ireland) sexual in nature by physical action: that is, roaming the trails and fields at night seeking out young lovers and halting dancing by their threatening presence. This outward form of intrusion into island affairs is resented by most folk, as is the inward intrusion through priestly remonstrances; they question the right of the young, virginal, inexperienced, and sexually unknowledgeable curates to give advice in this sphere.

Church influence is also exerted through missions which visit Inis Beag every three to five years. On these occasions, two Redemptorist priests (occasionally Franciscans, Dominicans, or Passionists) spend a week on the island, where they conduct mass each morning and deliver long sermons in the chapel every afternoon or early evening. Everyone, even old people and mothers with young infants, is urged to attend to receive the "blessings of the mission." To some, this means shortening the time in purgatory for themselves or a deceased relative (an indulgence used to enforce church discipline). To others, absence carries with it the penalty of damnation, just as viewing an eel or small fish in the sacred well, appropriated from the Druids, promises salvation in an equally magical fashion. A mission usually has a theme, the variations of which are explored with high emotion and eloquence by the visiting clerics in their exhortations. The most common theme is "controlling one's passions," but two others have often been addressed in the missionizing effort: abstaining from intoxicating drink and maintaining the faith as an emigrant. Collections are made by children to support the endeavor, and a list of

contributors and their respective donations is displayed publicly. This technique of social control is also used by the curate at the several yearly offerings. A mission creates an emotionally charged atmosphere on the island, which continues for weeks after the departure of the clerics.

The seeds of repression are planted early in childhood by parents and kin through instruction supplemented by rewards and punishments, conscious imitation, and unconscious internalization. Although mothers bestow considerable affection and attention on their offspring, especially on their sons, physical love as manifested in intimate handling and kissing is rare in Inis Beag. Even breast feeding is uncommon because of its sexual connotation, and verbal affection comes to replace contact affection by late infancy. Any form of direct or indirect sexual expression – such as masturbation, mutual exploration of bodies, use of either standard or slang words relating to sex, and open urination and defecation – is severely punished by word or deed. Care is taken to cover the bodies of infants in the presence of siblings and outsiders, and sex is never discussed before children. Several times my wife inadvertently inquired as to whether particular women were pregnant, using that word before youths, only to be "hushed" or to have the conversation postponed until the young people could be herded outside. The adults were so embarrassed by the term that they found it difficult to communicate with her after the children had departed. She once aroused stupefaction among men on the strand when she attempted unsuccessfully to identify the gender of a bullock about to be shipped off.

It is in the home that the separation of sexes, so characteristic of Inis Beag life, is inaugurated among siblings in early childhood. Boys and girls in the family remain apart not only when interacting with the parent of the same sex at work, but when playing in and near the cottage and traveling to and from school. Parents and their older offspring read popular religious journals, found in most homes, many of the articles in which deal with sexual morality of the Irish Catholic variety.

One sociologist (Berger 1963: 66–92) classifies social control methods as those which involve physical violence or its threat (e.g., political and legal sanctions), those which result in economic pressures (e.g., occupation and market place relations), and, finally, those which govern our "morality, custom, and manners" (e.g., persuasion, ridicule, and gossip). I will not consider political and economic manipulation; more significant are other techniques that I have labelled secular social control. Inis Beag, as much as any human community, is characterized by gossip, ridicule, and opprobrium. Influenced by nativism, primitivism, and structural-functional theory, writers and social scientists have painted a distorted picture of culture and personality equilibrium among Irish peasants. Actually, the folk are neither glorified Celts nor "noble savages," and dysfunctional sociocultural forms, mental aberrations (neuroses, psychoses, and psychosomatic disorders), and exaggerated defense postures abound.

Inis Beag people are ambivalent about gossip; they welcome every opportunity to engage in it, yet detest the practice when they are its victims. When asked to cite the major deficiencies of their way of life, islanders usually place the prevalence of malicious gossiping near the top of their list. Boys and men hide themselves in the darkness or behind fences to overhear the conversations of passersby; they maintain close scrutiny of visitors during the summer, both day and night, in order to discover them in "compromising" situations. Parties are organized at the last moment and persons will leave the island without any previous announcement – often to emigrate or enter the hospital or join a religious order – in order to circumvent gossip. Rumors run rife in Inis Beag, especially when they concern, for example, the "nude" sun bathing of a visiting actress (bared shoulders and lower thighs) or the "attack" on a Dublin girl late at night by an island youth (an effort to hold her hand while under the influence of stout). Over a dozen efforts on our part to determine the truth behind the most pernicious rumors of this genre revealed sexual fantasy at their core in every case.

The force most responsible for limiting the potential social activities of women – which would make their lot much easier and possibly stem the tide of emigration – is the fear of gossip: "If I went for a walk, they'd wonder why I wasn't home tending my chores." Even couples who might otherwise disregard religious teachings and the wrath of the priest do not court, because it might be observed and reported through gossip to the entire population.[6] An islander must carefully regulate his own words and actions in the presence of others so that the fires of factionalism are not ignited. Equally feared are informers of the curate and relatives or close friends of persons in an audience who might be offended by a heedless remark brought to their attention by the listeners.

It is sometimes heard in Ireland, from those aware of, and willing to admit, the fact, that the inability of most Irish to "share themselves" with one another, even husbands and wives, is a heritage of the fear of gossip – a fear that one's intimate revelations will become common knowledge and lead to censure and "loss of face." A more likely explanation, according to those of Freudian bent, is the Oedipus configuration, which numbers among its many effects the following: the prevalence of romantic attachments and the rarity of conjugal love; the lack of sexual foreplay, marked by little or no concern with the female breast; the brevity of the coital act and the frequent spurning of the woman following it; the need to degrade the woman in the sexual encounter and the belief that the "good" woman does not like sex, and, conversely, that the sexually disposed woman is by virtue of the fact "bad." All of these widely reported phenomena bespeak the overwhelming influence of the mother image.

Ridicule and opprobrium, as well as satire in song and tale, are effective control mechanisms in light of the emphasis placed by Inis Beag folk on saving face. Most islanders could not believe that I was author of the ballad referred to in footnote 4 because several stanzas attack my character; they find it difficult to conceive of anyone publicly proclaiming their own faults, under any circumstances. Opinions, once formed, are clung to tenaciously, even in light of obviating circumstances, since to alter them would be an admittance that they were ill advised in the first instance. The folk pride themselves on being able to judge a stranger's character immediately on meeting him, and this initial impression is rarely modified no matter how long their interaction continues. A seldom revealed tradition of satirical balladry exists in Inis Beag, but its employment is infrequent and then calculated according to singer and audience so as not to offend directly. Apprehensiveness and anxiety about real and imagined ego assaults by others are dominant personality traits of the islanders.

Historical and Cultural Implications

I have already touched tangentially on some of the historical and broad cultural implications of sexual puritanism, in Ireland as well as Inis Beag. In this final section, I will examine the perennially addressed phenomena of late marriage, celibacy, and emigration, in their island setting, with special reference to the factor of sexual repression.

In a population of 350, 116 persons are married, 13 are widows, 3 are widowers, and 33 males over twenty-three years of age and 21 females over seventeen are single. Since marriage occurs between twenty-four and forty-five for men and eighteen and thirty-two for women, on the basis of past statistics, only 18 men and 9 women are eligible for marriage. As mentioned earlier, the average marriage age for males is thirty-six and for females twenty-five. My wife and I isolated almost two dozen interrelated causes of late marriage and the prevalence of bachelor and spinsterhood. The most emphasized cause in Ireland is the pattern of inheritance: one son, usually the eldest, must wait until the father is ready to pass on his patrimony and his own siblings have married or emigrated. In an attempt to alleviate the situation somewhat, a law today requires that to receive the "old-age" (pension) a man at seventy must will his property to a son, or other appropriate person. This cause is important in Inis Beag, although primogeniture is not so well defined (of those sons inheriting property, 47 percent are first born, 42 percent second, 8 percent third, and 3 percent fourth and later). Inis Beag fathers are loath to surrender their

land and control of the household to their sons and will often play off the sons, one against another, in order to achieve favored treatment for their wives and themselves in their waning years. Occasionally this procedure "backfires": the sons, acting in concert, emigrate together, and an increasing amount of land lies idle because of this.

Equally loath to disturb the family status quo, island mothers will often resist incoming daughters-in-law, who threaten not only their commanding position but the loss of their sons' affection. Mothers whom we have interviewed in Inis Beag and elsewhere in Ireland display the extreme of Oedipal attachment when they rejoice in their sons' decision to join the priesthood; not only are spiritual blessings and prestige brought to the family as a result, but their sons are at last removed from potential wives. Yet the Inis Beag man who wants to marry and is prevented from doing so by domineering and jealous parents is the subject of much gossip. Outwardly, at least, his plight is considered a "shame."

To the man in his late twenties and thirties who is secure in his home and has established regularized patterns of conduct (and has a mother who acts in most ways as a wife surrogate), the general responsibilities of marriage, and specifically its sexual responsibility, are factors militating against his seeking a spouse. Some men who have land, the consent of their parents, and willing "sweethearts" will balk at a match because they are too happy "running with the lads," and if persuaded to marry, they will try to retain as much of their bachelor role as possible within marriage. It was hinted to my wife and me on several occasions that particular island celibates almost married several times in succession, only to find the sexual commitment too difficult to make at the last moment.

Three other causes of late marriage and the single estate in Inis Beag must be mentioned. Girls are more dissatisfied with their future lot than are boys and men and are emigrating at ever younger ages, thus sharply reducing the number of eligible females. During the 1950–1959 period, the average age at which girls emigrate dropped below twenty-one years. Each year more of them attend schools on the mainland and thus are more exposed to stimuli which promote emigration. Mothers are puzzled at the increasing exodus of their daughters, since women today have a far easier time than they did a generation or two ago; but some are glad to see them escape the drudgery and boredom of island existence. Since late marriage has been a persistent phenomenon in Ireland since the great famine, it has become institutionalized and serves as an expectation for young people. We heard Inis Beag adults assert that marriage should be postponed to conform to island mores; this usually was buttressed by a rationale of males not having "enough sense" to marry until they are nearly forty years of age. Reflected in this rationale is the male age-grading conceptualized by the folk: a man is a "boy" or "lad" until forty, an adult until sixty, middle-aged until eighty, and aged after that (exhilarating to the American anthropologist approaching forty who comes from a society obsessed with the "cult of youth"). A final cause, often articulated by the islanders, is the fact that divorce is impossible in Ireland, therefore the choice of a spouse must be well considered. It appears, however, that this argument is usually used as a rationalization for late marriage, when other causal factors are, in reality, responsible – certainly when "considering" covers two or more decades!

The population of Inis Beag has dropped from a high of 532 persons in 1861 (up 76 from the prefamine census a decade earlier) to 497 in 1881, 483 in 1901, 409 in 1926, 376 in 1956, and 350 when my wife and I were there two years later. Today, there is grave concern over the future of the island, and some folk hold that within another generation or two Inis Beag will have gone the way of the Blasket Islands. Although my wife and I isolated almost two dozen causes for the phenomena of late marriage and celibacy, over thirty interrelated causes pertain to emigration (many of those at work in the marital sphere also stimulate emigration). Once again, I will address only the principal causes and stress the role of sexual repression, dealing first with internal factors and then external ones promoting emigration.

Among internal causes, the previously considered inheritance pattern, parents who want to maintain the family status quo for various reasons, and the girls' and young women's increasing dissatisfaction with their lot figure as prominently in the emigration picture as the marital. Some Inis Beag men claim that the reason male youths are leaving the island is economic depression, caused by the collapse of kelp-making and the fishing industry. But this cause is untenable when one examines the increase in government subsidies, remittances from relatives abroad, and taxation and land rental policies; these have far more than made up for the loss of previous revenue. Real income has increased substantially, despite recent inflation, and young men are very much aware of this fact. Just as late marriage has become institutionalized over the past century, so has emigration since the first large-scale migration of islanders in 1822. Emigration is a way of life, which will stimulate some folk to leave in spite of other conditions which might lead an observer to advise their remaining.

By far the most important reason for Inis Beag's long dwindling population is the total cultural impact of sexual puritanism and the secular "excesses" of the clergy. Blanshard writes, "When all the reasons for a flight from Ireland have been mentioned, there still remains a suspicion that Irish young people are leaving their nation largely because it is a poor place in which to be happy and free. Have the priests created a civilization in which the chief values of youth and love are subordinate to Catholic discipline?" (Blanshard 1954: 154). What "remains a suspicion" to Blanshard is fully confirmed by a wealth of data from Inis Beag, only limited amounts of which have been reported in this chapter. Even though sexual repression and fear of the clergy prevent the folk from being outspoken in this matter, it is constantly broached among themselves.

Paramount among external factors stimulating emigration are prosperity on the mainland and abroad, the impact of the mass media of communication, the increasing number of tourists visiting Inis Beag, the return of former emigrants, and the fact that, with an increase in incomes and scholarship funds, more island children are going to the mainland for their schooling each year. America has been a land of freedom and prosperity to the Irish since before the famine, and, until the Second World War, most islanders migrated there never to return. But the growth of prosperity in England following 1946 shifted the stream of emigration in that direction, for not only were jobs plentiful across the Irish Sea, but large, viable ethnic communities served by Irish clergy had sprung up in big cities. And it was possible to visit Ireland frequently, as the distance and cost are slight compared to a journey across the Atlantic. It is common for youths vacationing in Inis Beag from England to talk others into returning with them. The latter declare that they will soon come back to the island to settle permanently, hopefully with "great riches," but they seldom return. Since the war, a number of "Yanks" have also returned home, and their stories of life in America make the youthful islanders restive. Tourists who remain for weeks and months in Inis Beag and come to know many folk also sow the seeds of discontent.

Television was introduced into Inis Beag during 1963, and the two sets now installed always have ready and willing audiences. Almost every cottage has a radio, and, although the islanders seldom read books, a wide assortment of domestic and foreign magazines and newspapers find their way into most homes. These mass media also are an emancipating force making for restiveness and discontent, as they allow the islanders to glimpse behind the "lace curtain" at what appears to be a happier and freer world. Television and radio programs are censored, but, even so, the morality expressed in them – especially the sex and violence drenched American ones – presents a striking contrast to locally conceived moral precepts. A censor from Inis Beag would most certainly create more discontinuities in films with his shears than do his much maligned "secularized" colleagues in Dublin.

Most of what I have written in this essay is to be found expressed in the works of such older Irish writers as James Joyce, Sean O'Casey, Austin Clarke, and Patrick Kavanaugh, and such younger ones as William Murray, John McGahern, Edna O'Brien, John Broderick, Brian Moore, and Benedict Kiely. Irish review-ers of the writings of the younger authors often criticize them for portraying an Ireland of the distant past. But, although conditions there are changing quite rapidly, sexual repression is still a force active enough to command the attention of creative artists and social scientists.[7] The subtle influences of nationalism, religion, and sexual puritanism were very apparent in the revisions suggested by most of the twenty-six "unbiased" scholars of Irish descent – in Ireland, England, and America – to whom I submitted the first version of this article for comment.

NOTES

1 For other reports on Inis Beag, consult Messenger 1962, 1968, and 1969.
2 The culture described herein is that of 1959–1960 and excludes important changes which have occurred since then, such as those resulting from the introduction of television, a summer language school for pupils from the mainland, and free secondary education.
3 Twenty-nine percent of those islanders of marriageable age are single. This rises to a high of 37 percent among first and second generation Inis Beag emigrants, indicating the actions of more than just economic causes. Irish scholars, for obvious reasons, tend to stress economic and other (climate, race, English oppression, the famine, loss of the Irish tongue, etc.) monistic causes in their analyses of culture and personality phenomena. Inadequate statistics for second and third generation migrants from Inis Beag suggest that the celibacy rate lowers markedly only when descendants of immigrants dissociate themselves from Irish ethnic communities and Irish-American priests. Ethnographic research is sorely needed among Irish of several generations in the countries to which they have migrated to probe this and other phenomena.
4 Among various projective techniques employed, including having islanders read and comment about print materials, the author composed a ballad which was performed on several occasions, so that audience reactions might be observed. [Eds.]
5 Strict varieties of Catholic Theology.

6 The fear of being observed, as well as repression, may account for the apparent lack of sexual contact with animals. This practice may be common among mainland peasants, if one is willing to accept as evidence the existence of a genre of dirty jokes popular there, and hearsay among certain scholars concerning confessional materials.

7 I am confident that one of the major "lines of attack" on my ethnography by Irish nativist reviewers will be that the community described is atypical and conditions in urbanized Ireland no longer bear any resemblance to those in Inis Beag. Since 1957, I have been much criticized by African elitists for describing in my writings a primitive culture which they claim is no longer characteristic of that developing continent.

REFERENCES

Arensberg, C. M. and Kimball, S. T.
  1968 *Family   Community   in   Ireland*. Cambridge: Harvard University Press.
Bales, R. F.
  1962 "Attitudes Toward Drinking in the Irish Culture." In *Society, Culture, and Drinking Patterns*, eds. David J. Pittman and Charles R. Snyder, pp. 157–187. New York: John Wiley and Sons, Inc.
Berger, P. L.
  1963 *Invitation to Sociology: A Humanistic Perspective*. Garden City: Anchor Books.
Blanshard, P.
  1954 *The Irish and Catholic Power*. London: Derek Verschoyle.
Coxhead, E.
  1961 *Lady Gregory*. London: MacMillan and Co., Ltd.
de Freine, S.
  1965 *The Great Silence*. Dublin: Foilseachain Naisiunta Teoranta.

Delargy, J. H.
  1957 "Folklore." In *A View of Ireland*, eds. James Meenan and David A. Webb, pp. 178–187. Dublin: Hely's Limited.
Humphreys, Fr. A. J.
  1966 *New Dubliners*. New York: Fordham University Press.
Lewis, O.
  1960 *Tepoztlan: Village in Mexico*. New York: Holt, Rinehart and Winston, Inc.
McCarthy, J.
  1964 *Ireland*. New York: Time Incorporated.
McGahern, J.
  1965 *The Dark*. London: Faber and Faber.
Messenger, J. C.
  1962 "A Critical Reexamination of the Concept of Spirits." *American Anthropologist*, 64, No. 2: 267–272.
Messenger, J. C.
  1968 "Types and Causes of Disputes in an Irish Community." *Eire-Ireland*, 3, No. 3: 27–37.
Messenger, J. C.
  1969 *Inis Beag: Isle of Ireland*. New York: Holt, Rinehart and Winston, Inc.
Murray, W. C.
  1965 *Michael Joe*. New York: Appleton-Century.
O'Brien, Fr. J. A., ed.
  1953 *The Vanishing Irish*. New York: McGraw-Hill Book Company.
Opler, M. K. and Singer, J. L.
  1956 "Ethnic Differences in Behavior and Psychopathology: Italian and Irish." *The International Journal of Social Psychiatry*, 2, No. 1: 11–23.
O'Suilleabhain, S.
  1963 *A Handbook of Irish Folklore*. Hatboro: Folklore Associates, Inc.
Tracy, H.
  1953 *Mind You I've Said Nothing*. London: Methuen and Co., Ltd.

Part VII
Virgin Birth

Introduction

It was in 1826 that the founder of embryology, Karl Ernst Ritter von Baer, discovered the ovum, and its precise significance and function were debated until later in the nineteenth century. In *Coming into Being Among the Australian Aborigines* Ashley Montagu notes that the association of intercourse with pregnancy was scientifically proven as late as 1850, "when Newport discovered and described the penetration of the ovum by the spermatozoon under its own movements" (1974: 291). Elsewhere, he notes that when Antony van Leeuwenhoek presented his discovery of spermatozoa to the Royal Society of London in 1677, there was incredulity as to the number of animalcules in the ejaculate. Despite Leeuwenhoek's assertion that a spermatozoon fertilized the ovum, many scientists regarded spermatozoa as parasites until 1850 (Montagu 1969: 197). One might add that at the beginning of the last century Havelock Ellis and his contemporaries were still speculating as to whether menstruation was a form of heat. Montagu felt it necessary in 1937 to disprove the hypothesis that humans had a rutting season.

During the same Victorian century that biologists finally learned "the facts of life," claims of primitive ignorance of details of physiological paternity appeared in the writings of early social anthropologists. McLennan and Morgan both saw such ignorance along with matrilineal descent as an obvious corollary of rampant promiscuity. Such convictions led to the misinterpretation of data by early fieldworkers such as Lorimer Fison and A. W. Howitt, who misinterpreted marriages between members of moieties and marriage classes in Australia as a form of group marriage (inasmuch as a man would have secondary rights to other women in his wife's group) pointing back to recent promiscuity and primordial ignorance:

> For, when a man has no exclusive right to his wives; when even strangers from a distant tribe, who are of a class corresponding to his, may claim a share in his marital rights;

Sexualities in Anthropology: A Reader, edited by Andrew P. Lyons and Harriet D. Lyons

when a woman is married to a thousand miles of husbands, then paternity must be, to say the least of it, somewhat doubtful. But there can be no possibility of mistake as to maternity, and therefore it seems natural enough that children should "follow the mother," as several of our correspondents put it. (Fison and Howitt 1967[1880]: 73)

From all over the continent came stories of people who supposedly disavowed the role of men in fathering their own children (there were other cases where this was not so). The most important accounts came from W. E. Roth in Queensland and, above all else, from Baldwin Spencer and F. J. Gillen, pioneer fieldworkers who visited the Aranda of central Australia, and explained (Spencer and Gillen 1968[1899]) how Aranda obtained their totems. Aranda women were impregnated by spirit children (*kuruna*) who inhabited places and spaces near totem sites where ancestors had wandered in the Dreamtime. Spirit children were associated with various animals and had been created by Numbakulla (Divinity) in the Dreamtime. The male had no physiological role in conception. Awareness of pregnancy might be imparted in dreams or after consuming food. Each ancestral site had different totemic associations; the child's totem was based not on heredity but rather on the particular location (which might be accidental) where the mother was impregnated, often while asleep.

The leading evolutionist Sir James Frazer was inclined to believe that the Aranda were indeed unaware of physiological paternity. He believed that they were at an earlier stage than Europeans in mental evolution, but there were other reasons for "so outstanding an ignorance of natural causation": "[T]he interval which elapses between the act of impregnation and the first symptoms of pregnancy is sufficient to prevent him from perceiving the connection between the two" (1905: 455). Moreover, the Aranda allowed intercourse between pre-pubertal children, and unsurprisingly that did not lead to pregnancy.

Even before Frazer wrote these words in *Fortnightly Review*, the evolutionary framework which supported matriarchal theory, primitive promiscuity, and ignorance of physiological paternity was in trouble. Emile Durkheim, Northcote Thomas, and Edward Westermarck were extremely skeptical that there could be any population who could be unaware of such biological facts. Bronislaw Malinowski's doctoral thesis endorsed Westermarck's attacks on the notion of primitive promiscuity, asserting that some form of the family existed in all societies. However, *Baloma: The Spirits of the Dead in the Trobriand Islands*, Malinowski's first major publication on the Trobriands, which appeared in 1916 after his first field trip, revived the idea of primitive ignorance, or, as he later preferred to call it, *nescience*. Although some details in his account were to vary over time (did or did not the Trobrianders understand the facts of life with respect to pigs and other animals?), the essential details remained the same (see the extract from the 1932 edition of *Sexual Life of Savages* reproduced in this section). Trobrianders believed that the dead go to the isle of Tuma. Periodically, they tire of life in Paradise, and are transformed into spirit children, which are washed ashore on Kiriwina. A spirit child enters the body of a woman of its sub-clan, impregnating her and assuring the *dala*'s (matrilineal sub-clan's) perpetuity. The father's intercourse with the mother merely "prepares the way" for the entry of the spirit child. *Momona* (sperm) does not fertilize. The father can mold the form of the child by sleeping with the mother during pregnancy. Readers of the Malinowski extract will note his stories about origin myths, clan ancestresses who gave birth without sexual intercourse, the ugly lady in Omarakana village who gave birth to children although no man would go near her, and the Trobrianders'(partial) extension of their beliefs about paternity to the pig population.

Although Malinowski maintained that Trobrianders did not recognize the biological role of the father, his social role in raising the child was very important. He was the object of affection for both female and male children. If a recognizable form of the family existed in a matrilineal society that did not acknowledge paternity and accorded the father the authority that normally accompanied such an acknowledgment, that very fact demonstrated the family's universal strength. However, inasmuch as the mother's brother rather than the father was the locus of jural authority, and the father could therefore inspire an unmixed emotion of love (rather than a mixture of love and fear of authority), the "family romance" that Freud assumed to be essential (the Oedipal stage and complex caused by the male child's jealousy of, and ambivalence toward, his father) did not exist there (see Malinowski 1927).

As noted in Part VI, the Trobrianders allowed their daughters some sexual freedom before marriage. Despite this fact, there were not a lot of illegitimate babies, a fact that they could point to when asked to justify their belief that intercourse did not cause conception.

Malinowski's ideas about Trobriand ignorance embroiled him in some controversy. He particularly attracted the ire of a British colonial magistrate, Alex Rentoul, who had adjudicated a number of Trobriand adultery cases, and insisted that Trobrianders knew the facts of life. In the apparent absence of other forms of contraception Trobriand women demonstrated both their knowledge and their physical agility in a remarkable way:

> I have been informed by many independent and intelligent natives that the female of the species is specially endowed or gifted with ejaculatory powers, which may be called upon after an act of coition to expel the male seed. It is understandable that such powers might be increased by use and practice, and I am satisfied that such a method does exist. (Rentoul 1931: 153)

Whether or not Rentoul should have given credence to such stories (they may in fact have been colonial folklore), he convinced Jack Driberg and Edward Evans-Pritchard who had studied with Malinowski. The schism was bitter. One consequence of the hubbub was that Malinowski felt compelled to refine his position, and he did so in a "Special Preface" to the third edition of *Sexual Life of Savages*:

> The Trobrianders do not suffer from a specific complaint *ignorantia paternitatis*. What we find among them is a complicated attitude towards the facts of maternity and paternity. Into this attitude there enter certain elements of positive knowledge, certain gaps in embryological information. These cognitive ingredients again are influenced by beliefs of an animistic nature, and influenced by the moral and legal principles of the community. (1932: lix)

This was indeed the viewpoint of one of Malinowski's students, M. F. Ashley Montagu, who crossed the Atlantic in the late 1920s, and wrote a doctoral thesis under the supervision of Ruth Benedict that was published as *Coming into Being Among the Australian Aborigines* (extracted below). In order to defend Malinowski, he turned to the work of Lucien Lévy-Bruhl, who had written many books suggesting that primitive peoples did not always distinguish between physical and metaphysical links between themselves and the rest of creation. Montagu argued that Aboriginal beliefs about totemism might, accordingly, entail something more than "ignorance" of the facts of life.

Montagu collected a formidable amount of Australian data to advance his hypothesis of *nescience* (willful not-knowing) rather than ignorance of physiological paternity and to defend Malinowski against critics. He thought that it was likely that adolescent girls in Australia and the Trobriands could indeed have sexual intercourse frequently without getting pregnant, because there was evidence of a period of reduced fertility for a few years after menarche.

Over the years contradictory evidence appeared. Some scholars, such as Phyllis Kaberry (1936), supported Malinowski. Others, such as Ronald and Caroline Berndt, received different accounts from different Australian groups. Subsequent ethnography in the Trobriands (starting with H. A. Powell's 1956 thesis for the University of London, as quoted by Leach on p. 201 in this volume) indicated that Malinowski may have relied too greatly on accounts of dogma from men, and that he would have given a different account had he talked more to women.

Edmund Leach, whose essay is reproduced here, was, like Montagu, a student of Malinowski. However, he was incredulous that Malinowski should have been so willing to follow the lead of nineteenth-century Scottish evolutionists who were "soaked in the classics" and imbued with "paternalistic imperialist values" (see below, p. 200), and that some contemporary scholars such as Melford Spiro were prepared to accept Malinowski's account. Given the fact that people everywhere had "an almost obsessional interest in matters of sex and kinship" ignorance of physiological paternity seemed implausible in all cases. Statements about conception of the type Malinowski and others analyzed are elements of dogma concerning social relations and perceived relationships between people and their god(s). As such, they follow social formulas, and give few clues as to the inner, intellectual, and emotional worlds of those who enunciate them, whatever some distinguished Victorian scholars like Edward Tylor and James Frazer may have thought. In the Trobriands, God is not involved, but there are spirit children who are reborn as living humans belonging to the matriline of the woman who becomes pregnant. The woman, an ordinary mortal, is married to a mortal husband. The husband "opens the way" but does not beget the ordinary child whose appearance he influences by lying with his wife. In Christian belief, the Holy Spirit actually begets Jesus, son of God, through Mary, who is abnormal inasmuch as she is a virgin, but Joseph is the social father of the exceptional child who belongs to the patriline of David.

Ashley Montagu hoped to include an appendix refuting Leach in a second, expanded edition of his book on Australian sexual knowledge in 1974, but there was no space. Another important paper was written by Carol Delaney in 1986, relating the Virgin Birth story to "folk theories of procreation" and gender roles, including metaphors such as "seed" (active and male) and "field" (passive and female) in farming societies in the Middle East, such as the biblical Hebrews and contemporary rural Turks. Delaney criticizes Leach for making comparisons that ignore major differences between cultures. She is less critical of Montagu's attempt to relate statements about conception to particular cosmologies and ideologies, but is concerned that his underlying beliefs about natural gender differences cause him to speculate that patriarchal ideas of fatherhood and motherhood may have preceded any particular encodings of them in myth and dogma.

There is surely no harm in admitting that statements about sex by members of diverse cultures may not be accurate in terms of modern biology (as we have already indicated, this was and, to some degree, still is the case in modern societies). At the same time we have to be aware that those statements must be related to local cosmologies and ideologies of gender if we are to make sense of them. The discussion of Sambia ideas about sex in the article by Herdt in Part X, below, shows us that to understand folk concepts we must go beyond giving a "Yes" or "No" to Malinowski or Leach. The Sambia "understood" that sperm creates babies, but their ideas about where sperm came from had more to do with their rituals of masculinity than with anything in a modern biology book.

REFERENCES AND FURTHER READING

Delaney, Carol
    1986   The Meaning of Paternity and the Virgin Birth Debate. Man (N.S.) 21(3)494–513.
Fison, Lorimer and A. W. Howitt
    1967[1880]   Kamilaroi and Kurnai. Oosterhout NB: Anthropological Publications.
Frazer, Sir James G.
    1905   The Beginnings of Religion and Totemism Among the Australian Aborigines. Fortnightly Review 84:452–466.
Kaberry, Phyllis M.
    1936   Spirit-Children and Spirit-Centres of the North Kimberley Division, West Australia. Oceania 6:392–400.
Kaberry, Phyllis M.
    1939   Aboriginal Woman: Sacred and Profane. London: Routledge.
Malinowski, Bronislaw
    1913   The Family Among the Australian Aborigines. London: University of London Press.
Malinowski, Bronislaw
    1916   Baloma: The Spirits of the Dead in the Trobriand Islands. Journal of the Royal Anthropological Institute 46:353–430.
Malinowski, Bronislaw
    1927   Sex and Repression in Savage Society. London: Routledge.
Malinowski, Bronislaw
    1929   The Sexual Life of Savages in North-Western Melanesia. London: Routledge.
Malinowski, Bronislaw
    1932a   The Sexual Life of Savages in North-Western Melanesia. 2nd edition. London: Routledge.
Malinowski, Bronislaw
    1932b   Pigs, Papuans and Police Court Perspective. Man 32:33–39.
Malinowski, Bronislaw
    1967   A Diary in the Strict Sense of the Term. Trans. N. Guterman. London: Routledge & Kegan Paul.
Montagu, M. F. Ashley
    1969   Sex, Man and Society. New York: Putnam's.

Montagu, M. F. Ashley
    1974[1937]   Coming into Being Among the Australian Aborigines: A Study of the
    Procreative Beliefs of the Native Tribes of Australia. With a Foreword by Bronislaw
    Malinowski. Rev. and exp. 2nd edition. London: Routledge & Kegan Paul.
Rentoul, Alex
    1931   Physiological Paternity and the Trobrianders. Man 31:152–154.
Spencer, Baldwin and F. J. Gillen
    1968[1899]   The Native Tribes of Central Australia. New York: Dover Publications.

15

Ignorance of Physiological Paternity

Bronislaw Malinowski

The correlation of the mystical with the physiological aspects in pregnancy belief – of the origin of the child in Tuma[1] and its journey to the Trobriands with the subsequent processes in the maternal body, the welling up of the blood from the abdomen to the head and down again from the head to the womb – provides a co-ordinated and self-contained, though not always consistent, theory of the origin of human life. It also gives a good theoretical foundation for matriliny; for the whole process of introducing new life into a community lies between the spirit world and the female organism. There is no room for any sort of physical paternity.

But there is another condition considered by the natives indispensable for conception and childbirth, which complicates their theory and blurs the clear outline of their belief. This condition is related to sexual intercourse, and brings us face to face with the difficult and delicate question: are the natives really entirely ignorant of physiological fatherhood? Is it not rather a fact of which they are more or less

aware, though it may be overlaid and distorted by mythological and animistic beliefs? Is it not an instance of empirical knowledge possessed by a backward community, but never formulated because it is too obvious to need explicit statement, whereas the traditional legend which is the basis of their social structure is carefully expressed as a part of the body of authoritative dogma? The facts which I am about to adduce contain an unambiguous and decisive answer to these questions. I shall not anticipate the conclusion, which, indeed, as we shall see, will be drawn by the natives themselves.

A virgin cannot conceive.

Tradition, diffuse folk-lore, certain aspects of custom and customary behaviour, teach the natives this simple physiological truth. They have no doubt about it, and it will be seen from what follows that they can formulate it tersely and clearly.

This statement was volunteered by Niyova, a sound informant in Oburaku: "A virgin does not conceive, because there is no way for the

Extracts from Bronislaw Malinowski, *The Sexual Life of Savages*, reprint of 3rd edition, Boston: Beacon Press, 1987|1932|, pp. 153–172. Reprinted with permission of Taylor & Francis UK.

Sexualities in Anthropology: A Reader, edited by Andrew P. Lyons and Harriet D. Lyons
© 2011 Blackwell Publishing Ltd.

children to go, for that woman to conceive. When the orifice is wide open, the spirits are aware, they give the child." [...]

I received a great number of similar declarations, all expressing the view that the way must be open for the child, but this need not necessarily be brought about by sexual intercourse. The point is quite clear. The vagina must be opened to remove the physiological obstacle, called simply *kalapatu* (her tightness). Once this has been done, in the normal way by sexual intercourse, there is no need for male and female to come together in order to produce a child.

Considering that there are no virgins in the villages – for every female child begins her sexual life very early – we may wonder how the natives arrived at this *conditio sine qua non*. Again, since they have got so far, it may appear difficult to see why they have not advanced just a little further and grasped the fertilizing virtue of seminal fluid. Nevertheless, there are many facts to prove that they have not made this advance: as certainly as they know the necessity of a mechanical opening of the vagina, so they do not know the generative power of the male discharge. It was in discussing the mythological tales of mankind's beginnings on earth and fantastic legends of distant lands, to the account of which I shall now proceed, that I was made aware of this subtle yet all-important distinction between mechanical dilation and physiological fertilization; and was thus enabled to place native belief regarding procreation in its proper perspective.

According to native tradition, mankind originated from underground, whence a couple, a brother and a sister, emerged at different specified places. According to certain legends, only women appeared at first. Some of my commentators insisted upon this version: "You see, we are so many on the earth because many women came first. Had there been many men, we would be few." Now, whether accompanied by her brother or not, the primeval woman is always imagined to bear children without the intervention of a husband or of any other male partner; but not without the vagina being opened by some means. In some of the traditions this is mentioned explicitly.

Thus on the island of Vakuta there is a myth which describes how an ancestress of one of the sub-clans exposed her body to falling rain, and thus mechanically lost her virginity. In the most important Trobriand myth, a woman, called Mitigis or Bolutukwa, mother of the legendary hero Tudava, lives quite alone in a grotto on the seashore. One day she falls asleep in her rocky dwelling, reclining under a dripping stalactyte. The drops of water pierce her vagina, and thus deprive her of virginity. Hence her second name, Bolutukwa: *bo*, female, prefix, *litukwa*, dripping water. In other myths of origin the means of piercing the hymen are not mentioned, but it is often explicitly stated that the ancestress was without a man, and could, therefore, have no sexual intercourse. [...]

Moving into another mythological dimension – into present-day legends of countries far to the north – we find the marvellous land of Kaytalugi, peopled exclusively by sexually rabid women. They are so brutally profligate that their excesses kill every man thrown by chance upon their shores, and even their own male children never attain maturity before they are sexually done to death. Yet these women are very prolific, producing many children, male and female. If a native is asked how this can be, how these females become pregnant if there are no men, he simply cannot understand such an absurd question. These women, he will say, destroy their virginity in all sorts of ways if they cannot get hold of a man to torture to death. And they have got their own *baloma*,[2] of course, to give them children. [...]

There are some convincing present-day instances which show that the natives believe that a girl can be with child without previous sexual intercourse. Thus, there are some women so ugly and repulsive that no one believes that they can ever have had intercourse (save, of course, for those few who know better, but who are very careful to keep silent from shame). There is Tilapo'i, now an old woman, who was famous for her hideousness in youth. She has become blind, was always almost an idiot, and had a repulsive face and deformed body. Her unattractiveness was so notorious that she became the subject of a saying: *Kwoy Tilapo'i* ("have connection with Tilapo'i"), a form of abuse used in mild chaff. Altogether she is an infinite source and pivot of all kinds of matrimonial and obscene jokes, all based on the presumed impossibility of being Tilapo'i's lover or prospective husband. I was assured, over and over again, that no one ever could have had connection with her. Yet this woman has had a child, as the natives would triumphantly point out, when I tried to persuade them that only by intercourse can children be produced.

Again, there is the case of Kurayana, a woman of Sinaketa, whom I never saw, but who, I was told, was "so ugly that any man would be ashamed" to have intercourse with her. This saying implies that social shame would be an even stronger deterrent than sexual repulsion, an assumption which shows that my informant was not a bad practical psychologist. Kurayana, as thoroughly chaste as anyone could be – by necessity, if not by virtue – had no less than six children, five of whom died and one of whom still survives.

Albinos, male and female, are considered unfit for sexual intercourse. There is not the slightest doubt that all the natives feel real horror of and disgust for these unfortunate beings. Yet there are on record several instances of albino women who have brought forth a numerous progeny. "Why did they become pregnant? Is it because they copulate at night time? Or because a *baloma* has given them children?" Such was the clinching argument of one of my informants, for the first alternative appeared obviously absurd. [...] As a means of testing the firmness of their belief, I sometimes made myself definitely and aggressively an advocate of the truer physiological doctrine of procreation. In such arguments the natives would quote, not only positive instances, such as those just mentioned, of women who have children without having enjoyed any intercourse; but would also refer to the equally convincing negative aspect, that is, to the many cases in which an unmarried woman has plenty of intercourse and no children. This argument would be repeated over and over again, with specially telling concrete examples of childless persons renowned for profligacy, or of women who lived with one white trader after another without having any baby.

Words and Deeds in Testimony

Although I was never afraid of using a leading question, or of eliciting the natives' point of view by contradicting it, I was somewhat astonished at the fierce opposition evoked by my advocacy of physiological paternity. Only late in my Trobriand career did I find out that I was not the first to attack this part of native belief, having been preceded by the missionary teachers. [...]

We must realise that the cardinal dogma of God the Father and God the Son, the sacrifice of the only Son and the filial love of man to his Maker would completely miss fire in a matrilineal society, where the relation between father and son is decreed by tribal law to be that of two strangers, where all personal unity between them is denied, and where all family obligations are associated with mother-line. [...]

But apart from any doctrinal difficulty, the missionaries are earnestly engaged in propagating sexual morality as we conceive it, in which endeavour the idea of the sexual act as having serious consequences to family life is indispensable. The whole Christian morality, moreover, is strongly associated with the institution of a patrilineal and patriarchal family, with the father as progenitor and master of the household. In short, a religion whose dogmatic essence is based on the sacredness of the father to son relationship, and whose morals stand or fall by a strong patriarchal family, must obviously proceed by confirming the paternal relation, by showing that it has a natural foundation. Only during my third expedition to New Guinea did I discover that the natives had been somewhat exasperated by having an "absurdity" preached at them, and by finding me, so "unmissionary" as a rule, engaged in the same futile argument.

[...]

Motago'i, one of my most intelligent informants, in answer to a somewhat arrogantly framed affirmation that the missionaries were right, exclaimed: –

"*Gala wala*! *Isasopasi*: *yambwata yambwata*
Not at all! They lie: always   always
nakubukwabuya   momona   ikasewo
unmarried girls   seminal fluid it is brimful

litusi   gala."
children theirs not.

Which may be freely rendered: "Not at all,
the missionaries are mistaken; unmarried
girls continually have intercourse, in fact
they overflow with seminal fluid, and yet
have no children."

Here, in terse and picturesque language,
Motago'i expresses the view that, after all, if
sexual intercourse were causally connected
with child production, it is the unmarried girls
who should have children, since they lead a
much more intensive sexual life than the
married ones – a puzzling difficulty which
really exists, as we shall see later on, but which
our informant exaggerates slightly, since
unmarried girls do conceive, though not nearly
as frequently as anyone holding the "missionary views" would be led to expect. Asked in
the course of the same discussion: "What,
then, is the cause of pregnancy?" he answered:
"Blood on the head makes child. The seminal
fluid does not make the child. Spirits bring at
night time the infant, put on women's heads
– it makes blood. Then, after two or three
months, when the blood [that is, menstruous
blood] does not come out, they know: 'Oh, I
am pregnant!'"

An informant in Teyava, in a similar discussion, made several statements of which I
adduce the two most spontaneous and conclusive ones. "Copulation alone cannot produce a
child. Night after night, for years, girls copulate. No child comes." [...]

My favourite informant gave a clear, though
somewhat Rabelaisian, statement of the native
point of view: –

"Takayta,   itokay   vivila   italagila
We copulate   she gets up   woman   it runs
                                         out

momona –   iwokwo."
seminal fluid –   it is finished.

In other words, after the traces of sexual
intercourse have been removed, there are no
further consequences.

[...] To a South Sea native, as to a European
peasant, his domestic animals – that is, his
pigs – are the most valued and cherished
members of the household. And if his earnest
and genuine conviction can be seen anywhere,
it will be in his care for the welfare and quality
of his animals. The South Sea natives are
extremely keen to have good, strong, and
healthy pigs, and pigs of a good breed.

The main distinction which they make in
the matter of quality is that between the wild
or bush-pigs, and the tame village pigs. The
village pig is considered a great delicacy, while
the flesh of the bush-pig is one of the strongest
taboos to people of rank in Kiriwina, the transgression of which they hold in genuine horror
and disgust. Yet they allow the female domestic pigs to wander on the outskirts of the village and in the bush, where they can pair freely
with male bush-pigs. On the other hand, they
castrate all the male pigs in the village in order
to improve their condition. Thus, naturally, all
the progeny are in reality descended from wild
bush sires. Yet the natives have not the slightest inkling of this fact. When I said to one of
the chiefs: "You eat the child of a bush-pig,"
he simply took it as a bad joke; for making fun
of bush-pig eating is not considered altogether
good taste by a Trobriander of birth and standing. But he did not understand at all what I
really meant.

On one occasion when I asked directly how
pigs breed, the answer was: "The female pig
breeds by itself," which simply meant that,
probably, there is no *baloma* involved in the
multiplication of domestic animals. When I
drew parallels and suggested that small pigs
are brought by their own *balomas*, they were
not convinced; and it was evident that neither
their own interest, nor the data supplied by
tradition, went far enough to inspire any concern as to the procreation of pigs.

Very important was a statement volunteered
to me by Motago'i: "From all male pigs we cut
off the testes. They copulate not. Yet the
females bring forth." Thus he ignored the possible misconduct of the bush-pigs, and adduced
the castration of domestic hogs as final proof
that intercourse has nothing to do with breeding. On another occasion, I instanced the only
two goats in the Archipelago, one male and
one female, which a trader had recently
imported. When I asked whether the female

would bear any young if the male were killed, there was no uncertainty about the answer: "Year after year she will breed." Thus they have the firm conviction that if a female animal were entirely cut off from any male of the species, this would by no means interfere with her fecundity.

Another crucial test is provided by the recent importation of European pigs. In honour of the first man who brought them, the late Mick George, a Greek trader and a truly Homeric character, they are called by the natives *bulukwa Miki* (Mick's pigs), and they will give five to ten of the native pigs in exchange for one of them. Yet when they have acquired it, they will not take the slightest precautions to make it breed with a male of the same superior race, though they could easily do so. In one instance when, having several small pigs of European race they castrated all the males, they were reproved by a white trader, and told that by so doing they lowered the whole breed. But they simply could not be made to understand, and all over the district they continue to allow their valued European pigs to mis-breed.

[...] In man, spirits are the cause of pregnancy: in animals – it just happens. Again, while the Trobrianders ascribe all human ailments to sorcery, with animals disease is just disease. Men die because of very strong evil magic; animals – just die. But it would be quite incorrect to interpret this as evidence that the natives know, in the case of animals, the natural causes of impregnation, disease, and death; while in man they obliterate this knowledge by an animistic superstructure. The true summary of the native outlook is that they are so deeply interested in human affairs that they construct a special tradition about all that is vital for man; while in what concerns animals, things are taken as they come, without any attempt at explanation, and also without any insight into the real course of nature.

Their attitude to their own children also bears witness to their ignorance of any causal relation between congress and the ensuing pregnancy. A man whose wife has conceived during his absence will cheerfully accept the fact and the child, and he will see no reason at all for suspecting her of adultery. One of my informants told me that after over a year's absence he returned to find a newly-born child at home. He volunteered this statement as an illustration and final proof of the truth that sexual intercourse has nothing to do with conception. And it must be remembered that no native would ever discuss any subject in which the slightest suspicion of his wife's fidelity could be involved. [...]

Children born in wedlock during a prolonged absence of the husband, will yet be recognized by him as his own children, that is as standing to him in the social relation of child to father. An instructive parallel to this is supplied by cases of children born out of wedlock, but during a liaison as exclusive as a marriage. In such a case, the physiological father would be obvious to us; yet a Trobriander would not recognize the children as his, and further, since for a girl it is dishonourable to bear children before she is married, he might refuse to marry her.[...]

Thus of children born by a married woman, her husband is the father *ex officio*, but for an unmarried mother, there is "no father to the child". The father is defined socially, and in order that there may be fatherhood there must be marriage. And traditional sentiment regards illegitimate children, as we have said, as improper on the part of the mother. Of course there is no implication of sexual guilt in this censure, but, to the native, to do wrong is simply to act contrary to custom. And it is not the custom for an unmarried girl to have babies, although it is the custom for her to have as much sexual intercourse as she likes. When asked why it is considered bad, they will answer:

[...]

"Because there is no father to the child, there is no man to take it in his arms." In this locution, the correct definition of the term *tamala* is clearly expressed: it is the mother's husband, the man whose rôle and duty it is to take the child in his arms and to help her in nursing and bringing it up.

Fatherless Children in a Matrilineal Society

This seems a convenient place to speak about the very interesting problem of illegitimate children, or, as the natives word it, "children born by unmarried girls," "fatherless children." Several questions must, no doubt, have already obtruded themselves on the reader. Since there is so much sexual freedom, must there not be a great number of children born out of wedlock? If this is not so, what means of prevention do the natives possess? If it is so, how do they deal with the problem, what is the position of illegitimate children?

As to the first question, it is very remarkable to note that illegitimate children are rare. The girls seem to remain sterile throughout their period of licence, which begins when they are small children and continues until they are married; when they are married they conceive and breed, sometimes quite prolifically. I express myself cautiously about the number of illegitimate children, for in most cases there are special difficulties even in ascertaining the fact. To have prenuptial children is, as I have said, by an arbitrary ruling of doctrine and custom, considered reprehensible. Thus, out of delicacy towards people present, out of family interest or local pride, the existence of such children is invariably concealed. Such children are often adopted by some relative, and the elasticity of kinship terms makes it very difficult to distinguish between actual and adopted children. [...] I was able to find roughly a dozen illegitimate children recorded genealogically in the Trobriands, or about one percent. [...]

Thus we are faced with the question: Why are there so few illegitimate children? [...] One thing I can say with complete confidence: no preventive means of any description are known, nor the slightest idea of them entertained. This, of course, is quite natural. Since the procreative power of seminal fluid is not known, since it is considered not only innocuous but beneficient, there is no reason why the natives should interfere with its free arrival into the parts which it is meant to lubricate. Indeed, any suggestion of neo-Malthusian appliances makes them shudder or laugh according to their mood or temperament. They never practise *coitus interruptus*, and still less have any notion about chemical or mechanical preventives.

But though I am quite certain on this point, I cannot speak with the same conviction about abortion, though probably it is not practised to any large extent. I may say at once that the natives, when discussing these matters, feel neither fear nor constraint, so there can be no question of any difficulties in finding out the state of affairs because of reticence or concealment. My informants told me that a magic exists to bring about premature birth, but I was not able either to obtain instances in which it was performed, nor to find out the spells or rites made use of. Some of the herbs employed in this magic were mentioned to me, but I am certain that none of them possess any physiological properties. Abortion by mechanical means seems, in fine, the only effective method practised to check the increase of population, and there is no doubt that even this is not used on a large scale.

So the problem remains. Can there be any physiological law which makes conception less likely when women begin their sexual life young, lead it indefatigably, and mix their lovers freely? Some such solution of the difficulty seems to me the only one, unless I have missed some very important ethnological clue. I am, as I have said, by no means confident of my researches being final in this matter.

It is amusing to find that the average white resident or visitor to the Trobriands is deeply interested in this subject, and in this subject only, of all the ethnological problems opened to him for consideration. There is a belief prevalent among the white citizens of eastern New Guinea that the Trobrianders are in possession of some mysterious and powerful means of prevention or abortion. This belief is, no doubt, explicable by the remarkable and puzzling facts which we have just been discussing. It is enhanced by insufficient knowledge, and the tendency towards exaggeration and sensationalism so characteristic of the crude European mind. [...]

Fecundity in unmarried girls is discreditable; sterility in married women is unfortunate. The same term *nakarige* (*na*, female prefix, *karige*, to die) is used of a childless woman as of a barren sow. But this condition brings no shame on the person concerned, and does not detract from the social status of such a woman. [...]

According to native ideas, a woman who is pregnant must, at a certain stage, abstain from all intercourse and "turn her mind away from men". She then needs a man who will take over all sexual rights in regard to her, abstain from exercising even his own privileges from a certain moment, guard her from any interference, and control her own behaviour. All this the brother cannot do, for, owing to the strict brother-sister taboo, he must scrupulously avoid even the thought of anything which is concerned with his sister's sex. Again, there is the need for a man to keep guard over her during childbirth, and "to receive the child into his arms", as the natives put it. Later it is the duty of this man to share in all the tender cares bestowed on the child. [...]

Though the natives are ignorant of any physiological need for a male in the constitution of the family, they regard him as indispensable socially. This is very important. Paternity, unknown in the full biological meaning so familiar to us, is yet maintained by a social dogma which declares: "Every family must have a father; a woman must marry before she may have children; there must be a male to every household."

The institution of the individual family is thus firmly established on a strong feeling of its necessity, quite compatible with an absolute ignorance of its biological foundations. The sociological role of the father is established and defined without any recognition of his physiological nature.

NOTES

1 An island where Trobrianders believed the dead resided until they were reincarnated.
2 Matrilineal ancestral spirits, believed to enter women's bodies to be reborn.

16

Tradition, Experience, and Belief

Ashley Montagu

Man is mind, and the situation of man as man is a mental situation.
> Karl Jaspers, Man in the Modern Age, 1933.

In the preceding chapters the evidence relating to the procreative beliefs of the Australian Aborigines has been considered at some length, the myths, the traditions, and the beliefs. We have seen what these myths and traditions are, and also something of the source from which they derive. We saw that wherever in Australia generally intercourse is in some way associated with pregnancy it is generally considered to be one of the conditions, not a cause, and sometimes a dispensable condition, of pregnancy. Intercourse, we found is customarily considered incapable of producing pregnancy. The effective cause of pregnancy, *and nothing else*, is the immigration into a woman of a spirit-child from some specifically known external source, such as a totem centre, an article of food, a whirlwind, and the like. The spirit-child is in origin entirely independent of its future parents. Whether or not a woman shall be entered by a spirit-child is generally considered to be dependent entirely upon the will of the spirit-child itself. Whether the belief in incarnation or in reincarnation was dominant or non-existent in any particular tribe we found to make little distinguishable difference to the observed fundamental belief that children were not the result of the congress of the sexes. Where animals are regarded as having souls they are believed to come into being in the same way as humans do, where they are denied any spiritual qualities, as among the Tully River natives of North Queensland, they are said to be the result of intercourse, or what is more likely, simple physical reproduction. This latter view represents a special form of the doctrine of supernatural birth which, in the absence of the belief in the original transformation of animal and plant life into human beings, together with the general totemic beliefs of the Central Australian type, accounts for the birth of men in such a way that animals and plants are necessarily excluded from the process.

It is clear, then, that the conceptional beliefs of the Aborigines in general represent but a

Ashley Montagu, *Coming into Being Among the Australian Aborigines*, 2nd edition, London: Routledge Kegan Paul, 1974, pp. 377–386. Reprinted with permission of Taylor & Francis Books UK.

Sexualities in Anthropology: A Reader, edited by Andrew P. Lyons and Harriet D. Lyons
© 2011 Blackwell Publishing Ltd.

special case of the belief in supernatural birth. This belief has virtually a world-wide distribution and assumes a large variety of forms. These forms and their distribution have been exhaustively dealt with by Hartland in his two works, *The Legend of Perseus* and *Primitive Paternity*.

We have also seen how the beliefs of the *Alchera* type, in eliminating or rendering unnecessary any notion of a physiological role played by individuals in the generation of a child, give a non-biological purely social meaning to the concept of parenthood and to the terms 'father' and 'mother'.

Whether the nescience of the causal relationship between intercourse and childbirth is a result of a primitive unawareness of the facts as Frazer, Hartland, and others believe, or whether this nescience has been secondarily produced by a social dogma which has caused a shift in emphasis to take place which completely obscures the part that intercourse may formerly have played in the native conception of procreation, as Lang, Read, Westermarck, and others believe, are questions which it has seemed to us impossible to answer with complete certainty. Whether the nescience gave rise to the dogma or the dogma to the nescience can be matter for speculation only. Such questions, it would appear to us, are falsely posed. Are we not in putting such questions, committing the error of introducing our own categories of Aristotelian thought into a situation in which they do not apply? The nature of the Aborigines' conceptual world is so thoroughly different from that of civilized Western man, it does not readily yield to what Lévy-Bruhl called 'simplist intellectual analysis'.[1] Such intellectual exercises are not only misconceived and doomed to failure but, what is worse, are likely to lead to explanations which, while perfectly congruent with our own patterns of thought, are quite inapplicable to that of the Aborigines. The question as to which preceded the other, the nescience or the dogma, is, I think falsely broached because it altogether fails to take into consideration the possibility that both the nescience and the dogma may actually be historically and culturally one and the same thing; that the dogma is the nescience, and the nescience is the dogma; or, at least, inseparable parts of one another, and in origin and development contemporaneous with one another, since they are part and parcel of one another. I do not see the necessity of assuming the priority of one to the other, and no very good reason has ever been adduced in its support by those who have made the assumption, though much erudition and ingenuity have been expended upon the question. Certainly it is possible to envisage a change in the shift of emphasis during the course of the development of the conceptional beliefs of the Aborigines from a condition in which intercourse was regarded as playing a more important role than it does today in the production of conception to one in which it was finally allowed to play little or no role at all in the procreative process; but this is purely speculative and, as far as we are concerned, unimportant. What the 'facts' may formerly have been there is now no means of telling. What the 'facts' are today it is difficult enough to determine, and our chief concern in this work has been with these latter, and with the attempt to determine their most probable meaning. In the present chapter our task will be to discuss the mechanism, the means by which the particular variety of the Aboriginal conceptional beliefs or 'facts' are maintained and confirmed.

The power of the human mind to transform 'facts', the data of experience, and to reinterpret as necessity arises and occasion demands is one of the most striking of all cultural processes, and there can be little doubt that such processes have played an appreciable part in all that is comprised within any particular Australian Aboriginal culture. A fact, as we see it, an idea or a belief, is essentially a judgment about something, and as such one of the chief characteristics of such judgments is that they are capable of undergoing modification and even complete change. Reason, imagination, emotion, are all brought to bear by the Aborigines upon their experience. By the use of these agencies it is not difficult to see how modifications, and even the reasons for them, may in the course of time bring about changes in social dogma and in individual belief.

In view of these considerations it is quite possible that the Aborigines have gradually succeeded in suppressing or in attenuating the emphasis that may possibly formerly have been placed upon intercourse in relation to conception, in conformity with the development of the official doctrines. It is possible but, as we have seen, there is no adequate evidence that this was ever the case.

Without, then speculating further concerning the possible origin of the conceptional beliefs of the Aborigines let us now inquire into the manner in which these beliefs function, how the individual comes to believe in them, and in what way these beliefs are maintained and reinforced by his own experience.

In describing the *Alchera* beliefs and social organization of the Arunta we saw something of the emotionally charged world in which the Central Australians live, a world consisting to a very large extent of spirit forces and influences, of occult powers and magic properties, concerning which there exists a body of traditional teaching which serves to give these phenomena their meaning and value. Into this world the individual is born as an experiencer and heir to the teachings which serve to give his experience its meaning. The variety of ways in which this teaching, the body of traditional knowledge, is acquired must be understood if we are to obtain any understanding of the nature of the process which produces the harmony between tradition, experience, and belief.

The all-pervasive spirit-nature of the Aboriginal world begins to make itself felt almost from the moment of the individual's birth, for from that moment, as well as being the product of spirit factors, he becomes the object of spirit practices and himself becomes closely associated with certain spirit charges and spirit objects with which he soon comes to establish a deeply emotional relationship. Gradually almost every object in the outside world and almost every one of his subjective states assumes a spiritual meaning for him, for he comes to life and grows up in a world which owes its being to spiritual powers and is operated and regulated by spiritual processes in which men seek to participate in order that they may, among other things, have some share in the regulation of that world.

Apart from such early instruction as he receives in the religious doctrines of the tribe, the more serious instruction is left until the time when the individual is considered to be capable of receiving it, which is usually some time after the attainment of puberty. Such instruction is formally concluded after a series of protracted ceremonies and ordeals have been passed through; before this period in his development, the individual is busy acquiring the techniques of living, in learning how to track animals, to read spoors, to distinguish the cries of birds, to make simple weapons, to dig for grubs and burrowing animals, and so on. His secular activities are pursued in an environment that is characterized by a dominant and all-pervasive belief in the operation of spirit forces. There are sacred places which he must never approach and which are shrouded in deep mystery, there are numerous other places which are the abode of certain spirits, the rocks, the gorges, the trees, the waterholes, the clouds, the sky, the sun, the stars, and the moon, all these are associated with spiritual powers, and for well understood very definite reasons.

Writing of the Arunta, Miss Olive Pink puts it very graphically:[2]

No one who has not experienced it can appreciate the vivid reality of the partially historic myths. The whole country through which we passed was apparently only mulga scrub, a few gum trees, a low or high range here and there, or some open plains, yet it is made a scene of much activity by aboriginal history embodied in myths, such as the journeys of 'dream-time' people travelling in various directions, whose roads we bisected or rode parallel with, or who were 'sitting down', that is, camping permanently and performing ceremonies, or 'finishing' and going into the ground ... So vivid are the tales that the investigator has the feeling of an inhabited area with much activity around: people hurrying hither and thither, or living normal lives like blackfellows did only a few generations ago in this very tribe.

On the march, a woman with her children will at times separate from her husband and take a very roundabout course to reach the same destination; the children eventually learn that this is because the locality which they have taken such pains to avoid is the location of a sacred place peopled by spirits, and so powerful that it is death for a woman or a child to approach it. Additional explanations are offered, and the mythological history of these and similar events to a certain extent illuminated, and for the rest the imagination of the child is relied on to supply what it can. When, as happens at certain intervals during the course of the year, the men depart from the camp to take part in the celebration of their totemic ceremonies, when a youth is to undergo the ordeal of initiation, the children witness and often participate in certain preliminary and subsequent activities which imaginatively interpreted against what background of knowledge they already possess serve to produce in them emotional states which are of lasting duration. When from the distant ceremonial ground the children hear the mysterious sounds which they observe to inspire such awe in the women and other children who have heard them before, and learn that the sounds are made by some great mysterious spirit who is about to swallow or has already swallowed one of the novices who used, perhaps, formerly to play with them; when they observe the difference in the deportment and in the appearance of the returned novice whom they may glimpse in the men's camp to which he is now permanently removed, the nature of the spiritual world becomes more real and more deeply impressive than ever.

Without entering into further detailed discussion of the many other elements of experience that condition the child's mind in Australia, it would seem so far clear in what manner experience is built into the mind, and how deeply it is ensconced in emotion and mystical bases. It should also be evident that under such conditions the play of the child's imagination in relation to the mystical events with which it is everywhere surrounded will form one of the strongest factors in producing a single system of workable beliefs. The fact that everyone else believes the same things in the same way makes the acquisition of these beliefs uncomplicated and inevitable.

As the child passes into adolescence and eventually proceeds through the various stages of initiation he acquires a broader and deeper knowledge of the nature of his world, of the place of the tribe within it, and of the individual within the latter, of the origin of the tribe and of himself, and of the traditions telling of these origins, of the nature of his world as it at present functions. During the course of the protracted ceremonies of initiation, which take place at intervals over an extended period of time, this knowledge is acquired by him in such a manner that it, together with all that he has formerly known, assumes for him a more profound meaning than was ever before possible. The extraordinarily mysterious nature of the rites, the practices, and the ceremonies in which he participates, the ordeals through which he passes, and all that he sees and hears are so surcharged with spiritual significances, and are emotionally, imaginatively, and intellectually so impressive, that ever afterwards the effective associations thus established for the structure and functioning of his universe are to him a living and ever-present reality.

The experiences through which the individual passes during the initiation ceremonies are deeply religious ones during which he comes into the closest touch with the spirit-forces with which his world is filled. The impenetrable veil of the non-appearing which lies behind the appearance which constitutes his experience is raised for him, he is admitted into the inner mysteries, the penetralia of things, and the essence of the non-appearing is made available to him.

Thus does the content of his mind, relating to his view of the world, come to acquire the deeply mystical character it possesses. The content of knowledge thus acquired serves as the measure to which all the data of experience are referred for judgment, and since the traditional teachings consist to a very large extent of judgments and interpretations of the nature of experience, that experience is therefore already prejudged, and so it comes about that the traditions which give experience its meaning are by that experience, through the medium of the individual, confirmed and supported. Tradition and experience are reciprocally and mutually supporting, and the result is that the individual's beliefs are constantly receiving the confirmation of this dual endorsement.

We must be careful here, however, not to draw too fine a distinction between things that are not quite so finely distinguished by the natives themselves. While it is true for classificatory purposes that there exists a body of traditional knowledge which is in the keeping of the elders and the initiated men of the tribe, the distinction is an artificial one, for what com- prises this knowledge is largely lived and expe- rienced by each individual for himself whether what is experienced is perceptible to sense or not. We perceive the world according to the kingdom that is within us, and the kingdom that is within us, the content of our minds, is determined by the culture which has constructed and furnished it, hence, what reality is con- ceived to be is culturally determined. The man- ner in which this enculturation is produced among the Aborigines we have to some extent been able to see. The traditional teaching, there- fore, is no mere body of esoterically idolized doctrines, but it is at once a testament of belief which each individual progressively lives and experiences for himself, a vital force which is inseparable from the life of the individual, an interactive relationship which maintains the individual and which the individual in turn serves to maintain.

There can have been little conscious specu- lation involved in the Aboriginal's acquisition of his knowledge of the world. The Aborigines are as intelligent as any other people – even their spirit-child beliefs attest to that fact – but in the spiritual environment in which they grow and develop, it is not so much with refined intellectual analysis that they are called upon to respond, but rather with the affective responses of emotion and imagination. One is neither encouraged nor required to speculate or critically examine the beliefs in which, like everyone else, one has been reared. Traditional teaching is there ready made to provide the Aboriginal with all that he needs to know. As Boas has said, 'the traditional material with which man operates determines the particular type of explanatory idea that associates itself with the emotional state of mind. Primitive man generally bases these explanations of his customs on concepts that are intimately related to his general view of the constitution of the world ... the origin of customs of primitive man must not be looked for in rational processes.'[3] This, of course, applies with equal force to the religious beliefs of primitive man.

From the standpoint of its consistency and organization as a workable cosmology, the traditional account of the nature of the Australian world is deeply impressive. It would,

however, be an error to assume that because it is intellectually so impressive it was therefore arrived at through the operation of intellectual processes which sought to give a rational explanation of the world in which man has his being. We are not concerned here with the origin of the cosmological beliefs of the Aborigines, but in considering them in their present form there can be little doubt that, as far as the individual is concerned, that form was not arrived at as a result of intellectual processes of reasoning, but rather that it is the result of processes of a nature more or less purely imaginative in character. The mythical environment of spirit-forces in which the Aboriginal lives is the great conditioner of his beliefs. It is the great 'illusory major premise' from which, with entire logic, he deduces his beliefs, the conclusions, that have been drawn out of what has previously been packed into the major premise.[4] That in the course of the historical development of the traditional beliefs individual thinkers, 'wise men' have, within the limits of the spirit-universe of feeling-permeated thought, served to bring about modifications in the traditional beliefs is more than likely, and that these were the result of some conscious reflection. It is also probable that such reflec- tion was largely influenced by the affective- imaginative universe of thought within which it functioned. We know that the Aboriginal in his 'profane moments' dispassionately reflects upon and discusses the traditional beliefs in a rational and logical manner, but his reason and his logic operate upon premises which serve only to sustain those beliefs.

Beliefs upon which the whole of one's exist- ence, as well as that of one's fellows, has been founded do not represent conclusions arrived at in the course of discussion or reflection, but represent rather the bequest of the hard-earned wisdom of earlier generations for the benefit of the group and of the individuals comprising it. Tested by each generation for itself, and by each individual for himself, these beliefs have passed every conceivable test of worthiness. They are beliefs that have been verified repeat- edly, and the Aboriginal, a confirmed pragma- tist, has every reason to believe that they work, and that therefore they are true. This is the acid test of experience which above all else serves to confirm for the Aboriginal the truth of the traditional teaching and of his own beliefs. Were his objectively patterned experience to fail in confirming him in the beliefs that he has socially acquired he could not and would not believe in them.

Having grasped the *meanings* with which his culture has endowed his world, their truth is confirmed and corroborated for him by his own experience of that world. Thus does the more personal and immediate part of his experience of the world come to enhance the truth, and increase the value, of the traditional view of it. It is in this way that he comes, as an apparently free and independent agent, to confirm for himself the truth of the traditional teaching concerning the nature of things. Since his world is thus finally accounted for at every point, there is, of course, never a necessity for the expression of a serious doubt or opinion concerning the nature of things as he knows them. Nor is there normally any occasion for anyone ever to inquire into things of which no one else knows, for everyone of adult years knows everything there is to know, or, what amounts almost to the same thing, needs to know. The world of the Aborigines is a *closed* and self-contained world in which everything proceeds according to laws which define the boundaries of all that is experienced within it. The beginnings and ends are all accounted for and properly classified in relation to one another. The body of knowledge at the disposal of the individual in such a world comprises for him the principles, the laws, the standards, according to which experience must necessarily function; that this experience is socially biased through and through is not much to the point here; what *is* to the point, however, is that experience can only function in certain ways if it is to be true experience. Experience which does not function according to the prescribed culturally established laws has no place in primitive culture. Normally such experiences could not, in any case, be, for all experience which could possibly fall within the universe of individual apprehension would long ago have been accounted for. Abnormal experiences such as those provided by the strange beliefs of the white man simply do not approach to within the periphery of the closed world of the Aboriginal; such beliefs are

outside his world, and thus outside his experience. Once such a foreign element has penetrated into his world it means the loss of its integrity, its dissolution. Unless an experience fits into the pattern of the world as he knows it that experience can have no place in his world, for it is meaningless. If the new experience can be made to fit into the scheme of his system, the traditional beliefs and judgments which are his principles, the new experience is readily incorporated into that system, otherwise it is simply *nonsense*, in the strict meaning of that word. Thus, all experience normally functions within a specific configuration, a configuration always determined by cultural necessity. To these principles the individual is for ever referring his new experiences, and perpetually fitting these experiences to them. Like everyone else he tends very strongly to believe in that which fits in with some pre-existing pattern. The common man of the civilized world proceeds in precisely the same way. The critical thinker proceeds by the converse method of adjusting his principles or beliefs in the light of new experiences. What is already known, what is accepted as truth, 'is held subject to use, and is at the mercy of the discoveries which it makes possible ... truths already possessed may have practical or moral certainty, but logically they never lose a hypothetic quality.'[5] For the Aboriginal, however, a truth never possesses this hypothetic quality. For him it is an eternal verity, a complete and unchanging certainty. The question of probability never arises, since everything he knows and experiences confirms the validity of his beliefs.

In his own thought the native is perfectly logical, and in relation to his own system of beliefs, his own framework of reference, his conclusions are perfectly valid. Like the philosopher he deduces results in accordance with what is implied in his own standards or measures, and through these he arrives by a logically faultless route at knowledge, or what is the same thing, for him as for ourselves, *justifiable belief*. 'Common sense' is for him what it is for us, that which is in common agreed upon as obvious to sense. It is common sense to the Aboriginal that children are the result of a woman having been originally entered by a spirit-child. Among ourselves it is common sense to believe that children are the result of an act of intercourse. If this is not so, then we are using a meaningless term and common sense does not perhaps have a real but a putative existence. Certainly common sense is demonstrably not the innate quality of the human mind some have imagined it to be, an irreducible 'reality' which causes it to judge all things in a similar manner.[6] Common sense represents a process of inference. What the nature of that inference will be depends largely on what happens during the passage of whatever it is that passes through the alembic of the mind. This is the reason why common sense is so often wrong. It is not that the data are at fault, but the mind through which they are perceived that is at fault. If this is true then it is clear that the inferences of common sense will depend almost entirely upon what is in the minds of those making them, and that the nature of the inferences will vary with the kind of apperceptive equipment with which the process of inference is made. The apperceptive equipment of the Aboriginal with respect to the datum of childbirth constrains his common sense to see only the effects of certain causes, spirit-children entering women in certain ways as a result of certain conditions and causes. The apperceptive equipment of the average bearer of Western culture inclines him to see in the similar datum of experience the effect of a cause which he believes to have been initiated by intercourse and possibly also the will of God. It is perhaps unnecessary to add that as far as his actual knowledge of the matter is concerned, it is quite as much a superstition as the beliefs held by the Aborigines. Common sense, in short, like every other aspect of thought, is a culturally conditioned trait.

[...]

NOTES

1 *How Natives Think*, 15.
2 'The landowners of the northern division of the Aranda tribe, Central Australia', *Oceania*, 6, 1936, 282–3.
3 *The Mind of Primitive Man*, 227.
4 W. G. Sumner and A. G. Keller, *The Science of Society*, New Haven, 1928, ii, 786; R. Karsten, *The Origins of Religion*, 22–48.
5 J. Dewey, *Experience and Nature*, 154.
6 See W. J. Perry, for example, 'Theology and physical paternity', *Man*, 32, 1932, 175–6.

SELECT BIBLIOGRAPHY

Boas, Franz
   1929 [orig 1911] The Mind of Primitive Man. New York: Macmillan.
Dewey, John
   1929 Experience and Nature. New York: Dover.
Frazer, Sir James G.
   1910 Totemism and Exogamy. 4 vols. London: Macmillan.
Hartland, Edwin Sidney
   1894–1896 The Legend of Perseus. 3 vols. London: D. Nutt.
Hartland, Edwin Sidney
   1909–1910 Primitive Paternity. 2 vols. London: D. Nutt.
Karsten, Rafael
   1935 The Origins of Religion. London: Kegan, Paul, Trench, and Tribner Ltd.
Lang, Andrew
   1905 The Secret of the Totem. London: Longmans, Green and Company.
Lévy-Bruhl, Lucien
   1926 How Natives Think. London: George Allen and Unwin, Ltd.
Pink, Olive
   1936 The landowners of the northern division of the Aranda tribe, Central Australia. Oceania 6:275–305.
Read, Carveth
   1918 No Paternity. Journal of the Royal Anthropological Institute 48:146–154.
Sumner, William Graham Sumner, and Albert Galloway Keller
   1928 The Science of Society. New Haven: Yale University Press.
Westermarck, Edward
   1922 [1891] The History of Human Marriage. 3 vols. London: Macmillan.

17

Virgin Birth

Edmund Leach

There are three partners in every birth: God, father and mother.
Talmud *Kiddush* 30 b.

The so-called primitive ignorance of pater-nity is nothing else but a very imperfect knowledge that intercourse is a necessary though not sufficient condition of the women being 'opened-up' as my Trobriand friends put it.
Malinowski in Ashley-Montagu (1937:31).

This lecture contains three themes which fol-low logically one upon another even though my presentation requires that they be slightly jumbled up. In the first place I review the classic anthropological controversy about whether certain primitive peoples, notably the Australian aborigines and the Trobrianders, were or were not 'ignorant of the facts of phys-iological paternity' when first encountered by early ethnographers. I conclude, as others have concluded, that they were not. Secondly, I take note of the fact that the anthropologist's belief

in the ignorance of his primitive contemporar-ies shows an astonishing resilience in the face of adverse evidence and I consider why anthro-pologists should be predisposed to think in this way. Thirdly, I suggest that if we can once lay aside this prejudice about ignorance and prim-itiveness we are left with some important prob-lems for investigation. Doctrines about the possibility of conception taking place without male insemination do not stem from innocence and ignorance: on the contrary they are con-sistent with theological argument of the great-est subtlety. If we put the so-called primitive beliefs alongside the sophisticated ones and treat the whole lot with equal philosophical respect we shall see that they constitute a set of variations around a common structural theme, the metaphysical topography of the relation-ship between gods and men. Limitations of time will prevent any elaboration of this latter theme.

[...]

What is really at issue is the technique of anthropological comparison which depends in turn upon the kind of 'meaning' which we

Extracts from Edmund Leach's essay, Virgin Birth, from *Proceedings of the Royal Anthropological Institute*, 1966: 39–49. Reprinted with permission of Wiley-Blackwell.

Sexualities in Anthropology: A Reader, edited by Andrew P. Lyons and Harriet D. Lyons
© 2011 Blackwell Publishing Ltd.

are prepared to attribute to ethnographical evidence.

When an ethnographer reports that 'members of the X tribe believe that …' he is giving a description of an orthodoxy, a dogma, something which is true of the culture as a whole. But [some anthropologists] desperately want to believe that the evidence can tell us much more than that – that dogma and ritual must somehow correspond to the inner psychological attitudes of the actors concerned. We need only consider the customs of our own society to see that this is not so. For example, a high proportion of English girls go through the *rite de passage* of a Church of England marriage service. In the course of this the husband gives the girl a ring, her veil is removed, her flowers are thrown away, a priest lectures her on the importance of childbearing, and she has rice poured over her head – a set of performances roughly analogous to those reported by W. E. Roth (1903) of the Tully River Blacks. But all this tells me absolutely nothing about the inner psychological state of the lady in question; I cannot infer from the ritual either what she feels or what she knows. She may be an outright atheist. Alternatively she may believe that a church marriage is essential for the well-being of her future children. Certainly her ignorance of the precise details of the physiology of sex is likely to be quite as profound as that of any Australian aborigine. On the other hand, the English marriage ritual does tell the outside observer a great deal about the formal social relations which are being established between the various parties concerned, and this is true of the Australian case also.

It would not be profitable to thrash over the details of the Australian material again. I will simply make the following summary points in justification of my position. [...]

1   There are two classically established reasons for supposing that the Tully River Blacks were not ignorant of the facts of physiological paternity in any simple sense. These are

(a)   that they freely admitted to Roth that the cause of pregnancy in animals other than man is copulation,

(b)   Hartland (1894–6; 1909–10) assembled a vast collection of mythological tales from all over the world which related to the magical conception of ancestral heroes and hero-deities.[1] Some of these stories resemble very closely indeed the account given to Roth by the Tully River Blacks of how *ordinary* human births occur. Hartland thought that such stories were survivals from a state of primeval ignorance. Almost everyone would now reject such an interpretation. But if the existence of European tales about ladies who became pregnant after eating magical fish is not now held to imply that Europeans are, or were, ignorant of the facts of physiological paternity, why should such stories have this implication in the case of the Tully River Blacks?

2   A third reason for rejecting the supposition of simple minded ignorance is the judgement of the more recent ethnographers. Meggitt (1962) for example remarks that the answers which a Walbiri makes to questions about conception depend upon who is asked and in what circumstances. 'In ritual contexts, men speak of the action of the *guruwari* (spirit entities) as the significant factor; in secular contexts they nominate both the *guruwari* and sexual intercourse. The women, having few ritual attitudes, generally emphasise copulation' (Meggitt 1962: 273).

3   Outside Australia the only society for which 'ignorance of physiological paternity' is commonly thought to have been well established is that of the Trobriand Islands. Malinowski's original statements on this point were very dogmatic. He asserted that 'knowledge of impregnation, of the man's share in creating the new life in the mother's womb, is a fact of which the natives have not even the slightest glimpse'. But later on he became much more guarded. The 1932 version was: 'The Trobrianders do not suffer from a specific complaint *ignorantia paternitatis*. What we find among them is a complicated attitude towards the facts of maternity and paternity. Into this attitude

there enter certain elements of positive knowledge, certain gaps in embryological information. These cognitive ingredients again are overlaid by beliefs of an animistic nature, and influenced by the moral and legal principles of the community...' (Malinowski 1932: 21). As much surely could be said of any people in the world?

We should also note that in his original account Malinowski stated that the Trobrianders, like the Tully River Blacks, recognised the significance of copulation in animals though not in men. [...] Despite the fame of Malinowski, the Trobriand Islands do *not* provide a supporting case illustrating the possibility of total ignorance of the facts of life.

Where does this get us to? Ignorance is a relative matter and obviously we are all ignorant in some degree particularly about sex. But I think that anyone who reads through the Australian ethnographic evidence with a mind reasonably free from prejudice must agree, not only that the balance of evidence is *now* heavily on the side that the aborigines were not 'ignorant about the facts of paternity' in any simple sense, but that the balance of evidence has *always* been that way. That being so the fact that a long line of distinguished anthropologists, which includes Frazer and Malinowski as well as Professor [Melford] Spiro, have taken the opposite view is a very intriguing fact. Spiro's attitude is in fact typical. He is positively *eager* to believe that the aborigines were ignorant and he accepts their ignorance as a fact without investigating the evidence at all; at the same time he displays an extreme reluctance to believe that the products of aboriginal thought can be structured in a logical way. This, of course, is a very ancient tradition. In anthropological writing, ignorance is a term of abuse. To say that a native is *ignorant* amounts to saying that he is childish, stupid, superstitious. Ignorance is the opposite of logical rationality; it is the quality which distinguishes the savage from the anthropologist. When Professor Spiro writes that 'Religion persists because it has causes – it is caused by the expectation of satisfying desires' (Spiro 1966: 117) he is simply rephrasing the old Frazerian argument that hope springs eternal

even in a context of total illusion. It is the same argument as that which affirms that if men perform magical rites before the start of a fishing expedition it is *because* they are deluded into believing that fish can be influenced by words and actions at a distance and they go on believing this *because* they desire to catch fish. In other words religion and magic persist in a context of ignorance.

Now the interesting thing about this argument is that it is applied only to *primitive* contexts. Frazer, who had such unbounded contempt for the ignorant savage magician, offered no objection to the nightly recital of Latin grace in Trinity College Hall. One cannot legitimately interpret the reading of grace as evidence that the parties concerned are either superstitious or devout; why then should we make different assumptions when 'ignorant natives' engage in 'meaningless ritual'? If an Australian aboriginal woman announces her pregnancy by bringing into camp a frog of a particular kind or by vomiting after taking food from her husband this is not evidence that she believes these actions to be the 'cause' of her pregnancy in a physical sense. They are signs not causes. Grace in a college hall 'says' that the meal is about to begin or that it has just ended; the actual word content is totally irrelevant. Similarly the ritual actions described by Roth serve to 'say something' about the social situation and the social condition of the parties involved, they do not express the sum of aboriginal knowledge.

I am here reminded of the fact that while the ordinances of the University of Cambridge indicate that young men obtain degrees because they sit examinations, they do not specify that any prior knowledge is required to achieve this desired end. Yet Cambridge undergraduates are not ignorant of the realities of the situation. The relationship between ritual and copulation in aboriginal theories about the causes of pregnancy appears to be of a strictly analogous kind.

But in any case, as I have said already, what seems to me interesting is not so much the ignorance of the aborigines as the naïveté of the anthropologists. It seems evident that Western European scholars are strongly predisposed to believe that *other people* should believe in versions of the myth of the Virgin Birth. If *we* believe such things we are devout: if *others* do so they are idiots. It is into this aspect of the matter that I should now like to enquire.

Let me first state my personal bias. I find it highly improbable on common-sense grounds that genuine 'ignorance' of the basic facts of physiological paternity should anywhere be a cultural fact. It is true that since human gestation lasts nine months and the first evidence of pregnancy can only be experienced several weeks after the act of intercourse which caused it and since in any case intercourse is a necessary but not sufficient cause of pregnancy, it is by no means absurd to suppose that there might be human groups which are quite ignorant of the role of the male; but consider the probabilities.

Human beings, wherever we meet them, display an almost obsessional interest in matters of sex and kinship. Presumably this has always been the case. Human beings have existed on earth for a very long time during which they have displayed collective problem solving intelligence of an astoundingly high order. Ethnography admits that with a very few exceptions all cultural communities now existing are fully aware of the physiological connexion between copulation and pregnancy. The exceptional groups, which are alleged to be ignorant of this connexion, appear to be fully the equal of their more knowledgeable neighbours in such matters as technical ingenuity, complexity of kinship organisation and so on. Moreover, the allegedly 'ignorant' groups are not living in lonely isolation in some fabulous ethnographical Shangri La, they are groups which have close political and economic ties with other peoples who are not 'ignorant of physiological paternity'.

My inference from all this is one of scepticism. If certain groups, such as the Trobrianders, have persuaded their ethnographers that they were ignorant of the facts of life, then it is because that 'ignorance' was for these people a kind of dogma.[2] And if the ethnographer in question believed what he was told it was because such belief corresponded to his own private fantasy of the natural ignorance of childish savages.

We meet with alleged ignorance of physiological paternity among peoples whom ethnographers rate as very primitive. This 'ignorance' is deemed a mark of the 'primitiveness'. In contrast the miraculous birth of divine or semi-divine heroes is a characteristic of the mythology of the 'higher' civilisations. Dionysos, son of Zeus, is born of a mortal virgin, Semele, who later became immortalised through the intervention of her divine son; Jesus, son of God, is born of a mortal virgin, Mary, who ...; such stories can be duplicated over and over again. They do not indicate ignorance.

The Frazer-Hartland generation of anthropologists tended to adopt two mutually inconsistent attitudes to such stories. On the one hand since virgin birth is plainly a non-rational concept, the stories could not have been invented by sensible civilised people – they were survivals from an earlier primitive stage of society. On the other hand it was implied that theology of the 'higher religions' was not amenable to anthropological investigation at all. Only the Catholic Fathers associated with the journal *Anthropos* could consider the possibility that the religions of primitive peoples might have theological merit in their own right.

It is a striking fact that the five volumes which Hartland devoted to the discussion of Virgin Birth (Hartland 1894–96, 1909–10) contain scarcely a single reference to Christianity and the corresponding volumes of *The golden bough* (Frazer 1906), despite their cynical tone, make no attempt to fit the details of Christian theology into a cross-cultural schema which also includes 'primitive' materials.[3]

Now in its Christian context the myth of the Virgin Birth does *not* imply ignorance of the facts of physiological paternity. On the contrary, it serves to reinforce the dogma that the Virgin's child is the son of God. Furthermore, the Christian doctrine of the physical-spiritual paternity of God the Father does not preclude a belief in the sociological paternity of St Joseph. Medieval Christians thought of St Joseph as a cuckold ... 'Joseph was an old man, an old man was he' ... but the authors of the Gospels of St Matthew and St Luke combine their account of the Virgin Birth with a pedigree which places Jesus in the direct line of patrilineal descent from David *through Joseph*. In other words the kind of interpretation which I put on Roth's evidence and which Professor Spiro finds so novel and unacceptable has been orthodox among Christians for about 1600 years. The myth, like the rite, does not distinguish knowledge from ignorance. It establishes categories and affirms relationships.

Ethnographers of the late nineteenth and early twentieth centuries were predisposed to discover cases of ignorance of physiological paternity by their reading in the theoretical works of McLennan, Morgan *et al*. McLennan's fantasy of the beginning of civilisation was of a society in which men mated promiscuously and the only kinship recognised was that through females. Common motherhood, he argued, is a fact very readily recognised whereas the recognition of paternity would require reflection and rational thought and would therefore be a much later development. The evolutionist doctrine that systems of matrilineal descent represent an 'earlier stage' in the evolution of human society than systems of patrilineal descent was tied in to this idea that matrilineal kinship is more obvious than patrilineal kinship. It was not argued that ignorance of physiological paternity must *now* prevail in all matrilineal systems, but only that it must have prevailed in the 'original' human societies and that these original societies would on that account have been matrilineal. This whole set of ideas predisposed ethnographers who were searching for 'very primitive' peoples to think they might discover matriliny and ignorance of physiological paternity in close conjunction. Moreover, even when the matriliny wasn't obvious, this particular type of ignorance could be taken as the ultimate mark of primitiveness, and would thus confirm the anthropologist in his hope that he had discovered a fossilised living specimen of primeval man – which is precisely what the ethnographers of Australian aborigines imagined they *had* discovered.

Evolutionism in its crude nineteenth century form is no longer the fashion but versions of the evolutionist argument are constantly being revived. This ties in with the fact that the quest for the ultimate primitive who is *quite different* from civilised man appeals very strongly to certain anthropologists. My own prejudices go all the other way. The data of ethnography are interesting to me because they so often seem directly relevant to my own allegedly civilised experiences. It is not only the differences between Europeans and Trobrianders which interest me, it is their similarities. This of course is a Malinowskian precept, but let us try to put it into practice. Let us go back to the Christians.

In the Christian case a careful distinction is made between Jesus' legal status *as a man* and his essential nature *as a god*. As a man he is the legal son of Joseph the husband of Mary and in this legal sense he belongs to the lineage of David. In contrast, his divine essence derives from the fact that the male component of his conception was 'the holy spirit' which entered Mary's body by an unnatural route. The details of this were at one time the subject of much learned speculation, the general consensus being that Mary was impregnated through the ear.

The distinction between legal status and substance appears also in the matrilineal Trobriand case in the reverse sense. A Trobriand child is of the same legal lineage as the holy spirit (the *baloma*) which magically enters the mother's body by an unnatural route at the moment of conception but the child's human substance and appearance derives from the mother's husband.

However, when the child is divine rather than human there is another factor which comes in besides the split between *pater* and *genitor* and that between descent and filiation. In the theology of Christianity it is not sufficient that Jesus as mediator should be ambiguously both human and divine, Mary must *also* function as a mediator and must therefore have anomalous characteristics when considered as a human being. And what could there be that is more anomalous than a human being who is sinless and a mother who is a virgin?

This is a point of some subtlety. If we take the whole range of materials relating to what *we* consider to be supernatural births we find, at one extreme, cases of the Trobriand type, where virgin births yield normal children from normal mothers. Next, we get myths of magical pregnancy in which, say, an old woman long past the age of childbearing is finally granted a child – as with the biblical stories of the birth of Isaac or of John the Baptist. Here the implication is that while the child is predestined to be a hero, the mother will remain a normal human being. Finally, at the other extreme we meet with virgin mothers of the Christian type where *both* child *and* mother are thoroughly abnormal.[4]

Theologians delight in paradox of this kind and the trouble with early anthropological discussion of the topic was simply that the anthropologists could not bring themselves to believe that their primitive informants might be armed with the ingenious sophistication of a Jesuit priest. But can we go any further than that? Can we offer any general explanation as to why people should maintain a dogma which seems to reject the facts of physiological paternity, or is each case peculiar to itself?

Tylor, Frazer and the latter day neo-Tylorians assume that statements of dogma start out as mistaken attempts to explain cause and effect in the world of nature. Dogma then persists because these mistaken ideas satisfy psychological desires. As a vulgar positivist I repudiate such speculation about causes which are inaccessible to observation or verification. It may seem surprising that men persist in expressing formal beliefs which are palpably untrue but you won't get anywhere by applying canons of rationality to principles of faith. All that the analyst can usually do is to observe the circumstances in which the untrue dogma is now affirmed and study the context of this affirmation in other ways. As with the recital of grace in College Hall we learn what the recital 'means' by studying the situation, not by studying the words.

Is there then anything which a dogma of Virgin Birth 'says' about the society in which it is affirmed? Well, let us consider first the simple logic of the matter. The Christian myth is compatible with a social system that is essentially patriarchal, in which it is taken for granted that the rulers are so vastly superior to the ruled that class difference almost ossifies into caste, a society in which the lords never marry into the lower classes, but in which they will graciously deign to take slave concubines and elevate their sons to the ranks of the elite. Such societies have in fact repeatedly emerged in Christendom, notably in Byzantium and

eighteenth century Brazil, both countries where the cult of the Virgin was exceptionally well developed. It would need a lot of careful research to discover whether this correlation is other than accidental but it does seem to be a striking feature of Catholic colonialism (which distinguishes it sharply from the Protestant variety) that the rulers, with their bias towards Mariolatry have tended to pull their half-caste sons into the ranks of the elite. In contrast, the Protestant colonists who generally speaking tend to reject the myth of the virgin birth have always pushed their bastards into the ranks below, insisting that the status of ruler-god is exclusive to the pure-blooded. God and Jesus fit well enough into the English Public School ethos; the Virgin-Mother has no place at all.

I fully realise that many people will find this sort of treatment of Christian ideology quite shocking and even more objectionable than Weber's celebrated tie-up between Protestantism and the rise of Capitalism, but I am quite serious. The British nineteenth century evolutionist anthropologists were mostly Presbyterian Scots soaked in a study of the classics and sharing, as far as one can judge, most of the paternalistic imperialist values characteristic of the English ruling class of the period. Their theories reveal a fantasy world of masterly men who copulated indiscriminately with their slave wives who then bore children who recognised their mothers but not their fathers (McLennan 1865: ch. 8). This fantasy had some indirect resemblance to features of American chattel slavery, but it bears no resemblance whatever to the recorded behaviour of any known primitive society or of any known species of animal. It was justified simply by *a priori* reasoning. In the beginning men would have been unable to recognise a causal connexion between coitus and parturition so that although men would dominate and satisfy their lusts by violence the only form of recognised kinship would be consanguinity through female links. The result was a theory appropriate to Protestant not Catholic imperialists.

McLennan's arguments were accepted by his friend Robertson Smith who passed them on to Frazer who passed them on to a host of admiring ethnographic correspondents. The whole argument was recapitulated in quite explicit form by Hartland and swallowed hook, line and sinker by Malinowski. That was back in 1913 and, as we have already seen, Malinowski later modified his position very considerably. But he retained his high regard for aristocracy and even at the end of his life he still thought of 'culture contact' as a kind of patronage extended by paternalistic colonial powers towards their more primitive subjects. The ignorance of the Trobrianders was a necessary element in their continuing primitiveness.

By 1932 Malinowski's theory of Trobriand ignorance had been partly abandoned but there was still the matter of Trobriand mythology. There was for example, 'The marvellous land of Kaytalugi ("satiated copulation") peopled exclusively by sexually rabid women. They are so brutally profligate that their excesses kill every man thrown by chance upon their shores, and even their own male children never attain maturity before they are sexually done to death. Yet these women are very prolific, producing many children, male and female', Malinowski (1932: 156). Notice how closely this Trobriand version of the Land of the Amazons resembles the anthropologists' own fantasies. McLennan's imagination ran to rabid men raping promiscuously their servile females; the Trobrianders' fancy devised a world of rabid women raping promiscuously their servile males. McLennan's dream emerged from the context of a patriarchal ruling class which expressed horror at the thought of any marriage between an upper class male and a lower class female; the Trobriand version belongs to a society with virilocal matriliny, likewise class stratified, in which women are given as tribute to political leaders.

Professor Spiro will be wholly unimpressed. He will still ask: But how can you *prove* that these associations of facts are relevant? Well, quite frankly, I don't claim to prove anything at all. In my vulgar positivist fashion I just want to put the pieces of the jig-saw together. When the pieces fit, I am interested. I think this sort of thing tells us something about Trobrianders and also about factors which have influenced the development of anthropological theory. But I agree that we learn no more about the Trobriander's factual ignorance than we do about McLennan's.

But I still haven't fully explained what I am trying to say. Since the whole business of belief in virgin mothers and ignorance of paternity has been the subject of a vast literature, what can be the point of my just recapitulating odd snippets?

Well partly I am interested in the problem of method. We are dealing here with statements which we know to be untrue; how should we interpret ethnographical statements about palpable untruth? There are various kinds of answer which can be offered to such a question. If we are Tylorians, we accept statements of belief at their face value. We can then follow the footsteps of Frazer and Hartland and assemble huge archives of apparently similar untrue beliefs from all over the world. We then have to ask: Why do all these people believe in something which is untrue? And if you imagine that there must be a straightforward single answer to such a question I think your only way out is to say that these false beliefs rest on childish ignorance. This was the answer offered by the evolutionists and by the Malinowski of 1913 and, in modified form, by Professor Spiro in 1966.

If we are not Tylorians we can say what Powell's Trobriand informants said. There are different kinds of truth. Which is also what good Catholics say: 'We know that virgins do not conceive; but we also know that the Holy Mother of God was and ever shall be an immaculate Virgin.' This is the sort of answer offered by religious people and it is an answer which I can respect. But I do not think it is the sort of answer which should be offered by professional anthropologists in the course of their professional duties. We are social analysts not theologians. From an anthropological point of view non-rational theological propositions can only serve as data not as explanation. So we are pushed back to vulgar positivism. What sort of positivist analysis is appropriate to the sort of ethnographical data which I have been discussing? [...]

Let me try to pull the various threads of my argument together. The crux is this. From many sources we learn of legends, traditions, ritual practices which seem to imply a belief that women may sometimes be made pregnant by means other than insemination by a human male. The simplest way of 'explaining' such a belief is to say that it is due to the ignorance of the believer. Many anthropologists have argued this way and some are still inclined to do so. They seem to gain reassurance from supposing that the people they study have the simple-minded ignorance of small children. That Frazer should have thought that way is understandable, that my contemporaries should do so is extraordinary.

An alternative way of explaining a belief which is factually untrue is to say that it is a species of religious dogma; the truth which it expresses does not relate to the ordinary matter-of-fact world of everyday things but to meta-physics. It is plain, for example, that Christians who say that they 'believe' in the doctrine of the Virgin Birth or in the closely related doctrine of the Immaculate Conception are not ordinarily arguing from a position of ignorance; on the contrary these are doctrines which are compatible with positions of extreme philosophical sophistication. This type of explanation is to be preferred to the other. Frazer's childish savage should be eliminated from anthropological discussion once and for all; in his place we should put a slightly muddle-headed theologian no less ingenious than the Bishop of Woolwich or even the cleverest of my anthropological colleagues.

The problem with which this muddle-headed theologian is concerned lies at the core of speculative philosophy. What is the difference between the physical and the metaphysical?[...]

The relationship between the here-now and the other can also be represented in other ways, for example as one of class status and power – the gods are perfect and powerful, men are imperfect and impotent; or as one of normality and abnormality – hence the supernatural births and immortality of divine beings.

But the disjunction of the two worlds is not enough, there must also be continuity and mediation. Cross cutting the idea that impotent men are the descendants of potent gods we have the incestuous dogma that gods and men may establish sexual connexion. Dogmas of virgin birth and of the irrelevance of human male sexuality appear as by-products of such a theology; I do not claim that they are thus *caused*, but this is where they fit in, and this is the case in primitive as well as in sophisticated societies.

This lecture has necessarily been very incomplete but the main points which I would like to put across are these:

1 Anthropological theories often tell us more about the anthropologists than about their subject matter.
2 Let us remain sceptical and positivist. Try to see connexions between the facts as we know them. Don't inject magical causal explanations from outside.
3 It is time that we finally abandoned the traditional distinction between the stupidity of savages and the theology of civilised men. Stories about ignorance of paternity among primitive peoples are of the same kind as stories about the virgin birth of deities in the so-called higher religions. And in neither case are the story-tellers stupid. If we are to understand such stories we need to consider them all together as variations on a single structural theme.
4 If anthropologists are to justify their claim to be students of comparative religion, they need to be less polite. So far they have shown an extraordinary squeamishness about the analysis of Christianity and Judaism, religions in which they themselves or their close friends are deeply involved. Roth's Bulletin No. 5 on the North Queensland Aborigines was an ethnographic document of considerable interest; so is Chapter 1 of the Gospel according to St Matthew. Serious anthropologists should treat the two works on a par; both are records of theological doctrine.

NOTES

1 Ishida (1964) reports on a wide range of oriental materials which were not available to Hartland.
2 The evidence for 'dogma' is very clear. In 1909 the Bishop of North Queensland complained to Frazer that ignorance of the relation between intercourse and pregnancy 'forms a fact which has to be reckoned with in the introduction of a higher standard of morality among the aborigines, for they do not naturally accept the

true explanation of conception and childbirth even after their admission to the mission stations' (Frazer 1909). In later references to the bishop's statement Frazer cites only the above remarks but the aboriginal reluctance to accept the European viewpoint seems to have been a male peculiarity. The bishop also told Frazer: 'We often have girls who are sent to the mission *enceinte* and we never dwell on any wrongfulness of their condition. We have no trouble afterwards, neither have we found, at any rate for many years, that the girls persist in the belief ... that copulation is not the cause of pregnancy'. Even more striking is Fortune's account (Fortune 1932: 239) of how he tried to stage a debate between Dobuans who maintained the role of the father and Trobrianders who denied it. 'But the head of every Dobuan in the room immediately was turned away from me towards the wall. They affected not to hear the conversation; but afterwards when they had me alone they were furious with me.' The argument was plainly about doctrine not about knowledge. Theologians who debate the doctrine of transubstantiation cannot usefully be accused of ignorance of the elementary facts of chemistry.

3 Two pages from the end of his three volume work Hartland remarks: 'I cannot hide from myself the important bearing that some of the subjects dealt with in these pages may have upon Christian controversy'; but his heretical daring gets no further than that. Frazer is equally cautious. Frazer (1906: 349–50) draws attention to the writings of a variety of authors who have seen similarities between the Cult of Isis and the Cult of the Virgin Mary, but he scarcely comments on this point. Book 2 Chapter 1 of this work, which is indexed 'Stories of Virgin Birth' never mentions Christianity at all.

4 All the numerous 'mother goddesses' of the Ancient World seem to have been classified as 'virgins'. There may be complex problems of translation here. In the Trobriands, a widow, after the conclusion of her mourning, becomes a 'marriageable maiden' and is classified as such. It is at least possible that the title of 'virgin' accorded to such goddesses as Aphrodite signified their sexual availability rather than their physiological condition. Incidentally the original Hebrew of Isaiah vii: 14 which is quoted in Matthew i: 23 refers to a 'maiden' rather than to a 'virgin'.

REFERENCES

Ashley-Montagu, M. F.
1937 *Coming into being among the Australian aborigines*. London: Routledge.

Austin, L.
1934 Procreation among the Trobriand Islanders. *Oceania* 5, 102–18.

Diodorus
see Oldfather, C. H., *Diodorus of Sicily*. English translation (10 vols.) Loeb Classical Library. (1932, vol. 1: 84–87, 274–75.) London: Heinemann.

Fortes, M.
1953 The structure of unilineal descent groups. *Am. Anthrop.* 55, 17–41.

Fortune, R. F.
1932 *Sorcerers of Dobu*. London: Routledge.

Frazer, J. G.
1905 The beginnings of religion and totemism among the Australian aborigines. *Fortnightly Rev.* n.s. 78, 162–72, 452–66.

Frazer, J. G.
1906 *Adonis, Attis, Osiris*. 2 vols. in 1 (later Vol. 5 and 6 of Frazer 1914.) London: Macmillan.

Frazer, J. G.
1909 Beliefs and customs of the Australian aborigines. *Man* 9, 145–7.

Frazer, J. G.
1910 *Totemism and exogamy*, 4 vols. London: Macmillan.

Frazer, J. G.
1914 *The golden bough*, 3rd edn. 12 vols. London: Macmillan.

Geertz, C.
1966 Religion as a cultural system. In *Anthropological approaches to the study of religion* (ed.) M. Banton (Monogr. Ass. social Anthrop. 3.) London: Tavistock Publications.

Hartland, E. S.
1894–6 *The legend of Perseus*. 3 vols. London: David Nutt.

Hartland, E. S.
1909–10 *Primitive paternity*. 2 vols. London: Folk Lore Society.

Ishida, E.
1964 Mother-Son deities. *Hist. Rel.* 4, 30–68.

Kaberry, P. M.
1936 Spirit children and spirit centres of the North Kimberley Division, West Australia. *Oceania*, 6, 392–400.

Kaberry, P. M.
1939   *Aboriginal woman*. London: Routledge.
Leach, E. R.
1961   Golden bough or golden twig? *Daedalus* Spring 1961: 371–87.
Malinowski, B.
1913   *The family among the Australian aborigines*. London: London University Press.
Malinowski, B.
1932   *The sexual life of savages in north western Melanesia*. (3rd edition with special foreword.) London: Routledge.
McLennan, J. F.
1865   *Primitive marriage*. London: Quaritch.
Meggitt, M. J.
1962   *Desert people*. Sydney: Angus & Robertson.
Pinkerton, J.
1808–14   *A general collection of the best and most interesting voyages & travels in all parts of the world*. 17 vols. London: Longman, Hurst, Rees & Orme.
Powell, H. A.
1956   *An analysis of present day social structure in the Trobriands*. Thesis, London.
Purcell, B. H.
1893   Rites and customs of Australian aborigines. *Z. Ethnol.* **25**, 286–89.
Radcliffe-Brown, A. R.
1931   The social organisation of Australian tribes (*Oceania Monogr.* **1**). Melbourne: Macmillan.
Roheim, G.
1932   Psycho-analysis of primitive cultural types. *Intern. J. Psycho-Anal.* **13**, 1–224.

Roth, W. E.
1903   *Superstition, magic and medicine*. (N. Queensl. Ethnogr. Bull. 5) Brisbane: Vaughan.
Schmidt, W.
1952   Der Konzeptionsglaube australischer Stämme. *Intern. Arch. Ethnogr.* **46**, 36–81.
Spencer, B. & Gillen, F. J.
1899   *The native tribes of Central Australia*, London: Macmillan.
Spiro, M. E.
1966   Religion: problems of definition and explanation. In *Anthropological approaches to the study of religion* (ed.) M. Banton (Monogr. Ass. social. Anthrop. 3). London: Tavistock Publications.
Stanner, W. E. H.
1933   The Daly River tribes: the theory of sex. *Oceania* **4**, 26–8.
Strehlow, C.
1907–21   *Die Aranda und Loritja Stämme in Zentral-Australian*. Frankfurt: Baer.
Talmud
Kiddush 30. b. See Epstein I, *The Babylonian Talmud: Seder Nashi VIII Kiddushin* (1936 p. 149, translated H. Freedman). London: Soncino Press.
Thomson, D. F.
1933   The hero cult, initiation and totemism on Cape York: the knowledge of physical paternity. *J. R. anthrop. Inst.* **63**, 505–10.
Warner, W. L.
1937   *A black civilisation*. New York: Harper.

Part VIII

The Attack on Margaret Mead

Introduction

Anthropology rarely makes the front pages of major newspapers, but that is precisely what happened early in 1983 when Harvard University Press announced the publication of *Margaret Mead and Samoa: The Making and Unmaking of an Anthropological Myth*. The book was the result of many years of labor by its author, Derek Freeman of Australian National University. At the time it finally appeared Mead had been dead for more than four years. Freeman, whose reputation was primarily based on his fieldwork with the Iban in Borneo, had been a teacher in Western Samoa between 1940 and 1943 and had also returned there in the 1960s.

Freeman claimed that in her first ethnography, *Coming of Age in Samoa* (1928), Mead had completely misrepresented the culture of Samoa in order to implement the "cultural determinist" political and scientific agenda of her mentor, Franz Boas, and to show that heredity counted for naught in social behavior. Boas had supposedly become a dogmatic anti-hereditarian in the course of his struggle against ideas of racial difference, and was now unfortunately, thought Freeman, inclined to doubt better-grounded ideas of universal genetic and behavioral similarity. Mead's study was undertaken so that she could show that Samoa was a "single negative instance" disproving the common assertion by hereditarian psychologists that adolescence was universally a time of storm and stress. Her study was supposedly judged to be a great success and was one of the main pillars of Boasian cultural determinism.

Whereas Mead had portrayed Samoan adolescents as "laid back" and lacking in ambition because they did not have to make anxious choices about their careers, Freeman saw them (particularly the males) as ambitious, status conscious and obsessed, like most Polynesians, with rank. Mead's Samoa was one with little adolescent crisis and little crime, but Freeman had crime statistics for the Samoan Islands that pointed to a relatively high but "normal" incidence of adolescent crime. Whereas

Sexualities in Anthropology: A Reader, edited by Andrew P. Lyons and Harriet D. Lyons
© 2011 Blackwell Publishing Ltd.

Mead's Samoan adolescents were perceived as sexually free, Freeman's followed puritanical rules.

Mead had described a world of clandestine, frequent, and relatively tolerated sexual encounters between adolescents. Among the group of adolescent girls she studied in the small island of Ta'u, about 50 percent had had premarital sex and a much larger percentage had masturbated and indulged in adolescent play. Because premarital sex was condoned rather than explicitly encouraged, young men who wished to have sex with a young girl might indulge in sleep crawling or *moetotolo*, that is to say intercourse (sometimes a "playful" form of rape, in which the visitor feigns to be the girl's boyfriend) which is performed just a few feet from the girl's sleeping family.

One exception to this rule was the *taupou,* and Mead was a friend of the only *taupou* left in Ta'u: Fa'apua'a, who was 25 and therefore no adolescent. In pre-Christian times the institution of the *taupou* or ceremonial virgin may have set the pattern for adolescent girls of high rank. *Taupous* were the daughters of high chiefs destined for dynastic marriage and effectively chaperoned until that point. At marriage, the *taupou* was publicly deflowered by her bridegroom, who ruptured her hymen with a finger and displayed the resultant blood to the spectators. Other high-ranking young women also had their virginity tested. Mead noted that in embarrassing cases the test could have been faked by a sleight of hand substitution of chicken for human blood. However, under Christian influence, these customs gradually disappeared and public defloration was banned. Mead noted that the banning of defloration undermined the cult of virginity and the traditional marriage complex. The Samoans had indeed adopted Christianity, but Christianity had not permeated all aspects of their social life. Pre-marital sexual freedom had probably increased since missionization.

According to Freeman, virtually all these statements were falsehoods. Most Samoan girls were virgins at the time they married and there was a strong code of sexual honor. *Moetotolo* did occur and was less benign than Mead implied, and violent rape was a more serious problem than she indicated. Before Christianity the *taupou*'s premarital chastity was the model all adolescent girls had followed. Puritanical values had been strengthened rather than weakened by Christianity.

How had Mead got Samoa so wrong? Freeman believed that, in addition to wearing the blinkers of Boasian ideology, she was a poor fieldworker who was only in Ta'u for five months, and that she spent a good bit of that time collecting data for a broader project on social organization that she had arranged with E. G. Handy of the Bishop Museum. She was possibly influenced by reading about other parts of Polynesia, including Handy's portrait of sexual freedom in the Marquesas. She relied on one male informant but, unlike Freeman who was an honorary chief, possessed no key to the understanding of the male power structure. There was an additional possibility, that she was the victim of a hoax. Samoans are supposedly proud of their prowess in recreational lying, *taufa'ase'a*. Indeed, Harriet Lyons was told in 1965 by a friend who had been engaged to a Samoan that there were rumors that Mead had been the target of skilled jokers. In 1999, in a second book on Samoa, *The Fateful Hoaxing of Margaret Mead,* Freeman identified two of Mead's friends (they were all roughly the same age), the *taupou* Fa'apua'a and Fafoa, as the deceivers. He interviewed Fa'apua'a in the late 1980s, and she admitted to the hoax. He believed that

Mead's principal source of information was the two young women, and not the 68 adolescents and younger women whom she interviewed. In the 1999 article from *Current Anthropology* that is reproduced in this section, Freeman explained the position he had taken in his 1998 book and defends himself against critics such as Martin Orans.[1]

The storm unleashed by Freeman's first book commenced the moment it appeared and did not cease with his death in 2001. Freeman was sympathetic to the claims of sociobiology, and held views on the nature versus nurture question which were disliked by most social anthropologists, but found a sympathetic reception on the political right. In 1999, the Intercollegiate Studies Association that included former members of the Reagan administration listed *Coming of Age in Samoa* at the head of a list of the 50 most pernicious books of the twentieth century.[2] Meanwhile, critics of anthropology and the social sciences in general saw the debate as proof positive of the sloppiness of our disciplines.

On the other side, North American anthropologists who had criticized Mead for being too conservative on issues like gender and imperialism, cultural materialists who had a disdain for psychological anthropology, along with many experts on Polynesia who felt that she always had tended to exaggerate and popularize, all rallied to Mead's defense. They were upset by Freeman's rhetoric and his supporters.

As historians of anthropology[3] the editors of this volume are puzzled by Freeman's assertion that Boas and his disciples in the US saw Mead's first ethnography as a crucial defense of their "cultural determinist" position. For better or worse, they did not, and some of them such as Robert Lowie were quite critical of her. She was not idolized by the American anthropological profession, and was denied the position at Yale or Harvard that she desired. In Britain she was viewed as an exemplar of the novelistic tradition of ethnographic writing that Evans-Pritchard and his disciples disdained. There were many anti-hereditarian anthropologists in the British Commonwealth who did not admire Mead.

Freeman's critics were quick to observe that he was describing British Samoa after 1940 (and as a trained anthropologist after 1966) whereas Mead had described an isolated island in American Samoa in 1926, and that Mead's gender allowed her to see a different side of Samoan life from Freeman. It is also clear to modern readers of Mead's entire text that, for all the sometimes florid rhetoric to be found there, the appendix detailing in very cursory form the sexual experiences of two dozen "adolescents" (some were 18 years old) she knew from the mission school would not appear sensational to someone who knows anything about North American high schools in recent decades. There is no need to assume that all her information came from a *taupou* who would supposedly be shielded from many realities when young and who had long since become a zealous Christian.

The most telling contributions to the debate came from scholars who have done fieldwork in Samoa. In 1987, Lowell D. Holmes, who had done a restudy of Ta'u in the 1950s, published a revised collection of his writings as *The Quest for the Real Samoa*. Holmes, like Freeman, felt that Mead's comprehension of rank and politics left something to be desired, but that nonetheless she understood Samoa better than Freeman, and her portrait of Samoan sexuality, although exaggerated, was basically correct. Other scholars of Samoa who have made significant contributions to the controversy and to our general understanding of Samoan sexuality are Bradd Shore,

Jeanette Marie Mageo, Penelope Schoeffel Meleisea, and Paul Shankman. Schoeffel, who is married to an indigenous Samoan scholar and UNESCO official, has published historical material concerning *taupous*, pre-Christian customs and contemporary sexual norms that should really lay the controversy to rest. Shankman's book, *The Trashing of Margaret Mead* (2008), covers both familiar and new ground most lucidly. In this volume we reproduce what Schoeffel and Shankman tell us about *taupous* and the complex details of the recent history of heterosexuality in Samoa.

The *taupou*'s virginity was indeed maintained until marriage, but that did not necessarily imply that virginity was valued in itself; rather, that the young woman was being preserved as a gift for someone of high chiefly rank. As Schoeffel notes, many other young girls of all ranks went through less prestigious deflorations with chiefs. Such was the privilege of male nobility, and it constituted an honorable loss of virginity, often before marriage. Once this was done, the girl could respectably offer her sexual services to visitors to her community. So the defloration became a declaration of availability. Both Schoeffel and Shankman note that Samoan marriage customs differed according to rank. The marriage of a *taupou* involved a defloration ceremony, feasting, and gifts of mats; a low-rank marriage might involve an unceremonious elopement and the subsequent approval of families. In all cases, the marriage tie was loose. Early missionaries were not impressed with Samoan morals. Obviously they did not like the fact of defloration ceremonies. They were also upset by "filthy" dancing and supposedly licentious behavior. Missionization did bring some changes. Besides the abolition of public defloration, chiefs lost other privileges such as polygamy. In consequence there were very few *taupous*. Shankman notes that sexual hospitality to visitors did not cease. The port town of Apia, capital of Samoa (formerly Western Samoa), was known for its nightlife in the late nineteenth century. During World War II, American soldiers fathered some 1,300 children in relationships with Samoan women. None of these reports shows that Samoans are particularly different from anybody else, but they do cast doubt on Freeman's assertions that there was and still is a "cult of virginity" in Samoa.

NOTES

1   In the second part of the article, which we do not reproduce here, Orans and James Côté respond to Freeman, and he closes with a rejoinder.
2   The list of 50 worst books also includes (at number 3) the first volume of the Kinsey Report (1948), Havelock Ellis's *Studies in the Psychology of Sex*, and a book by the American birth control advocate, Margaret Sanger, who was a friend of both Havelock Ellis and Malinowski.
3   The editors should also note that they were friends of two people in Mead's close circle. We met Mead on a number of memorable occasions, but doubt she remembered who we were.

REFERENCES AND FURTHER READING

Brady, Ian, ed.
    1983   Speaking in the Name of the Real: Freeman and Mead on Samoa. American Anthropologist 85(4):908–947.

Brady, Ian, ed.
1994 Adolescent Storm and Stress: An Evaluation of the Mead–Freeman Controversy. Hillsdale, NJ: Lawrence Erlbaum.
Côté, James E.
2000 Was *Coming of Age in Samoa* Based on a 'Fateful Hoaxing'? Current Anthropology 41(4):616–620
Freeman, Derek
1983 Margaret Mead and Samoa: The Making and Unmaking of an Anthropological Myth. Cambridge, MA: Harvard University Press.
Freeman, Derek
1999 The Fateful Hoaxing of Margaret Mead: A Historical Analysis of Her Samoan Research. Boulder, CO: Westview Press.
Freeman, Derek
2000 Was Margaret Mead Misled or Did She Mislead on Samoa, AND Reply to Orans and Côté. CA Forum on Theory in Anthropology: Sex and Hoax in Samoa. Current Anthropology 41(4):611–616, 620–622.
Holmes, Lowell D.
1987 Quest for the Real Samoa: The Mead/Freeman Controversy and Beyond. South Hadley, MA: Bergin and Garvey.
Mageo, Jeannette
1994 Hairdos and Don'ts: Hair Symbolism and Sexual History in Samoa. Man n.s. 29(2) June:407–32.
Mageo, Jeannette
1998 Theorizing Self in Samoa: Emotions, Genders, and Sexualities. Ann Arbor: University of Michigan Press.
Mead, Margaret
1928 Coming of Age in Samoa: A Psychological Study of Primitive Youth for Western Civilization. New York: William Morrow.
Orans, Martin
1996 Not Even Wrong: Margaret Mead, Derek Freeman and the Samoans. Novato, CA: Chandler and Sharp.
Orans, Martin
2000 Hoaxing, Polemics and Science. Current Anthropology 41(4):615, 616.
Shore, Bradd
1981 Sexuality and Gender in Samoa: Conceptions and Missed Conceptions. *In* Sexual Meanings: The Cultural Construction of Gender and Sexuality. Sherry B. Ortner and Harriet Whitehead, eds. Pp. 192–215. Cambridge: Cambridge University Press.

18

Sex and Hoax in Samoa: Was Margaret Mead Misled or Did She Mislead on Samoa?

Derek Freeman

In a letter from Samoa dated February 1892, Robert Louis Stevenson wrote: "It is hard to reach the truth in these islands" (Colvin 1911:14). It is equally hard, or so it would seem, to establish the truth about Margaret Mead's Samoan researches of 1925–26. Thus, Martin Orans and I, having separately studied the Mead Papers in the Manuscript Room of the Library of Congress, have reached conclusions which are, in Orans's words, "profoundly different" (Orans 1996:15; Freeman 1998). This profound difference is principally over the evidence that Mead was in March 1926 hoaxed by her Samoan traveling companions. My purpose here is to examine this issue, which lies at the heart of the Samoa controversy, in substantive detail.

The methods followed by Orans and myself have been radically different. Accepting the ordinary scientific requirement "that propositions must in principle be verifiable and should be accepted or rejected by consideration of their fit with observations" (Orans 1996:10), Orans restricts his attention to Mead's fieldnotes and to assessing their "adequacy and fit" in relation to her book of 1928, *Coming of*

Age in Samoa (personal communication, April 28, 1993).

In concentrating on Mead's texts in this way Orans, so he says, is specifically not producing a "history" of Mead's Samoan researches. Further, integral to his "scientific" approach is the singular stance of being "not concerned" with any "appraisal" of Mead herself, even though it was her brain that produced the texts he is studying (personal communication, May 24, 1993; 1996:131).

By following this approach, Orans reaches the conclusion that Mead's work in Samoa is both "profoundly unscientific" and "seriously flawed," being "filled with internal contradictions and grandiose claims to knowledge that she could not possibly have had" (1996:132). With this conclusion I am in full accord, and if Orans had confined his attention to the investigation of Mead's fieldnotes in relation to her published writings on Samoa, he would have produced a genuinely valuable study. But, quite unaccountably, given his avowed punctiliousness about the requirements of science, Orans, without ever having consulted the crucially significant historical sources, launches headlong, in chapter 5 of

Derek Freeman, Was Margaret Mead Misled or Did She Mislead on Samoa? Sex and Hoax in Samoa, from *Current Anthropology*, vol. 41, no. 4 (Aug–Oct 2000): 609–614. © 2000 by The Wenner-Gren Foundation for Anthropological Research. Reprinted with permission of The University of Chicago Press.

Sexualities in Anthropology: A Reader, edited by Andrew P. Lyons and Harriet D. Lyons
© 2011 Blackwell Publishing Ltd.

his book *Not Even Wrong*, into argumentation about the history of Mead's Samoan fieldwork.

He does this by advancing a series of hypothetical arguments against the view that on March 13, 1926, while engaged in ethnological research on the island of Ofu, Mead was hoaxed by her Samoan traveling companions, Fa'apua'a and Fofoa. The chief of these arguments has to do with what he calls "simple logic." According to Orans, Mead knew that there were restrictions on the sexual behavior of adolescent females, and therefore she could not possibly have been hoaxed into believing that, in secret, they were sexually promiscuous. His reliance on this "simple logic" is complete. Thus, when, in 1993, my highly competent Samoan research assistant, Unasa, Dr. L. F. Va'a, was preparing to travel to Fitiuta in American Samoa to question Fa'apua'a in detail for a second time about her hoaxing of Mead, I offered Orans the opportunity to have Dr. Va'a put to Fa'apua'a, on his behalf, any questions he would like to ask her. My offer was formally declined (personal communication, September 2, 1995). Orans did this, he told me, because "one does not investigate empirically, logical impossibilities." Thus, although Orans had not investigated either Mead's personality or her historical situation, he knew categorically, and without investigation of any kind, that she could not possibly have been hoaxed. This attitude, like Orans's other hypothetical arguments, I found, as I told him at the time, "quite Byzantine" (Freeman to Orans, personal communication, August 12, 1995).

In contrast, my own approach to Mead's Samoan researches has been strictly historical. Thus, I accept the view of R. G. Collingwood (1978[1939]:112) that "historical knowledge is the re-enactment in the historians' mind of the thought whose history he is studying." And I have followed the precept of G. R. Elton (1967:66) that a historian "should never consider less than the total of the historical material which may conceivably be relevant to his enquiry." Accordingly, I have over many years assiduously collected all of the evidence I could find on the personality and values of the young Margaret Mead.

Let me now turn to the historical analysis of Margaret Mead's Samoan fieldwork. What I want to do is to present an analysis securely based on the relevant primary sources and to leave it to my readers to decide whether they prefer this historical account to Orans's "simple logic," which, in my view, has led him into far-reaching error.

Margaret Mead's passionate desire as a 22-year-old student at Columbia University was to undertake ethnological research in the remote Tuamotu Islands of Polynesia. Instead, she had imposed upon her by Franz Boas, the "father of American anthropology," a study in American Samoa, "to see how much adolescent behavior is physiologically determined and how much it is culturally determined." This, as Mead has recorded, was a topic she "didn't even want to study." On the eve of her departure, however, she wrote to Boas, whom she regarded as "the greatest mind she had ever encountered," saying of the research she would be doing for him in Samoa, "I am going to try very hard to make it a success in every way." She well realized that Boas believed that her research "would indicate that culture was very important" (Freeman 1998:32; Mead 1976:40, 42; interview, KVZK TV, Pago Pago, November 1971; Mead to Boas, July 14, 1925, Papers of Margaret Mead, Manuscript Division, Library of Congress [hereafter PMM]).

On April 30, 1925, Mead, with the support of Franz Boas, was appointed to a National Research Fellowship in the Biological Sciences for the year 1925–26, to carry out in Samoa "a study in heredity and environment based on an investigation of the phenomena of adolescence." Boas, who was the sponsor of this research, was made her supervisor. His strict instruction to her was that she was not, while in Samoa, to engage in any ethnological research (Freeman 1998:52).

By fateful happenstance, when she was still in the U.S.A. Herbert Gregory, director of the Bishop Museum, put to her the proposal that she might, while in Samoa, undertake ethnological research. By this suggestion Mead was much intrigued. When she called at the Bishop Museum in Honolulu, en route to Samoa, she was promised by Gregory that any ethnological research she might do in Samoa would be published as one of the Bishop Museum's prestigious bulletins. For the ambitious young Margaret Mead this was an irresistible inducement. On November 1, 1925, before she had reached Manu'a, where she was due to give all of her time to the problem Boas had assigned to her, she wrote to Edward Craighill Handy, its senior ethnologist, formally agreeing to work on an ethnology of Manu'a for the Bishop Museum. About this quite major development Boas was not informed (Freeman 1998:56, 223).

After taking up residence on November 9, 1925, in the U.S. Naval Dispensary on the island of Ta'ū, Mead devoted almost all of December to "a detailed census of the 856 inhabitants and the one hundred households of the villages of Lumū, Si'ufaga and Faleasao," in which all of the girls she was proposing to study lived (Freeman 1998:153).

In a letter dated November 29, 1925, she had told Boas that any discussion of sex would have to wait upon "the obtaining of greater linguistic practice." On December 16, however, she interviewed To'aga, the English-speaking wife of Sotoa, the high chief of Lumā, about both female virginity and marriage in Manu'a. She was told, as is recorded in her fieldnotes, that "virgins formerly left their hair long on top and shaved at the sides" and that "if a girl eloped or became pregnant her head was shaved that all might know of her disgrace." To'aga then went on to say that at the marriage of a *taupou*, or ceremonial virgin, "the tokens of virginity are taken by the boy's *tulafale* (or talking chief)," while in "the marriage of an ordinary girl, the ceremony takes places in the house; only the family and the boy's friends are present and some elderly man, chosen by the boy, performs the ceremony." This was not the Samoa that she had been expecting (Mead to Boas, November 29, 1925, PMM; Mead, interview with To'aga, December 16, 1925, PMM).

In 1924, when working on her Ph.D. thesis at the American Museum of Natural History, Mead had studied Edward Craighill Handy's monograph *The Native Culture of the Marquesas*. It contains a graphic account of how in the Marquesas both sexes "run wild for a few years after adolescence," an

impression she had also been given by her reading of Melville. It was reinforced at the Bishop Museum in August 1925 when she was given formal instruction about things Polynesian by Edward Craighill Handy. In her interview with To'aga on December 16, 1925, she was given her first glimpse of a sexual system unlike anything she had previously encountered. This, for the young and inexperienced Margaret Mead, was disquieting. She did not know quite what to believe.

Thus, in her report of January 6, 1926, to the National Research Council (PMM), written *before* she had made any investigation of the sexual behavior of the adolescent girls of Manu'a, Mead correctly reports that in the case of a *taupou*, and also at the marriage of a girl of lesser rank, the "representative of the bridegroom is permitted to test the virginity of the bride." But she then, quite unaccountably, adds that "along with this institution" there is "an extensive tolerance of premarital sex relations." For this supposed state of affairs, which is totally at odds with the Samoan practice of testing the virginity of females at marriage, there is, in her fieldnotes, *no warrant of any kind*. We are thus dealing with a preconception about Polynesian sexual behavior that Mead had brought with her to Samoa.

On New Year's Day 1926, the island of Ta'ū was struck by a devastating hurricane. It "destroyed every house" in a nearby village and seriously disrupted for some three weeks the research on adolescent girls that Mead was waiting to begin. When she wrote to Boas on January 16, 1926, she was in a distraught state. She had, she said, "no idea" whether she was "doing the right thing or not" or "how valuable" her "results" would be. It all weighed "rather heavily" on her mind. "Will you," she asked her supervisor, "be dreadfully disappointed in me?" And her letter ended with the agitated words: "Oh, I hope I won't disappoint you in this year's work" (Mead to Boas, January 16, 1926, Papers of Franz Boas, American Philosophical Society, Philadelphia [hereafter PFB]). The possibility that she might disappoint Boas, whose views about the high importance of culture she wholeheartedly accepted, had become a source of acute anxiety to her.

On January 19, 1926, Mead made her first dated entry in the loose-leaf folder in which she recorded her notes on the sexual behavior of adolescent girls. The dated notes in this loose-leaf folder (PMM) continue until February 16, 1926. They comprise some 50 pages, each measuring 7 1/2 by 5 inches. The notes themselves are highly unsystematic, fragmentary, and anecdotal. Furthermore, they provide abundant evidence that because Samoan girls were, as Mead says of one of them, "very secretive," she was having extreme difficulty in collecting any kind of reliable information.

In her letter to Boas of February 15, 1926, although she had still not made a "special investigation" of the sexual behavior of her adolescent girls, Mead again asserted that there was "great promiscuity between puberty and marriage." There is, once again, no warrant for these assertions in Mead's fieldnotes books or in her loose-leaf folder. Indeed, of the 26 girls on whom there are brief notes in her loose-leaf folder, all of them having reached puberty, no fewer than 15 are said to have had no heterosexual experience, and the notes on the other girls of her sample are frequently based on mere hearsay (Mead to Boas, February 15, 1926, PMM).

Ordinarily, most of the girls Mead had selected for study were at school and "inaccessible except for about two hours a day." This situation had changed when the school closed after the hurricane of January 1, 1926. It was to reopen on March 1, 1926. The final fortnight of February 1926 was thus the last chance that Mead had for concentrated research on her adolescent girls. Yet, when the opportunity unexpectedly arose, she abandoned further research on these girls and traveled on February 20, 1926, to Fitiuta at the eastern end of Ta'ū, there to engage in ethnological research for the Bishop Museum.

By March 7, 1926, she had only eight weeks left to her in Manu'a, and the investigation of the adolescent girl as a study in heredity and environment was, without question, the research to which all of her energies needed to be given. Yet, the very next day, March 8, 1926, when a whale-boat arrived from the offlying island of Ofu, Mead, "lured by thoughts

of ethnological gain," at once hired it to take her there for a ten-day visit. Her aim was to complete her ethnology of Manu'a for the Bishop Museum (Freeman 1998:122, 134).

Once again Mead was abandoning research on her adolescent girls, none of whom could be contacted from Ofu or Olosega. Further, she had, since leaving for Fitiuta on February 20, 1926, conducted no further enquiry into their sexual behavior. She was thus in no position at all to provide Boas with any kind of answer unless she could somehow or other obtain significant additional information (Mead, Bulletin 14, March 24, 1926, PMM).

For Mead, who was desperately afraid that she might "dreadfully disappoint" Boas, this was a source of considerable anxiety as she proceeded with her ethnological research for the Bishop Museum. She was, however, accompanied whenever she went by Fa'apua'a and Fofoa, the two Samoan "girls," as she calls them, that she had brought with her to Ofu and Olosega as her traveling companions.

Then, on March 13, 1926, as is known from the sworn and carefully tested evidence of Fa'apua'a as well as from Mead's own account, when the three of them were alone, traveling together on the island of Ofu, Mead grasped the opportunity to try to obtain from Fa'apua'a and Fofoa the kind of information that she hoped would enable her to answer Boas's problem. She had been led to believe by Boas that informants such as Fa'apua'a and Fofoa could speak for the culture by which they had been shaped.

According to the sworn testimony of Fa'apua'a, Mead put to Fofoa and herself the preposterous proposition (so it seemed to them) that, despite the great emphasis on virginity in the *fa'aSamoa* and within the Christian church, unmarried Samoan girls were, *in secret*, sexually promiscuous. In so doing Mead was seeking to substantiate the imagined claim in her report of January 6, 1926, made before she had done any research on the subject, that in Manu'a there was "an extensive tolerance of premarital sex relationships." If only she could obtain from Fa'apua'a and Fofoa a clear confirmation concerning the premarital promiscuity that she supposed secretly existed in Manu'a, she would have established a "cultural pattern" that would allow her to reach what she so desperately needed: an acceptable solution to the problem Boas required her to investigate under the terms of her research fellowship.

In Samoa, as Albert Wendt (1983) has noted, it is not acceptable in ordinary conversation to discuss sexual matters in public. And so, in their bashfulness at Mead's brashness, Fa'apua'a and Fofoa, having conspiratorially pinched one another, whispered their agreement with all that their American friend had suggested to them, telling her with due embellishment that they, like other young women and adolescent girls, regularly spent their nights with members of the opposite sex. In saying this, they were, as a prank, engaging in the Samoan custom of *taufa'ase'e* behavior (or "recreational lying") and telling Mead the exact reverse of the truth (Wendt 1983:14). The letter that Mead wrote to Boas the very next day is unlike any other that she wrote to him from Samoa. In her letter of February 15 she had listed the mass of information she would need for the completion of her problem. Then, quite suddenly, on March 14, having done no work at all on her adolescent girls during the previous month, she elatedly announced to Boas that she had found "the sort of thing" he "wanted." She hoped that it would please him. Samoa, she reported, had a society in which "sexual life begins with puberty in most cases" and in which "fairly promiscuous intercourse obtains until marriage." And, as no attempt was made to curb this sexual promiscuity, there was an absence of stress (Mead to Boas, March 14, 1926, PFB).

This was the very information with which Fa'apua'a and Fofoa had hoaxed Mead on the previous day. It can be traced to no other source in Mead's fieldnotes. It was certainly inconsistent with what she had been told by To'aga and others, but by applying the theory of cultural patterning which she had learned from Franz Boas and Ruth Benedict and in which she fervently believed, it was very much the kind of information she was looking for. Above all, it presented her with the kind of solution that would be acceptable to Boas, whose approval she so greatly desired.

The young Margaret Mead was not mistaken. When her excited letter of March 14 reached New York, Boas was indeed pleased and at once wrote to her. Addressing her as "My dear Flower of Heaven," he told her how glad he was that she had been able to "do so well" with her "difficult problem" as to "feel able" to state her results "so succinctly" (Freeman 1998:232).

There can be no adequate accounting for the exceptional contents of Mead's letter to Boas of March 14, 1926, other than in terms of her hoaxing by Fa'apua'a and Fofoa on the previous day. This hoaxing is fully attested to by the sworn testimony of Fa'apua'a. But, most important, there is also the definitive evidence of Mead's own revealing account of the time that she spent with Fa'apua'a and Fofoa on the islands of Ofu and Olosega. It is contained in a little-known book entitled *All True! The Record of Actual Adventures That Have Happened to Ten Women of Today*. Both Orans and Côté have completely neglected this all-important source of information. The "adventure" by "Dr. Margaret Mead" is entitled "Life as a Samoan Girl" (Mead 1931). It begins with a wistful reference to "the group of reverend scientists" who had sent her to study the adolescent girls of Samoa with "no very clear idea" of how she was "to do this." It continues with a vivid description of her stay in Vaitogi and ends with an account of her journey to Ofu and Olosega in March 1926. Fa'apua'a and Fofoa, her companions on this journey, she refers to as the "two Samoan girls, Braided Roses and Born-in-three-houses," and she describes how these "two Samoan girls" (in fact they were both 24 years of age, slightly older than Mead herself) accepted the "great squares" of bark cloth that were presented to her after she had, on Ofu, danced as a ceremonial virgin. Mead then writes, "In all things I had behaved as a Samoan, for only so, only by losing my identity, as far as possible, had I been able to become acquainted with the Samoan girls, receive their whispered confidences and learn at the same time the answer to the scientists' questions" (Mead 1931:94, 113, 117). The relevant historical evidence thus points unremittingly to the circumstance that it was from her "two Samoan girls," Fa'apua'a and

Fofoa, that Mead derived the intensely gratifying and highly misleading information that led her to write to Franz Boas in the terms that she did on March 14, 1926.

Further telling evidence of her hoaxing is revealed in the actions Mead took soon after she had announced to Boas her answer to his problem. In January 1926 she had asked Boas, "If I simply write conclusions and use my cases as illustrative material will it be acceptable?" When she wrote to him on March 14, she was awaiting "with great interest" his reply to this pivotal question. She was due to remain for another six weeks in Manu'a. How she would spend her time would depend on Boas's reply (Mead to Boas, January 5, 1926, PMM; March 14, 1926, PFB).

She was still on the island of Ofu when Boas's letter of February 15 reached her on March 18, 1926. He had answered her momentous question in the affirmative, thus granting her the option to "simply write conclusions" and to use "cases" as "illustrative material." This approval transformed Mead's appreciation of her situation. The very next day she wrote to Boas again. After receiving his letter "on presentation of results," she had decided, she told him in a hurried note written on March 19, 1926, to "finish up" her work "in the next month – to terminate her fieldwork a month earlier than originally planned and head for the south of France (Freeman 1998:229; Mead to Boas, March 19, 1926, PFB). From her questioning of Fa'apua'a and Fofoa she had identified, she was convinced, the covert "pattern" of adolescent sexual behavior in Samoa. And, with this achieved, there was, she felt, no need for further detailed investigation. The conclusive evidence for this is contained in the five pages of entirely new entries that she made in her loose-leaf folder on March 24, 1926.

Perhaps the most unfortunate aspect of Orans's research in the Manuscript Room of the Library of Congress is his failure to investigate Margaret Mead's correspondence with Herbert Gregory, Edward Craighill Handy, and others of the Bishop Museum of Honolulu. Thus, Orans gives no account at all of the research on the ethnology of Manu'a (amounting to about two months in all) that Mead

undertook for the Bishop Museum during her five months in Manu'a. It was this ethnological research, undertaken in contravention of the explicit instructions she had been given by both Boas and the National Research Council, that, more than anything else, determined the fateful course of her Samoan researches. Of this crucially important historical situation, Orans makes no mention whatsoever.

His failure to research adequately the actual history of Mead's doings in Samoa is also evident in other ways. One of Orans's principal arguments is that "after the March voyage and the alleged duping, there are entries in the binder dated March 21 and March 24, indicating that her investigation of sexuality continued" (Orans 1996:99). There is, in fact, no entry in Mead's loose-leaf folder (or binder) dated March 21, 1926, for on that day she was confined to bed with tonsillitis and under treatment by Dr. Lane. Further, the long entry dated March 24, 1926, has nothing whatsoever to do with the continued investigation of sexuality. It is clearly headed "Cases to Use as Illustrations" and is a listing of cases that might be used, in her report to the National Research Council, to illustrate the conclusions which she had already reached. As the relevant historical documents show, after her hoaxing by Fa'apua'a and Fofoa, Mead engaged in no further systematic investigation of the sexual behavior of adolescent girls. The planned "special investigation" during April 1926 of the "sexual life" of the adolescent girl of which she had written to Boas on February 15, 1926, was, in the event, never undertaken.

Mead's official report on her fieldwork in Manu'a is entitled "The Adolescent Girl in Samoa." After Franz Boas had pronounced himself "completely satisfied" with it, it was dispatched on April 24, 1927, to the National Research Council and, on May 10, 1927, approved for publication as *Coming of Age in Samoa* (Mead to Lillie, April 24, 1927, PMM; Elliot to Mead, May 10, 1927, PMM).

In this report, as in *Coming of Age in Samoa*, Mead lists living as a girl "with many lovers as long as possible" as one of "the uniform and satisfying ambitions" of the Samoan girl, and in *Coming of Age in Samoa* she writes of the deferring of marriage "through as many years of casual love-making as possible" (1928:157, 195). To this mistaken view of Samoa she adhered for the rest of her life. Thus, in 1950 she described Samoa as one of the "best studied examples" of "premarital freedom," and during a major interview published some two years before her death in 1978 (Mead 1976:42) she was still attributing the easy nature of adolescence in Samoa to "freedom of sex."

All of these generalizations about "premarital promiscuity" in Samoa are entirely in accord with the letter she wrote to Boas on March 14, 1926, the day after she had been hoaxed by Fa'apua'a and Fofoa – a hoaxing which gave rise to what may be properly called "the Mead myth" about Samoa. It is crucially important to realize, however, that Mead – as is the case with any individual who has been successfully hoaxed – was oblivious of what had happened to her.

If, as Orans would have us believe, Mead was not hoaxed by Fa'apua'a and Fofoa, the situation changes, for then, as Orans states, it is evident that Mead "knew better" and that, as he says, she was "more misleading in some important matters than misled" (1996:142; personal communication, August 30, 1992). If this is what really happened, we are obviously dealing with conscious and, therefore, deliberate falsification of ethnographic evidence. This, I need hardly say, is a very serious charge indeed, and especially when Mead is said, by Orans, to have engaged in this kind of behavior in respect of her venerated supervisor Franz Boas. If Orans is to be believed, Mead becomes guilty of outright deception and one of the most wanton pretenders in the history of anthropology. This notion I unhesitatingly reject. As I told Orans when I first heard of this view of his (personal communication, April 28, 1993), "I would as soon believe in unicorns!" If Mead had indeed been involved in deliberate falsification she would never have made her Samoan papers available for public scrutiny in the Library of Congress.

Mead gave credence to the untruths and hyperbole of Fa'apua'a and Fofoa because, in accord with her fervent belief in Boas's theory of cultural patterning, her "two Samoan girls," with whom she had become so well

"acquainted," had serendipitously provided her, at a time when she was desperately in need of it, with just "the sort of thing" that she "understood" Boas "wanted." Then, with the arrival a few days later of Boas's letter giving her the option to "simply write conclusions," she suddenly realized that she could do exactly this on the basis of the information she had been given by Fa'apua'a and Fofoa and the "cases" she had already collected. Thus, Mead's activities during her final days in Manu'a all relate to the way in which the "whispered confidences" of Fa'apua'a and Fofoa had enabled her to find an answer to the problem to which Boas had very much wanted a clear-cut solution. On March, 24, 1926, as soon as she had sufficiently recovered from a severe attack of tonsillitis, she filled five pages in her loose-leaf folder with "Cases to Use as Illustrations." In her last bulletin from Manu'a, which was also written on March 24, as well as announcing she would be arriving in the south of France on June 25, 1926, she wrote of "all the holes" there were to patch in her ethnology of Manu'a. It was in this way, then, that she spent her time while waiting to depart from the island of Ta'ū.

Mead had come to Samoa as a fervent believer in Boas's theory of cultural conditioning. She had been brought up "to believe that the only thing was to add to the sum of accurate information in the world." In the judgment of William F. Ogburn (Ogburn to Board of Fellowships in the Biological Sciences), she had been "wonderfully well trained along lines of precision and accuracy." She was, all the available evidence indicates, a highly conscientious individual. In her letter to Boas of January 16, 1926, she reported that her life in Manu'a was "one long battle" with her "conscience" as to whether she was "working correctly" and "hard enough" and gave agonized expression to her fear that she might "disappoint" him. Less than three months later, after she had dispatched to Boas her letter of March 14, succinctly stating her solution to the problem he had imposed upon her, her state of mind had changed completely (Freeman 1998:160; Mead to Boas, January 16, 1926, PFB).

Another of the defects of Orans's account is that, while in the Manuscript Room of the Library of Congress, he failed to research

Mead's copious correspondence with her paternal grandmother, Martha Mead. Martha Mead had lived with Margaret's family from the time of Margaret's birth in 1901 and become "the most decisive influence" in her life. It was to her that Mead confided her innermost thoughts and feelings, ending her letters to her with such words as these: "Whenever I see something new, or curious or beautiful my first impulse is to tell you about it" (Mead to Martha Mead, June 12, 1926, PMM). The 15 letters that Mead wrote to her paternal grandmother from Samoa are thus an invaluable source of information.

When Mead wrote to her grandmother on April 7, 1926, her days were "simply a procession of ceremonial farewells," and with "so little to do" there was even time for her to write a short story about the faraway valley in rural Pennsylvania where she herself had come of age – a story entitled "The Conscientious Myth-Maker." She was waiting for the naval boat by which she would leave Manu'a, and she ended her letter to her grandmother with the words "I am leaving here with a very clear conscience. My work is finished satisfactorily, I think, and I can start off on a real holiday" (Mead to Martha Mead, April 7, 1926, PMM).

Her last letter from Samoa to Franz Boas was also written on April 7, 1926. Her "fear of failure," she told Boas, had left her. She thanked him again for his letter of February 15, in which he had approved her plan to "simply write conclusions" and use her cases as "illustrative material." This, she said, had "considerably relieved her anxiety." It made her very happy to know that she would soon be back with Boas again. She was "finishing up" her "stay in the field," she told him, with a "good taste" in her "mouth" (Mead to Boas, April 7, 1926, PFB).

These two letters record the state of Mead's mind as she was about to leave Manu'a. The tremendous pressure on her not to disappoint Boas, together with her fervent belief in his ideas, had operated to cause her, despite what she had previously been told by To'aga and others, to accept the "whispered confidences" of Fa'apua'a and Fofoa and to write to Boas as she had on March 14, 1926.

In contrast, Orans's view that Mead was not hoaxed by Fa'apua'a and Fofoa but "knew better" and even went so far as to "mislead" Franz Boas is a view which in no way tallies with the known historical facts about Mead's actions in Manu'a from March 13, 1926, onwards. Equally, it fails to account for the fixed belief about premarital promiscuity in Samoa to which Mead adhered for the rest of her life.

Another of the crucially important historical documents that Orans failed adequately to research in the Manuscript Room of the Library of Congress is entitled "The Adolescent Girl in Samoa." Although it is clearly identified as such in her letter to Dr. Frank R. Lillie of April 24, 1927 (PMM), Orans did not recognize this document of over 200 typewritten pages as Mead's official report to the National Research Council (Orans 1997: 211). In the introduction to this report, which Orans fails to consider, Mead poses the question: "Are the attitudes, the conflicts, the perplexities, the ambitions of the adolescent girl correlates of a special period of physiological development or are they rather to be attributed to the civilization in which she lives?" And, on its penultimate page, she concludes that what we are dealing with is "a flexible generalized human organism with great and diverse potentialities which, born into a particular civilization, is relentlessly shaped and moulded by the patterns of that society" (Mead, "The Adolescent Girl in Samoa," 1927, PMM). This is an admirably clear conclusion in propositional form and is thus fully open to refutation.

This undeniable fact impugns Orans's idiosyncratic claim that because Mead is "so mistaken" as to be "not even wrong" her findings are "invulnerable to refutation" (Orans 1996:156).

I would merely note that in my 1983 book *Margaret Mead and Samoa: The Making and Unmaking of an Anthropological Myth*, I presented a cogent refutation of exactly the conclusion that Mead reached in her official report of 1927 to the National Research Council. In 1998, in *The Fateful Hoaxing of Margaret Mead: A Historical Analysis of Her Samoan Research*, I presented a detailed history of Mead's anthropological activities from 1922, when, at Barnard College, she became a student of Franz Boas, to the publication in 1928 of *Coming of Age in Samoa*.

The history I have recorded here contains the momentous evidence of Mead's own account of her relationship with Fa'apua'a and Fofoa of March 1926, an account which has only come to light since the publication, late in 1998, of *The Fateful Hoaxing of Margaret Mead*. This evidence is of decisive significance for any critical assessment of the unhistorical suppositions that have been advanced by Orans. It is also definitive evidence, incognizantly provided by Mead herself, that mercifully brings to closure the protracted controversy over her Samoan fieldwork.[1]

Readers of CURRENT ANTHROPOLOGY are thus in a position to decide for themselves whether, in the case of Mead's Samoan researches, they prefer what Stephen Jay Gould has called "the determining and unerasable signature of history" to the hypothetical "logic" of Martin Orans.

NOTE

1 The evidence from Mead's 1931 "Life as a Samoan Girl" has been added to the second edition of *The Fateful Hoaxing of Margaret Mead* (1999).

REFERENCES

Collingwood, R. G.
  1978[1939] An Autobiography. Oxford: Oxford University Press.
Colvin, S., ed.
  1911 The Letters of Robert Louis Stevenson. Vol. 4: 1890–1894. London: Methuen.
Elton, G. R.
  1967 The Practice of History. Sydney: Sydney University Press.
Freeman, Derek
  1983 Margaret Mead and Samoa: The Making and Unmaking of an Anthropological Myth. Cambridge, MA: Harvard University Press.
Freeman, Derek
  1998 The Fateful Hoaxing of Margaret Mead: A Historical Analysis of her Samoan Research. Boulder, CO: Westview Press.
Handy, E. S. Craighill
  1923 The Native Culture in the Marquesas. Bernice P. Bishop Museum Bulletin 9. Honolulu, Hawaii.
Mead, Margaret
  1928 Coming of Age in Samoa. New York: Morrow.
Mead, Margaret
  1931 Life as a Samoan Girl. *In* All true! The Record of Actual Adventures that have Happened to Ten Women of Today. New York: Brewer, Warren and Putnam.
Mead, Margaret
  1976 What We Can Learn Today from "Savages." Psychology Today, August.
Orans, Martin
  1996 Not Even Wrong: Margaret Mead, Derek Freeman, and the Samoans. Novato, CA: Chandler and Sharp.
Orans, Martin
  1997 Freeman and Orans. Brief Reply. Journal of the Polynesian Society 106:211.
Wendt, A.
  1983 Three Faces of Samoa: Mead's, Freeman's, and Wendt's. Pacific Islands Monthly, April.

19

Sexual Morality in Samoa and Its Historical Transformations

Penelope Schoeffel

This essay aims to provide some historical and ethnographic elucidation of how sexual mores have been transformed in Samoa over the past 170 years. Samoan sexual behaviour has attracted extensive scholarly interest and controversy since Margaret Mead's 1928 (1969) case study of adolescent Samoan girls. Mead's finding that unmarried girls were free to engage in premarital sexual adventures was invoked scientifically for the next fifty-five years to demonstrate the flexibility of human sexual norms. However in 1983, Derek Freeman challenged her finding, asserting that Samoans placed high value on the chastity of unmarried girls. There is an extensive literature on the ensuing controversy. This essay will not revisit the debate, but two contributions to it must be noted, Shankman's (1996, 2005) critiques of Freeman's use of historical sources on Samoan sexual conduct. The emphasis here differs considerably, but in its historical focus, will add to Shankman's exegeses. The essay examines how the social construction of marriage and its association with female virginity has changed since the 1830s.

Historically, Christian cultures have associated female purity with family honour, a belief with ancient roots also found in Jewish and Islamic cultures; but in pre-Christian Samoa the virginity of young women was offered to the chiefs. The honour was in the gift, and the dishonour brought upon her family by a girl who had inappropriately lost her virginity (pa'umutu) was that of lese majeste. Virgins of high rank were publicly deflowered during their marriage ceremony, while virginity of girls of all ranks was taken in private rites. Marriage was for sex and reproduction; a transient state for those of high rank – and perhaps for most people. Those of lower rank did not formally marry at all in a formal sense, but cohabited by mutual consent. The strongest ties of affection were not between spouses but between blood kin and the deepest bonds of loyalty were between sisters and brothers. From the 1830s, the Christian

Penelope Schoeffel, Sexual Morality in Samoa and its Historical Transformations, from A Polymath Anthropologist: Essays in Honour of Ann Chowning, *Research in Anthropology and Linguistics*, vol. 6 (2005): 69–75, University of Auckland. Reprinted with permission of University of Auckland and the author.

churches tried to effect a moral transformation, promoting conjugality and premarital chastity. Conjugality is the cornerstone of Samoan society and in its Christian culture 170 years later, and premarital female virginity is firmly linked to family honour. The sexual conduct of men however, is largely exempt from opprobrium, despite the teaching of the church.

Filthy Songs and Naked Dancing

Pili sat in the water and listened
Looking toward the entrance, which
the maiden may have sought,
lit by a torch of burning twigs.
Hotly, he reached for her crotch;
with his mouth he snapped for her blood.
He caught the bird.
He captured it, the young one.
And so Sina got him as her man
The girl that he had taken below
    (Pili's Song. Krämer 1994 [1902]: 587,
    author's gloss of Samoan text)

One of the great tropes in popular representations of the Pacific is the missionary, sweating in his black coat, banning dancing, covering nakedness, and suppressing the sexual freedom of innocent islanders. Missionary accounts of their goals for the religious transformation of Samoa certainly show that the eradication of what they perceived as sexual immorality was high on their list of priorities. Although John Williams, the pioneer of the London Missionary Society in Samoa, was no prude by the standards of his day, he was disgusted by customs surrounding the courtship and marriage of chiefs and the lascivious display of young female bodies. In his eyes, abolition of disapproved sexual conduct was as imperative as the abolition of warfare. Writing in 1832, Williams recorded that he and Makea, the Christian *ariki* of Rarotonga, held a meeting with the chiefs of the ruling faction in Samoa to discuss Christian morality. Williams told the gathering that many things forbidden by the Christian religion were also condemned by Samoans; however as Christians they would have to ban certain customs, such as dancing naked, which he termed "filthy". On another occasion, Williams instructed the Tahitian and Rarotongan missionaries he had brought to teach the Samoans that while they should not ban all traditional amusements, they must advise the chiefs to prohibit "...those dances that were manifestly obscene such as dancing naked, singing their filthy songs & such like..." (Moyle [ed.] 1984:124, 142).

The "filthy" practices Williams condemned were integral to the prevailing political and moral order. *Ali'i* were held to be the earthly manifestations of the gods, an exalted class who maintained their status through endogamous marriage within a network of ancestrally connected aristocratic families spanning the Samoan archipelago. Men and some women of the highest ranks were expected to enter into a series of unions, as many as possible, with the object of begetting a child to link their lineages and polities to others of importance. Sexually explicit songs (see Moyle 1975) were sung at marriage festivities in celebration of aristocratic fertility; these songs extolled the hymeneal blood of virgins and the act of procreation, the ejaculation of semen, the quickening of the womb, and the hoped-for conception of a chiefly child combining the *mana* of its parents' ancestral gods. The objective of chiefly marriage was not a conjugal relationship, but a mating to create a new chiefly lineage. The term *usu* used in the standard formula of Samoan genealogies indicates the primacy of the sexual union; for example *'sa usu* Tui Manu'a *ia* Sina' – 'Tui Manu'a conquered/had sexual intercourse with Sina' (Milner 1966:304). As Williams observed on several occasions in 1830 and 1832, dances were held when a party from one village visited another for courtship or marriage ceremonies. Unlike Turner (Moyle [ed.] 1984:125), who associated night dancing with "all kinds of obscenity", Williams found most Samoan dancing quite unobjectionable, including those performed at night. What shocked him were dances he said the Samoans called *sa'e*. (Moyle [ed.] 1984:246–47, see also Mageo 1999:119–240 who provides extensive but undocumented speculation on these practices). The "filthy" dances were competitive erotic performances held at night between the young people of host and guest polities, typically in conjunction with the rites of chiefly courtship and marriage, and undoubtedly intended to encourage sexual encounters between ordinary young men and women from different and often distant polities.

In Samoan morality, sexual encounters and marriage within the local polity was undesirable, even improper. Accordingly, spouses should be found outside, from other polities. Consistent with the Samoan principle of *feagaiga* (see Schoeffel 1995) which gave cultural primacy to the sexual brother-sister relationship, young men and women from the same village were ideally as brothers and sisters to one another (Schoeffel 1979, Tcherkézoff 1993). Marriage and sexual unions within the village were disruptive of its social hierarchy and moral order, and also defeated the purpose of marriage for the creation of wide-ranging alliances. Accordingly, when chiefs went travelling for courtship and marriage, so did their followers; the ensuing chiefly rites provided a venue for two or more polities to come together in an atmosphere of supernaturally charged sexual licence. Each young man went out hoping to sexually "conquer" a young woman from a rival polity, perhaps to bring her home to serve his family and bear his children, at least for as long as he could hold her.

Virginity as a Gift

When a chief married, the virginity of his aristocratic bride was the most important of the treasures she brought with her as marriage gifts (Schoeffel 1999). The central rite of the ceremony was her public defloration, which most missionary observers found too disgusting to record in detail, although the practice was fully described by several mid-19th century foreign observers. The hymen of the bride was ruptured by the chiefly groom himself or, in the case of the highest-ranking chiefs, by his orator, using the fingers. The bride then displayed herself naked to the crowd of rejoicing onlookers, blood running down her legs. The gift of virginity allowed the highest-ranking chiefs to act the part of the gods that they represented on earth; gods associated with fertility, abundance and renewal. The act of defloration resonated with legends of super-

natural male power and of sexually conquering gods, whose progeny founded chiefly lineages – for example Pili, son of Tagaloa of the heavens, was cast out down to earth where, manifest as a lizard or an eel, he deflowered the aristocratic virgin Sina with his phallic tail (see the quotation above). But Williams observed that ritual defloration was not merely reserved for chiefly marriages, but was widely practiced for young women of all ranks:

It is also a common thing for young women to be publicly deprived of their virginity by a young respectable Chief in the same way as in the marriage ceremony. This is considered an honour & no person objects to marry a young woman who has been thus treated. The Chief who ruptures the Hymen will frequently give the young woman a great name which will gain her respectability but I suspect the reason why this singular custom prevails is the young females are tired of submitting to the restraints their virginity imposes on them & being thus honourably deprived of their virginity they have full liberty to gratify their wishes & also escape the disgrace of being looked upon as common prostitutes. (Moyle [ed.] 1984:256)

A private enactment of the defloration ritual was described by the French explorer La Perouse in 1787. His crew had been received hospitably by a village on Savai'i and one of the sailors had asked for a young woman to have sex with:

I have to relate ... that the very small number of young and pretty females ... soon attracted the attention of several Frenchmen, who in spite of my prohibition, endeavoured to form a connection with them. The looks of the Europeans expressed desires which were soon divined; some old women undertook the negotiations; the altar was prepared in the handsomest hut in the village; and all the blinds were let down, and the inquisitive excluded. The victim was then laid in the arms of an old man, who exhorted her, during the ceremony, to moderate her expression of her pain; while the matrons sang and howled; the ceremony being performed in their presence, and under the auspices of the old man, who served at once as priest and alter. (Irwin 1965:136; see Tcherkézoff 2004).

Young virgin women of all ranks were offered to high-ranking men and their privilege of deflowering virgins is comparable to the putative *droit du seigneur* of medieval Europe. However, once no longer virgins, the sexual behaviour of unmarried women was of little social consequence; they were expected to behave with sisterly propriety and circumspection towards men of their village, but were free – indeed expected – to have sexual relations with male visitors as a part of local hospitality. The term '*pa'umutu*' literally refers to a girl who has lost her virginity, in the sense that her virginity has been improperly taken. Nowadays it is a derogatory term, used of promiscuous women and prostitutes, but it is unlikely this term had such pejorative connotations in pre-Christian Samoa. In 1835 an officer of the whaling ship *Emerald* described the young Samoan women who entertained his crew. They wore scented oil, he wrote, and were girded with tapa, tied so as to display their pubic region, and they were "… in no way bashful towards strangers and always willing to grant favours" (Richards 1988:49). Such exchanges between hosts and guests were undoubtedly considered a normal avenue of reciprocity at the time. The following year, in 1836, the missionary George Platt recorded that while visiting a village in the company of other evangelists, he had to repel young women intent upon sharing their beds. As Platt understood the matter:

> … it is the custom here for the women who have no husbands (virgins excepted) to sleep with & find pillows and mats for their guests. They appear to be common property … when we told them to go … they informed us that they intended to sleep there & asked us where they should go … [but] the native teacher told them we were sacred and it was not our custom.[1]

It is likely that the house he occupied belonged to the women who sought to entertain him. The "virgins excepted" to whom Platt refers, were the girls including the *taupou*, reserved for the defloration rite. In the villages of important chiefs, unmarried women of all ages lived in a special house, the *fale tali malo*, allocated to the ceremonial virgin (*taupou*) of the village and other girls of high rank, and visitors were accommodated in this house. *Taupou* were selected on the basis of high-ranking matrilateral and patrilateral ancestry and bestowed with a title derived from the name of a famous ancestress. Installation to such a title, a lavish affair, similar to the installation of a chief to a high *ali'i* title, marked her as a candidate for dynastic marriage (see Keesing 1937, Shankman 1996 for more detailed accounts). Unmarried men in each village of importance also had their own house, one allocated to the young male heirs-apparent to high titles, who were termed *manaia* (a term connoting physical beauty) and were also invested with special ancestral titles.

Christian Conjugality

The *ali'i*, having embraced the new faith in haste, soon discovered that it threatened their sacred status, one that was soon to be usurped by clergymen. The clergy were referred to as *feagaiga*, a term for the sacred contractual bond between sister and brother, and sororal and fraternal descent lines, and they were also given honorific forms of address formerly reserved for the highest ranking chiefs (see Schoeffel 1995, 1999). Christian morality, with its doctrines of premarital chastity and monogamous, faithful marriage threatened many of the institutions that upheld the political system and the exclusivity of the chiefly class, as well as the system of marriage and alliance. It was therefore slow to take root, even though formal Christian religiosity quickly became an integral part of Samoan culture. To promote the Christian concept of marriage, the churches had to create models of conjugality in the person of the village-based pastor and his wife. Trained for their roles in theological colleges and girls' schools, the couple was expected to demonstrate ideals of Christian conjugal demeanour and gendered roles in each village parish. So powerful was this model of imparting Christian values that it was adopted by the Catholic Church. Although its celibate clergy lived on mission stations and served whole districts, its local leadership was provided by village-based catechists and their wives on the Protestant model.

Between 1830 and 1900 there was recurrent tension between leading chiefs and the churches over serial marriages, even though some of the great figureheads of the era, such as Malietoa Laupepa and Mata'afa Iosefa, were renowned for their piety (Gilson 1970). But, as time passed, the custom of formally conferring titles on high-born young women fell into decline. With acceptance of Christian teaching on monogamy, the expense of formally installing an aristocratic virgin could no longer be offset by the certainty of her advantageous marriage (Keesing 1937). Yet aspects of the old matrimonial system survived well into the 20th century. Neffgen (1975:13) writing in 1916, recorded that women and men of the highest rank still made many strategic marriages, setting aside former spouses to take new ones, "despite all missionary endeavours". Even in the 1940s, according to Fuluiole Peseta Meleisea (pers. comm. May 1996), there was residual tension between the church and the ranking chiefs. Now in her 90s, Fuluiole related that her family disapproved of her marriage to a district chief because of strong ties they had to the Congregational Church and its ministry. The daughters of the clergy, she said, were not permitted to marry chiefs, because chiefs had traditional obligations which were likely bring them into conflict with Christian precepts.

By the 20th century, old values of virginity, mediated by Christian moral teaching on chastity, became a new cultural ideal for all unmarried women. Under the relentless pressure of Christian moral authority, polygamy had given way to monogamy and conjugality, and in tandem with these changes, old political institutions were transformed into the *matai* system of modern Samoa. People no longer revered the holder of high titles as the descendants of the gods, for now everyone was equal in the eyes of Jehovah; clergymen became the new sacred chiefs and all were aristocrats *manqué*. Men and women could elevate their status by achievement, all men could expect to hold titles eventually, and the highest achievers could attain nationally exalted titles on the

basis of the most remote genealogical connection (Meleisea 1995; Olsen 2000; Schoeffel 1995, 1999; Tcherkézoff 2000).

Sex and the Single Samoan in a 20th Century Christian Community

Open affection in public to a young female was seen by the relatives of the girl as an attack or threat to their traditional responsibilities... her virginity... is paramount in Samoan traditions. ...the brothers are therefore vested with the traditional task of protecting their young virgin sisters at all cost, from other young smooth talking natives who are there to try and exploit her virginity.... in a warrior culture, it then creates a male sub-culture where it becomes a challenge for the native male to try and exploit as many young virgins as possible.... Sexuality was also used as revenge.... The challenge of eyeing someone else's virgin sister, while at the same time trying to protect your own sisters... makes the environment very secretive. It was a conducive environment for the outbreak of violence, paybacks, ambush and killings. Our native male sexuality was a high risk thrill. (Malopa'upu Isaia 1999:150, see also Copp 1950)

In the mid-1970s I conducted ethnographic research on gender in Samoa. This was a time when emigration to New Zealand and America was gaining momentum, but it was before mass migration had begun to have significant cultural and economic impacts. The study focused on a small, rural coastal village, remote from the town, which I shall call Vaima'a. Relations between Vaima'a and the seven other villages in the district were characterised by strong rivalry. Spatially and architecturally, Vaima'a was as open as a fishbowl. Its 16 extended family households all had *falesamoa* and most lived in them. *Falesamoa* are traditional open sided houses with domed, thatched roofs supported by rows of posts set in cobblestone floors. Most houses in Vaima'a were clustered around the *malae*, an open space covered with sand with a cement cricket pitch at its centre. A stroll through the village allowed any interested observer to see what other people were doing at any time of day, and neighbours could hear and observe one another at all hours.

A council of twenty-one *matai* of various ranks governed the village conservatively, by a consensus-based process of decision-making. The council was the arbiter of morality. Modern fashions that were considered immodest or unseemly were prohibited, for example the wearing of shorts, jeans and miniskirts by women, or the wearing of long hair and beards by men. Sexual immorality (including pregnancy outside marriage, adultery, sexual assault) was forbidden. Wrongdoers were punished with fines, which were levied on the *matai* representing the family of the wrongdoer. The ultimate punishment by the council was to banish the offender from the village. By Samoan law, offences classed as criminal acts had to be reported to the police, but there were instances in which the reports were not made, due to the shamefulness of the offence and the collective desire of the council to keep the matter quiet. The Congregational Church punished known sexual offenders by expelling them from communion for a specified period, and thus from the core membership of the church. However such exclusion usually followed rather than preceded punishment by the council. The pastor took advice from his deacons, all of whom were leading *matai* of Vaima'a. As in all villages, Vaima'a had a women's committee, and all adult women (defined as those past the age of puberty who were no longer attending school) were required to attend its weekly meetings. The leaders of the committee occasionally publicly reprimanded members who had committed moral offences and enforced a few moral rules of its own, for example against malicious gossip; however punishment of moral offences were usually the prerogative of the council.

Wrongdoing (typically defined as sexual laxity in females, selfishness, disobedience and disrespect) was privately punished by ridicule, rejection, exclusion and sometimes beatings. The fear of these sanctions, and the acute sense of shame induced by discovery of misdeeds, encouraged secretiveness, even deviousness, in relation to the fulfilment of personal desires (Freeman 1983; Gerber 1975; Ochs 1988;

Schoeffel 1979; Shore 1977, 1982, 1996). However private punishment was moderated by every family's desire to conceal the misdeeds of its members from public scrutiny. Moral rectitude was also associated with high social status, and this was most strongly emphasised in the elite households, at least, in the behaviour of their daughters.

Formally, people in Vaima'a acknowledged Christian principles that both men and women should be chaste before marriage and faithful afterwards. But informally, it was believed that all but elderly men were potential sexual predators, and that it was the duty of women, rather than of men, to be chaste and faithful, and of families to guard the reputations of their daughters. The weight of social disapproval for moral lapses fell heavily on women, whose behaviour, especially the conduct of young single women, was closely scrutinised. Ideally women and girls stayed in the village where everyone's eye was upon them. In contrast, men and boys went outside the circumscribed sphere of the village to work in their plantations and to fish; they moved about freely and there was little public scrutiny of their actions outside the village, nor concern about what they did. If a boy was known to have made a girl from another village pregnant, his conduct was ignored (unless he was a candidate for acceptance into theological college). But any observed attention by a man to a woman who was not of his immediate family was regarded with suspicion, especially if they were unmarried. If a young woman was seen openly talking to a young man not of her family she could be punished and her brothers might attack the young man. Up to the early 1970s, according to established Christian practice, most unmarried young women were sent to sleep in the Congregational Church pastor's house. It was assumed that no man would encroach upon such sacrosanct premises (even though jokes were told about men who had tried it in their youth).

Ideally, if a young man wanted to marry, he was supposed to bring a gift to the family of a girl he fancied, and to make his proposal to her parents or *matai*. But this ideal was seldom – if ever – practised. Instead, a kind of sexual guerrilla warfare prevailed. As Malopa'upu Isaia recalls (quoted above) young men regarded sexual conquest as a "high risk thrill" and in Vaima'a, predatory sexual behaviour was not confined to youths. Several older men were reputed sexual predators, although only one case came into the public domain during the period of the study. According [to] Freeman (1983:226–53), young men believed that the way to get a wife for themselves was to forcibly take the virginity of the girl they had chosen; typically by *moetotolo* (sleep crawling), a term referring to rape by stealth. Noting that most Samoan marriages began with a sudden elopement (this was so in Vaima'a), Freeman speculated that many such elopements followed the forcible defloration of the girl. The practice of surreptitious rape, Freeman found, involved "culturally transmitted male practices" that he had witnessed being communicated by one individual to another within a group of Samoan males (Freeman 1983:249).[2]

As a woman, the writer was never privy to what men or youths believed and discussed in Vaima'a, however several incidents occurred during the study suggesting Freeman was correct. On one occasion the pastor was approached by a youth from a neighbouring village who asked him to forbid a forthcoming wedding ceremony. The pastor sent him away with a scolding, but the youth responded by standing outside the pastor's house and shouting across the *malae* for all to hear that "[the bride-to-be] is my wife!", before making a hasty retreat. On another occasion, a schoolgirl of about seventeen years was found to have disappeared from her parents' house during the night. When her mother searched for her next morning, she found her daughter helping with the cooking in a house in another part of the village. The girl had been taken there during the night by the son of the house, and her mother made no attempt to bring her daughter home. It was rumoured that the boy had successfully committed *moetotolo*, forcing the girl to go to live with him as his wife. Cohabitation thus publicly acknowledged is regarded as marriage and was not punished.

Marriage was not the *rite de passage* that it is in many other societies, because true adulthood was only achieved when a *matai* title was bestowed, elevating the status of both a man and his wife in the community. Young couples did not set up their own households, they lived with the family of the man or the woman; ideally post-marital residence should be virilocal. In-marrying spouses are outsiders who are expected to serve the family of their husband or wife, and are excluded from its formal decision-making processes. It is considered more fitting for a woman than for a man to take this part, but many men opted to live with the family of their wives, and some young couples shuttle between their respective families for years before settling down. Tensions between spouses typically centre upon questions about how their services and resources should be allocated between their respective families. These tensions undermine the ideals of Christian conjugality, and young couples often separate in the early years of their union.

Pregnancy resulting from cohabitation was acceptable, even if the union was of brief duration. But if a single girl was found to be pregnant, moral outrage was expressed, followed by punishment. During the study period, two unmarried women became pregnant. In one case the woman was beaten by her brother (see the quotation from Malopa'upu above), and in both cases their families were fined by the council and thus publicly humiliated. Illegitimacy (*tōifale*) refers to the pregnancy rather than to the resulting child, who is always accepted by the mother's family and may subsequently be acknowledged by the father's family as well (although in so ancestor-focused a society, illegitimacy can be a severe disadvantage). The term is literally 'to be pregnant in the house' and refers to the family ('the house') of the illicitly pregnant woman. Unmarried women who became pregnant were considered fools who had given themselves lightly, because it was assumed that if their lovers had cared for them, they would have asked the girls concerned to elope, thus avoiding disgrace. In one case a young woman was pregnant by her married lover, who told her he would not acknowledge paternity. She refused to publicly name him as father of her child, fearing even greater shame from his denial. A single girl having an affair with a married man takes many risks, not the least of which might be punishment by the relatives of their lover's wife. Such was the fate of a young woman of Vaima'a living in town who had an affair with a married man. She was given a severe beating and had her head shaved. The disgrace of *tōifale* might be life-long as women known to have had illegitimate pregnancies were unlikely to find eligible husbands. The families of prospective suitors would not accept a daughter-in-law who had been illegitimately pregnant. Accordingly, it was common for families to try to conceal the shame of *tōifale* by adopting the child and sending its mother to live with relatives in another village, or overseas.[3]

The higher the rank and status of a family, the greater the effort they made to maintain the reputation of their unmarried daughters, the highest ideals of female conduct being associated, as in the past, with high rank. While there were several illegitimate pregnancies among girls from low-ranking families, there were none in the families of the village's ranking *ali'i*, or in those of its pastor and catechist. Further, although few young men and women married in church, those who did included all the daughters of the two highest ranking families. In several instances, the sons of these families eloped but never their sisters.

Moral Continuities in Migrant Communities

Fings da kirl should know
Don wear your hair out
Don show your shoulder...
Don sleep in da lavalava only
Don sleep by yourself
Don walk by yourself specially in the dark...
              From a poem by Tusiata Avia (2004)

As a concluding observation, many people from Vaima'a have settled in New Zealand, a sexually liberal society, where it might be expected that moral values of migrants from Samoa would change rapidly. However a study of Samoan men and women living in Auckland, New Zealand (Anae *et al.* 2000) carried out twenty-four years after the Vaima'a study shows a remarkable continuity, particularly among Samoans who were socialised in Samoa. The study showed that rank distinctions in

sexual conduct have been submerged by those of gender, and aspects of the cultural rationale for distinctively Samoan moral values, such as *feagaiga*, for example, were barely understood by young people (Park and Morris 2004). However, the prevailing moral values were continuities of older patterns, constraining unmarried girls to preserve their virginity, while expecting men and youths to quest for heterosexual adventures wherever they could find them. Among Samoans in New Zealand and around the world today, as in Samoa, these ancient paradigms endure: the desirable but sexually unattainable *taupou*, and the dashing, sexually conquering *manaia*.

ACKNOWLEGEMENTS

I am indebted to my inspiration, Professor Ann Chowning, who taught me at the University of Papua New Guinea in 1972–73, awakening my interest in both Anthropology and this topic. I am also, as always, indebted to my mentor Professor Judith Huntsman for rescuing the first draft of this essay, and also to Dr Ilana Gershon for her valuable comments and suggestions on the second draft.

NOTES

1 The reference is from Platt's 1835–36 Journal "Raiatea to Hervey and Samoa Islands". FM4 LMS Archives, Mitchell Library, State Library of New South Wales, Sydney.

2 Shore (1996) observes that young Samoan men are brought up to revere their sisters which may well pose psychosexual difficulties in adolescence that underpins these cultural behaviour patterns.

3 A more disturbing aspect of contemporary moral values is suggested by Samoan suicide data since the 1980s. Samoa has a comparatively high suicide rate on the basis of international comparison and the rate is highest among youth. For example between 1990 and 1996, 144 deaths were recorded as resulting from suicide; 97 were of people aged between fifteen and twenty-nine years (Data provided by the Samoa Department of Health, 1998). Much of the discussion of Samoa has addressed social change and the pressures on youth rather than

gender issues, although suicide attempts and deaths are higher among females than males in the age group fifteen to twenty-four. A possible explanation of female motivation – but one that is difficult to demonstrate – is *tōifale*.

REFERENCES

Anae, M., N. Fuamatu, I. Lima, K. Mariner, J. Park and T. Saalii-Sauni
2000   *Tiute ma Matafaioi a nisi Tane Samoa i le Faiga o Aiga: The Roles and Responsibilities of Some Samoan Men in Reproduction*. Auckland: Pacific Health Research Centre, The University of Auckland.

Avia, Tusiata
2004   *Wild Dogs Under My Skirt*. Wellington, Victoria University Press.

Copp, John Dixon (ed.)
1950   *The Samoan Dance of Life. Narrative of Fa'afouina I. Pula*. Boston: Beacon Press.

Freeman, Derek
1983   *Margaret Mead and Samoa: The Making and Unmaking of an Anthropological Myth*. Canberra: Australian National University Press.

Gerber, Eleanor
1975   The Cultural Patterning of Emotions in Samoa. Unpublished Ph.D. thesis, University of California, San Diego.

Gilson, R.P.
1970   *Samoa 1830 to 1900: The Politics of a Multicultural Community*. Melbourne: Oxford University Press.

Irwin, George
1965   *Samoa: A Teacher's Tale*. London: Cassell.

Keesing, Felix
1937   The taupo [sic] system of Samoa: A study of institutional change. *Oceania*, 8(1):1–14.

Krämer, Augustin
1994   [1902]. *The Samoa Islands*. Volume I. Translated by Dr Theodore Verhaaren. Auckland: Pasifika Press.

Mageo, Jeannette Marie
1999   *Theorizing Self in Samoa. Emotions, Gender and Sexualities*. Ann Arbor: The University of Michigan Press.

Malopa'upu, Isaia
1999   *Coming of Age in American Anthropology: Margaret Mead and Paradise*. Universal Publishers/uPUBLISH.com.

Mead, Margaret
1969   [1928]   *Coming of Age in Samoa: A Study of Adolescence and Sex in a Primitive Society*. New York: Morrow.

Meleisa, Malama
1995   "To whom god and men crowed": chieftainship and hierarchy in ancient Samoa. In J. Huntsman (ed.), *Tonga and Samoa: Images of Gender and Polity*. Christchurch: Macmillan Brown Centre for Pacific Studies, pp. 19–34.

Milner, G.B.
1966   *Samoan Dictionary. Auckland*: Polynesian Press.

Moyle, R.M.
1975   Sexuality in Samoan art forms. *Archives of Sexual Behaviour*, 3:231.

Moyle, R.M. (ed.)
1984   *The Samoan Journals of John Williams 1830 and 1832*. Canberra: Australian National University Press.

Neffgen. H.
1975   [1916]   Samoan Sketches. Unpublished typescript in possession of the author. Wellington: Maori Unit.

Ochs, Elinor
1988   *Culture and Language Development: Language Acquisition and Language Socialisation in a Samoan Village*. Cambridge: Cambridge University Press.

Olson, M.D.
2000   Articulating custom: The politics and poetics of social transformations in Samoa. *Journal of Legal Pluralism*, 45.

Park, Julie and Carolyn Morris
2004   Reproducing Samoans in Auckland "in different times": Can habitus help? *Journal of the Polynesian Society*, 113(3): 227–62.

Platt, George
1836.   Journal   Raiatea to Hervey and Samoa Islands, July 28, 1835 – August 22 1836. Unpublished manuscript, London Missionary Society Archives. Microfilm. Mitchell Library of NSW, FM4/333.

Richards, Rhys
1988   *Samoa's Forgotten Whaling Heritage. American Whaling in Samoan Waters 1824–1876*. Wellington. Western Samoa Historical and Cultural Trust.

Schoeffel, Penelope
1979   Daughters of Sina: A Study of Gender, Status and Power in Samoa. Unpublished Ph.D. thesis, Australian National University.

Schoeffel, Penelope
1995   The Samoan concept of *feagaiga* and its transformation. In J. Huntsman (ed.), *Tonga and Samoa: Images of Gender and Polity*. Christchurch: Macmillan Brown Centre for Pacific Studies, pp.85–106.

Schoeffel, Penelope
1999   Samoan exchange and "fine mats": An historical reconsideration. *Journal of the Polynesian Society*, 108(2):117–48.

Shankman, Paul
1996   The history of Samoan sexual conduct and the Mead Freeman controversy. *American Anthropologist*, 98(3):555–67

Shankman, Paul
2005   MS. Virginity and Veracity: Rereading Historical Sources in the Mead–Freeman Controversy. Unpublished paper presented to the Association of Anthropologists in Oceania.

Shore, Bradd
1977   A Samoan Theory of Action: Social Control and Social Order in a Polynesian Paradox. Unpublished Ph.D. thesis, University of Chicago.

Shore, Bradd
1982   *Sala'ilua: A Samoan Mystery*. New York: Columbia University Press.

Shore, Bradd
1996   *Culture in Mind: Cognition, Culture and the Problem of Meaning*. New York: Oxford University Press.

Tcherkézoff, Serge
1993   The illusion of dualism in Samoa. "Brothers-and-sisters" are not "men-and-women". In T. del Valle (ed.), *Gendered Anthropology*. London and New York: Routledge, pp.54–87.

Tcherkézoff, Serge
2000   The Samoan category of *matai* 'chief': A singularity in Polynesia? Historical and etymological comparative queries. *Journal of the Polynesian Society*, 109(2):151–90.

Tcherkézoff, Serge
2004   *First Contacts in Polynesia: The Samoan Case (1722–1848) Western Misunderstandings about Sexuality and Divinity*. Canberra and Christchurch: Journal of Pacific History and the Macmillan Brown Centre for Pacific Studies.

Turner, George
1984 [1884]   *Samoa: A Hundred Years Ago and Long Before*. Suva: Institute of Pacific Studies, University of the South Pacific.

20

Virginity and the History of Sex in Samoa

Paul Shankman

The *taupou* system occupies a central place in the Mead–Freeman controversy. Its very existence, according to Freeman and many Samoan critics of Mead, showed that virginity was more than an abstract value; it was part of a *system* of *institutionalized* virginity, where the *taupou* played an important role in Samoan culture and provided a role model for other girls. For Freeman, the *taupou* was one of Samoa's "most sacrosanct traditional institutions." He stated that in pre-European times female virginity was "very much the leitmotif of the pagan Samoans," and even in the late twentieth century, Freeman argued, "the sexual mores of the pagan Samoans are still, in many ways, extant."[1]

In pre-European Samoa a young woman, usually the adolescent daughter of a high-ranking chief, was appointed to the role of *taupou*; she represented the chief's political authority and the prestige of the village as a whole. Her marriage to another high-ranking chief could cement new political alliances. She was therefore an important figure in village political life. Beyond her valuable role in forging alliances, the *taupou* was also leader

of the village's association of unmarried women (*aualuma*) that entertained prestigious visitors. The *taupou* made kava for meetings of the village council, was a hostess and dancer, ate special food, wore distinctive dress, and did not engage in the heavy labor of her unmarried female counterparts. She was the pride of her village. At her marriage, there were elaborate gift exchanges between the families of the bride and groom. And she was required to demonstrate her chastity in a public defloration ceremony as part of the formal arranged marriage.[2]

Freeman provided an explicit description of the defloration ceremony:

The exchange of property having taken place, the bridegroom seated himself on the ceremonial ground of his village. The young woman was then taken by the hand by her elder brother or some other relative, and led toward her bridegroom, dressed in a fine mat edged with red feathers, her body gleaming with scented oil. On arriving immediately in front of him she threw off this mat and stood naked

Paul Shankman, Virginity and the History of Sex in Samoa, from *The Trashing of Margaret Mead: Anatomy of an Anthropological Controversy*, University of Wisconsin Press, 2009, pp. 175–189, 263–264. © 2009 by the Board of the Regents of the University of Wisconsin System. Reprinted by permission of The University of Wisconsin Press.

Sexualities in Anthropology: A Reader, edited by Andrew P. Lyons and Harriet D. Lyons
© 2011 Blackwell Publishing Ltd.

while he ruptured her hymen with "two fingers of his right hand." If a hemorrhage ensued the bridegroom drew his fingers over the bride's upper lip, before holding his hand for all present to witness the proof of her virginity. At this the female supporters of the bride rushed forward to obtain a portion of the smear upon themselves before dancing naked and hitting their heads with stones until their own blood ran down in streams, in sympathy with, and in honor of, the virgin bride. The husband, meanwhile, wiped his hands on a piece of white barkcloth which he wore around his waist for the rest of the day as a token of respect for his wife. With the bride's ceremonial defloration accomplished, the marriage was usually consummated forthwith, with the utmost decorum, in a screened-off part of a house.[3]

However, if the bride was not a virgin, she was cursed as a prostitute, and the marriage was nullified. Sometimes she was beaten by her relatives, even to death.[4]

Freeman argued that the value of virginity embodied in the *taupou* extended beyond her to all adolescent girls, and this "cult of virginity" continued after European contact. Christianity transformed and reinforced the values of the *taupou* system so that, in Freeman's view, "after the mid 19th century, when a puritanical Christian morality was added to an existing traditional cult of virginity," Samoa was a society in which this religiously and culturally sanctioned ideal strongly influenced the actual behavior of adolescent girls.[5]

Freeman's extensive discussion of the *taupou* system was intended to refute Mead's portrayal of the *taupou* as a girl of high rank whose virginity was closely guarded but who was the exception rather than the rule in terms of virginity. Mead argued that, apart from the *taupou* and other daughters of high-ranking chiefs and despite the ideology of virginity for all girls, adolescent girls from lower-ranking families could and did engage in clandestine premarital sex. Instead of reinforcing a pre-existing ideal of virginity, as Freeman would have it, Christianity and colonial government led to a relaxation of the severe traditional standards for the *taupou* in part by completely banning the defloration ceremony. Apart from the virginity of the *taupou*, to which Samoans

were committed, Mead believed that they were skeptical of Christianity's message about chastity for all Samoans and that they participated in what, by American standards of the 1920s, were permissive premarital relationships.[6]

Freeman agreed that changes in the *taupou* system had occurred, the banning of the defloration ceremony being the most obvious one, but the value of virginity for all girls remained. Chastity was now upheld by Christian Samoans, and the village pastor now guarded adolescent girls, who often resided in his home under his guidance and protection. The village and the church enforced a system of punishments for those who strayed from the fold, as did individual families. Freeman stated that the values of the *taupou* system began to break down as Samoans started to migrate overseas in the 1950s, but for the previous one hundred years or more the values of the *taupou* system had remained intact and enforced sexual restrictiveness.[7] Thus, according to Freeman, the *taupou* system was in effect before, during, and after Mead's research in the 1920s. So Samoa could not have been sexually permissive, despite Mead's assertions to the contrary.

While Mead and Freeman agreed on the importance of virginity for the *taupou*, they disagreed on virtually everything else – how widely the value on her virginity was held, the role of Christianity, and the actual behavior of adolescent girls. Because Samoa has a reputation for tradition and continuity, Freeman's depiction lent itself to an interpretation involving cultural conservatism and resiliency. Mead's depiction, on the other hand, suggested that as a result of missionization and colonialism, the *taupou* system attenuated and declined. So how persistent was the *taupou* system after European settlement began? What kinds of changes occurred? And how closely was the ideal of chastity observed at different times during the colonial period?

Mead's View of the *Taupou* and Her Use of History

In her 1927 National Research Council report, "The Adolescent Girl in Samoa," Mead discussed the decline of the *taupou* system in a chapter entitled "Samoan Civilisation As It Is To-day." The chapter also dealt with other changes in Samoa that occurred as a result of European contact.[8] But in terms of historical detail, the chapter got in the way of what she wanted to convey in *Coming of Age in Samoa.*

Mead wanted to present Samoa in a readable manner, without having to shift awkwardly back and forth between different historical time frames. By excluding history and other external factors, she could achieve a more uniform, if artificial, presentation. This kind of representation, known as "the ethnographic present" among anthropologists, was a commonly used literary tool. It factored out the "contaminating" effects of the past and highlighted what appeared to be a relatively untouched present. Yet the stylistic virtue of using the ethnographic present was also its weakness. It presented a culture in a timeless, enduring manner, as if it were forever traditional and unchanging.

Mead wanted to use the ethnographic present to organize the body of *Coming of Age.* So, in the transformation of her report into a book, she shifted the chapter on historical change to an appendix.[9] Mead knew that it was next to impossible to present a single, coherent picture of the culture without distorting history. Things did change. Thus, she noted that the culture of a Samoan adolescent girl's parents was different from the girl's own culture. But for the sake of the unity of the book, different time frames were lumped together, including "customs which have fallen into partial decay under the impact of western propaganda and foreign example."[10] The *taupou* system was one of those customs.

In the body of *Coming of Age*, Mead wrote about how, traditionally, the *taupou* differed from other girls and how she was deflowered in a public ceremony: "From this free and easy experimentation, the *taupo* [sic] is excepted. Virginity is a legal requirement for her. At her marriage, in front of all the people, in a house brilliantly lit, the talking chief of the bridegroom will take the tokens of her virginity. In former days, should she not prove to be a virgin, her female relatives fell upon her and beat her with stones, disfiguring and sometimes fatally injuring the girl who had shamed their

house." Mead footnoted this discussion by observing, "This custom is forbidden by law, but is only gradually dying out."[11]

She then continued her discussion of the *taupou* and other high-ranking daughters of chiefs:

These girls of noble birth are carefully guarded; not for them are secret trysts at night or stolen meetings in the daytime. Where parents of lower rank complacently ignore their daughters' experiments, the high chief guards his daughter's virginity as he guards the honour of his name, his precedence in the kava ceremony or any other prerogative of his high degree. Some old woman of the household is told to be the girl's constant companion. The *taupo* may not visit in other houses in the village, or leave the house alone at night. When she sleeps, an older woman sleeps beside her. Never may she go to another village unchaperoned. In her own village, she goes soberly about her tasks, bathing in the sea, working in the plantation, safe under the jealous guardianship of the women of her own village. She runs little risk from the *moe-totolo*, for one who outraged the *taupo* of his village would formerly have been beaten to death, and now would have to flee from the village. The prestige of the village is inextricably bound up with the high repute of the *taupo* and few young men in the village would dare to be her lovers. Marriage to them is out of the question.... For tradition says that the *taupo* must marry outside her village, marry a high chief or a *manaia* [heir apparent] of another village. Such a marriage is an occasion for great festivities and solemn ceremony. The chief and all of his talking chiefs must come to propose for her hand, come in person bringing gifts for her talking chiefs. If the talking chiefs of the girl are satisfied that this is a lucrative and desirable match, and the family are satisfied with the rank and appearance of the suitor, the marriage is agreed upon. Little attention is paid to the opinion of the girl.[12]

So Mead had a good understanding of the pre-European *taupou* system and described it in a manner similar to Freeman.

In "Samoan Civilisation As It Is To-day," now an appendix to *Coming of Age*, Mead described the changes that had occurred in the system in the nineteenth century, including less punitive sanctions of the *taupou* for an affair:

> Deviations from chastity were formerly punished in the case of girls by a very severe beating and a stigmatising shaving of the head. Missionaries have discouraged the beating and head shaving, but failed to substitute as forceful an inducement to circumspect conduct. The girl whose sex activities are frowned upon by her family is in a far better position than that of her grandmother. The navy has prohibited, the church has interdicted the defloration ceremony, formerly an inseparable part of the marriages of girls of rank; and thus the most potent inducement to virginity has been abolished. If for these cruel and primitive methods of enforcing a stricter regime there had been substituted a religious system which seriously branded the sex offender, or a legal system which prosecuted and punished her, then the new hybrid civilisation might have been as heavily fraught with possibilities of conflict as the old civilisation undoubtedly was.[13]

Mead did not see the church as reinforcing the *taupou* system, as Freeman did. The church was influential in promoting the ideal of virginity, especially for young women who went to live with the pastor, but Mead viewed the *taupou* system as a system of marriage that Christianity sought to replace almost in its entirety. However, neither Mead nor Freeman provided more than a brief review of how the *taupou* system worked or how it changed after the Europeans arrived. A more detailed review of the evidence may help resolve some of these issues in the controversy.

Before the Missionaries Arrived

The *taupou* system was, according to Mead, a system of marriage that governed the relationships of daughters of high-ranking chiefs, idealizing their virginity and protecting them from unwanted seduction. As noted earlier, each village had its own set of chiefs (*matai*), organized as a village council and incorporated into a broader hierarchy of chiefs.[14] In pre-European Samoa, chiefly prestige

was partly inherited and partly achieved. Chiefs could not simply rest on the status of a title after it was conferred; they had to earn prestige by forging alliances, participating in ceremonial exchanges of wealth, successfully waging war, and gaining new titles through strategic marriages. *Taupou* marriages were vital in all of these political activities. Chiefs used the *taupou* as a social asset to promote political alliances with other chiefly families in a system that allowed high-ranking chiefs to have multiple wives, sometimes a dozen or more. The more important the chiefly title, the more marriages he could contract and the greater his upward mobility and prestige.

Because the Samoan political system was not centralized, consisting instead of shifting, warring alliances, and because chiefly marriages were essential to alliance formation, high-ranking families were especially concerned with controlling their daughters' sexual conduct so that they could be used to cement alliances.[15] If the *taupou* passed the virginity test, the marriage transaction was completed and the alliance solidified. If not, there would be no marriage. After marriage, her role as a *taupou* ended. She was now the wife of a chief, and these marriages were not necessarily permanent. Chiefs taking new wives could discard old ones, and former *taupou* would return to their own villages with their children. They could not marry again without permission of their husbands.

If the *taupou* system was vital for high-ranking chiefs, it was far less relevant for lower-ranking chiefs and for untitled men and women. For them, *avaga* marriages based on elopement and individual choice rather than on prior family arrangement and elaborate gift exchange were the norm. Although virginity was nominally valued for young women of all ranks, in practice the lower the rank, the less the value on virginity.[16] Marriage for lower-ranking families was also typically monogamous. So there were two marriage systems in practice, the *taupou* system for elite chiefly families and *avaga* for almost everyone else.

Most girls were not *taupou* and did not have the opportunity to become *taupou* because of their lower rank. Among them there was enough premarital sex to draw the attention of early missionaries. John Williams, the missionary who brought Christianity to the islands in the 1830s, believed that Samoans were more like the permissive Tahitians he had encountered than the restrictive Tongans in terms of their "lascivious habits."[17] Williams traveled widely in the South Pacific and was a keen observer. He reported that non-*taupou* enjoyed a "roving commission" in sexual matters before marriage.[18] So, important as the *taupou* was, her behavior was not followed by many other girls.

The restrictions on the *taupou* and her proper conduct did not prevent women from the erotic singing and dancing that European observers found obscene. Williams witnessed occasions that included erotic "night" dances, and he provided the following account of them: "The young virgin girls taking the lead they now enter the house entirely naked & commence their dance. The full grown women then follow after. Then come the old women all of whom are entirely naked. During their dancing they throw themselves in all imaginable positions in order to make the most full exposure of their persons to the whole company.... During the whole of the time of performing the females are using the most vile, taunting, bantering language to the men."[19] Needless to say, Williams and other missionaries were shocked by this and many other aspects of Samoan culture. There was undoubtedly a great deal about Samoan culture that they did not understand.[20] Nevertheless, from their perspective, they had not encountered a culture committed to chastity for all men and women but rather a culture in which "indecent" sexual activities were common enough to become the missionaries' highest priority for reform.

Missionary Reform

The initial impression of a number of early Christian missionaries was that Samoa was a pagan culture filled with godlessness and immorality. Although they considered Samoans a "race" worthy of Christianity and superior to many other non-Western cultures, "sinful" sexual activities were common enough and public enough to receive the missionaries' fullest attention.

While approving of the ideal of virginity as symbolized by the *taupou*, missionaries did not approve of many aspects of the *taupou* system and other aspects of Samoan sexual conduct. They strongly condemned political marriages, multiple marriages, prostitution, adultery, ease of divorce, erotic dancing and singing, ease of sexual access in living arrangements, sexual activities during intervillage visits, and, of course, public defloration.[21] The missionaries were very interested in assuring that virginity become the ideal for all young women, not just the *taupou*, and that men remain faithful to their wives. Anthropologist Penelope Schoeffel, reviewing the early historical accounts of the *taupou* system, found that "in the past, only high-ranking women had been bound by the rules of chastity; and chiefly polygamy and philandering by men had been encouraged. Under the new Christian order, restrictions were applied to all Samoans, irrespective of rank, who wished for salvation."[22]

Williams and his missionary associates began converting Samoans in the 1830s. He initially thought that, given the low status of women and the chiefly prerogative of polygynous marriages, evangelizing Samoans would be difficult.[23] Yet within three decades they had converted in impressive numbers.[24] The process was so swift and seemingly complete that it was easy to mistake it for wholesale acceptance. Freeman, for example, speaks of the merger between the Samoan "cult of virginity" and a puritanical Christian morality reinforcing the value of chastity for all girls.[25] In reality, though, the two were often at odds, if not open conflict, over a number of matters, especially sexual conduct.

The missionaries moved to abolish public defloration, multiple marriages by chiefs, political marriages of any kind, adultery, fornication, and other acts of "immorality." They also sought to discourage a variety of activities that supported the *taupou* system as an institution. "Night" dances were prohibited and were to be replaced by churchgoing and hymn singing. Even mild forms of dance were forbidden. Although these prohibitions were later relaxed, they undermined the responsibilities of the *taupou* and the role of the unmarried women's association in public entertainment. Kava drinking, thought by missionaries to be a form of intoxication, was also banned for a time, and this too eroded the role of the *taupou*, who was responsible for making it.

Despite missionary teachings, allegedly sinful practices continued among large segments of the population, leading to frustration on the part of the missionaries. George Turner, a Wesleyan missionary who began working in Samoa in 1841, wrote: "Chastity was ostensibly cultivated by both sexes; but it was more a name than a reality.... There were exceptions, especially among the daughters of persons of rank, but they were exceptions, not the rule."[26]

There were so few missionaries that they could not realistically attempt far-reaching changes overnight. And there were many other temporary European visitors to Samoa who were more interested in vice than in virtue. The Reverend A. W. Murray recorded that, during the mid-nineteenth century, as many as six whalers with "lawless" crews of thirty men each could anchor at any one time in the port of Apia. The missionaries were almost helpless in the face of these men and their Samoan partners. Murray explained: "There they were – men of our own colour, speaking the same language with ourselves, and some of them our own countrymen, and claiming to be Christians, while giving themselves up to the most shameful immoralities, and telling the natives all manner of lies, so far as they could make themselves understood.... [W]e mourned over the moral havoc they wrought, and the influence in drawing the people away from schools and services."[27]

During the late nineteenth century, the increasing European population in the port town led to a number of relationships between Samoan women and European men. There were marriages, but many more were short-term unions.[28] Apia was the second busiest port in the South Pacific, and in the latter part of the nineteenth century Europeans and a growing group of poorer, rowdy "part-Europeans" clustered in an area called the Beach, known throughout the region for its grog shops and dance halls. Prostitution, gambling, and drink were all available, much to the missionaries' dismay. Writing in 1892, author Robert Louis Stevenson, who lived in Samoa at

the time, bemoaned that until recently "the white people of Apia lay in the worst squalor of degradation."[29] The port town was referred to as a "little Cairo" and a "hell in the Pacific." Samoans were supplying dancing girls and were rumored to be giving women in exchange for muskets.[30]

Samoans actively sought relationships with Europeans that they hoped would lead to marriage or at least a relationship that could benefit their families. This was simply an extension of pre-European custom.[31] But Europeans took advantage of members of the unmarried women's association who had become available for interethnic unions. This gave Samoan women "a bad reputation in the South Seas regarding their morals," according to Augustin Krämer, a German surgeon and observer of the period.[32] While this reputation was undeserved due to a misunderstanding of Samoan custom, it was nevertheless widespread. And there were increasing numbers of part-European children throughout the islands.

The *Taupou* System in Decline

By the end of the nineteenth century, the *taupou* system was in decline. The public defloration of *taupou* was not only forbidden by law but becoming extinct in practice. In the 1890s Krämer found that there were very few public deflorations remaining and that many *taupou* were eloping so that they might have a greater choice in marriage partners. Few true virgins remained, mostly among the very young. Krämer even observed that, in those rare public deflorations that did occur, the hymeneal blood of the *taupou* might be counterfeited in order to preserve the spirit if not the letter of the virginity-testing ceremony.[33]

Krämer did not approve of public defloration, but he found the idea of counterfeiting hymeneal blood to be morally reprehensible. Yet he did not blame Samoans but rather the missionaries for this distortion of Samoan custom. In a comment very similar to Mead's he stated: "Naturally, without wanting to say that the custom of public defloration must be maintained, one must however reproach the missionaries who have not been able to offer an alternative to the people.... In any case, also in this respect, the 'old Samoa' is finished."[34]

By the 1890s the *taupou* system of marriage was vanishing. Polygyny was no longer a public practice, while monogamy meant that there was no longer a need for many *taupou*. The abolition of multiple marriages by high chiefs created a surplus of candidates for the position of *taupou* and decreased their political usefulness. Anthropologist Felix Keesing, who visited Samoa shortly after Mead's research in the 1920s but prior to Freeman's in the 1940s, wrote: "In the old days a fresh taupo would be married off probably every two to four years. Since the number of high-born chiefs and chiefs-elect suitable for such matches was limited, the new monogamous marriage system brought what might be called a glut in the taupo marriage mart: many maidens but few available husbands of suitable rank."[35]

Taupou were expensive to appoint, maintain, and marry. Because there were fewer marriages of high-ranking chiefs, fewer *taupou* were appointed. If these young women were unable to marry, what good were they? Keesing asked in 1937:

What then of the taupo institution in the modern era of mission work, commercial development, schools, and Western political control?

The visitor to present day Samoa passes through village after village without encountering a full-fledged taupo. From the writer's own inquiries and experience of travel, he would judge that the great majority of chiefs entitled to maintain a taupo no longer do so. Even where a taupo is found, as in socially conservative areas like Manu'a [where Mead worked] and in the case of very high chiefs like Malietoa and Mataafa, her activities have become attenuated.[36]

Mead found that, while there were several chiefs who could have appointed *taupou* in Manu'a, only one *taupou* was actually appointed, her friend Fa'apua'a, and she was a woman in her midtwenties, not an adolescent girl. Even where *taupou* were still appointed, their role was limited. Although still a hostess, dancer, and political representative of her village and family, she had fewer responsibilities

than in pre-European Samoa. The unmarried women's association had declined in importance as well.

Freeman believed that the *taupou* system and Christianity merged and that this merger reinforced the value placed on virginity. At the level of public ideology, this may have been true, but as a system of marriage, the *taupou* system was attenuating. During his years in Samoa, Freeman never witnessed a public defloration ceremony himself because by the 1940s there were none.[37] They had ceased to occur decades earlier, with only an occasional private defloration taking place.

Replacing the *taupou* system was a new and different system of monogamous Christian marriage advocated by missionaries. Virginity as a religious ideal became accepted public belief for all young women, with premarital and extramarital sex strongly condemned. In theory this was true for men as well. In practice, though, Christian weddings were rare and mostly for higher-ranking families, while *avaga* marriages continued for the majority of families. In the village of Sa'anapu, for example, Freeman reported that of sixty-four marriages he recorded, only four began with a church ceremony. The other sixty were *avaga* marriages, although a number of couples had a Christian ceremony at a later date.[38]

World War II and Sexual Permissiveness

By the 1940s the role of the *taupou* had been transformed from an essential part of the traditional Samoan political and economic system to a far less significant part of a changing culture. Freeman argued that there was "general stability of Samoan culture" in the first half of the twentieth century, including sexual conduct.[39] Yet he neglected the most important event of the period – World War II.

The war years were a period of major change in the islands, including a dramatic increase in unions between outsiders and Samoans. Tens of thousands of American military personnel occupied both Western Samoa and American Samoa from 1942 through 1945, overwhelming the Samoans themselves.

Although the islands were not the site of military action, with the exception of one relatively harmless Japanese submarine attack, both sets of islands had major military bases.

W. E. H. Stanner, an anthropologist and postwar observer, described the situation in wartime Western Samoa as follows:

> Before the main body of troops moved to forward areas in 1943–44 there may have been as many as 25,000 or 30,000 troops in Western Samoa at any one time. The turnover, of course, was much higher because of transfer of units and movement of reinforcements. The troops were dispersed throughout the islands, many defended zones were constructed, and there was an enormous temporary building programme. The troops concentrated in camps or bivouacs along the coastline, in the main areas of native settlement, so that segregation was impracticable.... The Samoan islands experienced immensely heightened activity, intimate contact with Europeans *en masse*, and economic "prosperity," all in a degree greater than in any previous period in their history.[40]

The military needed Samoan labor and Samoan products; 2,600 Samoans were initially employed by the Americans. Samoans also quickly became effective small traders, restaurant and café owners, and brewers of crude but potent spirits, leading to increases in Samoan income. Historian Mary Boyd commented: "Wine, beer and spirits were manufactured from cocoa washings and sold at great profit. Gambling, drinking, promiscuity, and prostitution flourished. Samoan relations with the Americans were notably more friendly, hospitable and generous than with New Zealanders."[41]

In terms of Samoan culture, according to Stanner, "some native ceremonies were cheapened, and in cases debauched, to attract gift-bearing Americans. A few *matai* [chiefs] appointed new *taupo* virgins, as often as not girls lacking the technical attributes, to assist hospitalities." More generally, "during the military occupation men fraternized very freely with native people, approaching them, accosting them, using their houses as sprawling huts, doing violence to one cherished courtesy after another with complete indifference. The barriers were down, and easy association became epidemic."[42]

Wartime interethnic unions were common. Stanner found:

> A great deal of sexual promiscuity occurred between Samoan or part-Samoan women and American troops. Responsible Samoans said that actual prostitution was restricted to a very small group of women. Romantic, at least friendly, relationships are very common. One mission society reported that in Upolu alone there were 1,200 known instances of illegitimate children by American soldiers from Samoan girls. The official statistics were not revealed, but put the number of known illegitimate children much lower. Only a few incidents were caused by the jealousy of Samoan men, and not much was made of them by either side. Some villages were said to have set up a special curfew for their girls, and at Falefa (near Apia) no troops except officers on business were allowed to enter *fale* [houses]. With troops so widely dispersed in an area so densely settled it is impossible to prevent familiar association. Many soldiers regularly visited girlfriends within the villages, by no means only with single intention, but the entrance-gates to the airport, it was said, became known among Samoans as "the gates of sin." At least one *matai* [chief] was summarily expelled from his church congregation and from the society of the village on suspicion of procuring girls for prostitution.[43]

The well-known author James Michener reported in a discreet but detailed manner his own participation in one such relationship. As a lieutenant, Michener was responsible for base security. Early in his Western Samoan tour of duty he found a base where, during the day, sixty to seventy-two American men were on duty, yet at night there were only six. Concerned about security, Michener learned that military vehicles took the men to villages at dusk, where they were dropped off to meet their Samoan girlfriends for the evening. Michener saw firsthand that these evening arrangements were openly welcomed by Samoans. In the morning, servicemen were picked up and returned to their base. Michener himself was invited by a high-ranking Samoan chief to enter into such a relationship with his daughter and to father her child. As a result of his involvement, Michener felt so compromised that he never reported these relationships to his superior officers.[44]

These accounts of wartime Samoa suggest that relationships between American servicemen and Samoan women developed quickly and often, although many villages away from bases and roads had little contact with American troops. Where relationships took place, young women were allowed and even encouraged by their families to enter into them, with contact to a large degree under the control of parents and the village. There were relatively few overt conflicts between families and American troops. Although Samoans were perfectly capable of secluding their daughters and punishing them for affairs with Americans and for having children with them, they did not do so for the most part. This pattern of permissive sexual conduct during World War II is very difficult to reconcile with Freeman's portrait of a "severe Christian morality" and a culture in which "female virginity was probably carried to a greater extreme than in any other culture known to anthropology."[45] It is also at odds with Freeman's assertion that major changes in Samoan sexual conduct did not begin to occur until the 1950s.

Because the wartime occupation of Western Samoa began in 1942, perhaps the best opportunity to view these changes would have occurred shortly before and immediately after that date. Freeman arrived in Western Samoa in April 1940 as a schoolteacher and departed in November 1943. He was therefore in a position to have observed or at least known of these relationships. As a New Zealander whose country was the governing power in Western Samoa at that time, Freeman served in the Local Defense Force and would go on to serve in the Royal New Zealand Volunteer Naval Reserve. Yet the war and its effects on Samoa, including the relationships between American military personnel and Samoan women, were not discussed in Freeman's work. At that moment, when the world's political future was in great peril and when premarital sexual activity in Samoa was perhaps most apparent, Freeman's focus was elsewhere. He maintained that it was then he realized that he would "one day have to face

the responsibility of writing a refutation of Mead's Samoan findings."[46]

Does History Matter?

Because Freeman's critique of Mead was primarily a historical critique based on what Samoan sexual conduct was like before, during, and after the time that Mead did her research, an extended look at the history of Samoan sexual conduct is important in evaluating Freeman's argument. The historical data just reviewed indicate major problems with Freeman's reconstruction of the history of the *taupou* system. Historically, Samoa was less restrictive than Freeman allowed, and there were more variability and permissiveness in some areas of Samoan sexual conduct than he discerned. Especially puzzling is the absence of any discussion of interethnic relationships during World War II in the islands.

Could there be a problem with the sources Freeman used? Most of the sources used here were known to and employed by Freeman in *support* of his argument about the maintenance of the *taupou* system. Yet he neglected passages in source after source that did not conform to his argument. These problems were noted in an article I published in 1996 that included much of the material reviewed in this chapter.[47] Freeman was outraged by the article and sent me a five-page handwritten letter in which he threatened to ruin my career. He also recommended that I immediately come to the islands to offer a ceremonial apology to Samoans for having misrepresented their history.[48] Freeman later published a reply to my article titled "All Made of Fantasy: A Rejoinder to Paul Shankman," declaring that I did not know what I was talking about. Yet Freeman did not refute any of the article's major arguments about the decline of the *taupou* system. Why not?

After Freeman's death in 2001 I had the opportunity to read his postgraduate diploma thesis, "The Social Structure of a Samoan Village Community," which was based on his Samoan fieldwork in the early 1940s, a source that had been previously unavailable to interested scholars. As noted earlier, this was Freeman's most important ethnographic work on the islands, and I was surprised by the data in it. Although Freeman had scoffed at my argument about the decline of the *taupou* system, in his thesis he stated that by the 1940s "the *taupou* system has now become *virtually defunct* in Western Samoa."[49]

To illustrate this point he noted that in the village of Sa'anapu there were five high-ranking families that possessed *taupou* titles. Yet "in 1943 none of these five *taupou* titles was occupied." When necessary, a girl from one of the extended families would be temporarily appointed *taupou* but not maintained on a full-time basis. Freeman then listed the reasons for the decline of the *taupou* system in Sa'anapu:

> Principal among the reasons for this change has been the rigorous suppression of customs associated with it by the Christian missions. Economic factors have also operated. Like a *malai* [chief], a *taupou* is obliged to have her title ratified by the other lineages of her village community. This is established at a feast (*saofa'iga*) provided by the *taupou*'s lineage. Such a feast is a serious drain on a lineage's resources. Again, following the introduction of money into the Samoan economy, marked discrepancies have developed in the value of the property (*oloa* and *toga*) exchanged at marriage ceremonies. This has resulted in a situation in which a *taupou*'s lineage and village gain nothing from her marriage or formal election.

As for *taupou* marriages, they had become so infrequent that Freeman commented: "This type of marriage, now relatively rare, does not here concern us."[50]

So Freeman knew about the decline of the *taupou* system from his own fieldwork. His unpublished thesis had provided an important ethnographic account of this decline, yet his unpublished account differed from his published statements about the importance of the *taupou* system before, during, and after Mead's fieldwork in Samoa in the 1920s. And Freeman continued to insist on the viability of the *taupou* system in the 1920s even after my article appeared. In 1998 he wrote: "In fact, in Samoa in those days there was a virginity cult with ritual defloration at marriage."[51]

Freeman certainly knew the history of Samoa, and he gave great weight to his expertise in that area, stating that his work "would involve much research into the history of early Samoa."[52] Furthermore, he believed that "if I had not systematically completed my researches in the way that I have described, my refutation [of Mead] would certainly not have the cogency that it does."[53] He commented that his refutation of her work was "based on most carefully researched evidence, meticulously checked by native scholars, of a kind that could be submitted to a congressional or royal commission." Furthermore, he said that he used so many different sources that they could not "possibly have been affected by any projection of my personality."[54] The issue, though, is not the number of sources or their overall reliability; rather, it is *how* the sources were used.

Freeman not only misrepresented the historical work of others but neglected his own personal experiences in the islands during World War II and his unpublished work on the *taupou* system. To what extent these omissions were conscious and deliberate or unconscious and inadvertent is unclear. What is clear is that Freeman himself, not his sources, misrepresented and distorted the historical record so as to favor his interpretation of the *taupou* system and his critique of Mead. Mead's interpretation of the decline of the *taupou* system, however brief, is more in accord with the historical record presented here.

NOTES

1 Freeman, *Mead and Samoa*, 227, 253, 232, 236.
2 This portrait of the *taupou* is drawn from Freeman, *Mead and Samoa*.
3 Freeman, *Mead and Samoa*, 230–31.
4 Freeman, *Mead and Samoa*, 236; Mead, *Coming of Age*, 275, 98.
5 Freeman, *Mead and Samoa*, 350, 239.
6 Mead, *Coming of Age*, 274.
7 Freeman, *Mead and Samoa*, 350.
8 Mead, "The Adolescent Girl."
9 Mead, *Coming of Age*, 266–77, app. 3.
10 Mead, *Coming of Age*, 259.
11 Mead, *Coming of Age*, 98.

12 Mead, *Coming of Age*, 100–101.
13 Mead, *Coming of Age*, 273–74.
14 *See Goldman, Ancient Polynesian Society*, chap. 11, for a general outline of Samoan social and political structure.
15 Freeman, *Mead and Samoa*, 229–30.
16 Freeman, *Mead and Samoa*, 236.
17 Williams, *Samoan Journals*, 233.
18 Williams, *Samoan Journals*, 233.
19 Williams, *Samoan Journals*, 247–48.
20 Tcherkézoff details these possible misunderstandings in *"First Contacts."* See also Schoeffel, "Sexual Morality."
21 Gilson, *Samoa 1830–1900*, 96; Davidson, *Samoa mo Samoa*, 35.
22 Schoeffel, "The Samoan Concept," 103.
23 Williams, *Samoan Journals*, 283.
24 Daws, "Great Samoan Awakening"; Tiffany, "Politics."
25 Freeman, *Mead and Samoa*, 239.
26 Turner, *Nineteen Years*, 184.
27 Murray, *Forty Years' Missionary Work*, 41.
28 Shankman, "Interethnic Unions."
29 Stevenson, *A Footnote to History*, 26.
30 Gilson, *Samoa 1830 1900*, 179, 180.
31 Meleise'a, *The Making*, 157.
32 Krämer, *Die Samoa-inseln*, 36 (*The Samoa Islands*, 47n88).
33 Krämer, *Die Samoa-inseln*, 36 (47n87).
34 Krämer, *Die Samoa-inseln*, 36 (47n87).
35 Keesing, "The Taupo System," 7.
36 Keesing, "The Taupo System," 5.
37 Freeman's 1948 thesis ("Social Structure of a Samoan Village Community") makes this apparent.
38 Freeman, "Social Structure of a Samoan Village," 108.
39 Freeman, "Reply to Ember's Reflections," 914.
40 Stanner, *South Seas*, 325–26.
41 Boyd, "The Record," 185.
42 Stanner, *South Seas*, 326, 327–28.
43 Stanner, *South Seas*, 327.
44 Michener, *World Is My Home*, 38–40. On wartime interethnic unions in American Samoa see Mageo, "Spirit Girls."
45 Freeman, *Mead and Samoa*, 250.
46 Freeman, *Mead and Samoa*, xiv.
47 Shankman, "History of Samoan Sexual Conduct."
48 Freeman, personal communication, 1998.
49 Freeman, "Social Structure of a Samoan Village," 245, my emphasis.
50 Freeman, "Social Structure of a Samoan Village," 245, 108.
51 Freeman, "In Praise," 87.
52 Freeman, *Mead and Samoa*, xiv.
53 Freeman "Inductivism," 112.
54 Freeman, "Reply to Ember's Reflections," 915, 911.

REFERENCES

Boyd, Mary
  "The Record in Western Samoa to 1945." In *New Zealand's Record in the Pacific Islands in the Twentieth Century*, edited by A. Ross, 115–88. London: Longman Paul, 1969.
Davidson, James W.
  Samoa mo Samoa: The Emergence of the Independent State of Western Samoa. Melbourne: Oxford University Press, 1967.
Daws, A. Gavan
  "The Great Samoan Awakening of 1839." *Journal of the Polynesian Society* 70(1961): 326–37.
Freeman, Derek
  Dilthey's Dream: Essays on Human Nature and Culture. Canberra: Pandanus Books, 2001.
Freeman, Derek.
  "Inductivism and the Test of Truth: A Rejoinder to Lowell D. Holmes and Others." *Canberra Anthropology* 6, no. 2 (1983): 101–92.
Freeman, Derek
  "In Praise of Heresy." In Freeman, *Dilthey's Dream*, 79–92.
Freeman, Derek
  Margaret Mead and Samoa: The Making and Unmaking of an Anthropological Myth. Cambridge, MA: Harvard University Press, 1983.
Freeman, Derek
  "A Reply to Ember's Reflections on the Freeman–Mead Controversy." *American Anthropologist* 87, no. 4 (1985): 910–17.
Freeman, Derek
  "The Social Structure of a Samoan Village Community." Postgraduate diploma thesis in anthropology, London School of Economics, 1948. Mandeville Special Collections Library, Geisel Library, University of California, San Diego. Reprinted as *The Social Structure of a Samoan Village Community*, edited and introduced by Peter Hempenstall. Canberra: Target Oceania, 2006.

Gilson, Richard Phillip.
  Samoa 1830–1900: The Politics of a Multi-Cultural Community. Melbourne: Oxford University Press, 1970.
Goldman, Irving
  Ancient Polynesian Society. Chicago: University of Chicago Press, 1970.
Keesing, Felix M.
  "The Taupo System of Samoa: A Study of Institutional Change." *Oceania* 8, no. 1 (1937): 1–14.
Krämer, Augustin.
  Die Samoa-inseln. Stuttgart: E. Schweizerbart, 1902. Translated by Theodore Verhaaren as *The Samoa Islands: An Outline of a Monograph with Particular Consideration of German Samoa*, vol. I, *Constitution, Pedigrees and Traditions* (Honolulu: University of Hawai'i Press, 1994).
Mageo, Jeanette Marie
  1996 Spirit Girls and Marines: Possession and Ethnopsychiatry as Historical Discourse in Samoa. American Ethnologist 23: 61–82.
Mead, Margaret
  "The Adolescent Girl in Samoa." Report to the National Research Council, 1927. Unpublished manuscript, Library of Congress.
Meleise'a, Malama
  The Making of Modern Samoa. Suva, Fiji: Institute of Pacific Studies, 1987.
Michener, James
  The World Is My Home: A Memoir. New York: Random House, 1992.
Murray, Rev. A. W.
  Forty Years' Missionary Work in Polynesia and New Guinea from 1835 to 1875. London: James Nisbet, 1876.
Schoeffel, Penelope
  "The Samoan Concept of *Feagaiga* and Its Transformation." In *Tonga and Samoa: Images of Gender and Polity*, edited by J. Huntsman, 85–106. Christchurch, New Zealand: Macmillan Brown Centre for Pacific Studies, 1995.
Schoeffel, Penelope
  "Sexual Morality in Samoa and Its Historical Transformations." In *A Polymath Anthropologist:*

Essays in Honour of Ann Chowning, edited by C. Gross, H. D. Lyons, and D. A. Counts, 63–69. Auckland: Dept. of Anthropology, University of Auckland, 2005.
Shankman, Paul
  "Fear and Loathing in Samoa." *Global Reporter* 1, no. 2 (1983): 12.
Shankman, Paul
  "The History of Samoan Sexual Conduct and the Mead–Freeman Controversy." *American Anthropologist* 98, no. 3 (1996): 555–67.
Shankman, Paul
  "Interethnic Unions and the Regulation of Sex in Colonial Samoa, 1830–1945." *Journal of the Polynesian Society* 110, no. 2 (2001): 119–47.
Stanner, W. E. H.
  The South Seas in Transition. Sydney: Australian Publishing Company, 1953.
Stevenson, Robert Louis
  A Footnote to History: Eight Years of Trouble in Samoa. London: Cassell, 1892.
Tcherkézoff, Serge
  "First Contacts" in Polynesia, the Samoan Case (1722–1848): Western Misunderstandings about Sexuality and Divinity. Jointly published by the Journal of Pacific History (Canberra, Australia) and the Macmillan Brown Centre for Pacific Studies, Canterbury University, New Zealand, 2004.
Tiffany, Sharon W.
  "The Politics of Denominational Organization in Samoa." In *Mission, Church and Sect in Oceania*, edited by J. Boutilier, D. R. Hughes, and S. W. Tiffany, 423–56. ASAO Monograph, 6. Lanham, MD: University Press of America, 1978.
Turner, Rev. George.
  Nineteen Years in Polynesia. London: John Snow, Paternoster Row, 1888.
Williams, John.
  The Samoan Journals of John Williams: 1830 and 1832. Edited by R. Moyle. Canberra: Australian National University Press, 1984.

Part IX
Genital Cutting

Introduction

There are a number of problems in anthropology which provide exceptional challenges to cultural relativism, and many of them have to do with sex. Among these, the issue of culturally mandated operations on female and male genitalia has proved a particularly thorny one.

For men, these practices have included the removal of the foreskin (circumcision), practiced most prominently by Jews, Muslims, and in many African societies; the slitting of the foreskin, practiced in some Polynesian cultures; and subincision, the slitting open of the urethra, practiced in addition to circumcision in some Australian aboriginal societies. Circumcision was traditionally absent among European Christians

For women, genital cutting has been largely an African practice, though it is also found in a few locations in the Arabian Peninsula and Indonesia. It has involved surgery of various levels of severity, from the excision of part or all of the clitoris to infibulation, the removal of the entire clitoris and inner labia and stitching together of the outer labia. Both the male and the female operations can involve pain, health risks, and altered sexual response, but in recent years most public debate has concerned practices performed on girls and young women.

For many centuries before the development of anthropology as a discipline, Jewish circumcision had been a rallying point for Christian anti-Semitism, even being linked to accusations of child murder. Circumcision also reinforced the image of Muslims as "other," though it did not attract as much notice in Europe as Jewish practices did.

Some trends in nineteenth-century anthropology drew writers' attention to genital surgery, an interest which expanded to include female and male genital cutting in Africa. For some writers, these practices were evidence of primitive tendencies to pay more attention to bodily than to cerebral matters, part of the image of the "oversexed savage." Even though both male and female circumcision were believed to

Sexualities in Anthropology: A Reader, edited by Andrew P. Lyons and Harriet D. Lyons
© 2011 Blackwell Publishing Ltd.

reduce rather than increase sexual desire, this was believed by some to be a necessary curb on excessively developed libidos. Richard Burton, who traveled in both Africa and Arabia, was of the view that female operations were needed to reduce the sexual desires of otherwise voracious women to be compatible with the enervated organs of males whose natural lasciviousness had been reduced by circumcision. Bodily manipulations of all sorts were also viewed as part of a general tendency toward fetishism and magical thinking, alleged to have preceded the development of science.

There was also some interest among nineteenth-century medical practitioners, the emerging class of experts on sexual matters, in genital surgery as a health measure for Western populations. There was a brief vogue in England and the US for clitoridectomy as a cure for masturbation, but the medical use of male circumcision became much more entrenched, particularly in North America (outside Quebec) where, by the mid-twentieth century, it was almost universal, believed to prevent illnesses ranging from local infections to some cancers in both men and their female partners.

For most of the twentieth century there was a tendency among anthropologists to seek non-sexualized, blander explanations for ritualized genital surgery, insofar as they discussed it at all. This was spurred by some of the same motives which led to a more general de-sensationalizing of sexuality for much of this period: desire for scientific accuracy and a concern for the reputations of both anthropologists and their ethnographic subjects. British functionalists who worked in Africa were obliged to discuss male and female circumcision; when they did, they tended to stress its significance in the maintenance of social order. Malinowski's student, Dr. Jomo Kenyatta, who became Kenya's first president, made such an argument in defense of both customs in his ethnography, *Facing Mount Kenya* (1965[1938]). The French ethnographers Marcel Griaule and Germaine Dieterlen, writing about the Dogon of Mali (1965), recorded mythical accounts of the origins of circumcision and clitoridectomy, without an attempt to evaluate the operations from outside the point of view of their informants, who were mainly male ritual specialists.

In the 1970s, the emerging feminist movement began to take an intense interest in female genital cutting (usually called female genital mutilation or FGM in this discourse) and some authors, like Mary Daly (1978) and Alice Walker (1992), accused anthropologists of a cover-up of the torture and castration of young girls. Feminist anthropologists have found themselves challenged to develop an approach to female genital cutting which balanced concern for women's well-being with a desire to avoid the racism and ethnocentrism of the past. Harriet Lyons wrote an early article on this topic (1981) and, 25 years later, was asked to survey the anthropological literature that had developed in the interim. The article in this section is the result. It surveys writings by anthropologists and others on the topic of female genital cutting, both in the context of ethnographic research and in response to policy issues that have arisen in Europe and North America, as well as in Africa, in relation to these operations. In particular, it discusses debates over whether sexual response, including orgasm, remains possible after ritual cutting, an issue which seems to be less closed than some anti-FGM campaigns would suggest. It also discusses why clitoridectomy became a major issue among Western feminists.

Lyons's article takes the position that female genital cutting is not a single "thing" – that it has different meanings in different places, or even for different people in the same place. One of the authors quoted, Claudie Gosselin (2000), documents the varying attitudes toward excision, ranging from support to activist opposition, within a single community in Mali. This complexity goes some way toward a solution to the anthropologist's dilemma, since there is no longer a single "cultural" meaning, demanding a uniform position of relativism, but it is an incomplete solution. The problems posed by painful, sometimes dangerous, operations being performed mainly on women in or from the African continent remains, and with it the twin dangers of appearing to condone a situation which some Africans, both men and women, now oppose, or joining in a critique which is perceived by some Africans as racist and interfering.

It should be noted that in recent years there has been a movement in North America to end routine medical circumcision of male infants, and rates have dropped considerably. There have been issues concerning the perception of this movement as creating an uncomfortable climate for Jews and Muslims, though an anthropologist of Jewish origin, Leonard Glick (2006), has written a history of Jewish circumcision which advocates cessation of the practice, and he is far from the only Jewish scholar to write in that vein.

The dilemmas posed by sexual surgery for anthropologists are twofold: why should such practices exist at all and what attitudes should anthropologists take toward them? As yet, these problems are unsolved, but viewing them within the broader context of the history of the anthropology of sexuality suggests some interesting directions for study.

REFERENCES AND FURTHER READING

Burton, Captain Sir Richard F., trans.
  1885   The Book of the Thousand Nights and a Night. Benares: Kamashastra Society.
Daly, Mary
  1978   Gyn/Ecology: The Metaethics of Radical Feminism. Boston: Beacon Press.
Glick, Leonard
  2006   Marked in Your Flesh: Circumcision from Ancient Judea to Modern America. New York: Oxford University Press.
Gosselin, Claudie
  2000   Feminism, Anthropology and the Politics of Excision in Mali: Global and Local Debates in a Postcolonial World. Anthropologica 42(1):43–60.
Griaule, Marcel
  1965   Conversations with Ogotemmeli. Oxford: Clarendon Press.
Griaule, Marcel and Germaine Dieterlen
  1965   Le Renard pâle. Paris: Institut d'Ethnologie.
Kenyatta, Jomo
  1965[1938]   Facing Mount Kenya. New York: Vintage Books.
Lyons, Harriet
  1981   Anthropologists, Moralities, and Relativities: The Problem of Genital Mutilations. The Canadian Review of Sociology and Anthropology 18(4):499–518.
Walker, Alice
  1992   Possessing the Secret of Joy. New York: Harcourt, Brace, Jovanovich.

21

Genital Cutting: The Past and Present of a Polythetic Category

Harriet D. Lyons

Introduction

In 1975, Rodney Needham suggested that some phenomena encountered by anthropologists, like certain kinds of descent systems, might be best understood as polythetic classes – categories whose members bear overlapping family resemblances to each other, as well as to members of other classes, but do not exhibit the sort of single and exclusive defining feature which conventional monothetic definitions assumed. In 1981, the current author wrote one of the first articles drawing attention to the conflicts faced by feminist anthropologists attempting to maintain a relativist attitude toward traditional operations on the female genitals. I suggested that some of the difficulties in discussing genital cutting stemmed from monothetic understandings, which saw genital cutting as essentially about sex, or essentially about control, or solely as neutral or even as an honorific status marker. Interpretations in terms of sexuality or control stressed castration and/or subordination of women and were not easily reconciled with anthropological relativism.

Such interpretations were historically linked to negative stereotypes about African sexuality. Understandings that viewed "female circumcision" as a benign rite of passage preserved relativism but downplayed the physical, sexual, and psychological damage cited by opponents of such practices, inside and outside Africa. I suggested that some of the obstacles to productive discourse might be overcome by viewing genital surgery as a polythetic category, with both sexual and nonsexual meanings, and both positive and negative effects, and with due allowance for cross-cultural variation in the "bundles of relationships" which comprised the practices contentiously labeled "female circumcision" or "female genital mutilation."

Such an approach, I hoped, might facilitate cross-cultural dialogue, requiring neither blanket acceptance or nor blanket condemnation, and allowing the discovery of common areas of experience, while acknowledging difference in others. In the literature on this topic which has emerged since 1981, polythetic understandings, whether labeled as such or not, have informed some of the best

Harriet Lyons, Genital Cutting: The Past and Present of a Polythetic Category, from *Africa Today*, vol. 53, no. 4: 3–17. Reprinted with permission of Indiana University Press.

Sexualities in Anthropology: A Reader, edited by Andrew P. Lyons and Harriet D. Lyons

work. Such approaches have enhanced anthropologists' understanding of genital cutting and their own role in debates about its future. While polythetic approaches to this topic have advanced debate, I have come to realize that there remain dilemmas that they cannot solve. Indeed, I now argue that the fact that genital surgeries are best seen as polythetic categories may itself be an index of the reasons why the problems they present remain so intractable.

Health, Sickness, Pleasure, and Pain in the Analysis of Female Genital Cutting

My rationale for arguing for a polythetic definition of female genital surgeries was a hope that such a definition would enable us to avoid the allochronicity that has historically been a major problem in this discourse. My argument was that much of the ethnocentrism which had permeated discussions of female genital operations had come from monothetic approaches, which had defined them in terms of those aspects of the operations which appeared to present the greatest differences between "us" and "them." Sexuality, pain, and health were areas where Westerners, especially Western feminists, were most at risk of appearing ethnocentric.

As several writers on this topic have pointed out (see, for example, Bell 2005; Gosselin 2000; Walley 1997) the clitoris became, during the second wave of feminism in the West, a key symbol of the movement itself. Insistence upon clitoral gratification was an act of resistance against a regime of male experts who had insisted that female health and maturity required a redirection of female desire toward acts that facilitated male pleasure. The removal of the clitoris seemed to many feminist writers, like Mary Daly (1978) to be completely at odds with the newly claimed right to female pleasure and sexual agency. Although some writers, like Daly herself, saw analogies between African genital surgery and Western gynecological practice, the issue of allochronicity was not eliminated. Most of the desexualizing medical horrors (including a Victorian

vogue for clitoridectomy itself) cited in such discussions were safely in the past, so far as Western medicine was concerned. Even the ones which were still being perpetrated were the subject of feminist critique, and thus already "old-fashioned" to those with a raised consciousness. By contrast, operations which Daly described as "unspeakable atrocities" were assumed to be very much part of the African present.

The experiments of Masters and Johnson, in which women experienced orgasm under laboratory conditions, were widely believed, in the 1970s, to have "proved" that all orgasm was centered in the clitoris. It was thus taken for granted that women who had undergone genital cutting could not experience it. In fact, this has turned out to be a problematic assumption. Gruenbaum (1996:462) has noted that some infibulated women in the Sudan give convincing accounts of their experience of orgasm. For that matter, Marie Bonaparte, a disciple of Freud, who explored clitoridectomy as a means to encourage the transference of sexual sensation to the vagina, concluded on the basis of interviews with African women that excised women continued to experience orgasm (Bonaparte 1953: 191–208). There are numerous possible explanations for this. The clitoris extends well under the surface; infibulators have been known to leave an intact clitoris under the fused outer labia; other erogenous zones may become more sensitive in the absence of the clitoris; the vagina may be a source of more pleasure than Masters and Johnson encouraged us to believe; mental stimuli and/or responses learned from sexual experience prior to undergoing genital cutting may be significant in producing orgasms.

Boddy (1989) suggests that the whole issue of sexuality may be somewhat distorted by Western assumptions that sexuality is necessarily about genital pleasure. For her informants in the Sudan, adult female sexuality was about wombs and giving birth.

The issue of pain is probably the one that draws the most visceral reaction from Westerners learning about female genital cutting for the first time. Few of them have not imagined themselves as little girls held down while being cut, and possibly stitched, enduring a long and painful healing and, as infibulated women being cut open to facilitate defloration, and repeatedly cut and sewn to allow for childbirth. Physical pain as a rallying point for feminist opposition to genital cutting is not without allochronistic implications: Foucault noted ([1975] 1995) that the West, under modern regimes of power, has largely rejected pain as a mode of control in favor of subtle forms of persuasion and surveillance. Accordingly, the deliberate infliction of pain – even if pain itself is not the goal – can be seen as both shocking and old-fashioned. This is true even in contexts where Westerners deliberately seek pain: the literature on sado-masochism suggests that anachronism (dungeons, archaic costumes, even language) is an important part of its imagery. Again, objection to genital cutting on the grounds of suffering was to place the very women with whom one sought to identify in another, more backward, frame of time.

Western women seem to lack a place in their imaginary for identification with an aspect of painful initiation rituals that is widely cited in the literature. The opportunity to gain social status by a demonstration of courage and endurance in the face of physical suffering has been cited by many writers (e.g., Kratz 2002b; Shweder 2002;) as an important part of the positive value associated with female and male initiation rituals, cross-culturally. The earning of status through the endurance of pain in modern Europe and European North America has largely been associated with male experience, particularly in connection with warfare and sports. This may be part of the reason that painful male rituals provoke in Westerners less of what Shweder (2002) calls the "yuck factor" than do female ones.

Among feminists sensitive to issues of relativism, the effects of genital cutting on women's health have often seemed to be the least treacherous ground on which to protest. Health outcomes seem to be reassuringly objective. Surely one could wish to improve African women's health without fear of ethnocentrism or allochronicity. For many years, I have recommended Olayinka Koso-Thomas's book *Female Circumcision: A Strategy for*

Eradication (1987) because the author proposed a plan that began with the establishment of clinics for treating the medical complications resulting from genital operations. It was suggested that these clinics might eventually serve as centers for educating women concerning the health implications of female genital cutting as well as sources of employment for midwives and other traditional circumcisers. Koso-Thomas argued that even if these results did not ensue, or did not do so for a very long time, there would be immediate treatment for women whose health had been compromised by female genital cutting. This seemed to me, for years, to be a sensible, nonsensationalist suggestion by a female African physician; however, Claudie Gosselin, whose work is a model of finely textured polythetic approaches, is highly critical of it, in a way that suggests that medical approaches may be no less allochronistic than any others. Gosselin cites Koso-Thomas as one of a number of medical sources who contrast the medical "facts" about female circumcision with the traditional reasons given for the practice, in a manner Gosselin characterizes as designed to "ridicule and invalidate them one by one through a medical analysis" (Gosselin 2000:48–49). In another source which could be said to advocate a polythetic approach, and which is critical of many aspects of allochronicity in the West's response to female circumcision, Walley notes that media reports which highlight the health risks of genital operations tend to be written from a perspective which depicts Western medicine as exemplary of "culture-free reason and rationality" in contrast to a superstition-laden rest-of-the world, including the West's own past (Walley 1997:421). Melissa Parker, recollecting her observation of female genital cutting in the Sudan, reports "remembering" the next day that the blade was blunt and rusty, when, in fact, she had been too far away to see the condition of the blade (Parker 1995:518).

So entrenched is the image of female genital cutting as the antithesis of everything Western medicine perceives (or wishes) itself to be that it can be invoked as a taken-for-granted exemplar of that which Western medicine must avoid, as in the following comment about the current vogue for bariatric surgery:

> A particularly incendiary topic is weight-loss surgery (stomach stapling or more radical measures like rerouting the intestine). Activists regard such procedures as a human rights abuse akin to female genital mutilation. (Kipnis 2005)

We see then that the health arguments against female genital cutting, whatever their validity within their own terms of risk/benefit analysis, are no more exempt from charges of allochronicity than any others; indeed they may be less so. There has been, in any case, some debate about the magnitude of the health consequences themselves (see Mackie 2003; Obermeyer 1999, 2003), though no one doubts that they are real, particularly in the case of infibulation. This situation is somewhat altered by a recent report in *The Lancet* concerning a large-scale population study sponsored by the World Health Organization (a long-time opponent of female genital cutting), which demonstrated significantly elevated rates of mortality and morbidity among mothers who had undergone female genital cutting and their infants. Large studies of this kind would seem to be precisely the kind of evidence which Obermeyer found surprisingly absent from the many claims of negative effects of female genital cutting on health. In contrast, the final sentence of the article incorporates a long-standing trope about African priorities: the assumption that women's well-being is a matter of concern in African cultures mostly insofar as it affects their reproductive capacity:

> FGM remains a pressing human rights issue and reliable evidence about its harmful effects, especially on reproductive outcomes, should contribute to the abandonment of the practice. (WHO Study Group on Female Genital Mutilation and Obstetric Outcome 2006: 1841)

What I thought polythetic approaches might accomplish, when I wrote my original paper, was to find meanings for the operations that might allow for common ground between feminist anthropologists in the West and African women. I thought that if one could understand the full range of meanings of female genital surgery in a given culture, one might find area(s) of common ground. In particular, I suggested, very tentatively, that the tendency to sexualize women more than men was something shared by Western and African collective representations and might thus form a larger issue into which genital operations might be "dissolved." In retrospect, this particular proposed deployment of female genital cutting as a polythetic category has a number of flaws. Methodologically, it doesn't solve the relativist's dilemma, since it implies that sympathetic understanding of the other is dependent on perceived sameness, not on appreciated difference; moreover, research since 1981, much of it approaching female genital cutting polythetically, has found more valuation of circumcised women in terms which go beyond the sexual (or reproductive) than I would have anticipated.

Arguments for a Polythetic Approach

The growing corpus of research does indeed reveal that it is intellectually valid to treat female genital cutting as a polythetic category, even if doing so does not solve the moral issue. The multiple meanings of female genital cutting practices, sexual and nonsexual, have become more evident over the years. Common meanings include removal of male aspects of female genitalia; improving the aesthetic appearance of the genitalia; preventing rape; preventing women from having unauthorized relations with men; preventing masturbation; promoting physical or spiritual purity and cleanliness; making initiates eligible for religious participation; providing spiritual protection; testing courage and empowering those who show it; teaching women to submit to men; teaching young women to submit to senior women; carrying out the teachings of creation myths; avoiding fatal contact between the clitoris and infants' heads during childbirth (reported by one author, though not others, to be the sole explanation found among the Yoruba [Orobuloye, Caldwell, and Caldwell 2000:74]);

focusing women's sexuality on reproduction; resisting colonialism and postcolonial Western domination; and supporting a generalized adherence to tradition. Almost always, several of these (and/or other) explanations appear together in accounts of any given instance of female genital cutting, though none appears everywhere – the very definition of a polythetic category. Kratz (2002b) and Shweder (2000, 2002) have written particularly elegantly about the multiplicity of meanings which female genital cutting holds for those who practice and experience it; both suggest that providing such accounts is an important goal for scholars concerned with it.

In addition to our growing knowledge of the complex signification attached to genital cutting, it has become increasingly evident that communities in which genital surgeries occur are not monolithic in their attitudes; if a society can't be described as "polythetic," it can certainly be said to be "polyvocal." Claudie Gosselin (2000) describes women's opinions in Mali as ranging from active support for excision, to advocacy for its abolition, to acceptance without any great enthusiasm. Moreover, even a single individual may speak in several voices about female genital cutting: Walley (1997) notes that the attitudes toward it expressed by young, recently circumcised Kenyan women varied according to context, from pride and excitement to regret over lost sexual sensation.

Fuambai Ahmadu, an anthropologist who grew up partly in the United States and partly in Sierra Leone, has written of her own operation, for which she consented to return to her family's village toward the end of her undergraduate career in the United States. Her account has been portrayed as essentially positive (see Shweder 2000, 2002), but a close reading reveals it to be much more nuanced. It speaks of "unimaginable agony" (Ahmadu 2000:293), though she blames this on insufficient time for a locally injected anesthetic to work. She notes that other women assured her that she would not suffer a loss of sexual response and that Kono notions of female sexuality include vaginal orgasm (2000:304). She reports that she and other women who had had sexual experiences before they were initi-

ated did not notice any decrease in sexual response after the operation (2000:305). She does not provide any data on postoperative sexual response among women without previous sexual experience.

Ahmadu writes that women's authority among the Kono is enhanced, not lowered, by clitoridectomy. She argues for an approach that is polysemous, polyvocal, and alert to the complex cultural embedding of female genital cutting. She accepts that the historical trajectory is leading toward the abolition of genital cutting, and her ultimate recommendation is that girls and women be allowed to make up their own minds – and be given access to anesthetics and antibiotics.

In fact, access to medicalized genital cutting is itself a contentious issue, with activists claiming that to medicalize genital surgery is to legitimize it. Ahmadu notes that the operations *are* legitimate to those who practice them, so that warnings against legitimating them are denials of reality as women in cultures which practice female genital cutting experience it. Shweder compares genital cutting to abortion – an analogy that is likely to disturb many Western feminists. Both abortion and genital cutting, he argues, can be dangerous under certain circumstances. Most feminists, however, do not seek to ban abortion: they seek to make abortion safe, as Shweder thinks should be the case with female genital cutting (Shweder 2002:229). On a practical level, antibiotics and anesthetics for female genital cutting, though increasingly popular, would seem, like many other medical interventions in Africa, to be, in all likelihood, disproportionately available to relatively privileged individuals and communities.

Shweder argues for a truly polythetic analysis, in which, on the one hand, notions of "good" and "bad" bodies should be examined within their complex local contexts, and, on the other, practices like genital cutting should be dissolved into much broader categories, including means of achieving socially acceptable bodies. He includes virtually all medical and ritual bodily practices in this analysis. He reminds readers that parents in the West frequently force their children to undergo unpleasant procedures which cause them suffering, including, for many children, school attendance (Shweder 2002:245). In contrast, he notes that the West's dogma of individual freedom allows "autonomous" Western adults to choose to undergo nipple piercing, sex-change operations, and even cosmetically motivated clitoridectomies (Shweder 2002:242). He warns that the visceral response he calls the "yuck factor" is mutual: one culture's ideal body is another's object of disgust (Shweder 2002:222–226). Of recent anthropological writers on the topic he is perhaps the most supportive of the retention of traditional practices and most challenging to those who attempt to reconcile cultural sensitivity with a residual aversion to female genital cutting.

Emerging Issues: Diaspora and Asylum

In recent years, much of the literature (and controversy) surrounding female genital cutting has focused on diasporic communities in Europe and North America, some of whose members have either sought genital surgery for their daughters in their new homes, or brought girls back to their country of origin to be circumcised. Female genital cutting has been specifically banned in several such jurisdictions, including the United States. In some other countries, laws against assault and child abuse have been interpreted as banning female genital cutting without any specific legal statute. Some countries prohibit the transport of minors to be operated upon in other jurisdictions. Cultural tradition has been offered as a defense against prosecution in several cases where charges have been laid, though movements to eliminate female genital cutting, often led by women from countries where the practice is widespread, have grown up in diasporic communities.

Another topic which has brought discussion of female genital cutting into Western legal circles is that of asylum (see Coffman 2007). Should women be entitled to refugee status to escape being cut, or are the rights of Africans, especially African women, violated by assumptions that their traditional practices are violations of human rights, especially

when stereotyping publicity surrounds cases deemed particularly newsworthy? Anthropologists have written about these concerns and served as expert witnesses, and key contributions to the resulting literature have specifically called for the kind of understandings we might label "polythetic." Asylum cases can be particularly difficult for anthropologists, who are likely to sympathize with African women seeking asylum, particularly if they have been detained or otherwise mistreated by immigration authorities, but anthropologists are likely to be acutely aware that the success of such cases may depend upon reinforcing images of Africa as patriarchal, backward, and even brutal. Kratz (2002a), for example, has compared the media coverage and legal strategies surrounding two well-known asylum cases in the United States, those of Fauziya Kassinga of Togo and Adelaide Abankwah of Ghana. She argues that as female genital cutting became more familiar to the U.S. public, and opposition to it became more entrenched, lawyers and reporters paid less attention to debate and nuance within African discourses, leading to an increase in negative stereotyping and allochronistic images of African culture (Kratz 2002a:324–335). Piot, in contrast, reminds us of the dangers of the complexity and nuance inherent in the polythetic interpretations which he otherwise admires. A reading which is not simpleminded, he warns, is sure to "be cited and invoked by the INS [Immigration and Naturalization Service], rendering the best anthropological work subject to appropriation by conservative forces" (Piot 2006:233).

Female Genital Cutting: Polythetic or Overdetermined?

There are other caveats to be observed in approaching female circumcision from a polythetic perspective. One is that the concept of a polythetic category bears not a little resemblance to the notion of overdeterminism, though Needham, who suggested that many anthropological conundrums were due to treating polythetic concepts as if they were monothetic ones (Needham 1975:349–369), might well have found such a comparison disturbing, since he never showed an enthusiasm for Freudian analysis of sociocultural data. Indeed, Piot (2006:233) has described female genital cutting as an "overdetermined issue." The concept of overdeterminism (or overdetermination) has been used in two contexts in which surface content is held to hide multiple strands of meaning, some of them threatening to conscious reality. In *The Interpretation of Dreams* ([1910] 1913), Freud argued that dream symbols were overdetermined, insofar as they had multiple meanings and recurred in multiple contexts, from the most mundane and accessible to the most psychically menacing and repressed. Althusser ([1995] 1996) applied the notion of overdetermination to Marxian economics, arguing that some effects were the result of multiple causes, rather than a simple relation between base and superstructure; but perhaps even more than in Marx, those causes were obscured by false consciousness. If we apply the concept of overdeterminism to female genital cutting, the very multiplicity of meanings which we find may tell us that there are things which are hidden from the consciousness of those who talk about it, things which may well be threatening to personal and cultural self-perceptions.

From a Freudian perspective, which has been more or less banished from feminist discussions of female genital cutting (though Brown [1963] and Bonaparte [1953] employed psychoanalytic concepts in earlier analyses and Bettelheim [1952], famously or infamously applied Freudian concepts to analysis of male initiation), there is much that might be hidden under the overt cultural explanations of surgery on the female genitals – mostly things that would be unacceptable to Western feminists and Africans alike. Penis envy and castration fears are classic psychoanalytic interpretations of overdetermined symbols. Walley, in discussing the apparently inconsistent accounts of female circumcision given by Kenyan adolescents, suggests that a psychoanalytic approach to these interpretations may not be inappropriate, and does not see this mode of analysis as inconsistent with a sociological understanding.

Given the legacy of both Freud and Erving Goffman, it seems evident that each self has a public as well as a private side and many more layers within it, from the conscious to the deeply unconscious. (Walley 1997:412)

Whether or not we are willing to consider Freudian approaches to the motivations of people who practice female genital cutting, the vehemence of Western reactions to the operations can also be said to be overdetermined, in view of the multiplicity of reasons we offered for opposition to the practices of others: health, pain, alleged destruction of sexuality. Parker has commented particularly insightfully on the emotional baggage Westerners have brought to the discussion, noting that the ability to give and receive clitoral orgasm has become a virtual moral duty in the West (Parker 1995:519.) Here, our overdetermined response may make it reasonable to invoke another psychoanalytic concept, that of countertransference, the emotional response which is said to occur in therapy when the unconscious defenses of the analyst are disturbed by the material presented by the patient. Countertransference has been alternately viewed by psychoanalysts as a barrier and as an aid to understanding. In the context of female genital cutting, many argue that the emotional responses of those "over here" have gotten in the way of understanding the practices of those "over there"; however, by interrogating our own responses, as analysts are encouraged to do, we may be able to understand why we, as anthropologists, find it so difficult to arrive at a satisfactory conclusion on this issue. After all, female genital cutting should not present us with an insoluble problem, if our analytical tools are anywhere near as good as we have billed them. Applied anthropology sells itself as being good at examining a situation holistically to determine the benefits and harms of cultural practices and changes to those practices, whether a new factory or a new fertilizer. Why should female genital cutting be different? To some degree, it is not. Boddy (1989), Gosselin (2000), Gruenbaum (1996, 2001), Parker (1995), Prazak (2000), Shaw (1995), and Walley (1997) have produced just such textured, careful analyses of particular local situations. Nonetheless, general solutions elude us, and I think most of us are frustrated that this is so.

The Conscription of Female Genital Cutting

In *"Anthropologists, Moralities and Relativities"* (1981), I suggested that the sexuality of others was a screen onto which Europeans have projected their own fears and desires. In our recent book, *Irregular Connections: A History of Anthropology and Sexuality* (2004), Andrew Lyons and I developed the notion of "conscription" to describe the process by which anthropological subjects have been recruited into more than two hundred years of Western debates on sexuality. Such conscription has often been characterized by shifting attention to multiple aspects of a single phenomenon. It is therefore one corollary of polythetic categories. With regard to "third-sex" phenomena, for example, anthropologists have foregrounded homosexuality, ritual inversion of categories, or gender flexibility, according to current preoccupations. All these components, and more, are part of this particular polythetic category, but which of them was the focus of attention of a particular generation of anthropologists may tell us more about the observers than the observed. The recent history of female genital cutting suggests that there has been a considerable degree of conscription, though in this case the process has not been one-sided.

The initial feminist "discovery" of "female genital mutilation" conscripted Africans into several discourses. The demand for clitoral pleasure was only one aspect of the moment in feminist history when Western attention was turned to African traditional practices. Another feature of that period in feminist discourse was an accusation that feminists were concerned with issues which would primarily benefit privileged, mainly white, women in the First World. A campaign against a perceived harm to African women could be seen as an answer to this challenge, as well as an assertion that the denial of the clitoris and the control of women's bodies by men were indeed global

issues. Moreover, the consciousness-raising exercises which recruited many women in Europe and North America to feminism taught them to see sexual politics in what they had previously experienced as "personal problems," "human nature," or even "sacred truth." If they could have been oblivious to the pervasive power of the patriarchy, so could African women who insisted that genital operations were under the control of women, not of men. This distinction was important, since it allowed the configuration of African women as victims, not agents of mutilation, and therefore as sisters, not oppressors. This configuration, moreover, enabled the acclaimed African-American writer Alice Walker to incorporate opposition to female genital cutting into a novel, *Possessing the Secret of Joy* (Walker 1992), a coauthored nonfiction book, *Warrior Marks: Female Genital Mutilation and the Sexual Blinding of Women* (Parmar and Walker 1993), and a film, *Warrior Marks* (Parmar 1993), which she produced, all widely used in women's-studies and gender-studies programs. Diverse meanings and forms of the polythetic category of female genital cutting were selectively melded into a unified class of "female genital mutilations" (FGM). Among the characteristics of this monothetic construct were a tendency to make the relatively rare form of infibulation stand for all the operations, a stress on men's demands for circumcised brides and female chastity (which are by no means universal), and a dismissal of local explanations for the practices as mere varieties of a common false consciousness, and therefore something that need not be taken seriously.

For their part, many African women saw feminist campaigns as the latest stage in a long history of colonial cultural interference and evidence of an unhealthy, indeed immoral Western obsession with sex and genitalia. L. Amede Obiora, for example, in an article that is particularly critical of Walker, argues that some feminist perspectives employ "a double standard that reinstates the very silencing and stigmatization of women which feminism was supposed to challenge" (Obiora 1997:49). Such perceptions have the potential to fuel resistance, not only to Western intervention, but also to African activism against female circumcision. Obiora herself supports activists who take account of community sensibilities, but warns that those who do not do so are likely to fail in their endeavors (Obiora 2006:241).

Anthropologists have found themselves caught in the middle of this dialogue. Their professional credibility depends upon sensitivity to ethnocentrism and an ability to convey local voices accurately, including the multiplicity of those voices. They find themselves addressing this issue at a moment when the foundational concept of "culture" (and hence cultural relativism) is under suspicion, accused of distancing the very "others" whose "culture" one is enjoined to respect (for a particularly influential iteration of this argument, see Abu-Lughod 1991).

Conclusion: The Future of a Polythetic Category?

At the very least, the meanings of female genital cutting, like the rest of what many of us continue to call culture, for want of a better word, are undergoing continual change – another aspect of their polytheticism. Shaw (1995) has documented changes in the symbolic role of female initiation among the Kikuyu, including its famous deployment as a focus of resistance to colonialism. Miroslava Prazak has noted (personal communication) that the Kikuyu are now abandoning female genital cutting at a faster rate than other groups in Kenya, partly as a result of their relatively privileged status, and speculates that other ethnic groups may see in retention of the practice a mode of resistance to Kikuyu domination. References to African women's surprise on learning that their European interlocutors are not circumcised are something of a trope in the relativist literature (see, for example, Shweder 2002:221–222). Such claims, however, are beginning to seem decidedly allochronistic. Most Africans are by now surely aware of European attitudes and praxis in this regard. Obiora, critical of Walker and other feminists for their cultural insensitivity, now thinks that "it is plausible to argue that anti-circumcision campaign is an idea whose time has come" (Obiora 2006:241). In her

afterword to a 2006 collection of articles on activism against female genital cutting within African and diasporic communities, Obiora notes that the only certain cultural reality is change itself (Obiora 2006:239). In the same volume, Audrey Macklin opens her article with an ironic contrast between Western academic debates about female genital cutting and local activists' voices:

> The question that preoccupies most Western academics when they address female genital mutilation (FGM) is whether the national or international community should tolerate the practice. Yet the salient issue for most human rights activists working from within the communities where FGM has been prevalent is not *whether*, but *how*, to eradicate the practice. (Macklin 2006:207)

The more polythetic the category of female genital cutting becomes, the harder it becomes to take a position beyond the advice to "leave it to the locals." This position, however, may be arguing anthropologists out of a job. Is there any point then, in the polythetic understanding which I advocated in 1981? I think I was not wrong, insofar as we have produced a valuable cautionary tale about the construction of "female genital mutilation," "female circumcision," or "genital cutting" as public and professional issues. Ethnographers that have worked closely with circumcised women, with circumcisers, and with local activists against circumcision have produced work which is far more nuanced and multitextured than was once the norm for work in this field.

Polythetic analysis of female genital cutting may force us into more-textured analyses of the categories into which we dissolve it, like ritual. Mary Daly, in the work which disturbed me enough to provoke my original article, accuses Arnold Van Gennep of stimulating a patriarchal cover-up by asserting that circumcision (male, in this case) was a trivial marker of social status (Daly 1978:172–173; Lyons 1981:499–500). Victor W. Turner (1967, 1968) wrote about male circumcision (and the trials undergone by female initiates who are not cut) among the Ndembu of Zambia in ways that showed the "social status" marked by initiation to be a complex one, with negative as well as positive aspects. Miroslava Prazak, when she was an undergraduate, before either she or I had written about female genital cutting, remarked of the pictures of Jonestown on the covers of *Time* and *Newsweek*, "It's just like Woodstock; only they're all dead." She thus forced her listeners to notice both the mortality in ritual and the ritual in mortality, an encapsulation of Bakhtin's image of carnival (Bakhtin [1965] 1968), which goes further than Turner in acknowledging the grotesque – something like Shweder's "yuck factor" – in much ritual. Her memoir (Prazak 2000) of accompanying a young girl in Kenya to her circumcision, which at first the girl had resisted with the anthropologist's encouragement, has some echoes of this awareness. A good account of female genital cutting can show both the blood under the chairs, and the pride of the girl being greeted by joyous crowds on her way home, as well as the possibility that the procedure will be less imperative when the girl's daughter comes of age.

Perhaps such accounts can show us a way to answer the charge of an undergraduate of a new generation, a recent graduate of the University of Waterloo called Pamela Yuen, who challenged a class which was vociferously arguing for a relativist position on female circumcision, perhaps because that's what they thought the instructor wanted to hear. This dissenting voice, very quietly, said, "If twenty-five years from now Africans have abolished female circumcision, anthropologists are going to seem to have missed the boat."

REFERENCES

Abu-Lughod, Lila
   1991   Writing against Culture. In *Recapturing Anthropology: Working in the Present*, edited by Richard Fox. Santa Fe: School of American Research Press.
Ahmadu, Fuambai
   2000   Rites and Wrongs: An Insider/Outsider Reflects on Power and Excision. In *Female "Circumcision" in Africa: Culture, Controversy, and Change*, edited by Bettina Shell-Duncan and Ylva Hernlund. Boulder, Colo.: Lynne Rienner.

Althusser, Louis [1995]
   1996   Contradiction and Overdetermination. In *For Marx*, translated by Ben Brewster. London and New York: Verso.
Bakhtin, Mikhail [1965]
   1968   *Rabelais and His World*, translated by Helene Iswolsky. Cambridge, Mass.: MIT Press.
Bell, Kirsten
   2005   Genital Cutting and Western Discourses on Sexuality. *Medical Anthropology Quarterly* 19(2):125–148.
Bettelheim, Bruno
   1952   *Symbolic Wounds: Puberty Rites and the Envious Male*. New York: Collier Books.
Boddy, Janice
   1989   *Wombs and Alien Spirits: Women, Men, and the Zar Cult in Northern Sudan*. Madison: University of Wisconsin Press.
Bonaparte, Marie
   1953   *Female Sexuality*. New York: International Universities Press.
Brown, Judith K.
   1963   A Cross-Cultural Study of Female Initiation Rites. *American Anthropologist* 65:837–853.
Coffman, Jennifer
   2007   Producing FGM in US Courts: Political Asylum in the Post-Kasinga Era. Africa Today 53(4): 59–84.
Daly, Mary
   1978   *Gyn/Ecology: The Metaethics of Radical Feminism*. Boston: Beacon Press.
Foucault, Michel [1975]
   1995   *Discipline and Punish: The Birth of the Prison*, translated by Allan Sheridan. New York: Vintage.
Freud, Sigmund [1910]
   1913   *The Interpretation of Dreams*, translated by A. A. Brill. New York: Macmillan.
Gosselin, Claudie
   2000   Feminism, Anthropology and the Politics of Excision in Mali: Global and Local Debates in a Postcolonial World. *Anthropologica* 42(1): 43–60.
Gruenbaum, Ellen
   1996   The Cultural Debate Over Female Circumcision: The Sudanese Are Sorting This One Out for Themselves. *Medical Anthropology Quarterly* 10(4):455–475.
Gruenbaum, Ellen
   2001   *The Female Circumcision Controversy: An Anthropological Perspective*. Philadelphia: University of Pennsylvania Press.

Kipnis, Laura
2005 America's Waist: The Politics of Fat. *Slate*. Retrieved 1 July 2006 from http://www.slate.com/id/2128999/?GT1=7407.

Koso-Thomas, Olayinka
1987 *The Circumcision of Women: A Strategy for Eradication*. London: Zed Press.

Kratz, Corinne A.
2002a Circumcision Debates and Asylum Cases: Intersecting Arenas, Contested Values, and Tangled Webs. In *Engaging Cultural Differences: The Multicultural Challenge in Liberal Democracies*, edited by Richard. A. Shweder, Martha Minow, and Hazel Rose Markus. New York: Russell Sage Foundation.

Kratz, Corinne A.
2002b Circumcision, Pluralism and Dilemmas of Cultural Relativism. In *Applying Anthropology: An Introductory Reader*, edited by Aaron Podolefsky and Peter J. Brown. Boston: McGraw Hill.

Lyons, Andrew P., and Harriet D. Lyons
2004 *Irregular Connections: A History of Anthropology and Sexuality*. Lincoln, Nebraska: University of Nebraska Press.

Lyons, Harriet D.
1981 Anthropologists, Moralities and Relativities: The Problem of Genital Mutilations. *Canadian Review of Sociology and Anthropology* 18(4):499–518.

Mackie, Gerry
2003 Female Genital Cutting: A Harmless Practice. *Medical Anthropology Quarterly* 17(2):135–158.

Macklin, Audrey
2006 The Double-Edged Sword: Using the Criminal Law Against Female Genital Mutilation in Canada. In *Female Circumcision: Multicultural Perspectives*, edited by R. M. Abusharaf. Philadelphia: University of Pennsylvania Press.

Needham, Rodney
1975 Polythetic Classification: Convergence and Consequences. *Man* N.S.10(3): 349–369.

Obermeyer, Carla Makhlouf
1999 Female Genital Surgeries: The Known, the Unknown and the Unknowable. *Medical Anthropology Quarterly* 13(1):79–106.

Obermeyer, Carla Makhlouf
2003 The Health Consequences of Female Circumcision: Science, Advocacy and Standards of Evidence. *Medical Anthropology Quarterly* 17(3):394–412.

Obiora, L. Amede
1997 The Little Foxes That Spoil the Vine: Revisiting the Feminist Critique of Female Circumcision. *Canadian Journal of Women and Law* 9(1):46–73.

Obiora, L. Amede
2006 Afterword: Safe Harbor and Homage. In *Female Circumcision: Multicultural Perspectives*, edited by R. M. Abusharaf. Philadelphia: University of Pennsylvania Press.

Orubuloye, I. O., Pat Caldwell, and John C. Caldwell
2000 Female "Circumcision" among the Yoruba of Southwestern Nigeria: The Beginning of Change. In *Female "Circumcision" in Africa: Culture, Controversy, and Change*, edited by Bettina Shell-Duncan and Ylva Hernlund. Boulder, Colo.: Lynne Rienner.

Parker, Melissa
1995 Rethinking Female Circumcision. *Africa, the Journal of the International African Institute* 65(4):506–523.

Parmar, Pratibha
1993 *Warrior Marks*. 54 min. Women Make Movies.

Parmar, Pratibha, and Alice Walker
1993 *Warrior Marks: Female Genital Mutilation and the Sexual Blinding of Women*. New York: Harcourt Brace Jovanovich.

Piot, Charles
2006 Representing Africa in the Kasinga Asylum Case. In *Female Circumcision: Multicultural Perspectives*, edited by R. M. Abusharaf. Philadelphia: University of Pennsylvania Press.

Prazak, Miroslava
2000 Witnessing a Rite of Passage: Circumcision Rites among the Kuria. *Benningtoni Magazine*, Retrieved July 1 2006 from http://www.gonomad.com/features/0103/prazak_circumcision.html.

Shaw, Carolyn Martin
1995 *Colonial Inscriptions: Race, Sex and Class in Kenya*. Minneapolis: University of Minnesota Press.

Shweder, Richard A.
2000 What about "Female Genital Mutilation?" and Why Understanding Culture Matters in the First Place. *Daedalus*. Retrieved 1 July 2006 from http://www.findarticles.com/p/articles/mi_qa3671/is_200010/ai_n8920226/print.

Shweder, Richard A.
2002 "What About Female Genital Mutilation?" and Why Understanding Culture Matters in the First Place. In *Engaging Cultural*

Differences: The Multicultural Challenge in Liberal Democracies, edited by Richard A. Shweder, Martha Minow, and Hazel Rose Markus. New York: Russell Sage Foundation.

Turner, Victor W.
1967   *Mukanda*: The Rite of Circumcision. In *The Forest of Symbols: Aspects of Ndembu Ritual*. Ithaca and London: Cornell University Press.

Turner, Victor W.
1968   *The Drums of Affliction: A Study of Religious Processes among the Ndembu of Zambia*. Oxford: Clarendon Press and International African Institute.

Walker, Alice
1992   *Possessing the Secret of Joy*. New York: Harcourt Brace Jovanovich.

Walley, Christine J.
1997   Searching for "Voices": Feminism, Anthropology and the Global Debate over Female Genital Operations. *Current Anthropology* 12(3):405–438.

WHO Study Group on Female Genital Mutilation and Obstetric Outcome
2006   Female Genital Mutilation and Obstetric Outcome: WHO Collaborative Prospective Study in Six African Countries. *The Lancet* 367:1835–1841.

Part X
Gay, Lesbian, Bisexual, Transgender

Introduction

The period between 1935 and 1970 was one in which relatively little ethnography or theory was written about the comparative anthropology of heterosexuality. The "silence" with respect to same-sex and minority sexualities was even more emphatic. There were exceptions. In 1940 Ruth Landes stressed the role played by homosexual and "effeminate" men in some candomblé rituals, and received criticism for so doing. *Patterns of Sexual Behavior*, a book that Clellan Ford and Frank Beach assembled in 1952, using the statistics and ethnographic gobbets that constituted the new Human Relations Area Files, contained a chapter on homosexuality. There was a little more writing on Amerindian ritual transvestites or berdaches (e.g., Angelino and Shedd 1955) and a description of anal intercourse in Marind-Anim initiation by Jan Van Baal (1966), the anthropologist who had headed the Dutch administration of West Papua shortly before the Indonesian takeover. *Human Sexual Behavior*, the 1970 essay collection edited by Robert Suggs and Donald Marshall, contained an article by the ethnomusicologist, Alan Merriam, on the *kitesha*, a male transvestite role among the Basongye of Kasai in the Congo (he was not clear as to whether gender role reversal included sexual relations with other men: see Murray and Roscoe 2001[1998]: 144–6). Unfortunately, that volume ended with a shrill denunciation of the new gay liberation movement by Suggs and Marshall, expressing both their opinion that homosexuality was a pathology and their fears that a "homintern" was about to take over America!

If there was relatively little written by anthropologists as such, there were significant contributions by scholars in other disciplines. The most famous were the two volumes published by the Indiana University biologist, Alfred Kinsey, and his associates on *Sexual Behavior in the Human Male* (1948) and *Sexual Behavior in the Human Female* (1953). They revealed that more than 90 percent of young Americans masturbated, that 37 percent of American men had had at least one homosexual experience, and that 10 percent had been exclusively homosexual for at least three years of their lives. Rather than there being a sharp division between heterosexual and homosexual behavior in both sexes, there was in fact a continuum. Kinsey had a surprisingly large number of supporters, but he was attacked on several grounds. His sample was supposedly biased, because 25 percent of his data came from prisons, and because he was concealing his own sexual secrets. His approach was an application of loveless behaviorism, inhuman by design, according to critics like Margaret Mead and Geoffrey Gorer. Shortly before his death, McCarthyite forces in Congress accused him of "communism" and succeeded in chopping his federal funding. By contemporary standards Kinsey was unsophisticated, but his importance as a trailblazer was undeniable. Only one of his main associates, Paul Gebhard, was an anthropologist, and there was surprisingly little anthropology in the Kinsey Reports. Gebhard did write an introduction to the Suggs and Marshall collection, which was sponsored by the Kinsey Institute.

In a remarkable essay, Gayle Rubin (2002), herself a pioneer in feminist anthropology, has traced the importance of the Chicago School in Sociology (led by Robert Park and Ernest Burgess) in creating a tradition of American urban ethnography which students of sexual subcultures later followed, and has drawn attention to the role of John Gagnon and William Simon in legitimizing the sociology of sex and publishing a volume (*Sexual Deviance*, 1967) that contained three essays on urban gay culture in cities in the US and Canada. According to Rubin, symbolic interactionism provided an appropriate theoretical perspective for many pioneering studies such as Kenneth Plummer's *Sexual Stigma* (1975). Although she is herself clearly influenced by Michel Foucault in some of her writing, Rubin stresses that it is a mistake to assume that modern sexuality studies in the *constructionist* tradition merely implement a Foucauldian program.

The chapter from Esther Newton's *Mother Camp* contained in this section explicitly acknowledges the significance of the notion of *stigma* in the writing of the symbolic interactionist, Erving Goffman. Newton's book, a revised version of a 1968 Chicago doctoral thesis, was first published in 1972 and marks the beginning of the new wave in anthropological studies of sexuality. Newton studied female impersonators, concentrating her study on stage impersonators who considered themselves to be professional performers, emulating famous stars, rather than street fairies who were part-time players and hustlers. Note her explanation of the double act of concealment in drag – the exaggerated female dress imperfectly hiding the male body, and the male body concealing the female soul within it. To some gays drag is never amusing because it exposes the humiliation of a spoiled identity. However, it may be exceptionally funny in certain contexts only because its humor is derived from parody of that very "effeminacy" for which gays are stigmatized. Drag performances are exemplars of camp, a style that depends on inappropriate juxtapositions, well-executed transgressive performances, and outrageous humor. There are unwritten social rules in the subculture for the construction of camp humor and drag performance.

Foucault's *History of Sexuality, Volume One* appeared in French in 1976 and in English translation two years later. Its primary importance was that it saw sexuality as constructed out of talk, a discourse that varied according to location and social setting around an armature of power. Like priests in times past, therapists, sexologists, psychiatrists, and social workers in times present did most of the talking and classifying of the new sexual subjects. In an ironic introduction Foucault noted that the Victorian repression of sex whose reality virtually everyone accepted was at best partial truth, inasmuch as there was continual talk in appropriate registers about sexual norms and the categories of deviance. The liberation that followed the supposed ending of repression was another partial illusion inasmuch as one person's "freedom" might result in another's problematization, categorization, and therapy. As the nineteenth century ended, new categories of perversion were created. Foucault was not particularly interested in the cross-cultural study of sexualities, and his influence on the anthropology of sexuality is diffuse. Few have asked whether or not indigenous regimes of "biopower" existed in traditional societies that were comparable to our own, although such a perspective could be applied to initiates' training in sex in several societies. It is doubtful whether any anthropological investigation of indigenous sexuality in a colonial or postcolonial setting fits Foucault's framework, which reflected realities in France and Europe. Foucauldian perspectives have been applied by the late literary critic, Edward Said, to metropolitan, imperial representations of "Oriental" political life, social life, and sexuality. Within anthropology, Ann Stoler has used a Foucauldian perspective to explain attempts made by the Dutch colonial power to maintain a gendered and racialized form of social segmentation in Indonesia. But Foucauldian ethnographies of contemporary cultures took a while to appear.

In the meantime, in 1979, Kenneth Read, earlier known for his ethnographic work in the New Guinea Highlands, published *Other Voices*, an ethnography of the gay bar culture of a port city in the Northwest of the USA. Two years later, his student, Gilbert Herdt, published his first memorable account of male initiation rituals among the "Sambia," a people of southeast Papua New Guinea, *Guardians of the Flutes*. The Sambia, a patrilineal and patriarchal group that enforced rigid forms of gender separation, believed that Sambia adolescents unassisted could not produce enough semen to ensure fertility. It was therefore necessary for them to be inseminated by older youths through compulsory fellatio. Sambia men married late. Once they did so, same-sex relations were regarded as inappropriate. Herdt described the procedures at initiation as "ritualized homosexuality." Here was evidence of a culture that prescribed actions which many in Western cultures regarded as "against human nature." The use of the term "ritualized homosexuality" occasioned some criticism, inasmuch as it could be argued that the relationships between boys and youths were involuntary and not particularly erotic. Herdt has also been accused of over-emphasizing the exchange of semen, thereby failing to draw comparisons with the exchange of liquids like milk and coconut juice in other Melanesian rituals (see Elliston 1995). In the article reproduced here, Herdt replaces "ritualized homosexuality" with "boy insemination," but goes on to explain Sambia sexual representations in some detail. He asks a question of a type that is surprisingly rare in modern ethnography, namely what erotic feelings, what sexual excitement may or may not be present in Sambia initiation. Aside from their initiation rituals the Sambia also have a cluster of cases of 5-alpha-reductase deficiency, which is a genetic mutation in males that results in the formation of ambiguous genitalia while the fetus is still in the womb. Some infants with ARD are treated as female and so identify, but virilization at puberty may lead to problems. Herdt and his collaborators, who included the late psychoanalyst Robert Stoller, studied a number of these cases, including Sakulembei, the "turnim man," who underwent initiation, but could not undertake the youth's role as "fellated" rather than fellator. He was homosexual by inclination but did marry. His wife bore a child to another man.

A distinction should be made between cases of natural, biological "intersex" such as Sakulembei and other transsexual or transgender phenomena which are usually cultural in nature. Transvestism either in ceremonial or non-ceremonial contexts may or may not be associated with same-sex or heterosexual intercourse, and it may or may not mark a change in gender identification. Institutionalized cross-gender roles in indigenous North America are usually associated with important religious and ceremonial statuses. Some anthropologists, such as Georges Devereux, who discussed both male-female and female-male transvestism among the Mohave, have insisted that berdaches engaged in same-sex intercourse. However, the literature is more ambiguous, and sometimes the ritual and work roles of the berdache or "two spirit"[1] person are stressed more than sexual activity. That is why Harriet Whitehead, in "The Bow and the Burden Strap," regarded gender role rather than sexual orientation as the factor that determined the berdache role. It has been claimed that berdaches such as the Mohave *alyha* (male to female) and *hwame* (female to male), the *nadle* of the Navajo (who might sometimes be "intersex" or "hermaphrodite"), Albanian sworn virgins who reject marriage in favor of permanent chastity, and Indian *hijras* (see below) may constitute third (or fourth or fifth) genders in societies that do not insist on a two-gender model (see Herdt 1994). The existence of third genders is somewhat problematic, if only because a category like "gender" is rather difficult to translate. Recognition or a degree of toleration of certain named roles and their incumbents may or may not mean that they are accorded semantic or social equivalence with "male" or "female."

Hijras may entertain at Hindu weddings, and may also earn their living in much less prestigious ways as prostitutes. They are transsexuals in the sense that they have undergone castration. Most anthropologists are aware of *hijras* through the ethnography of Serena Nanda (1990), but they may not be aware that there are groups of *jankhas* in some of the same Indian cities. Some *jankhas* wear women's clothing and have sex with men, but they are not castrated (Cohen 1995).

It is easy to romanticize the lives of those occupying such gender positions, particularly in Brazil where some transvestites such as Roberta Close have attained prominence in the entertainment industry and many *travestis* play a role in Carnaval. One can see them as virtuous agents of resistance to patriarchal rule. Don Kulick's work, including the early article we reproduce here and his fine ethnography, *Travesti* (1998), serve as corrections to such viewpoints. The *travestis* of Salvador (Bahia Province, NE Brazil) often use silicon to enhance their breasts and buttocks, hiding their penises and male genitals. They are often prostitutes and petty thieves who occupy a stigmatized status in Brazilian society, blamed for extreme acts of violence that they do not commit and subjected to violence at the hands of clients, police, and homophobic members of the general public. According to Kulick, they routinely rob and sometimes assault their clients, and their "resistance" consists not of satire or defiance of customary norms but rather of actions that blackmail through threats of humiliation, e.g., threats to expose clients who withhold money as passive homosexuals rather than penetrators (the passive role in anal sex is particularly shameful in some Latin societies, whereas the active role is less marked). It should be noted that *travestis* identify as male homosexuals, but despite female attire and silicon enhancements they do not identify as women or transsexual.

Labels and epithets (gay, lesbian, intersex, same-sex, sex, sexuality, gender, homosexual, homosocial, heterosexual, heterogender, transsexual, transgender, transvestite, heteronormative, third sex, third gender, autosexual, allosexual, not to mention "berdache" and "two spirits") pervade the new anthropology of sexuality. They are not insignificant because they reflect the ways in which individuals and groups are classified, invoked, attacked, and defended in a variety of social contexts (social, medical, legal, etc.) by themselves (self-identification), by individuals like themselves, in the discourse of larger groups of which they are members, by other groups and by anthropologists or other "experts." Some terms are mutable; some are contested. For example, terms like the German "Urning" or the English "homosexual" and "invert" are products of the late nineteenth century. Certainly, the idea of homosexuals as a biological category or a form of self-identification as a member of such a group dates to that period in time. That is the meaning of the common but often misunderstood expression, "there was no such thing as homosexuality before the 1870s." As Tom Boellstorff has noted in *The Gay Archipelago* (2005), a change in labels may mean a change in worldview, but the fact that the same label is used in two places does not mean that it necessarily refers to exactly the same thing. In Indonesia the terms "gay" and "lesbi" denote modernity and a cosmopolitan outlook. There men with same-sex partners expect to marry heterosexually, because it is the norm for them as much as for anybody else.

As David Valentine notes, subcultural, working-class insiders who frequent the gay ball circuit in New York City may prefer to use a different label from that assigned to them by outsiders such as social workers, academics, and bourgeois gays and lesbians. The Latino, Afro-American population he studied included butch lesbians and fem queens (male-bodied) who were identified by outsiders as "transgender" in addition to butch queens and lesbian fems. The outsiders wanted to make a distinction between gender/transgender and sexuality, but the insiders do not wish to do so. They identify themselves as "gay."

Two of the articles in this section deal with same-sex sexualities in modernizing Southeast Asian nation-states. Megan Sinnott discusses media coverage of "transgendered sexual identities" – "toms," "dees" (corresponding roughly to Western butches and fems), and "gays" – in Thailand. According to Sinnott, all these groups are victims of an "internal Orientalism," to apply Said's expression. Teenagers who hug members of the same sex in malls and discos are seen as products of corrupt Western culture that threatens Thai values. On the other hand, same-sex sexualities may be seen as products of gender segregation in the school system, of a lack of modernity. Another increasingly common newspaper villain is the corrupt politician or military officer who preys on young boys. This image, according to Sinnott, is used to stereotype all alternately gendered people.

In Indonesia, according to Tom Boellstorff, the predominance of Islam in the nation-state creates problems for "gays" and "lesbis" inasmuch as gay and Islamic identities simply do not mix – they are an "ungrammatical" combination. Islam condemns heterosexual adultery, but the adulterer does at least fit into the moral hierarchy, whereas there is no recognized place for the "gay" or "lesbi" who is quite simply excluded and ignored by the Islamic system of social classification (albeit homosexuality is occasionally condemned by clerics). One can be an adulterous Muslim, but one cannot have a gay Muslim identity – there is no mosque for gay and lesbian worshippers. It should be noted that although the terms "gay" and "lesbi" have an obvious origin, the models for socialization in these cultures are Indonesian. Globalization has not brought about an erasure of difference with respect to sexualities.

NOTE

1   There is some controversy over the terminology to use when referring to people occupying tra-ditional Native American transgendered roles. The term "berdache" is considered insulting and inaccurate by many contemporary writers and activists, as it was originally a French term for catamite. The term "two-spirit" is preferred by many authors, but thought by others to overem-phasize the religious aspects of the role. We have tended to retain the terms used by the writers we discuss.

REFERENCES AND FURTHER READING

Angelino, Henry, and Charles Shedd
   1955   A Note on Berdache. American Anthropologist 57:121–126.
Boellstorff, Tom
   2005   The Gay Archipelago: Sexuality and Nation in Indonesia. Princeton: Princeton University Press.
Boellstorff, Tom
   2007   Queer Studies in Anthropology. Annual Review of Anthropology 36:17–36.
Cohen, Lawrence
   1995   The Pleasures of Castration: The Postoperative Status of Hijras, Jankhas, and Academics. *In* Sexual Nature, Sexual Culture. Paul R. Abramson and Steven D. Pinkerton, eds. Pp. 276–304. Chicago: University of Chicago Press.
Cole, Sally C.
   2003   Ruth Landes: A Life in Anthropology. Lincoln, NE: University of Nebraska Press.
Devereux, Georges
   1937   Institutionalized Homosexuality of the Mohave Indians. Human Biology 9:498–527.
Elliston, Deborah
   1995   Erotic Anthropology: "Ritualized Homosexuality" in Melanesia and Beyond. American Ethnologist 22(4)November:848–67.
Ford, Clellan S, and Frank A. Beach, eds.
   1952   Patterns of Sexual Behavior. New York: Paul B. Hoeber.
Foucault, Michel
   1980[1976]   The History of Sexuality, vol. 1: An Introduction. Trans. Robert Hurley. New York: Vintage Books.
Gagnon, John H., and William Simon, eds.
   1967   Sexual Deviance. New York: Harper and Row.
Herdt, Gilbert
   1981   Guardians of the Flutes: Idioms of Masculinity. New York: McGraw-Hill.
Herdt, Gilbert
   1990   Mistaken Gender: 5-Alpha Reductase Hermaphroditism and Biological Reductionism in Sexual Identity Reconsidered. American Anthropologist 92(1):433–447.

Herdt, Gilbert, ed.
1994   Third Sex, Third Gender: Beyond Sexual Dimorphism in Culture and History. New York: Zone Books.
Herdt, Gilbert, and Robert J. Stoller
1989   Intimate Communications: Erotics and the Study of Culture. New York: Columbia University Press.
Kinsey, Alfred C., W. B. Pomeroy, and C. E. Martin
1948   Sexual Behavior in the Human Male. Philadelphia: W. B. Saunders Co.
Kinsey, Alfred. C., W. B. Pomeroy, C. E. Martin, and P. H. Gebhard
1953   Sexual Behavior in the Human Female. Philadelphia: W. B. Saunders Co.
Kulick, Don
1998   Travesti: Sex, Gender and Culture Among Brazilian Transgendered Prostitutes. Chicago: University of Chicago Press.
Landes, Ruth
1940   A Cult Matriarchate and Male Homosexuality. *Journal of Abnormal and Social Psychology* 35:386–397.
Lyons, Andrew, and Harriet Lyons
2004   Irregular Connections: A History of Anthropology and Sexuality. Lincoln, NE: University of Nebraska Press.
Merriam, Alan
1971   Aspects of Sexual Behavior Among the Bala (Basongye). *In* Human Sexual Behavior: Variations in the Ethnographic Spectrum. Donald S. Marshall and Robert C. Suggs, eds. Pp. 71–102. Studies in Sex and Society. New York: Basic Books.
Murray, Stephen O., and Will Roscoe
2001[1998]   Overview: Central Africa. *In* Boy-Wives and Female Husbands: Studies in African Homosexualities. S. O. Murray and W. Roscoe, eds. Pp. 141–148. New York: Palgrave.
Nanda, Serena
1990   Neither Man nor Woman: The Hijras of India. Belmont, CA: Wadsworth.
Newton, Esther
1972   Mother Camp: Female Impersonators in America. Englewood Cliffs, NJ: Prentice Hall.
Plummer, Kenneth
1975   Sexual Stigma: An Interactionist Account. London: Routledge Kegan Paul.
Read, Kenneth E.
1979   Other Voices: The Style of a Male Homosexual Tavern. Novato: Chandler & Sharp.
Rubin, Gayle
2002   Studying Sexual Subcultures: Excavating the Ethnography of Gay Communities in Urban North America. *In* Out in Theory: The Emergence of Lesbian and Gay Anthropology, Ellen Lewin and William L. Leap, eds. Pp. 17–68. Urbana: University of Illinois Press.
Said, Edward W.
1978   Orientalism. New York: Vintage Books.
Sinnott, Megan
2004   Toms and Dees: Transgender Identity and Female Same-Sex Relationships in Thailand. Honolulu: University of Hawaii Press.
Stoler, Ann Laura
1995   Race and the Education of Desire: Foucault's History of Sexuality and the Colonial Order of Things. Durham, NC: Duke University Press.
Stoler, Ann Laura
2002   Carnal Knowledge and Imperial Power: Race and the Intimate in Colonial Rule. Berkeley, CA: University of California Press.

Suggs, Robert C., and Donald S. Marshall
    1970   Epilogue: Anthropological Perspectives on Human Sexual Behavior. *In* Human
    Sexual Behavior: Variations in the Ethnographic Spectrum, Donald S. Marshall and Robert
    C. Suggs, eds. Pp. 218–243. Studies in Sex and Society. New York: Basic Books.
Valentine, David
    2007   Imagining Transgender: An Ethnography of a Category. Durham, NC: Duke
    University Press.
Van Baal, Jan
    1966   Dema: Description and Analysis of Marind-anim Culture. The Hague: Nijhoff.
Van Baal, Jan
    1993   Lesbian/Gay Studies in the House of Anthropology. Annual Review of Anthropology
    (22):339–367.
Weston, Kath
    1998   Long Slow Burn: Sexuality and Social Science. New York and London: Routledge.

22

Role Models

Esther Newton

The Actress

Female impersonators, particularly the stage impersonators, identify strongly with professional performers. Their special, but not exclusive, idols are female entertainers. Street impersonators usually try to model themselves on movie stars rather than on stage actresses and nightclub performers. Stage impersonators are quite conversant with the language of the theatres and nightclubs, while the street impersonators are not. In Kansas City, the stage impersonators frequently talked with avid interest about stage and nightclub "personalities." The street impersonators could not join in these discussions for lack of knowledge.

Stage impersonators very often told me that they considered themselves to be nightclub performers or to be in the nightclub business, "just like other [straight] performers."

When impersonators criticized each other's on- or off-stage conduct as "unprofessional," this was a direct appeal to norms of show business. Certain show business phrases such as "break a leg" (for good luck) were used routinely, and I was admonished not to whistle backstage. The following response of a stage impersonator shows this emphasis in response to my question, "What's the difference between professionals and street fairies?" This impersonator was a "headliner" (had top billing) at a club in New York:

Well (laughs), simply saying … well, I can leave that up to you. You have seen the show. You see the difference between *me* and some of these other people (his voice makes it sound as if this point is utterly self-evident) who are working in this left field of show business, and I'm quite sure that you see a *distinct* difference. I am more conscious of being a performer, and I think generally speaking, most, or a lot, of other people who are appearing in the same show are just doing it, not as a lark — we won't say that it's a lark — but they're doing it because it's something they can drop in and out of. They have fun, they laugh, have drinks, and play around, and just have a good time. But to *me*, now, playing around and having a good time is [sic.] important to me also; but primarily my interest from the time I arrive at the club till

Esther Newton, Role Models, from *Mother Camp, Female Impersonators in North America*, University of Chicago Press, 1979, pp. 97–111. Reprinted with permission of The University of Chicago Press and the author.

Sexualities in Anthropology: A Reader, edited by Andrew P. Lyons and Harriet D. Lyons

the end of the evening – I am there as a performer, as an entertainer, and this to me is the most important thing. And I dare say that if needs be, I probably could do it, and be just as good an entertainer … I don't know if I would be any more successful if I were working in men's clothes than I am working as a woman. But comparing myself to some of the people that I would consider real professional entertainers – people who are genuinely interested in the show as a show, and not just as I say, a street fairy, who wants to put on a dress and a pair of high heels to be seen and show off in public.

The stage impersonators are interested in "billings" and publicity, in lighting and make-up and stage effects, in "timing" and "stage presence." The quality by which they measure performers and performances is "talent." Their models in these matters are established performers, both in their performances and in their off-stage lives, insofar as the impersonators are familiar with the latter. The practice of doing "impressions" is, of course, a very direct expression of this role modeling.

From this perspective, female impersonators are simply nightclub performers who happen to use impersonation as a medium. Many stage impersonators are drab in appearance (and sometimes in manner) off stage. These men often say that drag is simply a medium or mask that allows them to perform. The mask is borrowed from female performers, the ethos of performance from show business norms in general.

The stated aspiration of almost all stage impersonators is to "go legit," that is, to play in movies, television, and on stage or in respectable nightclubs, either in drag *or* (some say) in men's clothes. Failing this, they would like to see the whole profession "upgraded," made more legitimate and professional (and to this end they would like to see all street impersonators barred from working, for they claim that the street performers downgrade the profession). T. C. Jones is universally accorded highest status among impersonators because he has appeared on Broadway (New Faces of 1956) and on television (Alfred Hitchcock) and plays only high-status nightclubs.

The Drag Queen

Professionally, impersonators place themselves as a group at the bottom of the show business world. But socially, their self-image can be represented in its simplest form as three concentric circles. The impersonators, or drag queens, are the inner circle. Surrounding them are the queens, ordinary gay men. The straights are the outer circle. In this way, impersonators are "a society within a society within a society," as one impersonator told me.

A few impersonators deny publicly that they are gay. These impersonators are married, and some have children. Of course, being married and having children constitute no barrier to participation in the homosexual subculture. But whatever may be the actual case with these few, the impersonators I knew universally described such public statements as "cover." One impersonator's statement was particularly revealing. He said that "in practice" perhaps some impersonators were straight, but "in theory" they could not be. "How can a man perform in female attire and not have something wrong with him?" he asked.

Skip Arnold, an important informant, at home.

The role of the female impersonator is directly related to both the drag queen and camp roles in the homosexual subculture: In gay life, the two roles are strongly associated. In homosexual terminology, a drag queen is a homosexual male who often, or habitually, dresses in female attire. (A drag butch is a lesbian who often, or habitually, dresses in male attire.) Drag and camp are the most representative and widely used symbols of homosexuality in the English speaking world. This is true even though many homosexuals would never wear drag or go to a drag party and even though most homosexuals who do wear drag do so only in special contexts, such as private parties and Halloween balls.[1] At the middle-class level, it is common to give "costume" parties at which those who want to wear drag can do so, and the others can wear a costume appropriate to their gender.

The principal opposition around which the gay world revolves is masculine-feminine. There are a number of ways of presenting this opposition through one's own person, where it becomes also an opposition of "inside" = "outside" or "underneath" = "outside." Ultimately, all drag symbolism opposes the "inner" or "real" self (subjective self) to the "outer" self (social self). For the great majority of homosexuals, the social self is often a calculated respectability and the subjective or real self is stigmatized. The "inner" = "outer" opposition is almost parallel to "back" = "front." In fact, the social self is usually described as "front" and social relationships (especially with women) designed to support the veracity of the "front" are called "cover." The "front" = "back" opposition also has a direct tie-in with the body: "front" = "face"; "back" = "ass."

There are two different levels on which the oppositions can be played out. One is *within* the sartorial system[2] itself, that is, wearing feminine clothing "underneath" and masculine clothing "outside." (This method seems to be used more by heterosexual transvestites.) It symbolizes that the visible, social, masculine clothing is a costume, which in turn symbolizes that the entire sex-role behavior is a role – an act. Conversely, stage impersonators sometimes wear jockey shorts underneath full stage drag, symbolizing that the feminine clothing is a costume.

A second "internal" method is to mix sex-role referents *within* the visible sartorial system. This generally involves some "outside" item from the feminine sartorial system such as earrings, lipstick, high-heeled shoes, a necklace, etc., worn *with* masculine clothing. This kind of opposition is used very frequently in informal camping by homosexuals. The feminine item stands out so glaringly by incongruity that it "undermines" the masculine system and proclaims that the inner identification is feminine.[3] When this method is used on stage, it is called "working with (feminine) pieces." The performer generally works in a tuxedo or business suit and a woman's large hat and earrings.

The second level poses an opposition between a one sex-role sartorial system and the "self," whose identity has to be indicated in some other way. Thus when impersonators are performing, the oppositional play is between "appearance," which is female, and "reality," or "essence," which is male. One way to do this is to show that the appearance is an illusion; for instance, a standard impersonation maneuver is to pull out one "breast" and show it to the audience. A more drastic step is taking off the wig. Strippers actually routinize the progression from "outside" to "inside" visually, by starting in a full stripping costume and ending by taking off the bra and showing the audience the flat chest. Another method is to demonstrate "maleness" verbally or vocally by suddenly dropping the vocal level or by some direct reference. One impersonator routinely tells the audience: "Have a ball. I have two." (But genitals must *never* be seen.) Another tells unruly members of the audience that he will "put on my men's clothes and beat you up."

Impersonators play on the opposition to varying extents, but most experienced stage impersonators have a characteristic method of doing it. Generally speaking, the desire and ability to break the illusion of femininity is the mark of an experienced impersonator who has freed himself from other impersonators as the immediate reference group and is working fully to the audience. Even so, some stage impersonators admitted that it is difficult to break the unity of the feminine sartorial system. For instance, they said that it is difficult, subjectively, to speak in a deep tone of voice while on stage and especially while wearing a wig. The "breasts" especially seem to symbolize the entire feminine sartorial system and role. This is shown not only by the very common device of removing them in order to break the illusion, but in the command, "tits up!" meaning, "get into the role," or "get into feminine character."

The tension between the masculine-feminine and inside-outside oppositions pervade the homosexual subculture at all class and status levels. In a sense the different class and status levels consist of different ways of balancing these oppositions. Low-status homosexuals (both male and female) characteristically insist on very strong dichotomization between masculine-feminine so that people must play out one principle or the other exclusively. Low-status queens are expected to be very nellie, always, and low-status butch men are so "masculine" that they very often consider themselves straight.[4] (Although the queens say in private that "today's butch is tomorrow's sister.") Nevertheless, in the most nellie queen the opposition is still implicitly there, since to participate in the male homosexual subculture as a peer, one must be male inside (physiologically).

Recently, this principle has begun to be challenged by hormone use and by the sex-changing operation. The use of these techniques as a final resolution of the masculine-feminine opposition is hotly discussed in the homosexual subculture. A very significant proportion of the impersonators, and especially the street impersonators, have used or are using hormone shots or plastic inserts to create artificial breasts and change the shape of their bodies. This development is strongly deplored by the stage impersonators who say that the whole point of female impersonation depends on maleness. They further say that these "hormone queens" are placing themselves out of the homosexual subculture, since, by definition, a homosexual man wants to sleep with other *men* (i.e., no gay man would want to sleep with these "hormone queens").

In carrying the transformation even farther, to "become a woman" is approved by the stage impersonators, with the provision that the "sex changes" should get out of gay life altogether and go straight. The "sex changes" do not always comply, however. One quite successful impersonator in Chicago had the operation but continued to perform in a straight club with other impersonators. Some impersonators in Chicago told me that this person was now considered "out of gay life" by the homosexuals and could not perform in a gay club. I also heard a persistent rumor that "she" now liked to sleep with lesbians!

It should be readily apparent why drag is such an effective symbol of both the outside-inside and masculine-feminine oppositions. There are relatively few ascribed roles in American culture and sex role is one of them; sex role radiates a complex and ubiquitous system of typing achieved roles. Obvious examples are in the kinship system (wife, mother, etc.) but sex typing also extends far out into the occupational-role system (airline stewardess, waitress, policeman, etc.). The effect of the drag system is to wrench the sex roles loose from that which supposedly determines them, that is, genital sex. Gay people know that sex-typed behavior can be achieved, contrary to what is popularly believed. They know that the possession of one type of genital equipment by no means guarantees the "naturally appropriate" behavior.

Thus drag in the homosexual subculture symbolizes two somewhat conflicting statements concerning the sex-role system. The first statement symbolized by drag is that the sex-role system really is natural: therefore homosexuals are unnatural (typical responses: "I am physically abnormal"; "I can't help it, I was born with the wrong hormone balance"; "I am really a woman who was born with the wrong equipment"; "I am psychologically sick").

The second symbolic statement of drag questions the "naturalness" of the sex-role system *in toto*; if sex-role behavior can be achieved by the "wrong" sex, it logically follows that it is in reality also achieved, not inherited, by the "right" sex. Anthropologists say that sex-role behavior is learned. The gay world, via drag, says that sex-role behavior is an appearance; it is "outside." It can be manipulated at will.

Drag symbolizes both these assertions in a very complex way. At the simplest level, drag signifies that the person wearing it is a homosexual, that he is a male who is behaving in a specifically inappropriate way, that he is a male who places himself as a woman in relation to other men. In this sense it signifies stigma. At the most complex, it is a double inversion that says "appearance is an illusion." Drag says, "my 'outside' appearance is feminine, but my essence 'inside' [the body] is masculine." At the same time it symbolizes the opposite inversion: "my appearance 'outside' [my body, my gender] is masculine but my essence 'inside' [myself] is feminine."

In the context of the homosexual subculture, all professional female impersonators are "drag queens." Drag is always worn for performance in any case; the female impersonator has simply professionalized this subcultural role. Among themselves and in conversation with other homosexuals, female impersonators usually call themselves and are called drag queens. In the same way, their performances are referred to by themselves and others as drag shows.

But when the varied meanings of drag are taken into consideration, it should be obvious why the drag queen is an ambivalent figure in the gay world. The drag queen symbolizes all that homosexuals say they fear the most in themselves, all that they say they feel guilty about; he symbolizes, in fact, *the* stigma. In this way, the term "drag queen" is comparable to "nigger." And like that word, it may be all right in an ingroup context but not in an outgroup one. Those who do not want to think of themselves or be identified as drag queens under any circumstances attempt to disassociate themselves from "drag" completely. These homosexuals deplore drag shows and profess total lack of interest in them. Their attitude toward drag queens is one of condemnation combined with the expression of vast social distance between themselves and the drag queen.

Other homosexuals enjoy being queens among themselves, but do not want to be stigmatized by the heterosexual culture. These homosexuals admire drag and drag queens in homosexual contexts, but deplore female impersonators and street fairies for "giving us a bad name" or "projecting the wrong image" to the heterosexual culture. The drag queen is definitely a marked man in the subculture.

Homosexuality consists of sex-role deviation made up of two related but distinct parts: "wrong" sexual object choices and "wrong" sex-role presentation of self.[5] The first deviation is shared by all homosexuals, but it can be hidden best. The second deviation logically (in this culture) corresponds with the first, which it symbolizes. But it cannot be hidden, and it actually compounds the stigma.

Thus, insofar as female impersonators are professional drag queens, they are evaluated positively by gay people to the extent that they have perfected a subcultural skill and to the extent that gay people are willing to oppose the heterosexual culture directly (in much the same way that Negroes now call themselves Blacks). On the other hand, they are despised because they symbolize and embody the stigma. At present, the balance is far on the negative side, although this varies by context and by the position of the observer (relative to the stigma). This explains the impersonators' negative identification with the term drag queen when it is used by outsiders. (In the same way, they at first used masculine pronouns of address and reference toward each other in my presence, but reverted to feminine pronouns when I became more or less integrated into the system.)

The Camp

While all female impersonators are drag queens in the gay world, by no means are all of them "camps." Both the drag queen and the camp are expressive performing roles, and both specialize in transformation. But the drag queen is concerned with masculine-feminine transformation, while the camp is concerned with what might be called a philosophy of transformations and incongruity. Certainly the two roles are intimately related, since to be a feminine man is by definition incongruous. But strictly speaking, the drag queen simply expresses the incongruity while the camp actually uses it to achieve a higher synthesis. To the extent that a drag queen does this, he is called "campy." The drag queen role is emotionally charged and connotes low status for most homosexuals because it bears the visible stigmata of homosexuality; camps, however, are found at all status levels in the homosexual subculture and are very often the center of primary group organization.[6]

The camp is the central role figure in the subcultural ideology of camp. The camp ethos or style plays a role analogous to "soul" in the Negro subculture.[7] Like soul, camp is a "strategy for a situation."[8] The special perspective of the female impersonators is a case of a broader homosexual ethos. This is the perspective of moral deviance and, consequently, of a "spoiled identity," in Goffman's terms.[9] Like the Negro problem, the homosexual problem centers on self-hatred and the lack of self-esteem.[10] But if "the soul ideology ministers to the needs for identity,"[11] the camp ideology ministers to the needs for dealing with an identity that is well defined but loaded with contempt. As one impersonator who was also a well known camp told me, "No one is more miserable about homosexuality than the homosexual."

Camp is not a thing. Most broadly it signifies a *relationship between* things, people, and activities or qualities, and homosexuality. In this sense, "camp taste," for instance, is synonymous with homosexual taste. Informants stressed that even between individuals there is very little agreement on what is camp because camp is in the eye of the beholder, that is, different homosexuals like different things, and because of the spontaneity and individuality of camp, camp taste is always changing. This has the advantage, recognized by some informants, that a clear division can always be maintained between homosexual and "straight" taste:

He said Susan Sontag was wrong about camp's being a cult,[12] and the moment it becomes a public cult, you watch the queens stop it. Because if it becomes the squares, it doesn't belong to them any more. And what will be "camp art," no queen will own. It's like taking off the work clothes and putting on the home clothes. When the queen is coming home, she wants to come home to a campy apartment

that's hers – it's very queer – because all day long she's been very straight. So when it all of a sudden becomes very straight – to come home to an apartment that any square could have – she's not going to have it any more.[13]

While camp is in the eye of the homosexual beholder, it is assumed that there is an underlying unity of perspective among homosexuals that gives any particular campy thing its special flavor. It is possible to discern strong themes in any particular campy thing or event. The three that seemed most recurrent and characteristic to me were *incongruity, theatricality*, and *humor*. All three are intimately related to the homosexual situation and strategy. Incongruity is the subject matter of camp, theatricality its style, and humor its strategy.

Camp usually depends on the perception or creation of *incongruous juxtapositions*. Either way, the homosexual "creates" the camp, by pointing out the incongruity or by devising it. For instance, one informant said that the campiest thing he had seen recently was a Midwestern football player in high drag at a Halloween ball. He pointed out that the football player was seriously trying to be a lady, and so his intent was not camp, but that the *effect* to the observer was campy. (The informant went on to say that it would have been even campier if the football player had been picked up by the police and had his picture published in the paper the next day.) This is an example of unintentional camp, in that the campy person or thing does not perceive the incongruity.

Created camp also depends on transformations and juxtapositions, but here the effect is intentional. The most concrete examples can be seen in the apartments of campy queens, for instance, in the idea of growing plants in the toilet tank. One queen said that *TV Guide* had described a little Mexican horse statue as campy. He said there was nothing campy about this at all, but if you put a nude cut-out of Bette Davis on it, it would be campy. Masculine-feminine juxtapositions are, of course, the most characteristic kind of camp, but any very incongruous contrast can be campy. For instance, juxtapositions of high and low status, youth and old age, profane and sacred functions or symbols, cheap and expensive articles are frequently used for camp purposes. Objects or people are often said to be campy, but the camp inheres not in the person or thing itself but in the tension between that person or thing and the context or association. For instance, I was told by impersonators that a homosexual clothes designer made himself a beautiful Halloween ball gown. After the ball he sold it to a wealthy society lady. It was said that when he wore it, it was very campy, but when she wore it, it was just an expensive gown, unless she had run around her ball saying she was really not herself but her faggot dress designer.

The nexus of this perception by incongruity lies in the basic homosexual experience, that is, squarely on the moral deviation. One informant said, "Camp is all based on homosexual thought. It is all based on the idea of two men or two women in bed. It's incongruous and it's funny." If moral deviation is the locus of the perception of incongruity, it is more specifically role deviation and role manipulation that are at the core of the second property of camp, *theatricality*.

Camp is theatrical in three interlocking ways. First of all, camp is style. Importance tends to shift from what a thing *is* to how it *looks*, from *what* is done to *how* it is done. It has been remarked that homosexuals excel in the decorative arts. The kind of incongruities that are campy are very often created by adornment or stylization of a well-defined thing or symbol. But the emphasis on style goes further than this in that camp is also exaggerated, consciously "stagey," specifically theatrical. This is especially true of *the* camp, who is definitely a performer.

The second aspect of theatricality in camp is its dramatic form. Camp, like drag, always involves a performer or performers and an audience. This is its structure. It is only stretching the point a little to say that even in unintentional camp, this interaction is maintained. In the case of the football player, his behavior was transformed by his audience into a performance. In many cases of unintentional camp, the camp performs to his audience by commenting on the behavior or appearance of "the scene," which is then described as

"campy." In intentional camp, the structure of performer and audience is almost always clearly defined. This point will be elaborated below.

Third, camp is suffused with the perception of "being as playing a role" and "life as theatre."[14] It is at this point that drag and camp merge and augment each other. I was led to an appreciation of this while reading Parker Tyler's appraisal of Greta Garbo.[15] Garbo is generally regarded in the homosexual community as "high camp." Tyler stated that " 'Drag acts,' I believe, are not confined to the declassed sexes. Garbo 'got in drag' whenever she took some heavy glamour part, whenever she melted in or out of a man's arms, whenever she simply let that heavenly-flexed neck … bear the weight of her thrown-back head."[16] He concludes, "How resplendent seems the art of acting! It is all *impersonation*, whether the sex underneath is true or not."[17]

We have to take the long way around to get at the real relationship between Garbo and camp. The homosexual is stigmatized, but his stigma can be hidden. In Goffman's terminology, information about his stigma can be managed. Therefore, of crucial importance to homosexuals themselves and to non-homosexuals is whether the stigma is displayed so that one is immediately recognizable or is hidden so that he can pass to the world at large as a respectable citizen. The covert half (conceptually, not necessarily numerically) of the homosexual community is engaged in "impersonating" respectable citizenry, at least some of the time. What is being impersonated?

The stigma essentially lies in being less than a man and in doing something that is unnatural (wrong) for a man to do. Surrounding this essence is a halo effect: violation of culturally standardized canons of taste, behavior, speech, and so on, rigorously associated (prescribed) with the male role (e.g., fanciful or decorative clothing styles, "effeminate" speech and manner, expressed disinterest in women as sexual objects, expressed interest in men as sexual objects, unseemly concern with personal appearance, etc.). The covert homosexual must therefore do two things: first, he must conceal the fact that he sleeps with men. But concealing this *fact* is far less difficult than his second problem, which is controlling the *halo effect* or signals that would announce that he sleeps with men. The covert homosexual must in fact impersonate a *man*, that is, he must *appear* to the "straight" world to be fulfilling (or not violating) all the requisites of the male role as defined by the "straight" world.

The immediate relationship between Tyler's point about Garbo and camp/drag is this: if Garbo playing women is drag, then homosexuals "passing" are playing men; they are in drag. This is the larger implication of drag/camp. In fact, gay people often use the word "drag" in this broader sense, even to include role playing which most people simply take for granted: role playing in school, at the office, at parties, and so on. In fact, all of life is role and theatre – appearance.

But granted that all acting is impersonation, what moved Tyler to designate Garbo's acting specifically as "drag"? Drag means, first of all, role playing. The way in which it defines role playing contains its implicit attitude. The word "drag" attaches specifically to the outward, visible appurtenances of a role. In the type case, sex role, drag primarily refers to the wearing apparel and accessories that designate a human being as male or female, when it is worn by the opposite sex. By focusing on the outward appearance of role, drag implies that sex role and, by extension, role in general is something superficial, which can be manipulated, put on and off again at will. The drag concept implies *distance* between the actor and the role or "act." But drag also means "costume." This theatrical referent is the key to the attitude toward role playing embodied in drag as camp. Role playing is *play*; it is an act or show. The necessity to play at life, living role after superficial role, should not be the cause of bitterness or despair. Most of the sex role and other impersonations that male homosexuals do are done with ease, grace, and especially humor. The actor should throw himself into it; he should put on a good show; he should view the whole experience as fun, as a camp.[18]

The double stance toward role, putting on a good show while indicating distance (showing that it is a show) is the heart of drag as camp. Garbo's acting was thought to be "drag" because it was considered markedly androgynous, and because she played (even overplayed)

the role of femme fatale with style. No man (in her movies) and very few audiences (judging by her success) could resist her allure. And yet most of the men she seduced were her victims because she was only playing at love – only acting. This is made quite explicit in the film "Mata Hari," in which Garbo the spy seduces men to get information from them.

The third quality of camp is its *humor*. Camp is for fun; the aim of camp is to make an audience laugh. In fact, it is a *system* of humor. Camp humor is a system of laughing at one's incongruous position instead of crying.[19] That is, the humor does not cover up, it transforms. I saw the reverse transformation – from laughter to pathos – often enough, and it is axiomatic among the impersonators that when the camp cannot laugh, he dissolves into a maudlin bundle of self-pity.

One of the most confounding aspects of my interaction with the impersonators was their tendency to laugh at situations that to me were horrifying or tragic. I was amazed, for instance, when one impersonator described to me as "very campy" the scene in "Whatever Happened to Baby Jane" in which Bette Davis served Joan Crawford a rat, or the scene in which Bette Davis makes her "comeback" in the parlor with the piano player.

Of course, not all impersonators and not all homosexuals are campy. *The* camp is a homosexual wit and clown; his campy productions and performances are a continuous creative strategy for dealing with the homosexual situation, and, in the process, defining a positive homosexual identity. As one performer summed it up for me, "Homosexuality is a way of life that is against all ways of life, including nature's. And no one is more aware of it than the homosexual. The camp accepts his role as a homosexual and flaunts his homosexuality. He makes the other homosexuals laugh; he makes life a little brighter for them. And he builds a bridge to the straight people by getting them to laugh with him." The same man described the role of the camp more concretely in an interview:

Well, "to camp" actually means "to sit in front of a group of people" ... not on-stage, but you *can* camp on-stage ... I think that I do that when I talk to the audience. I think I'm camping with 'em. But a "camp" herself is a queen who sits and starts entertaining a group of people at a bar around her. They all start listening to what she's got to say. And she says campy things. Oh, somebody smarts off at her and she gives 'em a very flip answer. A camp is a flip person who has declared emotional freedom. She is going to say to the world, "I'm queer." Although she may not do this all the time, but most of the time a camp queen will. She'll walk down the street and she'll see you and say, "Hi, Mary, how are you?" right in the busiest part of town ... she'll actually camp, right there. And she'll swish down the street. And she may be in a business suit; she doesn't have to be dressed outlandishly. Even at work the people figure that she's a camp. They don't know what to *call* her, but they hire her 'cause she's a good kid, keeps the office laughing, doesn't bother anybody, and everyone'll say, "Oh, running around with Georgie's more fun! He's just more fun!" The squares are saying this. And the other ones [homosexuals] are saying, "Oh, you've got to know George, she's a camp." Because the whole time she's lighthearted. Very seldom is camp sad. Camp has got to be flip. A camp queen's got to think faster than other queens. *This* makes her camp. She's got to have an answer to anything that's put to her....[20]

Now *homosexuality* is *not* camp. But you take a camp, and she turns around and she makes homosexuality funny, but not ludicrous; funny but not ridiculous ... this is a great, great art. This is a fine thing. ... Now when it suddenly became the word ... became like ... it's like the word "Mary." Everybody's "Mary." "Hi, Mary. How are you, Mary." And like "girl." You may be talking to one of the butchest queens in the world, but you still say, "Oh, girl." And sometimes they say, "Well, don't call me 'she' and don't call me 'girl.' I don't feel like a girl. I'm a *man*. I just like to go to bed with you *girls*. I don't want to go to bed with another man." And you say, "Oh, girl, get you. Now she's turned butch." And so you camp about it. It's sort of laughing at yourself instead of crying. And a good camp will make you laugh along with her, to where you suddenly feel ... you don't feel like she's made fun of you. She's sort of made light of a bad situation.

The camp queen makes no bones about it; to him the gay world is the "sisterhood." By accepting his homosexuality and flaunting it, the camp undercuts all homosexuals who won't accept the stigmatized identity. Only by fully embracing the stigma itself can one neutralize the sting and make it laughable.[21] Not all references to the stigma are campy, however. Only if it is pointed out as a joke is it camp, although there is no requirement that the jokes be gentle or friendly. A lot of camping is extremely hostile; it is almost always sarcastic. But its intent is humorous as well. Campy queens are very often said to be "bitches" just as camp humor is said to be "bitchy."[22] The campy queen who can "read" (put down) all challengers and cut everyone down to size is admired. Humor is the campy queen's weapon. A camp queen in good form can come out on top (by group consensus) against all the competition.

Female impersonators who use drag in a comic way or are themselves comics are considered camps by gay people. (Serious glamour drag is considered campy by many homosexuals, but it is unintentional camp. Those who see glamour drag as a serious business do not consider it to be campy. Those who think it is ludicrous for drag queens to take themselves seriously see the whole business as a campy incongruity.) Since the camp role is a positive one, many impersonators take pride in being camps, at least on stage.[23] Since the camp role depends to such a large extent on verbal agility, it reinforces the superiority of the live performers over record performers, who, even if they are comic, must depend wholly on visual effects.

NOTES

1 In two Broadway plays (since made into movies) dealing with English homosexuals, "The Killing of Sister George" (lesbians) and "Staircase" (male homosexuals), drag played a prominent role. In "George," an entire scene shows George and her lover dressed in tuxedos and top hats on their way to a drag party. In "Staircase," the entire plot turns on the fact that one of the characters has been arrested for "going in drag" to the local pub. Throughout the second act, this character wears a black

shawl over his shoulders. This item of clothing is symbolic of full drag. This same character is a camp and, in my opinion, George was a very rare bird, a lesbian camp. Both plays, at any rate, abounded in camp humor. "The Boys in the Band," another recent play and movie, doesn't feature drag as prominently but has two camp roles and much camp humor.

2 This concept was developed and suggested to me by Julian Pitt-Rivers.

3 Even one feminine item ruins the integrity of the masculine system; the male loses his caste honor. The superordinate role in a hierarchy is more fragile than the subordinate. Manhood must be achieved, and once achieved, guarded and protected.

4 The middle-class idea tends to be that any man who has had sexual relations with men is queer. The lower classes strip down to "essentials," and the man who is "dominant" can be normal (masculine). Lower-class men give themselves a bit more leeway before they consider themselves to be gay.

5 It becomes clear that the core of the stigma is in "wrong" sexual object choice when it is considered that there is little stigma in simply being effeminate, or even in wearing feminine apparel in some contexts, as long as the male is known to be heterosexual, that is, known to sleep with women or, rather, not to sleep with men. But when I say that sleeping with men is the core of the stigma, or that feminine behavior logically corresponds with this, I do not mean it in any causal sense. In fact, I have an impression that some homosexual men sleep with men *because* it strengthens their identification with the feminine role, rather than the other way around. This makes a lot of sense developmentally, if one assumes, as I do, that children learn sex-role identity before they learn any strictly sexual object choices. In other words, I think that children learn they are boys or girls before they are made to understand that boys *only* love girls and vice versa.

6 The role of the "pretty boy" is also a very positive one, and in some ways the camp is an alternative for those who are not pretty. However, the pretty boy is subject to the depredations of aging, which in the subculture is thought to set in at thirty (at the latest). Because the camp depends on inventiveness and wit rather than on physical beauty, he is ageless.

7 Keil, *Urban Blues*, pp. 164–90.

8 This phrase is used by Kenneth Burke in reference to poetry and is used by Keil in a sociological sense.

9 Erving Goffman, *Stigma* (Englewood Cliffs, N.J.: Prentice-Hall, 1963.)

10 I would say that the main problem today is heterosexuals, just as the main problem for Blacks is Whites.

11 Keil, *Urban Blues*, p. 165.

12 I don't want to pass over the implication here that female impersonators keep up with Susan Sontag. Generally, they don't. I had given him Susan Sontag's "Notes on 'Camp'" (*Partisan Review* [Fall, 1964]: 515–30) to see what he would say. He was college educated, and perfectly able to get through it. He was enraged (justifiably, I felt) that she had almost edited homosexuals out of camp.

13 Informants said that many ideas had been taken over by straights through the mass media, but that the moment this happened the idea would no longer be campy. For instance, one man said that a queen he knew had gotten the idea of growing plants in the water tank of the toilet. But the idea is no longer campy because it is being advertised through such mass media as *Family Circle* magazine.

How to defend *any* symbols or values from the absorbing powers of the mass media? Jules Henry, I believe, was one of the first to point to the power of advertising to subvert traditional values by appropriating them for commercial purposes (*Culture Against Man*, New York: Random House, 1963). But subcultural symbols and values lose their integrity in the same way. Although Sontag's New York *avant garde* had already appropriated camp from homosexuals, they did so in the effort to create their own aristocracy or integrity of taste as against the mass culture.

14 Sontag, "Notes on 'Camp,'" p. 529.

15 Parker Tyler, "The Garbo Image," in *The Films of Greta Garbo*, ed. Michael Conway, Dion McGregor, and Mark Ricci (New York: Citadel Press, no date), pp. 9–31.

16 Tyler, "The Garbo Image," p. 12.

17 Ibid. p. 28.

18 It is clear to me now how camp undercuts rage and therefore rebellion by ridiculing serious and concentrated bitterness.

19 It would be worthwhile to compare camp humor with the humor systems of other oppressed people (Eastern European Jewish, Negro, etc.).

20 Speed and spontaneity are of the essence. For example, at a dinner party, someone said, "Oh, we forgot to say grace." One woman folded her hands without missing a beat and intoned, "Thank God everyone at this table is gay."

21 It's important to stress again that camp is a pre- or proto-political phenomenon. The anti-camp in this system is the person who wants to dissociate from the stigma to be like the oppressors. The camp says, "I am not like the oppressors." But in so doing he agrees with the oppressors' definition of who he is. The new radicals deny the stigma in a different way, by saying that the oppressors are illegitimate. This step is only foreshadowed in camp. It is also interesting that the lesbian wing of the radical homosexuals have come to women's meetings holding signs saying: "We are the women your parents warned you against."

22 The "bitch," as I see it, is a woman who *accepts* her inferior status, but refuses to do so gracefully or without fighting back. Women and homosexual men are oppressed by straight men, and it is no accident that both are beginning to move beyond bitchiness toward refusal of inferior status.

23 Many impersonators told me that they got tired of being camps for their friends, lovers, and acquaintances. They often felt they were asked to gay parties simply to entertain and camp it up, and said they did not feel like camping off stage, or didn't feel competent when out of drag. This broadens out into the social problem of all clowns and entertainers, or, even further, to anyone with a talent. He will often wonder if he is loved for himself.

23

Notes and Queries on Sexual Excitement in Sambia Culture

Gilbert Herdt

Introduction

Sexuality is typically understood in Western European and North American discourse to result from internal drives and biological forces in the individual, whereas, conversely, the meaning systems of the great majority of non-western societies often view sexuality as a product of social practices or relations in the cultural world. Such an ideal contrast is of course never perfectly accounted for in either tradition; however, the dual perspectives of these traditions pose important questions for the anthropology of sexuality and the local construction of sexual culture. The aim of this contribution is to examine this difference and to raise certain questions and observations arising out of the study of the Sambia of Papua New Guinea (Herdt 1981; Herdt and Stoller 1990). One of the most critical of these questions asks: what is 'sexual excitement'? In western discourse we understand this to be an essential process in the individual body; the stimulus in society may, however, provide the means to socially control the sexuality of individuals and groups, as Foucault (1980) has

suggested. Furthermore, we must ask: Who or what holds the power to generate sexual excitement within the person and the actor in the village, the small face-to-face encounter, the intimate group? A further goal of this paper, then, is to rethink the western category 'sexual excitement' as this might form a larger comparative project in social study.

The history of anthropological studies of sexuality, beginning in the nineteenth century, typically regarded the sexual as a product of biological evolution (Robinson 1976). To a lesser extent, until the time of Malinowski's (1927) functional theory of culture, the sexual was thought to be a biological driven individual desire that was functionally satisfied within kinship and family organization, the aim of which was reproduction (Vance 1991; Herdt 1994). Subsequent social and cultural theory in anthropology rejected this idea and its biologism, and along with it, sexuality as an area of study was largely dropped for two generations, with the exception of Margaret Mead's (1935) New Guinea works (Vance 1991). Armchair ethnologists and philosophical accounts of sexuality, such as Freud's *Totem and Taboo* (1913), opened

Gilbert Herdt, Notes and Queries on Sexual Excitement in Sambia Culture, from *Etnofoor*, vol. 7, no. 2 (1994): 25–41. Slightly adapted/edited for this Reader. Reprinted with permission of Amsterdam Institute for Social Science Research (AISSR).

Sexualities in Anthropology: A Reader, edited by Andrew P. Lyons and Harriet D. Lyons
© 2011 Blackwell Publishing Ltd.

the question of sexuality in cross-cultural perspective, in spite of the prudishness of the times and the orthodoxy of studying social things *sui generis* (Tuzin 1991). However, the Freudians were to undermine the comparative project of sexuality by reducing all forms to a common presumed structure of the Oedipal complex.

It was in fact Malinowski's (1929) *The Sexual Life of Savages*, that Trobriands' masterpiece, which effectively challenged the Freudian and western model, initiating the steady but slow process of viewing sexuality as a legitimate part of the study of culture and society. Malinowski demonstrated better than any previous single study the limitations of the western biological/egocentric model. Trobrianders do not understand sexual excitement as a pure product of the self isolated in the lone individual apart from social relations and the cultural world, Malinowski would show. A variety of ethnographic works during the past generation have added to the comparative record and supported Malinowski's basic insight (reviewed in Herdt and Stoller 1990; and see Lindenbaum 1992). Recent work on sexuality has attempted to go beyond the notions of Foucault (1980) that all erotic forms and sexual excitement are but a social construction or an enlargement of the discourse on sexuality, that would control and suppress agency and desire in culture (see for examples, Miller 1993). Other studies have demonstrated the limitations of a simple 'cultural influence model' of sexuality that posits that sexual excitement and relations are only a product of the social surround (Vance 1991). Sexuality, we are beginning to 'rediscover,' is neither purely a product of culture nor of individual strivings and drives and power relations; the picture is more complex, especially as one takes into account the entire structure of sexuality across the lifecourse in societies (Gagnon 1989).

The comparative study of societies and meaning systems, the province of anthropology, thus remains deficient in the domain of sexual culture. The concept of sexual culture is now meant to conceptualize that domain of beliefs, rules, and meanings surrounding sexual conduct in a particular society and historical period (Parker 1991). Until recently, sexual culture was largely omitted from ethnographies. The reasons typically cited for this omission include the taboo on sex in society and science (Gagnon 1989), the difficulties of eliciting accurate sexual information in the absence of observation (Herdt and Stoller 1990), the fact that sexual acts are usually private in most cultures around the world (Mead 1961), and the ethical problems of participating directly in sexual relations with informants (Bolton 1992). For example, the inadequacies in theory and the gaps in method and practice in the anthropological study of sexuality surely obstructed the study of AIDS/STDs over the past decade, and hindered the construction of culturally sensitive AIDS education and prevention (Herdt 1992). These challenges remain present; nevertheless, a new generation of studies is emerging to creatively tackle the relevant issues (see Brummelhuis and Herdt, 1995).

The study of sexual excitement and sexual relations is particularly problematic for anthropology, both for historical reasons issuing from the early modern period of European culture, and for anthropology as a theoretical and methodological field. Premodern historical formations located sexuality differently than the ideologies of today, both with respect to same-sex and opposite-sex relations and desires, since it has been argued that their world view was based upon a category system of four genders (man, woman, whore, and sodomite; Trumbach 1994). It has been argued that the rise of the public health clinic, coincident with the institutionalization of folk and medical notions of the sexual in the nineteenth century, resulted in a profound secular shift in views: sexuality was then thought to originate inside the agent or the individual self, increasingly locating the site of erotic excitement away from the social world or real-life forces that would determine it (Foucault 1973, 1980). In the important work of Van der Meer (1994) on eighteenth century Netherlands, however, we are beginning to see the limitations of a Foucaultian view that would ascribe all sexual classification and desires to the medical sexological model of the later modern period. Freud (1905), for instance, believed that both sexual drives and sexual preference, rooted in the biological bisexuality of human development, issued from within the body, or the unconscious, of the actor. Certainly Freud and sexology in general had not yet repudiated the nineteenth century idea that the sexual classification of the person (male or female) and even the gendered identity of the human being (masculine or feminine) must be dimorphic, an idea that anthropology was to implicitly challenge through accounts of such cultural forms as the North American Indian *berdache* (Herdt 1991). Today 'biological force' explanations of sexuality remain intact in many fields; typically, they are focused on the conception of sexuality as a production of internal forces and mechanisms rather than of social and cultural affairs (Herdt 1994). Such claims are increasingly contested in cross-cultural and historical study.

Over the past twenty years or so, Foucault (1980) systematically questioned these views regarding the history of sexuality, suggesting that social practices as 'technologies' of desire and discourse serve to capture and continuously control the energies of actors and their sexuality in society. The 'repressive hypothesis,' in Foucault's well known critique of Freud, was a displacement from the social-historical sphere to the individual mind. The suppression of sexual diversity in society was simultaneously accompanied by a discourse on sexuality that made power increasingly dominated by sexual forms and relations. Thus, Foucault critiqued 'repression' as a mechanism of the unconscious (Herdt 1992), although he did not directly contradict the idea that the 'unconscious' exists, primarily because the individual actor in Foucaultian models is deprived of agency (Herdt 1993). The effect of Foucault's work was to shatter the idea that an essential sexuality existed apart from 'society,' and this opened the way for a rewriting of social histories of sexuality. This, in turn, was a boon to anthropological models. All work on the erotic and gender in cultural context was immediately subject to cultural criticism when it ignored variations across time or space. A rush of work then came from feminist writers, from gay and lesbian accounts, and later from the new and urgent sexuality studies triggered by the AIDS epidemic in all corners of the world (Herdt and Lindenbaum 1992). A new position emerged. Among many of the sexual cultures of the non-western world, it was argued, the power to create and consummate sexual excitement exists in and only through the

Other, typically regarded as the opposite sex, which may be regarded in the local community as either a 'friendly' or a 'hostile camp.' But whatever the attitude regarding social relations with prospective erotic partners, sexual excitement should not be seen as a biological event inside the actor; its locus is the time and space world, via the actions and incitements of another person.

Thus we arrive at the present, still formulaic and largely programmatic, theoretical position: the important secular shift has enabled but not yet fully taken hold in ethnographic accounts of the sexual. Thus, the omission of sexual desire, attraction, and sexual relations from ethnographic study is still present in accounts and because of the understanding of these conceptual changes it seems more glaring than ever. In the past, as the late Robert Stoller, an eminent American psychoanalyst and sex researcher once remarked, anthropologists seemed to have assumed that when sexual desire or excitement was needed to make social relations 'work,' the 'culture' somehow supplied 'it' automatically in the minds and bodies of the actors, regardless their agency or desires. There is a methodological reason, of course. Few ethnographers have had either the theoretical interest, training, or opportunity to undertake the kind of study that is necessary to provide the missing material of sexual excitement and desire (Herdt and Stoller 1990). Contemporary efforts to document sexuality remain emergent and tenuous, even among the new cohort of younger fieldworkers ready to study these issues of sexuality (Vance 1991).

Notes on Sambia Sexual Culture

In the New Guinea Highlands, the power to 'control' sexuality has long been interpreted as a problematic feature of local cultural models of 'sexual antagonism' in these societies. Classical social and culture theory regarded socio-sexual relations within the context of the struggle for political cohesion in these village polities (Allen 1967; Langness 1967). Later it was suggested that the body and its fluids, as well as shells and other exchange valuables, became a cultural 'location' or symbolic site of power and control in relations between the sexes, and perhaps even in male/male homoerotic relations (Lindenbaum 1984; Strathern 1988). Among the Sambia, there are numerous expressions of the struggle for the cultural regulation of sexuality and the body (Herdt 1982, 1993), and while the main outlines of these have been examined elsewhere, primarily in Herdt and Stoller (1990), some general issues merit reiteration here.

Sambia, one of several Anga-speaking peoples, organized in hunting and gardening economies around small villages that form a tribe numbering more than 2,000 people in the Eastern Highlands of Papua New Guinea. Most elements of culture and social organization were constructed around the nagging destructive presence of warfare in the area. Descent is patrilineal and residence is patrilocal, for example, to maximize the cohesion of the local group as a warriorhood. Hamlets are composed of tiny exogamous patriclans that facilitate marriage within the group and exchange with other hamlets, again based upon the local politics of warfare. Traditionally, all marriage was arranged; courtship is unknown; social relationships between the sexes are not only ritually polarized but often hostile. Like other Highlands societies, these segmentary descent groups are associated with a men's secret society that ideologically disparages women as dangerous creatures who can pollute men and deplete them of their masculine substance. The means of creating and maintaining the village-based secret society was primarily through the ritual initiation of boys beginning at age seven-to-ten and continuing until their arranged and consummated marriages, many years later. The warriorhood is guaranteed by collective ritual initiations connecting neighboring hamlets. Within a hamlet, this warriorhood is locally identified with the men's clubhouse, wherein all initiated bachelors reside. Married men also frequent the clubhouse constantly; and on occasion (during fight times, rituals, or their wives' menstrual periods) they sleep there. The account of Sambia culture and society has been published elsewhere and need not be repeated here (Herdt 1981).

Sexual development, according to the cultural ideals of the Sambia lifeplan, is viewed as fundamentally distinct for men and women. Sambia conceive of the development of maleness and femaleness in fundamentally different ways. Biological femaleness is considered 'naturally' competent and innately complete; maleness, on the other hand, is considered more problematic, since males are believed incapable of achieving adult reproductive manliness without ritual treatment. Girls are born with female genitalia, a birth canal, a womb, and behind that, a functional menstrual-blood organ or *tingu*. Feminine behaviors such as gardening and mothering are also thought to be by-products of their natural *tingu* functioning. As the *tingu* and womb become engorged with blood, puberty and the menarche occur; the menses regularly follow, and they are linked with the women's child-bearing capacities. According to the canonical male view, all a woman then needs is a penis (i.e., semen) in facilitating adult procreation by bestowing breast milk (transformed from semen) and thus enabling childbirth. According to the women's point of view, however, women are largely competent and produce their own breast milk – a point of conflict between the two gendered ontologies. This gives rise to a notion that women have a greater internal resilience and health than males, and an almost inexhaustible sexual appetite. By comparison, males are not competent at birth or later, until they achieve manhood, and thus they require constant interventions of ritual to facilitate maturation. All males have a semen organ (*keriku-keriku*) it is believed, but in boys, this is immature and empty and it will not activate without ritual assistance. The purpose of ritual insemination is to fill up the organ, and hence to masculine the boys' body, ultimately masculinizing his phallus. In short, Sambia sexual culture operates on the basis of a strongly essentializing model, of sexual development, yet it incorporates many ideas of social support and cultural creation of the sexual due to the role of ritual and the supporting structures of gendered ontologies throughout the lifecourse of men and women.

The sexual appetite of men is not matched by the growth of the male body or its abilities to sustain sexual aggression. The growth of males is believed to be slower and more difficult than that of females. Men say that boys lack an endogenous means for creating manliness. Males do possess a *tingu* organ but it is believed 'dry' and nonfunctional. They say that a mother's (contaminating) birth,

menstrual, and vaginal fluids impede masculine growth for the body until he is separated
by initiation from the women's world. Males
posses a semen organ but unlike the female
menstrual blood organ it remains small, hard,
and empty since it contains no semen of its
own and cannot manufacture any. Though
semen is believed to be the spark of human life
and, moreover, the sole precipitant of biological maleness (strong bones and muscles, and
later, male secondary sex-traits: a flat abdomen,
hairy body, mature glans penis), Sambia hold
that the human body cannot naturally produce
semen. It must be externally introduced, which
is the ritual function of fellatio. 'Excess' sperm
is stored in the semen organ for adult use. In
short, biological maleness is distinct from the
mere possession of male genitalia, and only
repeated inseminations begun at an early age
and regularly continued for years confer the
reproductive competence that culminates in
sexual development and manliness.

There are four functions of semen exchange.
These ritual practices (which I once called 'ritualized homosexuality' but now prefer to call
'boy-inseminating rites'; Herdt 1993a) have
several critical purposes necessary to the reproduction of Sambia culture and sexual structure. These included: (1) the cultural purpose
of 'growing' boys through insemination
thought to substitute for mother's milk; (2) the
'masculinizing' of boy's bodies, again through
insemination, but also through ritual ordeals
meant to prepare them for warrior life; (3) the
provision of 'sexual play' or pleasure for the
older youths, who had no other sexual outlet
prior to marriage; and (4) for the transmission
of semen and soul substance from one generation of clansmen to the next, which was vital
for spiritual and ritual power to achieve its
rightful ends (Herdt 1984). These elements of
institutionalized boy-inseminating practices
are the object of the most vital and secret ritual
teachings in first-stage initiation, which occurs
before puberty. The novices are expected to be
orally inseminated during the rituals and to
continue the practice on a regular basis for
years to come. The semen transactions, however homoerotic they may be, are rigidly structured; novices may only act as fellators in
private sexual interactions with older bach-

elors, who are typically seen as dominant and
in control of the same-sex contacts. The
adolescent youth is the erotically active party
during fellatio, for his erection and ejaculation
are necessary for intercourse, and a boy's oral
insemination is the socially prescribed outcome
of the encounter. Boys must never reverse roles
with the older partners, nor take younger partners before the proper ritual initiations. The
violation of such rules is a moral wrong that is
sanctioned by a variety of punishments. Boy-
inseminating, then, is a matter of sexual relations between unrelated kin and must be seen
in the same light as the semen exchanges of
delayed sister exchange marriage: hamlets of
potential enemies exchange women, and participate in semen exchange of boys, which is
necessary for the production of children and
the maturation of new warriors.

Sexual Excitement

What meanings attach to 'sexual excitement'
for the Sambia? Study of sexual excitement by
clinical investigators in the United States has
consistently shown that sexual excitement,
while distinctive for each individual in certain
respects, is nonetheless culturally shaped by
gender (Stoller 1979). The category of 'excitement' (kalu-mundereingdapinu) is subject to the
intense genderization so apparent in many other
areas of Sambia culture (Herdt 1981). It will
thus come as no surprise that among the Sambia,
the meanings and emotions of sexual excitement are also heavily gendered, with the expression of these meanings in line with the gender
ontologies of men versus women. These ontologies are given support by the ritual practices and
ideology of the men's secret society. Several
principles of Sambia sexual arousal may be outlined in brief. It should also be noted that these
principles generally take the male subject as the
locus of sexual action, typically denying female
sexuality the same agency as the male actor.

The hallmark of Sambia sexual theory is the
primacy of looking and the social basis of all
sexual interaction. First, sexual arousal occurs
only in and through the gaze (chembdu, to
look) by looking at another person. For Sambia,
the canonical idea of sexual excitement is that

one experiences sensations only after looking upon another, whether in the time/space world, or on another plane, most typically in a dream. Sambia believe that the gaze arouses sensations which pass through the eyes, down through the body, and into the genitals. (For a similar Melanesian theory, see Malinowski's 1929 sketch of Trobriand sexual theory.) Only gazing upon another person typically stimulates arousal; that is, Sambia do not have a cultural meaning that arousal may occur when one is alone or that the actor might be aroused by his or her own body, since no other is present to stimulate. When arousal occurs in the absence of another person, as when someone is sleeping or lying alone or sitting idly, it is not construed as being 'erotic' but for men is generally dismissed as the result of needing to urinate. (Urination typically ends the arousal.)

Second, the emergence of arousal suggests, then, that its aim is to achieve sexual congress with another, usually a flesh-and-blood person (whether man or woman, boy or girl) or a spirit (typically, an experience that is dreaded, even if men report retrospectively that it is exciting). Thus, Sambia do not have an idea of masturbation, as explained below, nor do they imagine that auto-stimulation to orgasm exists in human beings or could possibly be sexually satisfying.

Third, all arousal will take the other as its object, even in non-waking states, such as in dreams or trance (in shamans, for example; Herdt 1989). Direct experience with a flesh-and-blood person is preferred; but when the dreamer or spirit of the person encounters others during the state of sleep, their interaction, typically spirits or ghosts, may also arouse sexual excitement (Herdt 1989). This sexual encounter may produce results (such as ejaculation) which are manifest in the physical body of the sleeper, as in the case of a wet dream (*wunjaalyu*); a matter of shame for initiates, who are not supposed to have sexual intercourse before the proper initiation. This point suggests that sexual excitement in conscious waking life is generally under intense social control in the cultural surround.

Fourth, adult men may experience sexual excitement with either boys or women, and no distinction in the category of sexual excitement is made with regard to the gender of the object

of arousal. The other must of course be a sexually appropriate partner, meaning that they must not be tabooed by kinship relation, which in either case is interpreted as incest. However, there is a distinction typically made in the nature and intensity of the orgasm experienced, since among adult men it is generally reported that women are more sexually exciting than boys. Thus, men compare the 'sexual heat' of women's vaginas to that of boys' mouths, finding the latter less 'hot.' (For details, see Herdt 1984.)

Fifth, however, heterosexual adultery and premarital sexual relations in most cases are severely punished, thus leading to a strong regulation of thought as well as feeling directed to the prohibited categories of sexual partners. Of course, such ideas of sexual culture are mitigated by the fact that violations of kin norms do occur, with cases of extended family incest in male/female relations and cross-cousin incest in male/male relations, and these seem to be sexually exciting in spite of the taboos. While other factors are important in sexual culture, these are sufficient for understanding the problem of how the cultural regulation of the gaze results in a kind of repression of power in Sambia culture.

Ideas and feelings regarding sexual excitement are strongly gendered for the sexes and may be thought to constitute separable sexual ontologies. The anthropologist Hallowell (1955) served to define this area of ontology and culture better than any other scholar, and his fine and sensitive ethnographies of the Ojibwa and other American Indian peoples were instrumental in showing how their cultural being could become infused with many of the meanings of the erotic we would identify with 'desires.' The idea of sexual excitement in gendered ontologies must entail all the necessary constituents that create the desire for a genuine and satisfying life as a man or a woman; concepts of the whole person, time, space, and social and physical action; a vision of having a certain social and spiritual being; of locating this ontological being in a body that is like the ones represented in the symbolic media of ritual and myth and drama which occupy social space.

For men, they emphasize their being through concepts of the phallus and erection. A 'sex drive' discourse among men is prominent, in which they talk of arousal, especially penile arousal, as being auto-volitional, and beyond the control of the person. The penis, in short, is an independent agent, in this cultural imagination, one that frequently leads men into trouble, according to the Sambia view. (A view, incidentally, shared by other tribal peoples; Gregor 1985.) Among women, however, the forms of arousal are regarded as more closely related to their role as wives and sexual partners of their husbands. This does not mean (as Sambia men are wont to say: Herdt and Stoller 1990) that women do not experience sexual excitement, and orgasm specifically; it means that their discourse does not invite the 'penis as independent agent' meaning so common among adult men. In a more general way, sexual excitement is thought to result largely from the interpersonal interaction and exchanges between unrelated persons, especially in private and intimate contexts. This holds true of all relations between eligible actors, whether the same or opposite-sex.

The power of interpersonal relations is acute in looking and gazing upon another. Indeed, the gaze is filled with the power to infect and influence the other, even to bend the will of the other, especially in male/female relations. Thus to look or gaze (*chemdu*) is an aggressive act, the results of which are to initiate sexual intercourse by a kind of control over the actors, who profess to be disempowered by the other. Such is true of men's erotic gaze at women; but also of women's to men; and likewise of the homoerotic gaze directed from an older youth to a boy. This enigma – that a practice associated with power (the gaze) is felt to create a state of powerlessness in the actors involved – implicates some of the most vital and symbolically significant dynamics of sexuality and power relations among the Sambia and related traditions of the Melanesian circle (Herdt 1981, 1984). Thus we face the questions of examining through some notes and queries this problematic of the construction of sexual excitement through gazing in Sambia culture.

Sexuality, in short, is always an expression of the structure of particular relationships across time: in the case of the same sex, it is usually casual and non-exclusive; in marital relationships it is usually intense and exclusive. Semen is a major sign of how this system operates for males, a token of themselves, and how they can transmit identity to younger males. Not only ritual but myth charters their conceptions in sacred and secular arenas of social action.

Let us enter into the Sambia sexual ontology further by examining the example of self-stimulation, which typically would be constructed as the category 'masturbation' in our culture. The comparison between Sambia sexual culture and western culture is problematical, since masturbation has such distinct meanings and vicissitudes in each distinct subculture and historical tradition. In the United States, for example, while the Kinsey study showed the normative first sexual experience of the white middle-class adolescent male was self-arousal to orgasm soon after puberty (Gagnon 1971), females had a different experience, and ethnic minorities were not considered. A concept of masturbation in individual development of this kind does not exist for the Sambia, either as individuals or as a sexual culture (Herdt and Stoller 1990). In Sambia sexual theory, as we have seen, arousal and erotic experience occur through the glance and only with another, who is typically a warm-bodied sexual partner in the time and space world. Thus it is not surprising that 'masturbation' as a marked category of Sambia sexuality is unthinkable. Again, this does not suggest that children or even adults do not on occasion fondle their genitals; however, *they never do so to the point of orgasm and ejaculation* – which is the implicit meaning of the category in the United States. The account of this suggests that all sexual intercourse should be trained upon either the growing or the reproduction of another, and will, therefore, even in the case of sexual relations for pleasure, be consummated by reference to that other and not to arousal within the self (see also Herdt 1984; Herdt and Stoller 1990). Of course we need to realize the difference between petting and orgasm. But when we contrast this with the typical and average sexual development in, say, the United States, and specifically among boys, it is clear that adolescent sexual behavior begins in masturbation (Gagnon 1971). This suggests that the self is in some sense the object of its own desires; or to be more precise, we might say that the source of mental attraction, while it exists in the outer world, is filtered through the mind of the agent, but is consummated in the body of the agent, making a tripartite schema:

Sexual image (subjective representation) ⇒ bodily arousal ⇒ sexual arousal (with or without a partner)

By comparison it follows that the Sambia model would look like this:

Sexual gaze ⇒ sexual image ⇒ sexual interaction

In short, whereas the western biopsychological model begins in the internal image and ends in arousal (but not necessarily with another person), the Sambia view begins with the interpersonal gaze and ends with the socio-sexual relation, since it is not possible for Sambia to conceptualize sexual interaction with the self, even with the self as a proxy for another person. The sexual occurs only with the other.

Let us examine the effects of socio-sexual interaction on the body and the ontology of masculinity, focusing upon the aspect of semen accumulation and semen depletion in male development. Semen depletion is a key to understanding the male ontology and sexual excitement. Since maleness is based on a fantasized accumulation of a semen pool inside the body, the depletion of that precious fluid threatens not only maleness but existence itself. As I once suggested, this results in an idea of male atrophy: that is the phenomenon induced by ritual and suffered by men (Herdt 1980). The boy's body is like an empty reservoir that must be filled up; once filled, the semen organ sustains existence by supplying semen; yet when diminished continually without replenishment, the source of maleness – and thus, life itself, evaporates – so only debilitation and death can result. Here is contained the terrible dilemma of Sambia masculinity. The masculinization of the boy through insemination results in heterosexual reproduction – and their erotic pleasures – which in themselves require repeated ejaculations for 'growth' or 'babies.' But this also depletes one's only reserve of vitality. Someone's loss is thus someone else's gain: the psychological reality of depletion is difficult if not insufferable, and it has resulted in many compromises in defending one's personal fund of semen, especially regarding women. Regulation of heterosexual intercourse is a primary defense. But another is

also vital: adult men practice secret, customary ingestion of white tree sap in the forest. Men say that this tree sap 'replaces' ejaculated semen 'lost' through heterosexual intercourse. So men regularly drink tree sap after coitus in order to replenish maleness (Herdt 1981).

To enter into a different area of sexual culture, the male ideology of female ontology and sexual excitement: men deny in general the existence of female orgasm (Herdt 1981). Adult men are reluctant even to extend the categorical status of sexual orgasm – marked as *imbimboogu* in Sambia discourse – to the female experience under any condition, including the women's arousal in sexual intercourse with their husbands (Herdt and Stoller 1990). They will, however, generally regard a man's ejaculation as an orgasm or *imbimboogu*, and will extend even the male orgasmic experience into sleep, as in the wet dream, which is a rather thoroughgoing extension of the category. But are the men willing to extend their own feelings of sexual excitement to boys in the act of ritual insemination? In order to study the issues of sexual excitement further, we may now enter into a current debate on the interpretation of Sambia age-structured relationships.

No issue in recent reviews of the anthropological literature in Melanesia has inspired more debate than the basic question of whether – or to what extent – sexual feelings and erotic desires are motives or consequences of these cultural practices (reviewed in Herdt 1993; Knauft 1993). Does the boy desire sexual intercourse with the older male? Is the older male sexually attracted to the boy? How much is power and domination involved? Should we think of these relations as sexual and is 'desire' the proper concept with which to gauge the ontology of the budding boy? Or do other factors, such as ritual or kinship, produce the sexual attraction and excitement (conscious or unconscious) necessary to produce arousal and uphold the tradition (Herdt 1991)?

Boys and Men

Transforming Sambia boys as neutered objects into the erotic objects of older men's sexual relations is the task of ritual and the implicit aspiration of the male ontology in ritual development.

Once boys are initiated (between the ages of seven and ten) and their 'female' traces are removed through painful rites, they are inseminated through oral intercourse so they can grow, become strong, and reproduce. All younger males between the ages of seven and fourteen are inseminated by older bachelors, who were once themselves semen recipients. The younger initiates are the semen recipients until their third-stage 'puberty' ceremony; afterward they are semen donors to a new crop of younger initiates. The Sambia prescriptive rule allows youths, aged fifteen and older, to inseminate younger initiates for years, until the older males marry and father a child. According to the men's sacred lore and the dogmas of their secret society, the bachelors are 'married' to the younger recipient males – as symbolized by secret ritual flutes (themselves empowered by female spirits). Ritual 'death' and 'rebirth' are basic to boy-insemination: out of the symbolic processes of initiation a new person/self is born. To be more precise: the characteristic essences and signs of masculinity are formed, among which the growth of the penis leading to the 'birth' of the glans penis at puberty takes precedence over all else. The homoerotic relationships of boys, conducted for years, vitalize the process. Age-structured relationships are ideologically concerned with the ritual reproduction of the boys, with making them into men. With father-hood, sexual relations with boys are to cease by ritual edict; the men's marriages and duties to their children would be compromised by boy relations, Sambia men say. Thus, sexual relations are bounded clearly by culture, suggesting that the male system of ontological objects and excitement can be socially regulated.

The anticipation of this social control occurs early in how male ontology restricts the erotization of the boy's body and the shift of the erotic of boys into public arenas. Ritual insemination of boys is hidden from women and children; the secrecy is part of the male discourse on privilege and power. The sexual excitement of the older youth is based on his fetishization of the boy's mouth as a sexual orifice; so that he is uninterested in the body or personality of the boy. During intercourse, it is reported by initiates that most bachelors avoid touching the boy's genitals, or psychological

involvement with him as a whole person. All homoerotic inseminations are purported to have nutritive functions in 'growing' (i.e., masculinizing) boys, as well, so that the older male's account of his behavior, while accepting his pleasure, also stresses his obligation and duty to the men's society in the act of giving semen to the boy. Following marriage, when a youth's wife reaches the menarche, he should de-escalate his involvement in homosexual practices; and, with the achievement of father-hood, the vast number of Sambia men leave behind relations with boys, though they may yearn for the earlier period when they were free of responsibilities to their wives and families.

The experiences of same-gendered, age-graded insemination, first begun in ritual, thus fan out into an entire ontology of the boy-transforming-into-man, in secular contexts of all sorts that create a seamless relationship between body and psyche, sexuality, and sociality. This is the achievement of the Sambia system of sexual excitement. It is not ritual that 'grows' someone, but a man's semen; however, the ritual metaphor becomes an omnibus representation for thinking and talking about transforming a man's sexual partner into a cultural producer in all major areas of advantage: warfare, ritual, and marriage for reproduction. According to the male view of life, males and females differ in most respects of their being, [...] The [...] ritual development of the male is designed to create and reproduce their [Sambia] distinctive ontology and sexual culture.

Conclusion

The founding of modern anthropology was based in no small measure on the problem of the comparison of human groups, issuing from work conducted in Melanesia and the island of New Guinea in particular, since the last century, a part of colonial history which generally omitted sexuality and power from the record. The omission is curious but has no doubt to do with the problems inherent in how sexuality was suppressed at home and in the colonies as well (Herdt 1984; Knauft 1993). Melanesian studies might be said to have opened with the 'problem of comparison' created by the *Cambridge Expeditions to the Torres Straits*, that multi-disciplinary natural history river boat survey undertaken at the beginning of this century (*Reports* 1901–1935). However, it was fieldwork that forged anthropology – as dramatically and brilliantly presented in Malinowski's (1921) ethnographies of the Trobriands off the Southeastern coast of the island – that carried cultural study far beyond those of his teachers and mentors who had conducted the riverboat reports a generation earlier. By entering into the village, ambitiously and uncompromisingly making native language and culture study the new standard for the representation of the Other, anthropological science was greatly advanced, even in sexuality study, by that masterpiece, *The Sexual Life of Savages*. How many decades had to pass before anthropology was to rediscover sexuality (Vance 1991; Herdt and Stoller 1990).

Yet for all of recent work, the understanding of sexual excitement and attraction and the aesthetics of desire remains virtually nil in anthropology. Nearly a hundred years following the famed Cambridge expeditions a new generation of anthropologists have thus come to question not only the natives' ideas about sexuality and culture, but the very construction of transparent categories, as instantiated by that riverboat crew who would objectify and quantify the natural history and customs of Melanesia, leading to the science of comparison known as anthropology. The reasons for the hiatus in anthropology concern the very distinctive construction of sexuality in western culture – a reduction of the whole person to the sexual act and ironically the elimination of the sexual act from social relations, so that sexuality can be imagined to occur in the condition of arousal with the self as Other.

As Foucault (1973, 1980) has argued the relationship between the emergence of state control and the regulation of sexuality in social life, the extent of the power of the gaze was not only to objectify the other, but to create Otherness – a kind of alienation of the actor from his or her body and mind. A cultural ontology of the clinic and public health and the reduction of the whole person to the symptom or disease emerged; its cultural reality embodied the idea that to be gazed upon was to concede that the power to know stems from the act of seeing and the power to see or to gaze lies not in the self but in the practitioners. The argument is intriguing and is compelling in the western context. It is easy to see how sexuality could have come to be regarded as a 'disease' in this discourse, and how psychoanalysis and sexology emerged to 'treat' or 'cure' it. Only in the later part of this century, through the results of reform movements and the emerging embodiment of sexuality again, are we seeing a return to a model of psyche and social life that enables anthropology to rediscover sexuality (Vance 1991).

Nearly a century has passed since anthropology began the project of comparing cultures, but within this field, the comparative study of sexuality and sexual culture is much newer. In New Guinea it comes in the wake of colonial and scientific models eclipsed by new Pacific nations and scientific paradigms that debunk the project of comparativism and indeed the very fabric of anthropology itself, the stepchild, as it were, of old. It is fitting, therefore, that we should turn to issues of sexuality in answering the question, 'How can anthropologists describe and compare ethnographic regions?' (Knauft 1993:3).

For example, the anthropological study of age-structured homoerotic relations – the canonical mode of sexual relations between males in Melanesia – was typically conducted in the naive context of mixing western prejudices with local knowledge and ontologies and practices, but without the critical benefit of explicit comparisons to sexual cultures in other parts of the world, including those of western nations. This is problematical, however, since anthropological concepts utilized – especially 'homosexuality' itself – contain the marked categories and unmarked or implicit assumptions that preoccupied western discourse at the time. Thus, the categorical 'homosexual' as instantiated in nineteenth century medical discourse and as used in New Guinea descriptions, including my own, is overburdened with the intellectual baggage of the past, and I have discarded it in favor of 'boy inseminating rites' (Herdt 1993). By the early 1980s, and the discovery that a variety of Papuan peoples participated in a symbolic complex of ritual sexual beliefs and practices, it was possible to launch a new comparative project, *Ritualized Homosexuality in Melanesia* (Herdt ed. 1984), whose aim was the positive comparison of these groups. What a sea of changes has occurred that both the colonial figures and the "ethnographers" and their scientific world view are called into question and by turns reconstructed in the new anthropology of sexuality.

From these notes and queries on Sambia sexual culture it has been possible to raise the larger issues of comparison between western and non-western cultures. A recent collection on 'third sexes' and 'third genders' grapples with such a grand question by investigating the assumption of western culture that all people and all communities divide the world into twos, the dyad of male and female (Herdt ed. 1994). If we examine concepts of third sex across history and cultures, the variations on the western model are so impressive that they cannot help but persuade us of an ethnocentrism in the 'core' emic concept of sexuality as defined in the west. Here is but another example of how the project of anthropology to forge an understanding of the spectrum of human possibilities is leading to new questions and answers. Nearly a century has passed since the accounts of ritual sexuality became a matter of scientific concern to western life and we still understand little of this complex divergence between the western and non-western areas of meaning in sexual excitement and sexual culture. But at last we have entered a new historical era in which the kinds of descriptions and comparisons necessary to understand the varieties of sexual life begin to make sense of a much larger and more interesting sexual world than that imagined by western culture in the past.

REFERENCES

Allen, Michael
   1967   *Male Cults and Secret Initiations in Melanesia*. Melbourne: Melbourne University Press.
Bolton, Ralph
   1992   Mapping Terra Incognita: Sex Research for AIDS Prevention – An Urgent Agenda for the 1990s. In: G. Herdt and S. Lindenbaum (Eds.), *The Time of AIDS*. Newbury Park, CA: Sage Publications. Pp. 124–159.
Brummelhuis, Han ten and Gilbert Herdt (Eds.)
   1995   *Culture and Sexual Risk*. New York: Gordon and Breach.
Foucault, Michel
   1973   *The Birth of the Clinic*. New York: Pantheon Books.
Foucault, Michel
   1980   *The History of Sexuality*. Trans. R. Hurley. New York: Viking.
Freud, Sigmund
   1905   [1953] Three Essays on the Theory of Sexuality. *Standard edition of the complete psychological works of Siegmund Freud* 8. London: Hogarth Press.
Freud, Sigmund
   1913   [1955] Totem and Taboo. *Standard Edition*, Vol. 13:1–164. Ed. and trans. J. Strachey. London: Hogarth.
Gagnon, John
   1971   The Emergence of the Sexual in Early Adolescence. In: J. Kagan and R. Coles (eds), *Twelve to Sixteen. Early Adolescence*. New York: Norton. Pp. 231–257.
Gagnon, John
   1989   Disease and Desire. *Daedalus* 118: 47–77.
Gregor, Thomas
   1985   *Anxious Pleasures*. Chicago: University of Chicago Press.
Hallowell, A.I.
   1955   *Culture and Experience*. New York: Schocken Books.
Herdt, Gilbert
   1980   Semen Depletion and the Sense of Maleness. *Ethnopsychiatrica* 3:79–116.
Herdt, Gilbert
   1981   *Guardians of the Flutes*. New York: McGraw-Hill Book Co.
Herdt, Gilbert
   1984   Ritualized Homosexuality in the Male Cults of Melanesia, 1862–1982: An Introduction. In: G. Herdt (Ed.), *Ritualized Homosexuality in Melanesia*. Berkeley: Univ. of California Press. Pp. 1–80.
Herdt, Gilbert
   1987   *Sambia: Ritual and Gender in New Guinea*. New York: Holt, Rinehart and Winston.
Herdt, Gilbert
   1989   Self and Culture: Contexts of Religious Experience in Melanesia. In: G. Herdt and

M. Stephen (Eds.), *The Religious Imagination in New Guinea*. New Brunswick, NJ: Rutgers University Press. Pp. 15–40.

Herdt, Gilbert
1990   Secret Societies and Secret Collectives. *Oceania* 60:361–381.

Herdt, Gilbert
1991   Representations of Homosexuality in Traditional Societies: An Essay on Cultural Ontology and Historical Comparison, Part I. *Journal of the History of Sexuality* 2:602–632.

Herdt, Gilbert
1992   Introduction. In: G. Herdt and S. Lindenbaum (Eds.), *The Time of AIDS*. Newbury Park, Ca: Sage Publications. Pp. 3–26.

Herdt, Gilbert
1993a   Introduction. In: G. Herdt (Ed.), *Ritualized Homosexuality in Melanesia*. Berkeley: University of California Press. Pp. vii–xliv.

Herdt, Gilbert
1993b   Sexual Repression, Social Control, and Gender Hierarchy in Sambia Culture. In: B. Miller (Ed.), *Sex and Gender Hierarchies*. New York: Cambridge University Press. Pp. 193–211.

Herdt, Gilbert and Shirley Lindenbaum (Eds.)
1992   *The Time of AIDS*. Newbury Park: Sage Publications.

Herdt, Gilbert and Robert J. Stoller
1990   *Intimate Communications: Erotics and the Study of Culture*. New York: Columbia University Press.

Knauft, Bruce
1993   *South Coast New Guinea Cultures*. New York: Cambridge University Press.

Langness, L.L.
1967   Sexual Antagonism in the New Guinea Highlands: A BenaBena Example. *Oceania* 37:161–77.

Lindenbaum, Shirley
1992   Knowledge and Action in the Shadow of AIDS. In: G. Herdt and S. Lindenbaum (Eds.), *The Time of AIDS*. Newbury Park: Sage Publications. Pp. 319–34.

Malinowski, Bronislaw
1922   *Argonauts of the Western Pacific*. New York: Dutton.

Malinowski, Bronislaw
1927   *Sex and Repression in Savage Society*. Cleveland, OH: Meridian Books.

Malinowski, Bronislaw
1929   *The Sexual Life of Savages*. New York: Dutton.

Mead, Margaret
1935   *Sex and Temperament in Three Primitive Societies*. New York: William Morrow.

Mead, Margaret
1961   Cultural Determinants of Sexual Behavior. In: W.C. Young (Ed.), *Sex and Internal Secretions*. Baltimore, MD: Williams and Wilkins. Pp. 1433–479.

Miller, Barbara D. (Ed.)
1993   *Sex and Gender Hierarchies*. New York: Cambridge.

Parker, Richard *et al.*
1991   Sexual Culture, HIV Transmission, and AIDS Research. *Journal of Sex Research* 28:75–96.

Reports
1901–1935   *Reports of the Cambridge Anthropological Expedition to the Torres Straits*. 6 vols. Cambridge: Cambridge University Press.

Read, K.E.
1952   Nama Cult or the Central Highlands, New Guinea. *Oceania* 23(1):1–25.

Robinson, Paul
1976   *The Modernization of Sex*. New York: Harper and Row, Publishers.

Stoller, R.J.
1979   *Sexual Excitement*. New York: Pantheon Books.

Strathern, Marilyn
1988   *The Gender of the Gift*. Berkeley: University of California Press.

Trumbach, Randolph
1994   London's Sapphists: From Three Sexes to Four Genders in the Making of Modern Culture. In: G. Herdt (Ed.), *Third Sex, Third Gender*. New York: Zone Books. Pp. 111–36.

Tuzin, Donald
1991   Sex, Culture and the Anthropologist. *Social Science and Medicine* 33:867–74.

Van der Meer, Theo
1994   Sodomy and the Pursuit of a Third Sex in the Early Modern Period. In: G. Herdt (Ed.), *Third Sex, Third Gender*. New York: Zone Books. Pp. 137–212.

Vance, Carole S.
1991   Anthropology Rediscovers Sexuality: A Theoretical Comment. *Social Science and Medicine* 33(8):875–84.

Williams, F.E.
1936   *Papuans of the Trans-fly*. Oxford: The Clarendon Press.

24

Causing a Commotion: Public Scandal as Resistance Among Brazilian Transgendered Prostitutes

Don Kulick

The political scientist James Scott's 1990 book *Domination and the arts of resistance* is a widely reviewed and influential attempt to theorize power and how groups articulate resistance to domination. Drawing his examples widely from anthropology, history, literature and linguistics, Scott argues that powerless groups in society frequently do not openly express their opposition to the dominant: not because they are the dupes of hegemonic power, as some social theorists have argued, but, rather, because open resistance is practically impossible, for the dominant are often so powerful that the consequences of open resistance would be too severe to bear.

Scott explains that in such situations, there are four principal varieties of oppositional or resistant discourse open to subordinate groups (1990:18–19). These are, in increasing order of open conflict: (1) appeals to the public self-image of dominant groups, whereby subordinate groups attain rights and privileges by obsequiously appealing to the dominant group's own presentations of itself – the King as protector, the slaveowner as facilitator of

Christian teaching, etc.; (2) an offstage counter-discourse that members of the subordinate group can develop in private, but not articulate in interaction with members of the dominant groups; (3) purposely ambiguous practices of subversion such as rumour, innuendo, tropes and euphemisms that criticize the dominant order without appearing to do so; and (4) open conflictual interactions, where what Scott calls the normally veiled, 'hidden transcript' of the subordinate group ruptures normal decorum and extrudes into the public realm.

A key idea in Scott's book is that the 'hidden transcripts' of subordinate groups will articulate ideas and values that 'reverse and negate' (1990: 44) those which are generated by the dominant group and which structure normal social interaction between the two groups. So if what Scott calls the dominant, official 'public transcript' holds that slaves are morally, socially and mentally inferior to their owners, for example, then the hidden transcript will articulate the opposite, and will be animated by desires of social reversal – what Scott, drawing on the work of Christopher

Don Kulick, Causing a Commotion: Public Scandal as Resistance Among Brazilian Transgendered Prostitutes, from *Anthropology Today*, vol. 12, no. 6 (Dec 1996): 3–7. Reprinted with permission of Wiley-Blackwell.

Hill and others, discusses as fantasies of a 'world upside down' (1990: 36–44, 156–182). In this theoretical model of resistance, then, the subordinate group's own language is 'contrapuntal': 'the repository of assertions whose open expression would be dangerous' (1990: 25, 40), and resistance is the repetition and enactment of those oppositional assertions either covertly, or, in rare instances, openly and defiantly.

The arguments about hegemony, power and the dynamics of resistance that Scott develops in *Domination and the arts of resistance* have been widely discussed by political scientists, sociologists and historians, and the ideas are gaining currency within an anthropology increasingly concerned with articulating people's ability and desire to resist hegemonic and often violent economic and cultural forces. Recently, however, the linguistic anthropologist Susan Gal (Gal 1995), in a lengthy review essay, has severely criticized Scott, arguing, among other things, that his notion of a 'hidden transcript' is shallow, and that his understanding of the relationship between language and resistance wrongly assumes that linguistic forms such as euphemism, indirection and tropes are transparent, context-independent windows onto a resistant consciousness.

Travestis

My goal here is to extend the critical examination of Scott's work begun by Susan Gal. In this paper, I will explore issues of domination, resistance and violence, but I will be doing so by analysing a type of opposition of the weak that differs from anything Scott considers in his book. The examples will be taken from my current work on transgendered prostitutes in the Brazilian city of Salvador. What I will demonstrate is that the transgendered prostitutes among whom I work resist dominant depictions of them and their lives, but not by countering those portrayals with alternative, oppositional, offstage-generated, 'hidden' ones of their own design. Instead, they oppose and resist hegemonic notions of gender and sexuality that degrade them by drawing on precisely those notions, and using them to

their own advantage in their interactions with members of the dominant group (in this case: males who are perceived to be 'normal', heterosexual men). Not only is this a type of oppositional practice not anywhere considered by James Scott, but it also calls into question some of Scott's basic understandings of what 'hidden transcripts' are and how they are deployed.

My data for this discussion are drawn from my 8 month long linguistic anthropological work among Brazilian transgendered prostitutes living in the city of Salvador, capital of the northeastern state of Bahia.[1] Transgendered prostitutes, called *travestis* in Brazilian Portuguese, are males who, sometimes beginning at ages as young as 8, begin wearing cosmetics and androgynous clothing. By the time they are in their early teens, many of these males are already wearing feminine clothing, cosmetics and hairstyles, and they are already consuming or injecting large quantities of female hormones, which are easily and cheaply purchased over the counter at any pharmacy in Brazil. The hormones are intended to modify the males' bodies to look more feminine. By the time they reach their late teens, many travestis have, in addition to consuming female hormones, begun injecting industrial silicone into their bodies (industrial silicone is a kind of plastic used to make automobile dashboards). The purpose of the silicone injections is to augment buttocks, hips, thighs and sometimes breasts, so that these become abundantly feminine. The majority of travestis in my acquaintance have injected between 2 and 5 litres of industrial silicone into their bodies. One very well-known travesti in Salvador, however, had 12 litres. And one travesti who no longer lives in Salvador is said to have 18 litres.

Travestis exist in virtually all towns of any size throughout Brazil, and in the large cities of Rio de Janeiro and São Paulo, they number in the thousands. Most travestis in large cities work as prostitutes, and in Salvador, virtually all travestis work as street prostitutes. One important fact about travestis to have clear from the beginning is that unlike northern European and North American transsexuals, almost no travesti self-identifies as a woman.

That is, though travestis habitually adopt female dress, hairstyles, cosmetics, names, address forms and linguistic pronouns, and though they irrevocably modify their bodies to attain stereotypically feminine forms, travestis do not consider themselves to be women, and the idea that they might be transsexuals – 'women trapped in men's bodies' – is vigorously rejected by virtually all of them. Another significant difference between transsexuals and travestis is that whereas the majority of North American and northern European transsexuals self-identify as heterosexual, all travestis self-identify as homosexual (*veado* or *bicha* in the vernacular).

Targets of Violence

As homosexuals and as transgendered street prostitutes, travestis find themselves obliged to reassert continually their rights to occupy urban space, and they lead their lives aware that they may, at any moment, suddenly become the target of verbal harassment and/or physical violence from anyone who feels provoked by their presence in that space. All this means that violence is an integral part of a travesti's daily existence. While working on the streets at night, travestis are continually harassed by policemen, and by passers-by in cars and busses. Much of this harassment takes the form of verbal abuse, but policemen also assault, rob and brutalize travestis; gangs of young men sometimes severely bash them; and people speeding by in cars often throw at them objects such as rocks and bottles. Sometimes they even shoot them.

Even when she[2] isn't working, a travesti walking down a city street will tend to attract attention, and she must be continually prepared to confront abusive remarks from men and women, or physical violence from males who feel themselves to be provoked by the presence of travestis in public space.

Violence against travestis is so widespread and common that it receives regular attention in the Brazilian press, but usually only when a travesti corpse is discovered (although many times even this will elicit no mention in local newspapers) or when there is a wave of mur-

ders, such as when the *Folha de São Paulo* ran a series of reports after 16 travestis in São Paulo had been shot in the head during the first three months of 1993. Also relatively common in Brazilian newspapers are reports about crimes committed by travestis. These reports uniformly portray them as vicious, armed, drug addicted, AIDS-spreading criminals who lure men into dangerous situations and then assault them, often disturbing the public peace and causing pandemonium in the process. The newspaper article below, which appeared in the largest daily newspaper in Salvador (*A Tarde*), in August 1995, is a kind of concentration of these themes. The only detail lacking in this article that frequently appears alongside texts about travestis is a line drawing depicting ridiculously masculine looking males in wigs pulling one another's hair or brandishing menacing knives at frightened men.

Travesti attacks young man with a razor in Pituba

During more than 15 minutes of total pandemonium, motorists stopped their cars to observe the actions of the bloody battle provoked by the travesti known as 'Karine', who frequents the Our Lady of the Light Square, in Pituba, to attract customers. The victim, who attempted to flee from well-aimed blows of a razor, was Roberto Carlos de Conceição Santos, 26 years old, from São Gonçalo dos Campos.

The event occurred at about 10 p.m. on Tuesday. The Our Lady of the Light Square was bustling with the presence of numerous travestis and prostitutes, who every night until daybreak afflict this dignified area of the Pituba neighborhood, not even respecting the presence of the soldiers stationed at the Military Police post there. 'Karine', a lanky mulata, 1.80 metres tall, in high heels, probably drugged, was inviting men to take part in amorous encounters. Incredible as it may seem, despite the threat of AIDS and a series of other dangerous diseases, men continue to frequent this locale to seek out travestis.

Chase

'Karine's' insistence finally attracted Roberto Carlos, who had already been in the area for more than an hour watching the travestis [!]. The two approach one another, according to a witness, and hold a quick dialogue. After this, the two disappear for several minutes, and, when there were fewer people about, 'Karine' reappears, running after Roberto Carlos, armed with a razor. The young man attempts to flee, but receives a deep blow to his right shoulder, even cutting his shirt. Blood begins flowing quickly, and people begin to scream, attracting the attention of passers-by and motorists.

Having already removed her high heels, 'Karine' continues chasing Roberto Carlos and strikes him again, this time in the back. The young man throws himself into the middle of the road, with his shirt soaked with blood, and 'Karine' keeps up her chase. A third deep cut is made on the right arm of Roberto, who is unable to continue fleeing.[3]

This article, like the vast majority of newspaper articles about travestis, appeared in the crime pages, which constitute a special section of every Brazilian newspaper. Generally speaking, whenever travestis do appear in the news, they are featured there as dangerous criminals, as in the article above, or as corpses (often photographed in lurid close-up).[4] An interesting linguistic difference between these two journalistic depictions of travestis is that whenever they are accused of committing violence, this is always clearly spelled out in headlines. So, for example, a headline will read 'Travesti attacks young man with razor at Pituba' [Travesti ataca rapaz a navalhadas na Pituba], as it does in the example above, or 'Reporter wounded by travesti' [Repórter foi furtado por um travesti], or 'Assassinated with a knife in a car by a travesti' [Assassinado a faca no automóvel pelo travesti]).

In stark contrast to this, reports of violence against travestis are often either without agents (so we get, for example, '16th travesti in 90 days murdered in São Paulo' [Assassinado em São Paulo o 16° travesti em 90 dias]; 'August begins with the taste of blood: First victim is travesti' [Agosto começa com gosto de sangue: Primeira vítima é travesti], and 'Three are killed at Ponto Negra' [Três são mortos em Ponta Negra]), or the agentive, subject position of the sentence is filled with an instrument – a knife, or a gun, or a blow – not a person. (For instance, 'Death in Pigalle: Brazilian assassinated with shots from a hunting rifle' [Morte

em Pigalle: Brasileiro assassinado com tiros de fuzil de caça], or 'Floripedes, the travesti, murdered with blow' [Floripedes, o travesti, assassinado a murro]). Thus in the case of reports about violence committed by travestis, agency and responsibility are underscored and foregrounded. Reports about violence inflicted on travestis, in contrast, often elide the agency of those responsible for the violence, or displace it onto weapons, in ways that leave in the background the perpetrators of the crimes (cf. Henley et al. 1995).

In any case, my point here is that regardless of whether they are seen as perpetrators of violence or its victims, there is an extremely salient link in the Brazilian popular imagination between travestis and violence. To be a travesti, so the story goes, is to lead a violent life, live in a violent, criminal milieu, commit violence against others, and risk being the victim of violence oneself.

But what about the objects of this discourse? What do travestis themselves think about all this? What is their relationship to violent acts?

Perpetrators of Violence

I learned very quickly in my work with various travestis that violence is a continual topic of concern and conversation. Travestis in Salvador spend a great deal of time discussing brutal police acts against them, and they continually keep one another informed about the current state of the street in all four areas of the city where they work. A police sweep along the highway at Pituba (the suburb mentioned in the newspaper article quoted above) will have travestis hopping into taxis and heading for the other areas in which travesti prostitution occurs. Similarly, repeated violent acts by known criminals or by gangs of males in Barra (another area where travestis work) will send the travestis who work there to Ajuda, or Pituba, or Aflitos for the rest of the evening, and maybe for several nights after that, until things return to normal. Whenever one travesti asks another how the street in a particular area of the city is (Como tá a rua?), she is asking both whether there is sufficient movimento (traffic) there to make money, and whether there is a risk of violence at the hands of police and others.

In addition to concerns about their personal safety, however, travestis also talk a great deal about the violence that they inflict on the clients who buy their sexual services. The overwhelming majority of travestis in Salvador habitually rob their clients (and only their clients, despite widespread beliefs that travestis assault anyone they set eyes on). Indeed, even though I was initially drawn to travestis because I did not understand *them* (i.e. I did not understand why they modified their bodies or how they constructed their identities as gendered persons), the people I gradually came to see as somehow even more puzzling than travestis were the clients, who returned time and again to travestis, despite the fact that they could virtually count on being pickpocketed, assaulted or coerced into giving the travesti all the money they carried (and frequently their watches and other valuables as well).

Men who pay travestis for sex are males of all ages, races and social classes. I spent virtually every night during my eight month fieldwork in the company of travestis working in different parts of Salvador, and taking note of the men who pulled up in their cars or who went with travestis off into dark alleys or cheap hotel rooms, I was unable to discern any one type of man who could be considered the 'average' client. The only thing that the overwhelming majority of clients seem to have in common, all travestis are agreed, is that they self-identify as heterosexual and maintain relationships with women. Beyond that, they range from about 13 to about 60 years old (the majority being between about 17–45 years old), they are white, black and everything in between, and they can be extremely poor or extremely wealthy and everything in between.[5] Different parts of Salvador attract different clients: so the highway running through the middle class suburb of Pituba attracts more middle-class men in cars than do the narrow streets and alleys in the centre of the city, where clients tend to be poorer and on foot. Travestis in Salvador are very familiar with the sexual and economic topography of their city, and they work different parts of the

city depending partly on how far from their rooms they feel like travelling and partly on how much money they need or want to make in a night.

Pickpocketing

Regardless of who they are and where they encounter them, travestis rob their clients. This happens in one of several ways. The most common way is by pickpocketing them. Pickpocketing (known variously in travesti slang as *azuelar, dar a Elza, dar uma churria, beijar,* which literally means 'kiss', or *dar uma dedadinha,* 'insert a little finger') can occur with truly magical speed as a travesti stands massaging a potential client's penis while negotiating a sexual encounter on the street: I have seen one particularly skilful travesti remove a potential client's wallet, count the money, take most of it, replace a tiny amount of money plus the man's identity card, and put the wallet back in his pocket it in matter of seconds, all the while she was keeping him distracted by squeezing his penis with one hand (while she slipped his wallet out of his back pocket) and turning her back to him to rub her bottom against his crotch (in order to examine the contents of the wallet)

Pickpocketing also commonly occurs while a travesti performs oral sex on a client in the client's car. Here the trick is to get the client to lower his trousers so that they are on the floor, and for the travesti to position herself across the client's lap in such a way that her body, and especially her hair, which she will repeatedly fluff up and toss in the direction of the client's face – this is known as *jogar o cabelo* – will obscure the client's view of what the travesti is doing with her hands while her mouth is busy performing other services. Similar pickpocketing occurs during other forms of sex, in hotel rooms, in the travesti's own room, or on the beach at night. Generally speaking, anywhere a client lowers his trousers or removes his clothing (travestis know that many men keep their money in their shoes, so those are often removed and examined at some point during a sexual encounter) is a situation in which a travesti will attempt to extract money.

Assault

A second form of robbery against clients is direct assault (also *azuelar,* or *grudar, pegar*). This occurs if the travesti judges that the client is *mole,* soft. Usually the travesti has also determined that her client doesn't have a weapon, or, alternatively, she has already located a weapon in the client's car or clothing, and she has taken it herself. When the travesti is reasonably sure that she can overpower her client, she will grab his shirt at the neck and press him up against a wall or his car door, demanding money. This inevitably occurs at the conclusion of the sexual encounter, most commonly right after the client has paid the price that he and the travesti had agreed upon before the encounter. As one travesti explained to me when we were talking about assaulting clients: 'If a man opens his wallet for me, Don, and pays me 50 [*reais* – approximately US$50], and he has more than that [in the wallet], he's gonna give me it all' (*Se o homem abrir a carteira pra mim Don e me pagar cinqüenta, e ele tiver mas do que equele, ele vai me dar tudo*).

In assaulting their clients, travestis sometimes employ knives or razors or small nail-scissors, and one of my closest travesti friends sometimes uses a syringe that she fills with tomato extract and presses against the necks of clients, telling them that the red fluid inside is HIV-infected blood. No travesti in Salvador uses guns to assault clients, largely because they know that armed assaults are regarded by police and the courts as much graver than assaults with other weapons, and if they are caught in the possession of a firearm, the consequences for themselves would be serious indeed.

Travestis frequently cooperate with one another in assaulting clients, in a system known as *fazer a portinha* (lit. 'do the car door'). This occurs when a client, after sex, drives a travesti back to the place where he picked her up (all travestis insist on this). As he stops the car for her to get out, the travesti will yank the key from the ignition and make her demands. At this point, one or more other travestis will come to their colleague's assistance and position themselves in front of the door on the driver's side, thereby blocking the driver's exit, and adding a further degree of menace to the situation. If the driver gives the travesti more money, his key will be returned and he will be allowed to drive away. If he resists, he will be openly struggled with and robbed.

Giving a Scandal

The third means of extracting more money from a client is the one that most interests me in this article, because of the challenge it represents to James Scott's understandings of power and resistance. This third means of extracting money from a client is one that travestis refer to as *fazer um rebucetê,* or as *dar um escândalo –* give a scandal. A scandal consists of a travesti publicly attempting to shame a client into compliance with her demands for more money. Scandals will be given if pickpocketing has been unsuccessful, if direct assault is for some reason impossible, if the client has discovered that the travesti has robbed or attempted to rob him and becomes aggressive, or if the client has no more money or valuables than have already been given to (or taken by) the travesti, but has been discovered to have an automatic teller bank-card or a chequebook (travestis will accompany clients to bank teller machines and wait for them to withdraw money. They also accept cheques for their services). In each of these cases, a travesti may decide to give a scandal.

A scandal consists of loud, abusive cries at the client that he is a *maricona safada* or *maricona desgraçada* (a 'disgusting faggot' or 'disgraceful faggot') who has engaged the services of a travesti and who, afterwards, is refusing to pay the agreed upon price. The key lexical item here, one that features prominently in all scandals, is *maricona*; a word that contains the culturally weighty assertion that the referent is a homosexual who enjoys being anally penetrated. Regardless of whether or not the client was in fact penetrated during sex with the travesti, the travesti will announce that she has 'eaten [penetrated] the ass' (*comi o cu*) of the client, and she will expand and embellish that announcement with details of how the client 'sucked [her] dick' (*chupou meu pau*), and how he wanted to be called by female names during sex. Extended scandals frequently also involve the travesti removing or threatening to remove all her clothing as she stands half-inside or beside the client's car (if a travesti has left the client's car to give a scandal, she will have also taken the car key or the client's identity card with her) or just outside the hotel room where she has had sex with the client.

The threatened or actual disrobings, and the language that foregrounds penetration, and oral sex performed by the client, are all craftily designed to draw public sharp attention to a very particular feature of the travesti's anatomy: her penis. Now in their day-to-day lives, travestis employ a number of practices (such as pulling the penis between the legs and wearing tight underpants to keep it in place there) to conceal their penis, even from their live-in boyfriends (Kulick n.d.). In scandals, however, the penis is removed from concealment and vigorously brought forth, both linguistically and, sometimes, physically as well. The reason for this revelation, of course, is to draw public attention to the fact that a male has had sex with another male. Travestis give scandals on the assumption that a client will be so mortified at the thought of being publicly revealed to have had sex with a male that he will hurriedly comply with the demands for more money just to get away and avoid an even bigger scandal that could have serious repercussions for his private and professional life. Nine times out of ten, travestis are correct in their assumptions, and the client being publicly shamed quite quickly acquiesces by giving the travesti his watch, or by writing her a cheque or by suddenly discovering more money hidden somewhere in his car.

What is important to perceive here is the cultural background against which travesti assumptions about scandals exist. The reason why scandals have coercive power – the reason why they make pragmatic sense and why they work – is because it is considered to be profoundly disgraceful in Brazil for a male to perform oral sex on another male, or, even worse, for a male to be anally penetrated by another male.

One of the main reasons for this disgrace is because sexuality and gender are configured in

such a way in Brazil that to perform these acts means that one is no longer a man. As anthropological studies of gender in Latin American and Mediterranean countries have abundantly demonstrated, males in those countries who allow another male's penis to enter their own body, either orally or anally, become symbolically resignified and regendered. They are no longer 'real' men – they become feminized men, homosexuals. And in that capacity, they often become the targets of all the many violent practices that have been developed in those countries to stigmatize and harass males who fail to maintain appropriate gendered behaviour.

In publicly calling a client a *maricona* during a scandal, therefore, a travesti accomplishes four significant discursive significations. First, she publicly engenders herself as a person in possession of a penis – that is, as a male. Second, she therefore announces that the ostensibly heterosexual client who has paid her for sex is, in fact, *homo*sexual. Third, because sexuality and gender are configured in such a way in Brazil that to be a *maricona* is to no longer be a man, a travesti's words during a scandal simultaneously engender the client: he stops being a man and becomes reconfigured as feminine. But fourth, because the person who has penetrated him (i.e. the travesti) is an effeminate homosexual herself, scandals proclaim that the client is just as homosexual and even more feminine than a travesti. The pragmatic punch packed by a scandal is, thus, potent indeed.

Scandals and Resistance Theory

The key thing to note here is that when travestis reconfigure their ostensibly heterosexual male clients as feminized homosexuals in this way, and use the label *maricona* to abuse and shame them, they are purposefully drawing on precisely the same attitudes and invoking precisely the same kinds of language that are continually drawn on and invoked by others to repress *them* as homosexuals and as transgendered individuals, and that motivate the violence directed against *them* by policemen, passers-by in cars, and gangs of young men.

Such a discursive strategy is extremely difficult to account for in terms of the theory of resistance that James Scott attempts to work out in the book with which I began this paper. Travesti *escândalos* fit nowhere into Scott's typology of how subjugated groups resist those who dominate them. Referring back to the first three varieties of oppositional discourse that Scott discusses in his typology, and that are listed at the beginning of this paper, it is clear that there is nothing obsequious, veiled or ambiguous about scandals. Quite the opposite. And even though scandals could be considered to be an example of Scott's fourth type of resistant discourse – discourse that is openly confrontational – they differ significantly from what Scott has in mind here, because they do not give voice to some otherwise 'hidden transcript' which opposes or challenges the public attitudes that result in travestis and other homosexuals being routinely discriminated against, assaulted and murdered. On the contrary, in these scandals, travestis enunciate and employ exactly those attitudes in order to coerce their clients into acceding to their demands for more money.

Instead of offering up some oppositional, inverted view of social order, what travestis who have scandals are doing is expanding the sphere of their own subordinate, abject status so that it moves to envelop individual members of the group who uphold the structures that keep travestis and other homosexuals marginalized and dominated. Scandals *abjectify* members of the dominant group. They appropriate the language of the dominant and use it to draw the dominant into the despised realm of the dominated. They resist by turning the dominant language against members of the dominant group: asserting that the dominant are secretly just as sexually perverse and transgendered as those whom the dominant employ violent discursive and practical arsenals to oppress.

There is a dynamic at work in travesti scandals that Scott does not consider in his work. Indeed, given Scott's insistence that subordinate groups resist the representations generated by the powerful, one kind of subordinated group whose existence cannot be broached in his framework is the subordinated group that has great investment in maintaining the structures which keep it subordinated. And given

Scott's understanding of resistant discourse as a 'hidden transcript' that articulates inverse, oppositional values, one kind of resistant discourse whose dynamics cannot be explained is the invocation of the public transcript by members of repressed groups to resignify the strong and draw them into the realm of the weak.

One of the criticisms most frequently levelled at attempts to understand resistance is that they tend to romanticize their object of study. Although James Scott is a sophisticated scholar who is obviously aware of this danger, in the end I must agree with Susan Gal (1995:420) that his understanding of resistance is heavily sugar-coated. The examples that Scott examines are, without exception, examples of resistance by groups whose interests resonate deeply with traditional liberal ideals of equality, freedom and justice for all. It is surely satisfying and certainly it is politically fortifying to be able to uncover hidden resistance in the everyday practices of slaves, peasants, workers, 'untouchables' and colonial subjects. But by concentrating only on such groups, Scott loads his dice. By choosing not to examine the resistance offered by oppressed groups whose goals may not always fit snugly with North American liberal political agendas, he not only ignores an entire spectrum of empirical data; he also fatally cripples any attempt to articulate a general theory of resistance.

The type of resistance I have described in this paper repels liberal attempts to understand it. One would be hard pressed to see anything particularly lofty in it. It does not strive for a 'world upside down', a society in which oppression will vanish and equality will reign. On the contrary, it depends for its effectiveness on structures and attitudes that maintain oppression and affirm inequality. It actively reproduces the structures that subordinate those who employ it. It is not pretty. But it is resistance nonetheless. It is a set of practices employed by a violently oppressed group of people to survive and maybe even prosper in a society that despises them and regularly hurts and kills them. What it offers us, in its raw, shameless and utterly non-progressive way, is a challenge to our current theories, and an acrid corrective to any perspective on resistance that imagines it to be necessarily noble.

NOTES

Research support for fieldwork in Brazil was generously provided by the Swedish Council for Research in the Humanities and Social Sciences (HSFR) and the Wenner-Gren Foundation for Anthropological Research.

1 This paper is based on eight months of anthropological fieldwork and archival research in the city of Salvador. Located in the state of Bahia in northeastern Brazil, Salvador is the third largest city in the country, with a population of over two million people. In September 1994, January-April 1995, and July-October 1995, I conducted fieldwork in Salvador, living with travestis and visiting them nightly at their various points of prostitution. In addition to socializing with them more or less continually, I also recorded and transcribed a total of about 18 hours of naturally occurring conversation between travestis and others, and I conducted sixteen in-depth interviews (fifteen of the interviews are with individual travestis, and one is with the *marido*, or husband, of a travesti). These interviews lasted between one and a half and ten hours. All in all, my transcribed corpus of travesti speech is about 50 hours. All tapes of naturally occurring speech and several of the interviews were transcribed by myself together with Keila Simpsom, my travesti colleague and teacher. The majority of the interviews were transcribed by Inês Alfano, a professional transcriptionist. The transcripts prepared by Ines Alfano were subsequently checked (by listening to the tapes and going through the transcripts) by Keila Simpsom and myself.

2 As I noted above, travestis adopt female address forms and linguistic pronouns, even though they do not self-identify as women. The logic behind these linguistic forms, and, indeed, behind any other dimension of travesti gendered self-identification, is extremely complex, and is analysed in detail in another paper. I use feminine pronouns and possessives when discussing travestis not only in deference to their own linguistic practices, but also because I believe that travestis' linguistic practices perceptively and incisively enunciate core messages that are generated by their culture's arrangements of sexuality, gender and biological sex. For a detailed discussion of all this, see Kulick n.d.

3 Several days after this article (which is a translation of the Portuguese original) appeared in the paper, I met Karine on the street at night and recorded an interview with her about the incident refered to here. Her version of events differs dramatically from the newspaper's. 'Look', she told me and several fellow-travestis who had gathered to listen, 'it's like this. I was there on my corner working [*batalhando* literally "battling"], right? And he came up and asked for 5 reais [approx US$5]. I said I don't have 5 reais. And he said "you don't huh" and went away'. The man, whom Karine knew to be a petty criminal that had previously robbed other travestis and female prostitutes who worked in the area, returned later, accompanied by another man, and brandishing a club to which nails had been attached. He again demanded money, at which point Karine, feeling threatened, removed a small knife from her purse ('we have to defend ourselves, right?') and stabbed him. Karine was appalled at the report in A Tarde. 'They lied', she explained. 'It wasn't a razor. And he wasn't a client. He wasn't somebody who came to me wanting to pay for sex. He was a street criminal (*um marginal de rua*)'. Karine was apprehended by the police after this incident, but released after she paid them a small bribe (*um acuezinho*).

Since I did not witness the incident described by Karine and A Tarde, I can only speculate as to which of these two highly divergent accounts might be closer to 'the truth'. Based on everything I know about travestis, however, I find it extremely unlikely that a travesti would chase a client down the street and out into traffic just to stab him. As I document throughout this paper, travestis are not interested in injuring clients. They are only interested in robbing them, and there are a number of well developed ways of doing that, none of which involve running after them down city streets and stabbing them. I also know that it is not at all uncommon for men to try to rob travestis and female prostitutes who work in Pituba. And in addition to all this, I know, too, that the newspaper A Tarde is infamous in Salvador for its regular, virulent attacks on gays and travestis. The newspaper's profoundly homophobic attitude is evidenced fairly clearly by the tone in which the article about Karine is written. So my own educated guess, based on all this, is that Karine's own version of this incident is the much more believable one, and that the piece in *A Tarde* is one of the many instances of journalistic reports about travestis where interest in promoting and reinforcing derogatory stereotypes overrides concern to provide accurate information.

4 It is important, however, to not give the impression that travestis only ever appear in the news in this way. There are other images of travestis that circulate in Brazil, namely those that depict travestis as glamorous and mysterious objects of desire. Images underscoring the desirability of travestis reach a kind of frenzy every year during the famous Carnival celebrations that take place throughout the country in late February or early March. They are also present whenever famous travestis such as Roberta Close, Valéria, Thelma Lipp, or Jane di Castro are portrayed in the media. Indeed, the fact that travestis are depicted as both despicable and desirable throughout Brazil is another example of the pungent combination of patriarchal repression and steamy sensuality that so typifies the nation (and that so occupies everyone trying to 'understand' Brazil).

In this paper, however, I want to cut through the romantic images of travestis and emphatically foreground the fact that those travestis who work on the street as prostitutes are the victims of continual and brutal violence. I stress violence in this way both to reflect the experiences of my travesti friends in Salvador, and also because I am aware that many Brazilians, particularly in conversations with non-Brazilians, tend to play down the violence and play up the romance when they talk about travestis, in order to argue that Brazil is an unusually tolerant society. My point is that as far as the day-to-day lives of travestis through-

out Brazil are conc[...] tolerance at all. Only[...] abuse, and violence.

5 I have been unable to inter[...] a conversation with, any cli[...] The main reason for the comp[...] bility of clients is that public reve[...] fact that one has had sex with a t[...] for an overwhelming majority of men,[...] ful and embarrassing in the extreme: in[...] this shamefulness is precisely what *escân[...]* *los* depend on for their effectiveness. My[...] travesti co-worker Keila Simpsom is fond of[...] saying that if a survey were taken of all Brazilian men, it would conclude that not a single one of them has ever had sex with a travesti, since no one would ever admit to doing so.

REFERENCES

Gal, Susan
1995 Language and the 'arts of resistance'. *Cultural Anthropology* 10(3):407–424.
Henley, Nancy M., Michelle Miller, and Jo Anne Beazely
1995 Syntax, semantics, and sexual violence: agency and the passive voice. *Journal of Language and Social Psychology* 14 (1–2):60–84.
Kulick, Don, n.d.
Penetrating gender: Brazilian transgendered prostitutes and their relevance for an understanding of sexuality and gender in Latin America. Under review at *American Anthropologist*.
Scott, James C.
1990 *Domination and the arts of resistance: hidden transcripts.* New Haven and London: Yale U. P.

25

...igion and Desire: ...slim and *Gay* ...onesia

...om Boellstorff

Of Anthropology, Islam, and Incommensurability

Work in the anthropology of religion has long concerned itself with the relationship between orthodoxy and practice as well as the problem of making intelligible widely divergent religious beliefs (Tambiah 1990). Such problems of "cultural translation" (Asad 1986) within and across religious traditions have been important to anthropology from its beginnings (Frazer 1915; Tylor 1958) and through many key moments of consolidation and innovation – for instance, in the work of Clifford Geertz, to whom I return at the end of this article. As anthropologists adjust to a world powerfully redefined – like it or not – in terms of a "War on Terror," we confront a range of official and popular ideologies that portray religion, particularly Islam, as the source of unbridgeable difference. How can fundamentally conflicting understandings of religion and ultimate order regarding issues from jihad to same-sex marriage be understood and lived side by side in a diverse world?

Elizabeth Povinelli has diagnosed the problem posed by such fundamental conflicts of worldview as one of "incommensurability" (Povinelli 2001). Noting an increasing ethnographic emphasis on incommensurability, from the contradiction of "other modernities" in China (Rofel 1999) to the paradox of spirit possession in a globalizing Thailand (Morris 2000), Povinelli draws on philosophers of language to link incommensurability to the question of translation and its failures. In this article, I explore a case where cultural translation appears to meet its incommensurable limit: *gay* Muslims in Indonesia. (I keep *gay* in italics throughout because *gay* is a concept that partially translates the English concept "gay," without being reducible to it.)

In examining *gay* Muslims' sense of inhabiting incommensurability, I do not imply that other religions are more tolerant than Islam, as the enthusiasm for banning same-sex marriage amongst certain Christian groups in the United

Tom Boellstorff, Between Religion and Desire, Being Muslim and *Gay* in Indonesia, from *American Anthropologist*, vol. 107, no. 4 (2005): 575–585. Reproduced by permission of the American Anthropological Association and the author. Not for sale or further reproduction.

States clearly indicates. My interest lies rather in responses to circumstances in which public norms render *gay* and Muslim "ungrammatical" with each other. From the voices amplified from mosques five times a day to fasting during the month of Ramadan to living openly as a husband and wife, Islam in Indonesia (as in many other parts of the world) is not just a matter of personal belief and prayer; it constitutes a public sphere that includes the nation itself. Heterosexually identified Indonesian men find a longstanding, voluminous, and public Islamic discourse addressed to their transgressions and concerns. Sex between men, in contrast, is unintelligible: *Gay* Indonesians find above all the silence of incommensurability.[1] On the relatively rare occasions when Islamic figures speak of male homosexuality, it is typically in terms of absolute rejection: "Homosexuality is clearly a social illness, a morally evil trend that must be eliminated, not a human right to be protected as [Western] gays now claim."[2] Male homosexuality does not bifurcate into the meritorious and sinful: It is incomprehensible as a form of sexual selfhood, and this incommensurability is a fundamental difference between how *gay* Muslim Indonesians and heterosexually identified Muslim Indonesian men experience their sexualities.[3] This incommensurability is further strengthened by the fact that although both homosexuality and heterosexuality in contemporary Indonesia operate on global and national spatial scales, no local tradition or *adat* sanctions contemporary *gay* subjectivities, which are distinct from ritual transvestite practices (Boellstorff 2005: Chapter 2). Yet *gay* Muslims exist: So how do these Indonesians resolve the apparently incommensurate statuses of being *gay* and being Muslim?[4]

The special challenge of incommensurability in regard to male homosexuality (rather than those proscribed forms of male heterosexuality, like adultery, glossed as *zina*) becomes evident in relation to this public character of Islam in Indonesia, as in other Muslim majority countries. In his book *Sexuality in Islam*, the influential Tunisian scholar Abdelwahab Bouhdiba notes that:

Anything that violates the order of the world is a grave "disorder," a source of evil and anar-

chy. That is why zina (adultery) arouses such strong, unanimous condemnation. However, in a sense, zina still remains within the framework of order. It is a disorder in order: it does not strictly speaking violate the fundamental order of the world; it violates only its modalities. It is, in its own way, a form of harmony between the sexes. It is a false *nikah* (marriage), it is not an anti-nikah. It recognizes the harmonious complementarity of the sexes and its error lies in wishing to realize it outside the limits laid down by God. (Bouhdiba 1998:30–31)

Bouhdiba emphasizes that "Islam remains violently hostile to all other ways of realizing sexual desire, which are regarded as unnatural purely and simply because they run counter to the antithetical harmony of the sexes ... in Islam, male homosexuality stands for all the perversions and constitutes in a sense the depravity of depravities" (Bouhdiba 1998:31). Not all Muslims agree with Bouhdiba, but it is important to acknowledge the dominance of such views in Indonesia and elsewhere. For Bouhdiba, forms of proscribed heterosexuality, as forms of "false marriage," remain comprehensible within an Islamic framework; to use a linguistic metaphor, they are false utterances like "the earth is square." Male homosexuality, however, is not just false but ungrammatical, like "earth happy twelve the": For Bouhdiba and most Indonesians, sex between men is incommensurable with Islam.

This fundamental difference is starkly evident in the scholarship on Indonesian Islam, which correctly emphasizes Islam's public character (Gade 2004; Hefner 2000). For instance, in one of the most comprehensive studies of Indonesian Islamic thought in recent years, John Bowen notes that his "primary objects of study are socially embedded forms of public reasoning" (Bowen 2003:5). Yet although he emphasizes that "the constant element in the narrative concerns gender, the equality of rights and relationships among men and women" (Bowen 2003:5), the topic of homosexuality is entirely absent from his study. Similarly, M. B. Hooker's study of Islamic judgments makes only a single brief reference to a 1998 judgment forbidding male and female homosexuality (Hooker 2003:185). Robert Hefner's important

Civil Islam: Muslims and Democratization in Indonesia (2000) also ignores homosexuality. That these three (and many other) recent and comprehensive studies of Indonesian Islam make so little mention of homosexuality accurately reflects how, to date, homosexuality has been incommensurable with Islam as a public discourse in Indonesia.

If, as Bowen and many others have noted, Islam in Indonesia is not a unified dogma but a set of debates, what is significant is that with rare exceptions, homosexuality is not even debated in Indonesian Islam. (Compare this with the predominant place of homosexuality as the Christian Right's "perfect enemy" [Gallagher and Bull 2001].) It is not that there are not *gay* Muslims; as discussed below, most Indonesian *gay* men follow Islam. Nor is it that being *gay* is never public. Although for the most part the "*gay* world" exists as a kind of distributed network – a largely invisible archipelago – amidst the "normal world" of Indonesian national culture, there are cases in which male homosexuality appears in the mass media or other public venues. However, there has been virtually no context in which Islam and male homosexuality have come together in the public realm. Indonesians find ubiquitous public display of proper heterosexuality and frequent debate over improper heterosexuality, but there are no *gay* Muslim publics. Herein lies the incommensurability of being *gay* and being Muslim.

Spatial Scales and National Belonging

The incommensurability between Islam and male homosexuality in Indonesia is shaped by local and national spatial scales. Indonesia, the fourth most populous nation on earth, is home to more Muslims than any other country. Islam has spread through the archipelago since at least the 13th century, primarily through the trade networks that linked many coastal communities to each other and, via the Straits of Malacca, to the great commercial system linking the Far East with South Asia, Africa, the Arab world, and Europe (de Graaf 1970). The Dutch were the dominant colonial power in the region for the 350 years preceding World War

II; during this time, colonial officials like Snouck Hurgronje called for working against Islam as a potential political movement and strengthening understandings of it as a set of localized religious beliefs (Steenbrink 1993). This meant, above all, identifying Islam with discrete local customs (adat). To this day, "ethnolocality" is consistently framed as a starting point, the origin – however contested and reconfigured – of authenticity that is subsequently placed into dialogue with national and global spatial scales (Boellstorff 2002). This grounding in ethnolocality often leads to a shared frame of reference for modern-day Indonesian and modern-day Indonesianist alike: "I start from the level of the village disputes and work upwards" (Bowen 2003:6, see chapter 3).

Gay Muslims face a particular challenge because being *gay* is incommensurable with ethnolocality, this "level of the village" that is so important to notions of Islamic "selfhood" and "community" in the contemporary archipelago. It is self-evident to *gay* Indonesians (and other Indonesians) that the concept *gay* is not learned from one's elders or from traditional beliefs, and to date there have not been individuals terming themselves *gay Jawa* or *gay Bugis* or organizing communities based on such identifications: Being *gay* is a foundationally national concept linked to globalizing notions of homosexual subjectivity. *Gay* Muslims cannot retreat to "the level of the village" and must find other spatial scales in which to inhabit the incommensurable space of being *gay* and Muslim.

Islam is one of several official religions in Indonesia (the others are Protestantism, Catholicism, Buddhism, and Hinduism: all globally recognized religions rather than localized or "animist" traditions). Despite this concession to national unity, because nearly ninety percent of Indonesians are Muslim, an Islamic ethos predominates in national popular culture and many regions of the archipelago: Every president has been Muslim and it is widely understood that it could not be otherwise. The vast majority of my *gay* interlocutors have been Muslim. From the existence of a department of religion to the requirement that all Indonesians have an approved religion on their identity cards and marry within their faith, the state links publicly recognized religion to national belonging (Bowen 2003:178–185, 246–252).[5] In postcolonial Indonesia, every citizen is to have a religion just as they are to have a gender: It is an essential attribute of being modern. Having a sexuality is also modern: Worldwide, sexuality typically plays an important role in notions of proper citizenship (Bunzl 2004; Mosse 1985). Leslie Dwyer notes in her study of Indonesian family planning that "sexuality and gender may be reified as essential, non-negotiable attributes of national identity" (Dwyer 2000:27). Although family planning discourse focuses on women's sexuality, it shapes notions of "proper masculinity" as well, so that " 'to make sense as a man in Indonesia' one must get married and function effectively as a dutiful husband and provider. ... the importance of adequately performing one's familial duties and obligations is now linked to notions of progressiveness and good citizenship" (Howard 1996:13,172). Religion, nation, and gendersexuality, thus, represent three points in a triangle that posits the heteronormative nuclear family household as the foundational unit of nation, piety, and proper citizen selfhood.

Because *gay* Muslims almost never find themselves in environments where they can be openly *gay* and Muslim at once, in what ways do they find not the resolution of incommensurability, but its habitation? I have never encountered a *gay* Muslim who had not thought carefully about the relationship between his faith and his homosexual desires, and *gay* Muslims often discuss questions of religion amongst themselves, although such conversations do not typically take place in official sites like mosques. Most *gay* Indonesians understand Islam to emphasize heterosexual marriage (and having children in that marriage) as the only acceptable basis for a pious life. Yet although *gay* Muslims find the domain of religion conflated with what they term the *dunia normal* (normal world), as they move through what they term the *dunia gay* (gay world) these Indonesians do not leave their faith behind. Inhabiting apparently incommensurate spaces of religion and *gay* subjectivity becomes largely a matter of

individual exegesis – albeit exegesis often shared with *gay* friends. It is for this reason that I focus on individual narratives in this article; such narratives accurately portray how most *gay* Indonesians link homosexuality and Islam.

If the question of religion is not surprising to *gay* Muslims, neither is it surprising to Western audiences: Some of the most common questions I am asked are "how do *gay* Indonesians deal with being Muslim?" and "does Islam in Indonesia accept homosexuality?" These are not just the questions of a layperson. From the earliest sustained Western scholarship on Islam in the archipelago by colonial officials like Snouck Hurgronje to mid-20th century writing (e.g., Siegel 1969) to more recent work (e.g., Beatty 1999; Bowen 1993, 2003; Hefner 1985, 2000; Siapno 2002), there has been great interest in how Islam shapes social relations, law, and governance – even if, as noted earlier, homosexuality is virtually absent in this scholarship.

Another common question I am asked is "how are there Indonesians calling themselves *gay* at all?" Indeed, it is only in the last 30 years that some Indonesians have started calling themselves *gay*, and only in particular, limited circumstances – a significant difference from the much longer history of gay identification in much of the West, including the United States (Chauncey 1994). Many Indonesians still do not know of the term *gay*, or if they do, they sometimes think it is an English version of the better-known terms *banci* and *béncong* (male transvestites, for whom the more respectful term is *waria*). Among those Indonesians who do know of their *gay* fellow citizens, many portray them as selfish and exclusive. In reality, most *gay* Indonesians are working class and learn of the concept *gay* through mass media or friends, rather than from travel outside Indonesia or meeting gay Westerners. Given this situation, it is not surprising that anthropological work on Islam in Indonesia has paid virtually no attention to homosexuality. However, this article offers more than an improved understanding of *gay* lives, worthy as such a goal may be. My hope is that the example of *gay* Muslims can contribute to anthropological conversations concerning cultural responses to incommensurability, a topic of increasing importance as globalization becomes experienced less as an impending process and more as a de facto state of affairs.

Doctrine

Most *gay* Muslims understand Islamic orthodoxy to be incommensurate with sex between men, but no orthodoxy provides a complete roadmap for faith; each represents "a structure of ideas and practices that penetrates but does not encompass the lives of its practitioners" (Barth 1993:177). Although some *gay* Muslims recall hearing from religious authorities that homosexuality was sinful, the overarching concern with sexuality that they encounter is the proper channeling of heterosexuality into marriage. Islam is often referred to as a "sex-positive religion" in the sense that sexuality is regarded as a gift from God and the right of every person: "In the quranic view of the world, physical love impinges directly on the social order" (Bouhdiba 1998:9–10). In Islamic thought in Indonesia as elsewhere, the central concept organizing sexuality is that of marriage, which has historically been seen as a contract between families, not just two individuals.[6] The sins against marriage in Islamic doctrine are typically adultery, premarital sex, and prostitution, not male homosexuality, because sex between men is assumed not to lead to children. If male homosexuality is mentioned, it usually takes the form of incidental references rather than sustained commentaries, as reflected in the scholarly literature on Islam in Indonesia.

This emphasis on heterosexual marriage and the de-emphasis of male homosexuality is shared by the Indonesian nation-state, whose "family principle" (*azas kekeluargaan*), promulgated through a range of policies including a pervasive family planning regime, stresses that the nation is made up of heterosexual nuclear families, not individual citizens (Suryakusuma 1996). National belonging and heterosexuality are mutually defining and supporting, and those who fall outside official sexual norms are failed citizens. Marriage in Muslim communities throughout Indonesia is usually seen as the very foundation of sociality, determining boundaries

of kinship and ethnicity, assuring social reproduction (because children are presumed to be the result of heterosexual couples), and literalizing one's relationship to the divine (Idrus 2004). Marriage is typically a key element of Muslim orthopraxy. It is not simply an expression of sexual desire or a sign of being pious, but a practice that makes one a more pious Muslim (see Mahmood 2001). Given the dual emphasis of Islam and the nation on heterosexual marriage, it is not surprising that so many *gay* Indonesians marry (Boellstorff 1999). It is not inaccurate to speak of a "religious-familial complex" in which kinship and faith are part of a single cultural domain. In his study of mostly Muslim *gay* men in Jakarta, Richard Howard found that they "recognized that they carried within themselves a divinely inspired nature (*kodrat*) as men, which could only be fulfilled through marriage and the continuance of the life cycle" (Howard 1996:3).

As heterosexual marriage tends to be the positive concept organizing sexuality, so adultery (zina) tends to be the negative one. In the Qur'an and most Islamic writings, *zina* is defined primarily in terms of illicit sex between a man and woman. Anal sex between men *(liwath)* is viewed as a sin in the Qur'an but in a rather oblique manner: Lot *(Luth)* is mentioned, but the cities of Sodom and Gomorrah are not, and in contrast to the detailed attention given to adultery, male homosexuality is not one of the abominations for which specific punishments are listed (Murray and Roscoe 1997:307).

Many scholars see in the Islam of the Mediterranean and Arab worlds a generalized "will not to know" in which sex between men, although officially frowned on, is tolerated so long as its practitioners do not make their acts or desires publicly visible. Such interpretations seem generally valid in the Indonesian case. If asked directly, most Indonesian Muslims will say that Islam disapproves of sex between men, and even liberal writers conclude it has been strongly forbidden in Islam (e.g., Fadhilah 2004). In recent years, there have been scattered incidents of "political homophobia" in which Muslim groups attack *gay* men attempting to claim public space (Boellstorff 2004a).

In practice, however, male homosexuality has not represented a major concern in Indonesian

Islamic thought: The typical perceived opposite of normative heterosexual marriage is the failure to marry or heterosexual sex outside the marriage bond. In Indonesia it is sometimes unclear as to whether sex between men counts as adultery (zina). For instance, the popular Indonesian Islamic sex manual *Bimbingan Seks Islami (Islamic Sexual Guidance)* states that "some experts in Islamic jurisprudence are of the opinion that male homosexuality is the same as zina, with the result that its penalty is the same as for zina" (Asrori and Zamroni 1997:192). However, the chapter on adultery *(pezinaan)* flatly states that "Zina is sexual relations between a man and a woman outside of marriage" (Asrori and Zamroni 1997:197). The authors posit that zina is damaging because it makes the lineage of children born from the zina uncertain and poses the threat of adverse affects to the fetus from sexually transmitted diseases (Asrori and Zamroni 1997:203), neither of which is relevant to sex between men. Significantly, the authors claim that zina is on the rise in Indonesia and attribute this to the influence of Western media, globalization, urbanization, and modernity (Asrori and Zamroni 1997:198–200). They do not mention male homosexuality as increasing or link it to globalization. It is simply included in the litany of things that can lead people away from marriage and its sinfulness lies in this characteristic. Because *gay* Muslims find little information on sex between men beyond silence or denunciation, it is primarily through interpretation that they inhabit these incommensurate spaces of religion and desire.

Interpretation

Seeing being gay as sinful

Gay Muslims find themselves in a doctrinal environment that speaks little of sex between men, but it is also an environment in which notions of "interpretation" *(ijtihad)* are debated and enacted on a variety of levels, from judicial decisions to personal notions of "virtue" and "sin" (Bowen 2003). Acts of interpretation are also held to be central to being a modern citizen: One votes, one consumes, and in

contemporary Indonesia one now typically chooses one's heterosexual marriage partner through love rather than "arrangement,"which is increasingly deemed backward and undemocratic (Boellstorff 2004c). It is through acts of interpretation, not reference to established conventions in Islamic thought, that the majority of my *gay* interlocutors have arrived at the conclusion that being *gay* is either not sinful or a comparatively minor sin, so long as they marry women and have children.

Before turning to the apparently predominant view among *gay* men that sex between men is not necessarily sinful, I wish to examine the interpretive practices of those *gay* Muslims who do feel that they are sinning: even in these cases, there exist struggles with incommensurability. At one extreme are those who see their sexuality as a serious sin. One *gay* Muslim in Bali, citing the story of Lot, felt that "being *gay* is a big sin in Islam, one of the sins that cannot be forgiven" (conversation with author, February 12, 1998). A young Muslim man in Surabaya underscored that "you know, being *gay* is a sin – a big sin" (conversation with author, September 23, 1997). Reflecting the relative de-emphasis of male homosexuality in Indonesian Islamic thought, many of these *gay* Muslims who feel they are sinning cannot recall where sex between men is prohibited in the Qur'an, or they combine narratives, as in one *gay* man's rendition of the story of Lot *(Nabi Luth)*:

> The people of Lot in Sodom were *gay*, lesbian, and transvestite. One day an angel came to Sodom disguised as a very handsome man. The people of Sodom wanted to have sex with the angel. Lot tried to offer his daughters instead, but the people of Sodom were not interested. So God told Lot to build a big boat and fill it with all the animals of the earth, because he was going to flood the earth. And he flooded the earth, and the people of Sodom were drowned. (Conversation with author, September 3, 2000)

My *gay* Muslim interlocutors who felt they were sinning cited the story of Lot and Sodom more than any other as they struggled to interpret their homosexual desires. Another frequently cited story concerned King David as a prophet who fell in love with a man (some say he married the man as well) and was then cursed by God. In Surabaya, one *gay* man combined the stories of Lot and David:

> Once there was a city called Sodom. There, men had sex with other men and women had sex with women. Now the prophet David was instructed by God to bring them back, so they would become normal again. So at that time, God sent two angels to Sodom in the guise of two very handsome men. They went to the room of prophet David in Sodom. And once they were there, everyone started saying "there are these two very handsome men in the house of David." So they all rushed to the house of David and wanted to force themselves in. The angels went out, and they helped David escape from Sodom. But because they didn't want to change back, that city of Sodom was cursed by God. And all of the *gay* people there were turned into ash and the city was destroyed. (Conversation with author, October 20, 1997)

Syncretic narratives like these reflect how many *gay* Muslims perceive prohibitions against sex between men in a rather diffuse manner. A few *gay* Muslims who thought being *gay* was sinful saw their desires for men as having a divine origin, the injunction being to control desires at odds with God's plan for the world. One such Javanese *gay* Muslim believed *gay* people were created as "a test from God, to see if we can overcome it and still marry and have children" (conversation with author, December 11, 1997). A Sumatran *gay* Muslim believed that "in Islam all people are created with feelings of love towards women and towards men. How large those feelings of love are is dependent on the person" (conversation with author, February 5, 1998). Many *gay* Muslims who saw being *gay* as sinful subscribed to environmental etiologies, as in the case of the following man, living in Bali but originally from rural East Java.[7] He felt he became *gay* after being seduced by a boy five years older than him:

> I remember being happy about the way it felt. I think that's when I started having feelings for men; I don't think it was something that started from birth, and for that reason I don't agree

with your Muslim friends who say that *gay* people were created that way by God. Back then I didn't know the word *gay*, but I had heard the word *homoseks*, and I knew that it was a big sin under Islam. I still feel that way; I feel that it is a big sin. But I also feel that I have to enjoy my life. I can't help it that I like being with men and don't like being with women. What can I do about it? So I just go on sinning. (Conversation with author, March 3, 1998)

Many of these *gay* Muslims located sinfulness in practices, as in the following example:

> The sin is from the *gay* activities. In my opinion, all religions are against being *gay*. But whether it's a sin or not depends on what you do. For instance, if you have lots of sex partners, that's a sin, not the *gay*ness itself.... For instance, say you become *gay*. There are people who become *gay* only here [points to his heart]. They don't actually have sex. They're just happy when they see people of the same sex. And I think that's not a sin ... Especially in Islam, marriage must come first. It's not supposed to be sex first. But the times demand that style ... And there are other people who are worse than me, who commit rape or murder. (Conversation with author, May 2, 1998)

Muhammad, from a rural part of South Sulawesi, shared this view of sin as arising from acts. Married to a woman, Muhammad nonetheless frequented places in the city of Makassar where *gay* men congregated. He reconciled marriage and what he saw as innate homosexual desires through behavior management:

> Well, yes, it is a sin. But I don't do it too much. I have tried to stop; I'm always praying to God and fasting, asking that I won't be like this anymore. But the feelings are still there in my heart, and eventually they just can't be held in anymore; after one to three months they get too strong [points to his chest]. So I have to let it out. (Conversation with author, April 14, 1998)

This view that the sinfulness of being *gay* lies in actions rather than status is why some *gay* Muslims avoided certain sexual practices, particularly penile–anal sex. One *gay* man from Makassar, Iwan, noted that "Even up to today, one thing I won't do is penetrate someone or be penetrated anally by them. Because I think that's even more of a sin. There are some people who say you're not an official *gay (gay resmi)* if you don't do that, but I don't care" (conversation with author, September 8, 2000). In this understanding, sexual acts, being the responsibility of the self, have greater import than homosexual desire, created by God. Hadi, a *gay* man from Surabaya, was from a devout family; both of his parents had already gone on the pilgrimage to Mecca, and he felt they would disown him should they ever learn he was *gay*. Hadi, like Iwan, worked to "reduce [his] sin as a *gay* person" (*mengurangi dosa saya sebagai gay* [conversation with author, November 12, 1997]). Unlike Iwan, however, he did this not through avoiding certain sexual practices, but by being a *gay* person who is "successful in his career" (*berhasil dengan karir* [conversation with author, November 12, 1997]). For Iwan and many other *gay* men, success in society could affect the domain of religion, mitigating the sinfulness of male homosexuality.

Seeing being gay as not sinful

The range of narratives presented above illustrates how many *gay* Muslims interpret their homosexual desires as being sinful. However, what I found most striking during fieldwork was that such views were not predominant among my *gay* Muslim interlocutors. Instead, most either did not see being *gay* as sinful or understood it to be a minor sin easily forgiven by God. Incommensurability was inhabited and understood as part of God's plan. It was meant to be that one was *gay*, yet also meant to be that being *gay* and being Muslim can never be made commensurate. The starting point for these *gay* Muslims was a belief in God's omnipotence and omniscience. Given that God is all knowing, all wise, and all merciful, many *gay* Muslims concluded they were created *gay* by God and, thus, that they were not sinning.

In these views, all forms of desire *(nafsu)* are planted in each individual by God and represent irresistible forces that cannot be denied, a common view among Indonesian Muslims (Brenner 1998:149–157; Siegel

1969). This was brought home to me on November 23, 1997, when I visited Ketut and Suhadi, a *gay* couple who shared a home with an elderly woman and a little male dog, Tika. Ketut, who was Balinese Hindu, had bought the dog several months earlier and lavished it with affection. His partner Suhadi, a Javanese Muslim, had grown to love the dog as well despite the fact that Indonesian Muslims rarely keep dogs as pets because they are seen as polluting *(najis)*. Tika was several months old and just coming into sexual maturity, playfully mounting the legs of anyone who stopped to pet him. Shaking his head, Ketut said, "Well, it's about time we get him castrated." Suhadi looked at Ketut with a mixture of revulsion and alarm. "It would be so sad that he wouldn't have *nafsu*. If we do that, would he still want to guard the house?" In this view, nafsu is a vibrant, essential aspect of being that can be temporarily controlled but not forever denied. For *gay* Muslims who do not see their subjectivities as sinful, homosexual desire, planted in one's soul at birth by God, represents a fate *(nasib)* that must be accepted, because "Nasib is the ultimate explanation for events in this life: that it was written as the will of God, that so should be" (Barth 1993:184). In the following excerpts, four *gay* Muslims, two Javanese and two Buginese, engage in this line of reasoning:

> In fact, it's a sin, right? But what can we do about it? God created me as *gay*. ... He created me to desire men, not women. God already knows all this, right? So we could also say that it's not a sin. Unless we do it wrong ... if we have sex with an authentic man [*laki-laki asli*], that's a sin [for both of us]. That man should think, "Gosh, I'm an authentic man; why am I having sex with another man?" That's a sin. But if we are made by God as homo ... if we have sex with each other – *gay* with *gay* – why is that a sin? He was the one who made us this way!... It's fate [nasib], right? (Conversation with author, August 24, 1997)

> I know that I was created the same as *hetero*. It's only that I desire men. I know that God knows my feelings, knows that I like men. So I think it's something that's ordinary and natural

[*lumrah dan wajar*]. ... I now realize that God has created everything, including *gay* people, so in fact it's not a sin. I didn't choose to be *gay*. Did you choose to be *gay*? Of course not. (Conversation with author, October 30, 1997)

After I read many books, I came to the belief that God has a different plan for me to have made me a *gay* person. And there is a kind of poetry that is good for me, that is good for you and for all *gay* people. "God has given me the ability to accept the things that I cannot change about myself, and has given me the ability to change the things that can be changed." Because *gayness* [*kegayan*] is inside of me. If it was just a thing like this [pointing to a chair], maybe I would have already thrown it away by now. But it's everywhere inside of my body. Inside of my nerves, inside of my blood. (Conversation with author, May 5, 1998)

Why do I think it's not a sin? Because it is God who creates us as *gay* ... if for instance we have a *gay* soul [*jiwa gay*], and we try to be like a *hetero* man, it's transgressing God's will for us [*justru keluar dari kodratnya kita*]. (Conversation with author, August 19, 2000)

Sometimes a sense of being *gay* as not sinful can even emerge from interactions with religious figures. Ardi, a *gay* man from near Medan in north Sumatra, was known for his skills in magic [*ilmu*], which he had learned at a syncretically minded Islamic boarding school (*pesantren*):

My religious teacher would speak in an indirect way. For instance, he knew that I was *gay*. I never told him directly, but he knew. And he never said anything about [it] to me directly, he never said that being *gay* was a sin or anything like that. But he did advise me not to take semen into my mouth or up my butt, because if I did it would weaken my ilmu. (Conversation with author, February 1, 1998)

That the incommensurability of being *gay* and Muslim is inhabited rather than superseded is indicated not only by Ardi's religious teacher's indirectness, but by the fact that Ardi planned on marrying a woman and living a "normal" life alongside, not in place of, his *gay* life. Indeed, the greatest concern of most of my *gay* Muslim interlocutors was typically not

the sinfulness of homosexuality, but their desire to marry heterosexually. This desire was powerfully shaped by religious and familial pressures but was not just an external imposition; for many it was another form of authentic desire. In the following narrative from Surya, a *gay* Muslim man living in East Java, both Islam and *gay* selfhood repeatedly surface around the issue of marriage. As Surya entered his early twenties, his parents and also his *gay* lover, Hendy, told him that it was his duty to marry and have descendants. Surya also wished to marry: "I felt that wanted to be normal" (*rasa ingin normal*):

So eventually I married a woman who was a villager and a religious fanatic [*fanatik agama*]. But I couldn't get an erection with her. I tried fantasizing about Hendy while having sex with her, but in order to put my penis into her I had to open my eyes, right? And as soon as I'd do that I'd go flat. So I tried and tried for a whole year. ... Eventually I told her about Hendy. She said it was against Islam, a sin [*dosa*], and I had to stop, but I told her I couldn't. She didn't understand that it's not a physical matter, it's a matter of the soul [*jiwa*]. ... She cried, "If you're like this, why did you marry me?" She was right because usually one marries for choice [*pada umumnya orang kawin pilihan*]. ... Once I got her pregnant I was so proud! I felt like I'd fulfilled my duty as a man. Now that I'm married, no matter what I have to take care of her and the child because according to Islam that's my responsibility. And fulfilling the sexual function is one of these responsibilities.... When she found out I was still seeing Hendy, she said I had two choices: get a divorce or stop seeing him. I told her that under Islam she couldn't initiate a divorce and I didn't want a divorce but I was still going to see Hendy. And he and I are still together to this day. (Conversation with author, October 12, 1997)

Note how for Surya choice is a defining feature of marriage, *gay* love, and faith – albeit one in which male privilege under his understanding of Islam makes his choice more consequential than his wife's attempt to force a different kind of choice. The shift from marriage based on arrangement to marriage based on choice and love is a key marker of being modern and properly national in Indonesia (Siegel 1997). Choice is how one consumes in a shopping mall, how one votes in a democracy, and how one implements "family planning," so important to state-sponsored ideologies of sexuality (Dwyer 2000). The importance of choice and love in the context of God's omnipotence even appears in many of the narratives from the minority of my *gay* Muslim interlocutors who claimed they would never marry, as in the following example:

If a man chooses a man and lives together with him, and that is what makes happiness, does that not count as a partner? God created day and night. Sun and moon. God also created man and woman. So why cannot a man with a man be understood as partners? I think that what's clear is that if they love each other, I think that's okay. (Conversation with author, August 29, 2000)

Those *gay* Muslims who say they will never marry usually come to that conclusion through acts of interpretation as careful as those of *gay* Muslims who do marry. Islamic law places all human actions within five categories: (1) obligatory acts like daily prayer and fasting (Arabic and Indonesian *wajib*); (2) commendable but not required acts like performing extra prayers (Arabic *mandub*, Indonesian *sunatrasul*); (3) acts toward which Islam is indifferent, like eating foods that are not forbidden (Arabic *mubah*); (4) reprehensible but not forbidden acts like divorce (Arabic *makruh*); and (5) forbidden acts like adultery and theft (Arabic and Indonesian *haram*).[8] Islamic jurists tend to regard marriage as required or *wajib*, but some claim that there are justifiable reasons why some people need not marry: "Marriage in Islam is a sacred contract which every Muslim must enter into, unless there are special reasons why he should not" (Ali 1990:445–446; see also Hallaq 1997:175). These "special reasons" can include not only financial and physical ability but also mental and spiritual ability. Some of my *gay* Muslim interlocutors reasoned both that marriage is sunatrasul (commendable, but not required) and that their homosexual desires make them physically and spiritually unfit for marriage:

In my opinion I've been this way ever since I was born; I was created this way. So I'm meant to be this way and I have to walk this path. None of us ask to be born this way, right? So it's definitely something that's meant to be. In my view, marriage is a duty [*kewajiban*] for Muslims only if they are capable [*mampu*]. And by mampu I don't just mean financially but spiritually, mentally, and physically as well. So by those criteria I'm not meant to get married and so it's not a sin that I don't marry. (Conversation with author, December 1, 1997)

What all these *gay* Muslims share is a sense that interpretation is necessary in the face of incommensurability between religion and desire. In the void created by the relative lack of Islamic discourse concerning male homosexuality, they feel they must use interpretation to forge answers, however imperfect and uncertain, to the question of how they should live. Even if engaging in these acts of interpretation in isolation from other *gay* men, all of my *gay* interlocutors understood *gay* as a national category of selfhood, linked to notions of gay selfhood found across the world. I recall a conversation in 2000 with Ali, a *gay* man living in Makassar, which occurred a couple of weeks after Anwar Ibrahim, deputy prime minister of Malaysia, had been accused of sodomy and sentenced to nine years in prison. I asked Ali if he or his friends were concerned that a similar event could happen in Indonesia. "There's been no influence here," Ali replied. "Malaysia is an officially Muslim country [*negara Islam*]. Indonesia is not a Muslim country, but a country founded on Pancasila [the Five Principles of the nation, including 'Belief in One God,' but not specifying Islam]" (conversation with author, August 16, 2000). For Ali, the fact that Islam was not Indonesia's official religion opened the door to inhabit the apparently incommensurate domains of religion and homosexuality that made the prosecution of the latter comprehensible in the Malaysian context. Yet even in a nation founded on Pancasila, most Indonesian Muslims understand Islam as a religion of calls to prayer, mosques, and collective rituals like the communal feast (*slametan*) – a religion that participates in a moral public sphere it construes in heterosexual terms. *Gay* Muslims also confront incommensurability with regard to community.

Community

My discussion thus far has intentionally presented the intersection of *gay* subjectivity with Islam in privatized terms. This is an accurate impression of the fundamental divide between religion and homosexuality that these Indonesians experience, because in Indonesia there is currently no way to be publicly *gay* and seen as a pious Muslim; it remains "ungrammatical." It is clearly not the case that *gay* Muslims do not think about the relationship between Islam and their sexualities; it is precisely that thinking about this relationship is, to a great degree, the only way they can experience the relationship at all. *Gay* Muslims do not necessarily feel excluded from their religion – I have never heard *gay* Muslims say they no longer felt they were Muslims because of their sexuality – but they imagine a life course of incommensurability in which they are *gay* in the *gay* world, marry heterosexually in the normal world, and find religious community in that normal world alone. Even many of those *gay* Muslims who do not feel that being *gay* is sinful, and who additionally do not plan on marrying heterosexually, expect to find religious community solely in the normal world. I know of no cases to date in which *gay* Muslims pray collectively and openly in a mosque or other formal venue.

It is not simply social disapproval that leads to a lack of *gay* Muslim community: A handful of *gay* Christian groups have existed in urban centers. Examining a meeting of one such group in a northern district of Surabaya in 1997 will help highlight the situation of *gay* Muslims. I disembarked from a pedicab one night before a storefront closed with a heavy metal gate. In front of the gate were 15 people, a mix of *gay* men, transvestites, and a few *lesbi* women. After waiting almost half an hour for the person with the keys to show up, we entered the building, a beauty college. We walked through a large room filled with desks: On each, a mannequin head awaited a student's careful powder brush. At the far end of the

room was a circular iron staircase; climbing it, we came to a room the same size as the one below, also filled with desks and heads. One wall was completely mirrored and the others sported posters detailing the latest makeup designs, happy customers with facial masks, and giant eyes displaying various eye shadow combinations. Everyone got to work clearing the tables from the room and setting out chairs in five long rows, facing a podium with a placard bearing the salon's address and the words "Prayer Alliance." Three transvestites, one *gay* man, and one *lesbi* woman – the leaders of the group – moved to the front of the room holding hands and praying audibly with bowed heads. Meanwhile, more *gay* men and transvestites entered; soon there were 30 people in the room gossiping, laughing, or praying with heads bowed and eyes closed.

The prayer circle ended and the leaders took their seats at the front of the room. A transvestite came up from the back of the room to operate an overhead projector; another moved to the podium to begin the service by singing to lyrics shown on the projector. Usually, a man accompanied the group with a guitar, but he was absent because he was marrying a woman the following day. Nevertheless, everyone sung with gusto, clapping their hands. The transvestite leading the singing shouted, "We have no music but still have the spirit to sing and praise God." The singing ended after 20 minutes and the transvestite asked if there was anyone who wanted to come forward and give testimony. One man told how he had feared he would be late because he worked in the factory on the outskirts of town, but that God had provided transport in the form of an unexpected ride. The testimony was followed by a sermon, focusing on the importance of following in God's footsteps. The meeting ended with songs, a closing prayer, and invitations to the next meeting in two weeks' time.

This Christian prayer group – significantly, it did not call itself a "church" – was sponsored by a local church but was not allowed to meet on its premises. In a nonpublic context, the group rendered Christianity and *gay* subjectivity commensurate, even though many participants wished to be "cured" and homosexuality was rarely openly discussed. Since the early

2000s, a few Muslim intellectuals have taken tolerant stances with regard to *gay* Muslims, calling for Indonesian Islam to publicly recognize homosexuality and even same-sex marriage (Al Qurthuby et al. 2004). Yet to my knowledge and the knowledge of my interlocutors, no Islamic analogues to the "Prayer Alliance" have existed in Indonesia to date, despite the common existence of informal Muslim study and prayer groups. One explanation for this state of affairs would be that Islam is more disapproving than Christianity of homosexuality. However, given the range of views in both religions this seems an overly hasty conclusion; at issue is, rather, how for Indonesian Muslims, unlike Indonesian Christians, proper religious practice should be public, not limited to the upper floor of a beauty college. This reflects both Islamic understandings of community (*umma*) and Islam's dominant position in contemporary Indonesia.

A *Gay* Slametan

The ethnographic materials presented in this article suggest that whether *gay* Muslims uphold heteronormativity (e.g., by seeing their homosexual desires as sinful, marrying heterosexually, or stating that they plan to marry) or destabilize it on some level (e.g., by seeing their homosexual desires as God given or saying that they will not marry heterosexually), to date no point of commensurability between the "languages" of Islam and *gay* subjectivity has been reached. Yet *gay* lives exist and are lived every day; what exists is a habitation, not a resolution, of incommensurability. This habitation of incommensurability recalls not translation but a process I have elsewhere described as "dubbing culture" (Boellstorff 2003). In dubbing, a topic of recent interest to the Indonesian state, the moving lips of persons speaking one language on a film or television show are set alongside a soundtrack in a different language. The incommensurability of the two languages is not translated in the usual sense; there is no resolution from one language into the other. Instead, the two languages are placed together like rails on a train track that unify only at some ever-receding horizon. It is impossible,

say, for a Japanese-language film dubbed into English to have actors whose moving lips exactly match the soundtrack – but this "failure" is presupposed by viewers. Similarly, the simultaneous habitation of the categories *gay* and Muslim is self-consciously incomplete.

Such processes might hold important lessons for an anthropology of incommensurability, helping to explain "the emergence of radical worlds in the shadow of the liberal diaspora" (Povinelli 2001:320). There may be things – concepts, poems, sublime ideas – that are untranslatable, but nothing is undubbable: "Dubbing" is a useful metaphor for inhabiting incommensurability. The narratives discussed above demonstrate how *gay* Muslims do not typically feel that being *gay* will ever be "utterable" in terms of religion and nation. Yet *gay* Muslims exist, inhabiting spaces of incommensurability between *gay*, Muslim, and Indonesian. The religious beliefs and practices of *gay* Muslims are "complementary, overlapping accounts" (Brodwin 2003:86) of faith, habitations of incommensurability involving movement between individual and community.

In *The Religion of Java*, Clifford Geertz identified the communal feast or slametan as central to Javanese experiences of Islam. Geertz notes that a slametan resolves incommensurability by acting as a "kind of social universal joint, fitting the various aspects of social life and individual experience together" (Geertz 1960:11):

A slametan can be given in response to almost any occurrence one wishes to celebrate, ameliorate, or sanctify. ... There is always the special food ... the Islamic chant, and the extra-formal high-Javanese speech of the host. ... Most slametans are held in the evening. ... Upon arrival each guest takes a place on the floor mats. ... When the host has completed the [formal introductory speech], he asks someone present to give the Arabic chant-prayer. ... The preliminaries completed ... the serving of the food begins. [Geertz 1960:11–13]

Arno's birthday slametan was held on November 28, 1997, in the little town where he lived about 20 miles outside Surabaya – coincidentally, Geertz's field site for *The Religion of Java*. Arno's friends came in from all over Surabaya (and his boyfriend all the way from Bali) to meet not at Arno's home, but the rented home of another *gay* man, tucked away on a small street on the far side of town. Its small front room had a low ceiling, lit by a single long fluorescent light bulb and decorated with a quotation from the Qur'an (the *ayat kursi*) alongside photos of the president and vice president. Here, Arno could hold his paradoxical gathering – a private slametan – safe from the eyes of family and neighbors, away from the public yet under the indifferent gaze of religion and nation.

Twenty-four men sat in a circle inside the crowded room, backs pressed to walls. Some of Arno's *gay* friends had been cooking all afternoon. From the kitchen, they emerged to place food in the center of the circle: rice, fried chicken, fried mashed potatoes, peanut sauce, and shrimp crackers. The room fell silent as one of Arno's friends began to speak, clearly but informally, in Indonesian rather than Javanese: "Well, we are here to celebrate Arno's birthday. He won't tell us exactly how old he is, but in any case we're here on his behalf." The assembled laughed gently. "So let's take a few moments to pray, each following our own beliefs and praying in our own way. Let's pray for the good fortune and health of Arno. Begin now." A few moments passed in silence with heads bowed. "Okay, that's enough. Now everyone please eat a lot!" Arno moved to the center of the circle and, taking a large pastry server in hand, cut off the tip of the rice mountain (*nasi gunung*), putting it on a plate with other food items. Everyone sat quietly: Arno was free to give this first serving to a person of his choice. Turning around on his knees, he approached his boyfriend and gave him the plate as they kissed each other on the cheeks. Approving murmurs reverberated around the circle. Plates were passed around and everyone moved in to eat.

Most slametans involve neighbors, but Arno's slametan grouped together men meeting on the basis of *gay* subjectivity. In place of Javanese narrative coupled with an Arabic chant, obligatory even in the Hindu slametans held by Tengger Javanese (Hefner 1985), these *gay* participants spoke Indonesian and prayed silently, "each in their own way." Inhabiting –

not resolving – incommensurability, Arno's slametan brought together *gay* men at the margins of the public. It made no appeal for social inclusion and did not invoke the potential of a *gay* Muslim public. Yet it drew from mainstream religious practice and also national discourses of individuality, national language, and religious egalitarianism. On another night, Arno would hold other events to celebrate his birthday with family members, coworkers, and neighbors. On this evening, a *gay* world of faith came into being in a little room around a mound of rice.

NOTES

Acknowledgments. Research in Indonesia was funded by the Social Science Research Council, the National Science Foundation, the Morrison Institute for Population Studies at Stanford University, and the Department of Cultural and Social Anthropology of Stanford University. I thank these institutions for their support. Helpful comments were provided by a range of colleagues: a special thanks to Lara Deeb, Bill Maurer, and two anonymous reviewers for *American Anthropologist*. All italicized terms are in Indonesian unless indicated otherwise.

1 Because of limitations of space, it is also not possible to discuss *lesbi* Muslims; "homosexuality" in this article refers to male homosexuality. From my own fieldwork and some published sources (e.g., Prawirakusumah and Ramadhan 1988:122, 250, 427), it is clear that many *lesbi* women are Muslim and struggle with questions of faith and belonging. This is a crucial area for research and I hope to discuss *lesbi* Muslims in a future publication. See Boellstorff 2005 and references therein for discussions of *lesbi* Indonesians.

2 *Republika* (2005). The phrase "gays demanding rights" apparently refers to Westerners.

3 "Bisexuality" is rarely discussed in Indonesia as a category of sexuality, even though in a behavioral sense it is quite prevalent. See Boellstorff 1999, 2005.

4 This article draws from two years of fieldwork conducted in Indonesia during 1992, 1993, 1995, 1997–98, 2000, 2001, 2002, and 2004, primarily in Surabaya (East Java), Makassar (South Sulawesi), and Bali. There are also, of course, *gay* Indonesians who

follow religions other than Islam, but because of limitations of space, I do not address them in this article, except for some references to *gay* Christians (Christianity is the next-largest religion in Indonesia after Islam). Additionally, I do not discuss the religious beliefs and practices of male transvestites (*warias*) in this article (see Boellstorff 2004b).

5 It lies outside the scope of this article to discuss events like the "Jakarta Charter," an attempt to constitutionally require Muslims to follow Islamic law.

6 See, for instance, M. Ali 1990:444–449; Esposito 1998:94; Idrus 2004; Waines 1995:94.

7 Howard (1996) claims that all of the *gay* men in his Jakarta sample, regardless of religion, saw becoming *gay* as the result of social relationships.

8 This five-fold division is termed *al-ahkam al-khamsah*. See Bowen 2003:14, Hallaq 1997:174–180; Waines 1995:76.

REFERENCES

Al Qurthuby, Sumanto Adib, M. Kholidul, et al., eds.
  2004 Indahnya Kawin Sesama Jenis (The beauty of same-sex marriage). Justisia 25:1.
Ali, Maulana Muhammad
  1990[1936] The Religion of Islam. Columbus, OH: Ahmadiyya Anjuman Ishaat Islam.
Asad, Talal
  1986 The Concept of Cultural Translation in British Social Anthropology. *In* Writing Culture: The Poetics and Politics of Ethnography. James Clifford and George E. Marcus, eds. Pp. 141–164. Berkeley: University of California Press.
Asrori, Ma'ruf, and Anang Zamroni
  1997 Bimbingan Seks Islami (Islamic sexual guidance). Surabaya: Pustaka Anda.
Barth, Fredrik
  1993 Balinese Worlds. Chicago: University of Chicago Press.
Beatty, Andrew
  1999 Varieties of Javanese Religion: An Anthropological Account. Cambridge: Cambridge University Press.
Boellstorff, Tom
  1999 The Perfect Path: Gay Men, Marriage, Indonesia. GLQ: A Journal of Gay and Lesbian Studies 5(4):475–510.
Boellstorff, Tom
  2002 Ethnolocality. Asia Pacific Journal of Anthropology 3(1):24–48.
Boellstorff, Tom
  2003 Dubbing Culture: Indonesian Gay and Lesbi Subjectivities and Ethnography in an Already Globalized World. American Ethnologist 30(2):225–242.
Boellstorff, Tom
  2004a The Emergence of Political Homophobia in Indonesia: Masculinity and National Belonging. Ethnos 69(4):4 65–486.
Boellstorff, Tom
  2004b Playing Back the Nation: *Waria*, Indonesian Transvestites. Cultural Anthropology 19(2):159–195.
Boellstorff, Tom
  2004c Zines and Zones of Desire: Mass Mediated Love, National Romance, and Sexual Citizenship in Gay Indonesia. Journal of Asian Studies 63(2):367–402.
Boellstorff, Tom
  2005 The Gay Archipelago: Sexuality and Nation in Indonesia. Princeton: Princeton University Press.
Bouhdiba, Abdelwahab
  1998 Sexuality in Islam. Alan Sheridan, trans. Los Angeles: Saqi Books.
Bowen, John R.
  1993 Muslims through Discourse: Religion and Ritual in Gayo Society. Princeton: Princeton University Press.
Bowen, John R.
  2003 Islam, Law, and Equality in Indonesia: An Anthropology of Public Reasoning. Cambridge: Cambridge University Press.
Brenner, Suzanne April
  1998 The Domestication of Desire: Women, Wealth, and Modernity in Java. Princeton: Princeton University Press.
Brodwin, Paul
  2003 Pentecostalism in Translation: Religion and the Production of Authority in the Haitian Diaspora. American Ethnologist 30(1):85–101.
Bunzl, Matti
  2004 Symptoms of Modernity: Jews and Queers in Late-Twentieth-Century Vienna. Berkeley: University of California Press.
Chauncey, George
  1994 Gay New York: Gender, Urban Culture, and the Making of the Gay Male World, 1890–1940. New York: Basic Books.

De Graff, H. J.
  1970 South-East Asian Islam to the Eighteenth Century. *In* The Cambridge History of Islam, vol. 2. A. P. M. Holt, Ann K. S. Lambton, and Bernard Lewis, eds. Pp. 123–154. Cambridge: Cambridge University Press.

Dwyer, Leslie K.
  2000 Spectacular Sexuality: Nationalism, Development and the Politics of Family Planning in Indonesia. *In* Gender Ironies of Nationalism: Sexing the Nation. Tamar Mayer, ed. Pp. 25–62. London: Routledge.

Esposito, John L.
  1998 Islam: The Straight Path. Third Edition. New York: Oxford University Press.

Fadhilah, Iman
  2004 Portret Homoseksual Dalam Wacana Fiqh Klasik (A portrait of homosexuality in the discourse of classical Islamic jurisprudence). Justisia 25:23–30.

Frazer, James George
  1915 The Golden Bough. New York: Macmillan.

Gade, Anna M.
  2004 Perfection Makes Practice: Learning, Emotion, and the Recited Qur'an in Indonesia. Honolulu: University of Hawai'i Press.

Gallagher, John, and Chris Bull
  2001 Perfect Enemies: The Battle between the Religious Right and the Gay Movement. Lanham, MD: Madison Books.

Geertz, Clifford
  1960 The Religion of Java. Glencoe, IL: Free Press.

Hallaq, Wael B.
  1997 A History of Islamic Legal Theories: An Introduction to Sunni usul al-fiqh. Cambridge: Cambridge University Press.

Hefner, Robert W.
  1985 Hindu Javanese: Tengger Tradition and Islam. Princeton: Princeton University Press.

Hefner, Robert W.
  2000 Civil Islam: Muslims and Democratization in Indonesia. Princeton: Princeton University Press.

Hooker, M. Barry
  2003 Indonesian Islam: Social Change through Contemporary Fatawa. Honolulu: University of Hawai'i Press.

Howard, Richard Stephen
  1996 Falling into the Gay World: Manhood, Marriage, and Family in Indonesia. Ph.D. dissertation, University of Illinois at Urbana–Champaign.

Idrus, Nurul Ilmi
  2004 Behind the Notion of Siala: Marriage, Adat and Islam among the Bugis in South Sulawesi. Intersections: Gender, History and Culture in the Asian Context, Issue 10 (August 2004). Electronic document, http://www.sshe.murdoch.edu.au/intersections/issue10/idrus.html#t23, accessed September 18, 2005.

Mahmood, Saba
  2001 Feminist Theory, Embodiment, and the Docile Agent: Some Reflections on the Egyptian Islamic Revival. Cultural Anthropology 16(2):202–236.

Morris, Rosalind C.
  2000 In the Place of Origins: Modernity and Its Mediums in Northern Thailand. Durham, NC: Duke University Press.

Mosse, George L.
  1985 Nationalism and Sexuality: Respectability and Abnormal Sexuality in Modern Europe. New York: Howard Fertig.

Murray, Stephen O., and Will Roscoe
  1997 Conclusion. *In* Islamic Homosexualities: Culture, History, and Literature. Stephen O. Murray and Will Roscoe, eds. Pp. 302–319. New York: New York University Press.

Povinelli, Elizabeth A.
  2001 Radical Worlds: The Anthropology of Incommensurability and Inconceivability. Annual Review of Anthropology 30:319–334.

Prawirakusumah, R. Prie, and Ramadhan K. H.
  1988 Menguak Duniaku: Kisah Sejati Kelainan Seksual (Revealing my world: A true story of sexual deviance). Jakarta: Pustaka Utama Grafiti.

Republika
  2005 Gays amongst Bandung's Students. Republika, June 4. Electronic document, http://www.republika.co.id/, accessed September 16.

Rofel, Lisa
  1999 Other Modernities: Gendered Yearnings in China after Socialism. Berkeley: University of California Press.

Siapno, Jacqueline Aquino
  2002 Gender, Islam, Nationalism, and the State in Aceh: The Paradox of Power, Co-optation, and Resistance. London: Routledge Curzon.

Siegel, James T.
1969 The Rope of God. Berkeley: University of California Press.

Siegel, James T.
1997 Fetish, Recognition, Revolution. Princeton: Princeton University Press.

Steenbrink, Karel
1993 Dutch Colonialism and Indonesian Islam: Contacts and Conflicts, 1596–1950. Amsterdam: Rodopi.

Suryakusuma, Julia I.
1996 The State and Sexuality in New Order Indonesia. *In* Fantasizing the Feminine in Indonesia. Laurie Sears, ed. Pp. 92–119. Durham, NC: Duke University Press.

Tambiah, Stanley Jeyaraja
1990 Magic, Science, Religion, and the Scope of Rationality. Cambridge: Cambridge University Press.

Tylor, Edward Burnett
1958[1871] Primitive Culture, vol. 1: The Origins of Culture. New York: Harper and Row.

Waines, David
1995 An Introduction to Islam. Cambridge: Cambridge University Press.

26

The Semiotics of Transgendered Sexual Identity in the Thai Print Media: Imagery and Discourse of the Sexual Other

Megan Sinnott

Introduction

Even a cursory scan[1] of Thai newspapers and magazines will undoubtedly reveal some story related to homosexuality, or transgender identity. What do these images and accounts signify? Are they accounts of real transgendered or homosexual people? Are they attempts to discipline transgendered/homosexual people through stereotypes and repression? Or do they serve another purpose? Elsewhere, Johnson (1997) has argued that transgendered men (*bantut*) in the Philippines, through their gendered performances, act as sites of 'cultural otherness' and 'self-transformation' in ethnic and national terms. This paper seeks to explore the homologies between this account and gendered sexual identities in Thai media discourse.

'Homosexuality' is not a well-recognized or often used category in popular Thai discourse. Gender, the qualities of femininity or masculinity, is the primary marker of what in the West is conceived of as homosexual identity, and those individuals who display attributes of a gender that are perceived to be in opposition to their sex have developed identities, such as *tom*, or *kathoey*, indicating a masculine woman and feminine man respectively. *Toms* and *kathoeys* are assumed to be homosexual, that is sexually interested in those of the same sex, by virtue of their gender identity. 'Homosexuality' distinct from gender identity is virtually absent in Thai discourse, including academic and medical perspectives that almost always equate same-sex desire with transgendered identity. This paper therefore uses the

Megan Sinnott, The Semiotics of Transgendered Sexual Identity in the Thai Print Media, from *Culture, Health and Sexuality*, vol. 4, no. 2 (2000): 425–440. Reprinted with permission of the publisher (Taylor & Francis Group http://www.informaworld.com).

terms 'transgendered sexuality' and Jackson's label of 'gendered sexualities',[2] rather than 'homosexual identities', in order to accurately reflect Thai folk perceptions of sexuality and gender.

While there are moments of convergence and divergence in the representation of Thai sexualized genders, all contain the element of homoeroticism as a key component, and this common feature serves as a unifying theme in this paper. The numerous terms used by Thais to refer to this constellation of gender identity and sexuality causes confusion to Thais themselves. Recently 'homosexuality'[3] has been partially incorporated in Thai discourse as an overarching concept for all gendered sexualities, but is generally used in particular contexts where transnationalism and/or authoritative scientific-sounding discourse is deployed. Therefore, when 'homosexuality' is referred to, it must be remembered that most Thais will interpret homosexual identity as essentially a gender identity.

Inspired by Foucault, much social research over the past decade has sought to analyse how discourses of sexuality have structured regimes of power. For example, Stoler's important work on discourses of sexuality and the formation of the colonized other in Indonesia provides a framework for the analysis of discourse and power both in Southeast Asia and elsewhere (1991, 1997). Here, however, the focus will be on transgendered sexuality as a key, iconic element in Thai public discourse. It will be argued that imagery of sexuality and gender as used and created by the Thai press operates as a kind of 'Orientalism' (c.f. Said 1978) in which the 'other' (in this case transgendered sexual identities) is used as an imagined discursive category to embody negative qualities of the self. This Orientalist discourse found in the Thai press is embedded in nationalist constructions of the 'Thai self', and myriad manifestations that it takes. These discourses are manipulated and contested by competing social forces which use the imagery of gendered sexuality to say various things, usually unpleasant, about their opposition or target. Thus, cultural conservatives may evoke images of gendered sexual identities to critique processes of industrialization and urbanization. Conversely, the image of transgendered sexuality may be evoked, reformulated and repositioned by political progressives to critique autocratic state centralism.

It is not only the use to which the imagery of trans/gendered sexuality is put that varies. The image itself is remarkably variable. For example, campy, unpredictable *kathoey*, hyper-masculine homosexual men, and profligate teenage cross-dressing girls – reveal the multi-referential nature of gendered sexuality in Thai discourse. The multiple imagery of gendered sexuality coexists with the multiple political uses to which it is put; these images can be discursively deployed to represent modernity and traditional ('backward') society, the state and the people as victims of the state. To illustrate these claims, this paper focuses on three issues recently discussed at length in the press. First, there has been discussion over 'modernization' in Thai society linked to *tom-dee* (female transgendered sexual identities discussed below). Second, there was coverage of the 1996 Rajaphat College ban on 'sexually deviant' students. Third, there were the 1997 *Tuy* sex crime cases. Beyond these cases, it is hoped to show how the appropriation of the image of transgendered sexuality as social critique has constructed a discourse of silence in which the transgenderism/homosexuality of individuals is rendered mute in 'respectable' portrayals of people not used for social/political discursive purposes. Friendly, non-sensationalistic media coverage of well-known homosexual/transgendered people most usually describes the subject's sexuality and gender in terms of culturally approved of, and gender normative models.

Transgendered Sexuality as Commentary on Modernity, Westernization and the Middle Class – *tom-dee*

Starting in the late 1970s, and continuing to the present, the media has produced a plethora of (threatening) images of growing transgendered (homo)sexuality in Thai society. These images have been associated with Westernization, passing fashions or fads, the middle class, and consumerist urban lifestyles – all aspects of that amorphous yet highly charged trope of 'modernity', and its close cousin, 'development'.[4] The primacy of concepts of 'modernization' and 'development' in Thai discourse is striking in a review of educational materials, media, and public attitudes. All types of social practices, especially sexual, have been argued for or against the case, on the basis of whether or not they are productive for 'national development' or 'national image'. For example, debates over polygamy, prostitution, women's rights, and family planning, are but a few of the issues that have been subsumed under the discourse of national development.[5] In the same way, the media filters the issue of gendered sexuality in Thai society through the discourse of modernity and development. Not only is the issue of gendered sexuality subsumed under the discourse of modernity, but also the media-produced image of transgendered sexuality becomes a stage for the expression of anxieties, aspirations, fears, and disillusionment associated with the experience of 'modernity'.

Newspapers and magazines have disseminated provocative images of a growing population of transgendered sexualities in Thai society, a dark underworld of sexual deviants, an unstoppable surge of teenage converts to the ways of homosexuality. The press sensationalized an apparently recent phenomenon – the emergence of *tom-dee*[6] identity, as well as of '*gay*' identified young men. Images of these youthful gender-benders have been splashed on the covers of magazines with stories inside describing the strange ways of the modern middle class youth.

The media identified the emblem of the 'western' consumer society, the shopping mall, as the primary site for these new *tom-dee*, and young *gay* men, inextricably linking their emergence with commodified entertainment. For example, in a recent 14 page 'expose' article, this sensational picture of the results of prosperity and development is provided:

Every day is the same, from the morning to night there are thousands of youths in groups there to buy things they want ... gathering in an atmosphere of continuous loud disco

music. The image of hugging, kissing, stroking between men and men and between women and women, is easy to see in this place ... In brief, these days the customers that supply fashion retail places with money are youths who have altered sexual tastes (*Phuen Chiwit* 1984, p. 19, T)[7]

The same article goes on to describe 'gay and lesbian bars' that are 'popping up like mushrooms in the rainy season'. The magazine describes the scene as a commodified free-for-all, with the objective of these commercial sites being to grab as much money as possible by selling expensive drinks, and possibly sex (*Phuen Chiwit* 1984, p. 19). These decadent transgendered/homosexual youth are explicitly associated with the new middle-class:

The dress, complexion, and abundant spending [of these kids], shows that most of them are the descendents of the well-to-do who have no time themselves to care for their children. (*Phuen Chiwit* 1984, p. 20, T)

An apparent consensus among journalists/columnists at the time intrinsically linked *tom-dee* identity to consumerist lifestyles and profligate spending of the middle class. Thai identity was often positioned in opposition to this 'Westernization' of urban youth. For example, a columnist for *Matichon* discussed an article that had earlier appeared on the subject of *tom-dee*:

[Kids] don't just walk around for fun. They buy clothes and expensive food, making for wasteful personalities. Kids don't think when they buy something expensive, they think the more expensive the better. [Parents] should teach their kids to know Thai culture too, or they will only know Western culture. (*Matichon* 16 October 1988, T)

The image of transgendered sexuality has been insinuated into the public discourse of modernization in contradictory ways. Transgendered sexuality has not only been associated with new middle class lifestyles, but has also been presented as a sign of the lack of modernization. For example, the press, and the academics it cites, associates transgendered sexuality with the traditional practices of sex-segregation, such as same-sex schools, and taboos on teenage dating. Politicians and journalists have argued that Western-style dating and mixing of the sexes is modern, and will prevent homosexuality and transgenderism. In 1994, the then Minister of Education suggested transforming all schools to co-educational, citing academics and psychologists as support, giving the reason that co-educational schools were psychologically healthier and helped prevent the sexual/gender 'deviance' that single-sex schools were believed to promote (*The Nation* 31 October 1994). The press, supported by academics, have also promoted Westernized psychological concepts such as 'emotional health' and 'modern' communication between parents and children in order to avoid homosexuality/transgenderism in one's own children:

> Raising children depends on the way you talk to them. You must be modern, so they can take care of themselves. But culture creates a lot of pressure, because old-fashioned beliefs are enforced, leading to more negative results than positive. (*City Life* July 1994, pp. 123–124, T)

However, efforts to convince parents to adopt 'modern' attitudes towards their daughters and allow dating and mixing of the sexes is still controversial, and efforts to de-segregate schools have met with only partial success.

The vexed relationship between the positively valued concept of 'being modern' and the more troublesome concept of 'Westernization' is reflected in the Thai public discourse of transgendered sexuality as a feature of Thai youth. The ambivalent relationship between negatively valued Westernization and positively valued 'modernity' is parodied by a columnist in an article sarcastically entitled 'Homosexuality, a Developed Country',

> People always say that in the developed countries there are so many gays that they are a majority. So I can almost write a theory that homosexuality comes from being a developed country. If Thailand is developed because of its homosexuality, I ask to change my household registration to Karen. (*Athit Wiwat* 1 November 1984, T)

The joke here is that the writer would rather live with the Karen, a minority ethnic group living in the rural or mountainous areas of Northern Thailand, perceived by Thais as the antithesis of modernity, than live in a 'Westernized' version of modernity.

Transgendered sexuality has also entered the discourse of 'national development', with the image of transgendered sexuality constructed as both a product of 'modernization' and a hindrance to the proper (masculine) development of the nation:

> Many of the nation's youth are engrossed in devouring the same sex like this – it is perverse sexual behaviour. It is disgusting that the deterioration of morality and ethics will have a negative impact on society at large, because [the homosexual youth] will grow up to be citizens who are weak, and unable to build a society that is beautiful. (*Phuen Chiwit* 1984, T)

The association of transgendered sexuality with modernity, and national development are constant themes in the press. The media has positioned the image of transgendered sexuality in a variety of ways to reflect the objective of the moment. The following discussion of two specific media stories further illustrate the ways that the press manipulate representation of transgendered sexuality to position the press and its readers in social-political debates – namely, the Rajaphat College's ban on 'sexual deviants' and the *Tuy* sex crimes.

Rajaphat

In December 1996, Rajaphat, the largest state-run college system in Thailand, announced a ban on 'sexually deviant' or 'homosexual' students. This official prohibition shocked local observers who had long assumed a 'tolerant' attitude towards homosexuality in Thai society. The ban also prompted a massive protest against the 'undemocratic' acts of the Ministry of Education (Rajaphat's governing body) and Rajaphat Institute. For the first time in Thai society, mainstream academics, psychologists, journalists and activists openly supported 'homosexual rights'. The extensive coverage the Thai press gave to the debate was instrumental in challenging Rajaphat and the Ministry of Education. However, closer inspection of the rhetoric deployed by the press during the debate reveals that the issue debated was not homophobia, or 'gay rights'. What the press was promoting was a challenge to the overly centralized state, and the autocratic and unresponsive bureaucracy. The ban and debate that followed occurred during the contentious passage of the People's Constitution and the challenge promoted by the media was framed in terms of the 'undemocratic' and 'unconstitutional' tendency of the bureaucracy, embodied in Rajaphat.

Rajaphat's actions had special significance in the politics of national development and democratization. Rajaphat Institute, as a teacher's college, is associated with national development, producing the teachers that will go to the rural areas throughout the country to educate the people as Thai nationals. Teachers are the primary bearers of the state, teaching the central Thai dialect, standard nationalist history, and nationalist symbols to the rural majority. Rajaphat, criticized for not meeting its nationalist mandate, framed the ban in terms of responding to the intense demands for educational reform that had hounded the Ministry for some time. Rajaphat claimed that homosexual teachers were poor role models for students, and referred to the ubiquitous academic and media reports claiming that homosexuality was a perversion, illness and abnormality – claims that had been made by the media with stupefying repetition.

The opposition to the ban, a coalition of human rights organizations and academics, charged the Ministry of Education, and Rajaphat, with violating the constitution, acting undemocratically, and against global trends. Well-known academics were given space in the press to express their views against Rajaphat's decision. Homosexuals, for example, were compared to other oppressed minority groups in need of protection from the state:

The new constitution gives importance to the needs of the people. For too long people, such as women, the handicapped, the poor, or people who deviate from the mainstream have

been neglected ... democracy is freedom from repression ... Rajaphat goes against the democracy movement. (Chalitaporn Songsamphan, *Matichon* 25 January 1997, T)

The media generally sided with the protestors, and published opinion pieces by various academics who opposed the ban, such as that above. However, unlike some of the guest opinions, the press itself maintained consistently negative attitudes towards homosexuals[8] themselves, while simultaneously challenging the politics of the Ministry of Education. The press challenged the Ministry on the basis that they were autocratically denying a certain group their rights to education. The press generally agreed that transgendered/homosexual people should not be teachers, as they were 'deviant', sexually and emotionally abnormal, but the media maintained that the government had no right to deny them education, for example:

People who are *gay, tut*, or *tom* does not mean that they shouldn't study to be teachers. If there are any hindering because there is fear that kids will take them as models, then there should begin to be selection for teachers ... not a hindering of people studying the field of education. (*Daily News* 28 January 1997, p. 23, T)

While the print media and many of the 'experts' interviewed did not challenge the negative portrayal of homosexuality and transgenderism, they agreed that banning homosexuals from Rajaphat Institute was a constitutional violation. Seri Swanphanan, Secretary of Thai Law Association, said the ban was against the constitution, as all citizens had equal rights to protection of the law. The 'problem of sexual deviance' must be solved at its source, the home, not at the end point, claimed the *Daily News* (25 January 1997, p. 12, T).

The association of homosexuality and gender identity with 'human rights' was a new discourse, and one that Rajaphat clearly did not anticipate. Rajaphat lost the debate because it lost control over the discourse of homosexuality. The primary aim of the ban had been against *kathoey/tut*, transgendered and/or effeminate homosexual men – the flamboyant screechy cross-dressers often portrayed in TV soaps and dramas. However, through the all-embracing, and technical sounding terms used in the debate, such as 'homosexuality' and 'sexual deviants' (*khon-biangbeen-thang-pheet*), the ban came to be understood as encompassing all types of homosexual and cross-gender identities. For example, a *Daily News* team editorial started out with defining the issue by including all categories of homosexuality, and linking these identities to gender deviance:

> *Tuts*, closet cases, *gay, tom, dee, katheoy*, these are all names used to call the people who have the psychology or behaviour that is deviant from ones true sex that nature has given one. Human beings have only two sexes, female and male, and also by nature women must be mates with men in order to propagate the species. (*Daily News* 27 January 1997, T)

The media confirmed the deviant, and essentially negative, meaning of transgenderism and homosexuality that Rajaphat promoted, and referred to the targets of the ban as 'sexual deviants'. Yet in time, and through the extensive and varied voices that were represented in this and other media stories, the ban came to be understood as including all kinds of homoerotic and transgender identity and behaviour. Moreover, Rajaphat's own confused use of homosexual/gender categories, indiscriminately referring to 'sexual deviants', 'homosexuals', the 'third sex', 'gays', etc., allowed for the construction of an all-inclusive category of people based on sexual preference – homosexuals, who according to international standards, and transnational movements, did indeed have 'rights'.[9] Violating the 'rights' of a group of oppressed people, according to international standards as well as the People's Constitution, was obviously not the image the institute had originally intended to promote! Instead, the original goal had been an image of cultural conservatism and moral integrity by banning an assumed non-vocal and non-political minority ('gender deviants') who were clearly widely disapproved of.

Rajaphat officials tried to defend their position against charges that they violated the rights of homosexuals, on the grounds that individual freedoms must take second place to needs of society:

> The future of our youth and country are important, it is right and appropriate to not allow homosexuals into the profession of teacher because teachers are role models ... Human rights are important, but the future of our country's youth is what we must choose. (*Thansetakit Weekly* 25–31 January 1997, T)

Government defence of the ban combined the previously common media claim that 'sexual deviance' was foreign, and a threat to Thai identity, with the position popular in psychiatric circles that transgendered people/homosexuals were violent. Deputy Minister of Education Suraphorn, for example, stated that:

> this group has a high rate of violence in disciplining children. There is a problem of sexual deviance in Bangkok, so the Ministry of Education believes we should maintain the Thai way of life rather than the foreign one. (*Khawsot* 22 January 1997, pp. 1–2, T)

Preventing 'deviants' from entering teacher-training, the original intention behind the ban, became a fiasco for Rajaphat. Rajaphat and the Ministry of Education officials who backed the ban were portrayed as backwards, prejudiced, ignorant demagogues, typical representatives of an unpopular, overly centralized government bureaucracy. The charge that Rajaphat was harming the nation's image by going against global trends eventually led to the successful challenge to the ban, so ending the Institute's (rather pathetic) efforts at public relations and image enhancement (*Matichon* 22 January 1990, p. 1, 4, *Matichon* 14 January 1997, p. 32).

In the process, Ministry of Education officials appeared to have been manoeuvred into a debate about 'gays and lesbians' and 'homosexual rights', topics they were only vaguely aware of. In a ludicrous attempt to fend off the intense criticism they had received, officials at one time suggested that separate educational facilities could be provided for 'deviant students', an idea that was quickly ridiculed and withdrawn. In September 1997, the month that the People's Constitution was passed, Rajaphat, surprised and overwhelmed, backed down and rescinded the ban. The Institute's officials, by this time realizing that banning 'homosexuals' was a politically incorrect thing to do, claimed the controversy occurred because of misunderstandings over terminology alone.

> The Institute misunderstood and used the wrong word. That's why it seems to violate human rights. What they meant to screen was 'sexually abnormal people', not 'sexual deviants'. (*Bangkok Post* 11 September 1997).

Importantly, the press had never aimed to promote a pro-homosexual/transgender stance through criticism of Rajaphat and the Ministry of Education. Indeed, the press and Rajaphat were not far apart in portraying negative images of homosexuality/transgenderism. The press's earlier exploitative and sensational reporting on crimes involving homosexuals/ transgendered people had in fact provided education officials with the initial justification for the ban. Rather than disagreeing with Rajaphat's homophobia, the press positioned itself and its readers as 'pro-democracy' in a political debate. The image of sexual/gender deviance thereby became a vehicle through which both Rajaphat and protesters argued about the meaning of development, democracy, and nation building, with debate over the ban on homosexuals being used as a vehicle to talk about changing visions of society. The People's Constitution set the tone for this debate, calling for an end to paternal, and autocratic rule by an arrogant bureaucracy.

Tuy

The *Tuy* sex crime cases, which occurred soon after the resolution of the Rajaphat case, reveal a curious reversal of sexual imagery in the press. *Tuy* imagery was less about 'transgendered' identity, than about a type of sexuality associated with exaggerated normative gender – an overly masculine man with homosexual behaviour. The sexualized gender of the *Tuy* is in sharp contrast to the Rajaphat case's portrayal of the 'sexual deviant' as an effeminate, victimized, minority group at the mercy of the bureaucracy (or as harmless, yet decadent middle class youth, such as in the early *tom-dee* portrayals).

In February 1999, Bangkok police raided a brothel in which teenage boys were working as prostitutes. Some of the boys, upon questioning, told the police that one of their male customers was a high-ranking politician with the nickname *Tuy*, a common nickname in Thai. The mystery of who the *Tuy* in question was, and the combination of politicians and homosexual commercial sex was a sensation in the press. The press unabashedly referred to *Tuy*'s homosexuality in the most offensive terms. The same papers that months before had defended the rights of homosexuals to education, now carried headlines like:

> Now known shit-packer *Tuy* is parliament officer ... face of shit-packing cross-dressing that pervert *Tuy* revealed. (*Thai Rath* 15 February 1998, p. 1, T)

And:

> Naked truth revealed. Sexual style of shit-packing *Tuy* makes hair stand on end. (*Thai Rath* 16 February 1998, p. 1, T)

The descriptive phrase 'at *thua dam*', literally meaning 'packing black beans' referring to anal homosexual sex, was added to the beginning of the name *Tuy* in most of the headlines, a practice that continued in the later *Tuy* cases as well. Eventually the police apprehended a politician for the crime, and the story faded from the papers. In the process, however, the name *Tuy* became a term used to refer to a certain kind of homosexual behaviour, that of an older man, or man in a respected senior position, taking advantage of that position through having sex with younger boys or men. For example, stories of monks who violated their vows by having sex with men or boys (either consensual or not) had often appeared in the sensationalist press. Headlines such as the following began to appear, with the term '*Tuy*-monks' being used to grab attention:

> *Tuy* Monk crops up again using Valium to sodomize sleeping kids. (*Daily News* 25 March 1998, p. 1, T)

In August 1998 the most sensational *Tuy* case of all broke – the case of 'Captain *Tuy*'.

A well-known male researcher was found murdered, and several army officers were quickly arrested for the crime. The police quickly surmised that all involved were homosexual and involved in a relationship. The police postulated that the victim, who had been raped and beaten to death, had threatened to blackmail the officers, or had been indiscreet, and was murdered in revenge. The police identified one primary suspect, an army captain, who was immediately labelled by the press as 'Captain *Tuy*'.

What started out as another sensational gay crime story was transformed into a political scandal and a focal point of cultural critique when Captain *Tuy*'s background was discovered. The press revealed that Captain *Tuy* had previously served a three-year prison sentence in Australia, and upon release had been escorted back to Thailand and reinstated in the military (against regulations) by a 'high placed friend'. The image of a 'perverse' and evil army officer protected by high placed friends resonated with press and public contempt of government cronyism and corruption. Even 'respectable' political papers such as *Matichon*, *Baan Muang*, and *Naewnaa* carried the Captain *Tuy* government corruption story as a front-page headline, daily for over a week. The political aspect of the story was emphasized, and the murder itself fell into the background. Demands from the press to know who had reinstated Captain *Tuy* back into the military were so intense that the Prime Minister himself, Chuan Leekpai, ordered an investigation. At one point, the ex-Prime Minister, Chawalit Yongchaiyut, was accused of being responsible for the reinstatement, a charge he denied. The association of the *Tuy* with political power is quite evident in the *Matichon* cover of its weekly journal: 'Bio of a *Tuy*'.

Eek! Bio of a *Tuy*, newest *Tuy* formula, government Mafia does a *Tuy* and then kills. (*Matichon Weekly* 1 September 1998, T)

The story that ran inside the magazine makes the connection between a *Tuy* and abuse of government power quite explicit.

It is important to recognize the broader context within which the term *Tuy* entered Thai vocabulary. The *Tuy* emerged as a media construction during a particularly scandal-plagued political and social context – for example, the mismanagement of the Bank of Thailand, logging scandals, and accusations of police shakedowns were hot issues at the time. This was the beginning of the era of Asian financial crisis, with a crippled Thai economy popularly believed to have been caused by political mismanagement and cronyism. There were demands for all types of reform, political, economic and social. The association of corrupt, autonomous centres of government power, such as the military, with the rapacious, decadent figure of the *Tuy* proved irresistible for the Thai press.

Like the *Tuy* stories before it, the Captain *Tuy* case eventually faded from the headlines, but the press has continued to use the term *Tuy*. For example, newspapers have more recently targeted the Thammakaya Buddhist sect for its alleged distortions of Buddhist teachings and unorthodox financing, running headlines with the word 'Thamma*tuy*' to conjure associations of 'perversion' and misuse of power (*Matichon Weekly* 15 December 1998). Media preference for using sensational images of homosexuality and transgenderism, in all the varied permutations this image can take, is therefore intimately linked to connecting the press and its readership, in broader political-social debates. The Thai media is, however, curiously silent about the sexuality of high-profile people who are widely known to be transgender/homosexual.

Discourse of Silence

Jackson (1997) among others has made the case that the homophobic attitude prevalent in Thailand is not primarily an attempt to control or discipline homosexuals. He notes that while many Thai academics have talked about homosexuality/transgendered sexuality as a problem in need of a cure, little effort has been made to enact laws or other forms of regulation. Of course such homophobic discourse is a type of control in itself, linking to the control of identity and the presentation of the self in public. As in other Orientalist discourses, Thai discourse of gendered homosexuality is about positioning the self in relation to an imputed set of negative characteristics belonging to an imagined entity. The placement of gendered sexualities in discourse as a marker of the other renders a silencing effect on positive portrayals of the self as transgendered/homosexual.

The coverage of Monrudii and Kop, two well-known female actors/models, offers a good example of the kind of muting of homosexual identity found in Thai press coverage. The couple was interviewed and asked if they were *tom-dee*. Kop replies.

If [Monrudee] were a man I would be prepared to live with her for the rest of my life. [L]ove between [Monrudee] and I, I think that we are doing as well as possible, we love each other, but it's not like *tom-dee* (*Siam Rath* 30 March 1998, T).

The magazine *Life and Home* recently ran the couple on their cover under the theme of 'Friends of the Heart'. In the accompanying text, Kop says she does not care if her 'friends' are men or women, but since society does not accept that women and men can be friends, she prefers women, '… being with a man there is a lot of slander, there is more risk than being with a woman' (*Life and Home*, 3, 1997, T). In both these articles, the relationship is never labelled as sexual, yet the individuals concerned are acknowledged being in a monogamous, romantic relationship which is widely interpreted as being *tom-dee* anyway. The theme of emotional closeness, and special friendship defines their relationship.

This theme of homosexuality (and its assumptions for gender identity) being recognized visually but muted verbally runs throughout the coverage of female same-sex couples. *City Life*, for example, ran a Valentine's Day issue on the subject of different kinds of love, and interviewed a *tom-dee* couple and a *gay* male couple. Unlike the movie stars, the ordinary women openly acknowledged that they were lovers (*faen*) yet never explicitly mentioned the sexual nature of their relationship and stressed once again their 'friendship'. In contrast, the *gay* men in the article said their relationship was about knowing what each other wanted sexually, saying that to have sex with a woman was flavour-less, like 'eating paper' (*City Life* 12 February 1995, T). The press provided sympathetic readings of both these men and women by construing their gendered sexual identity in stereotypical terms, void of any association with the types of sexuality and gendered identities used in media discourse of sexual otherness.

In these more sympathetic images, for example, women are (properly) asexual and emotionally sensitive. Men are in need of sexual diversity. These and other non-threatening images of gendered homosexuality currently appear on the cover of up-market magazines, and co-exist with the scathing vituperative of 'sexual deviance' and political/social mud slinging deployed elsewhere in the media. Foucault (1978) analyses the production of discourse that includes the production of silence; those images and words that are produced within the cultural logic but are constituted as unspeakable. In the space of the print media, in particular the print media aimed at middle-class audiences (compared with 'popular' tabloid-style media), sexuality and gender can be spoken of and represented in strictly controlled ways, but only to serve social/political agendas of the press.

Conclusions

The ubiquitous use of imagery of transgenderism and homosexuality in Thai public discourse can best be understood as a public discussion of qualities of the Thai self, rather than part of a consistent effort to suppress homosexuality or transgendered sexualities.[10] Through its appearance in the press, transgendered sexuality and homosexuality serves the discursive function of marking otherness, the point of transition between self and the other. Thais often insist that the issue of 'homosexuality' in society is not important, and in the sense that people generally are not concerned with the lives and realities of transgendered/homosexuals this seems to be true. However, gendered sexuality does serve an important function in contemporary discourse of self, alongside other images of non-self such as representations of ethnic minorities (see Krisadawan 1999). 'Deviant' groups thereby serve as a foil for the construction of the Thai self. They include the ubiquitous images of the sex-worker in Thai public discourse, as that which embodies the negative aspects of 'modernization', among other themes (see Mills 1993). In a different but related context, Thongchai's work on mapping in Siam explains that the use of boundaries is less about imaginary lines on the ground than about constructing spatial markers of otherness. The boundaries patrolled by the Thai Border Patrol Police are not the physical national limits, but the sense of Thai-ness that is to be found in hill tribe villages, rural communities, and even in the grounds of Thammasat University in Bangkok, among radical students (Thongchai 1994).

The media's use of the imagery of transgendered sexual identities and homosexuality is a type of Orientalist discourse in which images of the non-self, in the form of a disempowered other, are evoked in order to say something about the self, a process referred to as 'negative identification' by Thongchai (1994). Negative identification is useful for the exercise of political and social control because that which will be labelled as other can in principle embody any value: passivity or aggression, modernity or backwardness, for example. Representations of the stereotyped other are a standard form of discourse of self. The author Toni Morrison has explained how images of the black other are an integral part of the classic American literary tradition. The non-free, non-empowered, non-identified figure is necessary in order to identify the 'American' self as autonomous and individualistic. Morrison writes,

[T]here was a resident population ... upon which the imagination could play; through which historical, moral, metaphysical, and social fears, problems, dichotomies could be articulated. (1993, p. 37)

Like the image of transgendered sexuality/ homosexuality in Thai discourse, the black figure had no constant meaning, but could be contorted to meet the changing needs of the discourse of self,

[I]mages of blackness can be evil *and* protective, rebellious *and* forgiving, fearful *and* desirable – all of the self-contradictory features of the self. (1993, p. 59)

Discourse of homosexuality in the Thai press also uses the rhetoric of self and Other in its positioning in political/social debates. The homosexual marks the point of transition, an ever-changing boundary between self and Other. In the case of the young *tom-dee* and *gays*, homosexuality and transgenderism represent the uncertainty and anxiety related to the social transition to bourgeois modernity. The transgendered person and homosexual is most usually a young, brash, consumer-oriented offspring of the emerging middle class.

In the Rajaphat case, the transgendered/ homosexual is the vulnerable self, manifested in the image of the '*tut*', or '*kathoey*', in need of protection from an insensitive, and authoritarian state bureaucracy. The transgendered/ homosexual is here a proxy for people's rights in the desired political decentralization characteristic of the era of the 1997 constitution.

In contrast, in the *Tuy* sex crime cases, the sexualized gender/homosexual was a symbol of the governmental system itself, against which the population needed protection. The state power embodied in the figure of the *Tuy* was one based on cronyism and personal favours – the *Tuy* represented the traditional self, against which a new transparent and responsive government could be imagined. The homosexual imagery in the *Tuy* case was that of an almost hyper-masculine figure, a parody of the homo-social masculinity and aggression of the military.

Cultural iconography inherently contains contradictions and variation. John Fiske (1989, p. 5), in exploring the use of cultural symbols, explains, 'This semiotic richness ... means that they cannot have a single defined meaning, but they are a resource bank of potential meanings'. Thai public discourse on gendered sexuality/homosexuality is particularly rich in semiotic manipulation and creation, and this paper can only serve as only an introduction to the myriad themes of gender and sexuality in Thai public discourse that can be encountered.

The symbolic function of transgendered identity (at times inscribed as homosexual (*rakruampheet*) or third gender (*pheet thi saam*)) in embodying an Other through which cultural categories are reinforced or challenged, is perhaps a feature of the Indianized states of Southeast Asia and beyond. Johnson (1997,

p. 32) claims that the Philippine equivalent of the *katheoy*, the *bantut* has transformed from being 'metaphors of ancestral unity', evidenced in their pre-modern roles in royal and shamanistic ritual, to 'categories of crisis'. The transsexual–transgender–transvestite *bantut* symbolically embodies a national and ethnic other,

> The *bantut* [are] negatively defined not simply as a category of impotent men and unrealizable women, but as persons who have been overwhelmed by a potent cultural other, an alter-identity defined in terms of American style and the penetration of the Christian Philippines.

Johnson (1997, p. 32) concludes that the positioning of the *bantut* as exterior does not negate their use as 'figures of incorporation'. In Thai public discourse too, the transgendered/homosexual marks the point of crossing between imagined self and other, consistent with the general Thai concept of the inherent relationship between same-sex sexuality and gender inversion, being neither fully male nor female, and existing as a 'third sex'. Perhaps it is this gender ambiguity of the Thai imagined 'homosexual' – *katheoy, tom, dee,* or *gay* – that so easily evokes an image of the moment of social transition and cultural boundary crossing.

ACKNOWLEDGEMENTS

This paper is based on dissertation research on the topic of homosexuality in Thailand. I would like to recognize and thank the following for their support of the research: Peter Jackson, Mark Johnson, Kallayanee Techapatikul, Suphecha Baothip, Mattana Chetamee, Somjai Viriyabunditkul, Katherine Bowie, Ubonrat Siriyuvasak, Thongchai Winichakul, Tami Loos, Susan Hangen, the Fulbright Foundation; and the Center for Southeast Asian Studies, University of Wisconsin.

NOTES

1 This paper is based on three years research in Thailand on the subject of sexuality and sexual identity. Research for this paper included interviews with journalists at most major Thai newspapers. In addition, I interviewed columnists, academics, as well as approximately one hundred women identifying as *tom-dee*. The material for this paper is based on an analysis of approximately 150 articles from Thai newspapers and journals dating approximately from the early 1980s to the present.

2 See Jackson (1995, 1997), Morris (1994) for further detail on the history of Thai gendered and sexual identities.

3 The technical term for homosexuality, '*rakru-ampheet*' is of relatively recent origin, and smacks of academic jargon. The term used by most Thais to refer to what they recognize as homosexuality is '*pheet-thi-saam*' the third gender/sex, or '*phuying prapheet-thi-song*', literally the 'second kind of woman', referring to male transgendered homosexuals.

4 See Mills (1993) for discussion on the cultural meanings of 'modernity' in Thai society.

5 For example, see Loos (1999, pp. 238–301) for an analysis of how Siamese political elites in the early twentieth-century discredited political opposition by associating them with proclaimed 'primitive' practices such as polygamy, by accessing Western anthropological texts on social evolution, and the use of women's status as marker of social progress.

6 *Tom*, derived from the English word 'tomboy' means a masculine-identified woman. *Dee* refers to the feminine partner of the tom, derived from the word 'lady'. Same-sex sexual activity between women has long been recognized in Thai society, labeled as 'playing friends' (*len-phuen*), but there was no recognizable transgendered sexual identity before approximately the 1970s, with the emergence of *tom-dee*. There had long been a 'third gender' category that was once used to refer to either men or women who were cross-gendered, but now it has become to refer to men almost exclusively – the *kathoey*. A gender-normative man identifying as homosexual – *gay*, rather than a transvestite, was a new phenomenon, and I place the word in italics to indicate its specific Thai connotations.

7 All Thai sources were translated by the author and are marked with a 'T'.

8 There were notable exceptions to the general media homophobia, such as Pranee Srikamnert's articles for *Krungtheep Thurakit*.

9   Morris (1997) has suggested that the discourse of homosexuality in the Rajaphat case has helped bring about the reality of 'homosexuality' as a cultural category in Thailand. I would agree with her that the Rajaphat discourse did establish some academic definitions of homosexuality, but that these understandings of homosexuality are not embraced by *gays, tom-dee,* and *kathoey* for the most part. Even among many psychologists and academics, homosexuality remains an issue of gender deviance. In recently referring to male homosexuals, for example, the President of the Thai Psychiatric Institute referred to homosexuality as 'losing ones sex/gender', that is no longer being a 'real man' (*Matichon Daily* 30 January 1997, p. 9).

10 Although suppression is certainly the agenda of some academics, such as Wanlop Piyamanotham. 1992. '*Tom, gay, tut, dee*' in *Talking with a Psychologist,* Bangkok: Baphitkanphim Publishing (in Thai).

REFERENCES

Fiske, J.
(1989)   *Understanding Popular Culture* (New York: Routledge).
Foucault, M.
(1978)   *The History of Sexuality. Volume 1: An Introduction* (New York: Vintage Books).
Johnson, M.
(1997)   *Beauty and Power: Transgendering and Cultural Transformation in the Southern Philippines* (Oxford: Berg).
Jackson, P.
(1995)   *Dear Uncle Go: Male Homosexuality in Thailand* (Oakland, CA: Floating Lotus).
Jackson, P.
(1997)   *Katheoy*><Gay><Man: The Historical Emergence of Gay Male Identity in Thailand. In L. Manderson and M. Jolly (eds) *Sites of Desire, Economies of Pleasure: Sexualities in Asia and the Pacific* (Chicago: University of Chicago Press), pp. 166–190.
Krisadawan, H.
(1999)   *Competing Discourses on Hilltribes: Media Representations of Ethnic Minorities in Thailand.* Paper presented at the Seventh International Thai Studies Conference, Amsterdam, 4–8 July.
Loos, T. L.
(1999)   *Gender Adjudicated: Translating Modern Legal Subjects in Siam,* Unpublished PhD Dissertation, Cornell University.
Mills, M. E.
(1993)   '*We Are Not Like Our Mothers*': *Migrants, Modernity and Identity in Northeast Thailand.* Unpublished PhD Dissertation, University of California, Berkeley.
Morris, R. C.
(1997)   Educating Desire: Thailand, Transnationalism and Transgression. *Social Text,* 52/53, 53–79.
Morrison, T.
(1992)   *Playing in the Dark: Whiteness and the Literary Imagination* (London: Picador).
Said, E.
(1978)   *Orientalism* (Harmondsworth: Penguin Books).
Stoler, A.
(1991)   Carnal Knowledge and Imperial Power: Matrimony, Race, and Morality in Colonial Asia. In M. Leonardo (ed.) *Gender at the Crossroads of Knowledge: Feminist Anthropology in the Postmodern Era* (Berkeley: University of California Press), pp. 51–101.
Stoler, A.
(1997)   Educating Desire in Colonial Southeast Asia: Foucault, Freud, and Imperial Sexualities. In L. Manderson and M. Jolly (eds) *Sites of Desire, Economies of Pleasure: Sexualities in Asia and the Pacific* (Chicago: University of Chicago Press), pp. 27–47.
Thongchai, W.
(1994)   *Siam Mapped: A History of the Geobody of a Nation* (Honolulu: University of Hawaii Press).

27

The Categories Themselves

David Valentine

This forum seeks to consider the relationship between sexuality and gender. Still, for me, there is a question that needs to be asked before we can explore that relationship: among those human experiences in which we are interested, which count as "gendered" and which as "sexual"? Or, more simply, what exactly do we mean by "sexuality" and "gender"? Putting these terms in quotation marks highlights the fact that "gender" and "sexuality" are themselves categories that hold certain meanings. Like those of other categories, these meanings can shift, are historically produced, and are drawn on in particular social contexts.

In short, to ask about the relationship between "gender" and "sexuality" requires that we conceptualize them as distinct in the first place. In contemporary social theory, "gender" and "sexuality" are (like all categories) heuristics that generally and respectively describe the social meanings by which we figure out who is masculine and who is feminine and what those gendered bodies do with one another or feel about one another in a realm we call sex. Yet it is clear that these broad understandings are complicated by the ways that "gender" is inflected by our understandings of "sexuality," and vice versa. Hence this forum.

Asking about the relationship between "gender" and "sexuality," then, presents us with a dilemma: the question requires us to understand them simultaneously as discrete categories even as we recognize the interpenetration of experiences expressed through them. To return to the concern of my opening questions: how is it that, despite this dilemma, certain meanings have cohered around "gender" and certain ones around "sexuality"?

The separation of "gender" and "sexuality" has several, interrelated roots in recent history. In *How Sex Changed* Joanne Meyerowitz makes a convincing argument for the role of discourses and practices in the development of transsexuality in the United States as sources of the separation of biological sex, gender, and sexuality.[1] Drawing on late-nineteenth-century and early-twentieth-century European

David Valentine, The Categories Themselves, from *GLQ: A Journal of Lesbian and Gay Studies*, vol. 10, no. 2 (2004): 215–220. Copyright © 2004 Duke University Press. All rights reserved. Used by permission of the Publisher.

Sexualities in Anthropology: A Reader, edited by Andrew P. Lyons and Harriet D. Lyons
© 2011 Blackwell Publishing Ltd.

sexologists, U.S. doctors and researchers used the concepts of gender and sexuality to mark a difference between same-sex desire in gender-normative people (what we understand as homosexuality) and the desire to transition to another gender because of a deep sense of gender identity at odds with that ascribed at birth (what we understand as transsexuality). Meyerowitz notes that this schema was strengthened at least in part by those who desired new surgical possibilities for transforming their bodies and selves by denying not only homosexual desire (i.e., desire for people with similar embodiments prior to surgery) but sexual desire in general. Asexuality was, indeed, a primary criterion by which transsexual people were allocated a place in university-based gender identity clinics for sex reassignment surgery. The desire of gender-normative homosexual men and women *not* to have surgery, or their insistence that their core gender identity was in accord with their ascribed gender, further elaborated this model.

In feminist scholarship, too, the distinction between "gender" and "sexuality" has had a vital place. In the context of the "sex wars" of the 1980s, the separation of "sexuality" from "gender" was an essential part of a liberalizing move to recognize that oppressions do not apply evenly through the gendered categories of "woman" and "man" and that the separation of gender and sexuality as analytic categories enabled a more nuanced (and potentially liberatory) mode for understanding sexuality as something more than simply a tool of oppression.[2] Likewise, in mainstream gay and lesbian activism, the assertion of homosexual identification without the implication of gender-variant behavior has been essential to the gains of accommodationist groups seeking civil rights protections in the past thirty years.

What I have outlined so far is self-evident to contemporary social analysts, as is the recognition that gender and sexuality are inflected by other kinds of social differences: race, class, national origin, and age, to mention a few. However, what I am after here is a deeper observation: that the intersections of these experiences, as described and laid out in analytic categories, require the corralling of expe-

rience into discrete segments. This is, indeed, the basic problem of language: to describe something as seamless as lived experience, one needs categories. Yet a danger arises when those categories come to be seen as valid descriptions of experience rather than as tools used to apprehend that experience.

I am concerned, then, that the recent tendency to claim, as empirical fact, that gender and sexuality are separate and separable experiences results in a substitution of an analytic distinction for actual lived experience. For while this model describes some contemporary Western identities well, it is not the only model available. Indeed, the claim that bodily sex, social gender, and sexual desire are distinct categories stands in contrast to a much broader U.S. folk model of these experiences as a neatly aligned package. Their analytic separation has helped in, among other things, the analysis (and political validation) of queer, nonnormative identities and experiences, but it should be recognized that this is still only a model; it does not describe everyone's experiences.

And I am not necessarily concerned with Western heterosexual, gender-normative identities and experiences. Margaret Jolly and Lenore Manderson's discussion of desire and pleasure in Asia and the Pacific is instructive here. In considering contemporary critiques of Bronislaw Malinowski's collapsing of sexuality into reproductive heterosexuality and kinship, they argue: "The issue extends beyond the separation of sexuality and reproduction to the broader supposition that sexuality has ontological status in all times and places, that it is a thing that can be named and to which a set of behaviors, feelings, and desires can be attached."[3] That is, they propose that "sexuality" is not just about individual desire and that to understand it, we may need to look at things like reproduction, usually gathered into "gender," in those contexts where it is a significant aspect of what "sexuality" might signify for certain social actors. Thus Jolly and Manderson ask us to think about the ontological status of "sexuality" and "gender" in using those categories cross-culturally.

My own data indicate that such a critical question should also be directed at Western subjects who are assumed to be easily explained by the truth of a distinction that is itself culturally constructed. In New York City in the late 1990s, some people who were understood as "transgender" by social service agencies and activists either rejected that category or, often, did not use it to describe their own identities even though they knew it was used about them. Most of those who did not use it were young, poor, African American or Latina/o self-identified "gay" people, the same community made famous by Jennie Livingstone's film *Paris Is Burning* (1990). I put "gay" in quotes here because many people who see themselves as gay in this setting are not interpreted as such by the social service agencies under whose aegis I conducted my research. In the constellation of performative categories available at the balls, there are, indeed, strict distinctions between fem queens (male-bodied feminine people), butch queens (male-bodied masculine people), butches (female-bodied masculine people), and women or lesbians (female-bodied feminine persons). But the divisions, strictly enforced as they are, are seen at the balls to be united by the category "gay." At the ball, in other words, no matter what your embodiment, clothing, or behavior, everyone is considered to fall into a broader category of "gay".

In terms of more mainstream understandings of identity, though, this unity is rejected in favor of another distinction – between fem queens and butches ("transgender") and butch queens and lesbians ("gay"). These distinctions have real and institutional effects. Safer-sex outreach programs, social services, and, currently, federally funded AIDS research directed at the ball community are organized around the categories "gay" and "transgender." The rationale is based on the very distinction I am discussing: "transgender" identities are seen to flow from experiences of "gender" that are different from the "sexual" identity of "gay." The unity of the ball community as "gay" is not given credence precisely because fem queens and butches are, in theoretical and institutional terms, seen to have sources of identity that are ontologically distinct (residing in their "gender") from those of their butch queen and lesbian peers (who are seen to be united by their "sexual" identities). At root, this etic distinction relies on the analytic distinction between

"gender" and "sexuality," which overrides local understandings of those experiences we call gender and sexuality. The unity of the ballgoers as "gay" people is, I would argue, defined not by a distinction between "gender" and "sexuality" but by the conjunction of their disenfranchisement in terms of both class and racial memberships and their nonnormative "genders" or "sexualities."

As in Jolly and Manderson's discussion, the claim that the "gendered" practices of body transformation, cross-dressing, and the assertion of a nonascribed gendered identity are analytically separate from the "sexual" produces an effect in which the analytic model overrides understandings of self on the part of the young fem queens and butches of the balls. Indeed, such understandings, in which gender-transgressive practices and same-sex sexual desire are inextricable, are often decried by scholars as a kind of "misreading" or "false consciousness" or as "pre-modern."[4] Yet such conceptions of personhood exist historically and, I would add, persist in the modern West. To claim that fem queens and butches are "conflating" these experiences, or that they are holdovers of a premodern form of identification, is to make a modernist claim to progress and to the discovery of the truth of the separateness of "gender" and "sexuality."

The political stakes of this conceptual disjunction should be clear. In professing "gay" identities, the fem queens and butches become unrepresentable both in mainstream LGBT politics and in academic representations because they are claiming identities seen to be inherently false. This interpretation is licensed in turn by an analytic distinction between "gender" and "sexuality" that is seen to have ontological truth.[5]

The question "What is the relationship between gender and sexuality?" is therefore, for me, ultimately ethnographic and historical rather than purely theoretical, because this relationship is itself possible only in historical and cultural contexts where "gender" and "sexuality" have come to be – and are able to be – conceptualized as distinct arenas of human experience. The question requires us to think not simply about how these experiences intersect but about *which* lived experiences these terms might describe for historically and culturally located subjects.

I am certainly not calling for a return to a situation in which "gender" and "sexuality" cannot be conceived of as separate experiences or useful as analytic categories. After all, this distinction is not only relegated to the pages of scholarly journals but operative in (among other arenas) the cultural politics of civil rights activism, media representations, and (at least some) gay-, lesbian-, bisexual-, and transgender-identified people's self-understandings. But it is vital to recognize that it is also a modern (and modernist) technology of understanding the self that developed in the West in the mid- to late twentieth century. More important, it does not explain everyone's understanding of self in all times and places. In short, in much of the discussion about "gender" and "sexuality," the categorical power of these terms has come to be read as experiential fact; or, more succinctly, the experiential is subsumed and reordered by the categories we use to make sense of experience. Where this becomes dangerous is in the reordering of experience through analytic categories seen to be transparent and natural, a reordering that can, for all its progressive impetus, reproduce the invisibility and disenfranchisement of people who have had little voice, historically, in the debates and policies that have shaped their worlds.

We need, then, to think less about a relationship between "gender" and "sexuality" than about the constitution of those categories themselves as a historically located social practice. As with any relationship, it makes sense to think about the history of the parties involved before assessing what the relationship is.

NOTES

1 Joanne Meyerowitz, *How Sex Changed: A History of Transsexuality in the United States* (Cambridge, Mass.: Harvard University Press, 2002).

2 See Gayle Rubin, "Thinking Sex: Notes for a Radical Theory of the Politics of Sexuality," in *Pleasure and Danger: Exploring Female Sexuality*, ed. Carole S. Vance (London: Pandora, 1992), 267–319.

3 Margaret Jolly and Lenore Manderson, introduction to *Sites of Desire, Economies of Pleasure: Sexualities in Asia and the Pacific*, ed. Lenore Manderson and Margaret Jolly (Chicago: University of Chicago Press, 1997), 24.

4 See, e.g., Ken Plummer, "Speaking Its Name: Inventing a Lesbian and Gay Studies," in *Modern Homosexualities: Fragments of Lesbian and Gay Experiences*, ed. Ken Plummer (New York: Routledge, 1992), 3–25; and Gert Hekma, "'A Female Soul in a Male Body': Sexual Inversion as Gender Inversion in Nineteenth-Century Sexology," in *Third Sex, Third Gender: Beyond Sexual Dimorphism in Culture and History*, ed. Gilbert Herdt (New York: Zone, 1994), 213–39.

5 For a more developed version of this argument see David Valentine, "'We're Not about Gender': The Uses of 'Transgender,'" in *Out in Theory: The Emergence of Lesbian and Gay Anthropology*, ed. Ellen Lewin and William L. Leap (Urbana: University of Illinois Press, 2002), 222–45.

Part XI
Heterosexuality Today

Introduction

When anthropology "rediscovered sexuality" (Vance 1991), it primarily rediscovered same-sex sexualities. In the 1980s and early 1990s comparatively little work with any theoretical impact appeared concerning the cross-cultural study of heterosexuality, with the possible exception of Marjorie Shostak's *Nisa* (1981), the story of a San woman, and Thomas Gregor's account of heterosexuality and sexual antagonism among the Amazonian Mehinaku, *Anxious Pleasures* (1987). To disciples of Michel Foucault that would not be surprising, given his remarks that the new science of sexology had, ever since the 1880s, shifted the focus of discourse away from the married, fertile, heterosexual couple to the hysterical woman, the Malthusian couple, the masturbating child, and the "perverse" adult (Foucault 1977: 105). Foucault did not consider "savages" as a category of discourse, and his remarks reflect the former moral climate in France (arguably, the Malthusian couple is much less controversial today). However, because the anthropology of sexuality has always tended to reflect social currents in metropolitan countries, it is perhaps not surprising that gay and lesbian liberation as a social movement should be so prominently reflected in the design and completion of anthropological research projects and the creation of new theory about sexualities since the 1970s. Whatever the reason for the time lag, some interesting, new ethnographic work on heterosexuality has appeared since 1995.

Although the three articles we have selected discuss very different cultures and places (the Copper Inuit of Holman, now Ulukhaktok, in the Canadian Northwest; urban and rural Igbo in Southern Nigeria; and the young, partly detribalized, urban elite of Nairobi, Kenya), they all tell a story of increasing choice in the election of sexual and marriage partners, a valorization of romantic love (influenced by film, television, and other media), and a pursuit of "companionate marriage" as an ideal, at least during the

Sexualities in Anthropology: A Reader, edited by Andrew P. Lyons and Harriet D. Lyons
© 2011 Blackwell Publishing Ltd.

courtship process. All three articles raise interesting questions about sexual and marriage practices in the past and the way they were described, as well as the degree of social change in the past 50–100 years, and the causes and the consequences of such transformations. Only one of the articles (Stern and Condon) raises, albeit peripherally, the question of a biological base to romantic passion, but all three assume that "love" in some form or other is universal. Lastly, two of the articles (Smith and Spronk) address the problems of describing sexuality in the age of AIDS.

The distinction between sexual desire, romantic love, and companionate/lasting love is an important aspect of these analyses. Essentialists such as Helen Fisher (author of *Why We Love*, 2004) and William Jankowiak and Thomas Paladino (2008) argue that these are separable/separate states and that each of them has a distinct neurological and biological basis – for example, a release of the neurotransmitter oxytocin may accompany orgasm and may persist during a period of passionate love. While there are many who may be skeptical of such findings, there is no doubt that a belief in the existence of these three states is at the very least common to our own and other cultures. In contemporary Western societies, romantic love is supposed to form part of the courtship process which leads to marriage by individual choice. In societies where the marriage partner is prescribed and/or arranged by one's kin or future in-laws, romantic love is unlikely to accompany marriage, although it may have a place in pre-marital and extra-marital trysts (such as those celebrated by medieval troubadours). It has been argued (e.g., by Jankowiak) that romantic love is universal, but that is not strictly provable at the moment. However, there is no doubt that it is far more widespread than was formerly believed. The notion of companionate love and marriage was originally developed by sexologists and family planning advocates such as Marie Stopes early in the last century, as well as by social scientists like Elsie Clews Parsons and the American Judge Ben Lindsey. In contemporary parlance the companionate ideal involves the notion that self-realization is only possible through continued intimacy and love between partners who cohabit and share their life interests, rather than inhabiting separate spheres of social and familial space. Urbanization, industrialization, the breakup of the large extended family, changes in reproductive technology, mass media influences, and individualism have all played a role in such developments.

If romantic love and companionate marriage are favored by modern industrial conditions, what kind of sexual relationships, love, and marriage prevailed in premodern societies? As we have already noted, nineteenth-century travelers, missionaries, and evolutionary anthropologists exaggerated cultural differences, thereby "othering" non-European peoples. However, that does not mean that all differences were purely the work of fervid imaginations. As Stern and Condon observe, spouse exchange was a real institution among the pre-contact Copper Inuit, but spousal jealousy and male violence, caused by disputes over women, was also a reality in a society where brides were in short supply due to female infanticide. Most marriages were arranged, and involved alliances for survival in sparsely populated areas where there was a very small group of potential partners. Such institutions were ideal talking-points for cross-cultural voyeurs. Following writers such as Rasmussen and Jenness, Stern and Condon show that "infatuation" did occur between marriage partners, and sometimes between individuals involved in spouse exchanges. They believe that exchanges were frequently undertaken for reasons of political alliance and that they also may have worked as safety valves for partners in exchange marriages. In the early contact period, the missionaries proved effective in effecting the disappearance of many Inuit institutions, and monogamous, Christian marriages became the norm. In the 1980s and 1990s, when Stern and Condon did their fieldwork, Inuit had permanent settlements where they lived in prefabricated houses. They were part of the cash economy, bought food in stores, watched television, and visited other parts of Canada as tourists. For the first time there were enough adolescents in the community to create some sort of subculture. Premarital sex, romantic love, late marriage involving personal choice, divorce, and the choice of single motherhood were all now part of the picture.

Racist and ethnocentric portrayals of African sexuality have already been the subject of discussion in this Reader (see Magubane's article – Chapter 2). The fact that AIDS first became endemic in Africa caused both the scholarly community and laypeople to speculate whether or not Africans were indeed "different" in some significant way. Such speculation is perhaps inevitable, but micro-organisms themselves are innocent of sin and know nothing of "race," ethnicity, or sexualities. There is a randomness about epidemics that few appreciate. John and Patricia Caldwell and their research teams (e.g., Caldwell et al. 1989), many of whom were African, disclaimed all forms of racism, but did attempt a cultural explanation of differentials in AIDS incidence. They tried to link the high incidence of AIDS in Africa to a common "African family system" with the following characteristics: hoe rather than plough agriculture, barren land, no substantial surplus, ownership of services rather than land, kin groups based on unilineal descent rather than nuclear families, the lack of a female honor/virginity complex, the need to reproduce labor and maximize the number of children, polygyny, and lax rules about pre-marital and extra-marital sexuality extending to women. Some of these features, most of which originated in the rural economy, are indeed present in some African societies, but in many they have disappeared, if they were once there. AIDS rates differ from one part of the continent to another, and these differences may be explained by complex historical and epidemiological factors rather than just the absence or presence of any African family complex. In Southern Nigeria, where Daniel J. Smith worked, the incidence of AIDS has risen to between 3 and 5 percent of the population, significant but much lower than in some other parts of the continent. Smith does indicate which specific feelings and behaviors may enhance the risk of HIV infection in the course of an analysis of contemporary Igbo sexuality and morality.

Romantic love and marriage according to personal choice have been features of Igbo life in cities such as Onitsha since World War II, although it is only recently that they have become usual rather than exceptional. Smith indicates that most of his young informants had pre-marital sex with a partner to whom they were romantically attracted, and that the relationship between partners was egalitarian during the period of courtship and based on a companionate ideal. However, Igbo marriages were still patriarchal, centered round the extended family and the production of children. A double standard was condoned. Many married men took their young mistresses or "handbags" to sports clubs and traveled around with them. A feeling that one must not show distrust in one's partner (lover, husband, or "sugar daddy") and a belief that condoms destroy intimacy resulted in decreased condom use, a high rate of abortions, and an enhanced risk of AIDS.

Spronk's approach is quite unusual, inasmuch as she is concerned that the AIDS epidemic has distorted the focus of the anthropological study of sexuality to such a degree that some anthropologists are inclined to forget that for most people in Africa and elsewhere sex is a pleasurable activity. Most of her informants were second-generation city dwellers who were students or had middle-class jobs. They usually had pre-marital sex and married partners with whom they shared dreams of intimacy. They consumed not merely Western but also indigenous mass media that supported romantic love and companionate marriage. They were concerned about giving not merely love but also sexual pleasure to their partners. Indeed, their newly found freedom implied a duty to promote mutual intimacy and satisfaction, and there was, accordingly, some anxiety about performance. This is what the philosophers Michel Foucault and Judith Butler have called the paradox of subjectivation (*assujetissement*) – the processes that call sexual subjects/agents into being are also the means by which they are subordinated.

REFERENCES

Butler, Judith
    1993   Bodies that Matter: On the Discursive Limits of Sex. London: Routledge.
Caldwell, John. C., Caldwell, Pat, and Pat Quiggin
    1989   The Social Context of AIDS in Sub-Saharan Africa. Population and Development Review 15(2):189–234.
Fisher, Helen
    2004   Why We Love: The Nature and Chemistry of Romantic Love. New York: Holt.
Foucault, Michel
    1977   The History of Sexuality, vol. I: An Introduction. New York: Vintage.
Foucault, Michel
    1980   Power/Knowledge: Selected Interviews and Other Writings 1972–1977. Colin Gordon, ed. London: Harvester.
Gregor, Thomas
    1987   Anxious Pleasures: The Sexual Lives of an Amazonian People. Chicago: University of Chicago Press.
Jankowiak, William R., and Thomas Paladino
    2008   Desiring Sex, Longing for Love: A Tripartite Conundrum. *In* Intimacies: Love and Sex Across Cultures. William Jankowiak, ed. Pp. 1–36. New York: Columbia University Press.
Shostak, Marjorie
    1981   Nisa: The Life and Words of a !Kung Woman. Cambridge, MA: Harvard University Press.
Vance, Carole S.
    1991   Anthropology Rediscovers Sexuality: A Theoretical Comment. Social Science and Medicine 33(8):875–884.

28

A Good Spouse Is Hard to Find: Marriage, Spouse Exchange, and Infatuation Among the Copper Inuit

Pamela R. Stern and Richard G. Condon

His eyebrows wishing to meet
His eyebrows wishing to meet properly,
Wishing to meet, meet.
His armpit, its odor.
His eyebrows wishing to meet properly,
Wishing to meet, meet.
Its odor.
His eyebrows wishing to meet properly,
His eyebrows wishing to meet,
Wishing to meet, meet.
His armpit, its odor,
His eyebrows,

> Dance song performed by Jennie
> Kanayuk, a Copper Inuit girl

Introduction

Early accounts of arctic explorers, traders, and missionaries have created a stereotype of the Inuit as promiscuous and lusty in their sexual liaisons. The typical scenario is that of an Inuit man who displays his generosity to strangers by offering the sexual favors of his wife or daughters. The stereotype of sexual liberalism is as enduring an image of Inuit culture as snowhouses, raw-meat eating, and female infanticide. The fact that this stereotype has taken such a firm hold on the Western imagination probably says more about our own sexual voyeurism than about the true nature and function of Inuit marriage and spouse exchange.

As is so often the case with simple stereotypes, there exists a parallel but opposite myth. The contrasting myth presents the archetypal Inuit male consumed with fear and jealousy lest another man abduct his wife. Indeed, the precontact practice of selective female infanticide did result in a scarcity of women and thus a skewing of the sex ratio. The result was that competition between males for wives,

Pamela R. Stern and Richard G. Condon, A Good Spouse Is Hard to Find: Marriage, Spouse Exchange, and Infatuation Among the Copper Inuit, from *Romantic Passion*, William Jankowiak, ed., New York: Columbia University Press, 1995, pp. 196–218. Reprinted with permission of Columbia University Press.

Sexualities in Anthropology: A Reader, edited by Andrew P. Lyons and Harriet D. Lyons

occasionally leading to murder, was common-place in some areas. With both stereotypes women are presented as mere pawns of their men, giving freely of their bodies with a minimum of emotional attachment.

The reality of Inuit pairbonding and spouse exchange, however, is much more complex, although some facets of the stereotypes may ring true. We cannot deny the existence of spouse exchange (which some have inappropriately called wife exchange or wife lending), nor can we fail to recognize the importance of male competition for females. As is true of all societies, the sexual mores of the Inuit were mitigated by a host of demographic, social, and economic realities. That Inuit husbands would be concerned over the potential loss of their wives to a competitor while at the same time accepting their sexual liaisons with other men highlights one of the paradoxes of Inuit culture. Such an apparent paradox begs the question "What is the nature of Inuit marriage and to what extent is it based upon affection between partners versus a simple marriage for convenience?"

There is a great deal of evidence in the ethnographic literature to suggest that Inuit husbands and wives had strong affective ties to one another, although the high value Inuit placed upon emotional restraint could mask the expression of these feelings to the naive outside observer. While sexual attraction and infatuation could serve as the basis for pairbonding, it was unlikely that this was the rule. The demands of the harsh arctic ecosystem resulted in both high mobility and low population density. The scarcity of suitable marriage partners and the demand that young men and women make a rapid transition from childhood to adult responsibilities effectively limited opportunities for courting behavior or individual choice in pairbonding. In short, a good spouse was hard to find.

Traditional Inuit marriage, however arranged, had a particularly interesting feature – institutionalized spouse exchange. Many scholarly treatments of traditional Inuit marriage and sexual relations have attempted to make sense of this practice (see Balikci 1970; Burch 1970; Burch and Correl 1972; Damas 1971; and Guemple 1979). To Westerners accustomed to thinking of extra-marital sexual activity as necessarily illicit, the widespread acceptance of socially sanctioned extramarital sexual activity – apparently devoid of jealousy – is difficult to comprehend. For example, Diamond Jenness, who spent three years in extremely intimate contact with the Copper Inuit, recorded the following confession in his diary:

> There was an interesting insight into the customs of these Eskimos last night. After "supper" Itoqunna disappeared and Niq entered the house. ... She took Itoqunna's place and a little later turned in to bed. Itoqunna, I believe slept with Niq's husband Akhiatak – an exchange of wives for the night – very likely in connection with the change from the summer hunting of caribou on land to the winter's sealing on the ice. In the morning Niq turned out, mended the trousers of Haviuyaq's father, who sleeps in the other part of the house, and generally took the place of Itoqunna. A little later Itoqunna came in, said not a word but went into the other part of the house, trimmed the lamp, and appeared to wait for Niq to depart, which she did quietly a few minutes later. No words passed between the two women, but when Itoqunna entered, Haviuyaq laughingly asked me "Where is Itoqunna?" – alluding to my question of the night before, whereupon everyone laughed. I do not know if everyone exchanged wives last night, though Haviuyaq asked me if I still wanted to sleep alone. The custom is, of course, well known among savages from books, but strangely enough it shook my nerves more than anything else I have seen in the Arctic. ... I have not dared enquire yet whether it was in connection with the sealing – though I feel rather ashamed of my weakness in this respect as an ethnologist. (Jenness 1991:350)

Jenness recorded several other instances of spouse exchange between the two couples mentioned above, including an extended trip by Ahkiatak into the territory of Itoqunna's relatives. Although Itoqunna was married to Haviuyaq, she accompanied Ahkiatak in order to visit her kin *and* to assure Ahkiatak's welcome among strangers. Niq and Haviuyaq remained behind together. Upon completion of the trip each returned to his or her own spouse (Jenness 1970:85–86; Jenness 1991:357, 370).

These and other anecdotal accounts of Inuit sexual activity often leave the faulty impression that Inuit husbands and wives lacked the strong emotional attachments to each other that might be characterized in our culture as romantic love or infatuation.[1] In fact, some researchers have even suggested that the Inuit lack emotional attachment altogether (Lubart 1970). This argument is often supported by referencing high separation rates for Inuit men and women, either as a result of divorce or accidental death (see Burch 1970 and Heinrich 1972 for discussions of divorce among North Alaskan Inupiat). Thus, in this view, the rigors of life were so great for the Inuit that emotional attachments must necessarily be shallow, as concerns of the stomach must inevitably supersede concerns of the heart.

In attempting to understand Inuit spouse exchange, many researchers have sought purely economic explanations. These include the cementing of social ties between families already engaged in some kind of trading or hunting partnership (McElroy 1979), the extension of kinship networks (Damas 1971), and the creation of alliances between families of different regions (Burch 1970; Burch and Correl 1972). Whether an Inuit male seeks to solidify a hunting partnership through spouse exchange or desires safe passage through a strange territory by bringing along an exchange spouse who originates from that area, it is the alliance function of spouse exchange that takes precedence in most scholarly discussions. Burch (1970) emphasizes that spouse exchange must be viewed as an integral part of Inuit marriage in which most married couples engaged at some point in their lives. Diamond Jenness (1970:86), alone, considers lust and power in addition to the standard alliance explanations of spouse exchange.

Unfortunately, purely materialist explanations of Inuit marriage and spouse exchange serve to oversimplify the complex sexual, psychological, economic, and political motivations of Inuit couples in establishing spouse exchange relationships. Indeed, the personal motivations for creating such alliances may have varied from one circumstance to another and from one spouse to another. Who is to say that infatuation with another's spouse was not a critical motivating factor for many exchange relationships, even those that may have resulted in some kind of formal alliance?

Admittedly, it is difficult for outsiders to understand the emotional relationships and motivations of Inuit husbands and wives. At least two of the researchers in the best position to interpret the Inuit marital relationship, Diamond Jenness and Jean Briggs, have readily admitted that there is little that they understand fully (Briggs 1974:272; Jenness 1991). It has been our experience that Inuit are exceedingly reluctant to openly discuss any sort of emotional experience, even though they may be quite candid in their sexual joking. It is far easier to describe peoples' behaviors than to ascribe, with any degree of accuracy, the motivations to those behaviors. As a result, like Briggs and Jenness, we are left to interpret emotional states and motivations primarily from observable behavior and hope that our interpretations bear some resemblance to reality.

The authors have spent in excess of fifty-seven person months between 1978 and 1993 engaged in ethnographic fieldwork in the Copper Inuit community of Holman in the Central Canadian Arctic. During this period we have investigated a number of topics including adolescent development, health, and nutrition, reactions to extreme seasonal variation, and the impacts of rapid social change. Since 1987 we have been engaged in detailed oral history interviewing and genealogical data collection from community elders. Overall, our involvement in this community has entailed fairly intimate participation in and observation of community life. For this reason we feel reasonably qualified to make some observations regarding Inuit marriage and the kinds of changes it has undergone since the arrival of Euro-Canadian traders, missionaries, and government functionaries. Our data pertaining to the precontact era are mostly derived from the observations of researchers such as Diamond Jenness and Knud Rasmussen, while our data on the postcontact period (contact-traditional horizon, in the words of Helm and Damas 1963) come primarily from life history interviews conducted with Inuit elders. Lastly, information regarding courtship and marriage patterns since the late 1970s are based entirely upon our own extensive fieldwork.

The Inuit couples we know in Holman are no more homogeneous than our married friends and colleagues here in the South (who we admit are no more a representative sample than our Inuit informants). There are couples who seem to be happy with each other and couples whose relationships are clearly strained. There are couples who fight and couples who do not, couples who work and relax side by side and couples who spend little time together. Some of our Inuit friends have marriages that were arranged by parents against their wills, but have nonetheless come to value and appreciate their spouses. Other couples boast of having chosen one another without parental intervention. And still others admit to having married over the objections of their parents.

The circumstances leading to these marriages are as varied as the personalities involved in them. There is no doubt that precontact pairbonding and the spouse exchange relationships that eventually developed from those marriages were similarly varied. While traditional pairbonding was heavily influenced by the availability and economic competence of the potential partners, there was certainly room for infatuation based upon personality and physical appearance. While the amount of "room" for romance was probably small, Inuit society has always been characterized by a high degree of negotiability and flexibility. It is this flexibility that allowed for the expression of individual choice in all domains of Inuit life. In short, Inuit men and women could have passions. These passions could result in a young girl rejecting a marriage partner selected by her parents, they could lead a man to kidnap another man's wife, and they could motivate a woman to urge her husband to enter a spouse exchange relationship with an enticing trading partner. Far from being automatons oriented toward the brutish and sometimes tedious tasks of finding food and shelter, Inuit had individual personalities with varied agendas, or, to put it more simply, they were human.

In the text that follows we will try to discuss some of the changes that have occurred in Copper Inuit marriage and spouse exchange

practices over the past sixty to seventy years. Because we consider the Copper Inuit to be distinct from other Inuit groups, either to the east or west, we will make no attempt to generalize our observations to the entire Eskimo culture area.

Fieldsite

The residents of Holman are primarily descendants of the northernmost groups of Copper Inuit who occupied the western coast of Victoria Island: the Kanghiryuarmiut of Prince Albert Sound and the Kanghiryuatjagmiut of Minto Inlet. There are also a small number of "western" Inuit families from the Mackenzie Delta whose ancestors entered Copper Inuit territory in the 1930s and 1940s for the purposes of trading, trapping, and wage employment. The Victoria Island Copper Inuit were among the last groups to come into prolonged and direct contact with traders, missionaries, and government officials, and, hence, were the most recent group to experience the extreme changes in economic, social, and religious activities demanded by the outsiders. In our view the postcontact experience of these northern Copper Inuit differs from that of other Canadian and Alaskan Inuit in one major respect: the majority of the most dramatic acculturative changes have occurred within the memory of Holman's oldest residents.

No aspect of Copper Inuit life was left unchanged after contact with Euro-Canadians. Traders, missionaries, and the Royal Canadian Mounted Police (RCMP), each with their own agendas, entered Copper Inuit territory at virtually the same moment. Each group demanded changes in Inuit social organization and ideology. In addition, Euro-Canadians were a vector for a host of lethal diseases that, by themselves, would have been enough to change Inuit life forever.

During our 1982–83 fieldwork we came to the startling conclusion that divorce did not exist in Holman. Our genealogical, life history, and household census data indicated that from the 1940s onward couples who had established a coresidence *never* separated. A check with informants confirmed that there had, indeed, been two "divorces"[2] within their memories. All other marriages were not necessarily harmonious but, once established, did not end in divorce. While Roman Catholic and Anglican missionaries had successfully eliminated institutionalized spouse exchange, they were unable to affect basic attitudes regarding sexuality and sexual behavior. "Extramarital" sexual activity continued to be common, but without the reciprocity required of formal spouse exchange, leading at least one Holman elder, Albert Palvik, to assert that promiscuity never existed before the arrival of whites. Oddly enough, in their attempt to guide the Inuit from a "heathen" existence to a Christian life, the missionaries may have inadvertently contributed to an increase in illicit sexual activity by eliminating a culturally approved and open system of spouse exchange. Palvik's assertion of the recent origin of promiscuity certainly makes sense from an emic perspective. An extremely large number of children are reported by Holman residents to have resulted from extramarital affairs. This is testimony, at least to the community's belief, that sexual fidelity is not the key ingredient to a successful marriage.[3]

Upon returning to Holman in 1988 for another extended research visit, we documented a number of significant social, economic, and physical changes in the community. In addition to experiencing an increase in population, the community had a new multimillion dollar school building equipped with a large gymnasium. School attendance had improved so dramatically that truancy was no longer a problem. Television programming, which first became available in 1981, had increased from a single station (CBC North) to five channels, including an NBC station from Detroit, offering people an even bigger window to the outside world. Wage labor had become the primary economic activity and, consequently, store-bought food comprised a large percentage of most families' diets. People increasingly looked to the South rather than to the land for their leisure diversions, and many (especially younger) families chose to vacation in Yellowknife or Edmonton. Finally, in the process of updating our household census records, we discovered that there had been a number of divorces and separations.

While it is perhaps too soon to determine if Holman is undergoing a major shift in its marriage patterns, more recent data collected in 1992–1993 suggest that young adults, at least, are following a more Euro-Canadian style of pairbonding. Not only are many young adults deciding to delay pairbonding to a later age, but a large number of those who do form a domestic unit with a spouse often separate after a few years. Interestingly, this observation seems to conform to the nearly universal pattern of marriage and divorce identified by Fisher (1987, 1992). While we agree with Fisher's general observations, we feel that the biological/evolutionary case presented by her is insufficient to fully explain this behavioral change in Holman, nor does it account for the very different patterns of marriage operating in the precontact and postcontact periods. Fisher does, however, point out that economic, social, and historical factors can and do alter even those human behaviors that appear to be most strongly rooted in biology. As a result, we feel that it is important to identify these social and historical factors, an exercise that is best achieved by examining changes in marriage institutions within individual societies over a long period of time. In the remainder of this essay we hope to accomplish this task for Copper Inuit society by describing marriage (and extramarital) patterns for three historical periods: 1) contact to circa 1935, 2) circa 1935 to 1985, and 3) 1985 to the present. We make no claim that these are distinct historical periods with firmly delimited boundaries; they are simply convenient markers for discussing somewhat gradual but nevertheless distinct changes in Copper Inuit pairbonding.

Copper Inuit Marriage and Divorce: Contact to 1935

At the beginning of this century, when the first Euro-Canadian explorers, traders, and missionaries arrived in the Central Arctic, Copper Inuit marriage was an extremely informal affair. While it is clear that children were prepared for adult roles that were synonymous with marriage, no elaborate ceremonies existed to mark either the transition from childhood to adulthood or the establishment of a pair-bond. Nevertheless, marriage was clearly a significant marker of adulthood and was necessary, in the words of elder Sam Oliktoak, "in order to have a full life." In fact, an idiomatic expression meaning "a lonely man" translates literally as "one who is without a woman" (Rassmussen 1932:319).

Social and economic conventions mandated highly distinct but equally crucial roles for men and women. This mutual dependency, for both economic and reproductive purposes, necessitated that nearly all adults be married. There was little incentive and certainly no advantage to staying single. As has often been noted in the anthropological literature, the Copper Inuit region of the Central Arctic is an extremely harsh, unproductive environment. A spate of poor hunting luck or an accident could, and frequently did, result in starvation. Marriage for women signified security; for men, hunting success was synonymous with marriage. This is expressed most clearly in the following Copper Inuit dance song:

How here telling me to find subsistence.
Caribou when they take to the water despite
    my wish to secure them.
Only one its way, this one,
Of Marau to the lands, to the place possessing
    caribou down thither.
How here telling me to find subsistence.
Seals, they will not come to me, although one
    wishes to secure them.
Only one its way, this one,
Of Qoingnannaq to the lands, to the place
    possessing seals down thither.
A more abundant place than this one though
    being hard to find ...
To a place with seal-holes, a place with seals;
    when there are no seals one is always idle.
How here telling me to find subsistence.
Women, those, they will not marry me
    although I wish to get them.
Only one its road, this one,
Of Tamarsuin to the lands, though wishing
    to go.
A more abundant place than this though being
    hard to find ...
To a place with women, to a place with people;
    when there are no women one always dreams
    of them. (Roberts and Jenness 1925:451)

To some extent, it was probably easier to find "subsistence" than to find suitable marriage partners. Given the practice of female infanticide, there were a large number of bachelors in precontact Copper Inuit society. Extremely low population density throughout the region meant that as a youngster approached marriageable age there might be few or no suitable mates. Children of both sexes were betrothed at birth, but these commitments were rarely honored (Jenness 1970:158). Families were highly individualistic in their travels, and encountering a potential spouse for a son or daughter was often serendipitous. Consequently, individuals could not afford to be too choosy with respect to the selection of a mate. Most first marriages were arranged by parents, although it was not unusual for a young woman or man to reject the parents' choice of mate. But, given the absence of any sizeable adolescent peer group to function as a playing field for courting and sexual experimentation, parents were generally in a better position to locate potential spouses for their offspring. In spite of arranged marriage, it is clear that some couples were clearly infatuated with one another:

> Instances of genuine affection are not at all uncommon, even before a child is born to cement the union. Avranna and Milukkattak might often be seen stretched out on the bedskins in their hut pressing noses and caressing each other, wholly oblivious to the presence of other natives around them. Milukkattak would go out hunting with him, and sealing too at times, so that they might not be separated for a single hour. (Jenness 1970:160)

Other couples were not as emotionally involved and simply tolerated each other. The value traditional Inuit placed on tolerance, nondemandingness and noninterference (see Condon 1992; Honigmann and Honigmann 1965) undoubtedly pervaded the marital relationship as well. In many cases couples who were incompatible did not stay married more than a few days or weeks. The economic necessity of marriage encouraged flexibility. These included temporary unions between brothers and sisters (which occasionally involved sexual intercourse) as well as polygyny and, less commonly, polyandry.

Marriage for females generally occurred right around menarche, while for males it was delayed until they demonstrated the necessary hunting and survival skills *and* could locate a suitable mate. The first months or years of a marriage were really a trial period for the couple. If the man planned to take his wife to another region, he was expected to provide a modest brideprice to the woman's family. If, however, the couple planned to stay in the same vicinity, it was common for the young man to move into his in-law's household and to work with his father-in-law as a kind of brideservice. This one- to two-year period provided an opportunity for the couple to determine their compatibility and to mature into their adult roles before embarking out on their own. Divorce was common during the trial marriage period; both the man or woman could abandon the partnership at any time. The only requirement was that the brideprice, if one was paid, be returned. Many traditional unions were long and enduring, ending only with death. Both Jenness (1970:160) and Rassmussen (1932:51) report that divorce was exceeding rare after the birth of a child. Nevertheless, high accidental death rates, especially for males, and often large age differences between husbands and wives meant that most people married several times over the course of a lifetime. Young widows had fewer problems in remarrying than young widowers. Men as well as middle-aged and elderly widows, however, might have a long wait for another spouse if they remarried at all (Jenness 1970:163).

Despite the extreme hardships of a single life, individuals who found themselves in intolerable marriages took steps to remedy the situation. In the words of Frank Kuptana,

After my father, Iqalukpik, died, my mother remarried ... [but] she got tired and fed up with her second husband, Urhuraq, and feeling sorry for the way he treated me. So she left Minto Inlet because her husband would beat her up. ... My mother started her trip away from Minto when the land had no more snow, so that her husband couldn't go and track her down. My mother and I reached people near Read Island [three hundred miles to the south]. ... Me and my mom never saw my

[stepfather and his people] again. Well, they weren't able to track us down. He must have looked for us, but they never did find us. My mother must have known that there were people down around Read Island, so that's where we ran off to. ... There were quite a few people there. My mother and I were adopted by Kanayoks and those people looked after us. Then my mother married Qunmuktuk. ... That man, Qunmuktuk, was a very nice man. He sure was good to me. He showed me a lot of affection. ... That's how I remember him.

Although compatibility rather than infatuation was undoubtedly the critical element in pairbonding, Jenness (1970:163) reports that jealousy was a perennial source of conflict between husbands and wives, although one that rarely led to divorce. Given the Inuit emphasis on cooperation, and the value placed upon the avoidance of conflict within local groups, such jealousy may have been highly controlled. It is within this context that we must consider the practice of spouse exchange. Burch (cited in Briggs 1974) reports that, for North Alaska, spouse exchange relationships, rather than marriages, were often made on the basis of infatuation. It is reasonable to conclude that while most marriages were arranged on the basis of convenience, availability, compatibility, and potential alliances, spouse exchange relationships had the potential to be based upon more amorous concerns for *all* parties involved. Seen in this light, spouse exchange may be viewed not only as a technique for alliance formation, and the ultimate extension of the Inuit tendency to share everything in their possession, but also as a method to diffuse sexual tension and jealousy. It was also a legitimate avenue for the expression of sexual attraction. Spouse exchange provided a reciprocal and egalitarian method for extra-marital sex that neither threatened the critical marriage bond nor led to its dissolution. In fact, the occasional temporary exchange of partners might very well have resulted in a strengthening of the marriage bond. Why leave your husband for another when you can have your husband and share someone else's too?

In discussing the spouse exchange event cited at the beginning of this chapter, Jenness

(1991:352) observed that Itoqunna and Haviuyaq showed each other a great deal of affection "despite the temporary change in marital relations the other night." The woman Itoqunna is the focus of many of Jenness's observations of spouse exchange. She is also the subject of an improvised dance song dealing with infatuation. According to Jenness, the singer, Aquluk, observed Itoqunna gaze longingly across the room at the husband of a third woman (all three couples were present). When Itoqunna realized that she was being observed she looked down in embarrassment.

> Her husband, she feeling love for him,
> The woman she was smiling.
> Her husband when she felt love for him,
> Her husband, I began to gaze at her.
> Wishing to come – when she felt love for him,
> The woman, she looked down ashamed.
> Wishing to come,
> Myself [I], bending down
> To the drum, to the drum-stick,
> Myself, bending down [on account of their weight].
>   (Roberts and Jenness 1925:442)

Rasmussen (1932:140–144) also transcribed two songs in which a man expressed his desire and longing for the wives of other men. During at least one of the performances, the man claimed embarrassment when he discovered that the objects of his desire were present.

While many benefits may have resulted from spouse exchange relationships, it is quite likely that the practice served to prevent conflicts stemming from illicit sexual liaisons. If infatuation is a natural tendency of the human condition – and we suspect that it is – then legitimizing extramarital sex in a controlled fashion may have ensured the relative stability of the marital union and prevented sexual conflict and jealousy from undermining essential cooperative relationships within both households and local groups.

The Disappearance of Divorce, 1935–1985

The arrival of traders, missionaries, and the Royal Canadian Mounted Police (RCMP) led to dramatic changes in Copper Inuit marriage patterns. By the late 1920s introduced diseases, especially influenza and tuberculosis, are estimated to have decreased the Copper Inuit population at least one-third to as much as half (Usher 1965:67–8). This population decline probably made finding a spouse an even more difficult endeavor than had been the case previously.[4] Genealogical data supplied by our informants indicate that illness, rather than starvation or injury, had become the most common cause of death of both adults and children. These data indicate that large numbers of men and women died leaving no offspring.

The Inuit concept of marriage also changed after contact with whites. As the RCMP report of 1932 shows, people were easily converted to Christianity (both Anglican and Roman Catholic):

> The influence of the missionaries is very noticeable and at the camps visited the natives would show me their hymn books. The Minto Inlet natives held a service while I was their [sic], which consisted of singing six hymns. They observe sunday [sic] very closely and will not do a thing, spending most of the day singing hymns even if the camp is out of meat. (RCMP annual report, January 1935:5)

The preceding statement indicates a pattern typical of many Inuit camps throughout the Canadian Arctic after conversion to Christianity. Many Inuit believed that the decrees of the missionaries had the force of law as well as the force of the spiritual realm. As a result, they modified their behavior accordingly to avoid conflict. While precontact marriage involved only the consent of the parties involved and a period of trial marriage, missionaries were highly successful in pushing the Christian view of marriage as a sacrament that required a ceremony and a certificate. The marriage certificate that was issued became a tangible reminder that the missionaries had official backing. In the community of Holman today many couples frame and display their wedding certificates on their living-room walls. In our conversations with elders regarding marriage, those who had lost their marriage certificates took pains to point that out. "My marriage certificates are all gone.

My daughter was cleaning the house. She had put the box and the papers out to dry and they blew away. That's when my wife and I were out hunting seals in Prince Albert Sound" (Albert Palvik, cited in Condon fieldnotes, 1989).

As a result of missionary work the institution of marriage took on new meaning for the parties involved. Linguistic evidence from Holman supports this view. Traditionally, according to elders Mabel and Morris Nigiyok, people used a single Inuinaqtun term (*teteutimiulittut*) for a couple living together regardless of the length or permanence of the union. With the arrival of missionaries and the availability of Christian marriage ceremonies, a new term (*kattitiktut*) was applied to couples who were married by a minister and the former term was applied only to couples who were not formally married.

Conversations with Holman elders also indicate that after the missionaries arrived people's definition of marriage changed. Consider the following exchange between our research assistant, Julia Ogina, and an elder, Frank Kuptana:

JULIA: When did you get married?
FRANK: When I was becoming an adult. After I quit trapping with Iqutaqs and it was time for me to get a wife. Fred Kahak asked me to travel with them so I could marry Avilingak's (Kahak's wife) sister, Qiuvikhaq.
JULIA: Where did they take you after Kahak asked for you?
FRANK: I returned to Read Island and lived there for a while with Kahaks and Iqutaqs. They went to Read Island to visit and trade. That's when they asked me to come along and marry Qiuvikhaq. That's when they came to Read Island from Naluayok and when they were returning. That's when I went with them.
JULIA: When did you guys get married?
FRANK: We were married long ago by a minister called Mr. Webster.
JULIA: Where did you guys get married?
FRANK: We were married I think at Read Island. That man, Mr. Webster, used to travel a lot. He married a lot of people back then.

The new concept of marriage as representing a permanent and less casual commitment was undoubtedly reinforced by an incident that occurred around Minto Inlet in April 1935. The previous winter a young Copper Inuit woman and a Mackenzie Delta man had been living together in a traditional marriage arrangement. Although she had become pregnant, she was abandoned by her husband and returned to her parents' home. Fortuitously for the woman's family, this occurred immediately prior to the annual patrol of the Coppermine-based RCMP officer. The woman's father complained to Constable Albert "Frenchie" Chartrand, who convened a hearing to settle the dispute. After each family stated its case, Constable Chartrand decreed that the marriage was dissolved, but that the young man was required to turn over to the woman's family one-half of his trapping income for that year. The Hudson's Bay Company clerk, George Burnham, who recorded this incident (Burnham 1986:116), felt that Chartrand's ruling was acceptable to "all parties involved," but half of a year's trapping income must have seemed like an extremely heavy fine to people previously accustomed to walking away from unsuccessful marriages.

Throughout the 1930s to the 1950s, Holman Inuit resided in seminomadic hunting and trapping camps. Trading posts were moved around the region in accordance with administrative decisions made in Ottawa, London, and elsewhere. Often, as the trading posts moved so did the people. This was especially true as people became increasingly dependent upon southern trade items. The Christian holidays of Christmas and Easter became major ingathering periods at the trading posts that provided opportunities for matchmaking and marriage. At other times of the year Anglican and Catholic missionaries (sometimes, but not always, accompanied by RCMP) traveled by dogteam from their bases in Coppermine to outlying camps. The performance of baptisms and marriage ceremonies were a critical feature of these circuits. Often nuptials were performed for couples who had lived together for many years, but, undoubtedly, the forceful presence of the missionaries and other whites led to legal marriages between new couples who might not have remained together (see Matthiasson 1992:81–82 for an example of this from Baffin Island). The RCMP and the missionaries were often feared, and their decrees were generally respected. The former had the ability to admonish and arrest, while the latter had the force of a powerful deity *and* government laws behind their admonitions.

In 1939 both the Hudson's Bay Company and the Roman Catholic Mission established permanent locations at the site of the current community of Holman. Throughout the 1940s and the 1950s people used Holman much as they had the other trading posts: as a place to socialize, to seek medical attention and welfare rations as well as a place to exchange fox furs for imported goods. Few families settled there permanently before the early 1960s, when the federal government embarked on a housing program intended to entice people into the new town. It was during this period that the Anglican Church finally provided a year-round missionary in Holman. However, largely due to the efforts of earlier Anglican missionaries (especially the Reverend Harold Webster), nearly all of Holman's residents were already Anglican. The Roman Catholics, on the other hand, had been successful in converting only a handful of Copper Inuit. Competition between the two churches continued and, to some extent, accelerated after the arrival of the full-time Anglican missionary. The missionaries kept score in this competition by comparing performances of sacraments such as baptism, funerals, communion, and marriage.

Through the mid-1970s a formal marriage ceremony was viewed as an essential aspect of pairbonding, and nearly all young couples submitted to either a Roman Catholic or Anglican ceremony. The missionaries were also quite active in repressing the traditional practice of spouse exchange, although we have been unable to determine how long it took for these formal exchanges to drop out of use. More problematic for the missionaries during this period were premarital and extramarital sexual relations. The latter seemed to increase in response to the disappearance of spouse exchange as a legitimate social practice.

Even after most families moved into the settlement (population concentration was com-

pleted by the late 1960s), parents continued to be heavily involved in spouse selection, but not necessarily premarital sexuality. Most, although not all, of our middle-aged informants reported that their marriages were arranged by parents or, at the very least, that their parents had significant input. One of our informant couples, currently in their mid-forties, claims to have been the first couple to have an unarranged marriage and a southern-style ceremony complete with a white wedding gown and tiered cake. The wedding occurred in 1972. Though they appear to have been trendsetters, they did not live together prior to the wedding and their first child was born *after* the ceremony.

As in the precontact and immediate post-contact periods, nearly everyone married and eventually had children. During the early settlement period, however, especially after the construction of public housing in the early 1960s, there was a slight increase in the numbers of both never married and widowed women with children. Without the physical and economic security of the settlement, most of these women would probably have been remarried several times. The creation of the settlement and its associated system of public housing and social assistance allowed these women to remain relatively independent. The absence of a spouse (either by choice or by circumstance) did not, however, limit a woman's opportunity for a full sexual and reproductive life.

The concentration of people into the settlement also led to a new demographic phenomenon for the Copper Inuit and one that had significant implications for pairbonding and sexuality – an adolescent peer group. This process has been described in detail by Condon (1987, 1992). Improvements in medical care in the 1950s and 1960s led to a drop in infant mortality and a dramatic increase in the number of live births. By the late 1970s this birth cohort had reached their teenage years, essentially constituting the first large, adolescent peer group to exist in Copper Inuit society. This group of young Inuit was profoundly influenced by formal schooling, mass media exposure, and a settlement existence that provided both safety and security. Freed from the responsibilities and duties character- izing the childhoods of their parents and grandparents, these children and adolescents had relatively little to do other than spend their nonschool time engaged in impromptu sports and sexual liaisons. Most critically, the amount of time spent with and learning from parents declined dramatically as the peer group attained paramount importance.

For many of these new adolescents pair- bonding decisions were made without the imput of parents and were motivated by new criteria. Marriage was no longer an abso- lute economic necessity for either men or women, but it remained an important marker of adult status and, thus, was desirable. Men and women, for the most part, continued to maintain distinct, but complementary, roles. Men remained the hunters and, therefore, the providers of high-quality meat. Women maintained the household, cooked, sewed, and, quite frequently, earned the cash income that supported male hunting activities. Single women (and their children) had less reliable access to land foods than did married women and were often dependent upon gifts of fresh meat and fish from relatives.

Availability of housing also played a signifi- cant role in pairbonding. From the earliest days of the settlement until the mid-1980s Holman suffered from a shortage of housing. Young couples wishing to establish a separate household from parents often had to wait years for an available unit, a requirement that was unnecessary in the presettlement era when a new house could be easily fashioned from snow or skins.

By the mid- to late 1970s, church wed- dings ceased to be a critical element in the pairbonding process, indicating a departure from the experience of the preceding genera- tion. Not only were young people selecting partners on their own, but they were gener- ally living together for several years and hav- ing children long before the formal marriage ceremony. The typical pattern was as follows. A young couple would start to see one another on a regular basis. This frequently entailed sexual relations, but on an extremely clandes- tine basis. The secretive nature of premarital sexuality was not due to any fear that parents

would disapprove but reflected a concern that parental knowledge of such activities would lead to subtle pressures for the couple to establish a more permanent union. Once the young couple decided upon their compat- ibility, they would get "shacked up" (to use the local expression). This entailed either the young man or the young woman moving into the other's bedroom in the parents' home. When a housing unit became available, the young couple would set up a neolocal resi- dence. Frequently – only after several years of marriage and at least one or two children – the couple would decide to have a formal church wedding. Prior to the formal cere- mony the couple nevertheless considered themselves and were considered by others to be husband and wife.

For the teenagers and young adults of the 1970s and early 1980s, semisecretive, premari- tal sexual activity and subsequent bedroom pairbonding must have served the same pur- pose as trial marriages had during the tradi- tional period. Undoubtedly, sexual gratification was the purpose of many teenage sexual liai- sons. However, as a young person matured a (generally) exclusive sexual relationship, based on compatibility and affection, replaced the more promiscuous activities of youth. Since nearly all potential marriage partners were indi- viduals known since birth (now that the popula- tion was concentrated in the same location), "dating" in order to get to know one another was unnecessary. Parentally arranged marriage was also unnecessary since young people were no longer plagued by the scarcity and scatter- ing of nuptial resources. Boys and girls reported that they frequently had little to talk about and as a result generally spent their time together in sexual play, including intercourse: "Sometimes [when I want to have sex,] I just call up a girl and ask her to come over. After we have had tea for a while and talked a bit, I might say, 'Hey, you want to fool around?' And then we do it" (eighteen-year-old male quoted in Condon 1987:144–5). Most of the teens we interviewed in 1983, both boys and girls, cited personality rather than physical characteristics as desirable qualities in a potential spouse, even though physical attraction was clearly important for sexual partners. And, as in the previous period, compatibility rather than infatuation appeared to be the most important factor in the choice of a spouse.

The Current Situation: 1985–Present

Prior to the mid-1980s it was extremely rare to see couples, of any age, openly display any signs of affection in public. Hand holding, kissing, and hugging in public were considered inappropriate. Affection between courting couples and life-long partners was expressed in different and often more subtle ways: with a glance of the eye, an eyebrow flash, or the simple making of a cup of tea for a partner. We have interacted with older couples who obviously hold great affection for one another, although it was rarely expressed overtly. Beginning in the mid-1980s we noticed a distinct change in the public presentation of affection. Couples, both young and old, were observed walking hand in hand, hugging at the community hall, and kissing one another good-bye at the start of the workday. We suspect that these changes have been brought about, in part, by exposure to southern mass media, particularly television, with its ubiquitous displays of both positive and negative emotions.

Many of the courtship and marriage practices that developed in the 1970s have continued to the present. For nearly all couples formal marriage ceremonies are delayed until the couple has been together for several years. Most have one or two children at the time of their wedding. Several of our younger informant couples have mentioned sexual fidelity as a desirable characteristic, but we are uncertain if their views and behaviors in this regard differ greatly from those of their parents.

One consequence of the fact that Holman young adults are now making their own marriage decisions is that many are delaying the age of pairbonding, and an increasing number of men and women seek spouses from the neighboring, and larger, community of Coppermine. Young singles from both communities make frequent visits back and forth during holidays, usually staying with relatives, while searching for possible mates. While

intracommunity marriages have always been common, there has been a dramatic increase since the mid-1980s. Some of our young informants admitted that Coppermine Inuit are more exciting as partners because they do not suffer the stigma of familiarity. It also seems likely that, given the short courtship periods that these intracommunity relationships necessarily have, infatuation is a critical ingredient in pairbonding. It may also contribute to the current fragility of marriages.

In addition to an increase in both the average age of marriage and the number of intracommunity marriages, one of the most noticeable changes has been an increase in the number of single-parent households.[5] In 1987 we updated our household census and discovered a large number of separations and legal divorces – the first that we have been able to document for the settlement period. This was even more evident by 1992. Most of the couples affected were young people who had been together for short periods of time (less than two years), and many had at least one child. To some extent these relationships were clearly trial marriages, much like those of the precontact period. The difference was that while traditional trial marriages stabilized after the birth of the first child, this appears not to be the case in the modern period. While attitudinal changes brought about as a result of extensive exposure to southern television programming may be partly responsible, we suspect that economic conditions are a more critical factor. Unlike the precontact period, the essential economic interdependency of males and females in Copper Inuit society no longer exists. Several factors seem to be at work here. As the people have become more and more involved in the wage-labor and social welfare economy of Northern Canada, women find no particular economic advantage to marriage. During the early settlement era (and just prior), most of the cash needs of a family were generated by fur trapping – a male activity. Women contributed to the family economy, but often by supporting male subsistence hunting and trapping. Prior to the mid-1980s, there were very few wage-labor jobs in Holman that were sufficient to support a family not also reliant on hunting and trapping. Holman's incorporation as a hamlet in 1984 enabled a much larger number of people to find both skilled and unskilled wage-labor employment. The new jobs went to both men and women.[6] At the same time southern antifur sentiments, coupled with high equipment and fuel costs, destroyed fur trapping as a viable economic strategy. As a result, the presence of two adults in a household no longer ensures greater financial security. Finally, the presence of extended kin living nearby, rather than being spread out as they were during the traditional era, provides single mothers with access to desirable land foods and to babysitters.

Attainment of adult status, which was once synonymous with marriage, now can be achieved in other ways. In the traditional period marriage enabled young people to separate from their parents. It was this separation, and not the marriage, that established a person as adult. Within the settlement era housing shortages served the same purpose. Until very recently young people could not get a house apart from parents before they established their intention to marry by getting "shacked up." Even then, there was often a delay. A construction boom in the 1980s created a housing surplus that enabled older adolescents to move out of their parents' homes. As a result, a number of new households were formed by siblings in their late teens and early twenties, giving these youngsters a degree of social independence and autonomy not possible in their parents' homes. The surplus in housing may have also contributed to the reappearance of divorce. Having a place to go must clearly figure into any decision to leave a spouse. As Holman's population grows, however, it is unlikely that the current housing situation will continue. In fact, the Housing Corporation of the Northwest Territories recently announced plans to curtail new construction in Holman.

From the perspective of many young women in the community today, their lives are better as single mothers than as wives in marriages that are less than ideal. The increase in alcohol and drug abuse throughout the Canadian Arctic has unfortunately contributed to a growing tide of spousal assault. Repeated spousal abuse is an oft-cited reason for separations and divorce, and the changes in household composition we have noted are not surprising.

Although most of our data regarding separation and divorce come from unsystematic and informal interviews, both authors are quite familiar with many of these individuals and are therefore able to suggest motivations. A woman's motivations for leaving an abusive husband should be fairly obvious, especially when economic conditions allow. We suspect that these young women do not remarry right away (if at all) in part because of raised expectations concerning ideal marriage relations *and* recognition that their lives and those of their children are better in single-parent households. Both of these factors may also account for why many other young women now choose not to marry, but, nonetheless, decide to have children. The sexual lives of single women do not seem to be hampered by their choice to remain single. They often engage in a series of short-term relationships based upon infatuation or physical attraction rather than any concern for the compatibility that might lead to marriage. In short, just as in the traditional period, a good spouse is still hard to find.

Conclusion

Copper Inuit marriage customs have undergone some distinct changes as the Copper Inuit have adapted to the demands and realities of ever increasing integration into global society. Yet, a number of aspects of Inuit marriage have held steady. First and foremost among these is a quality that can be said to characterize Inuit culture overall, that is, its flexibility. Just as traditional Inuit were willing to accommodate a variety of marriage types in order to adjust to particular environmental and social circumstances, so their descendants modified their marriage practices, first to satisfy the demands of powerful outsiders and, more recently, to cope with changing economic and social conditions. Many Inuit continue to choose their spouses on the basis of compatibility rather than infatuation. While this may contribute to extramarital affairs, to our knowledge infatuation with someone other than an Inuk's spouse has not resulted in the dissolution of a single contemporary Holman marriage.

During the traditional period extremely low population density severely limited people's choices of potential mates. Consequently, they had few opportunities to develop unrealistic expectations of their marriages. As the attitudes of Euro-Canadian culture infiltrate Copper Inuit culture, either explicitly through mass media or surreptitiously through economic changes, there are greater opportunities to regret a marriage decision. Despite an increase in the numbers of single adults, the majority of Holman's young people continue to court and form pairbonds. Perhaps the only unfortunate consequence of having choices regarding mate selection is the opportunity to question the choice made.

NOTES

The Copper Inuit poem quoted in the epigraph that precedes this essay is from Roberts and Jenness (1925:468).

1   Throughout this essay we will use the word *infatuation* in the place of the term *romantic love*. While both terms bear the stigma of wide popular use, which lends them a Western cultural bias, we believe that is it possible to more narrowly define *infatuation*. We accept Fisher's (1992) construction of the term. In that sense infatuation refers to the uncontrollable, anxious, ecstatic, and often short-lived neurochemical reaction a person has for someone to whom he or she is sexually attracted. The attraction, however, extends beyond the mere sexual.

2   Neither of these were divorces in the legal/official sense. One involved a woman who was legally married running away from her husband to become the co-wife of another man. The separation occurred within the first few months of the marriage. The second case involved what is often referred to in the anthropological literature as a trial marriage. It, too, lasted less than a year.

3   It is important to note that the 1940s and 1950s coincided with the first TB surveys conducted in the Holman region. A number of men and women were evacuated to Charles Camsell hospital in Edmonton where many remained for years undergoing treatment. It is not surprising that the spouses left behind continued what could be called normal sexual lives, but with partners other than their spouses.

4   Indeed, it is quite possible that the marriage practices documented by the earliest anthropologists and explorers, especially in the Netsilik regions to the east (e.g., scarcity of marriage partners, competition over women, and high frequencies of bachelorhood), may have been considerably amplified by these dramatic population changes.

5   Not surprisingly, these single-parent households were primarily those headed by women. While most resulted from divorce or separation, a growing number were headed by women who had never married or lived with the fathers of their children.

6   There remains a shortage of full-time, wage-labor jobs in Holman and other Inuit communities. Most families continue to get by with a combination of social assistance, wage labor, and reciprocity.

REFERENCES

Balikci, A.
1970   *The Netsilik Eskimo.* Garden City, N.Y.: Natural History Press.
Briggs, J. L.
1974   "Eskimo Women: Makers of Men." In C. J. Matthiasson, ed., *Many Sisters*, pp. 261–304. New York: Free Press.
Burch, E. S., Jr.
1970   "Marriage and Divorce Among the North Alaskan Eskimos." In P. Bohannon, ed., *Divorce and After*, pp. 152–181. Garden City, N.Y.: Doubleday.
Burch, E. S., Jr., and T. C. Correl
1972   "Alliance and Conflict: Inter-regional Relations in North Alaska." In D. L. Guemple, ed., *Alliance in Eskimo Society*, pp. 17–39. Seattle: University of Washington Press.
Burnham, G.
1986   *The White Road.* Interlake Graphics, Inc.
Condon, R. G.
1987   *Inuit Youth.* New Brunswick: Rutgers University Press.
Condon, R. G.
1992   "Changing Patterns of Conflict Management and Aggression Among Inuit Youth in the Canadian Arctic: Longitudinal Ethnographic Observations." *Native Studies Review* 8(2):1–15.
Damas, David
1971   "The Problem of the Eskimo Family." In K. Ishwaran, ed., *Canadian Family: A Book*

of Readings, pp. 54–78. Toronto: Holt, Rinehart and Winston of Canada.

Fisher, Helen
1987 "The Four-Year Itch." Natural History 96(10):22–33.

Fisher, Helen
1992 The Anatomy of Love: The Natural History of Monogamy, Adultery, and Divorce. New York: Norton.

Guemple, D. L.
1979 "Inuit Spouse-Exchange." Ann Arbor: University Microfilms International.

Heinrich, A. C.
1972 "Divorce as an Alliance Mechanism Among Eskimos." In D. L. Guemple, ed., Alliance in Eskimo Society, pp. 79–88. Seattle: University of Washington Press.

Helm, J., and D. Damas
1963 "The Contact-Traditional All-Native Community of the Canadian North: The Upper MacKenzie 'Bush' Athapaskans and the Igluligmuit." Anthropologica 5(1):9–21.

Honigmann, J., and I. Honigmann
1965 Eskimo Townsmen. Ottawa: Canadian Research Centre for Anthropology.

Jenness, D.
1970 The Life of the Copper Eskimos. New York: Johnson Reprint.

Jenness, S., ed.
1991 Arctic Odyssey: The Diary of Diamond Jenness 1913–1916. Hull, Quebec: Canadian Museum of Civilization.

Lubart, J. M.
1970 Psychodynamic Problems of Adaptation: MacKenzie Delta Eskimos. Ottawa: Department of Indian Affairs and Northern Development.

McElroy, A.
1979 "The Negotiation of Sex-Role Identity in Eastern Arctic Culture Change." Occasional Papers in Anthropology 1:73–81.

Matthiasson, J. S.
1992 Living on the Land. Peterborough, Ontario: Broadview.

Rasmussen, Knud
1932 Intellectual Life of the Copper Eskimos. Report of the Fifth Thule Expedition, 1921–24, vol. 9. Ottawa.

Roberts, H. H., and D. Jenness
1925 Eskimo Songs. Report of the Canadian Arctic Expedition, 1913–18, vol. 14. Ottawa.

Royal Canadian Mounted Police.
1935 "RCMP Patrol Report, Coppermine Detachment." Ottawa: Public Archives of Canada.

Usher, P. J.
1965 Economic Basis and Resource Use of the Coppermine-Holman Region, N.W.T. Ottawa: Department of Northern Affairs and National Resources.

29

Love and the Risk of HIV: Courtship, Marriage, & Infidelity in Southeastern Nigeria

Daniel Jordan Smith

Marriage has been a staple of anthropological study in sub-Saharan Africa since the colonial period (Radcliffe-Brown and Forde 1950; Colson 1958; Schapera 1966). More recent reexaminations of nuptuality in Africa have been important catalysts for rethinking anthropological theory (Comaroff 1980). The study of marriage has been central for understanding kinship and social organization (Fox 1967; Mair 1969), the developmental cycle of the household (Goody 1962; Guyer 1981), the social and cultural underpinnings of demographic processes (Bledsoe and Pison 1994; Feldman-Savelsberg 1999), and the significance of gender as an organizing social force and category of analysis (Potash 1986; Goheen 1996). Part of the impetus for a shift toward analytical perspectives that pay greater attention to women's agency (Bozzoli 1991) and to the strategic and performative aspects of marriage processes (Murray 1976; Karp 1987) has come from the changing nature of marriage itself (Caldwell 1968; Harrell-Bond 1975; Parkin and Nyamwaya 1987). As the introduction to this volume demonstrates, changes in courtship practices, in rituals establishing marriage, in marital ideologies, in household gender dynamics, and in the importance of conjugality vis-à-vis other kinship relationships must be understood in the context of broader social transformations.

In this chapter, I examine how changing patterns of courtship and marriage are affecting HIV risk among Igbo-speaking people in southeastern Nigeria. In particular, I aim to explain how a complex intersection of changing marital ideals and practices combine with continuing gender inequality to shape patterns of sexual behavior and condom use across a spectrum of premarital, marital, and extramarital relationships. Similar to trends in many other parts of the world (e.g., Hollos and Larsen 1997; Hirsch 2003), men and women in Nigeria increasingly privilege the conjugal bond relative to other social relationships. The idea that marriage should be a partnership sustained by the private personal and emotional attachment of two people has grown significantly over the past several decades (Obiechina 1973; Smith

Daniel Jordan Smith, Love and the Risk of HIV, *from Modern Loves*, Jennifer Hirsch and Holly Wardlow, eds., Ann Arbor: University of Michigan Press, 2006, pp. 135–154. Reprinted with permission of University of Michigan Press and the author. Photos © Daniel J Smith.

Sexualities in Anthropology: A Reader, edited by Andrew P. Lyons and Harriet D. Lyons

2000, 2001). The rise of forms of marriage that have been described as companionate is sometimes interpreted as part of a larger movement toward individualism and gender equality. Indeed, among the population that I studied in Nigeria, most young women and many young men explicitly desired and promoted marital ideals that privilege conjugality, romance, and individual relationships as the bedrock of marriage, deploying these ideals in their negotiations with suitors and spouses as well as with their extended families. But these emerging ideals and patterns of marriage unfold in a context of continuing gender inequality, such that expectations about fidelity, romantic love, and intimacy are placing women at risk of contracting HIV from their partners. The combination of changing relationship ideals and behaviors and continuing gender inequality is making it difficult for women, married or not, to negotiate safe sex.

In sub-Saharan Africa, where 25 million people are estimated to be HIV positive (UNAIDS 2004), 55% of adult infections are in women (WHO 2000). For most women in Nigeria, as in much of the world, the behavior that puts them at greatest risk of infection from HIV is having sex with their husbands (Federal Ministry of Health 1999). In Nigeria, the most recent sentinel sero-prevalence survey of pregnant women (Federal Ministry of Health 2004) indicated that approximately 5% were HIV positive. Extrapolations from this data suggest that more than three million Nigerians are currently infected with HIV. Projections predict that in the next two to three years nearly five million Nigerians will be infected. The ethnographic study of sexual relationships, marriage, and gender dynamics elucidates how the rise of love as a relationship ideal combines with the social construction of male gender and its manifestation in multiple extramarital sexual relationships to shape patterns of HIV risk in Africa's most populous country.

Setting and Methods

The setting for the research that forms the basis for the analysis presented here is Igbo-speaking southeastern Nigeria. Igbos are the

third largest of Nigeria's nearly 250 ethnic groups, numbering approximately 20 million. I have lived and worked periodically in Nigeria since 1989. During that time, I conducted more than three years of field research in southeastern Nigeria in a semirural community located just eight miles from Umuahia, the capital of Abia State. Data for this chapter have been accumulated while undertaking a variety of research projects carried out over the past ten years. Research methods included participant observation, semistructured interviewing, extended case studies, village household surveys of women of reproductive age and their husbands, large sample surveys of secondary school and university students, and multiple interviews with adolescent and young adult rural-urban migrants. Over the years, I have spent most of my time doing participant observation, and it is, I think, the source of the most interesting and valuable data. Participant observation has meant attending all manner of local social events and ceremonies – marriage rites, burials, chieftancy installation ceremonies, family meetings, gatherings to resolve local disputes, child-naming ceremonies, and so on. But perhaps more important, it has entailed accompanying and spending time with people as they went about their everyday lives – farming, fetching water, cooking, trading in the market, drinking palm wine or beer, going to church, and traveling to town. It has also meant listening to, and often participating in, the conversations, negotiations, and gossip that unfolded in all of these different settings and contexts. Much of what I know about Igbo marriages and about Igbo sexual relationships, marital infidelity, and the negotiation of condom use comes from observation and participation in the kinds of informal conversations and exchanges of gossip that can best be achieved through extended fieldwork.

Romantic Love and Marriage in West Africa

The question of whether or not romantic love is universal has intrigued researchers for a long time (Murstein 1974; Kurian 1979; Endleman

1989; Jankowiak 1995). In one of the few anthropological studies of romantic love, Jankowiak and Fischer (1992) set out to test the question by examining Murdock and White's (1969) Standard Cross-Cultural Sample looking for the existence (or not) of romantic love in ethnographic data collected from nearly two hundred cultures. They preface their study with this assertion.

> The anthropological study of romantic (or passionate) love is virtually nonexistent due to the widespread belief that romantic love is unique to Euro-American culture. ... Underlying these Eurocentric views is the assumption that modernization and the rise of individualism are directly linked to the appearance of romantic notions of love. (Jankowiak and Fischer 1992:149)

Defining romantic love as "any intense attraction that involves the idealization of the other, within an erotic context, with the expectation of enduring for sometime in the future" (1992:150), Jankowiak and Fischer conclude from their analysis that romantic love *is* a cross-cultural universal, or at least that it is *nearly* universal. They stress, however, that even if some form of romantic love is nearly universal across cultures, there is a need to understand "its emic manifestations within a variety of cultural settings" (154).

Like a number of scholars (e.g., Hatfield and Rapson 1996), Jankowiak and Fischer distinguish between romantic love, which is defined as passionate and erotic, and what they call "companionship" love (1992:150), which emerges over the long evolution of a relationship. As indicated in the introduction to this volume, terms such as *companionate marriage* are sometimes defined in different ways by different scholars. Falling in love, marrying for love, and staying married because of love are not the same thing. Regardless of terminology, it is important to recognize and explain the ways in which ideas and expectations about love are implicated in the social construction of marriage in contemporary Igbo-speaking Nigeria. My findings support the argument in this volume's introduction that changes in marriage in Nigeria, as in many settings, are intertwined with larger trends such as the rise of more explicit notions of an individualized self, the growing importance of commodity consumption as a means of self-fashioning, and the emergence of discourses about gender relations as a way to claim (or contest) modern identities. Further, I show how these same dynamics contribute to the configuration of premarital and extramarital sexual relationships. Specifically, I explore how the contemporary construction of marriage articulates continuities and changes in gender dynamics, and particularly how male gender and the structure of gender inequality continue to be expressed in patterns of extramarital sexual behavior.

Evidence from Nigeria (Obiechina 1973; Okonjo 1992) and across Africa (Mair 1969; Little 1979; van der Vliet 1991) indicates that Africans are increasingly likely to select marriage partners based, at least in part, on whether they are "in love". The emergence of romantic love as a criterion in mate selection and the increasing importance of conjugality in marriage relationships should not be interpreted to mean that romantic love itself has only recently emerged in Nigeria. When I asked elderly Igbos about their betrothals, about their marriages, and about love, I was told numerous personal stories and popular fables that indicated a long tradition of romantic love. A number of men and women confessed that they would have married a person other than their spouse had they been allowed to "follow the heart". Scholars have documented the existence of romantic love in Africa long before it became a widely accepted criterion for marriage (Bell 1995; Plotnicov 1995; Riesman 1972, 1981). Uchendu (1965) confirms the existence of passionate love in his study of concubinage in traditional Igbo society. Interestingly, both men and women were reportedly accorded significant institutionalized extramarital sexual freedom and a related proverb survives to the present: *uto ka na iko* (sweetness is deepest among lovers). As Obiechina notes: "The question is not whether love and sexual attraction as normal human traits exist within Western and African societies, but how they are woven into the fabric of life" (1973:34).

Exactly when Nigerians in general and Igbos in particular began to conceptualize marriage choices in more individualistic terms, privileging romantic love as a criterion in the selection of a spouse, is hard to pinpoint. In some parts of Igboland and in many parts of Nigeria the social acceptance of individual choice in mate selection is still just beginning. Certainly these changes occurred first in urban areas among relatively educated and elite populations (Marris 1962; Little and Price 1973). Obiechina's (1973) study of Onitsha pamphlet literature indicates that popular Nigerian literature about love, romance, and modern marriage began to emerge just after World War II. Historical accounts suggest that elements of modern marriage began even earlier in the twentieth century (Mann 1985). By the 1970s, a number of monographs about modern marriage in West Africa had been produced (e.g., Oppong 1974; Harrell-Bond 1975).

In contemporary Igboland, young people increasingly value choosing their own spouses. In my village sample of just over 200 married women of reproductive age, over 60% reported that their marriages were choice marriages rather than arranged marriages, and, not surprisingly, the percentages were higher among younger women and lower among older women. The expectation to choose one's spouse is almost universal among young persons still in school. In my sample of 775 students drawn from 19 secondary schools, over 95% said they expected to choose their marriage partners themselves, and the expectation was universal among 420 university students I surveyed. Among married people who chose their own spouses and among young people anticipating choosing a spouse, love is frequently mentioned as one important criterion, though not the only one. Individual choice in mate selection and love as a relationship ideal are connected, but one is not the equivalent of the other.

Premarital Sex and Contemporary Igbo Courtship

To understand the emergence and spread of the expectation that marriage partners should be selected by individual choice based, at least in part, on romantic love, it is necessary to know something about premarital sexual relationships and patterns of courtship in contemporary Igbo society. Indeed, certain patterns and expectations about gender roles are established in premarital relationships, and these expectations create difficulties for women to negotiate safe sex after marriage, when the roles of wife and mother become paramount.

Premarital sexual relationships are increasingly common in contemporary Nigeria (Nichols et al. 1986), including in the Igbo-speaking southeast (Feyisetan and Pebley 1989; Makinwa-Adebusoye 1992; Smith 2000). Driven by the spread and acceptance of formal schooling as valuable for both boys and girls and the growth of nondomestic work opportunities for women, average age at marriage for females in southeastern Nigeria has increased from approximately sixteen years old at independence in 1960 to around twenty-one years old at present (Isiugo-Abanihe, Ebigbola, and Adewuyi 1993). A significant proportion of young women now remain single into their late twenties. Most men marry around the age of thirty, the later age at marriage for men attributed to their need to secure themselves economically in order to be able to pay bridewealth and support a family. Concurrent with and also contributing to later age at marriage, more and more single young people are migrating to Nigeria's cities (Oucho and Gould 1993; Gugler and Ludwar-Ene 1995). In the city, young people are less subject to the discipline of their village relatives and more likely to be exposed to peer and media messages about the appeal and acceptability of premarital sex.

Related to demographic changes such as age at marriage and levels of urban migration is a changing conception of the nature of male-female relationships. In addition to simply having more time before marriage to try sex, young people value male-female intimacy to a degree their parents and grandparents did not. Premarital sexual relationships are places where young people construct their identities, very often in self-conscious opposition to traditions they perceive as "bush", "backward", and "uncivilized" – their words, not mine (Smith 2000). Sex is being socially constructed as an appropriate expression of intimacy, but also as a statement about a particular kind of modern identity. The place of sex in this creation of a modern Igbo identity and the relationship between modern sexual identities and commodity consumption are very much evident in practices of courtship (Smith 2001; Cornwall 2002). The case briefly described here exhibits many of the patterns that are now common in contemporary Igbo courtship.

Chinyere Nwankwo met her husband Ike in the town of Owerri in southeastern Nigeria, where she attended a teachers college after completing secondary school in her village community. Ike was eight years her senior, and when they met he was doing very well as a building contractor – well enough to own a used car, a prized symbol of wealth and success. On their first date he took her to the disco at the Concorde Hotel, at that time the fanciest in town. In addition to being educated, Chinyere was a beautiful young woman and consequently had many suitors. Her courtship with Ike lasted almost two years. During that time they often dined out and went dancing together. Among the more memorable events of their courtship were a weekend outing to the Nike Lake resort near Enugu and a trip to Lagos during which they attended a performance by Fela Ransome-Kuti, a famous Nigerian musician. During their courtship, each bought the other Hallmark-like cards on birthdays, and for Ike's birthday, Chinyere baked him a cake. They went to many social events together and acknowledged to their peers that they were a couple. Not long into their relationship, Chinyere and Ike began sleeping together. Many months before they decided to marry, they were sexually intimate. Prior to approaching Chinyere's people and his own family about their getting married, Ike asked Chinyere. They agreed together to get married and then began the process of including their families.

For Chinyere and Ike, as for many unmarried young Igbos, sexual intimacy constituted an integral part of their relationship, a relationship that they thought of as a romance. Chinyere described her decision to marry Ike this way: "A lot of things are important in

deciding whom to marry. You need a good husband who can provide for the family and it's important to find a man who is progressive. I would never marry a man who just wanted a wife to cater to him like a servant. There are a lot of things, but if you are not in love what's the point, really?" Later, in talking more specifically about sex and intimacy she added: "For a good marriage husband and wife need to be compatible. Sex is part of it. A big part. If you are not compatible in bed how intimate can you really be?"

Premarital sex, symbolic commodities such as greeting cards, and public displays of being a "couple" are bound together in the performance of modern courtship in southeastern Nigeria. While young people engage in premarital sexual relations for a variety of reasons, what is striking is the degree to which most young Igbos expect and accept that sex is and should be a part of the process of courtship. Of course there are many competing and sometimes critical discourses about young people's sexual behavior in Nigeria (especially young women's sexual behavior), including those in the idiom of religious morality (Smith 2004a). Nevertheless, the degree of acceptance that sex is appropriate when two people are "in love" is most striking (Smith 2004b).

Equally important is recognizing the degree to which premarital romances tend to support a relatively egalitarian gender dynamic, at least with regard to expectations of fidelity. During courtship, when the couple's relationship is based primarily on their personal emotional relationship to each other, both persons feel an obligation to fidelity. While this obligation is not necessarily observed, an individual who cheats on his or her lover and gets caught knows there is a good chance that the other person will end the relationship. It was my impression that young unmarried Igbo men cheated more than young unmarried Igbo women, but not dramatically so. But most important for the case I want to make, the sanctions each faced were similar. Infidelity during courtship was a personal violation and the consequences had to be negotiated between the individuals involved. Of course young people often enlisted friends to plead their cases, but the grounds for "making up" almost always included a pronouncement of continued love. The patterns and consequences of infidelity that emerge after marriage are quite different, and they result from a very different construction of gender roles that emerges in marriage. The contrast between courtship and marriage is tied to the ways in which conjugal relationships are much more deeply embedded in larger kinship structures and relationships to extended family and community than premarital relationships (Smith 2001).

A final note about Igbo courtship and premarital sexual relationships is the way in which contraceptive use, particularly condom use, is (or is not) negotiated. Young people I interviewed in surveys in local secondary schools, at a local university, and in two large cities were split fairly evenly among those who thought that contraception was a man's responsibility, a women's responsibility, or a joint responsibility. But those numbers obscure the degree to which young people feared broaching the subject at all, an anxiety exacerbated by increasing awareness of the AIDS epidemic. Most contraceptive and condom negotiations took place under the aegis of concern over preventing unwanted pregnancies (Smith 2004a,b). Particularly in relationships self-described as romantic, few young people dared discuss condom use in the context of AIDS prevention because of the insinuation that they or their partners were unsafe (Smith 2003; cf. Preston-Whyte 1999 for South Africa, and Adih and Alexander 1999 for Ghana). While almost all young Igbos know that HIV/AIDS is transmitted sexually, a majority associated AIDS risk with various forms of immoral sexual behavior. Thus, to suggest condom use with a partner implies that one or the other has previously engaged in such wayward or promiscuous sex. In addition, there is a fairly widespread feeling among young Igbos (both men and women) that condoms inhibit intimacy, and it is precisely in love relationships that intimacy is most valued. Incredibly high rates of unsafe illegal abortions attest to widespread failure to use effective contraception in premarital relationships. Popular stories of young women resorting to abortion are legion in southeastern Nigeria and must be inter-preted with caution because these stories are part of a critical public discourse about the role of gender and sexuality in social change. Nonetheless, in my sample of 420 university students, 40% of the women who had engaged in sexual intercourse (which was 80% of the sample) reported having had an abortion. As I will explain, ideals of monogamy and intimacy combine with the continued paramount importance of fertility in marriage to inhibit women's ability to negotiate condom use, even in instances where women know or suspect their husbands are unfaithful.

Marriage, Parenthood, and Male Infidelity

There is no doubt that both the ideals and practices of Igbo marriage have changed over the past generation. The strength of the conjugal relationship has grown vis-à-vis other family and community relationships. Young couples are far more likely than their parents to share one bedroom, eat together, maintain a single household budget, and live in town away from the compound of the husband's family, which is the traditional place of residence. The quality of a young couple's personal relationship, including the degree of emotional intimacy and sexual compatibility, is more likely to figure in their private assessments of the state of their marriage than was the case with their parents.

But once a couple is married, and certainly once they have children, the importance of their personal relationship as a measure of the state of the marriage recedes in comparison to the tremendous emphasis on successful parenthood. The place of children in adult relationships is central to understanding the whole social fabric of Igbo society. As Meyer Fortes argued quite some time ago, it is "parenthood that is the primary value associated with the idea of family in West Africa" (1978:121). "Parenthood," Fortes says, "is regarded as a *sine qua non* for the attainment of the full development of the complete person to which all aspire" (1978:125). Having children is not only a means to individual personhood, but also a fulfillment of one's obligations to kin

Fig. 1 *Although many Igbo couples now marry for love, fertility and successful parenthood remain paramount social values. (Photo by Daniel J. Smith.)*

and community. Biological reproduction is also social reproduction. Once a couple has children together, particularly once they have a son, there are few socially acceptable reasons for them to divorce. Disputes and incompatibilities that lead to fissures and separations are almost always mediated by extended family members on both sides who see it as their duty to bring the couple back together—most often with the welfare of the children explicitly voiced as the obligation that must reunite the couple. Deteriorating personal relationships are not generally sufficient grounds for divorce. A married woman with children will be on much firmer ground in complaining about her marriage if she can show that her husband fails to support his children than if she complains of personal problems with him.

The striking thing that I want to describe and explain is the dramatic shift in gender dynamics between man and woman that occurs in the transition from courtship to marriage and parenthood (Smith 2001). A more patriarchal gender dynamic emerges after marriage. It is in the expectations about and consequences of marital infidelity that this inequality is most profound, and the sad irony is that even as women continue to deploy ideals of intimacy and love to influence their husbands' sexual

behavior, these very ideals prevent the negotiation of safe sex.

Sugar Daddies, Handbags, and Razor Blades: Gender and Marital Fidelity

In premarital relationships, the social rules about fidelity are largely the same for men and women, as I indicated earlier. In Igbo marriages the rules about fidelity are quite different. An older wealthy Igbo man once said to me, when I asked about the consequences of extramarital affairs for men and women: "If I catch my wife, she is gone; if she catches me, she is gone too." In other words, not only was it not acceptable for her to have extramarital sex, it was also not acceptable for her to object to his having extramarital sex. The levels of acceptance of extramarital sexuality are much more contested than my informant's bold statement suggests, but the idea that Igbo men can and do have extramarital partners is widely acknowledged. A man who cheats on his wife risks little social condemnation, assuming he continues to provide for his wife and children, and does not do something "foolish" like propose to leave his wife for his lover. In fact, among Igbo men there is a certain pride in taking lovers. It is primarily in the way that men construct masculinity in their male peer groups that taking lovers becomes so significant. Being able to have lovers is sign of continuing masculine prowess and of economic success, because, increasingly, women expect their lovers to "perform" economically as well as sexually (Cornwall 2002; Hunter 2002).

When I lived in the town of Owerri ten years ago, people used to lament (but also laugh about) the plethora of cars parked outside the gates of Alvin Ikoku Teachers College on Friday and Saturday nights – cars belonging to married men who were there to meet young female lovers. Patterns of marital infidelity are structured along the dimensions of age, gender, and social class. Alvin Ikoku Teachers College has male students as well. But it was inconceivable that married women would park en masse outside the college waiting for young male lovers. Nor was it possible to imagine that poor men would be waiting outside on foot or with their bicycles. The following example illustrates some of the ways that men's extramarital sexual relationships are organized along various dimensions of inequality.

John Ezigbo is forty-seven years old. A married father of five, he runs a successful business raising poultry and selling animal feed. Most every night John leaves his house about 5 P.M. bound for Umuahia Club, where he plays an hour of tennis, drinks a few beers, and socializes with the other well-to-do Igbo men who are members of the club. Many evenings, after a postgame beer, he drives off to pick up a young lady friend whom he brings back to entertain, offering her drinks and something to eat from the club's kitchen. Though spouses are honorary members once their husbands are inducted, John knows that he and his girlfriend will not encounter any wives at the club, women who might report him to his own spouse. There is an unwritten rule among the men that wives are not welcome, except on specially designated occasions. The club is a safe place to bring one's girlfriend.

John's girlfriends are typically secondary school graduates, who are either attending one of several tertiary institutions in town or seeking employment in some kind of urban office or business. All of them are young, educated, modern girls who wear makeup, straighten their hair, sport fashionable clothes, and see school and the city as means to a better life. John is one of the more blatant philanderers in the club. It is rare to see the same lady in his company for more than a few weeks.

Other men keep much more steady lovers; many do not bring their girlfriends to the club at all, preferring to keep their sexual affairs more private. Indeed, some men do not have extramarital lovers at all. But keeping outside women (that is, outside of marriage) is accepted, indeed socially rewarded, among elite Igbo men (cf. Karanja 1987; Hunter 2002; Luke 2005). Bringing a pretty young lady to the club is done proudly. Many men want their male peers to know that they have extramarital affairs. They tell each other stories about sexual conquests, sometimes including the graphic details. One of the wealthiest guys in the club, who also had the reputation of attracting the most beautiful women, was known by the nickname "One Man Show." No doubt there is much male bravado in all this. Surely some men exaggerate their sexual exploits to their own social benefit. But the fact that perceived extramarital sexual activity is socially rewarded is precisely what I want to emphasize. Most Igbo men share a sense that real manhood implies continued sexual desire and new sexual conquests after and outside marriage.

Perhaps not surprisingly, given the economic inequalities in Nigerian society, the ability to have new women is a marker of economic status as well as virility. Men who own cars, belong to social clubs, rent expensive hotel rooms, and have the resources to give women substantial amounts of money and gifts are by far the more desirable married lovers. Such attributes define "sugar daddy." Much as men expect sexual intercourse and an attractive partner to display to their peers, the young women require and exact from their married lovers any number of kinds of assistance (Cornwall 2002; Hunter 2002; Smith 2002). On dates or outings, young ladies pressure

Fig. 2 *Settings of mostly all-male sociality, such as this sports club, contribute to strong positive peer-group pressure about extramarital sexuality. (Photo by Daniel J. Smith.)*

their sugar daddies to buy them the most expensive beer, order them special food, and reserve rooms at the fanciest hotels. They routinely ask their sugar daddies for money to pay school fees, start businesses, help their parents, or assist with rent. They also expect their men to buy them gifts – clothes, shoes, jewelry, and even electronics and appliances.

Unlike in their premarital relationships with their wives, few sugar daddies, and indeed few of their lovers, view these relationships as romances. Most men like to see themselves as masters of these extramarital relationships, in charge of their lovers in the same way they want to be in charge of their married households and their money. In male discourse, young female lovers are objectified – discussed as if they are not persons. When the men of the sports club travel to neighboring towns and cities to play tennis tournaments – as they do eight to ten weekends a year – these trips are viewed as great opportunities to meet (and display) their young lovers. In anticipation of a weekend on the road, men ask each other whether they are "carrying a handbag," a reference to taking a young female lover. I often traveled with the club to these tournaments and was struck by how widely this term was used and recognized, in Igbo cities all over the

south-east. Even many of the young women knew the meaning of the term, and while they did not appreciate its derogatory connotations, they did not seem too bothered by it – perhaps because they knew very well that women have more power in these relationships than one would guess from male rhetoric.

Yet even men acknowledge, perhaps unwittingly, the degree to which young female lovers have some control over relationships with their sugar daddies. Men often complained that these young women would "bleed" them – manipulating them for money, and even, ironically, for sex. This brief dialogue in Nigerian Pidgin English is typical of married men's discussions about their young lovers.

Chuks: How e de go wit dat new girl from Alvin? E be like say you de busy too much.

Charles: Dat uman no de taya. These girls today na war-o. Di girl done bleed me finish. Na real razor blade.

Chuks: Take am easy-o.

The terms *bleeding* and *razor blade* in reference to sexual relationships have multiple meanings. First, there is the clear reference to economic extraction. Razor blades cut men to bleed them of their money. Second, and perhaps more interesting, is an implication that women are extracting sex; that somehow, even as men view themselves as the aggressors in sexual relationships, they see women as insatiable – reservoirs of bottomless and dangerous sexual desires that can wear men out. Finally, the terms are often used in connection with romance and love, such that women are able to manipulate men's hearts to get their own sexual and material gratification. Much as many men eschew the idea that they are vulnerable to love in these extramarital relationships, they participate in a common countervailing discourse in Igbo society that women have "love medicine" and are capable of manipulating men sexually and romantically.

"Razor blades" and "handbags" imply very different notions of women's agency, one active and dangerous, the other passive and under control, both objectifying, and neither particularly attractive. But these contrasting images reflect well the conflicting representations of women in Igbo men's discourse. And each is, to some extent, representative of the real status of unmarried young women in their sexual relationships with sugar daddies. They are clearly used by men; yet they clearly also use men.

Extramarital Sex and the Risk of HIV

Extramarital sexual relationships pose increasing risks given the spread of HIV/AIDS in Nigeria. When I first lived in Nigeria, from 1989 through 1992, few of the men I knew took seriously the risk of AIDS. Most men believed they were not personally at risk because they viewed AIDS as a "gay" disease, a white man's disease, or something that could only be contracted from prostitutes. Among these same men, other STDs were not taken to be too serious. Indeed, I remember one conversation with some male friends in which they told me that anyone who had not experienced gonorrhea at some time in his life was not yet a man. Easy access to over-the-counter antibiotics led to widespread self-medication for STDs (no doubt increasing drug-resistant strains). During fieldwork from 1995 through 1997, little had changed about people's

perceptions of their own risk for contracting HIV/AIDS, and many men in extramarital sexual relationships still preferred to rely on their girlfriends to prevent (or terminate) pregnancy rather than use "pleasure-inhibiting" condoms. While young women were certainly concerned about preventing pregnancy and about the possible effects on their own future fertility of contracting STDs, even among women who had such concerns, negotiating condom use proved difficult in these economically unequal relationships. However, over the past several years, I have noticed the beginnings of a change in the attitude toward AIDS. The change was due in part to widespread publicity in the wake of Nigeria's 1999 and 2003 sero-prevalence surveys. But it is probably more important that some people now knew or had heard about individuals with HIV/AIDS.

Still, in a great many of these extramarital relationships condom use remains difficult to negotiate. Even among the most educated and elite classes – like my tennis buddies – AIDS continues to be represented as a disease of immorality spread through reckless sex with wayward or evil strangers (Smith 2003). Yet almost all real sexual relationships are between people who know each other – one's lover is not a stranger. In sugar daddy relationships even negotiations for money take place in a personal or kinship idiom. Young women rarely ask directly for money for sex. Women often defer their requests for money specifically not to coincide with a recent sex act. A woman's requests are made in terms of needing money for rent or transportation, or even more characteristically so that she can help a sibling pay school fees or assist her parents with a problem in the village. Sugar daddies almost always know the community of origin of their lovers, and likewise the girls know the same about their men. After one's name, one's place of origin is the first question Igbos ask in ordinary conversation. People are always placed in the context of the networks of social relationships that constitute Igbo society. As disparagingly as my elite male Igbo friends seemed to talk about their "handbags," the reality is far more complex. Even as peer-reinforced ideas of masculinity seem to create in

Fig. 3 *Public health communication about HIV/AIDS in Nigeria has risen dramatically in recent years, including messages about the risks of extramarital sex. (Photo by Daniel J. Smith.)*

sugar daddies the need to possess and control their lovers as objects, other notions of manhood require that they fulfill social obligations to these lovers – obligations that the girls can manipulate by exploiting men's sense of themselves as patrons and providers.

I have provided ethnographic evidence primarily about elite men, relatively educated young women, and a distinctly urban-oriented population. One might wonder how sexual dynamics play out in courtship and marriage among poorer men and less educated women who live mostly in rural areas. Certainly the people I have focused on are not the lowest common denominator. Men who cannot afford to belong to a tennis club are not as well placed to secure young women aspiring to a better life. Nevertheless, similar patterns of sexual relations play out in courtship and marriage among less privileged Igbos. An old adage about social hierarchy in sub-Saharan Africa says that everyone is a patron to a lesser person and a client to a more powerful person (d'Azevedo 1962). A similar nesting of power characterizes patterns of sexual relationships, so that while the young lovers of my tennis buddies expect, for example, that their sugar daddies will offer them Guinness Stout to drink, sexual relationships among poorer peo-

ple are negotiated with, for example, Coca-Cola. In other words, while the level of expectations regarding economic support and conspicuous consumption is lower, sexuality and sexual intimacy are markers and means of being modern among poorer Igbos, just as they are among the more educated and well off. With regard to HIV/AIDS, the salient point is that because AIDS has been socially constructed as a fearful disease spread by immoral sexual relations with variously constructed others, few people see their own sexual liaisons as fitting into this risky category.

Love, Marriage, and HIV

To conclude, I want to bring attention back to the risks that this situation poses to married women and explain how it is that the very ideals that provide women with significant leverage over their husbands also prevent them from negotiating condom use. Igbo women know that, in general, married Igbo men often seek "outside" women. Many married women certainly suspect, and may even know, that their own husbands do so. When a woman discovers that her husband has a lover, it often leads to terrible rifts – especially among younger couples where the basis for marriage included pronouncements of love, feelings of intimacy, and promises of sexual fidelity. Young Igbo women want their husbands to be faithful. To keep their husbands in line, women deploy discourses about love and call upon Christian concepts of monogamy and fidelity (see van der Vliet 1991 for a similar account about South Africa). In addition, as more women in urban areas are employed outside the home, they are controlling economic resources that give them certain kinds of leverage in their marriages. Anecdotes I heard in conversations among friends suggest that men who are more financially dependent on their wives may be more cautious in initiating extramarital relationships. But overall, women's increasing participation in the formal economy has not dramatically changed the domestic division of labor and the dynamics of power in the household. Even among the most elite women, the roles of wife and mother remain highly valued.

In contemporary Igbo-speaking Nigeria, extramarital sexuality is largely conceived of as a contest between husbands who want to be and think they are entitled to extramarital sexual relationships and wives who mostly want to rein in their husbands' extramarital activities. In many cases the women's strategies, combined with the strength of conjugal relationships, are effective. Not all Igbo men cheat on their wives. But women find it difficult to appeal to their kinfolk and affines for help and can expect little sympathy from society if they leave a man simply because he has had sex outside the marriage, especially if he has been relatively discreet.

Marriages among the current generation in Igboland are likely to be contracted first between individuals, with love and emotional intimacy as part of the criteria of spousal choice, and with monogamy as the expectation. While most people are aware of the prevalence of male marital infidelity, and of the fact that HIV/AIDS is transmitted through sexual intercourse, a number of factors combine to make it difficult for women to negotiate condom use with their husbands. First, as I have emphasized earlier, despite the rise of a companionate marriage ideal, the collective interests in marriage as an institution continue to emphasize the importance of parenthood in social reproduction. Thus, for a woman to suggest condom use (or any other contraception) for the sake of preventing pregnancy is itself potentially problematic. But more to the point in the context of the AIDS epidemic, a woman's expectation that marriage should be based on love and intimacy, with sexual fidelity as the ideal, means that any suggestion that her husband use a condom can be interpreted by him as undermining intimacy and trust and implying his (or her) infidelity. The irony is that because women rely on ideals of love and intimacy to negotiate relationships with their husbands, trying to protect themselves through condom use is seen as undermining the very thing they wish to preserve. Rather than protecting women, love marriages may contribute to the risk of contracting HIV from their husbands.

REFERENCES

Adih, William, and Cheryl Alexander
    1999 Determinants of Condom Use to Prevent HIV Infection Among Youth in Ghana. Journal of Adolescent Health 14(1):63–72.
Bell, Jim
    1995 Notions of Love and Romance among the Taita of Kenya. *In* Romantic Passion: A Universal Experience? W.R. Jankowiak, ed. Pp. 152–165. New York: Columbia University Press.
Bledsoe, Caroline H., and Giles Pison, eds.
    1994 Nuptiality in Sub-Saharan Africa: Contemporary Anthropological and Demographic Perspectives. Oxford: Clarendon Press.
Bozzoli, Belinda
    1991 Women of Phokeng: Consciousness, Life Strategy, and Migrancy in South Africa, 1900–1983. Portsmouth, NH: Heinemann.
Caldwell, John
    1968 Population Growth and Family Change in Africa: The New Urban Elite in Ghana. Canberra: Australian National University Press.
Colson, Elizabeth
    1958 Marriage and Family among the Plateau Tonga of Northern Rhodesia. Manchester: Manchester University Press.

Comaroff, John, ed.
   1980   The Meaning of Marriage Payments.
   New York: Academic Press.
Cornwall, Andrea
   2002   Spending Power: Love, Money and
   the Reconfiguration of Gender Relations in
   Ado-Odo, Southwestern Nigeria. American
   Ethnologist 29(4):963–980.
d'Azevedo, Warren
   1962   Common Principles and Variant Kinship
   Structures among the Gola of Western Liberia.
   American Anthropologist 64(3): 504–520.
Endleman, Robert
   1989   Love   and   Sex   in   Twelve   Cultures.
   New York: Psyche.
Federal Ministry of Health, Nigeria
   1999   HIV/Syphilis Sentinel Sero-Prevalence
   Survey in Nigeria. Abuja, Nigeria: Federal
   Ministry of Health.
Federal Ministry of Health, Nigeria
   2004   2003 HIV Sero-Prevalence Sentinel
   Survey. Abuja, Nigeria: Federal Ministry of
   Health.
Feldman-Savelsberg, Pamela
   1999   Plundered Kitchens, Empty Wombs:
   Threatened   Reproduction   and   Identity   in
   the Cameroon Grassfields. Ann Arbor, MI:
   University of Michigan Press.
Feyisetan, Bamikale, and Anne Pebley
   1989   Premarital Sexuality in Urban Nigeria.
   Studies in Family Planning 20(6):343–354.
Fortes, Meyer
   1978   Parenthood, Marriage and Fertility in
   West Africa. Journal of Development Studies
   14(4):121–148.
Fox, Robin
   1967   Kinship and Marriage: An Anthro-
   pological Perspective. Baltimore, MD: Penguin
   Books.
Goheen, Miriam
   1996   Men Own the Fields, Women Own
   the Crops: Gender and Power in the Cam-
   eroon Grassfields. Madison, WI: University of
   Wisconsin Press.
Goody, Jack, ed.
   1962   The Developmental Cycle in Domestic
   Groups. Cambridge: Cambridge University
   Press.
Gugler, Josef, and Gudrun Ludwar-Ene
   1995   Gender and Migration in Africa South
   of the Sahara. In The Migration Experience in
   Africa. J. Baker and T. Aina, eds. Pp. 257–268.
   Uppsala: Nordiska Afrikainstitut.

Guyer, Jane
   1981   Household and Community in African
   Studies.   African   Studies   Review   2–3:
   87–137.
Harrell-Bond, Barbara
   1975   Modern Marriage in Sierra Leone:
   A Study of the Professional Group. Paris:
   Mouton.
Hatfield, Elaine, and Richard Rapson
   1996   Love and Sex: Cross-Cultural Perspec-
   tives. Boston: Allyn and Bacon.
Hirsch, Jennifer
   2003   A Courtship after Marriage: Sexuality
   and Love in Mexican Transnational Families.
   Berkeley,   CA: University   of   California
   Press.
Hollos, Marida, and U. Larsen
   1997   From Lineage to Conjugality: The
   Social Context of Fertility Decisions among the
   Pare of Northern Tanzania. Social Science and
   Medicine 45:361–372.
Hunter, Mark
   2002   The Materiality of Everyday Sex:
   Thinking beyond "Prostitution." African Studies
   61(1):99–120.
Isiugo-Abanihe, U. C., J. A. Ebigbola, and A. A.
   Adewuyi
   1993   Urban Nuptiality Patterns and Marital
   Fertility in Nigeria. Journal of Biosocial Science
   25:483–498.
Jankowiak, William R., and Edward Fischer
   1992   A   Cross-Cultural   Perspective   on
   Romantic Love. Ethnology 31(2):149–155.
Jankowiak, William R.
   1995   Introduction. In Romantic Passion:
   A Universal Experience? W. R. Jankowiak, ed.
   Pp. 1–19. New York: Columbia University
   Press.
Karanja, Wambui
   1987   "Outside Wives" and "Inside Wives" in
   Nigeria: A Study of Changing Perceptions of
   Marriage. In Transformations in African
   Marriage. D. Parkin and D. Nyamwaya, eds.
   Pp. 137–154. Manchester: Manchester
   University Press for the International African
   Institute.
Karp, Ivan
   1987   Laughter at Marriage: Subversion in
   Performance. In Transformations in African
   Marriage. D. Parkin and D. Nyamwaya,
   eds. Pp. 137–154. Manchester: Manchester
   University Press for the International African
   Institute.

Kurian, George, ed.
1979 Cross-Cultural Perspectives on Mate-Selection and Marriage. Westport, CT: Greenwood.

Little, Kenneth, and Anne Price
1973 Some Trends in Modern Marriage among West Africans. In Africa and Change. C. Turnbull, ed. Pp. 185–207. New York: Knopf.

Little, Kenneth
1979 Women's Strategies in Modern Marriage in Anglophone West Africa: An Ideological and Sociological Appraisal. In Cross-Cultural Perspectives on Mate-Selection and Marriage. G. Kurian, ed. Pp. 202–217. Westport, CT: Greenwood.

Luke, Nancy
2005 Confronting the "Sugar Daddy Stereotype": Age and Economic Asymmetries and Risky Sexual Behavior in Urban Kenya. International Family Planning Perspectives 31(1):6–14.

Mair, Lucy
1969 African Marriage and Social Change. London: Frank Cass.

Makinwa-Adebusoye, Paulina
1992 Sexual Behavior, Reproductive Knowledge, and Contraceptive Use among Young Urban Nigerians. International Family Planning Perspectives 18(2):66-70.

Mann, Kristin
1985 Marrying Well: Marriage Status and Social Change among the Educated Elite in Colonial Lagos. Cambridge: Cambridge University Press.

Marris, Peter
1962 Family and Social Change in an African City. Evanston, IL: Northwestern University Press.

Murdock, George P., and Douglas White
1969 Standard Cross-Cultural Sample. Ethnology 8(4):329–369.

Murray, Colin
1976 Marital Strategy in Lesotho: The Redistribution of Migrant Earnings. African Studies 35(2):99–121.

Murstein, Bernard
1974 Love, Sex, and Marriage through the Ages. New York: Springer.

Nichols, Douglas, O. A. Lapido, John Paxman, and E. O. Otolorin
1986 Sexual Behavior, Contraceptive Practice, and Reproductive Health among Nigerian Adolescents. Studies in Family Planning 17(2):100–106.

Obiechina, Emmanuel
1973 An African Popular Literature: A Study of Onitsha Market Pamphlets. Cambridge: Cambridge University Press.

Okonjo, Kamene
1992 Aspects of Continuity and Change in Mate-Selection among the Igbo West of the River Niger. Journal of Comparative Family Studies 13(3):339–360.

Oppong, Christine
1974 Marriage among a Matrilineal Elite. Cambridge: Cambridge University Press.

Oucho, J. O., and W. T. S. Gould
1994 Internal Migration, Urbanization, and Population Distribution. In Demographic Change in Sub-Saharan Africa. K. Foote, K. Hill, and L. Martin eds. Pp. 256–296. Washington, DC: National Academy Press.

Parkin, David, and David Nyamwaya, eds.
1987 Transformations in African Marriage. Manchester: Manchester University Press for the International African Institute.

Plotnicov, Leonard
1995 Love, Lust and Found in Nigeria. In Romantic Passion: A Universal Experience? W. R. Jankowiak, ed. Pp. 128–140. New York: Columbia University Press.

Potash, Betty
1986 Widows in African Societies: Choices and Constraints. Palo Alto, CA: Stanford University Press.

Preston-Whyte, Eleanor
1999 Reproductive Health and the Condom Dilemma: Identifying Situational Barriers to Condom Use in South Africa. In Resistance to Behavioral Change to Reduce HIV/AIDS Infection in Predominantly Heterosexual Epidemics in Third World Countries. J. Caldwell, P. Caldwell, J. Anarfi, K. Awusabe-Asare, J. Ntozi, I. O. Oruboloye, J. Marck, W. Cosford, R. Colombo, and E. Hollings eds. Pp. 139–155. Canberra: Australian National University Press.

Radcliffe-Brown, Alfred, and Daryll Forde, eds.
1950 African Systems of Kinship and Marriage. London: Oxford University Press.

Riesman, Paul
1971 Defying Official Morality: The Example of Man's Quest for Woman among the Fulani. Cahiers d'Etudes Africaines 11(44):602–603.

Riesman, Paul
1981 Love Fulani Style. In Anthropological Realities. J. Guillemin, ed. Pp. 9–25. New Brunswick, NJ: Transaction Books.

Schapera, Isaac
    1966 Married Life in an African Tribe.
    Evanston, Il: Northwestern University Press.
Smith, Daniel Jordan
    2000 "These Girls Today Na War-O": Pre-
    marital Sexuality and Modern Identity in
    Southeastern Nigeria. Africa Today 47(3–4):
    141–170.
Smith, Daniel Jordan
    2001 Romance, Parenthood, and Gender in a
    Modern African Society. Ethnology 40(2):
    129–151.
Smith, Daniel Jordan
    2002 "Man No Be Wood": Gender and Extra-
    marital Sex in Contemporary Southeastern
    Nigeria. Abfad Journal 19(2):4–23.
Smith, Daniel Jordan
    2003 Imagining HIV/AIDS: Morality and
    Perceptions of Personal Risk in Nigeria.
    Medical Anthropology 22(4):343–372.
Smith, Daniel Jordan
    2004a Youth, Sin, and Sex in Nigeria:
    Christianity and HIV-related Beliefs and

Behaviour among Rural-Urban Migrants.
    Culture, Health, and Sexuality 6(5):425–437.
Smith, Daniel Jordan
    2004b Premarital Sex, Procreation, and HIV
    Risk in Nigeria. Studies in Family Planning
    35(4):223–235.
Uchendu, Victor
    1965 Concubinage among the Ngwa Igbo of
    Southern Nigeria. Africa 35(2):187–197.
UNAIDS (Joint United Nations Programme on
    HIV/AIDS)
    2004 Report on the Global Aids Epidemic.
    Bangkok. http://www.unaids.org/bangkok2004/
    GAR2004_html/GAR2004_03_en.htm#P237_
    35114.
van der Vliet, Virginia
    1991 Traditional Husbands, Modern Wives?
    Constructing Marriages in a South African
    Township. African Studies 50(1–2):219–241.
World Health Organization
    2000 AIDS Epidemic Update. Geneva. http://
    whqlibdoc.who.int/unaids/2000/9291730084.
    pdf.

30

Beyond Pain, Towards Pleasure in the Study of Sexuality in Africa

Rachel Spronk

The global Aids epidemic exposed the deficiency of our knowledge about the complexity and variety of sexual behaviour. As a result, there has been an impressive increase in research activities aimed at responding to this discrepancy. In Africa this has meant that the study of sexuality is mainly conducted in relation to HIV infection. One of the major consequences of this is that sex becomes de-eroticised to an act devoid of meaning and as a result, sex is studied apart from its sensorial power. The challenge of sex research is to understand the ways that societal factors organise sex and sexuality. It is important to note that sex is, above all, about the senses, and many times people engage in sex for pleasure. If we do not pay due attention to the pleasurable and sensorial aspects of sex we will continue producing deficient knowledge about sexuality. In this article I will shortly reflect on the dominant trend of sexuality research in Africa, after which I will explore how to study sex beyond its painful realities and consequences and how to study its pleasurable capacities as well,

based on my research on love and sex in Nairobi, Kenya.

The State of Art Regarding Sexuality Research in Africa

There are two major flaws in the health-related approaches to studying sexuality. The first is that the term 'sexuality' has been used in a self-evident and instrumental manner, rather than being approached with due attention to the full variety and subjectivity of sexual behaviour.

Studying 'the' sexuality of teenagers, for example, can mean studying their discourse on sex, their experience of arousal, their gendered expectations, their sexual identity or their sexual relations. Studies that do not take into account the imprecision of the term 'sexuality' start from a flawed position that sees sex simply as an obvious incident or action (Weeks 2003). In reality it is far more complex than this. The word 'sex' refers to an act, a category, a practice, a gender. 'Sexuality'

Rachel Spronk, Beyond Pain, Towards Pleasure in the Study of Sexuality in Africa, from *Sexuality in Africa Magazine*, vol. 4, no. 3 (2007): 3–6, 8–14. African Regional Sexuality Resource Centre, www.arsrc.or. Reprinted with permission of ARSRC.

Sexualities in Anthropology: A Reader, edited by Andrew P. Lyons and Harriet D. Lyons
© 2011 Blackwell Publishing Ltd.

refers to the quality of 'being sexual', it is a concept depicting the social arena where power relations and moral discourses are played out, and it also refers to sexual desire. These different aspects of sexuality highlight the need to define the term 'sexuality' in concepts such as sexual practices, categories, desire, identity, etc., in order to clarify what is being studied.

A second related flaw is that a mainly ahistorical approach has been responsible for grossly simplifying notions of 'culture'. Much research has been limited by ideas that there is something peculiar about African cultures regarding sexuality (Arnfred 2004, Stillwaggon 2003). Cultural 'traditions' and 'taboos' are the first things researchers tend to look for, to account for sexual behaviour, overlooking the more mundane aspects of life such as the influence of poverty or the emotional weight of sex. One such common assumption is that African men engage in multi-partnered sexual relationships because of 'their culture'.

A historical analysis of sexuality in Kenya offers an alternative explanation which is that, since the colonial period onwards, many married couples could not live together due to laws controlling male labour migration. In such situations of separation women and men would have engaged in other sexual affairs, all likely to be against 'cultural' conventions because adultery was a crime amongst many groups in Kenya (Robertson 1997, White 1990). Since sexuality is often presented as embedded in 'age-old traditions', too little attention has been given to such historical and social explanations of particular contemporary sexual practices. This is especially important given the current colonization of the public debate in different African countries representing a glorified 'African' past where sexuality was trouble-free and healthy.

The challenge of sex research is to understand the ways that societal factors organise sex and sexuality, and finding out how these processes shape the experiences of people. How, then, do we study sexuality and at the same time respect the interface between the social context and personal experience?

'Better Sex Makes Happier Couples'

In Nairobi (where I did my research on the love and sex lives of young adults), public debates about sexuality getting out of hand due to the loss of ('African') morals have flared up from late colonialism (Mutongi 2000). Debates about sexuality tend to articulate social discontent about social change, particularly when gender and sexuality are shifting, because this occurs to the detriment of existing gerontocratic power structures (Robertson 1997, White 1990, Thomas 2003). The history of public debates about sexuality shows that current changes in gender and sexuality are part of a continual reconfiguration of gender and sexuality, despite common views that sexual morals or 'traditions' have been under pressure in the last decades only. Interestingly, the volatile discussions about sexuality in Nairobi occur side by side with a positive discourse on sexuality that has found a niche in the media. A discourse has come into being, praising the vitalising force and bonding intimacy that comes from sex in relationships (Spronk forthcoming). *Parents* magazine is known particularly, among married and unmarried people, for its weekly column called 'Sex' or 'Sexuality'. Sexual practices and principles are dealt with in explicit terms. Sexual positions and the type of gratification that can be expected are described, while the topics of foreplay, fantasy and sexual variation to enhance female pleasure are written about regularly. The rationale of *Parents'* editor is reflected in the statement that 'Better sex makes happier couples,' claiming that sex is 'a couple's primary way to show love' (November 2001). In contrast to the conventional and religiously inspired idea that 'sex is a marital duty,' which is interpreted among many female young adults as enforcing the sexual subordination of women, the 'modern' duty is the fulfilment of a mutual orgasm. I do not mean that people did not have sex for pleasure before, but that the positive language of sex – sex as love, intimacy, and pleasure – as it is espoused by magazines such as *Parents* provides a sounding board for couples to develop their sex lives.

The implication of mutual orgasm is that sexuality gains a new interpretation; female sexuality becomes redefined as pleasure and not necessarily as procreation, and male sexuality becomes partly redefined in relation to female pleasure. This approach is new, exciting and more engaging for both women and men compared to conventional perspectives on sexuality emphasizing the procreative aspects of sex. For many young adults, to have a fulfilling sex life has become a symbol for a truly contemporary person. This does not necessarily imply that it is perceived as a green light to sexual permissiveness. Depending on the person's morals, a sexual life is developed only in marriage, while for others it is possible in premarital relationships as well. Both women and men are advised and encouraged to 'work' on their sex life, as it 'enriches' their personal sexual experiences as well as their partner's. Personal and mutual sexual happiness becomes an asset of individuals, as well as a symbol for a successful relationship:

'These days, we want our part of pleasure. I mean… We, women, know what to buy in this world and there is no way I could make love with a man and be left unsatisfied. It sometimes happened [that a man did not know how to satisfy a woman properly], men are not yet [as] up to date as women, and then I was so so disappointed. I mean, I don't even consider explaining [to] him what to do with a woman. Imagine! Some don't even realise!' (Dana, aged 29)

'OK, as a modern man you have to know how to satisfy a woman, there is no way to … when you have sex, that only you get satisfied. You have to know what she likes, to postpone her coming, to tease her so that she begs you. Sometimes it's disturbing when you cannot make it, when you cannot satisfy a woman. I once had a girlfriend and she never had an orgasm, it disturbed me to have mine whereas she was left … nothing.' (Ruben, aged 28)

In general, young adults are searching for new definitions of sex. They want to give a positive meaning to sex in their premarital sexual relationships. Pamela, aged 22, for example, says: 'How can something be wrong when it makes me feel good?' In popular definitions of sexuality, sex is linked to love instead of to reproduction, ethnic compatibility or marriage as conventional discourse has it. What is most notable is that women, in contrast to conventional discourse, also recognise sex as natural, as an embodied element of growing into adulthood. They thus recognise sexual desire as crucial to their identity as women, instead of understanding sexual desire in relation to married motherhood. For men, sexual desire has always been understood as self-evident in conventional discourse; sex is normatively understood as individual achievement. But, as Ruben explains, there is now more to sex for men like him because his sexual potential is also connected to his partner's sexual pleasure. In the new definition of sexuality, then, sexual intimacy becomes a matter of the self as a sexual subject; intimacy becomes an intersubjective experience. 'Intimacy', therefore, is the name of the game. It has become a fashionable word in all popular self-help columns in Nairobian magazines advising on the art of good relationships. For young women and men, notions of romantic love and emotional intimacy are increasingly important criteria for selecting a lover or spouse. Their desire resonates with an emerging discourse on love that is shared among many factions of society, from religious understandings of marriage to popular understandings of dating.

In my research I worked out a step-by-step approach linking the personal and the contextual, and I was able to study sexuality from its diverse angles (Spronk 2005a, 2005b, 2006). The personal aspect of sex focuses on sexual meanings that are individual and often have an emotional basis and are experienced through the body. Young adult women and men, like others all over the globe, reflected positively about the fact that sex is above all about sensual pleasure or the promise of pleasure and physical thrill. Being sexually active implies being sexually attractive or 'wanted', which contributes positively to women's and men's sense of self-worth. The sex act is experienced as a moment of bliss, of physical energies that cannot be negated and sex is recognised as a powerful 'natural' force. Having sex makes people feel 'good!', 'happy', 'alive', 'in love', 'sexy', 'loved', 'strong', and much more, or as a woman expressed it: 'Making love connects my body and soul'. Many experienced sex as a vitalizing force, linking its power to its capacity as the source of life, literally and metaphorically. In 2001, Winnie Madikizela-Mandela's phrase 'sex makes the world go round' (which circulated in the Kenyan media) was often used to joke about and to answer my never-ending questions.[1] Sex is often perceived as a 'gut feeling' (referring to excitement, sensuality, and release associated with bodily sensations, and with more complex understandings like 'feeling wo/man' augmenting a gendered sense of self).

Whereas these meanings of sex are more centred on the individual, other meanings are relational, seeing sex as connected to love, affection, romance, in which sex is defined corresponding to one's relation to another person. For many people sex was a mutual pleasure that augments an emotional bond between lovers, whether it concerned a casual or committed relationship. Mutual orgasm as proof of success and/or intimacy in sexual relations has become an indicator among certain young adults. Moreover, experiencing orgasm is often explained to me as the primal urge to feel alive, to achieve the ultimate moment of self-awareness while simultaneously getting lost in the pleasure of orgasm. It is a positive experience for the individual as well as for the couple. Second, the intersubjective aspect of sex comes about because the moment of sex is a moment of exchange where the personal and the social merge.

Ambiguous Pleasures

For many women, experiencing femaleness through their bodies was a means to feel empowered and what they labelled as 'feeling sexy' was typically informed by wider shared notions of femininity. In spite of normative understandings that equate female sexuality with reproduction, they also actively appropriated sexual pleasure as an index of their gendered sense of self. However, when pleasure and mutual orgasm become a standard, then sex becomes a new kind of obligation, generating insecurity. Several women recounted fear of failing as a competent sexual partner, either because of this new standard or because of the

fact that they were never encouraged to perceive themselves as desiring sex for pleasure and therefore felt inhibited to do so. Most of the women as they got older became more sexually assertive, and bolder in taking a position against existing double standards. For all the men, having sex was a necessary aspect of being masculine, whereas for them also, the interpretation of sex as an emotional exchange of trust and companionship could lead to uncertainty because it contradicted the common sense idea that male sex is spontaneous. Some men's desire for sex was close to compulsion and for them sex was a means of feeling alive and virile, hence masculine. A minority of men resisted this hegemonic notion of male sexuality by drawing on the discourse on love, in the same way that a minority of women chose to delay sex till marriage. These experiences show that there is a thin line between pleasure and anxiety in sex; and that they are not unconnected or mutually exclusive emotions and experiences.

I believe that there can never be a purely physical, ecstatic or anxiety free sexual encounter. From the young adults' experiences (and underlined by other accounts described in the literature), it can be concluded that sex is almost always imbued with some degree of uncertainty, ambiguity or anxiety. Feelings of shame, fear of losing the partner, fear of disappointing, fear about violation of trust, anxiety about failure to enjoy sex or have an orgasm, and fear of arousing suspicion, all these were experienced by both women and men, and only serve to highlight the precarious and complex nature of a sexual encounter. For example, many women endlessly deliberated whether or not to initiate condom use because they feared to arouse the suspicion of their partner about being promiscuous. Other women recounted similar qualms, as well as a fear of violating trust by initiating condom use. Men recounted similar anxieties, though less often. Besides anxieties such as these that were related to social expectations, sex was also used to deal with a range of feelings, such as rejection, insecurity or anger, or to exert power or increase self-worth. For example, Thomas, aged 26 dealt with his fear of rejection, related to his experience with his first committed relationship, by having multiple relationships: once he sheepishly said that sex 'boosts my ego'. Njeri, aged 24, however, would never phrase it in such a way and instead explained how she enjoyed the fact that her boyfriend was 'hooked to her' because of their 'great sex life'. In her sexual life the interface of pleasure and anxiety becomes clear in the way she enjoyed sex with her partner to the full, which was important to her, despite the fact that the relationship was troubled with fights, mistrust and frustrations, which she claimed did 'not do me well'. It should be pointed out that pleasurable and anxiety evoking aspects of sex are not mutually exclusive and that, therefore, such uneasy aspects of sex should not be over-problematised. It highlights the fact that sex is fraught with ambiguity.

In sum, people's explanations about the importance of sex mostly relate to how sex augments a gendered sense of self. Gender ideologies influence how people understand themselves and how sex plays a role in their gendered identity. If sex is constitutive to people's feelings of being either 'woman' or 'man', then experiencing being feminine and masculine is partly related to normative expectations based on existing gender roles. Butler's notion of the 'paradox of subjectivation' (Butler 1997) is helpful in pointing out how women and men both advocate new interpretations of gender (because young adults unsettle, in different degrees, the patriarchal understanding of sex and gender) as well as reproduce normative understandings.

The hegemonic symbolic construction of women as moral caretakers, guardians of the family, and devoted wives, serves as the norm of femininity even when women deviate from it. It comes to women being encouraged to remain chaste and being severely judged when transgressing normative parameters. Women have therefore been compelled to adopt more secretive strategies when having sexual affairs compared to men. They have to be constantly negotiating between factors that are associated with deviance on the one hand, and aspects that would allow them to be considered respectable on the other. Nevertheless, women appropriated sexual pleasure as part of contemporary personhood, and many enjoyed doing so. In general, the older the women were,

the more boldly they pursued sex for pleasure, whether it was via short affairs or by finding out about sex toys or toy condoms.

Men generally had, and have, more leeway to deviate from the norm. Although men are also encouraged to remain chaste, mainly by the Christian discourse, they are also encouraged to be sexually active, which is endorsed by the patriarchal discourse equating male sexuality with virility and social achievement. Public discourse is highly contradictory when it comes to manhood and morality, and this also impacts on men's sexual behaviour and their relationships with women. Whereas they perceive sex as constitutive to their sense of masculinity, men should also exercise self-restraint and therefore there is a (undefined) limit to sex. A man should not appear to be addicted to sex, because this implies being dependent on women and thus not being self-reliant. On the other hand, a man should not fail in having sex and, above all, being a good lover. In patriarchal discourse being a skilful lover is not considered crucial to men's sexuality, while in the new discourse it is. The new discourse, however, implies that sex is not as spontaneous as it is conventionally understood to be; instead, it needs to be 'worked upon' as sexual skills, like other skills, require knowledge and practice. Many men recounted or hinted at their anxieties about failing to be skilful lovers. The new discourse on sex as central to emotional intimacy challenges conventional constructions of masculinity, and men struggle to balance and incorporate both in their lives as lovers. Nevertheless, the discourse of sex as being natural to men remains hegemonic and most men consider it their right to take pleasure in sex.

Young adult women and men in Nairobi maintain ambiguous attitudes towards each other because men occupy an ambiguous position in women's lives as lovers, friends and future husbands, as well as figures of authority and social control. As a result, both women and men communicate ambiguity towards their partners and potential partners. It turns out that many sexual affairs are not self-evident anxiety-free encounters. Especially in non committed relationships, sex is embedded in ambiguity because of social and cultural expectations, as well as the fear of arousing suspicion and violating trust. Further, Aids poses a realistic threat when having unprotected sex, which continues to happen although condom use is fairly high. The moralising discourses on Aids have further codified sex with a negative meaning in public discourse; 'bad' sex is 'immoral' sex, while 'good' sex has come to mean sex that conforms with normative cultural values. These social definitions of sex affect the very personal experience and sensations of sex.

Studying Sex in All its Meanings, Sensations and Connections

In order to be able to interconnect the personal and social aspects of sex, I propose to use sexuality as an analytical tool with three foci. First, sex is a vehicle for powerful sensations that are experienced very subjectively. In other words, sex is *personal* and sex is a medium for expressing a variety of feelings, emotions and needs in a person. In all the biographical narratives I collected, the effects of sexual desire and conduct on the person stood out from the power of sexual attraction as an uncontrollable force, to the bodily craving for sexual fulfilment. Women and men reflected differently about these experiences depending on their relationships, their view on sex or intimacy, or their anticipation of gendered expectations. In my research group of 49 people, the differences between individual people stood out. This is an important observation to make, since large scale studies, because of their methodology, cannot but generalise and therefore easily negate variety. Generalisation itself does not need to be problematic as long as the limitations of this approach are taken into account in the production of knowledge about sexuality.

Second, sex is more often than not an *inter-subjective* exchange between people; sex implies intimacy in the sense that mutually agreed sexual conduct always implies a degree of confidence or trust (Heald 2005). Sex carries a sense of emotional interaction that varies in its nature. The young adults' experiences show that sex is a means for the expression of different feelings, emotions and needs that are acted upon in relation with another person. People have sex for fun, to fulfil a desire for intimacy, as a physical

thrill, to achieve social status, to confirm a gendered sense of self, to exert power, to express love, to humiliate, to conform to expectations, and much more. The emotions and the nature of intimacy can differ. Despite the popular connotations of the term, 'intimacy' does not always imply feelings of monogamous romantic love – 'lovey-dovey' feelings, to use a man's words whose narrative showed how intimacy can imply friendship or financial care more than romantic love (Eerdewijk 2006, Tadele 2006). Perceiving sex as an inter-subjective exchange can be used as a direct call for further research studies to move beyond an essentialist analysis of sex as an obvious act.

Third, because sexuality is also a peculiarly sensitive conductor of social influences, cultural perceptions and political divisions, sexuality is also *socially* defined. These social aspects inform all the abovementioned emotions and exchanges. Every one of the biographical narratives I collected testifies to how social meanings frame people's behaviour, their understanding of themselves and their experience. The accounts of, for example, women's 'playing hard to get' to men's burden of needing to be seen as 'man enough', show how people acted in order to preserve their sexual reputation. Sexual ideology and practices are related to notions of gender, age, ethnicity or race, religion, social status, familial responsibility, ideas about intimacy, love and affection. Relations of power are typically translated into the organisation of sexuality (Arnfred 2004), such as different perceptions regarding chastity defined by gender. The different biographical narratives elaborate how people's sexuality developed in interaction with these social axes.

In short, epidemiological studies and/or studies from a health perspective on sexuality have tended to ignore the construction of gendered and sexual identities, the cultural meaning of sexual conduct, and the erotic significance of variant sexual practices in distinct social settings. There is no way of avoiding the fact that accounts of sex, intimacy and sexuality eventually come down to studying personal sensations. These sensations are comprised of the complex conjunction between physiological arousal, erotic practices and interpretative processes; they are thus situated at the threshold where body and discursive knowledge converge and merge.

The challenge of sexuality research in Africa is to bring into focus the experiential aspect of sex while continuing to work from a health perspective (which seems inevitable for as long as research remains dependent on 'development-related' finances, which is not the case for sexuality studies in the West). We should not compromise on a solid research epistemology despite pressures to do so such as the pressure to work towards solutions for so-called risk behaviour which tends to narrow down the research epistemology. This is easier said than done. It is why in this context Obbo calls for a certain degree of humility in the current explosion of Aids-related sexuality studies geared towards formulating answers and solutions (Obbo 1998). After more than two decades of Aids research, there is an urgent need to incorporate into the Aids paradigm that 'the hallmark of sexuality is its complexity: its multiple meanings, sensations and connections' (Vance 1984).

NOTE

1 Winnie Madikizela-Mandela is the well-known ex-wife of the former president of South Africa Nelson Mandela.

REFERENCES

Arnfred, S.E.
   (2004) Re-thinking Sexualities in Africa. Sweden: Almqvist and Wiksell Tryckeri.
Butler, J.
   1997 The Psychic Life of Power: Theories in Subjection. Stanford: Stanford University Press.
Eerdewijk, A.v.
   2006 Love and Money: the Intimate Relationships of Dakarois Girls. Etnofoor 19.
Heald, S.
   1995 The Power of Sex: Some Reflections on Caldwells' 'African Sexuality' Thesis. Africa 65, 491–506.
Mutongi, K.
   2000 'Dear Dolly's' Advice: Representations of Youth, Courtship, and Sexualities in Africa, 1960–1980. International Journal of African Historical Studies 33, 1–23.
Obbo, C.
   1998 Social Science Research: Understanding and Action. In Vivre et Penser le Sida en Afrique /

Experiencing and Understanding Aids in Africa (eds) C. Becker, J.-P. Dozon, C. Obbo & M. Touré. Dakar, Paris: Codesria, Karthala
Robertson, C.
   (1997) Trouble Showed the Way. Women, Men and Trade in the Nairobi Area, 1890–1990. Bloomington: Indiana University Press.
Spronk, R.
   Forthcoming. Media and the Therapeutic Discourse of Love in Middle-class Nairobi. In Locating Love in Africa, Rethinking Love from Africa (ed.) J. Cole and L. Thomas.
Spronk, R.
   2005a Female Sexuality in Nairobi: Flawed or Favoured? Culture, Health and Sexuality 7, 267–279.
Spronk, R.
   2005b "There is a Time to Fool Around and There is a Time to Grow Up". Balancing Sex, Relationships and Notions of Masculinity in Nairobi. In Rethinking Masculinities, Violence and AIDS (Eds) D. Gibson & A. Hardon. Amsterdam: Het Spinhuis Publishers.
Spronk, R.
   2006 Ambiguous Pleasures. Sexuality and New Self-definitions in Nairobi. Unpublished PhD thesis: University of Amsterdam.
Stillwaggon, E.
   (2003) Racial Metaphors: Interpreting Sex and AIDS in Africa. Development and Change 34, 809–832.
Tadele, G.
   2006 Bleak Prospects: Young Men, Sexuality and HIV/AIDS in an Ethiopian Town. Africa Studies Centre Series. Leiden: Brill Academic Publishers.
Thomas, L.M.
   2003 Politics of the Womb. Women, Reproduction and the State in Kenya. Berkeley: University of California Press.
Vance, C.S.
   1984 Pleasure and Danger: Toward a Politics of Sexuality. In Pleasure and Danger. Exploring Female Sexuality (ed.) C.S. Vance. London: Pandora.
Weeks, J.
   (2003) Sexualities, second edition. London: Routledge.
White, L.
   1990 The Comforts of Home. Prostitution in Colonial Nairobi. Chicago: The University of Chicago Press.

Index

Sexualities in Anthropology: A Reader, edited by Andrew P. Lyons and Harriet D. Lyons
© 2011 Blackwell Publishing Ltd.